M000289198

LIBRARY OF CONGRESS
SURPLUS
DUPLICATE

The Treasury of Precious Instructions: Essential Teachings of the Eight Practice Lineages of Tibet

Volume 5: Sakya
Part 1

The Tsadra Foundation Series

published by Snow Lion, an imprint of Shambhala Publications

Tsadra Foundation is a U.S.-based nonprofit organization that contributes to the ongoing development of wisdom and compassion in Western minds by advancing the combined study and practice of Tibetan Buddhism.

Taking its inspiration from the nineteenth-century nonsectarian Tibetan Buddhist scholar and meditation master Jamgön Kongtrul Lodrö Taye, Tsadra Foundation is named after his hermitage in eastern Tibet, Tsadra Rinchen Drak. The Foundation's various program areas reflect his values of excellence in both scholarship and contemplative practice, and the recognition of their mutual complementarity.

Tsadra Foundation envisions a flourishing community of Western contemplatives and scholar-practitioners who are fully trained in the traditions of Tibetan Buddhism. It is our conviction that, grounded in wisdom and compassion, these individuals will actively enrich the world through their openness and excellence.

This publication is a part of Tsadra Foundation's Translation Program, which aims to make authentic and authoritative texts from the Tibetan traditions available in English. The Foundation is honored to present the work of its fellows and grantees, individuals of confirmed contemplative and intellectual integrity; however, their views do not necessarily reflect those of the Foundation.

Tsadra Foundation is delighted to collaborate with Shambhala Publications in making these important texts available in the English language.

Sakya

The Path with Its Result

Part 1

THE TREASURY OF PRECIOUS INSTRUCTIONS:
ESSENTIAL TEACHINGS OF THE EIGHT PRACTICE
LINEAGES OF TIBET
VOLUME 5

Compiled by Jamgön Kongtrul Lodrö Taye

TRANSLATED BY
Malcolm Smith

SNOW LION

Snow Lion
An imprint of Shambhala Publications, Inc.
2129 13th Street
Boulder, Colorado 80302
www.shambhala.com

© 2022 by Tsadra Foundation

Cover art: Thangka "The Sakya Practice Lineage of Tibetan Buddhism."
Collection Eric Colombel. Photo: Rafael Ortet, 2018. © Eric Colombel, New York.

All rights reserved. No part of this book may be reproduced
in any form or by any means, electronic or mechanical, including
photocopying, recording, or by any information storage and retrieval
system, without permission in writing from the publisher.

9 8 7 6 5 4 3 2 1

First Edition
Printed in the United States of America

Shambhala Publications makes every effort to print on acid-free, recycled paper.
Snow Lion is distributed worldwide by Penguin Random House, Inc.,
and its subsidiaries.

LIBRARY OF CONGRESS CATALOGING-IN-PUBLICATION DATA
Names: Kong-sprul Blo-gros-mtha'-yas, 1813–1899, author. | Smith, Malcolm
(Buddhism practitioner), translator.
Title: Sakya. volume 1 / compiled by Jamgön Kongtrul Lodrö Taye; translated by Malcolm Smith.
Description: Boulder : Shambhala, 2022– | Includes bibliographical references and index.
Identifiers: LCCN 2021011443 | ISBN 9781611809664 (hardback)
Subjects: LCSH: Lam-'bras (Sa-skya-pa) | Sa-skya-pa (Sect)—Doctrines. |
Tripiṭaka. Sūtrapiṭaka. Tantra. Hevajratantrarāja—Commentaries.
Classification: LCC BQ7672.4 .K66 2022 | DDC 294.3/420423—dc23
LC record available at https://lccn.loc.gov/2021011443

Contents

Part Three: The Liberating Instructions

Foreword

In his vast work *The Treasury of Precious Instructions* (*gDams ngag rin po che'i mdzod*), Jamgön Kongtrul Lodrö Taye, that most eminent of Tibetan Buddhist masters, collected together all the empowerments, instructions, and practices of the eight great chariots of the practice lineages. Not only that, but he himself received the complete transmissions for all the practices, accomplished them including the retreats, and preserved them in his own mindstream. He then passed on the transmissions to his own students and all who requested them.

The Treasury of Precious Instructions exemplifies how Jamgön Kongtrul Lodrö Taye's whole life was dedicated to teaching and spreading the dharma, whether it be sutra or mantra, *kama* or *terma*, old or new translation school, free of sectarian bias. Without his supreme efforts, many traditions of Tibetan Buddhism would have been lost.

The teachings of the Buddha have now spread throughout the Western world, and there is a growing need for major texts to be translated into English so that Western dharma students and scholars have access to these essential teachings. I was, therefore, delighted to hear that having successfully published a translation in ten volumes of Jamgön Kongtrul Lodrö Taye's *Treasury of Knowledge* (*Shes bya kun khyab mdzod*), the Tsadra Foundation has embarked on a second major project, the translation of *The Treasury of Precious Instructions*, and I would like to express my gratitude to them.

May their work be of benefit to countless sentient beings.

His Holiness the Seventeenth Karmapa, Ogyen Trinley Dorje
Bodhgaya
February 21, 2016

Series Introduction

The *Treasury of Precious Instructions* (*gDams ngag rin po che'i mdzod*) is the fourth of the five great treasuries compiled or composed by Jamgön Kongtrul Lodrö Taye (1813–1900), also known as Karma Ngawang Yönten Gyatso, among many other names. Kongtrul was one of the greatest Buddhist masters of Tibet. His accomplishments were so vast and varied that it is impossible to do them justice here. The reader is referred to an excellent short biography in the introduction to the first translated volume of another of his great works, *The Treasury of Knowledge*, or the lengthy *Autobiography of Jamgön Kongtrul*. Even if his achievements had consisted solely of his literary output represented in these five treasuries, it would be difficult to comprehend his level of scholarship.

Unlike *The Treasury of Knowledge*, which is Kongtrul's own composition, his other four treasuries may be considered anthologies. Kongtrul's stated mission was to collect and preserve without bias the teachings and practices of all the lineages of Tibetan Buddhism, particularly those that were in danger of disappearing. The English publication of *The Treasury of Knowledge* in ten volumes and the forthcoming translations of this *Treasury of Precious Instructions* in some eighteen volumes can attest to the success of his endeavor, perhaps even beyond what he had imagined.

The Treasury of Precious Instructions is, in some ways, the epitome of Kongtrul's intention. He first conceived of the project around 1870, as always in close consultation with his spiritual friend and mentor Jamyang Khyentse Wangpo (1820–1892). The two of them, along with other great masters, such as Chokgyur Dechen Lingpa, Mipam Gyatso, and Ponlop Loter Wangpo, were active in an eclectic trend in which the preservation of the texts of Tibetan Buddhism was paramount.[1] It was with Khyentse's encouragement and collaboration that Kongtrul had created *The Treasury of Knowledge*—his incredible summation of all that was to be known—and compiled the anthologies of *The Treasury of Kagyu Mantra* and *The Treasury of Precious Hidden Teachings*. This next treasury expanded the scope by aiming to collect in one place the most important instructions of *all* the main practice lineages.

Kongtrul employed a scheme for organizing the vast array of teachings that flourished, or floundered, in Tibet during his time into the Eight Great Chariots of the practice lineages (*sgrub brgyud shing rta chen po brgyad*), or eight lineages that are vehicles of attainment. He based this on a much earlier text by Sherap Özer (Skt. Prajñārasmi, 1518–1584).[2] The structure and contents of that early text indicate that the seeds of the so-called nonsectarian movement (*ris med*) of the nineteenth century in eastern Tibet had already been planted and just needed cultivation. The organizing principle of the scheme was to trace the lineages of the instructions for religious practice that had come into Tibet from India. This boiled down to eight "charioteers"—individuals who could be identified as the conduits between India and Tibet and who were therefore the sources of the practice lineages, all equally valid in terms of origin and comparable in terms of practice. This scheme of eight practice lineages became a kind of paradigm for the nonsectarian approach championed by Kongtrul and his colleagues.[3]

The Treasury of Precious Instructions implements this scheme in a tangible way by collecting the crucial texts and organizing them around those eight lineages. These may be summarized as follows:

1. The Nyingma tradition derives from the transmissions of Padmasambhava and Vimalamitra during the eighth century, along with the former's illustrious twenty-five disciples (*rje 'bangs nyer lnga*) headed by the sovereign Trisong Detsen.
2. The Kadam tradition derives from Atiśa (982–1054) and his Tibetan disciples headed by Dromtön Gyalwai Jungne (1004–1063).
3. The Sakya tradition, emphasizing the system known as the "Path with Its Result," derives from Virūpa, Ḍombhi Heruka, and other mahāsiddhas, and passes through Gayadhara and his Tibetan disciple Drokmi Lotsāwa Śākya Yeshe (992–1072).
4. The Marpa Kagyu tradition derives from the Indian masters, Saraha, Tilopa, Nāropa, and Maitrīpa, as well as the Tibetan Marpa Chökyi Lodrö (1000?–1081?).
5. The Shangpa Kagyu tradition derives from the ḍākinī Niguma

and her Tibetan disciple Khyungpo Naljor Tsultrim Gönpo of Shang.

6. Pacification and Severance derive from Padampa Sangye (d. 1117) and his Tibetan successor, Machik Lapkyi Drönma (ca. 1055–1143).
7. The Six-Branch Yoga of the *Kālacakra Tantra* derives from Somanātha and his Tibetan disciple Gyijo Lotsāwa Dawai Özer during the eleventh century and was maintained preeminently through the lineages associated with Zhalu and Jonang.
8. The Ritual Service and Attainment of the Three Vajras derives from the revelations of the deity Vajrayoginī, compiled by the Tibetan master Orgyenpa Rinchen Pal (1230–1309) during his travels in Oḍḍiyāna.

The very structure of the *Treasury* thus stands as a statement of the nonsectarian approach. With all these teachings gathered together and set side by side—and each one authenticated by its identification with a direct lineage traced back to the source of Buddhism (India)—maintaining a sectarian attitude would be next to impossible. Or at least that must have been Kongtrul's hope. In explaining his purpose for the collection, he states:

> Generally speaking, in each of the eight great mainstream lineages of accomplishment there exists such a profound and vast range of authentic sources from the sutra and tantra traditions, and such limitless cycles of scriptures and pith instructions, that no one could compile everything.[4]

Nevertheless, he made a good start in *The Treasury of Precious Instructions*, which he kept expanding over the years until at least 1887. The woodblocks for the original printing—carved at Palpung Monastery, where Kongtrul resided in his nearby retreat center—took up ten volumes. An edition of this is currently available in twelve volumes as the Kundeling printing, published in 1971–1972.[5] With the addition of several missing texts, an expanded and altered version was published in eighteen volumes in 1979–1981 by Dilgo Khyentse Rinpoche. Finally, in 1999 the most complete version became available in the edition published by Shechen Monastery, which is the basis for the current translations.[6] The structure of this enhanced edition, of course, still centers on the eight lineages, as follows:

1. Nyingma ("Ancient Tradition"), volumes 1 and 2;
2. Kadampa ("Transmitted Precepts and Instructions Lineage"), volumes 3 and 4;
3. Sakya, or Lamdre ("Path with Its Result"), volumes 5 and 6;
4. Marpa Kagyu ("Precept Lineage of Marpa"), volumes 7 through 10;
5. Shangpa Kagyu ("Precept Lineage of Shang"), volumes 11 and 12;
6. Zhije ("Pacification"), volume 13, and Chöd ("Severance"), volume 14;
7. Jordruk ("Six Yogas [of Kalācakra]"), volume 15; and
8. Dorje Sumgyi Nyendrub ("Approach and Accomplishment of Three Vajras," also called after its founder "Orgyenpa"), volume 15.

Volumes 16 and 17 are devoted to various other cycles of instruction. Volume 18 mainly consists of the *One Hundred and Eight Guides of Jonang*, a prototype and inspiration for Kongtrul's eclectic anthology, and also includes his catalog to the whole *Treasury*.

Translator's Introduction

THIS VOLUME is the fifth in *The Treasury of Precious Instructions* series and the first of two that treat the teachings of the Sakya school. The Sakya school's principal teaching is known as Lamdre, or the "Path with Its Result." According to traditional Sakya sources, this system was first taught by Mahāsiddha Virūpa to Kāṇha, the lesser of his two disciples, some twelve hundred years or so following the Buddha's death, or parinirvāṇa. It was passed down as an oral tradition through a series of Indian siddhas and entered Tibet in the middle of the eleventh century. It was finally written down in 1141 C.E. by Sachen Kunga Nyingpo. While the details of that story are fairly well known, much less has been written about the Sakya tradition's portrayal of the rise of Secret Mantra Vajrayāna and the origins of the Hevajra cycle of tantras.

Hevajra is a prominent Buddhist deity influential throughout India and Southeast Asia. Representations have been found as far east as Cambodia, dating from the twelfth-century reign of Jayavarman VII,[1] and in Sumatra, where we find a fourteenth-century epigraph of devotion to the practice of Hevajra from the reign of King Ādityavarman.[2] Furthermore, Taranātha received a transmission of Hevajra from the Indian master Pūrṇavajra, who traveled to Tibet in the late sixteenth century. The influence of Hevajra in Tibet, Mongolia, and beyond has continued to the present day, with the *Hevajra Tantra* forming one of the basic texts of two major Tibetan Buddhist schools, Sakya and Kagyu.

Western scholars typically date the appearance of the *Hevajra Tantra* to the beginning of the tenth century C.E.[3] Traditional Sakya scholarship dates the dissemination of the *Hevajra Tantra* and its two main explanatory tantras to the encounter between Śrī Dharmapāla, an abbot of Nālanda University, and a ḍākinī known to us from the *Hevajra Tantra* as Nairātmyā ("she who lacks a self") at an unknown time, predating the founding of Samye Monastery in 762 C.E.

Tibetan sources generally consider the rise of Secret Mantra teachings in India to have begun with an Indian king referred to as "King Dza," mentioned in a tantra generally identified as the *Saṃvara Supplementary Tantra.*[4] Amezhab,[5] the seventeenth-century polymath and the twenty-seventh Sakya throne holder, relates that one hundred twenty years following the passing of the Buddha, Vajrapāṇi appeared to King Brilliant Moon (Rab gsal zla ba, a.k.a. King Dza) and conferred upon him the Compendium of the Principles of All Tathāgatas empowerment, and so on.

The traditional Sakya presentation of the later spread of the unsurpassed yoga tantras of Vajrayāna[6] is related by Sönam Tsemo, the fourth Sakya throne holder, in his *General Presentation of the Tantras.* Śākyamuni Buddha visited King Indrabhūti in Oḍḍiyāna and granted him the Guhyasamāja empowerment. King Indrabhūti attained full awakening during the empowerment. After Vajrapāṇi compiled the tantras, he gave them to the king and his subjects; all attained siddhi, and the country became vacant.

A great lake filled with nāgas arose in Oḍḍiyāna. The nāgas who lived in the lake were ripened by Vajrapāṇi and entrusted with the tantras he had collected. The nāgās gradually took on human form and established a city on the lakeshore. Those who practiced Vajrayāna became siddhas and ḍākinīs; those who did not became humans. Later on King Visukalpa in South India dreamed that if he journeyed to Oḍḍiyāna, he could attain awakening in a single lifetime. He traveled there and became the disciple of a woman from whom he received both the Guhyasamāja and the Compendium of the Principles of All Tathāgatas empowerments. He then returned to South India and promulgated the Vajrayāna, and from there it spread to the rest of India.

Turning to the Hevajra cycle of tantras specifically, one of the most important Sakya sources is Ngorchen Kunga Zangpo's *Marvelous Ocean*, which presents Bhagavān Hevajra in three ways: through the dharmakāya, the saṃbhogakāya, and the nirmāṇakāya. To summarize the first, the mind of Hevajra is the dharmakāya, the dharmatā nature of all phenomena. The saṃbhogakāya Hevajra is referred to as the cause Heruka, and the nirmāṇakāya Hevajra is referred to as the result Heruka (which has implications for understanding the cause and result Vajradhara sections in the Hevajra sādhana in part 2 of this volume). The saṃbhogakāya Heruka is described in the usual terms of the five certainties of the saṃbhogakāya:

the certain place is Akaniṣṭha Ghanavyūha; the certain teacher is the eight-headed, sixteen-armed Mahāvajradhara; the certain retinue is the bodhisattva Vajragarbha, and so on; the certain dharma is the Hevajra tantras; and the certain time is always.

In terms of the nirmāṇakāya Hevajra, Ngorchen then discusses the taming of the mundane devas, the prerequisite condition for the Hevajra tantras to arise in our world. He describes the universe as possessing four rulers: Brahma, the ruler of the form realm; Maheśvara, the ruler of the wider desire realm; Papayin Māra (a.k.a. Kamadeva), the ruler of the Paranirmitavaśavartin devas, the highest set of devas in the desire realm; and Rudra, the ruler from the peak of Sumeru on down and the ruler of the earth. They and their four wives (Gaurī, and so on), along with the eight arrogant gods (such as the desire realm's Brahma) and their wives, constantly engaged in intercourse out of desire, slew humans whose flesh they devoured out of anger, and were confused about the meaning of cause, result, and reality due to ignorance.

Because of the unvirtuous actions of the gods, the saṃbhogakāya cause Heruka entered the samādhi called "The Vajra Play of the Great Samaya of Various Intentions" and issued forth various maṇḍalas into the billion-world system in order to benefit those to be tamed. In India—or more broadly, this world—the Bhagavān emanated a maṇḍala composed of nine deities: the eight-headed, sixteen-armed form of Hevajra in union with Nairātmyā and the eight goddesses whose names match those of the wives of Rudra, and so on. The Bhagavān made the four rulers of the universe his seat, and the eight goddesses made the eight arrogant gods their seats. Rudra's main retinue was dominated by the principal deity, Hevajra in union with Nairātmyā, and Rudra himself was dominated by Ghasmarī. In the eight charnel grounds, Gaurī, and so on—the eight wives of the desire realm gods, such as Rudra, with their numberless retinue—tame the hateful through fear, the passionate through erotic apparitions, the ignorant with the sound of mantras, and so on.

After taming Rudra and his retinue, the Bhagavān teaches a retinue of those who have transcended the world in the celestial mansion called "The Bhaga[7] of the Vajra Queen." The tantras he teaches are the great *Hevajra Root King Tantra* in seven hundred thousand lines (the "large" tantra); the topical[8] *Hevajra Tantra* in five hundred thousand lines (the "small" tantra); the supplemental tantra, the *Ornament of Mahāmudrā*; the addendum to the supplemental tantra, the *Essence of Gnosis*; the unshared explanatory tantra, the *Ornament of Gnosis*; the shared commentary tantra, the *Saṃpūṭa Tantra* in three hundred sixty thousand lines; the essence tantra, the *Ornament That Definitively Explains Accomplishment;* and the result tantra, the *Lamp of Principles*. According to Ngorchen, all these tantras were taught prior to the advent of Śākyamuni Buddha.

As to the question of when and where the tantras were taught by the Bhagavān in this world, Ngorchen cites the account given in Alaṃkakalaśa's *Extensive Commentary on the Vajra Garland Tantra*. According to this account, the Bhagavān—Śākyamuni Buddha manifesting in the form of Hevajra—taught the large and small Hevajra tantras and the commentary tantras in Magadhā, India, in order to tame the four māras, but Alaṃkakalaśa declined to give further locations.[9]

When the question arises of who then will teach the tantras at a later time period, Ngorchen's account of the spread of Vajrayāna in human lands after the Buddha's parinirvāṇa is based on this citation from the *Ornament of Gnosis*:

> "Oh Bhagavān, in the future who will explain this tantra of the true secret to fortunate sentient beings?" The Bhagavān replied, "Śrī Vajrapāṇinātha will explain it."[10]

Ngorchen also cites a prediction found in the *Lamp of Principles*:

> The goddess asked, "By whom will this tantra of the great secret be known and explained?" The Bhagavān replied, "It will be known, explained, and clarified for sentient beings by Indrabhūti, the king of Oḍḍiyāna, in the place of the glorious vajra in the north."[11]

We are to understand that the compiler of the tantras is Vajrapāṇi, and as the *Lamp of Principles* also asserts, Indrabhūti is an emanation of Vajrapāṇi. In this way, not only are the teachings of the *Hevajra Tantra* and other tantras grounded in Śākyamuni Buddha's lifetime, but their means of transmission in the future is guaranteed by Vajrapāṇi.

Ngorchen then turns to how the three main Hevajra tantras were taught. Ngorchen cites the commentary composed by Kāmadhenupa concerning the origin of the *Hevajra Tantra* in two sections, the *Vajrapañjara Tantra*, and the *Saṃpūṭa Tantra* we have at present as the principal sources for the practice of Hevajra in the Tibetan tradition. Kāmadhenupa places the teaching of the *Hevajra Tantra* during the lifetime of Śākyamuni Buddha, which was taught to the bodhisattva Vajragarbha (and his retinue of eighty million heroes), the yoginī Nairātmyā (and her retinue, said to be equal to the atoms of Sumeru), and innumerable other devas and humans. After this the Bhagavān taught the *Vajrapañjara Tantra* and the *Saṃpūṭa Tantra.*

To answer the question of why the longer Hevajra tantras are no longer extant in human lands, Ngorchen turns to a passage in the *Vajrapañjara Tantra*. It explains that in the future, after the Buddha's parinirvāṇa, people will not be able to uphold the extensive tantras because they have little wisdom and short lives. Therefore, the root and explanatory tantras would be taught in condensed forms. The passage reads:

> "Bhagavān, why were [the tantras] condensed from the extensive forms? If in the Fortunate Eon bodhisattvas and ordinary people have short lives, how will they uphold them? How will they hear them? How will their minds be transformed? Bhagavān, why will the lives of ordinary people be short?"
>
> Vajradhara replied, "Some will become teachers and incur root downfalls. The behavior of others will be enjoyment of the ten unvirtuous actions. Others, ordinary people, will slay creatures. Some with craving will desire to possess a harem of women. For those reasons all tantras will not be taught in their extensive forms."[12]

The Hevajra Tradition in the Sakya School

The Sakya school specializes in the practice and exegesis of the *Hevajra Tantra*, developing its entire Vajrayāna curriculum around the root tantra, its respective commentarial tantras, and the Indian commentarial literature that grew up around the Hevajra Tantra cycle. The Sakya school concerns itself with four principal Hevajra lineages. Three of these traditions pass through Drokmi Lotsāwa Śākya Yeshe: the Virūpa tradition, the Ḍombhi Heruka tradition, and the Saroruha tradition. The Kṛṣṇa Samayavajra tradition passes through the eleventh-century translator Gö Khukpa Lhetse. It should be noted that in all these lineages, the person who reveals the *Hevajra Tantra* to Virūpa, Anaṅgavajra, and Samayavajra is none other than the ḍākinī Nairātmyā, who is consistently identified as a nirmāṇakāya.

Among these four lineages, the principal lineage to emerge was the

Virūpa tradition, also known as the Intimate Instruction tradition (*man ngag lugs*) or the Path with Its Result. The Path with Its Result begins with the hagiography (*rnam thar*) of the mahāsiddha Virūpa. However, there are at least two Virūpas known to us. The Virūpa of the Path with Its Result tradition is known as Śrī Dharmapāla,[13] who is identified as the author of *The Vajra Verses.* The other, a brahmin Virūpa,[14] is identified as a disciple of Princess Lakṣmiṃkāra[15] in the Jal tradition (*dpyal lugs*) of Vajravārāhī. It is possible there may be more Virūpas, but such an exploration is beyond the scope of this introduction.

There are three primary sources concerning the life of Śrī Dharmapāla Virūpa: the single verse of supplication to him found in the *Supplication to the Eighty-Four Mahāsiddhas*, the *Chronicle of the Eighty-Four Mahāsiddhas*, and the *Chronicle of the Indian Gurus.* While the latter two texts disagree on biographical details—the monastery in which Śrī Dharmapāla Virūpa resided, his main practice, and so on—all three agree on a key episode of Virūpa's hagiography: the notorious incident when Virūpa stopped the sun because he did not want to pay his bar tab. In addition, we may add a fourth source: the *Commentary on the Songs of Conduct* composed by Munidatta, which contains a version of Virūpa's song about the barmaid.

The *Chronicle of the Indian Gurus*, the principal hagiography, relates that Śrī Dharmapāla Virūpa was a member of the aristocracy, ordained into the Mūlasarvāstivāda lineage, and later initiated into the Cakrasaṃvara tradition by a preceptor named either Dharmamitra or *Vijayadeva[16] at Nālanda Monastery. Upon the passing of his preceptor, Śrī Dharmapāla Virūpa replaced him as Nālanda's grand preceptor. Amezhab notes that he was born one thousand twenty years after the parinirvāṇa of the Buddha. Abhayadatta's account gives Śrī Dharmapāla Virūpa's birthplace as the Tripura region[17] of Bengal during the early ninth-century reign of Devapāla and maintains that he was a monk at the Somapūri Vihara,[18] adding that he practiced Vajravārāhī for a period of twelve years, accumulating one billion mantras.

Ngawang Chödrak (1572–1641)[19] reports that the Zhije lineage maintains that Śrī Dharmapāla Virūpa was a direct disciple of Ācārya Āryadeva[20] and composed a commentary on Āryadeva's *Four Hundred Verses*, which links Śrī Dharmapāla Virūpa to the famed sixth-century Yogācāra master, Śrī Dharmapāla. While Śrī Dharmapāla's commentary on the *Four Hundred Verses* was never translated into Tibetan, his commentary is mentioned by Avalokitavrata.[21]

Ngawang Chödrak further reports that Śrī Dharmapāla Virūpa was Śāntarakṣita's teacher, according to the lineage lists given for the *Dhāraṇī of the Ten Stages* and the *Noble Dhāraṇī of the Mother of Planets*. The latter is a special Khön family lineage that begins with Śrī Dharmapāla Virūpa,[22] passes to Śāntarakṣita, then to Khön Nagendrarakṣita (kLu'i dbang po srung), and so on. Finally, Ngawang Chödrak states that King Trison Detsan invited Śrī Dharmapāla Virūpa to Tibet toward the end of his incredibly long life span.[23]

The second principal lineage, the Ḍombhi Heruka tradition, concerns the explication of the Hevajra tantras and does not possess a root text. Ḍombhi Heruka was the main disciple of Vīrupa.

The third principal lineage, the Saroruhavajra tradition, begins with Vilasavajrā,[24] an Indian woman identified as an emanation of Nairātmyā by Sachen in the *Chronicle of Ācārya Saroruhavajra*. She was the guru of Anaṅgavajra, and he in turn was the guru of Saroruhavajra, the source of the eponymous *Saroruha Sādhana*.[25] Saroruha, also known as Padmavajra, is the author of several other important works on the Hevajra cycle. The most significant is the *Padminī* commentary[26] on the two-section *Hevajra Tantra*. Kongtrul identifies Saroruhavajra with Padmasambhava.

The fourth principal lineage is the Samayavajra tradition. Samayavajra was a direct disciple of Nairātmyā and the author of the *Jeweled Garland of Yoga*, a commentary on the two-section *Hevajra Tantra*.[27] Samayavajra is also referred to as Kṛṣṇa Jr. (Nag chung), as opposed to the more famous Kṛṣṇācārya (Nag po spyod pa). Samayavajra's Hevajra maṇḍala rite serves as a major source of the empowerment of Hevajra translated here in part 2.

According to the *Catalog of the Hevajra Dharma Cycle*, the lineages of Ḍombhi, Saroruha, and Samayavajra contain a total of thirty-nine discrete texts.[28]

Apart from the Hevajra cycle just mentioned, there is another set of Sakya teachings called the Nine Path Cycles (*lam dgu skor*). Volume 5 of *The Treasury of Precious Instructions* concerns just one of those path cycles: Virūpa's Path with Its Result. The other eight path cycles will be presented in volume 6.

Path with Its Result

The preeminence in Tibet of the Path with Its Result as one of the eight great practice lineages is bound up with the prominence of the Khön clan (*'khon rigs*), one of the ancient clans of pre-Buddhist Tibet that has ruled the Sakya region in western Tsang since the eleventh century.[29] The political, social, and economic prominence of the Khön clan ensured the success of these teachings. We can be certain that they were lent prestige by the spiritual reputation of the five founding Sakya masters and the backing of the Mongolian emperor Kublai Khan. It should be noted that there were five other traditions of the Path with Its Result, descending either directly from Drokmi, or in the case of the Phakmo Dru lineage, from Sachen: the Drom, Zhama, Chegom, Jonang, and Phakdru traditions.[30]

The Path with Its Result is a heterogeneous system largely forged out of the translations of Drokmi, who in the latter part of his life lived in Mugulung in western Tibet, near the location of Sakya Monastery. Drokmi, a prolific translator, spent twelve years studying at Nālanda in India and is responsible, along with his guru, Gayadhara, for translating at least thirty-one texts in the Tibetan Buddhist canon, including the *Hevajra*, *Vajrapañjara*, and *Saṃputa* tantras. In addition, Drokmi translated many more works with other collaborators. It is no exaggeration to state that Drokmi was largely responsible for introducing the Hevajra system to Tibet in the eleventh century.

Drokmi's principal sponsor was Könchok Gyalpo (dKon mchog rgyal po, 1034–1102), a Khön scion and the founder of Sakya Monastery. The Khön, who were staunch Nyingma practitioners since the time of the Tibetan empire, focused mainly on the practices of Śrī Heruka from the *True Accomplishment Sādhana*[31] and Vajrakīlaya. Könchok Gyalpo's elder brother, Sherab Tsultrim, aware of the decline of the Nyingma tradition in western Tsang, encouraged his younger sibling to study with Drokmi. Although Könchok Gyalpo received the Hevajra empowerment and some teachings from Drokmi, he never received *The Vajra Verses*. Drokmi had a policy of never giving the Intimate Instruction teachings to disciples to whom he taught the commentaries, and vice versa. However, Könchok Gyalpo's son, Sachen Kungpa Nyingpo, the third Sakya throne holder, would receive Drokmi's complete teachings through intermediary gurus, and it is Sachen Kungpa Nyingpo's treatment of the Path with Its Result that is presented here.

This volume is divided into three major divisions: part 1, "The Core Collection of the Treatise and Manuals on the Path with Its Result" (*Lam 'bras gzhung khrid gces btsus*); part 2, "The Ripening Empowerment"; and part 3, "The Liberating Instructions." Part 1 focuses on Virūpa's *Vajra Verses*, which was not committed to writing until sometime after Sachen Kungpa Nyingpo began teaching it in 1141. *The Vajra Verses* is not in fact a collection of verses but consists of terse statements that require a commentary to fully understand. The remainder of part 1 contains the core collection (consisting of several short texts that outline *The Vajra Verses* and provide the fundamental framework for all later Path with Its Result literature) and the *Nyakma Commentary*.

Part 2 contains the sādhana, bali offering, maṇḍala rite, and the empowerment manuals necessary for bestowing the Hevajra at the Time of the Path empowerment in the Intimate Instruction lineage of Virūpa. Absent here are the Hevajra at the Time of the Path empowerment and the ḍākinī blessing of Nairātmyā or Vajrayoginī, which in this system are prerequisites for meditating on the paths of the three higher empowerments, according to the manuals presented in part 3. It is important to understand that the Path with Its Result presented here is not the full system. A number of important practices are omitted, such as the blessing for the Profound Path guru yoga, Virūpa's protection practice, and the uncommon bodhisattva vow rite from the Mahāyāna section of the Path with Its Result, which is traditionally bestowed at the commencement of the common Mahāyāna section in the common experiential appearance section in the *Three Appearances* manuals.

Part 3 contains the instructional manuals that follow the outline presented in chapter 5, *How to Give Instructions According to the Treatise: The Instructional Manual of the Path with Its Result, the Precious Oral Instruction*.

Kongtrul's selection of texts avoids the entanglement of the controversial division of the Path with Its Result transmissions into two separate textual lineages: the *Explanation for the Assembly* and the *Explanation for Disciples*. However, chapter 14 in part 3, *The Complete Clarification of the Hidden Meaning*, can be understood to be the basis for the *Explanation for the Assembly*. Chapter 17, *The Manual That Clarifies Symbols and Meanings*, can be understood to be the basis for the *Explanation for Disciples* because it contains teachings and practices on luminosity (*'od gsal*), dream yoga, and illusory body, which are excluded from the *Explanation for the Assembly*.

Acknowledgments

First, I would like to acknowledge my root guru, His Holiness Sakya Trichen Rinpoche, the forty-first Sakya throne holder, from whom I had the good fortune of receiving the teachings and transmissions of the Path with Its

Result. I would also like to recall the memory of the late His Holiness Dagchen Rinpoche, from whom I received the same. I owe a debt of gratitude to Khenpo Migmar Tseten, who guided me through my three-year retreat on the Path with Its Result cycle, has continually tutored me in Tibetan since 1990, and who patiently answered my questions concerning obscure terms in the colloquial language of his native Tsang province, which occasionally make an appearance in these manuals. I would like to express my appreciation to all the translators of Sakya works who have tread before me in this area of study. My work here has been made easier because of their trailblazing efforts. I would like to thank Osa Karen Manell, who worked with me through all phases of this project and whose exacting attention to detail improved the manuscript inestimably. I would also like to thank Anna Wolcott Johnson, our editor at Shambhala, whose advice was invaluable in polishing and preparing the manuscript for print. Finally, I would like to thank Eric Colombel and the staff of Tsadra Foundation for the opportunity to work on these texts that are so essential to the Sakya tradition.

Technical Note

The basic edition followed here is the Shechen edition[1] of the Palpung block prints; the page numbers in brackets reflect the pagination of that edition. However, because of the poor quality of the carving of the Sakya texts in the Palpung block prints, I have principally relied on the versions found in the *Explanation of the Path with Its Result for Disciples*, the *Explanation of the Path with Its Result for the Assembly*, and the *Collected Works of Sakya*. All canonical works are identified throughout with their Tohoku catalog numbers. There are two works that are not found in the Tohoku catalog; they are taken from the Peking Tengyur (Q) and the Narthang Tengyur (N). Titles of identified Sanskrit and Tibetan works that appear in the body of the texts have been translated into English, apart from a few well-known titles—*Hevajra*, *Vajrapañjara*, and so on—that have been left untranslated.

Sanskrit personal names and place-names—as well as the names of Indian Buddhist schools and nonhuman beings, such as yakṣas—have been left in Sanskrit, with translations in parentheses where needed. A few technical terms that do not have uniform or satisfactory English translations have been left in Sanskrit. I have opted to back-translate the anatomical terms *tsa* (*rtsa*), *lung* (*rlung*), *tikle* (*thig le*), and *khorlo* (*'khor lo*) to their corresponding Sanskrit terms *nāḍī*, *vāyu*, *bindu*, and *cakra*.

In all cases Sanskrit words and names have been rendered with full diacritics, with the exception of some words that have entered the English lexicon, such as samsara, nirvana, and so on. The mantras in the empowerment manuals were carefully corrected by Ngorchen Könchok Lhundrub according to the Indian manuscripts at his disposal. I have rendered the mantras as he presents them in the sādhana and empowerment texts. Tibetan personal names and place-names have been phoneticized following Tsadra Foundation's conventions.

The formatting of these translations follows the standard practice of rendering prose as prose and verse as verse. Footnotes represent annotations in the block prints. Endnotes belong to the translator.

PART ONE

The Core Collection of the Treatise and Manuals on the Path with Its Result

1. The Vajra Verses

The Treatise of the Precious Oral Intimate Instruction of the Path with Its Result[1]

Virūpa

The *Vajra Verses* is the fundamental text of the Path with Its Result tradition. Originally an oral tradition, this text was transmitted by the mahāsiddha Virūpa (eighth century) to the lesser of his two main disciples, the siddha Kāṇha.

The Vajra Verses was transmitted through three more Indian masters, Ḍāmarupa, Avadhūtīpa, and Gayadhara, who in turn transmitted them to Drokmi Lotsāwa (992/3–1043/1072?), the principal master who promulgated the Hevajra system in Tibet. After Drokmi, *The Vajra Verses* was transmitted through two more Tibetan masters: Setön Kunrik (Se ston Kun rig, 1029–1116) and Zhangtön Chöbar (Zhang ston Chos 'bar, 1053–1135). In 1141, *The Vajra Verses* was finally committed to writing by Sachen Kungpa Nyingpo (1092–1158), who was also the first person to compose commentaries on it.

Although the title of the text might lead one to believe that the text is composed in metered didactic verse, the text is written in prose throughout, apart from a single citation of the first line of a passage found in *Chanting the True Names of Mañjuśrī*. The content of *The Vajra Verses*, composed of terse statements that are often grammatically incomplete and difficult to understand without a commentary, primarily focuses on completion stage instructions and is notable for its detailed account of the varieties of yogic experiences that arise on the path, both below the path of seeing and on the path of cultivation. This focus on the experiential appearances of the path is directly related to the narrative of Virūpa's frustration with Cakrasaṃvara practice and his eventual encounter with Nairātmyā. Another key feature of *The Vajra Verses* is its presentation of the path in four interwoven themes: the four empowerments, the five paths, the thirteen stages, and the thirty-seven factors conducive to awakening, the last of which grounds the practitioner in the classical scheme of progress common to all Buddhist schools. Additionally, the text is divided according to three overarching themes: the path common to samsara and nirvana, the mundane path, and the transcendent path.

The Vajra Verses is included in all editions of the translated treatises, or Tengyur (*bstan 'gyur*), but lacks both a Sanskrit title and a colophon indicating where and by whom it was translated. The version presented here is found in both the *Treasury of Precious Instructions* (DNZ) and the *Collection of All Tantras* (G). It contains a topical outline whose author is unknown. The root text is also contained in the *Yellow Volume* (P), the volume of the Path with Its Result instructions compiled by Jetsun Drakpa Gyaltsen.[2] In the latter collection, *The Vajra Verses* does not possess the topical outline found here. *The Vajra Verses* has been translated several times.[3]

I. The Homage

I bow to the lotus feet of the sublime guru.

II. The Commitment to Explain

The concise discourse on the path and result shall be written down.

III. The Actual Explanation of the Meaning of the Treatise
A. The Expansive, Medium, and Narrow Explanations
1. The Seven Topics in the Path Common to Samsara and Nirvana
a. The Explanation of the Three Appearances

Impure appearances are for a sentient being in affliction.[4] Experiential appearances are for a practitioner in samādhi. Pure appearances are for a sugata in the ornamental wheel of the inexhaustible body, speech, and mind.

b. The Explanation of the Three Tantras

Because samsara and nirvana are complete in the all-basis, it is the root tantra.

In the body method tantra, and so on, there is the empowerment of the cause with the four threes: the seats, and so on. On the path, the creation stage, and so on, are explained with the four fives. Guard the samayas of equipoise, and so on. Mend violations with the vajra ḍākinī, and so on. One should please them with the five: the objects of desire, and so on. By meditating on the four empowerments in the four sessions of the path, the obscurations of great bliss cease in dependence on the body; since buddhahood manifests, it is the explanatory tantra.

The mahāmudrā result tantra is omniscience through the four empowerments of the result. {3}

c. The Explanation of the Four Authorities

The result is confirmed with the four authorities.

d. The Explanation of the Six Instructions

The poison of concentration is extracted with the trio: the absence of the fault of internal contradiction, and so on. Rely on diet, conduct, vāyu, bindu, and a consort. Since one is never separate from the bliss of the five pure essences and the experience of the five sense organs, rely on the amṛtas. The four nāḍīs of samsara, the cakras, the others, and the three for each stage—from first to last, up to the tenth stage—are released by freeing the knots of the nāḍīs.

The poison of the view is removed by meditating on the concepts of a purified intellect, the path of the elimination of engagement. Rely on amṛtas by not abandoning the five objects with the five consciousnesses. Since from the beginning pure phenomena arise as empty, they are released.

e. The Explanation of the Four Aural Lineages

Explain the four: the aural lineage of Secret Mantra, and so on.

f. The Explanation of the Five Dependent Originations

The limit of entities dependently originates in dependence on the extraordinary body. Other-dependence is dependent origination; it is the path of great awakening. The dependent origination of all phenomena is the authority of origin. The all-basis consciousness is pure great awakening. The path is totally perfected with the five dependent originations.

g. The Explanation of the Different Preventatives

The obstacles of the practitioner who deviates to the side of the method are prevented by stable faith, the protection wheel, mantra recitation, and mantra knots. They are prevented by never being separate from the meaning of the ocean of suchness, because phenomena are appearances of the mind, other-dependent origination, and reflections. {4}

Regarding wisdom, for the external māra, there are the two paths that multiply the views and conclusions into eight. For the inner [māra], there are the ten: the path, and so on. If one does not know the symbols, [obstacles] arrive; if known, [obstacles] are prevented. Prevent contamination, obscuration, and leaking bindu.

2. The Seven Topics in the Mundane Path

a. The Seven Further Topics in the Concise Explanation of the Cause of Samādhi

i. The Explanation of the Cause

After obtaining the four[5] results of disconnecting from the ordinary body, voice, and mind on the path of accumulation . . .

ii. The Explanation of the Remote Cause

The three ways of gathering the elements through the impartialities . . .

iii. The Explanation of the Proximate Cause

And the self-empowerment of vāyu and mind . . .

iv. The Explanation According to the Adjuncts of Awakening

When progressing on the path according to the thirty-seven factors conducive to awakening, the four bases of magic power of undistracted meditation ignite the fire of transcendent gnosis through the male and female karma vāyus and the genderless vāyu. The first gathering of the elements sunders the nāḍī, like the force of the winter wind.[6] The mind is still, there are dreams of horses, pain of nāḍī and vāyu arise, there are various nāḍī knots, and so on. Through the seven differentiations of arresting the ten vāyus, the fundamental vāyus, and so on, the secondary vāyus gradually cease internally and an abundance of bindus spread uniformly, permeating the body.

v. The Concise Explanation of the Samadhi that Arises from That [Path]

Based upon that, the mind abides within, the five consciousness gather within, the five aggregates are tamed, and the movement of gnosis is reversed.

vi. The Summary Explanation

The visions, dreams, and experiences of undistracted meditation, three by three, appear as all three realms, seemingly prior to concepts.

vii. The Explanation of the Three Ways of Path Instruction

When earth dissolves into water, a mirage [appears]; when water dissolves into fire, mist; when fire dissolves into air, fireflies; when air dissolves into consciousness, blazing lamps; and when consciousness dissolves into luminosity, there is an appearance of a cloudless sky. When earth, water, fire, air, and {5} the vāyu-mind gather uniformly, all three realms appear to be on fire. The water vāyu [inflates] the pores and cools the body. The air vāyu causes discursiveness; [dreams] of oneself flying and birds arise. The vāyus of the four elements move evenly, and various goddesses offer dances. The vāyus of the four elements [produce] a diversity of scents and flavors equal with space; all pores and the body are blissful.

There are the five amṛtas, the forms of the tathāgatas, and so on, from olibanum and the sun and camphor and the moon. In the subtle nāḍīs, there are tiny essences and stars. In the bearing nāḍīs, and so on, there are tree trunks. There are the five kinds of attachment and aversion and the nāḍīs of fear, misery, and ghosts. For the nāḍīs of tears, yawns and tears. When the vāyu and mind gather evenly in the syllables of the six realms that first form at the navel, there are experiences such as the movement and speech[7] of the six realms, being led to those, dreams, and appearing in all three realms. The samādhi of the concentrations arises from *oṃ*, and so on. When there is total dissolution into the *a* of the mother's space, the three realms are space. When there is dissolution into the palace of the great mother Prajñāpāramitā, and so on, the dharmakāya is experienced and subject and object are liberated. Clarity and lightness arise from *hūṃ*; self-originated gnosis is the perfectly immaculate space.

In the intermediate gathering of the elements, since the force of the vāyu wanes, the nāḍīs unravel, the bindu is painful, and the visions stabilize.

b. The Extensive Explanation Following the Concise Explanation

In brief, for rakṣa, and so on, there are rākṣasas, and so on. Like a droning sound and the pure divine eye, one thinks that the experiences of samādhi up to the peak of existence arise, endlessly illustrated through explanations—concealed from the fifth and the tenth.

c. The Explanation of the Path Free from Hope and Fear

The outer dependent origination of undistracted meditation is reversing the vāyu, and so on, three by three. The inner five ḍākinīs and five kāyas of the tathāgatas cause the dependent origination of great awakening; it is understood that accomplishments arise from oneself. {6} Since this is understood, thoughts of hope and effort are removed.

Since māras and deviations are understood as one's path and dependent origination, the faults should be taken as qualities. Heat should be naturally sustained because it arises in and out of order.

d. The Explanation of the Four Examinations

Since the devaputra māra, and so on, arrive on the path that deviates to the side of wisdom, prevent this with the four examinations.

e. The Explanation of the Path of the Foundation of Mindfulness

Regarding the four foundations of mindfulness of undistracted meditation, since objects cease, it is thought that one's pledged deity and the vowels are necessary. Since samādhi is uniform, it is the final gathering of the elements. Since one is free of the touch of the vāyu, the nāḍīs break up; the essences gather into the six sense gates and one also properly understands the six close mindfulnesses. One also perceives some nirmāṇakāyas.

f. The Explanation of the Result of That Path

The four correct renunciations of undistracted meditation are the understanding[8] arising after the three empowerments that arise from the nirmāṇakāya. For joy,[9] and so on, seek the nāḍī of a twenty-year-old[10] padminī.[11] Because of the types,[12] such as moving slowly, and so on, the mind enters into the tip of the avadhūti, the *aḥ* of the heart center. Body, voice, and mind adopt the vajra posture. Since the vāyu is controlled by the bindu and one cannot hear the sound of drums, and so on, the māras of contentment, and so on, are destroyed.

The path of the inner buddhas reaches the peak of existence. Patience for the nonarising of phenomena is difficult, but the patience of emptiness is the mind reversing into the central nāḍī. There is patience when the mind shifts. Since the phenomena of samsara are transcended and the path phenomena of nirvana are totally perfected, among all phenomena, [nirvana] is the highest.

g. The Explanation of the Summary of the Path

As such, there are faulty and faultless experiences. Once the vāyu and mind evenly gather above in the outer shape of *a*, the essence, nature, and characteristic arise as the paths.

3. The Transcendent Path

a. The First Conclusion {7}

i. The Explanation of the Demarcation of the Path of Seeing on the First Stage

In the transcendent path . . .

I) The Explanation of the Cause

The path arises as outer and inner dependent origination.

II) The Explanation of the Result

The nirmāṇakāya is naturally accomplished without effort.

III) The Explanation of the Path

Through the path of the creation stage . . .

IV) The Explanation of the Empowerment

One reaches the culmination of the vase empowerment that purifies the body.

V) The Explanation of the Signs

The nondeceptive signs are as follows: The seven limbs of awakening are the four palaces of the precious nāḍīs and the three principal ones. Once the body maṇḍala is seen, conceptuality comes and goes.[13] One can shake one hundred nirmāṇakāya buddhafields and hear [the dharma], make one hundred gifts, radiate one hundred lights, give explanations to one hundred inferiors, and enter into the equipoise of one hundred different samādhis.

If one sees the nāḍīs of the six realms—and, in particular, the one that supports the human realm—there is joy, fearfulness, shame, and disgust. At the moment when samsara and nirvana are inseparable, as the guru already taught at the time of the cause, there is realization, compassion arises, tears fall, one knows the various thoughts of others, and one laughs when various objects of desire are seen. Various magic powers are produced instantly by perceiving the inner buddhafields. Without seeing the inner, the outer will not be seen.

At that moment the liṅga is firm and, likewise, the bindu resides on the stage of the connate [joy] at the tip of the vajra. The body[14] is intoxicated[15] with bliss, and one is rendered unconscious. One does not recognize self and other.

The inner sign is the vāyu stopping at one finger length. The outer sign is the bindu stabilized in half of the secret place.

VI) The Summary

The path of seeing on the first stage.

ii. The Path of Cultivation

I) The Explanation of the Empowerments

Further, the empowerments, four by four, are received from[16] the nirmāṇakāya.

II) The Explanation of the Signs

In the path of cultivation, from the second stage onward, one can shake one thousand nirmāṇakāya buddhafields, and so on; qualities, and so on, increase; and the coming and going of conceptuality, and so on, cease. The inner sign is the vāyu stopping at six finger lengths. The outer sign is the bindu stabilized at the secret place, the navel, and the heart. One sees a saṃbhogakāya.

III) The Summary

The six stages on the path of cultivation. {8}

b. The Second Conclusion

i. The Explanation of the Cause

Further, the empowerments are received four by four from the saṃbhogakāya.

ii. The Explanation of the Path

From the path of self-empowerment . . .

iii. The Explanation of the Result

The saṃbhogakāya is naturally accomplished without effort.

iv. The Explanation of the Empowerment

One reaches the culmination of the secret empowerment that purifies the voice.

v. The Explanation of the Signs

The nondeceptive signs are obtaining mastery over the five faculties and the vāyus of the five pure essences, the five abilities and the gazes becoming unimpeded, seeing the seed syllables of the six realms in the bhaga maṇḍala and obtaining mastery over the six seed syllables, teaching the dharma in the language of sentient beings, and no impediment in the generic and intrinsic characteristics of phenomena. Once the eight outer syllables of the navel and the vowels and consonants are seen, there is no impediment in the twelve branches of the discourses of the dharma of the sutras; one is able to enjoy the five amṛtas and the six tastes. The transformation into the melody of Brahma is elucidated by the six lines "*A* is the supreme of all seed syllables,"[17] and so on. Above the seventh bhūmi, the victors[18] of the four cakras shake one billion saṃbhogakāya buddhafields, and so on.

The inner sign is the vāyu ceasing at ten finger lengths. The outer sign is the bindu stabilized at the throat.

vi. The Summary

The ten stages on the path of cultivation.

c. The Third Conclusion

i. The Explanation of the Cause

Further, the empowerments are received four by four from the dharmakāya.

ii. The Explanation of the Path

From the path of the maṇḍalacakra method that purifies the mind . . .

iii. The Explanation of the Result

The dharmakāya is naturally accomplished without effort.

iv. The Explanation of the Empowerment

One reaches the culmination of the gnosis of the wisdom consort empowerment that purifies the intellect.

v. The Explanation of the Signs

The nondeceptive signs [are as follows]: The five powers move the five vāyus of awakening or[19] the purest of the pure essences, and once the fundamental maṇḍala of bodhicitta is seen, the signs are exhibited. {9} Once the empowerment of the three kāyas and the five gnoses are obtained, when one sees the five amṛtas gather into the locations, one sees the deeds performed by buddhas to benefit others. When one sees the bindus gather into the nirmāṇacakra and the mahāsukhacakra, one sees the buddhas abiding in profundity in the place of Akaniṣṭha. When one sees the five amṛtas and the vāyus gather in the nirmāṇacakra of the navel, [one sees] the five saṃbhogakāyas. After entering the bhaga of the mother, one sees the secret proclaimed to the fortunate bodhisattvas. When one sees the purest pure essence of the mudra, there is no impediment to clairvoyance. When the pure essence is drawn into the nāḍī syllables, there is no impediment to magic power. When shifting to those again, one recalls past existences.

The inner sign is the vāyu ceasing at twelve finger lengths. The outer sign is the bindu stabilized in the whole crown.

vi. The Summary

The twelfth stage of the path of cultivation.

d. The Fourth Conclusion
i. The Brief Explanation
I) The Explanation of the Cause

Furthermore, the empowerments are four by four. The ultimate purification of the ultimate dependent origination is the ultimate path.

II) The Explanation of the Path

Through the path of the vajra waves, there is supreme accomplishment, mahāmudrā. For the person of the knowledge consort, existence is the pure path . . .

III) The Explanation of the Result

The svabhāvakāya is naturally accomplished without effort.

IV) The Explanation of the Empowerment

The fourth is the ultimate empowerment of body, speech, and mind.

V) The Explanation of the Signs

The nondeceptive signs [are as follows]: The eight-limbed path of the āryas is the pure eight consciousnesses, the attainment of the twofold result. This great stage gives joy, delights, and satisfies. That [laughter] shakes the ground in six ways. Sound resounds in the place of māras. The three realms are seen in the mudra's place. The ḍākinīs gather from afar. The eight topics of mastery arise, such as harima, and so on.

The inner sign is the prāṇa and āyāma placed in the avadhūti. The outer sign is the bindu stabilized in half of the uṣṇīṣa. {10}

VI) The Summary

The first half of the thirteenth stage . . .

ii. The Extensive Explanation
I) The Explanation of the Cause

The fourth is the ultimate empowerment of the mind.

II) The Explanation of the Signs

The nondeceptive signs [are as follows]: the single result is attained and the penetrator penetrates the dharmadhātu, the city of youths, with bodhicitta.

III) The Explanation of the Result

The result is the ability to shake all the dharmakāya[20] buddhafields, and so on.

iii) The Very Extensive Explanation

I) The Explanation of the Cause

Upon the attainment of the thirteenth stage, the consorts of the thirteenth stage[21] are summoned with the mind. The master is the concentrated essence of the sugatas of the three times. Through the dependent origination of receiving siddhi in the bhaga from the inseparability of the pledged deity with the guru, existence is the pure path.

II) The Explanation of the Result

The very pure svabhāvakāya is naturally accomplished without effort, the ultimate result.

III) The Explanation of the Signs

The nondeceptive signs [are as follows]: The result is the ability to shake all saṃbhogakāya buddhafields, and so on. The inner sign is the prāṇa and āyāma ceasing in the avadhūti. The outer sign is the bindu stabilized in the whole uṣṇīṣa.

IV) The Explanation of the Result of All Paths

The elimination of the defects and faults of cultivation through the dissolution of the four movements of outer and inner dependent origination is the thirteenth stage. There is omniscience. The thirteenth stage, Vajradhara, appears to be an arrangement of dependent origination. In buddhahood, the retinue attains buddhahood in a single group.

V) The Explanation That Summarizes the Treatise

Secret Mantra Vajrayāna is the empowerments of the cause, path, and result.

Though investigated with concepts,[22] realization lacks concepts; that is the appearance of gnosis.

B. The Profound, Mediocre, and Shallow Explanations

The profound path is the guru, samaya, and the analytical cessation of the body.

C. The Concluding Explanation of the Treatise {11}

The oral instruction and the intimate instructions of the Path with Its Result are complete.
samāptamithi[*]

[*]Here from among the eleven extant commentaries of the great Sakya guru, the principal one is *Nyakma* (*nyags ma*) and the large commentary is *For the Sons* (*S*). There are a great many others, both early and late, such as those authored by Zhankar [unidentified], Martön [dMar ston chos rgyal, thirteenth century], and so on.

2. The Summarized Topics of *The Vajra Verses*[1]

Jetsun Drakpa Gyaltsen

Jetsun Drakpa Gyaltsen (1147–1216) was the fifth throne holder of Sakya. The hagiography of Drakpa Gyaltsen[2] is very sparse because Sakya Paṇḍita (1182–1251) was forbidden to write on it extensively. The main features of Drakpa Gyaltsen's life are that he and his elder brother, Lopön Sönam Tsemo (1142–1182), received the Path with Its Result transmission in 1152 from their father. When Drakpa Gyaltsen was ten in 1157, he taught the Hevajra Tantra at Sakya to a large assembly. Following his elder brother's abdication in 1160, Drakpa Gyalsten was elevated to the throne of Sakya at the age of thirteen. As a lifelong, celibate upāsaka, he resided at Sakya for his entire life, overseeing the religious and mundane affairs of the Sakya complex until his death in 1216.

Drakpa Gyaltsen compiled the *Yellow Volume*, so named because it was wrapped in yellow silk. This text constitutes the most authoritative collection of instructions devoted to the explication of the Path with Its Result tradition, includes *The Nyakma Commentary* authored by Sachen contained in this volume, and supplies the earliest ancillary Sakya writings of the Path with Its Result. Apart from *The Versified Manual on How to Give the Instruction of the Path with Its Result in Accordance with the Text* and the outline composed by Ngorchen Kunga Zangpo, the texts in the core collection compiled by Kongtrul are drawn from the *Yellow Volume*. While this text is the first independent outline of *The Vajra Verses*, it is clearly based on the outline found at the beginning of Sachen Kunga Nyingpo's commentary, *For the Sons* (S).

This text is first presented as a pared-down, Western-style outline and then in full, in the order of the original Tibetan. The latter includes annotations composed by Jetsun Drakpa himself pointing the reader to the corresponding sections of *The Vajra Verses.*

I bow my head to the feet of the sublime guru.

I. The homage to the feet of the sublime guru and the commitment to explain the Path with Its Result
II. The text
  A. The explanation of the extensive, medium, and concise paths
    1. The extensive path
      a. The explanation of the path common to samsara and nirvana
        i. The path explained in the three appearances
        ii. The path explained in the three tantras
        iii. The path explained in the four authorities
        iv. The path explained in the six instructions
        v. The path explained in the four aural lineages
        vi. The path explained in the five dependent originations
        vii. The explanation of the different preventatives on the path of the practitioner who veers into method or wisdom
      b. The explanation of the path of the mundane dance upon the wheel
        i. The concise explanation of samādhi's cause of arising
        ii. The extensive explanation that follows the concise explanation {12}
        iii. The explanation of the path free from hope and fear
        iv. The explanation of the four examinations
        v. The explanation of the foundations of mindfulness
        vi. The explanation of the result of the foundation of mindfulness
        vii. The summary explanation
      c. The explanation of the path that transcends the mundane spinning of the wheel
        i. The explanation of the cause
        ii. The explanation of the signs
        iii. The explanation of the result
        iv. The summary

    2. The explanation of the medium path
    3. The explanation of the concise path
B. The explanation of the profound, mediocre, and average paths
    1. The profound path is the path of the guru
    2. The mediocre path is the path of samaya
    3. The average path is the dependent origination of the analytical cessation of the body

---

I bow my head to the feet of the sublime guru.

There are two topics in *The Vajra Verses*: the homage to the feet of the sublime guru and the commitment to explain the Path with Its Result and the text. In the latter, there is the explanation of the extensive, medium, and concise paths and the explanation of the profound, mediocre, and average paths.

[In the first,] there is the explanation of the extensive path,* the explanation of the medium path,† and the explanation of the concise path.‡

[In the first of those,] there are three topics: the explanation of the path common to samsara and nirvana, the explanation of the path of the mundane dance upon the wheel, and the explanation of the path that transcends the mundane spinning of the wheel.

[In the first of those three,] the path common to samsara and nirvana, there are seven sections: the path explained in the three appearances,§ the path explained in the three tantras,¶ the path explained in the four authorities,** the path explained in the six instructions,†† the path explained in the four aural lineages,‡‡ the path explained in the five dependent originations,§§

*The four stages of the root text.
†Five topics, such as the cause of samādhi, and so on.
‡Included within essence, nature, and characteristic.
§Sentient being . . .
¶The all-basis cause tantra . . .
**The result is confirmed with the four authorities . . .
††The absence of the fault of internal contradiction . . .
‡‡The aural lineage of Secret Mantra . . .
§§In dependence on the extraordinary body . . .

and the explanation of the different preventatives on the path of the practitioner who veers into method or wisdom.*

In [the second of the previous three,] the dance upon the wheel, there are seven sections: the concise explanation of samādhi's cause of arising,† the extensive explanation that follows the concise explanation,‡{12} the explanation of the path free from hope and fear,§ the explanation of the four examinations,¶ the explanation of the foundations of mindfulness,** the explanation of the result of the foundation of mindfulness,†† and the summary explanation.‡‡

In [the third of the previous three, transcending] the spinning of the wheel, there are four topics: the explanation of the cause,§§ the explanation of the signs, the explanation of the result, and the summary.

Thus, the extensive path is included within eighteen dharmas. The five topics for the medium path and the three topics for the concise path will not be written here.

[In the second of the two topics within the text,] the profound, mediocre, and average paths, the profound path is the path of the guru,¶¶ the mediocre path is the path of samaya, and the average path is the dependent origination of the analytical cessation of the body.

samāptamithi[3]

*Veering to the side of method . . .

†On the path of accumulation . . .

‡In brief, for the rakṣa . . .

§Undistracted meditation . . .

¶Wisdom . . .

**Undistracted meditation . . .

††The correct renunciations of undistracted meditation . . .

‡‡As such . . . arising on the path . . .

§§To be applied in order to the root text.

¶¶The result accomplished by that path is "The thirteenth-stage, Vajradhara, appears to be an arrangement of dependent origination" and "omniscience," and so on.

3. The Verse Summary of the Topics of the Commentary of the Precious Oral Intimate Instruction[1]

Sachen Kunga Nyingpo

The Verse Summary of the Topics of the Commentary of the Precious Oral Intimate Instruction is the first of the eleven commentaries[2] on *The Vajra Verses* written by Sachen Kunga Nyingpo (Kun dga' snying po, 1092–1158) between 1141 and 1158. *The Verse Summary* was clearly written down prior to *The Vajra Verses*, as indicated in the conclusion of the text.

The Verse Summary is generally known by its nickname, *Asengma*, because it was written for Aseng Dorje Tenpa (c. twelfth century), who was among the teachers of Phakmo Drupa (1110–1170) and Dusum Khyenpa (1110–1193).

This translation was prepared on the basis of the commentary written by Gorampa Sönam Senge (1429–1489). The outline to the text is a later addition, which does not appear in the *Yellow Volume*.

I. The Introductory Topic

The introductory topic is the praise *namo guru virṇani*.[3]

II. The Commitment

Freed from the darkness of the mind that perceives a self,
my mind has become slightly illumined

from the beams of the rising moon that free one from darkness,
the speech of the sublime, precious venerable one.

Having purified the continuum by listening to the sublime, supreme friend,
having donned the armor of accomplishment for the purpose of
awakening,
with the commitment of having received the oral transmission in the
presence of the sublime one,
supreme human, your command is weighty.

The speech of the omniscient is like the ocean:
deep, difficult to fathom, and endless.
Vajrayāna is taught with many intentions,[4]
impressed with the seal of vajra words.

The doctrine will be realized by followers
who depend upon the oral instructions[5] of siddhas,
such as Nāgārjuna who was predicted, and so on,
and Virūpa who was empowered by the ḍākinī, and so on. {13}

In your mind, you primarily hold the oral instructions of the path
of Virūpa, and so on.
Nevertheless, because of your unimpeded kindness,
I shall set down in writing what arises from my mind.

III. The Topic of the Text
A. The Five Paths Common to Samsara and Nirvana

The foundation of the path is prepared with the three appearances,
all experiences are understood with the three tantras,
doubts are eliminated with the four authorities and the four aural lineages,
and the stages of the path are demarcated with the five dependent
originations.

B. The Explanation of the Mundane Path

Be free of doubt and denial by making distinctions
through the three modes of gathering and the seven impartialities.

The proximate cause of samādhi will be realized
through realizing the three modes of holding the mind stable.

It is said that one can know any samādhi
through the arising of experiences in one's pure body.
[Heat] is naturally sustained
through the arising of heat, gradually or not.

Realize the different experiences of samādhi
through the three modes of giving instructions like a caravan leader.
Eliminate doubts about the demarcations of the path
through applying the three examples to the three gatherings.

Be free of hope and fear concerning other causes and conditions
through the three dependent originations that assemble in oneself.

C. The Thirty Protections Arising from the Removal of Obstacles

The practitioner who unifies method and wisdom
can have obstacles with the two, but none for one.

The protections are eight, eight, and sixteen.
There are eight for method, faith, and so on.
Wisdom is protected by the four kinds of examination.
The inner māra is repelled by the symbols of the four empowerments.

There are fourteen protections common to both.
One should understand how to remove the obstacles
to embarking upon the path, abiding on it,
slight stability in holding the mind, and increasing that stability.

D. The Seventy Intimate Instructions

Releasing nāḍī pain is crucial.
Reward vāyu pain and avert it.
It is said there are three [remedies] for immobile vāyu: {14}
releasing, empowering, and meditating on bliss.

E. The Six Oral Instructions

Use amṛta for the poison that arises in view and meditation.
One should know the six intimate instructions for releasing pain.

F. Removing Obstacles of the Four Cakras

Bliss and emptiness become supreme with the three aspects:
the blazing, movement, and stability of the bindu.

When it blazes, bindu pain arises.
Reverse it by holding, and stabilize it
with the four animal movements.
This renders the bindu motionless in the body.

In order to spread [the bindu] everywhere and stabilize it,
shake the body and spin the wheel,
throw lassos of wind with the four limbs,
and behave like a small child.

G. Summarizing and Explaining the Practice

The text of glorious Śrī Virūpa
summarizes the path of the four empowerments into eight: the [four] views and the [four] conclusions.
One must take faults as qualities
and take obstacles as siddhis.

H. Summarizing and Explaining the Removal of Obstacles[6]

If one knows any of the experiential appearances,
the māras and deviations self-liberate.

I. The Instruction for Following[7] the Intimate Instructions

Without doubt, if great effort is made,
supreme person, you will follow the conclusion.

IV. The Concluding Topics, the Reason for Brevity

Having dwelled in the collection of views of self,
I have also been lazy with respect to practice.
Also, venerable Virūpa's text
has not been set down in writing.
If it were set down, it would transgress the sublime one's command
and it would also break the command of the friend.
Witnessed by the ḍākinīs, I request their forbearance.

This summary of topics was composed by the venerable great lord of yogis, the great and glorious Sakyapa at the request of the bodhisattva bhikṣu of Dome,[8] Aseng.[9]
samāptamithi[*] {15}

[*]There are many earlier and later commentaries, such as those by Trulungpa Kunmön [Kun dga' smon lam, ca. thirteenth century] and Omniscient Sönam Senge [bSod nams seng ge, 1429–1489].

4. The Root Verses of the Illuminating Jewel

The View of the Inseparability of Samsara and Nirvana[1]

Jetsun Drakpa Gyaltsen

Drakpa Gyaltsen (1172–1216) composed *The View of the Inseparability of Samsara and Nirvana*, the seminal text that formulates the general view of the Sakya school and the specific Sakya approach to the Path with Its Result. This text also has a detailed autocommentary[2] that is the basis for the explication of the all-basis cause tantra in all later three tantras literature.

The view of the inseparability of samsara and nirvana is not an analytical view derived from hearing and reflection. It is an experiential view that is meditated on based on having received Vajrayāna empowerment.

The View of the Inseparability of Samsara and Nirvana summarizes three approaches to the inseparability of samsara and nirvana of the all-basis cause tantra via the twenty-seven connate dharmas, the three key points of practice, and the three tantras. The inseparability of samsara and nirvana of the path method tantra is outlined with respect to the ripening empowerment and the liberating path—the creation and completion stages. The inseparability of samsara and nirvana of the result tantra reconciles the contradiction between effortless accomplishment (*lhun grub*) and transformability (*gnas 'gyur*). This point of the noncontradiction of effortless accomplishment and transformability justifies the Sakya assertion that the all-basis cause tantra, the path method tantra, and the result tantra are inseparable. Indeed, for orthodox Sakyapas, the inseparability of the basis, path, and result is the very feature of Vajrayāna that distinguishes it from the Pāramitāyāna.

Homage to the excellent guru.[3]

Having first prostrated to the feet of the guru,
in the second line, I bow to Vajradhara.
Prostrating to the feet of the lord of yogis,
please protect me with compassion. (1)

Someone who realizes this well becomes a supreme buddha,
equal with the mind of Vajradhara.
With love for others, I shall write
the concise topics of the words of the inseparability of samsara and nirvana. (2)

From the nature—clarity, emptiness, and their unification—
there are coarse afflictions, vāyus, syllables, nāḍis, elements,
illnesses, and malevolent beings, three by three:
the innate twenty-seven causes. (3)

As such, if effortless accomplishment is thoroughly comprehended,
one will understand the characteristics of the causes and results of samara and nirvana.
Also, having thoroughly comprehended the outer and inner dependent originations,
one is able to destroy all illnesses and malevolent beings. (4)

Having been ripened, in the path of practice,
there are three natures for the trio of creation, completion, and gnosis.
When those are each divided in three,
they are the [three] innate [dharmas] of the path. (5)

Clarity is the nirmāṇakāya, emptiness is the dharmakāya,
and union is the saṃbhogakāya.
Also, each of those has three aspects. Considered in terms of
effortless accomplishment and transformability, they are the [three] connate [dharmas] of the result. (6)

The three key points of practice—
mind, illusion, and absence of inherent existence—

have thirty-two or thirty-seven examples.
For all, there is the preparation, main subject, and conclusion. (7)

For the key point of mind, there is sleep, substances, illness, and spirit deceptions,
optical illusions, ophthalmia, fire wheels, and rapid spinning.
The second key point is illusion, mirages, the moon in the water, lightning,
Harikela, a fairy castle, clouds, and rainbows. (8)

In the third key point, first there is dependent origination:
instruction, lamp, mirror, seal,
fire crystal, seed, sour, and echo.
Second is the explanation of inexpressibility: (9) {16}

the laughter of a child, the dream of a mute,
scratching a point, orgasm,
the wisdom of the third, intercourse,
the surge of enjoyment, and the maṇḍalacakra. (10)

The extensive explanation: in the beginning, there is the nature of the all-basis,
the manner of the support and the supported, the cause, the root,
how they are related, and the way samsara and nirvana are complete within the body and mind
through considering the three appearances. (11)

For the method: ripening, path, and experiences.
First, the maṇḍala empowerment, the substance empowerment, and so on,
and also the inseparability of samsara and nirvana in each of the three seats
should be received from one's glorious Guru. (12)

For the creation stage: the preliminaries, the support, the procedure of creation,
the color, hand implements, positions, with the branches,
and also each one's nature of inseparability of samsara and nirvana
should be explained with perfect loving intent. (13)

For the completion stage: since the result (the gnoses and buddhas) is perfectly complete
in samsara (body, speech, and mind),
mutually seal and realize cause and result,
and introduce the example gnosis. (14)

Creation and completion are considered to have six shared features.
If one wishes realization to increase more and more,
commitments, symbols, and so on should be perfectly applied.
One should investigate with a stainless mind. (15)

Incorrect views are abandoned on the basis of the experiences of samsara.
The sole vehicle is accomplished through the experiences of the path.
There will be supreme joy through the experiences of the result.
All dharmas are confirmed with the four authorities. (16)

When the natural cause is considered, it is effortlessly accomplished.
The limitless qualities are transformable.
Therefore, effortless accomplishment and transformability are noncontradictory.
This is the inseparability of samsara and nirvana of the result. (17)

By that limitless, untainted merit
from having summarized the view of the inseparability of samsara and nirvana
first demonstrated by the sublime Guru—
may all migrating beings obtain Śrī Heruka. (18)

When heard, attractive like the melody of the gods. {17}
When reflected upon, satisfying like the taste of amṛta.
When meditated, like immortality when taking elixir.
These three examples are given to you.

In glorious Sakya, the source of qualities,
on the fifteenth day of Mṛgaśirā in the Fire Tiger year (1206),
the vajra holder Drakpa Gyaltsen composed
The Illuminating Jewel, the essence of all tantras. (20)

The verse treatise in twenty stanzas, *The Illuminating Jewel: The View That Is the Essence of All the Tantras, the Inseparability of Samsara and Nirvana*, was composed by the Śākya upāsaka, the vajra holder Drakpa Gyaltsen.
ithi

5. How to Give Instructions According to the Treatise

The Instructional Manual of the Path with Its Result, the Precious Oral Instruction[1]

Jetsun Drakpa Gyaltsen

The *Vajra Verses* and its direct commentaries focus principally upon the uncommon experiential appearances of the Vajrayāna path but do not include detailed presentations of the impure appearances and the common experiential appearances. *How to Give Instructions According to the Treatise: The Instructional Manual of the Path with Its Result, the Precious Oral Instruction* remedies this absence by presenting a detailed overview of 1) impure appearances, which include the sufferings of samsara, precious human birth, death, impermanence, and karma; and 2) the common experiential appearances, which include relative bodhicitta and ultimate bodhicitta. The pure appearances of the sugatas are only cursorily explained.

How to Give Instructions According to the Treatise, also known as the *Jochakma* (*Jo lcag ma*), is taken from a collection in the *Yellow Volume* called *The Four Great Trees of the Treatise*. The other three texts within that collection are the *Instruction with the Six Key Points of the Intimate Instructions*, the *Instruction with the Eleven Key Points for the Diligent*, and the *Instruction for People of the Three Capacities: Best, Medium, and Average*. These latter three texts are the basis of Sönam Gyaltsen's *The Threefold Instruction*, the text in chapter 15.

How to Give Instructions According to the Treatise is the fundamental text for the signature literature of the Sakya tradition: *The Three Appearances* and *The Three Tantras*. The first commentaries to treat these two texts separately are Ngorchen Könchok Lhundrub's *The Beautiful Ornament of the Three Appearances*[2] (1543) and *The Beautiful Ornament of the Three Tantras*[3] (1552).

These latter two manuals form the basis of the contemporary presentation of the Path with Its Result and are its most important and widely used texts.

I prostrate to the feet of the compassionate venerable gurus and go for refuge.

Devoted disciples, listen to what the guru says. If one wishes to give instruction that is in accordance with the extensive manual of the treatise of the Path with Its Result, to begin, give instruction with the three appearances. Next, since all texts are included in the three tantras, give instruction with the three tantras.

I. Instruction with the Three Appearances

Now then, to give instruction with the three appearances, give instruction through impure appearance, experiential appearance, and pure appearance.

A. Impure Appearance

The three topics in impure appearance [are as follows]: With "a sentient being,"[4] since one examines the realm of sentient beings, one understands and meditates on the faults of samsara. With "in affliction,"[5] since the lower realms are generated by afflictions, meditate on the difficulty of attaining the freedoms and endowments occurring in those lower realms. With "impure appearance," since this arises from deluded appearance and karma, meditate with conviction in the causes and results of karma.

1. The Faults of Samsara

The three sections in the first topic are meditating on the suffering of suffering, the suffering of change, and the suffering of formations in samsara.

a. The Suffering of Suffering

First, one should contemplate the suffering of the three lower realms. With respect to hell beings, reflect on the suffering of the eight cold hells,

{18} the eight hot hells, the temporary hells, and the proximate hells. One should meditate for as many days as it takes to understand, "Birth in them is unavoidable."[6] Apply this to pretas and animals.[7]

b. The Suffering of Change

Next, reflect on the suffering of change: (1) the general suffering of change, and (2) the specific suffering of change.

i. The General Suffering of Change

The first is the absence of benefit in birth as Indra, the lord of the gods, since it is possible that even he can be born again as a hell being. There is also no benefit in being born a universal emperor, since even he can be born a pauper. There is also no benefit in being born as the sun and moon, since even those enter into darkness. There is no benefit to obtaining any of those births. Thus, reflect on the suffering of recurring change.

ii. The Specific Suffering of Change

When thoroughly examining a specific person, the wealthy become impoverished, the mighty become low, and so on. When one looks at local people, relatives, and the people of the nation, nothing remains as it was before. Meditate repeatedly until certainty in the suffering of change arises.

c. The Suffering of Formations in Samsara

Next, the reflection on the suffering of formations is as follows: There is no end to activities, because there is no end to preparations while we are aging and dying. Since life is passing by, there is no end to activities.

Those topics are "for a sentient being." If one reflects on and decides that wherever a sentient being is born there is no happiness, whatever one does becomes the dharma.

2. The Freedoms and Endowments

Next, meditate on the difficulty of attaining freedoms and endowments. The three sections are as follows: (1) the difficulty of attaining freedom and endowments, (2) the great benefit of attaining freedom and endowments, and (3) the fleeting duration of the attainment of freedom.

a. The Difficulty of Attaining Freedom and Endowments

The reflection on the difficulty of attaining freedom and endowments is reflecting on the difficulty for the inconceivable number of sentient beings who do not attain such a body of freedom and endowment, the inconceivable number of sentient beings who attain a body in the six realms, and those who do attain a human body.

b. The Great Benefit of Attaining Freedom and Endowments

This has three sections: {19} (1) reflecting on the very great benefit of this body of freedom and endowment that is able to attain higher realms in this and future lives, (2) accomplishing the nirvana of lower vehicles, and (3) accomplishing omniscient buddhahood in this life.

c. The Fleeting Duration of the Attainment of Freedom

This has three sections: (1) reflecting on the certainty of death, (2) reflecting on the uncertainty of the time of death, and (3) reflecting that at the time of death nothing else is of any benefit.

i. The Certainty of Death

This has three sections: (1) death due to disturbances in the inner and outer elements; (2) death due to disturbances by misleading obstructors; and (3) death due to disturbances by other malevolent beings, such as the male gods,[8] and so on.

ii. The Uncertainty of the Time of Death

This has three sections: (1) there is no certainty about longevity, (2) there are many negative conditions, and (3) positive conditions are rare.

iii. At the Time of Death Nothing Else Is of Any Benefit

This has three sections: apart from sudden conditions, when the time of certain death arrives, (1) it cannot be averted by substances, (2) it cannot be averted by mantras, and (3) it cannot be averted by dependent origination.

3. The Conviction in the Cause and Result of Karma

This has three sections: (1) unvirtuous karma, (2) virtuous karma, and (3) neutral karma.

a. Unvirtuous Karma

This has three sections: (1) reflecting on unvirtuous karma, (2) reflecting on the result of karma, and (3) reflecting on avoiding that result.

i. Reflecting on Unvirtuous Karma

Reflecting in great detail on the ten nonvirtues.

ii. Reflecting on the Result of Karma

Reflect on the result of unvirtuous karma; that is, reflect on the certainty that the three lower realms and all negative conditions in the higher realms arise from nonvirtue.

iii. Reflecting on Avoiding the Result of Karma

Reflect on avoiding that result; that is, reflect on the thought, "Therefore, I will not engage in nonvirtue."

b. Virtuous Karma

The three sections in virtuous karma are (1) reflecting[9] on virtuous karma, (2) reflecting on the result of virtuous karma, and (3) accomplishing virtuous karma.

i. Reflecting on Virtuous Karma

One must thoroughly reflect upon the ten virtues and the ten perfections.

ii. Reflecting on the Result of Virtuous Karma

The three higher realms and all abundance in the three higher realms arise from virtue; {20} that is, reflect on "enjoyments are accomplishment through generosity," and so on.

iii. Accomplishing Virtuous Karma

Reflect on accomplishing that virtue; that is, reflect on the thought, "Because such qualities exist, I should accomplish whatever virtue I can."

c. Neutral Karma

This has three sections: (1) reflecting on neutral karma, (2) reflecting on the result of neutral karma, and (3) reflecting on the accomplishment of neutral karma.

i. Reflecting on Neutral Karma

Neutral karma is eating, wearing clothes, sleeping, and so on, which are not connected with either unvirtuous or virtuous karma.

ii. Reflecting on the Result of Neutral Karma

Reflect on the result of [neutral karma]; that is, no result of any kind arises from that.

iii. Reflecting on the Accomplishment of Neutral Karma

Transform neutral karma into virtuous karma; that is, having generated bodhicitta beforehand, everything, such as eating and sleeping, is transformed into virtuous karma. As such, having carefully reflected upon those topics, one should have a thorough conviction in them.

B. Experiential Appearance

The second general topic is meditating on experiential appearance. That has two sections: "For a practitioner" is (1) the common practitioner, who meditates until the common appearances of experience arise in their continuum repeatedly, and (2) the uncommon practitioner, who meditates until there is repeated certainty in the experience that has arisen.

1. The Common Practitioner

This has three sections: (1) cultivating love, (2) cultivating compassion, and (3) cultivating bodhicitta.

a. Cultivating Love

This has three sections: (1) cultivating love for relatives, (2) cultivating love for enemies,[10] and (3) cultivating love for all sentient beings.

i. Cultivating Love for Relatives

Cultivate love for one's mother. Then, add one's relatives, and finally, add neutral beings. The way one cultivates those is to reflect on the thought, "Since my mother is very kind, may she be happy and possess the causes of happiness."

ii. Cultivating Love for Enemies

In the same way, there is not even a single relative who has not been one's mother.

iii. Cultivating Love for All Sentient Beings

Since there is not even one enemy or neutral being who has not been one's mother, reflect on the thought, "All sentient beings are my mother."

b. Cultivating Compassion

This has three sections: {21} (1) compassion with reference to sentient beings, (2) compassion with reference to phenomena, and (3) nonreferential compassion.

i. Compassion with Reference to Sentient Beings

Compassion with reference to sentient beings is the thought, "May the object, sentient beings who are tormented by suffering, be free from suffering and the causes of suffering."

ii. Compassion with Reference to Phenomena

Compassion with reference to phenomena is the wish, "Since the cause of suffering arises from ignorance, may all sentient beings be free from ignorance."

iii. Nonreferential Compassion

Even though no sentient being is truly established by nature, meditate upon nonreferential compassion toward all sentient beings and their grasping.

c. Cultivating Bodhicitta

This has three sections: (1) aspirational bodhicitta, (2) engaged bodhicitta, and (3) ultimate bodhicitta.

i. Aspirational Bodhicitta

This has three sections: reflecting on the thought (1) that one will attain the stage of perfect buddhahood for the benefit of all sentient beings, (2) that one will place all sentient beings on the stage of nirvana via the three vehicles, and (3) that one will gradually train those of the three kinds of dispositions and place all sentient beings equal with space on the stage of the buddhas.

ii. Engaged Bodhicitta

This has three sections: (1) cultivating the equality of self and others, (2) cultivating the exchange of oneself for others, and (3) training in those conducts.

A) Equality of Self and Others

Reflect upon the thought, "Just as I wish to abandon suffering, other sentient beings also wish to abandon suffering. Just as I wish to accomplish happiness, sentient beings should also be established in happiness."

B) Exchange of Oneself for Others

The cultivation of the exchange [of oneself for others] is reflecting on the thought, "May all the karma and nonvirtue of all sentient beings ripen upon me. Since my bodies, enjoyments, and virtue are offered to all sentient beings,[11] may all sentient beings equal with space be happy."

C) Train in Those Conducts

Therefore, having wished that all one's bodies, enjoyments, and happiness be offered to sentient beings and having accomplished whatever one can, {22} train in all bodhisattva practices.

2. The Uncommon Practitioner

The cultivation of certainty in the arising of the uncommon experiential appearances is the arising of inconceivable experiential appearances upon entering the profound Vajrayāna path. While there is no cause for rejoicing in conducive factors, despite the many inconducive factors that arise, there is also no cause for regret, because under the power of the mind various experiences will arise in dependence on one's nāḍīs, nāḍī syllables, amṛta elements, and essential gnosis vāyus. As such, the experiences are inconceivable, but when summarized they are fifteen: three paths, three heats, three dependent originations, three experiences, and three samādhis. However, the statement "These fifteen can be included in samādhi alone" is meant to be the seven proliferations concerning experience prior to the arising of experience. When experience has arisen once, identifying this experience as physical and that experience as mental should be sustained naturally.

C. Pure Appearance

The cultivation of pure appearance is meditating on the inconceivable qualities of the buddhas, such as recalling the ornamental wheel of the inexhaustible body, and so on, while meditating with special enthusiasm, "By all means,[12] this must be achieved at once!"

The explanation of the section on the three appearances is complete. Following that, give instruction with the three tantras.

II. Instruction with the Three Tantras

The three topics in the three tantras are (1) the characteristic of the cause, the composition of samsara; (2) the path, the method of meditating; and (3) the result, the stage of buddhahood.

A. The Cause

The first topic will not be discussed here, because it has already been discussed in the explanation of the impure appearances.

B. The Path

The three topics in the path are (1) the basis, abiding in samaya; {23} (2) the means of instructing a person; and (3) recognizing samādhi and presenting the divisions of the path for generating special certainty.

1. The Basis

Since samaya is the basis of all paths and the main path of the mediocre person, the twenty samayas must be maintained. Abiding in the empowerments and samaya are the basis of all paths. All people can be instructed by abiding in samaya.

2. The Means of Instructing a Person

The three topics in the means of instruction are (1) meditating on the inseparability of samsara and nirvana, the all-basis cause tantra, in order to eliminate proliferation with the view; (2) meditating on the body method tantra in order to generate the experiences of the path; (3) and meditating on the way the five kāyas of the result are realized.

a. The Inseparability of Samsara and Nirvana

The three sections in the first topic are (1) the brief explanation of the view of the inseparability of samsara and nirvana through the three connate dharmas, (2) the extensive explanation through the three dharmas of practice, and (3) the very extensive explanation through the three tantras.

i. The Brief Explanation

When disciples are given instruction, they must engage in supplicating the guru with strong devotion for several days. Then, when the introduction is given, all phenomena are included in mind. Generate certainty that there is no phenomenon that is not included in the mind and identify clarity at the outset. Then identify emptiness. That being so, meditate until certainty arises in the Buddha's introduction of both clarity and emptiness as inseparable, so-called union. Once that certainty arises, the explanation of the twenty-four connate dharmas eliminates proliferation. Thus, begin the meditation to repeatedly sever proliferation.

ii. The Extensive Explanation

Next, establish all phenomena as mind through the eight examples that establish all phenomena as mind, and begin the meditation to repeatedly arouse certainty that all phenomena are mind. Those meditations will sever the proliferation of the mind, since there is no creative agent—chance, Īśvara, molecules, and so on—apart from the mind. {24}

Then, begin the meditation to repeatedly arouse certainty that all phenomena are illusory through the eight examples that establish all phenomena as illusory. That absence of identity in the mind severs the proliferation about a so-called mind, because various results arise based on various causes and conditions through the power of the various transformations of the mind itself.

There are two sections in establishing that illusions lack intrinsic nature: establishing illusions as dependently originated and establishing illusions as inexpressible. Begin the meditation to repeatedly arouse certainty in dependent origination through the eight examples. Though a so-called illusion is not established by nature, since a cause will not become a result, nor will a result arise without depending on a cause, it is necessary to establish both the absence of going and coming and the absence of arising and ceasing.

Next, begin the meditation to repeatedly arouse certainty in inexpressibility through the eight examples that establish inexpressibility. Further, the experience of inexpressibility cannot be expressed through an affirmation or a denial that "It is like this." When the four primary examples for the repeated arousal of the experience that is free from clinging to inexpressibility are compiled, four dharmas at a time are confirmed on the basis of each individual example. When the primary example is extracted, certainty arises on the basis of confirming all phenomena.

iii. The Very Extensive Explanation

The three topics in the very extensive explanation through the three tantras are (1) the all-basis cause tantra, (2) the path method tantra, and (3) the result tantra.

A) The All-Basis Cause Tantra

One should meditate to generate certainty in the way samsara and nirvana are complete in the all-basis cause tantra through the seven topics.[13]

B) The Path Method Tantra

The three in the path method tantra are (1) generating certainty in the empowerment, (2) generating certainty in the path, and (3) generating certainty in experience.

1) Generating Certainty in the Empowerment

The three certainties generated in the empowerment are (1) the merger of samsara and nirvana in the maṇḍala, (2) the merger of samsara and nirvana in the empowerment, and (3) meditating on the merger of samsara and nirvana in the gnosis of the empowerment. {25}

2) Generating Certainty in the Path

The merger of samsara and nirvana in the path is generating certainty in the merger of samsara and nirvana in each path of the four empowerments.

3) Generating Certainty in Experience

The merger of samsara and nirvana in experience is meditating with special certainty on the cause and result of karma in dependence on the experiential appearance of impurity, accomplishing all paths as one vehicle in dependence on the experiential appearance of the path, and generating devotion in the stage of resultant buddhahood in dependence on the experiential appearance of the result.

Then, one should meditate with certainty on the inseparability of samsara and nirvana of the result through the absence of contradiction between effortless accomplishment and transformation. When one has aroused certainty in those topics, it is said one has reached the culmination of the view of hearing and reflection and a slight gnosis arises produced by meditation. This concludes the explanation of the instruction of the all-basis cause tantra.

b. The Body Method Tantra

Meditate on the body method tantra in order to generate certainty in the path. Then, prior to engaging in the practice, receive the empowerment for the time of the path from the guru and restore samaya. If the guru is not present, then one should draw the accomplishment maṇḍala and perform an extensive self-admittance. When one has avoided inconducive conditions and arranged conducive ones, then enter into the practice. Further, one should engage in the approach recitation of the creation stage with four hundred thousand repetitions of the mantra. One should also perform ten percent of those repetitions during the fire puja. Then, one should concentrate the mind, relying on the creation stage. Meditate on the deity's central eye and concentrate the mind. If the deity's central eye is clear, recognize it is clear and stop. If it is not clear, recognize it is not clear and stop, thus training on the path. Maintain the essence of the view that arises from within. If one wishes for the appearances to manifest as the maṇḍala, maintain this until appearances manifest as the maṇḍala.

Next, if one can, receive empowerment from the guru, and if one cannot, admit oneself into the maṇḍala. If one cannot do that, gather the accumulation of positive conditions and purify the obscuration of negative conditions in dependence on maṇḍala offerings, the one-hundred-syllable mantra, and so on. One should train the body again and again with either the extensive or concise training of the body. The measure of such training is that activities will not be difficult, there will be no illness, and the body will be comfortable and light. For some people, it is possible that samādhi will naturally arise at that time. {26} Whichever one performs, if one trains the body for a long while, then samādhi will arise for a long while and obstacles to samādhi will not arise.

Next, meditate on the seven vāyu yogas. Add the eighteen unification and inner heat visualizations and meditate. At these occasions one should enhance with the eight enhancements. The key points of the six oral instructions are also necessary at this occasion. Train on the path with the intimate instructions of inner heat, and meditate until one repeatedly gains the view, self-originated gnosis. As this first involves the gathering of the elements, the thirty protections and the removal of obstacles are necessary in these circumstances to instill greater confidence.

Next, meditate on the path of the third empowerment in dependence on either an actual consort or a gnosis consort. This is the middle gathering of the elements, the instruction on the path of the experience of bliss and emptiness of the bindu. Then, meditate on the vajra waves of the fourth empowerment. This is the final gathering of the elements, the instruction on the path of the non-defective, fundamental gnosis. These are intended for gradually instructing the person of average intelligence.

Some forgo the instruction on the three appearances but also sustain this with the view. However it may be, up to this point, by all means one must engage in meditation after arousing certainty. Up to this point, the classification of the person is not defined. Some only sustain this within the creation stage, but the position of Ācārya Yogeśvara Virūpa is that after one slightly stabilizes the visualizations of the creation stage, one should principally emphasize the training of the body and the vāyu. The visualizations of vāyu and inner heat are the so-called cause or path of samādhi. Since the view—self-originated gnosis—is called "samādhi," at that time it arises and is sustained. The view that was previously confirmed with hearing and reflection is defective. This [self-originated gnosis] is called "the non-defective view," "the example gnosis," or "path mahāmudrā." {27} Therefore, since a result will not arise without[14] a cause, make effort in the cause. In dependence upon the cause, the vāyu and the visualizations of inner heat, self-originated gnosis gives rise to path mahāmudrā.

Further, some classes of people should train in gentle inhalation for one year, after having trained for a single year in all the instructions that were previously explained. Then, they should train in meditating only on the waves of mental samādhi in dependence on forceful inhalation and unifying the vāyu. This is called "the engagement of supreme diligence."

This concludes the explanation of the means of instructing people.

3. Generating Special Certainty

With respect to generating a special certainty, there are three sections in recognizing samādhi and presenting the divisions of the stages of the path: (1) generating certainty with the four authorities and the four aural instructions, (2) recognizing samādhi and presenting the divisions of the path, and (3) the signs of accomplishing the maṇḍalacakra.

a. The Four Authorities and the Four Aural Instructions

The first is explicated in the treatise.[15]

b. Recognizing Samādhi and Presenting the Divisions of the Path

The second is the first, middle, and final gathering of the element.

c. The Signs of Accomplishing the Maṇḍalacakra

There are four sections in the maṇḍalacakra; that is, the first, second, third, and fourth conclusions. Since those have already been explained in the manner of instructing a person, it is necessary to investigate the signs of "which person arrives in which circumstance" and give instruction.

This concludes the explanation of the method of giving instruction on the path.

C. The Result

Since the resultant five kāyas—the buddhahood naturally accomplished without effort—will be understood in the context of the explanation of the result, it is not necessary here. While the way of giving instructions according to the treatise has not been written down previously, this was written in response to the many requests of my disciple, Kartön Jose Chakyi Dorje (lCags kyi rdo rje, twelfth century), a Lhodrakpa[16] of good family and lineage, who came with great difficulty from the border of Bhutan and Tibet. Through the merit produced by this composition, {28} may all sentient beings equal with space swiftly attain the stage of Mahāvajradhara's omniscient buddhahood and may our obstacles on the path of all yogas that accomplish the path be pacified.

*ithi**

*This is the root of all the instruction manuals. There are many commentaries that depend on this text, such as those composed by Lama Dampa [Bsod nams brgyal mtshan, 1312–1375], Tsarchen [Blo gsal rgya mtsho, 1502–1566], Ngorchen [Kun dga' bzang po, 1382–1456], and so on.

6. The Versified Instructional Manual on How to Give the Instruction of the Path with Its Result in Accordance with the Treatise[1]

Jetsun Drakpa Gyaltsen

The *Versified Instructional Manual on How to Give the Instruction of the Path with Its Result in Accordance with the Treatise* is a verse presentation of the longer *How to Give Instructions According to the Treatise*, in chapter 5, and generally covers the same topics. Widely cited as a proof text in the *Three Appearances* and *Three Tantras* manuals, it is not included in the *Yellow Volume* but is included in Drakpa Gyaltsen's collected works.

The *Versified Instructional Manual* sets out the earliest lines of the debate between the Sakya and Kagyu schools concerning the importance of receiving full empowerments—as opposed to only blessings—and the importance of completion stage practice with respect to the nature of mahāmudrā. Drakpa Gyaltsen notes that the profound intimate instructions are a slow path when divorced from the completion stage practice of uniting the vāyus, which is an implicit criticism of so-called Sutra Mahāmudrā. He also criticizes the notion of "a mahāmudrā that descends from above," echoing the Samye debate and foreshadowing Sakya Paṇḍita's sustained critique of the so-called white panacea (*dkar po cig thub*) teachings.[2]

Having paid homage to the assembly of glorious gurus,
in the second line, I bow to Vajradhara.

Listen to the essential meaning of all the treatises of sutra and tantra,
expressed with few words. (1)

The three lower realms are the place of the suffering of suffering,
likened to a cancerous lesion on a sore caused by leprosy.
If one reflects on this thoroughly, how can one bear it?
Thus, one must avoid unvirtuous karma. (2)

Further, there is change and formations in the three higher realms.
First, reflect on the change of higher to lower.
Second, reflect on where will there be an end to activity?
Therefore, first reflect on the faults of samsara. (3)

In an isolated location, meditate with concentration.
Since solitude cannot be attained if one associates with the childish,
one should meditate on the renunciation of people.
Through this, solitude will be attained and one will become averse to wrong livelihood. (4)

As such, once thoughts of the world are given up,
one should go for refuge to the Three Jewels.
Meditate on the bodhicitta of equalizing and exchanging oneself for others,
and also meditate on ultimate bodhicitta. (5)

As such, reflect that there is craving for this life, which is impermanent.
Impermanence should be recalled repeatedly
in between sessions,
because if not reflected upon constantly, time passes without purpose.(6)

Between sessions of meditating on the two bodhicittas,
one should recite sutras and be diligent in making offerings to the Three Jewels.
Having summarized the system of the perfections, {29}
these are the intimate instructions of the essential meaning.(7)

Also, if one's mind is not content with only those instructions,
those of greater intelligence should be interested in the profound training.

Those who wish to swiftly attain the stage of Mahāvajradhara
should be given the Vajrayāna. (8)

One should rely on and offer supplications
to a guru who possesses the lineage, knows the meaning,
guards the supreme samaya, is adorned with the intimate instructions,
whose continuum is moistened with compassion, and who understands many treatises. (9)

Having entered into the great maṇḍala through their permission,
one must take the four empowerments completely—
not just a minor empowerment—
because empowerment is the basis of mantra. (10)

One must then endeavor to purify
the root and branch samayas;
that alone will cause accomplishment within sixteen lifetimes
and is the basis of all paths. (11)

After a suitable person
has been taught the path of the creation stage and its branches,
they should undertake the recitation, purify their continuum with a burnt offering,
and then train their mind in the pure view. (12)

First, one should establish all entities as mind,
as there is nothing else not included in mind.
Contaminated by traces of delusion, one's mind
is like a horse or elephant in a dream, or ophthalmia. (13)

That mind lacks inherent existence and is illusory,
appearing simply through the assembly of various conditions,
like a mirage, the moon in the water, or a fire stick.
Can one describe the nature of this mind? (14)

Also, a so-called illusion lacks inherent existence
and arises in dependence.

When there is no arising, ceasing, or abiding,
what can be thought about in this inexpressible state? (15)

Inexpressible—there is no meaning to express here.
Unthinkable—there is no basis for thought.
If there is nothing to meditate on, what could be meditated on here?
{30}
If understood in this way, one will be without grasping. (16)

Having trained the mind through reflecting on the correct view,
one must then meditate by concentrating on the two stages.
Train the mind gradually with the creation stage,
or taking that as the basis, there are two approaches. (17)

The first[3] is meditating until one obtains the mental appearance
in the creation stage itself.
The second is meditating on the completion stage, having already
meditated on either the complete maṇḍala or the natural form.[4] (18)

The preliminaries for all profound completion stages
are the three purifications. Then train in vāyu.
Among the seven yogas, the primary one is holding the vase.
The path of buddhahood resides in the hold. (19)

This is the elixir of immortality,
the supreme medicine of agelessness.
This accomplishes many powers
and also stabilizes the dependent origination of the two stages. (20)

That is the explanation of the training in the preliminaries
of the two aspects of the completion stage:
the trio of the self-empowerment, inner heat, and subtle bindu;
and the actual karma consort and gnosis consort. (21)

All profound intimate instructions devoid of the union [of the vāyus]
are paths of gradual progress.
Since they do not swiftly cause accomplishment,
therefore, be devoted to the path of the union [of the vāyus]. (22)

The qualities of buddhahood reside in the union [of the vāyus].
It is important for practitioners who meditate on unification
to train for a long while beforehand in the training of the body.
After experience arises, it should be integrated with the view. (23)

One's mind (the cause tantra free of proliferation from the beginning),
the gnosis of empowerment (the view of the path),
and experiences are the same entity on the stage of buddhahood.
Thus, the buddhahood of realization is explained through the example
of the moon. (24)

Some say, "Mahāmudrā descends from above."
This is a claim some confused teachers have made before.
That is not mahāmudrā but instead is the concentration on the view.
{31}
Mahāmudrā arises from the power of meditation. (25)

As such, having attained heat through effort on the path of the two
stages
and having stabilized the signs through conduct,
after one accomplishes the stages,
the stage of Vajradhara is attained through connection with the
proximate causes. (26)

This was composed at Sakya by
the upāsaka Drakpa Gyaltsen,
due to the supplication of devoted Tratön Lodrö,
who was interested in the essential meaning rather than the extensive
meaning.(27)

By the virtue that arises from this well-written composition—
this explanation that extracts the innermost essence
and has twenty-seven verses (and this one, the twenty-eighth)—
may all migrating beings attain the stage of Vajradhara. (28)

I confess the collection of faults in the presence of the gurus and the Buddha. May this virtue be dedicated to all sentient beings and may all their obstacles be pacified!

7. The Summarized Topics of the Stages of the Path of the Three Tantras of the Versified Manual on How to Give the Instruction of the Path with Its Result in Accordance with the Treatise[1]

Ngorchen Kunga Zangpo

Ngorchen Kunga Zangpo[2] (Kun dga' bzang po, 1382–1429) is the most important Sakya master to follow the five founders of the Sakya school. Born, raised, and educated at Sakya Monastery, Kunga Zangpo rose to prominence as one of the principal defenders of the Path with Its Result tradition against polemical attacks from both within and without the Sakya tradition. Ngorchen was a Vajrayāna scholar of exceptional depth and clarity, and his writings on the systems of Hevajra, Cakrasaṃvara, Sarvavid, and so on, remain fundamental texts in modern Sakya Vajrayāna curricula. Renowned for his monastic discipline, Ngorchen felt compelled to establish Evaṃ Chöden, a monastic institution[3] independent of Sakya Monastery, free from the bustle and temptations of town life.

This text, *The Summarized Topics*, is a topical outline of Jetsun Drakpa Gyaltsen's *Versified Instructional Manual*. The text is presented below first as a Western-style outline, and then in full in the order of the Tibetan original. The latter includes parenthetical annotations of the verse and line number that correspond to Drakpa Gyaltsen's text, included as marginalia in the Tibetan.

I. The beginning section on the stages of the path
  A. The praise
  B. The commitment to explain
II. The stages of the path with its sections
  A. Training one's continuum with the path of the perfections
    1. Reflecting on the faults of samsara to be abandoned
      a. {31} Reflecting on the suffering of suffering
        i. The nature of suffering
        ii. The explanation of avoiding its cause
      b. Reflecting on the other sufferings
        i. The concise explanation
        ii. The extensive explanation
          I) Reflecting on the suffering of change
          II) Reflecting on the suffering of formations
      c. Explaining how to avoid evil companions.
    2. Meditating on the path to rely upon
      a. The preparation, the stage of going for refuge
      b. The main subject, the stage of cultivating bodhicitta
        i. Cultivating relative bodhicitta
        ii. Cultivating ultimate bodhicitta
      c. The conclusion, the stages of activity between sessions
        i. Reflecting on impermanence
        ii. Gathering accumulations
    3. The conclusion of those
  B. Entering the actual stages of the path of Vajrayāna following such training
    1. The way to rely on a guru, the foundation of the path
      a. The characteristic of a reliable disciple
        i. Ripening by empowerment
          I) Explaining the full rite as an authentic ripening empowerment
          II) Explaining that other rites are not valid ripening empowerments
        ii. Having been ripened, purifying one's continuum
          I) Purifying the samayas to protect
          II) Purifying one's continuum with the approach recitation
        iii. Meditating the path after purification

I) The instruction on the view to abandon clinging to all entities
A) Appearances as mind
B) Mind as illusory
C) Illusion as lacking inherent existence
1) Establishing illusions as dependently originated
2) Establishing illusions as inexpressible
II) The yoga of the two stages that has the nature of support and supported
A) The general yoga of the two stages
B) The individual yogas
1) The yoga of the creation stage
a) The concise explanation
b) The extensive explanation
i) The creation stage meditated by a beginner
ii) The completion stage meditated by one who has gained stability
2) The yoga of completion stage
III) Obtaining heat by abiding in the two stages
IV) The way of meditating the proximate cause because one abides in the conduct
b. The nature of a reliable guru
c. How one relies on that guru
2. Once one relies on a guru, training the mind in the stages of the path
a. The preliminary, purifying the three doors
b. The main section, training on the path
i. The main subject of the path
I) The self-empowerment
A) The intimate instruction of the pervading [vāyus]
B) The intimate instruction of the pervaded
II) The maṇḍalacakra
ii. The branches of that path
c. The conclusion, maintaining the view
i. The brief explanation
ii. The extensive explanation.
I) The presentation of our system
II) The refutation of the system of others
3. The result of training on the path

a. Heat as the preliminary for conduct
b. Once heat is attained, engaging in the conduct

III. The ultimate conclusion of the stages of the path
A. Who
B. Why
C. Where
D. How
E. Enumeration
F. Composition
G. The author's dedication of virtue

Homage to the venerable gurus.

There are three topics in the stages of the path of the three tantras of Śrī Hevajra: the beginning section on the stages of the path, the stages of the path with its sections, and the ultimate conclusion of the stages of the path.

There are two topics: the praise (1ab) and the commitment to explain (1cd).

There are two topics: training one's continuum with the path of the perfections and entering the actual stages of the path of Vajrayāna following such training.

The first topic has three sections: reflecting on the faults of samsara to be abandoned, meditating on the path to rely upon, and the conclusion of those (7cd).

There are three sections: {31} reflecting on the suffering of suffering, reflecting on the other sufferings, and explaining how to avoid evil companions. (4)

There are two in the first section: the nature of suffering (2ac) and the explanation of avoiding its cause.

There are two (3) in the second section: the concise explanation and the extensive explanation. Here there are also two subsections: reflecting on the suffering of change (3b) and reflecting on the suffering of formations (3c).

There are three sections in the second topic: the preparation, the stage of going for refuge (5b); the main subject, the stage of cultivating bodhicitta; and the conclusion, the stages of activity between sessions.

There are two items in the second section: cultivating relative bodhicitta and cultivating ultimate bodhicitta (5d).

There are two items in the third section: reflecting on impermanence (6) and gathering accumulations (7).

There are three topics in the main stages of the path of Vajrayāna: the way to rely on a guru, the foundation of the path; once one relies on a guru, training the mind in the stages of the path; and the result of training on the path (26d).

There are three sections in the first topic: the characteristic of a reliable disciple (8), the nature of a reliable guru (9), and how one relies on that guru.

There are three items in the first section: ripening by empowerment; having been ripened, purifying one's continuum; and meditating on the path after purification.

There are two further items in the first subsection: explaining the full rite (10ab) as an authentic ripening empowerment and explaining that other rites are not valid ripening empowerments (10c).

There are two further items in the second item: purifying the samayas to protect (11) and purifying one's continuum with the approach recitation (12ac).

There are four further items in the third item: the instruction on the view to abandon clinging to all entities, the yoga of the two stages that has the nature of support and supported, {32} obtaining heat by abiding in the two stages, and the way of meditating on the proximate cause because one abides in the conduct (26c).

There are three further items in the first item: appearances as mind (13), mind as illusory (14), and illusion as lacking inherent existence. Here there are two further items: establishing illusions as dependently originated (15) and establishing illusions as inexpressible.

There are two further items in the second item: the general yoga of the two stages (18ab) and the individual yogas.

Here there are two items: the yoga of the creation stage and the yoga of the completion stage.

There are two further items in the first: the concise explanation (18cd) and the extensive explanation. Here there are two further items: the creation stage meditated on by a beginner (19ab) and the creation stage meditated on by one who has gained stability (19cd).

There are three items in the first item: the preliminary, purifying the three doors (20ab); the main section, training on the path; and the conclusion, maintaining the view.

There are two items in the second item: the main subject of the path and the branches of that path (22).

There are two items in the first item: the self-empowerment and the maṇḍalacakra (22d).

There are two items in the first item: the intimate instruction of the pervader(18b) and the intimate instruction of the pervaded (22c).

There are two items in the third item: the brief explanation and the extensive explanation. Here there are two: the presentation of our system (24) and the refutation of the system of others (25).

There are two items in the third section: heat as the preliminary for conduct; (24c) and once heat is attained, engaging in the conduct (26b).

There are six sections in the third topic: who (27b), why (27d), where (27a), how (27d), enumeration (28d), composition (28a), and the author's dedication of virtue (28a).

The Summarized Topics of the Stages of the Path of the Three Tantras was composed by the Śākya bhikṣu Kunga Zangpo. May this be beneficial to the doctrine and all sentient beings. *sarvadā maṅgalaṃ bhavantu*

8. The Nyakma Commentary

A Commentary on The Vajra Verses, *the Treatise of the Path with Its Result, the Precious Oral Instruction*[1] *{36}*

Sachen Kunga Nyingpo

The *Nyakma Commentary* is the last of the Eleven Commentaries That Explain the Treatise.[2] Composed by Sachen Kunga Nyingpo at the request of Nyakzhi Darma Wangchuk Gyaltsen (sNyag bzhi dar ma dbang phyug rgyal mtshan, twelfth century), it is considered the preeminent commentary on *The Vajra Verses* for its completeness and brevity. Later commentaries on *The Vajra Verses* are considered to be elaborations on this.

The text is heavily annotated by Drakpa Gyaltsen, closely following the commentary, *For the Sons*. His annotations are incomplete and inaccurately carved in the Palpung block prints, and so are not included here. Rather, marginal notes found in the *Yellow Volume* are here included in footnotes, and annotations on those marginal notes are in the footnotes in parentheses. Pagination follows the Palpung block prints, and passages from *For the Sons* supplement the translation in the endnotes.

I prostrate with my head to the feet of the sublime guru.

To describe the subsidiary topics, "sublime guru" has four topics: outwardly, the sublime guru[3] totally eliminates doubts;* inwardly, the guru

*The body is shown to be the nirmāṇakāya through conferring the vase empowerment on the body.

teaches self-originated gnosis;* secretly, the guru teaches connate gnosis;† and ultimately, the vajra master guru teaches the utterly pure reality of all phenomena as reality.‡ Since all qualities are generated in one when the guru's lotus feet are touched, one bows with body, voice, and mind motivated by a special pure faith.

The "path" is enumerated into eight divisions: both the mundane§ and transcendent¶ path; both the path of the dance of the wheel** and the path of spinning the wheel;†† both the path categorized‡‡ by§§ heat¶¶ and the path categorized by signs;*** the entry††† and reversal of gnosis; and the entry and reversal of concepts.‡‡‡

The "result" has three modes: {37} (1) the five kāyas through the arrangement of dependent origination and completing all the accumulations, which are important for oneself, such as giving sight to the blind, and so on; (2) the many results important for others; and (3) the retinue attaining buddhahood in a single group, which is important for both oneself and others.

That being the case, there is the instruction of the path with its result;§§§ the instruction of the result with its path;¶¶¶ the instruction on knowing many things by knowing one thing;**** the instruction of removing obstacles to concentration by recognizing samādhi; the instruction of removing the obstacles of māra by recognizing obstacles;[4] the instruction of taking

*The voice is shown to be the saṃbhogakāya through conferring the secret empowerment on the voice.

†The mind is shown to be the dharmakāya through conferring the prajñā's gnosis empowerment on the mind.

‡The essential wisdom is shown to be the svabhāvakāya though conferring the fourth empowerment on the trio of body, voice, and mind.

§Application and preparation.

¶Seeing, meditation, and ultimate.

**The body, superior, and bodhicitta.

††The first stage and above.

‡‡Not deceptive if stabilized.

§§Three heats.

¶¶Deceptive if not stabilized.

***Three signs.

†††Minor benefit.

‡‡‡Concepts that inflict minor harm.

§§§Employing the result as the path.

¶¶¶Asserting transformation as gnosis.

****Everything is inner and secret dependent origination.

the faults as qualities;* the instruction of taking obstacles as accomplishments;† and the instruction that is like the gold-transforming elixir. Since permission for the concise discourse, which is of few words‡ and extensive in meaning, was obtained from the nirmāṇakāya,§ it is called the "concise discourse." In brief, *The Vajra Verses* is the epitome of the Tripiṭaka.¶ The meaning of "shall be written down" is like a precious wish-fulling gem.

Now, for the topics of the text, there are seven topics in the path common to samsara and nirvana. First, from the path explained as the three appearances, there is the impure appearance, the experiential appearance, and the pure appearance. Each of those three has three divisions: What is the basis? What is the cause? {38} What is the appearance?

Now then, the basis is "sentient beings." In general, they are included in the six realms. Specifically, this appearance is defined upon the continuum** of a single person. Though the cause is called an afflicted appearance, the appearance that is dominated by traces of karma and affliction is called "the impure appearance." There are two within impure appearance: appearances of delusion†† and appearances of karma.‡‡

The support is a "practitioner." There are three for that: a person who has a special body,§§ a person who has a totally purified¶¶ continuum,*** and a person who has aroused††† experience in their continuum. Though the cause is said to be "samādhi,"‡‡‡ by implication§§§ it is empowering the ten ḍākas

*The path free from hope and fear.

†One's body, and so on.

‡With many topics.

§Rje bstun ma.

¶The heart of the path.

**Who has not aroused experiences even though they have obtained empowerment.

††The appearance that comports with the six realms, even though the entity does not exist.

‡‡Like seeing the appearances of the happiness and suffering of the six realms or the semblance of water [as perceived in the six realms].

§§Their faculties are complete, and they are not arthritic, hunchbacked, and so on.

¶¶Purified by empowerment; that is, without obtaining the empowerment, the path cannot be taught.

***Purified by hearing, reflection, and training.

†††Fortunate karma, and so on.

‡‡‡Among the five dependent originations, the first three are on the mundane path; the second two [inner and secret] are arranged, but they are not arranged for the female of the tenth stage.

§§§Secret dependent origination.

and ḍākinīs of the vāyu and mind[*] in the palace[†] of the nāḍī syllables. The "experiential appearance" arising in one's continuum has three paths (clearing the entry, and so on): the path of clearing the entry,[‡] the path of eliminating attachment,[§] and the path of great awakening.[¶] The three experiences are the experience of the body,[**] the experience of the mind,[††] and the experience of dreams.[‡‡] The three dependent originations are the dependent origination of the reversal of the vāyu,[§§] the appearance[¶¶] of visions,[***] and dreams.[†††] The three heats are the heat of prior concepts,[‡‡‡] the heat of the gathering of the nine elements,[§§§] and the heat of the blazing and gathering of the bindus.[¶¶¶] The three samādhis[****] are the samādhi of various characteristics;[††††] the samādhi of the empty nature;[‡‡‡‡] and the samādhi of the essence, union. {39} As such, since all fifteen experiences arise in and out of order, samādhi is recognized and maintained[5] on the path.

The support is a "sugata,"[§§§§] of which there are four kinds: the sugata of outer shape,[¶¶¶¶] the one that went from the bliss[6] of the path of the two accumulations,[*****] the sugata of inner mantra, and the one that went from the bliss of the middle path.[†††††] The sugata of the secret empowerment is the one who went to bliss from the space of the mother.[‡‡‡‡‡] The sugata of

[*]Inner dependent origination.
[†]The experiences that arise are categorized by heat and categorized by sign.
[‡]Placing the mind on anything.
[§]The emptiness of that experience.
[¶]Union.
[**]Pain, and so on.
[††]Affliction, and so on.
[‡‡]Dreams of horses, and so on.
[§§]Such as flying, and so on.
[¶¶]Undefined, delusive appearances (such as ogres, and so on).
[***]Smoke, and so on.
[†††]One flies, and so on.
[‡‡‡]Abiding in previous sights and sounds.
[§§§]Seeing the sun and moon.
[¶¶¶]Bliss, and so on.
[****]Experience.
[††††]The form of the deity, and so on.
[‡‡‡‡]The emptiness of the object, and so on.
[§§§§]Having abandoned samsaric misery.
[¶¶¶¶]Three.
[*****]In connection with the creation stage.
[†††††]In connection with inner heat.
[‡‡‡‡‡]The path of the mudra.

ultimate suchness is the one who went to bliss from the path of the three doors of liberation.[*]

The "inexhaustible body" is the inconceivable secret of the body[†] and all bodies.[‡] Inexhaustible "speech" is the inconceivable secret of speech[§] and all speech.[¶] Inexhaustible "mind" is the inconceivable secret[**] of mind[††] and all minds.[‡‡] An "ornament" beautifies oneself and others. The "wheel" is the wheel of the activity of deeds. There is the one performing benefits[§§] and the one who is benefited.[¶¶] Also, both engage continuously in performing the benefit of sentient beings until samsara is emptied. Those explain the support. The implied explanation, the dissolution of the four movements[***] that arise from below, will not be explained here.

The appearance is the "pure appearance." In brief, one realizes that the different appearances of samsara and nirvana do not exist apart from one's gnosis. At that time samsara and nirvana[†††] are of one taste. The path and result[‡‡‡] are of one taste. Buddhas[§§§] and sentient beings[¶¶¶] are one continuum. {40} The object to renounce[****] and the antidote[††††] are of one taste. At that time there is neither anything to adopt nor reject, which is the meaning of "renunciation and attainment are nondual."

Now, in the path explained as the three tantras, there is the all-basis[‡‡‡‡]

[*] In connection with the vajra waves.
[†] According to sutra.
[‡] Supreme and common.
[§] Understood by all at the same time.
[¶] Explanations in the many languages of the six realms.
[**] The five gnoses.
[††] According to sutra.
[‡‡] A moment of [two omnisciences] about the nature of everything and the extent of everything.
[§§] The tamer.
[¶¶] The tamed.
[***] The so-called outer and inner dependent origination, and so on.
[†††] At the time of meditation, they are realized by one's single continuum.
[‡‡‡] When it is the time of accomplishment.
[§§§] Later.
[¶¶¶] Earlier.
[****] When one is a sentient being.
[††††] Samadhi.
[‡‡‡‡] The all-basis is a phenomenon that can produce the result.

cause tantra,[*] the body method tantra,[†] and the mahāmudrā[‡] result[§] tantra. Further, the all-basis[¶] is the "root tantra;" the body is the "explanatory tantra"; and the body, speech, and mind are the "result tantra."

When the subsidiary topics are discussed, the so-called "all-basis" becomes the basis for either samsara or nirvana through the distinction of being connected or not being connected with the method. "Cause" is used for the power that gives rise to a result.[**] "Tantra" is the uninterrupted continuum of the mind's cognizance,[††] the rosary of its intrinsic cognizance[7] from the state of a sentient being up to the state of Vajradhara. "Samsara and nirvana are complete" means that all phenomena of samsara are complete in the form of characteristics. All paths of nirvana are complete in the form of qualities. All phenomena of the result are complete in the form of potential.[‡‡] "It is the root[§§] tantra" means that since dependent origination is arranged on the body, the mind that is the cause of realization is the all-basis.[¶¶]

Now, the body method tantra is divided into five sections: the initial cause empowerment of method tantra; the twenty phenomena of the body, and so on; the explanation of the group of samayas; if samaya is broken, the explanation for mending the broken samayas of the five ḍākinīs; and the explanation of the principal path empowerment of the method tantra.

First, the "body method tantra" exists in the all-basis mind in the form of a seed or a cause.[***] {41} Since dependent origination is arranged on the body, it is the method for generating realization. "And so on" is a summary

[*]There are six topics here: (1) What is the support? (2) What is the supported all-basis? (3) How do they both exist (inseparably)? (4) The explanation of samsara and nirvana being complete (in three) within that all-basis. (5) The explanation of the all-basis as the cause tantra (the commentary). (6) The explanation of the all-basis as the root tantra (the object to realize).

[†]Dependently originated because dependent origination is arranged on the body.

[‡]Because the result is obtained in dependence on the method.

[§]The knowledge of this.

[¶]The category.

[**]The five kāyas.

[††]Since concepts (coarse and subtle) and suffering (hell) are complete in the all-basis, it is the cause tantra.

[‡‡]Since it is the case that the potential to accomplish the five kāyas exists in one's continuum, the all-basis is established as the cause tantra.

[§§]It is similar to the trunk of a tree.

[¶¶]The support and the supported.

[***]Like the support and the supported.

for "the body . . . is the explanatory tantra," which will be addressed below. The mind is the foundation of samsara and nirvana.* Since dependent origination can be arranged on the body, there is the potential for realization and comprehension.† The "four threes"‡ are which empowerment§ is obtained from which maṇḍala, which purifies which taint—the four groups of three. Within those, "the seats, and so on" are connected with the four maṇḍalas. Within that, the three seats are the seat of the buddhas and bodhisattvas, the seat of the knowledge consorts and goddesses, and the seat of the male and female wrathful ones. Therein, the buddhas¶ are in the middle of the seat, and the [individual] seats** of the bodhisattvas are in the cardinal and intermediate directions. For the knowledge consorts,†† the gnosis knowledge consorts are in the middle of the seat of the knowledge consorts; the physical knowledge consorts‡‡ are on the left of the seat of the vidyās; and the [individual] seats of the goddesses§§ are in the inner cardinal and intermediate directions, with the form of one taste, and so on. The [individual] seats of the male¶¶ and female wrathful ones are the outer cardinal and intermediate directions. This is also how the three seats are set up in the maṇḍala of colored powder. For the remaining three maṇḍalas, the three seats should be understood according to how they are meditated on as being complete. That is the explanation of the first topic, the maṇḍalas.

Second, from what is there an empowerment? The vase empowerment has eleven;*** the secret empowerment can be obtained from any of the three;††† the gnosis of the wisdom consort has two;‡‡‡ and from the five in

*The all-basis is the cause of samsara and nirvana.

†The explanatory tantra.

‡Now, the path from the empowerment of the method.

§First, explain the empowerment; without that, the path cannot be explained.

¶Any of the five families.

**Eight.

††Buddhalocanā, and so on.

‡‡At the time of empowerment, and so on.

§§Rupavajrā, and so on.

¶¶Ten.

***The five empowerments of the families; sixth, the perfect buddha; seventh, the vase empowerment; and eighth through eleventh, the permission, prediction, solace, and praise.

†††Obtained from the father, obtained from the mother, or obtained from the strength of liberation.

‡‡‡The support and the experience.

the fourth empowerment,* one obtains [the empowerment] from any of the five, such as the supported, and so on. {42}

Third, "which taint is purified" refers to purifying the taints of the body, voice, and mind, and the trio of body, voice, and mind together, making it possible to destroy ordinary concepts, meditate on the path, and so on, and create the fortune of obtaining the result of the four kāyas. Furthermore, if those [kāyas] are obtained on the basis of an actual mudra, this is the best; if obtained on the basis of a gnosis mudra, it is medium; and if obtained on the basis of words, it is average. The "empowerment of the cause," to begin, is obtained from the guru, like polishing a vessel or clearing land. Those explain "there is empowerment of the cause with the four threes, the seats, and so on."

Now, "on the path, the creation stage, and so on, is explained with the four fives" is the explanation of the twenty dharmas of the path, and so on, connected with empowerment: What is the path for each empowerment?† What is the view?‡ What is the conclusion?§ What is the time of death?¶ What is the result? There are five for each.

Therein, the five of the vase empowerment are the path, the shape of the creation stage; the view, the three essential natures; the conclusion, the inseparability of samsara and nirvana; the time of death, transferring higher; and the nirmāṇakāya that is naturally accomplished without effort. Therein, the path of the shape [of the creation stage] should be understood from the guru's instruction.

The three essentials of the view are the essential nature of the perspective of appearance,** the essential nature of the perspective of emptiness,†† and the essential nature of union.‡‡ For each of those, there is the dharmin that is the opposite of the appearances of ignorance;§§ the dharmatā that is free

*Word, meaning, path, result, and the supported.
†The first path of accumulation.
‡Heat on the path of application.
§The three transcendent paths.
¶The intermediate person.
**Form, and so on.
††Empty space, and so on.
‡‡Moon in water, and so on.
§§Cognizance connected with clarity.

from mental imputation; and also the differentiation of that single entity* through the principle of isolation.†

The conclusion is the inseparability of samsara and nirvana. On the six stages of the transcendent path: a one-billion-world universe can be placed in a mustard seed without one shrinking or the other enlarging; walls, {43} mountains, and so on, pose no impediment; the flow of rivers can be reversed; the bottom edge of the sun, moon, and so on, can be held; one can be turned into many; many can be turned into one; and so on.

If one is not able to follow the conclusion, there are three in the time of death to transfer higher: there is the time of death practice of transforming appearances, the time of death practice of the ball of light transference, and the time of death practice of transference with sound. Also, the stages of these practices should be understood from the guru's instruction.

The result—the nirmāṇakāya that is naturally accomplished without effort—will be explained during the time of the result, but it will not be discussed here. Those are the five sections of the vase empowerment.

The five sections of the secret empowerment are the path is the stage of self-empowerment, the view is self-originated gnosis, the conclusion is distinct and totally perfect, the time of death is luminosity, and the result is the saṃbhogakāya that is naturally accomplished without effort.

First, in general, though the omniscient one‡ has said there are inconceivable key points, [the path] is summarized in nine hundred and one key points.§ Those key points [of the path] can also be summarized in seventy-five key points.¶ When the intimate instructions of their practice are condensed, they are summarized into nine key points.

There are five that do not depend on cakras:** feeding the butter lamp, the thunderbolt of Brahma, the yoga of the nāḍīs, the churning wheel, and the yoga of the bindus. There are three that depend on cakras: depending on one cakra, depending on two cakras, and depending on four cakras. Since others depend on the intimate instructions, the rapid ones are condensed into nine.

First, the key point of the body is sitting in an upright position with the

*Included in a single cognizance.
†The different ways of defining it.
‡Intending the inclinations of those to be tamed and a single person's vajra body anatomy.
§Intending the vāyu yogas.
¶Intending the key points of the syllables.
**For rapid experience.

knees drawn to the chest. Four fingerbreadths below the navel, visualize an inverted, dark-red *kṣa* syllable. At the navel visualize a pale-red *aṃ*. Next, since the vāyu meets the lower tip [of the central nāḍī],* {44} the fire of the groin blazes. The *kṣa* blazes greatly; that strikes the *aṃ*. Amṛta descends in a fine stream, feeding the fire of the *kṣa*. Visualize in that way the blazing and dripping. The vāyu should be held as long as one can. Train on† the path. Maintain the view.‡ Heat will manifest§ naturally. There is no number or length of sessions. Examine the object of mental engagement.[8] Take stock of one's health.[9]

Second is hitting the target of bodhicitta¶ with the bow of vāyu** and the arrow of fire,†† which rapidly induces gnosis. There are no repetitions.‡‡ All experiences should be naturally sustained. There is no number or length of sessions, and so on.

Third, the key point is taking any posture of the body, cross-legged, and so on. While exhaling, the solar rasanā on the right with the nature of fire is visualized as red. While inhaling, the lunar lalanā on the left with the nature of water is visualized as white. While the breath remains inside, the central nāḍī is visualized with four characteristics: it is thin, like the stem of a lotus; it is straight, like the trunk of a plantain; it is clear, like a lamp of sesame oil; and it is red, like a lac tree flower.[10] Keeping this in mind, train in this again and again. Allow all experiences of heat to be natural. There is no definite length of the session, and so on.

Fourth, the key point of the body is sitting in an upright position with the knees drawn to the chest. In the center of the body, the red central nāḍī§§ travels from the navel to the crown, visualized as either thick or thin. Both nāḍīs on the right and left are white, visualized as either thick or thin, churning the central nāḍī; that is, the two nāḍīs are used like a churning rope to churn the central nāḍī.¶¶ For the vāyu, join the upper vāyu and the lower

*Opening and closing.
†Effort.
‡Experience.
§The fifteen experiences.
¶With a finger of flame.
**Taking the posture of the body and using the air element of the rectum.
††The fire element of the groin.
‡‡One session.
§§The churning rod.
¶¶That is like the churning rod.

vāyu forcefully.* {45} This should be encouraged with the quirt of diet† and behavior.‡ One trains on the path without a number or length of sessions. Maintain the view. Allow any experiences that arise to be natural.

Fifth, the key point of the body is any position: there is the conjoined sun and moon of the heart, the solitary hero of the navel, the essence of bliss in the secret place, and the seed of white hair at the ūṛnā. Corresponding with the vāyu, one should briefly request instruction from the guru in order to practice these. That is the explanation of the five divisions that does not depend on cakras.

Among those that depend on cakras, the first is the practice that depends on one cakra: The key point of the body is sitting in an upright position with the knees drawn to the chest. Also, all the other limbs of concentration are complete. There is the air element at the rectum and the fire element at the groin. At the navel, the sixty-four outer petals are without an array of syllables. The first syllables of the eight sets[11] are arranged to the right on the eight inner petals. In the center there is an extremely fine *aṃ*. All syllables are visualized as red. The two lower vāyus§ meet at the lower tip. The air element activates the fire element in the groin. The latter strikes the *aṃ* in the navel. From the *aṃ*, fire, which is red in color and hot in nature, is visualized blazing up about four fingerbreadths. The vāyu is held gradually. There is no number or length of sessions. As before, examine the object of mental engagement,¶ and so on. Train on the path, maintain the view, and allow all experiences of heat to be natural.

The practice that depends on two cakras is as follows:** Above the previously mentioned navel cakra, the eight petals of the heart cakra are without an array of syllables. In its center, imagine an inverted pale-blue *hūṃ*. Then imagine that both the *aṃ* and *hūṃ* pair are within the central nāḍī. Further, since the vāyu meets at the lower tip, a very slender flame blazes up from the *aṃ* to the *hūṃ*. A fine stream of bodhicitta drips from the *hūṃ* onto the *aṃ*. {46} Focus the mind on the form of the white and red blazing and dripping. The vāyu is held gradually. One should understand the length of the session,

*For as long as one is able.

†Nutritionally dense.

‡Cold.

§The mother of fire (*me ma*) from the right, and the mother of sleep (*gnyid ma*) from the left. [This note migrated into the body of D and P.]

¶Either one wishes to perform this or not.

**The signs, which include heat, are rapid.

and so on, as before. The arising of the visual appearance categorized under heat has five signs, and there are also secondary signs, for a total of ten. First, under the influence of the right nostril, there is smoke,* mirage,† fireflies,‡ butter lamps,§ and cloudless space.¶ The signs categorized by the left nostril are darkness,** rainbow, lightning, moonbeams, and sunbeams. These are either visual appearances or dream experiences. Allow all experiences to be natural.

Third, the practice that depends on four cakras is as follows:†† The key points of the body, and so on, are as before. Next, there is the visualization of the two active cakras: On the sixty-four outer petals of the navel cakra, two groups of vowels circle to the left, and the consonants—excluding *ha* and *kṣa*—circle to the right. The eight inner petals are the same as above. All seed syllables are red and upright. Then, on the eight petals of the heart cakra are *bhrūṃ*, *āṃ*, *jriṃ*, *khaṃ* in the cardinal directions and *māṃ*, *lāṃ*, *paṃ*, *taṃ* in the intermediate directions. All the seed syllables are black and inverted. On the sixteen petals of the throat cakra are the sixteen vowels circling to the left. In the center, there is *aṃ*. All the seed syllables are red and upright. On the thirty-two petals of the crown cakra are the vowels circling to the left, and there are sixteen consonants from *ka* to *ta* in their natural order[12] circling to the right. In the center, there is *haṃ*. All the seed syllables are white and inverted.

Next, the mother-of-fire[13] vāyu and the mother-of-sleep vāyu meet at the lower end, igniting the fire of the groin and striking the *aṃ* of the navel; that heated vāyu travels through the rasanā, burning the elements of the seed syllable in the heart. {47} Again, it travels through the rasanā, burning the elements of the seed syllable in the throat. Again, it travels through the rasanā, touching the *haṃ* of the crown. The *haṃ* melts into light, which descends through the left lalanā. It restores the seed syllable of the throat as before, causing it to expand. Again, [the light] travels through the lalanā, restoring the seed syllable of the heart as before, causing it to expand. Again, it moves into the lalanā, and because it strikes the *aṃ* of the navel, the *aṃ*

*From the earth vāyu.
†From the water vāyu.
‡From the fire vāyu.
§From the air vāyu.
¶From the space vāyu.
**These are in reverse order, beginning from the space vāyu.
††This is stable and covers all.

blazes greatly. After the central nāḍī opens slightly, it travels into the central nāḍī in the form of a lightning bolt. Also, the *hūṃ* of the heart and the *aṃ* of the throat are destroyed without the impediment of clinging, and through [the flame's] mere touch, a fine stream of amṛta descends through the central nāḍī. It gradually descends past the *aṃ*. No matter which* object of mental engagement arises between the throat and four fingerbreadths above the navel, focus on the blazing and dripping. Hold the vāyu as long as possible. All experiences should be naturally sustained. The rest is as before.

The practice that depends on the intimate instructions is as follows: The key point of the body is sitting in an upright position with the knees drawn to the chest. The other limbs of concentration are also similar. Then, visualize one's body as hollow. Imagine that the interior of the body is filled with a pale lamplight. Counting the vāyu and not counting totals twenty-four. The vāyu is held for the length of the session. Encourage with the quirt of diet and conduct. All experiences should be naturally sustained. There are four fixed sessions. The best† switch visualizations in three days; the medium,‡ five days; and the average,§ nine days. Next, imagine that there is a dark-red *raṃ* on the soles of both feet. Fire blazes from them, traveling through the nāḍīs of the ankles, entering the major nāḍīs of the thighs, and meeting in the secret place. Focus on the cinder that is sharp,¶ rapid,** intense,†† and violent. Everything else is the same as before.‡‡ {48} The way bindus struggle is the same as before. The way§§ the wheel is visualized is the same as before. The way the fire blazes upward is the same as before.¶¶ The way the fire blazes greater is the same as before.*** From that, fire blazes everywhere, as before. In all, the experience should be naturally sustained.

The view is the four self-originated gnoses:[14] the self-originated samādhi of affliction;††† the self-originated samādhi of concepts; the self-originated[15]

*As one wishes.
†Experienced rapidly.
‡Experienced slowly.
§Experienced with difficulty.
¶The tip.
**Motion.
††Hot.
‡‡The vāyu.
§§Two bindus are stacked on the tip of the flame, and the fire wheel revolves.
¶¶A handspan.
***Up to the crown.
†††Arises without depending on the condition of objects.

samādhi of[*] confusion;[†] and the clear[‡] and light[16] samādhi of great, self-originated gnosis.

The conclusion[§] is distinct and totally perfect. Qualities arise in one's continuum, such as the ability to understand the language of the four continents and six classes and to teach the dharma in those languages; the power of the vowels and consonants is obtained;[¶] the supreme of words[**] is accomplished;[††] conventions are examined;[‡‡] and the power over the four kinds[§§] of perfect personal knowledge is obtained, the melody of Brahma, and so on.

If one cannot follow the conclusion, then there is the time of death, luminosity. Having made the vāyu at the time of death a condition, all vāyus enter the central nāḍī. The samādhi of supreme emptiness and clarity arises.[¶¶] Since that is merged with the previous samādhi[***] of self-originated gnosis, one will follow the conclusion without a bardo, becoming a vidyādhara.

The result—the saṃbhogakāya that is naturally accomplished without effort—will be explained at the time of the result, but it will not be discussed here. Those are the five sections of the secret empowerment.

The five sections of the gnosis of the wisdom consort empowerment are the path is the path of the maṇḍalacakra method, the view is the four joys of connate gnosis, the conclusion is the minor seal of bliss and emptiness, the time of death is the arrival of Vajrasattva, {49} and the result is the dharmakāya that is naturally accomplished without effort.

First, there are two in the path: extensive and concise. There are five in the extensive explanation: equality in body and voice, equality in bliss, equality in being empowered, a pure vidyā, and a connection[†††] with the intimate instructions.

First, "equal in body and voice" means that both oneself and the mudra

[*]Everything is inside all bodies.
[†]Slightly unclear.
[‡]Supreme clarity and emptiness.
[§]Various conventions.
[¶]The cause.
[**]That which arises from that cause.
[††]Arises according to whatever one said.
[‡‡]One knows the Tripiṭaka, and so on.
[§§]Words, meaning, definitions, and eloquence.
[¶¶]Naturally.
[***]From the experience.
[†††]The doctrine.

meditate together on the deity using a four-limb sādhana, or instantly.* The voice† recites the root mantra, and so on. Also, a text[17] states:

> The thought of the deity's form
> and the thought of samaya‡ are the same.§

"Equality of desire" is one's¶ realization of connate gnosis in dependence on the knowledge consort and the desire for full awakening.** Also, the knowledge consort has the same desire as oneself; that is, she is equal in her desire for full awakening.

"Equality in empowerment"†† is empowering the space‡‡ and the secret.§§ The space of the mother vanishes,¶¶ and from emptiness, there is *āḥ*, from which arises an eight-petaled lotus with *āḥ* on its anthers, which is empowered by the father. The secret of the father vanishes,*** and from the stage of emptiness there is *hūṃ*, from which arises a five-tined blue vajra marked with a *hūṃ* in the center and an upright, dark-red *phaṭ* at the opening, empowered by an *aṃ* on the jewel.††† The jewel tip arises from *svā*.‡‡‡

The pure knowledge consort is of two types: the pure knowledge consort that arises from birth and the pure knowledge consort that arises from training. There are five for the first: the doe, the conch, the cow, the patterned one, and the variegated one. The characteristics of these can be best comprehended§§§ from¶¶¶ the guru's instruction. There are three in the knowledge consort that arises from training: {50} Since she trained in hearing**** and

*Equality of the body.
†Equality of the voice.
‡This empowers the body as the nirmāṇakāya.
§Generating the samaya; the entrance of the gnosis being; empowering the sense bases and the body, speech, and mind; and conferring empowerment.
¶To abandon concepts of the ordinary.
**The dharmakāya.
††This empowers speech as the saṃbhogakāya.
‡‡Of the mother.
§§Of the father.
¶¶To abandon concepts of the ordinary.
***To abandon concepts of the ordinary.
†††The projection of a string of pearls.
‡‡‡At the opening of the central nāḍī.
§§§The stages of arising.
¶¶¶Understand from elsewhere.
****All view and conduct.

reflection,[*] her continuum is purified. She is purified by empowerment.[†] She is purified by the samādhi of yoga.[‡] As such, the pure knowledge consort arises first. Then, the equality of body and voice is empowered by the nirmāṇakāya. Next, there is the equality of empowerment, the arising of the empowerment of the saṃbhogakāya. After that, there is the equality of desire, the arising of the empowerment of the dharmakāya.[§]

Fifth, the connection with the key point of the intimate instructions is first, descending; then, holding; next, reversing; after that, spreading; and finally, preventing degeneration.

First, the knowledge consort, the absolutely pure support, should be placed either near or far, and one should gaze on her form. Since the fire of passion burns hot, the bindus descend. Meditate on bliss, protect with a wide-open stare,[¶] and keep the secret.[**] Likewise, listen to her sound,[18] smell her scent, and taste her. Likewise, touch her on any point of the body. Since the fire of passion[††] burns, the bindu descends. Meditate on the bliss, protect with a wide-open stare, and keep the secret.[19] In all of those, maintain any experiences[‡‡] that arise spontaneously. As such, it is said, "The bindu descends and increases.[§§] It increases and is retained.[¶¶] It is retained and gradually reversed." The three are produced in connection.

In the first moment,[***] there is the gnosis of joy. After that, the *bola* and *kakkola* unite, and the bindu descends due to the fire of passion. Meditate on the bliss, protect through gazing with a wide-open stare, and keep the secret.

In the second moment,[†††] there is the gnosis of supreme joy. In those two, the bindu descends, and because the power of bliss increases, it is called "the heat of the blazing bindu." {51}Then, when one copulates, one is endowed with bliss and nonconceptuality. As before, the bindu descends. One should

[*]The vows of personal liberation.
[†]The complete four.
[‡]Abiding in the two stages.
[§]That is how the three kāyas are made into the path.
[¶]Cross both arms and stare upward with the eyes.
[**]Avoid intercourse.
[††]For any of the five objects.
[‡‡]Bliss and nonconceptuality.
[§§]Into many.
[¶¶]It is not lost.
[***]There is much activity, and the bliss is small.
[†††]Fewer activities and more bliss.

meditate on bliss and nonconceptuality, protect with a wide-open stare, and keep the secret.[*] Both are important.

In the third moment, there is the joy of separation from joy called "the heat of the moving bindu."[†] At that time, if it is difficult to retain the bindu, one should either hold the breath or protect the bindu with the six movements, and so on. If it is easy to protect, then protect in the fourth moment. At that time the sphincter becomes numb,[‡] heavy,[§] and clenches. Sometimes the feces, urine, and so on, cannot pass and cannot be held. The hair of the body stands up.[¶] When yawning or tearing, the bindu is retained. At that time one searches for the nāḍī in the totally purified support,[**] and with the three preliminary empowerments, since the vajra and lotus are united, the two nāḍīs are united,[††] the two bindus are united,[‡‡] the two vāyus[§§] are united, bliss and emptiness are unified, and a samādhi of unidentifiable bliss arises. Here, also maintain that samādhi. Protecting with wide-open eyes, and so on, and keeping the secret[¶¶] are both important. Now then, if one is going to protect with the six movements, one reverses the bindu with drying the ocean on Sumeru,[***] subduing the four continents,[†††] placing the apprehender of taste in its own place,[‡‡‡] leaving the supreme organ upward,[§§§] sounding a loud and long *hūṃ* with a strong voice, and shooting the *hūṃ* of samādhi with the bow of *phaṭ*.[¶¶¶] Then, one tightens the belt of the vāyu, {52} tosses the noose, and spins the body like the wheel of a wooden pestle. Through acting like a small child, the bindu is spread throughout the body.

In the fourth moment, there is the connate joy called "the warmth of the

[*] Protect against the loss of the bindu.
[†] Moving up slightly.
[‡] Because the bindu is retained.
[§] Because the bliss is strong.
[¶] Since the bliss is unbearable.
[**] This occurs at the time the padminī gives the prediction; one should administer ginger, and so on.
[††] The central nāḍīs.
[‡‡] Solar and lunar.
[§§] The downward-voiding vāyu.
[¶¶] Keeping the bindu.
[***] Pressing the belly to the spine.
[†††] Contracting the four limbs.
[‡‡‡] Placing the tongue on the palate.
[§§§] The eyes are wide open.
[¶¶¶] By guiding *hūṃ* with *phaṭ*.

stable bindu." The six ways of preventing its loss are mentioned below in the section on preventing leakage, and so they will not be mentioned here.

The concise path has a preparation:

> Having built up the tissues of the body[20]
> and engaged in physical conduct,[*] there is a sun on the right hand
> and a moon[†] on the left hand,[‡]
> which are crossed, covering the two knees.
> Make[§] nine long *hūs* and short *hus*[21] in front:[¶]
> three on the right and three on the left,
> exhaling three times and inhaling three times.[**]
> One should train in this cycle.[††]
> In three days the genitalia recedes into a sheath.[‡‡]

The main subject:

> Having performed the empowerment, and so on,
> slightly constrict the anal sphincter,[§§]
> suck strongly on both middle fingers,
> and stare upward with both eyes.
> This will retain the bindu.[¶¶]
> Also, strongly utter "ha."
> Also, one should perform the other physical yantras.[***]
> These two will retain the bindu.[†††]

To eliminate traces:[‡‡‡]

[*]Sitting in an upright position.
[†]Intermediate recollection.
[‡]Ordinary form.
[§]With the voice.
[¶]Of the body.
[**]Three times each: middle, right, and left.
[††]One should repeat this.
[‡‡]The best should train for a half a day, and so on, on very strong vāyu.
[§§]In order to retain the bindu after bliss arises.
[¶¶]By relying on the three key points of the body.
[***]To block the upper vāyu.
[†††]Up to this point, both the descending and retention of bindu are explained.
[‡‡‡]These demonstrate reversing and spreading the bindu.

Hi like an elephant, growl *hūṃ hūm* like a tigress,
retch* like predator, and sniff† like a fox.
Drawn up in stages through the navel, heart,
throat, and crown,‡
the bindu is distributed through the body§ with the mudra of
liberation.[22]

There are four things for those who are not skilled in that:¶ if one is not skilled in descent, the bindu will be quickly lost; if one is not skilled in retaining, {53} the bliss will be short-lived;** if one is not skilled in reversing, the bindu will be combined with urine;†† and if one is not skilled in spreading,‡‡ one will become ill. To introduce the four skills for remedying those, skill in descent is moving like a tortoise;§§ skill in retaining is the three movements of body, voice, and mind;¶¶ skill in reversing is the four animal behaviors;*** and skill in spreading is the mudra of liberation. Further, one should tighten the belt of vāyu, and so on, as in the extensive path. This concludes the demonstration of the path for the time being.†††

The view, the four joys of connate gnosis, includes the four joys that depend on a sequence, the four joys that depend on a location, the four joys that depend on an object to renounce, and the four joys that depend on an intrinsic nature.

The four joys that depend on this sequence are explained at the time of the path and are not explained otherwise. In the second of those, there are two in the joy that depends on location: depending on outer locations and depending on inner locations. For the first of those two, when it arises in parts of the body, it is joy. When it arises in most of the body, it is supreme joy. When it arises throughout the whole body, it is the joy of separation

*The sound *hag*.
†The sound *hig*.
‡Also understood as those.
§According to the technique.
¶Those that desire intercourse.
**As before.
††Since the fourth is not understood.
‡‡Using the mudra of liberation, and so on.
§§Slow motion.
¶¶Such as constricting the sphincter, and so on.
***The *hiṃ* of the elephant, and so on.
†††Here, *S* and other treatises also offer a very concise path.

from joy.* When all apparent entities arise as bliss, it is innate joy. For the second of those two, between the crown and the throat, there is joy;† between the throat and the heart,‡ supreme joy; between the heart and the navel, the joy of separation from joy; and between the navel and the secret place, connate joy.

The four joys that depend on an object to renounce are the gradual cessation of coarse§ concepts of subject and object is joy, the gradual cessation of coarse concepts of identity is supreme joy, {54} the cessation of the concept of the mudra is the joy of separation from joy,¶ and the cessation of the concept of the joy of the separation from joy is connate joy. Apply these to the body.

The bindu is the joy that is the minor experience of bliss.** The blazing of bliss is supreme joy. Nonconceptual bliss is the joy of separation from joy. The bliss that is nondual with emptiness is the connate joy. One should also apply the citations.††

The conclusion‡‡ is the eleventh stage, the minor seal of bliss and emptiness, and the twelfth stage, the arising of the realization that all phenomena of nirvana, and so on, are bliss and emptiness.

If one is unable to follow the conclusion, Vajrasattva's arrival at the time of death is that the nāḍī knots break from the condition of the vāyu of death, and the bindu, the element that supports the mind, gradually assembles. Since these slightly enter the central nāḍī, supreme bliss and emptiness arise at the moment of death; *vajra* is emptiness and *sattva* is bliss. After mixing that with the previously mentioned view of bliss and emptiness, one follows the conclusion, and so on.

The result—the dharmakāya that is naturally accomplished without effort—will be explained at the time of the result, but it will not be discussed here. These are the five topics of the gnosis of the wisdom consort empowerment.

*The scripture states, "All the causes and noncauses of bliss," and so on [*HT*, f. 15b, line 1].
†Any experience that arises.
‡Drawing down the bindu.
§"The first joy is the form of a migrating being," and so on [*HT*, f. 12a, line 3].
¶"Because the third joy itself is renunciation, the connate is said to be awakening" [*HT*, f. 12a, lines 4–5].
**"First is mere joy," and so on [*HT*, f. 12a, line 2].
††Which explain heat on the path of application with that view.
‡‡The transcendent path.

The five for the fourth empowerment are the path, the three vajra waves; the view, the four joys stabilized by the principle of the utter purity of all phenomena; the conclusion, vast bliss and emptiness; the time of death, transference through mahāmudrā; and the result, the svabhāvakāya that is naturally accomplished without effort.

For the first of those, after the preliminaries, such as physical training, and so on, perform the full nine limbs of concentration. After the preliminaries, such as prāṇa, āyāma, and so on,* the movement of the lower vāyu† is the wave of the body.‡ Next is the wave of the voice. {55} Following that, there is the wave of the mind, meditating in samādhi.

There are three in training on the path, based on either an actual padminī§ or a gnosis mudra:¶ the method tantras, the so-called wisdom tantras, and the individual tantras of both.

Further, there are three topics, such as the sameness of body and voice,** and so on. The activities are similar to the path of the third empowerment. Next, the moment the method and wisdom enter into union, the supreme, refined elements of both the father and mother arrive at the anthers.†† Then, [the elements] transform into a ray of light, which travel into the nāḍī on the right, the rasanā. The navel cakra becomes faint like the light at dawn, clearer and clearer like sunrise, and becomes hollow like an inflated lung. After it becomes entirely filled, there is no more room. Again the elements move through the right rasanā, arriving at the heart. Recall the three characteristics. Again the elements move through the rasanā, arriving at the throat. Recall the three characteristics. Again the elements move through the rasanā, shining from the right nostril in the form of a ray of light. The maṇḍala of the supreme deity shines through the door of the ray of light, conferring empowerment upon the continua of sentient beings. The sentient beings become the supreme deity. The two merge together, becoming the bindu of amṛta,‡‡ and enter one's crown aperture. Recall the three characteristics at the crown. Arriving at the throat, the elements possess the

*The other vāyu yogas, and so on.

†Retaining the breath.

‡Both gentle and forceful.

§Best.

¶Medium.

**Employing the three kāyas as the path.

††The place where the two nāḍīs meet.

‡‡Because one's continuum is able to transform into the three kaȳas.

radiance of one thousand suns.* The elements transform into five-colored light in the heart. After the elements emerge from the path of the nāḍīs at the navel, as before, [the element] abides in the space of the mother. The immobilization of the right wave† of the object is the door of liberation called "signless." This is the first result. Likewise, the above is also performed for the left nāḍī. The immobilization of the left wave‡ of the subject is the door of liberation called "aspirationless." This is the second result. {56} Likewise, the above is also performed for the central nāḍī. The immobilization of the wave§ of both subject and object is the door of liberation called "emptiness." This is third result. This is the demonstration of the purification of the method tantra.

The above should also be performed for the wisdom tantra. Apart from merely arising at the earholes from the right and left nostril, the element does not issue outward. Traveling through the central nāḍī, one makes the element leave and gather back into the crown aperture. If one does not, it is asserted to be the same. The application of the three immobilizations and the three doors of liberation are understood to be the same as before. Then, since one purifies the tantras of method and wisdom individually, that refined element, in the form of a ray of light, moves through the central nāḍīs of the father and mother, dissolving into the supreme uṣṇīṣa. Likewise, it dissolves into the mother's uṣṇīṣa. Both the father and mother should recall the effortlessly accomplished five kāyas. Any experience that arises is undetermined; whatever arises should be naturally sustained.

The view is the four joys stabilized by the principle of the utter purity of all phenomena. Further, it is stated:[23]

> Aging is conquered because the cause corresponds.¶
> Strength is bestowed because of ripening.**

*Controlling the central nāḍī and the abiding vāyu causes subtle concepts of subject and object to subside.

†Controlling the right nāḍī and exhalation causes the concept of object to subside.

‡Controlling the left nāḍī and inhalation causes the concept of subject to subside.

§Controlling the central nāḍī and the abiding of the breath causes the concepts of subject and object to subside.

¶At the navel.

**At the heart.

> There is increase because of a person's activity.[*]
> Immortality is bestowed because of stainlessness.[†]

In the first joy, the element becomes as beautiful and attractive[‡] as the essence of all migrating beings. In the second joy, it gives rise to slight clairvoyance. In the third, one is able to enjoy all the flavors[§] of the world. In the fourth, one exhibits slight magic power. Further, in the first joy,[¶] the samādhi of bliss and emptiness is minor; in the second,[**] it is medium; in the third,[††] it is great; and in the fourth, it becomes the greatest of the great.[‡‡]

The conclusion is great bliss and emptiness:[§§] {57} in the first half of the thirteenth stage, all of samsara and nirvana is the state of a single emptiness, with nothing to accept or reject and with nothing to abandon or adopt.

If one cannot follow the conclusion, there are three topics in the time of death, the transference of the mahāmudrā of the path: training, familiarity, and the application of the activity.

The training is training in the vāyu. On any first day [of the month], one should train in four definite[¶¶] sessions with seventeen rounds of prāṇāyāma vāyu. In the same way, one should train for a period of twenty-one days, increasing each repetition each day. On the final day, the repetitions of the prāṇāyāma vāyu increases to thirty-seven.[***] Then, one decreases by one on the first day. In the same way, since one decreases each repetition each day,[†††] this also becomes the gauge for twenty-one days. One trains the vāyu for forty-two days until the movement of the vāyu becomes clear[‡‡‡] and its form[§§§] definitely arises.

[*] At the throat.
[†] At the crown.
[‡] Qualities.
[§] Any kind.
[¶] That pervades one's continuum.
[**] As soon as it appears.
[††] Pervading only nirvana.
[‡‡] Pervading all samsara and nirvana.
[§§] As much as possible in the view.
[¶¶] Repeated as much as possible.
[***] Increase.
[†††] Decrease.
[‡‡‡] From where it moves.
[§§§] Color.

There are two in cultivation: cultivation with sound and cultivation with syllables. First, settle into the key point of the body, and so on. Draw up with twenty-one "hi ka." Rest with twenty-one* "ka hi."† As such, train for seven days with four defined sessions.‡

There are two in the cultivation with syllables: cultivation with the outer syllables and cultivation with the inner syllables. The outer occurs in the main subject.§ The inner resembles the extensive inner heat based on the four cakras. Nevertheless, in both the right and left nāḍīs, the sixteen upright red vowels and the sixteen pairs of white inverted consonants are arranged in descending order, alternating with one another, and blocking both the right and left nāḍīs. Further, at the time of āyāma,[24] those syllables are visualized in ascending order. At the time of prāṇa,[25] they are visualized in descending order. One should cultivate those for seven days in four defined sessions. {58]

There are four in applying this in activities: applying this to higher realms, applying this to other migrating beings, applying this to other continents and birthplaces, and applying this to mahāmudrā. The stages of this practice should be understood from the instruction of the guru.

The result, the svabhāvakāya, will be explained at the time of the result but is not discussed here. These are the five topics of the fourth empowerment.

As such, the path,¶ and so on, are explained in twenty topics for a person of average** capacity. The medium path, "guard the samayas of equipoise, and so on,"[26] includes the samayas of equipoise,†† the samayas‡‡ of continual practice,§§ the samayas of eating,¶¶ the samayas of protection,*** and the samayas of nonseparation††† for each empowerment.‡‡‡

Now then, for the vase empowerment, the samaya of equipoise is the

*Arising with color, and so on.
†The movement through *ka hi*.
‡Explained below.
§Explained below.
¶Arranging the five dependent originations on the body.
**Because of little training.
††The path.
‡‡The view.
§§Samādhi itself.
¶¶Because it benefits body and mind.
***Because it avoids negative conditions.
†††Because is supports positive conditions.
‡‡‡Because it is the cause of the arising of samādhi.

creation stage. The samaya of continual practice is the three essentials of the view. The samaya of eating is the pill of five amṛtas and the five meats. The samaya of protection is the twenty-two root and branch downfalls. The samaya of nonseparation is the vajra and bell.

For the secret empowerment, the samaya of equipoise is the nāḍīs and vāyu.* The samaya of continual practice is self-originated gnosis.† The samaya of eating is emptiness and clarity.‡ The samaya of protection is all conflicts§ with self-origination and vāyu.[27] The samaya of nonseparation is to never be separate from either strong or gentle vāyu yogas.¶

For the gnosis of the wisdom consort empowerment, the samaya of equipoise is the maṇḍalacakra. The samaya of continual practice is the connate. The samaya of eating is bliss. The samaya of protection is avoiding the six ways the bindu leaks. The samaya of nonseparation is the actual or gnosis mudra.

For the fourth empowerment, the samaya of equipoise is the three waves. The samaya of continual practice is the principle of utter purity. The samaya of eating is the bliss and emptiness of great bliss. The samaya of protection is the knowledge obscuration from among the two obscurations. {59} The samaya of nonseparation is never being separate from the actual padminī or the gnosis mudra.

There are four ways to prevent "violations" of those samayas: violations are prevented by all samayas arising properly in one's continuum, violations are prevented by recalling** them through their enumeration, violations are prevented through the arising of an experience,†† and violations are prevented‡‡ by special devotion to the guru.§§

There are two in violations: violations of samaya that lead to suffering in samsara and violations of samaya that cause long delays in progress on the path. The first is violating the fourteen root downfalls that one promises to keep during the vase empowerment. The second is called a "samaya

*The path.
†The view.
‡Because it is beneficial.
§Because conflicts are avoided.
¶Because it supports positive conditions.
**Because a beginner needs to cultivate them.
††Since all key points are complete in this.
‡‡To all samayas.
§§Because the profound path is the guru.

violation," because violating the remaining samayas causes long delays* in progress on the path and long delays in accomplishment. The method of mending those is "mend violations with the vajra ḍākinī, and so on."[28] The vajra ḍākinī[29] is the guru.† The gnosis ḍākinī is the saṃbhogakāya. The mother ḍākinī is the nirmāṇakāya. The flesh-eating ḍākinī is the lords of the charnel ground, and so on. The samaya ḍākinī‡ is one's vajra siblings.[30]

If those samayas are violated, then the mending of violations of the five ḍākinīs is fulfilling the commitments of the vajra ḍākinī when all samayas are violated, which are supplied below.

[The text says,] "One should please them with the five, the objects of desire, and so on." Present them with the enjoyment of the external five substances of desirable enjoyment, and so on, and the inner desirable enjoyments, adorned with a knowledge consort. If one violates the samayas of equipoise, it is necessary to please the gnosis ḍākinī. For that, bring the view to its culmination.§ If one violates the samayas of continual practice, {60} it is necessary to please the mother ḍākinī by bringing the meditation to culmination.¶ If the remaining three samayas are violated, it is necessary to please the flesh-eating ḍākinī and the samaya ḍākinī with the enjoyment of an oblation of flesh and blood and a feast, respectively. That is the explanation of mending violations when the twenty samayas, which are the limbs of the medium path, are violated.

Now, in order to explain the four empowerments of the path in connection with the shape—the main point of the method tantra—it is said, "by meditating on the four empowerments in four sessions of the path." Taking the extensive, medium, and concise empowerments should be understood from the guru's instruction.

"In dependence on the body" means that the empowerment at the time of the cause is taken upon[31] the body and also the empowerment at the time of the path is taken upon the body. Further, the five dependent originations are arranged upon the body. The paths and stages are traversed inside the body. That which is abandoned is abandoned by the body. Thus, this is stated in this way.

*Since the cause of samādhi and samādhi itself are abandoned.

†Because the guru is one taste with the deity.

‡Because of having the same samaya.

§Placing the mind.

¶Because a faultless experience arises.

"The obscurations of great bliss" are as follows: In general, the eight defects and flaws are the obscuration of knowledge. Also, objects are the union of appearance and emptiness, consciousness is the union of clarity and emptiness, and the body is the union of bliss and emptiness from the absence of flaws.* These three "cease" in the manner of one taste through supreme bliss and emptiness.

"Since buddhahood manifests" means since dependent origination is arranged on the body, the accomplishment of the four or five kāyas of the result manifest. "It is the explanatory tantra" means since the cause of realization is the fundamental mind and the agent of realization is arranging dependent origination on the body, the body is the explanatory tantra, because there is realization and comprehension.

Up to this point, the body method tantra has been explained.

Now, to explain the mahāmudrā result tantra, "the mahāmudrā result tantra is omniscience through the four empowerments of the result." Since accomplishment depends on a mudra,† the so-called "accomplishment of the mudra," or the "person of the knowledge consort," is great or supreme because there is nothing higher than this. The ultimate path, the proximate cause of such accomplishment, {61} is the "four empowerments of the result": the vase empowerment is the route of the nāḍīs,‡ the secret empowerment is the route of the syllables,§ the wisdom consort's gnosis empowerment is the route of the bindus,¶ and the fourth empowerment is the route of the vāyus.** The result accomplished with those four is omniscience. The quoted passage refers to the omniscience†† of the body; the omniscience‡‡ of speech; the omniscience§§ of the mind; and the omniscience¶¶ of body, speech, and mind, which are the accomplishments of the four kāyas and the five kāyas. As such, up to this point the path explained as the three tantras has been explained.

*Because the view of the fourth empowerment is flawless.

†Because the retinue is liberated in a single group.

‡The central nāḍī.

§Because the color, shape, and power are complete.

¶The refined element.

**The gnosis vāyu.

††Nirmāṇakāya.

‡‡Saṃbhogakāya.

§§Dharmakāya.

¶¶Svabhāvakāya.

Now, in order to swiftly traverse the path because a special confidence has been generated, from the path demonstrated as the four authorities, it is said, "the result is confirmed with the four authorities." The speech of the sugata is the authority of the authentic scripture,* the experience of the vajra master guru is the authority of the intimate instruction,† the experience of the practitioner themself is the authority of recollection,‡ and the dependent origination of the limit of entities is the authority of the chronicle.§ This is indicated only by "The result is confirmed with the four authorities"; that is, one should understand that the result is confirmed with the four authorities, the path is confirmed with the five fives, and the cause is confirmed with all of samsara.

Now, in order to swiftly generate¶ samādhi, and so on, there is the path explained in the six oral instructions.

[The text says,] "The poison of concentration is extracted with the trio: the absence of the fault of internal contradiction, and so on." These are the six: the trio of extracting the poison** of concentration, utilizing amṛta, and release; and the trio of extracting the poison of the view, the five amṛtas, and release. {62} Though the trio of concentration is mentioned first here in the treatise, the trio of the view is mentioned first in the direct realization. Thus, they have been transposed here.

[The text says,] "The poison of the view is removed by meditating on the concepts of a purified intellect, the path of the elimination of engagement." In general, there are two in the view: mere understanding that is presented as the view and experiential samādhi presented as the view.

The first is the view that eliminates the doubts of hearing and reflection,†† the view of biased opinion in individual treatises,‡‡ the intellectually inclined view,§§ the view equivalent to the perfection vehicle, and the view that is not separate from the meaning of the ocean of reality.¶¶ Though such

*The Hevajra Tantra, and so on.

†One's guru.

‡Mental experiences, and so on.

§The instruction on the dependently originated experience.

¶To swiftly remove obstacles.

**The all-basis cause tantra.

††This removes the poison of ignorance.

‡‡Cittamatra, and so on.

§§Because of clinging and devotion to the real, it is not superior to Vajrayāna.

¶¶Since it is never separate from clinging.

views are connected with understanding, since they are unable to pacify the poison of the flow of conceptuality,* they do not become the immaculate path and the truth will not be seen—just as when food with one hundred flavors is poisoned, it is not beneficial.

To remove that poison, it is said, "the path of the elimination of engagement." Now then, first perform the complete nine limbs of concentration. Then, since one meditates by coordinating vāyu and the mind,† such as with the prāṇāyāma vāyu, when the mind abides on that, it is the path of the elimination of engagement.‡ The nominal categorization§ of that is "the conceptuality of a purified intellect." That¶ is also called "proper mentation." If that is empty,** it is called "the path of eliminating attachment." Otherwise, when the mind remains on [meditative signs, such as] smoke, and so on, it is called "the path of awakening."†† Since these arise in and out of order, {63} the samādhi should be recognized and naturally sustained.

If those do not remove the poison of the view, since consciousness desires an object, like a thirsty person searching for water, one should rely on the object, amṛta. [The text says,] "Rely on amṛta by not abandoning the five objects with the five consciousnesses." Since consciousness is satisfied by objects, [consciousness] abides on those objects—beginning with the eye seeing amazing spectacles up to relying on tactile sensations. The name for the mind that previously did not abide [on those objects] is "the heat that precedes conceptuality." That mind that abides [on those objects] "relies on the amṛta" of various objects, one from among the eight enhancements.

[Qualm:] Since objects are transformed into amṛta, because all sentient beings rely on objects, all will be endowed with samādhi.

[Reply:] This is not so. [The text says,] "Since pure phenomena arose as empty from the beginning, they are released." The meaning of that is as follows: Objects that do not arise from the start are empty. Since their nature is the three doors of liberation, there is neither bondage nor liberation; they are only released into nonarising emptiness. Bondage and liberation depend solely upon skill or lack of skill in the method. If one understands the key

*The so-called poison of effort.
†When exhaling, think "exhalation," and so on.
‡Engagement with the flow of conceptuality.
§Because it is a conceptual antidote.
¶Meditation on the coordination of vāyu and mind.
**If it is intrinsically empty of a perceived object.
††Because the object, appearance, and emptiness are in union, and so on.

point of being natural, it becomes the heat that precedes conceptuality. If this is not understood, then conceptuality flows, called "the māra of the meditation stolen by conceptuality," turning into concepts of the ordinary. That being the case, in dependence on skill in the method, one should understand that objects are only released[32] in nonarising emptiness. This is the explanation of the trio of the view.

Now, from among the trio of concentration, [the text says,] "the poison of concentration is extracted with the trio: the absence of the fault of internal contradiction, and so on." As such, though the poison of the view has been extracted, if the poison of concentration arises, the knowledge obscuration with eight faults, one should extract the poison with the faultless trio. The meaning of that is as follows: for the essence, there are two faults on the side of appearance {64} and the side of emptiness,* which are included in reification and denial.

For self-originated gnosis, there are three faults: affliction, concepts, and confusion, which are included in lethargy and agitation. Those also are unable to remedy that which is to be abandoned.† It is difficult to distinguish ordinary afflictions,‡ and so on. Joy in the connate and utter purity possesses the first three faults, because it is included§ in craving.¶

The remover of those eight poisons is the faultless trio: for the essence,** union lacks the fault of contradiction; for great self-originated gnosis,†† clarity and emptiness lack the fault of contradiction; and for the connate‡‡ and utter purity, the bliss and emptiness of connate joy lacks the fault of contradiction. Though the eight faults are identified as samādhi, by means of the key point of being natural, the faultless trio arises and extracts§§ the poison. If the faultless trio does not arise, the method of arousing them must be understood from the guru's instruction.

When neither the faultless trio nor even the faults arise, one should rely on amṛta. Though there are seven ways to do that, when they are included in

*Because it is a samādhi on being.
†Afflicted concepts.
‡Since they arise resembling experiences.
§Because it becomes a path or a cause of the three realms.
¶"The first joy is the form of a migrating being," and so on [*HT*, f. 12a, line 3].
**The object.
††Consciousness.
‡‡"The first joy is the form of a migrating being," and so on [*HT*, f. 12a, line 3].
§§Since those eight faults are transformed into the path.

three, there are the five amṛtas that generate the samādhi that has not arisen, enhance samādhi that has arisen, and individually remove faults (totaling seven).* The first of those is "diet." One should avoid hot spice,[33] excess salt, mountain onions,[34] sour, hot chang,[35] and spoiled meat; that is, one should avoid rough food. One should rely on a "regular application of amṛta": a little garden onion, *Terminalia chebula* soaked in milk and continuously chewed, the intimate instruction for cooking in water and butter, the three fruits and honey,[36] and feces and honey. After one uses those in the procedure to cultivate bodhicitta, they become supreme amṛta. The "conduct" is to avoid fire, the sun, {65} smoke, and dust. The conduct to be relied upon is to be relaxed and easy. The "vāyu" is any of the seven kinds of intimate instructions† of the vāyu. The "bindu" is the supreme concentration with any‡ of the four yogas of the bindu. Relying on a "mudra" is the same as the path of the third consecration. Those will generate the samādhi§ that has not arisen. "The bliss of the five pure essences"¶ is used for enhancement. If one wishes for any bliss that arises to pervade the whole body or all appearances, this is cultivated by blocking the āyāma,** exhaling†† slightly through the prāṇa,[37] and gazing upward with the eyes. "Since one is never separate from . . . the experience of the five sense organs," faults are removed. Focus attention anywhere discomfort[38] arises. Then, with either a peaceful or forceful utterance, propel it into the door of the sense organ.[39] This gives rise to bliss in the body and samādhi‡‡ and removes faults.§§

As such, there is the explanation of releasing the occurrence of pain of the nāḍīs and vāyu,¶¶ since samādhi arises through relying upon amṛta. There are three for that: releasing [pain in the ṇāḍī] in the location of that nāḍī, releasing pain of the vāyu through giving a reward, and releasing that [pain] is the natural heat of the mind. The latter two are found below.***

*Seven explanations.

†Explained below.

‡In the section on inner heat above.

§Or will enhance it.

¶With the five amṛtas.

**The right nostril.

††The stale vāyu.

‡‡Such as lack of clarity in the eyes, and so on.

§§Lack of clarity of the sense organs, and so on.

¶¶If it occurs.

***In the section on the seventy intimate instructions of the vāyu yoga and in the section on freedom from hope and fear.

There are two in releasing the nāḍīs: releasing the nāḍīs of samsara and releasing the nāḍīs of nirvana. First, in general, there are the nāḍīs of the six realms: like a ball of yarn,[*] like a skein of thread,[†] like a coiled snake,[‡] {66} like an umbrella,[§] like a spreading tree,[¶] and like a snarl of hair.[**] Each of those should be released.[††]

Now then, "the four nāḍīs of samsara" are both the rasanā and the lalanā. Above the navel, they exist based in the right and left sides of the body. Below the navel, it is maintained that they divide into four: the right side, left side, front, and back. Further, there is the nāḍī that expels[‡‡] and holds olibanum[40] on the right side, the nāḍī that expels and holds camphor[41] on the left side, the nāḍī that expels and holds musk[42] in front, and the nāḍī that expels and holds the fourfold unguent[43] in the rear. Since those nāḍīs generate the body[§§] that is generated by karma and the mind that possesses subject and object, they are termed "the nāḍīs of samsara."

There are six cakras: the two cakras[¶¶] in which bodhicitta does not move and the four cakras[***] in which it does move. Further, there are twelve cakras for the twelve major joints.[†††] Thus, there are eighteen cakras.

When nāḍī pain arises, that pain should be released in those nāḍīs. "The others" refers to the other thirty-two nāḍīs and the other subtle nāḍīs.[‡‡‡] When pain arises, it should be released in those locations. Now, in releasing pain in the nāḍīs of nirvana, when the pure vāyu and mind are in the central nāḍī, there are thirty-two nāḍī-constricting knots. Each knot between the first stage (very joyful) and the twelfth stage (great gnosis) must be released.[§§§] Up to the tenth stage is the initial preparation, the main sub-

[*] The nāḍī cakra of the heart.
[†] Navel.
[‡] Throat.
[§] Crown.
[¶] The whole body.
[**] In all the fingers and joints.
[††] By focusing on the site of pain.
[‡‡] And the vāyu.
[§§] The physical body.
[¶¶] The moon of the father in the ūrṇā (the coil of hair between the brows) and the mother's olibanum in the secret place.
[***] The crown cakra, and so on.
[†††] There are thirty-two nāḍī petals that generate the four pathological elements: vāta, pitta, kapha, and rakta (blood).
[‡‡‡] The seventy-two thousand, and so on.
[§§§] In ascending order.

ject is enjoyment, and the conclusion is total completion and dissolution.[44] Thus, the knots are released three at a time. That being so, {67} "the three for each stage—first to last, up to the tenth stage—are released by freeing the knots of the nāḍīs."

As such, the six oral instructions have been explained.

Now,[*] in the path explained as the four aural lineages, "explain the four, the aural lineage of Secret Mantra, and so on": the river of empowerment never subsides, the lineage of empowerment is unimpaired, the stream[†] of oral instructions is without error, and the thought of devotion can satiate.

First, the empowerment at the time of the cause never subsides,[‡] the empowerment at the time of the path never subsides,[§] and the empowerment at the time of the result never subsides.[¶] In brief, this is the treatise that perfects the path by the empowerment. Second, Secret Mantra has the nature of four limits: the limit of practice,[**] the limit of experience,[††] the limit of empowerment,[‡‡] and the limit of the conclusion.[§§] Third is when many kinds of harm arise, such as māras, rākṣasas, obstacles, terror, fear, and so on. When those are recognized as the path, the obstructions to concentration are dispelled because samādhi is recognized.[¶¶] Since obstacles are recognized, the māras are dispelled. Since the faults are recognized as qualities, and since obstacles are taken as accomplishments, it is called "the oral instruction of recognition." Fourth, all obstacles and accomplishments and hope and fear are explained by the sublime guru to arise from the arrangement of the dependent origination of the nāḍīs and vāyus in one's body. A special confidence arises, and one begins to think of guru as a buddha.

Now, in the path explained as the five dependent originations, [there are]: {68} What is the basis[***] of arranging dependent origination? What is

[*] Since all accomplishments arise from the unbroken lineage of meaning.
[†] *Sarga.*
[‡] Either the profound, medium, or average empowerment from the guru.
[§] Either extensive or concise, and so on.
[¶] The dissolution of the four movements.
[**] Vāyu, and so on, from the complete limbs of concentration.
[††] Physical experiences, and so on.
[‡‡] Flexibility of the body.
[§§] The first stage and above.
[¶¶] Because the dependent origination of syllables is recognized.
[***] Dependence on a special body.

the limit[*] of dependent origination? What is dependent origination[†] itself? What arises[‡] from its four paths? What arises from the four[§] authorities? The meaning[¶] indicated and actualized by that dependent origination is the path, which is perfected through an origination that is dependent and relational,[**] explained in seven topics. That should be applied in stages to *The Vajra Verses*.

Now, the prevention of obstacles of the path of the practitioner who deviates to the sides of method or wisdom is as follows: There are eight preventatives for the four obstacles of the practitioner who deviates to the side of method. There are eight preventatives for the four obstacles of the practitioner who deviates to the side of wisdom. There are fourteen preventatives in common for both [kinds of] yogis. There are a total of thirty preventatives in the lower worldly path. That is explained by "the obstacles of the practitioner who deviates to the side of method."

"Deviating to the side of method" is deviating because of devotion and involvement[††] and deviating into experience.[‡‡] Such a person is attacked by the four obstacles during four time periods: When entering the path,[§§] there is the obstacle of mundane phenomena. When abiding on the path,[¶¶] there is the obstacle of external māras. When the mind is slightly stable,[***] there is the obstacle of māra's increasing strength. When the mind is stable, there is the obstacle of not recognizing samādhi.[†††]

There are two in the first: the obstacle related to relatives[‡‡‡] and the obstacle related to the guru and companions.[§§§] {69} The first is prevented by stable faith, which is prior to trivial and minor generosity. The second is

[*] The limit of entities.
[†] Other-dependence is dependent and relational.
[‡] Great awakening.
[§] The authority of the chronicle.
[¶] The great awakening of the pure all-basis.
[**] Dependent origination is totally complete in five: outer, inner, secret, true, and ultimate dependent origination.
[††] Faith in the form of the deity, and so on.
[‡‡] The vision of smoke, and so on.
[§§] Four sessions, and so on.
[¶¶] When experiences arise.
[***] Medium gathering of the elements.
[†††] Medium and average gathering of the elements.
[‡‡‡] Turning away from the path because of regret and being engaged in the trivial.
[§§§] Involvement in activities.

prevented by stable faith, which is prior to trivial generosity[*] and mental affection.[†]

The obstacle of external māras is definitely prevented by three things: the protection wheel of the vajra fence,[†] and so on; reciting the *sumbhani* mantra, and so on;[§] and the mantra knots that depend on the external condition of the guru and companions.[¶] Those are the four preventive methods for the obstacles of the method.

The obstacle of a māra's increasing strength is turned into the protection wheel,[**] prevented by recognizing that the one with the obstacle, the obstructing māra, and the obstacle itself are mind—recognized as illusory and recognized to lack inherent existence.[††] That being so, there are three preventatives of the obstacle of method through wisdom. Since the vāyu and mind gather evenly in the locations of *kṣa*, and so on, when the mind is stable,[‡‡] when many injuries occur, such as being struck by rākṣasas, piśācis,[§§] and so on, the obstructions[¶¶] to concentration are removed by recognizing samādhi.[***] Since the obstacles are recognized,[†††] the obstructions of māra are removed.

The recognition that takes faults[‡‡‡] as qualities[§§§] and the recognition that takes obstacles[¶¶¶] as accomplishments[****] pacify obstacles. In brief, it is said the eight preventatives can be included in three: the four preventatives of obstacles of method with method, the three preventatives of obstacles of method with wisdom, and the single preventative of an obstacle of method with dependent origination.

With respect to the so-called path of wisdom, and so on, there are two

[*]Things.
[†]Apologizing.
[†]That occur in general sādhanas.
[§]For confidence.
[¶]Granted by the powerful.
[**]The ultimate protection wheel.
[††]Any of these three.
[‡‡]The secret dependent origination.
[§§]External.
[¶¶]Which are not separate.
[***]As true samādhi.
[†††]Claiming it is not correct.
[‡‡‡]Because they are not recognized.
[§§§]Because they are recognized.
[¶¶¶]When they are not recognized.
[****]When recognized.

types of person: the one who deviates into the side of wisdom through devotion and involvement and the one who deviates into the side of wisdom through experience. Also, those two are attacked by four obstacles: the obstacle that generates harm* and {70} suffering, the obstacle that manifests form,† the māra of uttered sound,‡ and the obstacle of change of view and conclusions.§ The four preventatives for those are entered gradually; that is, with the four examinations. Those will be supplied below in connection with the passage concerning preventing the devaputra māra,[45] who arrives on the path of wisdom with the four examinations. The four examinations are the examination through experience,¶ the examination through samādhi,** the examination through mantra,†† and the examination through view and conclusion.‡‡

If the subsidiary topics are briefly mentioned, the so-called "external māra" is the misleader, who is only an obstacle of the dark side from the beginning. "The two paths that multiply the views and conclusions into eight" means the views and conclusions multiplied into eight on the two paths are the four obstacles.

Now, "the inner māra" is the four obstacles as before, which are prevented by the symbols of the four empowerments. Now, the inner māra is beneficial,§§ harmful,¶¶ and both destructive and caring. Therefore, it is called "the inner māra," and also called an obstructor. "The ten, the path, and so on," are also as before. "Prevented by knowing the symbols" means the symbols of the body:[46]

> Gather*** the five.††† Press the tip.[47]
> Touch the *e*[48] of the thumb and ring finger,‡‡‡

*Pain, and so on.

†Many.

‡Predictions, and so on.

§Claims that they are not so.

¶Prevention with the three protection wheels.

**When pain, and so on, arise at the time of meditating on the path.

††If one is imitated, [it is an obstacle].

‡‡If one does not recognize the four paths, [it is an obstacle].

§§If pleased.

¶¶If not pleased.

***Applied to the four empowerments, respectively.

†††The techniques.

‡‡‡When the guru places the bodhicitta on the tongue during the secret empowerment.

> the mudra of supreme awakening.[49]
> The index finger indicates space.[50]

The subsidiary symbols:[51]

> Display the separated fingers.
> Make the inseparable vajra fist.
> Display the raised three-tined vajra.
> The index finger indicates space.

The symbols of the voice are *ka la śa a*, *ya ra la wa*, {71} *e vaṃ ma ya*, and *oṃ āḥ hūṃ aṃ*. These four* should be understood as the four kinds [of symbols of the voice].† These definitely prevent obstacles. Those explain the two sets of eight preventatives from deviating into the side of method and wisdom in sixteen topics.

Now, among the fourteen preventatives that are common to both yogas, it is said "prevent contamination, obscuration, and leaking bindu"; that is, prevent the six contaminations,‡ the six leaking bindus,§ and the two obscurations.¶ Among those, the six contaminations are the contamination of samaya,[52] the contamination of spirits, the contamination of evil companions, the contamination of food, the contamination of place, and the contamination of corpses.

Among those six, the first is a major contamination, the middle four are medium contaminations, and the last is a minor contamination. The three grades of contamination will be understood in dreams and experience. By examining where there is impurity,** the major contamination is in the body, the medium contamination is on one's clothes, and the minor contamination is in one's dwelling or on one's skin. Further, the six contaminations should be understood separately in dreams or experience. The major contamination will deprive one of life. The medium contamination will generate suffering for body and mind and plunder samādhi. Also, when there is a minor contamination, it too will plunder samādhi.

*The four sets.
†One set for each of the four empowerments.
‡Primarily during the initial gathering of the elements.
§Primarily during the middle gathering of the elements.
¶Primarily during the final gathering of the elements.
**Bugs, ants, and so on.

To remove those contaminations, the major contamination is removed by taking empowerment,* the medium contamination is removed by offering feasts,† and the minor contamination is removed by washing.‡ With respect to removing the major, medium, and minor contamination of spirits, from the perspective of removing contamination by washing, the major contamination can be removed accordingly§ by performing a vase ritual: Pour ash from a wrathful fire offering, aconite root, powder of human bone, and white mustard seeds into a vase. Fill it with sweet-scented water and recite the essence mantra of the excellent deity many times. Then, the contamination is removed by washing during the three times. For the medium, use the ash from an increasing¶ fire offering. {72} For the minor, use the ash of a pacifying fire offering. To eliminate the contamination of contagious diseases, use the ash of a power fire offering, as prescribed by the rite.**[53] Also, in general, the six contaminations will be removed by empowerment, removed by feasts on specific days,†† removed by washing,‡‡ and removed by making sācchas§§[54] (half the sāccha is left in an isolated place, and half is cast into a large river). Moreover, contaminations can be removed by protecting the life of small creatures, confessing woefully¶¶ with the voice, and so on. Since these contaminations are primarily obstacles during the initial gathering of the elements, removing contamination is very important.

The six leaking bindus occur because bliss arises and overflows, because of spirits and dreams, combined with urine because of illness, because of passion aroused by the knowledge consort, because of weakening oneself with improper diet, and combined with perspiration because of one's behavior.

To prevent those, for the first there are the six kinds of movement, such as prevention through different strengths, the gentle and strong vocal inhalation. The second is using the ash of black gugul, human brain, white mustard seeds,*** and lotus blood, combining them well, and applying this [mixture]

*From the guru.
†To the samaya ḍākinī.
‡Also by reciting one's essence mantra.
§Seeds, medicine, and so on.
¶Substitute the third.
**Look elsewhere for this.
††Corresponding with the class of deity.
‡‡Reciting many mantras.
§§According to how they are molded.
¶¶The one-hundred-syllable mantra.
***First burn the mustard seed, then the gugul, and finally add the other two ingredients.

in the evening to the secret place and the waist. Further, make twenty-one knots on a black thread, recite the essence mantra of the excellent deity, and tie it around the waist. For traces, use the soiled clothes of a women. The others will be prevented by physical behavior* and methods that are shared with action tantra,† and so on. Third, in general, rely on a nutritious diet. Administer a small quantity of the dry powder of the three hot herbs[55] on an empty stomach. To keep warm, wrap the secret place and the waist with a strip of a predator skin,[56] and so on. {73} Apply moxibustion five or seven times on the point where the elbows reach when standing. This will definitely pacify [leaking bindu because of illness]. Fourth, prevent with the special method of staring.‡ The other two methods§ of prevention should be understood in detail from the guru.

The prevention of the last two leaking bindus is no different than the occasion of relying on the amṛta of diet and conduct. Since these two are also primary obstacles to the second gathering of the elements, it is extremely important to prevent it.

The two obscurations are the afflictive obscuration and the knowledge obscuration. The first is the incessant flow of concepts. Those are prevented with the trio of clearing the entry, and so on. The knowledge obscuration has eight faults even though there is samādhi. Those are prevented with the three faultlessnesses by means of the critical points of naturalness. If the three faultlessnesses do not arise, the method of generating them must be understood from the guru.¶ Those** show the fourteen shared methods of prevention, but in general there are thirty methods of prevention. As such, having divided the text into seven sections, the shared path of samsara and nirvana has been explained.

Now, in the teaching on the mundane path—the dance of samsara and nirvana—though that text is said to be divided into seven sections, the presentation of the general path has three systems of path instruction and two systems of progress. First, there is the path instruction with vāyu,[57] the path instruction with amṛta elements, and the path instruction with the nāḍī syllables.

*Seated upright with knees drawn to chest.

†Found separately.

‡With the eyes looking up.

§Diet and medicine.

¶Separately.

**For the three kinds of persons.

Below the mundane path, there is the path instruction with the vāyu for the harm inflicted* during the initial gathering of the elements, the path instruction with the vāyu that is neither harmful nor beneficial during the middle† gathering of the elements, and the path instruction with the vāyu that is beneficial during the final gathering of the elements.‡ {74} That concludes the mundane path.

On the transcendent path, there is the path instruction with immaculate vāyu,§ the path instruction with the vāyu of the five faculties,¶ the path instruction with the vāyu of the five powers,** and the path instruction of the total dissolution of the vāyu of the prāṇa and āyāma.†† Following the dissolution of the movement of the vāyu, it becomes only gnosis vāyu.‡‡

Second, the path instruction with element amṛtas is the path instruction with the unrefined element during the initial§§ gathering of the elements, the path instruction with the slightly refined element during the middle gathering of the elements, and the path instruction with the largely refined element during the final gathering of the elements. This concludes the mundane path.

In the transcendent path, there is the path instruction with the refined elements, the path instruction with the essence of amṛta, the path instruction with the very refined element, the path instruction of the extremely refined element, and the most refined element through the dissolution of the movement of the amṛta element.[58]

Third, in the path instruction with nāḍī syllables, there is the path instruction with syllables with the undefined, delusive appearances during the initial gathering of the elements, the path instruction with the syllables arising as defined, visual appearances during the middle gathering of the elements, and the path instruction with the syllables arising as very defined, clear appearances. This concludes the mundane path.

In the transcendent path, there is the path instruction with the slightly

*Major pain.

†Medium pain.

‡This removes the increase of pathological humors, and so on.

§Six bodhisattva stages, one through six.

¶Four bodhisattva stages, seven through ten.

**The first two stages of buddhahood, eleven and twelve.

††The first half of the thirteenth stage of buddhahood.

‡‡The thirteenth stage of buddhahood.

§§The pure and impure parts of the element are mixed together.

pure power of the syllables, the path instruction with the mostly pure power of the syllables, the path instruction with the pure power of the syllables, and the path instruction with the purest of the pure syllables. After the movements of the syllables dissolve, they transform into indestructible syllables.

Now, the two systems of progress on the path [are as follows]: there is progressing on the path according to the five paths from the perspective of conforming to scripture[*] and progressing on the path according to the thirty-seven factors conducive to awakening. First, there are four[†] in the path of accumulation: the outer path of accumulation of shapes, and so on.

In the path of application, there are three kinds of heat, such as preliminary conceptuality, and so on; {75} the two[‡] external and internal summits; the difficult patience toward the nonarising of phenomena,[§] the single patience of emptiness; and both the supreme dharma beyond the dharmas of samsara[¶] and the supreme dharma beyond the dharmas of nirvana.[**] The paths of accumulation and application conclude the mundane path.

There is the path of seeing because of three signs,[††] the path of cultivation because of eleven groups of three signs, and the consummate path because of the dissolution of four movements.

Second, if one progresses on the path according to the thirty-seven factors conducive to awakening, first, the four bases of magic power[‡‡] are the antidote to appearances arising as enemies. When emptiness arises as an enemy, there are the four foundations of mindfulness. There are the four correct renunciations when one faints from bliss. These twelve complete the mundane path.

Next, in the transcendent path, in the [first] six stages [one through six], there are the seven limbs of awakening.[§§] The five faculties exist for [the next] four stages[¶¶] [seven through ten], and the five powers exist for the

[*]The *Ornament of Direct Realization*.
[†]There is also an enumeration of three.
[‡]Realization.
[§]Because the vāyu gathers in the central nāḍī.
[¶]That which is abandoned.
[**]That which is accepted.
[††]The outer signs, and so on.
[‡‡]This is the reverse of the perfection vehicle, because it is a critical point of rapid progress on the path.
[§§]Enumerated on nāḍīs.
[¶¶]Enumerated on the vāyus.

two [penultimate] stages[*] [eleven and twelve]. Supported on the first half of the thirteenth bhūmi, the eight consciousnesses are the eightfold path of nobles. As such, the transcendent path concludes with the twenty-five factors conducive to awakening.

Now, among the subsidiary topics, which are explained sequentially, there is the so-called path of accumulation, which has four topics: [First,] the outer path of accumulation of shapes is the path of accumulation,[†] which begins from inviting the guru and deity, who are not different, into the space before one and making the five offerings.[59] [Second,] the inner[‡] path of accumulation of mantra is the path of accumulation that begins from gathering the vāyu and mind into the location of the navel. [Third,] the secret path of accumulation of empowerment {76} is the path of accumulation, which begins from gathering the vāyu and mind in the space of the mother.[§] [Fourth,] the consummate[¶] path of accumulation of reality is the path of accumulation of joy, and so on, which begins from gathering the vāyu and mind in the supreme anthers of a twenty-year-old padminī.

In brief, it is asserted that the so-called "path of accumulation" accumulates the causes of arousing samādhi. When the foregoing path prepares the heat[**] of the path of application, there are three heats: weak,[††] medium,[‡‡] and strong heat.[§§] Since the three gatherings of the elements are entered gradually, it is said, "after obtaining the four results of disconnecting from the ordinary body, voice, and mind." With respect to that, in general, at the time of the cause, four[¶¶] results arise. Four results[60] arise for the first conclusion, and four results arise for each conclusion.

The four results at the time of the cause [are as follows]: The disconnected result is disconnected from the ordinary body, voice, and mind.[***] The ripened result ripens for oneself, because it exists in the all-basis.[†††] The simul-

[*]Power over the vāyu.
[†]The creation stage.
[‡]Caṇḍālī.
[§]The mudra.
[¶]The waves.
[**]Preliminary conceptuality, and so on.
[††]Slight harm by external conditions in weak heat.
[‡‡]No harm or benefit in medium heat.
[§§]The result is produced in strong heat.
[¶¶]Primary.
[***]Appearances arising as the deity.
[†††]Such as understanding the language of animals.

taneous result that corresponds with the cause is experienced according to whatever actions were performed.[*] The result of a person's effort,[†] or the immaculate result, arises from a person's effort and abandons the negative factors to be abandoned. The first of those is the result from the gradual stabilization of the experience of heat: one's own body and others' bodies arise as deities, voices arise as mantras, and one's mind arises as an uninterrupted stream of samādhi. Then, at that moment, there is also the second result: one can understand any language of animals, one understands anything that is said, and one feels one cannot be impeded by any appearance. Then, at that moment, there is the third result: the bliss of the body is uninterrupted, and even conditions of suffering arouse bliss. Then, at that moment, there is the fourth result: temporary afflictions are averted, {77}the conceptual mind of the eight worldly dharmas gradually ceases, and any clinging is reduced.

There are four results that arise in the first conclusion. The first result is that one sees the faces of nirmāṇakāya buddhas; one appears as the excellent deity; the creation stage stabilizes, and one disconnects from the ordinary body; one explains the dharma to one hundred disciples with the voice, and one disconnects from ordinary voice; and a samādhi devoid of equipoise and post-equipoise arises in one's mind, and one disconnects from one's ordinary mind. Then, at that moment, the second result is that one is unimpeded by walls and mountains, one can place the three realms in a mustard seed without one getting smaller or the other larger, one can create many from one, one can reduce many to one, and so on. Then, at that moment, the third result is that the vāyu and mind are inserted into the central nāḍī, one is embraced by the queen on one's lap, and uninterrupted immaculate bliss arises. Then, at that moment, the fourth result, which is that any concepts of visual appearance and so on, are reversed, the power of the negative factors to abandon weaken, the power of antidotal gnosis increases, and the movement of concepts is countered.

The four results of the individual conclusions are the names of the result given in the four conclusions themselves. In the context of heat, those arise primarily as the first four. Thus, it begins there.

Now, in order to explain the cause of samādhi, the intrinsic nature of samādhi, and the benefits of samādhi,[‡] it is said, "the three ways of gathering

[*]Bliss arising through the condition of suffering.

[†]Because of weak attachment to the eight worldly dharmas.

[‡]Completing the five paths.

the element through the impartialities. . . ." The three ways of gathering the elements are the natural gathering of the elements of a karmically destined person,* the gathering of the elements of the empowerment of a devoted one,† and the effortful gathering of the elements by a diligent one.‡ When the seven impartialities {78} are applied to the first way of gathering the elements, the karmically destined person becomes active impartially,§ the vāyu¶ reverts impartially, the fire of inner heat blazes impartially, the nāḍīs are released impartially, the element gathers impartially, contaminated clairvoyance arises impartially, and uncontaminated clairvoyance arises impartially. There are seven for the devoted person and seven for the diligent person, making a total of twenty-one. If one possesses all twenty-one, one will follow the conclusion in this lifetime. If one possesses fourteen, one will follow the conclusion in the bardo. If one possesses only seven, one will follow the conclusion after sixteen lifetimes. The first in each of those three is the indirect cause of samādhi. The five in the middle in each of those three is the intrinsic nature of samādhi. The last in each of those three is the qualities or result.

Now, the explanation of the three ways of stilling the mind is the self-empowerment of vāyu and mind. The mind is stilled by reversing the vāyu. The mind is stilled through the self-empowerment of the vāyu and mind. The mind is stilled by mingling it evenly within the body. The example for the first is like water freezing or catching a horse. The example for the second is like fainting from poison, and so on. The example for the third is like pouring water into water or ghee into ghee. The first and the last are explained later. Here, the self-empowerment of the vāyu and mind will be explained. From the perspective of the corresponding citation, it is said, "When progressing on the path according to the thirty-seven factors conducive to awakening." "Awakening" refers to the abandonments and gnosis of the thirteenth stage. "Factor" refers to a cause. "Thirty-seven" refers to the enumeration, the presentation of dependent origination, vāyu, and so on.

Among those thirty-seven, from the perspective of a beginner quickly entering or making progress on the path, it is said, "the four bases of magic power of undistracted meditation." "Undistracted meditation" refers to

*Samādhi arises at the time of the cause empowerment, and so on.

†Devoted to the guru, and so on.

‡Four sessions.

§The cause.

¶The five revert in impartial samādhi.

the arrangement of dependent origination upon oneself {79} and every samādhi that exists. The "four bases of magic power" refers to the base of magic power of the earth vāyu due to generating a special samādhi* with the earth vāyu. That is mixed with the other three [vāyus].

With respect to that, the "karma vāyu" is defined as karma vāyu because it performs ten functions in the mundane path. In general, there are four† entering karma vāyus. When divided, there are ten. There are seven key points of practice and a total of seventy key points of intimate instruction. First, there is trembling‡ because of the male vāyu, shaking because of the female vāyu, stability because of the genderless vāyu, and many functions, such as jumping, running, and so on, because of the entry of the blazing fire of the transcendent gnosis.

"The first gathering of the elements" means that the vāyu and mind gather the samaya being and the gnosis being of the ten fathers and mothers§ in the manner of ḍākinīs in the four palatial meeting places. "Sunders the nāḍī like the force of winter wind" refers to the pain of the nāḍī and vāyu that arises because at that time there is no prior purification. For example, it is like feeling very cold in the winter.

The "mind is still"¶ refers to the mind being even. "Dreams of horses" refers to dream experiences. "Pain of nāḍī and vāyu arise" means harmful to the body. To explain the meaning of that, "the tenfold division" means there are five fundamental vāyus and five secondary vāyus, totaling ten. The seven keys points of practice for those [are as follows]: In general, the four vāyus in one person are exhalation,** inhalation, abiding, and holding. Thus, one breath has four vāyus. Now then, if the last topic†† is described first, after fully adopting the nine limbs of concentration, first begin from the āyāma.‡‡ Then, begin from the prāṇa.§§ Then, gradually give a reward.¶¶ Naturally

*The sign of smoke, and so on.
†Kinds.
‡For one or every person.
§In the four places.
¶It stays wherever it is directed.
**Also for each one, earth, and so on.
††The practice.
‡‡Exhalation.
§§Inhalation.
¶¶Long inhalation.

sustain all experiences.* Examine objects of mental engagement. Take the element's measure. {80}

Then, the instruction on exhaling the breath for stability and progress is the limb of releasing. The three parts are blocking the āyāma† and releasing through the prāṇa,‡ releasing through both to develop strength,§ and releasing¶ through the nostrils with sound. Moreover, the instruction on inhalation for stability and progress is the limbs of filling. There are two for that, filling noiselessly through the nostrils,** and blocking the āyāma and filling through the prāṇa.†† Further, the instruction of the abiding breath is the main entrance of the path for stability. Progress is the hold. Also, one must fully adopt the limbs of concentration: first draw up the lower vāyu, engage the upper vāyu, and then draw up the lower vāyu again—it is very important not to err in these three key points.‡‡ Focus one's consciousness on the *a* at the navel, and so on.

> For the most diligent, uninterrupted;
> for the more diligent, sixty-four;
> for the mediocre, thirty-two;
> but there is no specified number for the average.

Since all the experiences arise in and out of order, all heat should be naturally sustained. "Through the seven differentiations of arresting the ten vāyus, the fundamental vāyus, and so on" refers to the seventy key points of intimate instructions: the name for each vāyu, the place it is located, its function, the pain from arresting it, its samādhi, the faults of immobilization, and the method of treatment.

With respect to those, the first fundamental vāyu is named "life-sustaining" (*srog 'dzin*, Skt. *prāṇa*).§§ It is located in the aorta (the life nāḍī).

*Physical experience, and so on.
†The right nostril.
‡The left nostril.
§Thinking of the ūrṇā.
¶Mindfully.
**Imagine consciousness absorbs into the *aṃ* at the navel.
††Virūpa's qualities arose from this practice.
‡‡Do not mistake an even duration of movement with an uneven duration of movement. If the relaxed lower vāyu moves up, it is an error. If it moves inside, qualities will arise.
§§The water vāyu.

It prevents the disconnection of the body and mind and causes grasping to "I" and "self." When [this vāyu is] arrested, the pain is heart instability[61] and palpitations, there are sharp pains and aches in the upper body, and one is talkative. {81} The [associated] samādhi is emptiness and clarity that arises for a long while. If the prāṇa vāyu becomes immobile, it leads to vāyu in the heart.[62] There are three methods of treatment for vāyu in the heart: releasing, empowering, and meditating on bliss.

The second fundamental vāyu* is named "metabolic" (*me mnyam*, Skt. *samāna*). It is located in the gut. Its function is to metabolize food and drink and separate nutriment from waste. When arrested, the pain is bloating in the abdomen, the sound of grumbling, and so on. The [associated] samādhi of bliss and emptiness arises for a short while. If it becomes immobilized, it leads to ascites, and so on. The method of treating that is the same as before.

The third fundamental vāyu† is named "downward-clearing" (*thur sel*, Skt. *apāna*). It is located in the groin. Its function is expelling and holding olibanum and camphor and expelling and holding the fourfold unguent and musk. When arrested, the pain is pain and aches in the middle that come and go. The [associated] samādhi is emptiness and clarity that arises for a long while. If it becomes immobilized in the lower body, either there is uncontrollable diarrhea or feces and urine will be bound. The method of treating that is the same as before.

The fourth fundamental vāyu‡ is named "upward-moving" (*rgyen rgyu*, Skt. *udāna*). It is located in the throat. Its function is speaking, laughing, swallowing, and throwing up food. If it is arrested, there is swelling and pain in the throat. The [associated] samādhi is a clear and empty consciousness that arises for a long while. If it is immobilized, this can lead to internal cancers, and so on. The method of treating that is the same as before.

The fifth fundamental vāyu§ is named "pervading" (*khyab byed*, Skt. *vyāna*). It is located in the crown and the twelve major joints. Its function is leaping, running, lifting, setting things down, and so on. If it is arrested, there is pain in the head and all the joints. The [associated] samādhi arises in the form of bliss and clarity in the whole body. If it is immobilized, the limbs

*The earth vāyu.

†The air vāyu.

‡The fire vāyu.

§The space vāyu.

contract, one becomes hunchbacked, and so on. The method of treating that is the same as before.

That is the explanation of the thirty-five points of the intimate instructions of the fundamental vāyus.

Now, among the five secondary vāyus,[63] {82} the first is named "bearing" (*rgyu ba*, Skt. *vāha*). It is located in both eyes. Its function is perceiving superior, intermediate, and inferior forms. If that is arrested, there is pain in the eyes and the eye socket. The [associated] samādhi prevents harm by external objects and subsequently assists the gnosis of realization. If immobilized, it leads to blindness, and so on. The method of treatment is the same as before.

The second secondary vāyu is named "flowing" (*rab tu rgyu ba*, Skt. *pravāha*). It is located in both ears. Its function is perceiving superior, intermediate, and inferior sounds. If it is arrested, there is pain in the ear canal and it becomes slightly difficult to hear. The [associated] samādhi prevents harm by external objects and subsequently assists the gnosis of realization. If it is immobilized, it leads to deafness, and so on, and on occasion, blood may seep from the ear. The method of treatment is the same as before.

The third secondary vāyu is named "bearing with ease" (*shin tu rgyu ba*, Skt. *suvāha*). Its location is the nostrils. Its function is perceiving superior, intermediate, and inferior scents. If it is arrested, there is pain in the nose and septum. The [associated] samādhi prevents harm by external objects and subsequently assists the gnosis of realization. If immobilized, it leads to flat nostrils and the inability to smell. The method of treatment is the same as before.

The fourth secondary vāyu is named "eating" (*mngon par rgyu ba*, Skt. *abhyavāha*). It is located in the tongue and uvula. Its function is perceiving superior, intermediate, and inferior tastes. If it is arrested, there is swelling and pain of the tongue and uvula. The [associated] samādhi prevents harm by external objects and subsequently assists the gnosis of realization. If it becomes immobilized, it leads to muteness, and so on. The method of treatment is the same as before.

The fifth secondary vāyu is named "carrying" (*yang dag par rgyu ba*, Skt. *saṃvāha*). It is located in the nāḍīs, the skin, and all pores. Its function is perceiving superior, intermediate, and inferior tactile objects. If it is arrested, the whole body becomes hot, sore, and so on. The [associated] samādhi prevents harm by external objects and subsequently assists the gnosis of realization. If it becomes immobilized, it leads to skin diseases with scaling, itching, lesions, and so on. The method of treatment is the same as before. {83}

Now then, for the method of treatment, there are three sections in the first method, releasing: releasing pain at the site of the nāḍī,* giving a reward to the vāyu and releasing it,† and releasing by naturally sustaining the heat of mental experience.‡

There are six sections in empowering: the empowerment of the sublime guru,§ the empowerment of the excellent deity,¶ the empowerment of the outer and inner ḍākinī,** the empowerment of the words of the sutras and tantras of the profound Mahāyāna,†† the empowerment of various appearances,‡‡ and the empowerment of profound dependent origination.§§

There are two sections in the meditation on bliss: the meditation on bliss that depends on the wave of enjoyments above and the meditation on bliss that depends on the secret union below.¶¶

Now then, from among the subsidiary topics, the "various nāḍī knots" refers to the four palaces, which include the navel, and so on.

The seven differentiations are the seven that have already been explained, such as the name, and so on.

"The secondary vāyus gradually cease internally" refers to the five secondary vāyus, the vāha, and so on, that gradually cease internally through the power of arresting the five fundamental vāyus. That implicitly explains the blazing fire of inner heat.*** That sunders the nāḍīs. That "gathers the elements," from which the three signs are understood.[64] From the refined element, abundant bindus spread, like the butter of churned curd.†††

"Uniformly permeating the body" refers to the four bindus that both abide in the four palaces of the precious nāḍīs and are moved through the

*Focusing on the site.
†Inhale and focus on the site.
‡Because of pain during samādhi.
§Expressing devotion with the crown of one's head.
¶The entry of the gnosis being.
**Pleasing them with the feast.
††Confidence because of being amazed.
‡‡Because of amazing objects.
§§Because of purification of the body, and so on.
¶¶These are similar to searching through the condition of a distracted meditation.
***Great heat.
†††It is the supported.

power of meditation that merges in the manner of the samaya ḍākinī and the gnosis ḍākinī, which is the empowerment.* Because of that, "the mind abides within"† means the intellect is arrested. "The five consciousnesses gather within" means the eye, and so on, do not follow external objects. {84} Those explain both the essence of samādhi and the nature of samādhi. "The five aggregates are tamed"‡ explains the benefit. First, the temporary afflictions are slightly reversed, clinging to anything is diminished, and so on; also, the four flexibilities§ gradually arise. "The movement of gnosis is reversed" refers to the way samādhi arises. For a beginner, though a nonconceptual samādhi arises during the first gathering of the element, and so on, it is unstable. Since it is under the power of conceptuality, even though gnosis arises, gnosis is reversed. Since there is little benefit, it is like the sun in the midst of the clouds.

Now, in order to give a summary explanation through the distinctions¶ of the three heats that are the modes of the arising of samādhi, "undistracted meditation" is as before. "Visions" are smoke, and so on. "Dreams" are dreams of horses, and so on. "Experiences" are physical experiences, such as pain of the nāḍīs, vāyu, and so on. "Seemingly prior to concepts" refers to the three visions, and so on, the three gatherings of the nine elements, and the three blazings and gatherings of the bindu that are prior to concepts because of the divisions of the three heats, totaling nine. "Appearing as all three realms" refers to abiding in samādhi upon that, devoid of perception of other appearances.

Among the three kinds of path instruction, in order for the path instruction of vāyu to extensively explain samādhi, it is said, "when earth dissolves into water, a mirage," and so on. Further, there is the experience of arresting the five vāyus in their individual locations, the experience of increasing strength, the experience of arresting the four elemental vāyus equally, and the experience of arresting the sixteen parts equally. From that [earth element] dissolving into water, there is a mirage; that is, there are three experiences when that vāyu is arrested in its own location,** a mirage, [and so on]. One should understand that should be applied to the rest.

*The cause of samādhi. *S* clarifies this is the self-empowerment.

†The nature of samādhi.

‡The benefits of samādhi.

§The flexibility of vāyu, nāḍī, syllables, and amṛta.

¶Nine.

**The navel.

When those are arrested in the central nāḍī, the supreme place, {85} the mirage, and so on, become very clear and very stable. The progression of these* in the treatise should be heard from the guru.†

Now, in the experience of the increasing strength of the five elemental vāyus, "earth, water, fire, and air" exist in the manner of the samaya ḍākinī, abiding as the basis. "The vāyu-mind gathers evenly" is the empowerment in the manner of the gnosis ḍākinī. In particular, when empowered by the fire vāyu, the vision is an appearance of fire in all three realms, the dream is a dream of a great city being burned by fire, and the physical experience is the whole body feels hot and sore. Two are explained by implication.

"The water vāyu [inflates] the pores and cools the body" means that since the water vāyu increases in power, the physical experience of the body is feeling cold during the empowerment of one's continuum; the dream experience is dreaming of placing a boat on the ocean; the vision is seeing the four oceans, and so on. The last two are understood implicitly.‡ This is [systematically] supplied below.

"Equal with space, and all pores and the body are blissful" means that during the self-empowerment, because the strength of the space vāyu increases, the physical experience is that all pores and the body are satiated, feel blissful, and cannot be harmed by conditions of suffering.§ The mental experience is mostly emptiness. The dream experience is dreaming that one is unimpeded by any appearance. The last two are explained by implication.

When there is the self-empowerment of the air vāyu, so-called discursiveness is the mental experience. Even though consciousness does not move for a second, it causes an abundant, discursive flow of concepts and also interrupts sleep; sleep occurs for one hundred moments, in dreams one flies, and there are many small birds. {86} The physical experience is running like a horse. The last two are explained by implication.

*Their enumeration, measure, and force.

†There is no certainty in their respective presence or absence through outer and inner dependent origination and they should be applied in the same way—one should understand this up to "when consciousness dissolves into luminosity." When the space vāyu dissolves its own location, the crown, there is a vision that is like the sky free of clouds. In brief, so-called dissolution means that after that portion of the movement of each elemental vāyu is arrested, the movement of the other element vāyus is also arrested and dissolves, but it is not as if the vāyus merge together and then dissolve.

‡In the treatise.

§Such as fire, weapons, and so on.

The implied explanation of the experience of the earth vāyu* is that when there is the self-empowerment because the strength of the earth vāyu increases, the physical experience is all pores and the body become heavy, and one cannot lift [one's limbs or fingers]. The mental experience is seeing the golden ground and appearances arising as yellow. In the dream experience, one dreams that one is unable to cross a great plain. The last two are explained by implication.

In order to simplify *The Vajra Verses* with those, the experience of the fire vāyu is applied to the visions, and the other two experiences are explained by implication. The water vāyu and the space vāyu are applied to the physical experience and the other two experiences are explained by implication. The air vāyu is applied to the mental experience and the dream experience, but the physical experience and visions are explained by implication. The experiences of the earth vāyu are all explained by implication. As such, one should understand that there are fifteen experiences.

Now, in the enumeration of the even portions of the vāyu of the four elements, it is said, "the vāyus of the four elements move evenly and various goddesses offer dances." There are two hundred twenty-five vāyus for each of the four elements; nine hundred when taken together. In visions and dream experience, there will be goddesses presenting offerings with song and dance. Here, the physical experience is not described because this diminishes its importance. Because the elements are in sixteen even parts, it is said, "the vāyus of the four elements [produce] a diversity . . . ."† When the vāyus of the two movements are arrested evenly, having created the inner dependent origination, there is an external diversity. "Scents and flavors" refers to the arising of the thought that there are various scents and various flavors. Here, apart from strictly physical experiences, there are no visions and dream experiences. Also, these are an experience of the characteristic [clarity]‡ arising as a variety. Since the other experiences, the nature (emptiness) {87} and the essence (union) arise in and out of order, all heat should be naturally sustained.

Since the remainder of the path instruction with the vāyu in the transcendent path was already explained in the presentation of the general path and will be explained in the transcendent path, it is not mentioned here.

*In order to simplify *The Vajra Verses*.

†The ground, and so on.

‡Method.

Now,* in the path instruction with the amṛta elements, it is said, "the five amṛtas, the forms of the tathāgatas." At the time of the self-empowerment, because the five amṛtas are in equal proportion, any kind of tathāgata, their families, colors, and so on, arise in the three experiences. When there is the self-empowerment from the blood obtained from the mother, in particular, it is called "olibanum and the sun." In visions and dream experiences, one sees the suns of a billion worlds.† The physical experience is being circled by red light. When the strength of bodhicitta increases, the moon obtained from the father is called "camphor and the moon." In visions and dream experiences, one sees the moons of a billion worlds. The physical experience is being circled by white light.

"In the subtle nāḍīs there are tiny essences and stars" means the seventy-two thousand subtle nāḍīs branch off from the principal nāḍī, in which the subtle bindu increases. In visions and dream experiences, one sees the stars of a billion worlds. The physical experience is that many planets and stars arise from the pores. Those are the experiences of the characteristic arising as the diversity. The other two experiences are explained by implication. The rest of the path instruction with the amṛta elements will be understood in the transcendent path.

Now, in the path instruction with the nāḍī syllables, when the text is divided into sections, there is (1) the path instruction with the ordinary syllables, (2) the path instruction with the fourteen syllables, and (3) the path instruction with inconceivable syllables.

As for "In the bearing nāḍīs, and so on," {88} if it is asked what are the three experiences when the vāyu and mind gather uniformly in the great bearing nāḍīs,[65] they are mountains and rocks.[66] When gathering in the minor bearing nāḍīs,[67] there are "tree trunks"[68] in the three experiences.

"The five kinds of attachment and aversion" refers to when the vāyu and mind gather evenly in the syllables of the five afflictions at the heart center, *bhrūṃ*, and so on,[69] and the five afflictions arise of their own accord in one's continuum. Appearing to arise in the continuums of others,‡ one has a vision of destroying the five afflictions; that is, there is a vision of destroying the poison of desire, pouring out the fire of hatred, removing the darkness

*Second.
†This is not definite.
‡As delusions.

of ignorance, breaking down the great mountain of pride, and freeing the shackles of jealousy.

The "nāḍī of fear" is located inside of the two kidneys. When the vāyu and mind gather there, terror and fear arise in the mental experience and the dream experience. In the physical experience, there is fearful behavior. The "nāḍī of misery" is primarily located in the two big toes, and it is normally located in the two thumbs. When the vāyu and mind gather there, misery arises of its own accord in the three experiences. The "nāḍī of ghosts" is primarily located in the ring finger of both hands and normally located in the fourth toe of the two feet. When the vāyu and mind gather there, it seems as if one is oppressed by ghosts in the three experiences.

The nāḍī of yawns and "tears" is located externally below both kidneys. The two coiled nāḍīs of the eyes are located above. When the vāyu and mind gather there, there is only a physical experience: uninterrupted yawns and tears occur. Those explain the path instruction with the ordinary syllables, and [those] are the experience of the characteristic arising as a diversity. Since the other two experiences arise and vanish respectively, all heat should be naturally sustained.

Now,* in the path instruction with the fourteen syllables, {89} it is said, "when the vāyu and mind gather evenly in the syllables of the six realms that first form at the navel, there are experiences such as the movement and speech of the six realms, being led to them, dreams, and appearing in all the three realms."

With respect to that, when the vāyu and mind gather evenly into the seed syllable of the devas, the white *a*, the experience of the devas is being more joyous than before, and the thought arises, "I am a deva." "Movement" leads to physical behaviors, such as wearing flower garlands, and so on. Speech refers to speaking the language of the devas, Sanskrit, and so on. Also, those† arise in the mind.‡ Movement arises in the body. Speech arises in the voice. In the three kinds of visions, one sees the abode of the gods, the Vijaya palace; one sees the devas themselves adorned with all ornaments, such as deva boys and deva girls; and one sees oneself and others being led there. Since

*The support of mental traces.
†Experiences.
‡Because of empowerment.

any of those can also arise in dreams, there is a dream experience. Thus, there are seven experiences.

When the vāyu and mind gather evenly in the seed syllable of the human realm, the blue *nri*, the experience of humans is excessively enjoying the eight worldly dharmas more than before, engaging in the behavior of the dance of various countries, and [wearing] various kinds of garb. For speech, one speaks in various human languages and expresses various kinds of conversation, and in particular, there are the three experiences [that arise in the mind], Magadha, and so on. For the three visions, one will see the abode of humans and the four continents. In particular, one will see Magadha, and so on. One will see humans with different bodies, big noses, big ears, and so on. One sees oneself and others being led there. Since any of those can arise in the dream experience, there are seven experiences.

When the vāyu and mind gather evenly in the seed syllables of the asuras, yellow *su*, the experience of the asuras is becoming angrier and more irritated than before. The movement of the body is taking up clubs and weapons. The speech is producing many sounds, such as "Strike! Kill!" and so on. The three experiences that arise in the mind, and so on, {90} are the same as above. With respect to the three visions, one sees the place of the asuras, the crevices of Sumeru; the asuras fighting amongst themselves; and oneself and others being led there. Since any of those can arise in the dream experience, there are seven experiences.

When the vāyu and mind gather evenly in the seed syllable of the pretas, red *pre*, the experience of the pretas is that even though one eats, one is hungry; though one drinks, one is thirsty; or one has no appetite, and so on. The movement of the body is behaving with hunger and thirst. The speech is crying "*pre*" and conversing about food and drink. The three experiences that arise in the mind, and so on, are the same as before. The three visions are seeing the great city of the pretas, Kapila; seeing houses that are red and beautiful; seeing oneself as a preta, hungry and thirsty; and seeing oneself and others led to the city of pretas.[70] Since any of those can arise in the dream experience, there are seven experiences.

When the vāyu and mind gather evenly in the seed syllable of the animals, the smoke-colored *du*, the experience of animals is being stupid, with little concept of cleanliness, and so on. The movement of the body is many animal behaviors, such as that of dogs, cows, and so on. The speech is uttering many animal sounds. The three experiences that arise in the mind, and so on, are the same as above. The three visions are seeing the abodes of animals, such as the oceans, and so on; seeing oneself as an animal, such as crocodile, a large fish, and so on; and seeing oneself and others being led there. Since any of those can arise in the dream experience, there are seven experiences.

When the vāyu and mind gather evenly in the seed syllable of the hell beings, black *tri*, the experience of hell beings is the arising of more suffering from heat, cold, and so on. The movement of the body is the arising of behavior of suffering, such as the body doubling up with pain, and so on. The speech is uttering cries of misery, {91} such as wailing, and so on. The three experiences that arise in the mind, and so on, are the same as above. The three visions are seeing an iron house that is burning intensely, and so on; seeing oneself as a hot or cold hell being; and seeing oneself and others being led there. Since any of those can arise in the dream experience, there are seven experiences.

Though the characteristic of these is the experience of arising as a diversity, the nature of these is empty and the essence of these is union. Because these experiences arise in and out of order, all heat should be naturally sustained. If one purifies any one of these forty-two bases of purification, outer and inner parasites leave;* one obtains confidence that one will not go to lower realms; and one obtains the name "irreversible bodhisattva." This explains only the coarse order of some experiences in the desire realm.

"The samādhi of the concentrations arises from oṃ, and so on" means that when† the vāyu and the mind gather evenly in the *oṃ* of samādhi, the experience of the four concentrations of the form realm that arises includes a samādhi engaging a subtle conceptual and analytical‡ wisdom, a joyful and blissful samādhi, a samādhi free of joy and bliss,§ and a samādhi of total equanimity.¶ Because these experiences arise in and out of order, all heat should be naturally sustained.

"When there is total dissolution into the *a* of the mother's space, the three realms are space" means that when the vāyu and mind gather evenly into the *aḥ* syllable of the wisdom consort, the experience of the four bases

*The benefit to the body, and so on.

†Due to the self-empowerment.

‡Of any coarse or subtle entity.

§Physical bliss.

¶Free of eight characteristics. [*S* indicates this means being free from all joy and bliss.]

of the four realms arises. All phenomena* are these four: mere space, mere consciousness, nothing at all, and beyond existence and nonexistence.†[71] Because these are experienced in and out of order, all heat should be naturally sustained. {92} This explains only the coarse order of some experiences in the three realms.

Now, in the transcendent experiences, "when there is dissolution into the palace of the great mother Prajñāpāramitā and so on, the dharmakāya is experienced, and subject and object are liberated" means that when the vāyu and the mind gather evenly into the *aḥ* of the heart, the thought arises, "the concepts of subject and object to be abandoned are abandoned,"‡ and also, "I have obtained the great bliss of the dharmakāya."

"Clarity and lightness arise from *hūṃ*; self-originated gnosis is perfectly immaculate" means that vāyu and mind gather evenly in the *hūṃ* of union and the samādhi of self-originated gnosis arises. Clarity refers to the mind, and lightness refers to the body.§ Immaculate space is the example. Because these are experienced in and out of order, all heat should be naturally sustained. The foregoing completely explains any experiences of the first gathering of the elements.¶

"The intermediate gathering of the elements" refers to the assembly of the vāyu and mind, the five fathers** and five mothers†† in the four palaces,‡‡ and so on, becoming slightly purified and gathering. "Since the force of the vāyu wanes, the nāḍīs breakup" means that just as the cold touch of the wind wanes in the spring, the pain of the vāyus and nāḍīs§§ slightly diminishes. "The bindu is painful" means that because the blaze of the bindu¶¶ increases, pain mixed with bliss arises. Therefore, preventing leakage is very important. "The visions stabilize" means that since the elements are slightly

*Of samsara and nirvana.

†The inner dependent origination of these is not established.

‡Though the support is not abandoned.

§Like a ball of cotton.

¶Even though in general the variety of experiences is inconceivable.

**The five amṛtas.

††The five vāyus.

‡‡The nāḍī knots of the four cakras.

§§Because the nāḍīs become pliant.

¶¶During descent.

purified and the vāyu is slightly stable, one sees smoke, and so on, without being deceived.*

Now, in the extensive explanation that follows† the concise explanation,‡ "in brief, for rakṣa, and so on" means that the rakṣa syllable below the navel is the place§ of the rākṣasas and the place of all piśācas, {93} bhūtas, yāmas, yakṣas, and so on. When the vāyu and mind evenly gather there, in visions and dreams one will be beaten, threatened, and so on, by many rākṣasas, and so on. One must know the way to avert and part from these. Therefore, apply this below. "Like . . . and the pure divine eye, one thinks the experiences of samādhi up to the peak of existence arises" means that since the visions¶ are stable, there is the clairvoyance** of the contaminated eye. "A droning sound" means the supreme droning sound is the central nāḍī. When the vāyu and mind evenly gather there, it is like the sound of bees. The common sound abides in middle of the *aḥ* of the wisdom consort from the right ear. When the vāyu and mind gathers there, one hears any of the sounds of the three realms, whether near or far. The divine ear can be understood implicitly. "Endlessly illustrated through explanations" means that the path instruction is explicated with inconceivable syllables; that is, gradually drawn by the vāyu, the five amṛtas become pliable.†† That liberates the knots of the nāḍīs, and the nāḍīs become pliable. Because of that, various nāḍī syllables‡‡ arise, and the syllables become flexible. Through the power of that, the obstacles that disturb the body's elements are removed, and the kāya becomes flexible. In brief, among the four flexibilities, the power of the flexibility of the syllables and the amṛtas causes all phenomena of samsara and nirvana to arise in the experiential appearance. Thus, one is able to understand the intimate instruction of the akṣara[72] syllables, the intimate instruction of the undeluded meaning, and the intimate instruction of understanding many things by understanding one thing.§§ One is

*Usually.
†Extensive meaning.
‡Few words.
§The support of mental traces.
¶Mostly nondeceptive.
**Impeded.
††Gathering whatever can be gathered.
‡‡Shapes.
§§Through secret dependent origination.

able to understand the intimate instruction of the syllables never becoming exhausted by explanation even for ten million years* with a single phrase. "The fifth" refers to the conclusion of the five paths proclaimed in the perfection vehicle. {94} "The tenth" refers to a tenth-stage bodhisattva. Since they do not know of the four flexibilities and the intimate instruction of the meaning of the syllables, it is concealed from them, just as the sound "cow" is never heard on Nārīkela[73] Island.

That is the concise explanation of† the cause of samādhi, the samādhis,‡ and the path demonstrated extensively following the concise explanation.

Now, in the explanation of the path free from hope and fear, there are four topics: explaining the reason or validity of freedom from hope and fear; explaining the path of freedom from hope; explaining the path of freedom from fear; and because of those, explaining the path of naturally sustaining all heat. If the subsidiary§ topics are described, "undistracted meditation" is as above. "Outer dependent origination" is the outer dependent origination of outer, coarse appearances. Flying, and so on, is included in "reversing the vāyu, and so on." The vision of smoke, and so on, and the dream experience of horses, and so on, are "three by three"; that is, there are nine through the differences in the three kinds of heat. The cause that produces those is the inner dependent origination. The "inner five ḍākinīs" are the five vāyus.¶ The "five kāyas of the tathāgatas" are the five element amṛtas. The inner five ḍāka fathers and mothers arrive and go into the citadels of the four palaces. The samaya ḍākinīs** merge in the manner of the gnosis ḍākinī.†† The self-empowerment is "the cause of the dependent origination of great awakening," causing the dependent origination of the path of the thirteenth stage. That explains the validity of the freedom from hope and fear.

Now, because of that, to explain the path of freedom from hope,‡‡ it is said, "accomplishments," and so on. {95} "Accomplishments" is the four conclusions, the five kāyas, and so on. "Arise from oneself" is understood

*Samsara and nirvana.

†The vāyu and mind, the five fathers and the five mothers, the syllables, and . . . .

‡The physical experiences.

§The reason.

¶These are the support for the tissues of the body and the mind.

**Abiding in the basis.

††Arriving from above because of meditating.

‡‡Accomplishments are not bestowed from somewhere else.

from the five ḍākinīs and five male ḍākas.[74] First, this is understood[*] from the guru;[†] later, it is the measure of recalling one's experience.[‡]

"Thoughts of hope . . . are removed" refers to being free from hope of accomplishments from the external nirmāṇakāya of the victor. "Effort" refers to being free from the effort of making offerings to external deities, bali offerings, burned offerings, and so on.[§]

Now, in the path of freedom from fear,[¶] the practitioner who does not recognize "māras and deviations" is attacked by rākṣasas and piśācis, terrified and full of dread, haunted by ghosts, and so on, whereas for the practitioner who understands the path, those are the "path and dependent origination," like a narrow bridge or a boat on a river. Therefore, since samādhi is recognized, the obstructions of concentration are recognized. Since the obstacles are recognized, the obstructions of māras are recognized. Recognize that the "faults should be taken as qualities." This is called "the instruction for taking the obstacles as the accomplishments." Therefore, "heat should be naturally sustained because it arises in and out of order." Both hope[**] and fear[††] are {96} due to the arrangement of dependent origination, either in or out of order. Experiences arise in and out of order. This practitioner, who is free from accepting and rejecting, naturally sustains all heat.

Now, the path explained as the four examinations is as follows: "Since the devaputra māra, and so on, arrives on the path that deviates to the side of wisdom, prevent this with the four examinations." This will not be discussed here because one should specifically understand its means of application for disturbances in the section on preventing [deviations] with wisdom from

[*]Via hearing and reflection.

[†]This is included in four topics: the cause of hope and fear, freedom from hope because of that cause, the path of freedom from fear, and naturally sustaining all experiential heat because of freedom from hope and fear. There are two sections in the first topic: the outer dependent origination of reversing the vāyu, the visions; and the dream experience arisen in and out of order. As such, the dependent origination that continually produces [the three experiences], the vāyu and mind, the five ḍākinīs and five ḍākas, the nāḍī palaces, the kāyas, the samaya ḍākinī, and the empowerment through means of the gnosis ḍākinī is the cause of all visions of hope, visions of fear, and apparitional sounds. The doubt, "Aren't all these external?" is eliminated. The three topics can be understood by applying this to the root verses. This has been written down because the clarification is elsewhere.

[‡]Through cultivation.

[§]Because doubts are always eliminated.

[¶]Arising as an external obstacle.

[**]Experience in general.

[††]Inner experience.

the above section on the thirty different methods of preventing deviations into method and wisdom.

In brief, up to this point—from the perspective of making progress on the path with the vāyu—how to remedy appearances arising as enemies with the four bases of magic power has already been explained.

Now, in engaging in the four foundations of mindfulness, the remedy for emptiness arising as an enemy, it is said, "The four foundations of mindfulness of undistracted meditation" from the perspective of mind being the main principle. "Since objects cease," though there are nine emptinesses, five emptinesses arise in the experience of a practitioner: the emptiness of visible objects through the dissolution [of the vāyu and mind] into the *aḥ* of the wisdom consort, the emptiness free of subject and object to be abandoned through the dissolution into the *aḥ* of the heart center, the emptiness of the cessation of the six senses though the dissolution into the nāḍī of the equipoise of cessation, the emptiness of the samādhi of qualities through the air vāyu arising with the power of a razor, and the emptiness of fainting with bliss through dissolution into the outer shape of *a*.

It is said, "The first of those is empty of the faults of thing and name,* the samādhi of qualities is empty of śamatha and vipaśyana, the hut of concentration is empty of concentration, and the visible object to be abandoned is empty of diversity." The four foundations of mindfulness in the minor remedial conduct are "one's pledged deity": mindfulness of the body† and by implication, mindfulness of the deity (that is, {97} the summoning and entry of the gnosis being). Mindfulness of the mantra is the essence mantra of the excellent deity. "It is thought . . . the six ornaments are necessary" is from the perspective of the meaning of the syllables.[75] The meaning of this is stated in a text:

> Homage to guru Vajradhara,
> who purposefully bears the wheel . . .[76]

"Since samādhi is uniform" means that since only the experience of emptiness arose before, as such, one is free from the danger of emptiness arising as an enemy because appearance and emptiness were paired. The thought arises that appearances arise as the maṇḍalacakra of the excellent deity, all

*Coarse subject and object.
†As one's deity.

sounds arise as the mantra,* and the stream of bliss† is stabilized. At that moment this is given the name, "the creation stage is slightly stable." From such cultivation, the occasional or persistent thought, "This is stainless great bliss; this is seeing the truth; and this is following the conclusion," is the māra of contentment called "the danger of great lethargy that never wavers from that." This is the power of the vāyu and mind gathering in the outer shape of *a*. The remedy for that is entering into the four correct renunciations. Since the meaning of that is the four empowerments, there are four things that must be understood: When taking empowerments, from whom should they be taken? Who is the person who obtains them? What is the intrinsic nature of the empowerments? What are their benefits?

To describe the subsidiary topics, "it is the final gathering of the elements" means that when the gathered vāyu and mind are mostly pure, the five ḍākinīs and five ḍākas gather in the manner of the samaya ḍākinī and the gnosis ḍākinī. "Free of the touch of the vāyu" means the pain of the nāḍīs and vāyus is pacified and becomes beneficial.‡ "The bindus gather into the six sense gates" means that the refined elements gathering in the sites of the six sense bases, the eye, and so on, give rise to "the six close" mindfulnesses, {98} the contaminated clairvoyances, such as the ability to see visible forms regardless of whether they are near or far, and so on. "One perceives some nirmāṇakāyas" means that based on the dependent origination of the refined element,§ one can see as many as one to ten nirmāṇakāyas.

"Undistracted meditation" is the same as before. The "four correct renunciations" are the correct renunciation by abandoning all concepts referred to in "joy,¶ and so on, seek the nāḍī of the twenty-year-old padminī"; in the same way, all concepts are abandoned "because of the types [of movement], such as moving slowly, and so on; the mind enters . . ."; all concepts are abandoned because "body, speech, and mind adopt the vajra posture"; and all concepts are abandoned "because the vāyu is controlled by the bindu."

"From the nirmāṇakāya"[77] explains the person from whom the empowerment is received. The "understanding** arising after the three empower-

*Of one's deity.
†In the mind.
‡Body and mind.
§The person from whom the empowerment is received.
¶The basis of empowerment.
**The intrinsic nature of the empowerment.

ments"* is the support for the fourth empowerment, the experience of the four joys, stabilized by the predicted, young padminī karma mudra.

Now, in order to explain the intrinsic nature of that empowerment arising from the four dependent originations, it is said "joy, and so on." She is not joyless; joy is generated. She is not an unqualified consort; she is qualified. She is not disinterested; she is very interested and passionate. She does not lack empowerment; she is empowered. A padminī is a young woman of the lotus family, with images of eight-petaled lotuses on her palms and soles, and so on. Ten multiplied by two means two sets of ten, or twenty. "Seek the nāḍī" means to seek with the procedure of saddling.[78] It is said that the nāḍī is as thin as the stem of a lotus, as pointed as the tip of a spear, as sharp as the edge of a sword, and as smooth as the surface of a mirror. Thus, one who understands possesses these four qualities. This explains the first correct renunciation.

"The *āḥ* of the heart center"† is the support of the dharmakāya. "Arriving at the tip of the avadhūti" means that since the form of the bindu enters the tip of the central nāḍī, {99} from that, the *āḥ* moves up. "Moving slowly, and so on"‡ refers to the five fundamental vāyus. "Types" refers to purification. "Mind" refers to the central nāḍī, into which there is entry. This explains the second correct renunciation.

"Body" refers to the rasanā, "voice" refers to the lalanā, and "mind" refers to the central nāḍī. "Adopt the vajra posture" refers to the indivisibility of [the three nāḍīs], which transform into the syllable *tsha*. This explains the third correct renunciation.

"The vāyu is controlled by the bindu" refers to the refined element arriving at the juncture of the three nāḍīs, suppressing the vāyus of both the right and left nāḍīs. Because of this, contaminated bliss arises as the highest experience up to the stage when highest mundane phenomena arise. This explains the fourth correct renunciation.

"One cannot hear the sound of drums"§ means that at that moment, though there is contaminated bliss, since that is apprehended as immaculate bliss, one becomes unconscious. One cannot be awakened even by one hundred large drums, or by horns, cymbals, and so on. With respect to that,

*Of the empowerments.

†*Āḥ* is the inner dependent origination.

‡The dependent origination of the essential gnosis vāyu.

§The benefits.

there are several māras of contentment, such as contentment through the view, contentment through experiential samādhi, and contentment through instruction. Here, "the māra of contentment, and so on, is destroyed" means that once the māra of contentment—the immaculate bliss from the path of the four foundations of mindfulness on down—is destroyed, since the immaculate bliss of the four correct renunciations is uniform, that terminology is used because a special samādhi arises that approaches the first stage and all the māras of contentment are destroyed by the path of seeing itself. Since the samādhi that includes the three levels of heat arises in the three gatherings of the element, heat in the fourfold path of application is explained.

Now, in order to explain the remaining three phases of the path of application through the aspect of the qualities of heat, there is "the path of the inner buddhas." {100} "Inner buddhas" refers to the vāyu, mind, the five ḍākinīs, and the five ḍākas. "The peak of existence" refers to the tips of the right and left nāḍīs. The peak beyond that is arriving at the tip of the central nāḍī. That explains the second part of the path of application through the aspect of qualities.

"Patience for the nonarising of phenomena is difficult" means that though the samādhi of emptiness arises on the mundane path on down, great fear arises. At this occasion of the vāyu and mind gathering in the central nāḍī, though* a samādhi of realizing samsara and nirvana as empty arises, there is patience that is not frightened. The inner dependent origination is said to be "the mind reversing into the central channel. There is patience when the mind shifts." This is the third aspect of the path of application.

"The phenomena of samsara are transcended" means that though a samādhi arose in both paths of accumulation and application, since it does not have the power to stop the suffering† of existence and intense sensations, the highest phenomenon‡ beyond that, "nirvana,"§ is the immaculate first stage, and "the path phenomena of nirvana are totally perfected." Thus, the four aspects of the path of application are explained through the two highest dharmas.

Now, in the very condensed explanation of the treatise on the paths

*Because the path and realization are higher.

†Strong illnesses, and so on; that is, disturbances of the body's elements, spirits, and so on.

‡Abandoning the object to abandon.

§The arrangement of the dependent origination of qualities.

explained in that way, there are eight "faulty" [experiences] and three "faultless experiences." "The vāyu and mind evenly gather above in the outer shape of *a* . . ." means that having transcended the nāḍīs, syllables, bodhicitta, and the vāyus of the mundane path on down, [the vāyu and mind] enter the central nāḍī, marking the beginning of the transcendent path.

In order to include the samādhis of both previous paths* and the samādhi arising in the transcendent path into three, it is said, "the essence, nature, and characteristic arise as the paths." When applied in reverse order, {101} the characteristic† is diversity, the nature‡ is emptiness, and the essence§ is union.

Having divided up the treatise into seven sections, there is both the path of accumulation and [the path of] application. Having divided twelve of the factors conducive to awakening into the three gatherings of the element, the instruction of the mundane path is explained.

Now, in the transcendent path, there is also an explanation of the general path. According to the paths, there are three: the path of seeing, the path of cultivation, and the ultimate path. According to the factors of awakening, there are twenty-five. According to the stages, there are twelve and one-half. Though all paths are completely included there,¶ sometimes when divided into sections, it is included in four:** six stages are included in the vase empowerment, four stages are included in the secret empowerment, two stages are included in the wisdom consort's gnosis empowerment, and half a stage is included in the fourth empowerment.

In the first,†† the creation stage is stabilized. In the second, the self-empowerment is stabilized. In the third, the maṇḍalacakra is stabilized. In the fourth, the vajra wave is stabilized. Also, in the first,‡‡ there is empowerment in the nirmāṇakāya buddhafield. In the second, there is empowerment in the saṃbhogakāya buddhafield. In the third, there is empowerment in the dharmakāya buddhafield. In the fourth, there is empowerment in the

*The paths of accumulation and application.
†The visions, and so on.
‡The cessation of objects, and so on.
§The empty, apparent object, and so on.
¶The explanation of the presentation of the general path.
**According to the empowerments.
††According to the empowerments.
‡‡According to buddhafields.

svabhāvakāya buddhafield. In the first,* one realizes the body maṇḍala. In the second, one realizes the bhaga maṇḍala. In the third, one realizes the fundamental bodhicitta maṇḍala. In the fourth, one realizes the maṇḍala that includes the condensed essence of the sugatas. Further, in the first,† one follows the conclusion of the inseparability of samsara and nirvana. In the second, one follows the distinct and totally complete conclusion. In the third, one follows the conclusion of the small seal of bliss and emptiness. In the fourth, one follows the conclusion of the great seal of bliss and emptiness.

Now, from the perspective of each individual stage, the topics of *The Vajra Verses* should be described in four topics each: the explanation of the cause of each stage, the explanation of the signs, {102} the explanation of the result, and the explanation of the summary.

With respect to the first topic, there are two in the cause: the indirect cause and the direct cause. There are two in the indirect cause: the empowerment‡ and the path.§ The two in the indirect cause are obtaining the vase empowerment¶ from the guru at the time of the cause and meditating that one receives the vase empowerment** in four sessions at the time of the path. The path is the shape of the creation stage.†† There are two in the direct cause: outer dependent origination‡‡ and inner dependent origination. Outer dependent origination is receiving the four empowerments§§ from the nirmāṇakāya. Inner dependent origination is seeing the body maṇḍala.¶¶

There are three signs: The outer sign arises in the bindu. The inner sign arises in the vāyu. The nondeceptive sign arises in the mind.*** Now, to describe the subsidiary topics, "in the transcendent path" means that having transcended the paths††† of accumulation and application, one begins on the path of seeing. Now, in the explanation of the direct cause, "the path arises as

*According to the maṇḍala.
†According to the conclusion.
‡The vase empowerment.
§The creation stage.
¶With eleven sections.
**In extensive, medium, or concise form.
††The body maṇḍala.
‡‡The cause of accomplishing that stage.
§§Without defined sessions.
¶¶The nāḍī cakras.
***This one is first. [These three are numbered in reverse order in the margin notes: 3, 2, 1.]
†††Nāḍīs, syllables, amṛtas, and vāyus.

outer and inner dependent origination" means that in the mundane path on down, progress on the path is made with the three dependent originations. Here, from the perspective of the direct cause, outer dependent origination is taking the four empowerments* from the nirmāṇakāya. Inner dependent origination is seeing the body maṇḍala that arises from below.

"The nirmāṇakāya is naturally accomplished without effort" means the result abides in the cause, the nāḍīs. One who has the result,† the thirteenth stage, realizes the meaning of "all kāyas are the nirmāṇakāya." "One reaches the culmination of the vase empowerment" refers to the indirect cause, the empowerment. One should also understand by implication that the path is the creation stage.

Now, in the direct cause—inner dependent origination—"the seven limbs of awakening" refers to awakening and the gnosis of the first stage. {103} The limbs are the direct cause of that awakening: the shape of the palace of the nāḍī knots of the four cakras, existing as *e vaṃ ma ya*, and the three channels (the rasanā, lalanā, and central nāḍī), totaling seven. "Conceptuality comes and goes" refers to the way the object to be abandoned is abandoned. In general, on the transcendent path on up, one abandons twelve grades of concepts. However, all of those are not negative factors to be abandoned as causes of the suffering of existence and intense sensations. Rather, they are obscurations that cause delays in progressing in the realization of the stage of the vajra holder and progressing to one higher stage after another. In brief, since the strength of the object to abandon is weak and the strength of the antidote is strong, even though concepts arise, they immediately dissolve into gnosis. This is understood to be like the ocean and waves.‡

Now, the explanation of the signs, when the treatise is divided into sections, this is the fourth, which explains the qualities in seven sets of one hundred, specifically§ explained at the time of the first stage and the path of seeing. The different qualities that are explained elsewhere arise from the sixteen immaculate joys.¶ Now then, "one can shake one hundred nirmāṇakāya buddhafields" means that one can shake the Sahā[79] buddhafield, and so on. One can see the faces of those buddhas and "hear" their dharma. "Make one

*Without defined sessions.

†At the time of the conclusion.

‡They are not separate.

§The nāḍīs of the six realms, and so on.

¶At that moment the liṅga becomes firm, and so on.

hundred gifts" explains one hundred different kinds of gifts, such as giving away one's eyes, giving away one's head, and so on. "One hundred lights" means one hundred visions, and so on, such as radiating white and drawing back red. "Give explanations to one hundred inferiors" means explaining the dharma to one hundred different people to be tamed, who are inferior to oneself. "One hundred different samādhis" refers to entering into equipoise on one hundred different samādhis, like those that originate in the perfection of wisdom [sutra] supplied below, such as the samādhi of the hero's progress, the samādhi of the yawn of the lion, and so on.

"Various magic powers are produced in an instant" means that one displays one hundred magic powers, such as fire blazing from above and water welling up from below, {104} turning one into many and turning many into one, and so on.

The inner dependent origination, which produces the seven sets of one hundred qualities that appear externally in that way, is perceiving the inner buddhafields. "Perceiving the inner buddhafields" is the aforementioned seven limbs of awakening.

Now, in the presentation of the path of seeing and the first stage, "if one sees the nāḍīs of the six realms" means that once the secret dependent origination is created by seeing the blue letter *nri*, one "enjoys" the external experiential appearance without being deceived. Since one sees the meaning of the immaculate truth one did not see before, a special joy arises. "Fearfulness" means that because one has experienced all the suffering of hell beings, and so on, during one's time in the world, and one sees all the suffering there is for deluded migrating beings, fearfulness is the worry, "Though I am free from delusion and am not experiencing that suffering, I might experience it." "Shame and disgust" is the phrase for renouncing the samsaric behaviors undertaken when one was a deluded sentient being, such as marrying one's mother, taking the impure as pure, and so on.

Now, in the explanation of how the other special qualities of that first stage arise, it is said, "At the moment when samsara and nirvana are inseparable, as the guru already taught at the time of the cause, there is realization." That explanation of the twenty dharmas of the path, and so on, arises here in the first conclusion: one can place one billion worlds in a mustard seed without one becoming small or the other large; one can cause water to flow uphill; one can catch the bottom of the sun and moon; one is unimpeded by walls, mountains, and so on—many such things arise in one's continuum. "Compassion arises" means that compassion without reference to suffering sentient beings arises, and through the power of that, "tears fall." "One knows the various thoughts of others" means that among sentient beings, one can see the passions of humans {105} with the clairvoyance of an immaculate mind. "One laughs when various objects of desire are seen" means seeing the celestial mansion of immaculate gnosis that was not seen before and seeing the enjoyments without clinging to objects of desire,* such as Rupavajrā,[80] and so on.

Now, in the explanation of what the sixteen immaculate joys arise from, it is said, "At that moment the liṅga is firm and, likewise, the bindu resides on the stage of the connate [joy] at the tip of the vajra. The body is intoxicated with bliss, and one is rendered unconscious." "The liṅga is firm" means that once the vāyu and mind gather upward in the outer shape of *a*, the first knot of the central nāḍī is released. Since the refined element is stabilized in half of the cakra of the secret place, at that moment† the liṅga is rampant. "The tip of the vajra" means up to the first knot from the outer shape of *a*. "The stage of the connate" is the stage of the sixteen joys, which descend from above. The bindu stabilizes at the stage of the first, second, and third joys, which are stabilized in ascending order. "The body is intoxicated with bliss and rendered unconscious" means that when one obtains the wisdom of the first stage, the body is intoxicated with immaculate bliss, and the mind becomes unconscious because of blissful joy. "One does not recognize self and other" means that one abandons all concepts that are abandoned by [the path of] seeing. Those are the nondeceptive signs that arise in the mind.

"The inner sign is the vāyu stopping at one finger length" means the measure is an external finger length because both [the vāyu and the bindu] stop at one finger length both internally and externally. The enumeration is that eighteen hundred‡ [karma vāyus][81] dissolve into the central nāḍī.[82] "The outer sign is the bindu stabilized in half of the secret place" means that the first knot of the central nāḍī is released, and once half of the cakra of the secret place is filled with the refined element, it does not revert again.

The summary is "The first stage," called "Very Joyful" in conformity with scripture. Now, in the explanation of the five stages§ included in the vase empowerment, {106} it is said, "Further, the empowerments, four by four,

*Because it is the appearance of gnosis.
†Externally.
‡The number of vāyus in a two-hour period.
§On the path of cultivation.

are received from the nirmāṇakāya." ["In the path of cultivation, the second stage onward,"] as previously explained in the explanation of the cause from the four topics of the explanation of the cause, and so on, there is both the direct cause and the indirect cause. In the indirect cause, there is both the empowerment and the path. In the direct cause, one should understand as before, that there is both outer dependent origination and inner dependent origination.*

The explanation of the topic of the result is the nirmāṇakāya. There are three in the signs: First, from the perspective of the nondeceptive sign arising in the mind, "one can shake one thousand nirmāṇakāya buddhafields, and so on." One should understand to swap seven sets of one hundred qualities with seven sets of one thousand, seven sets of ten thousand, seven sets of one hundred thousand, seven sets of one million, and seven sets of ten million. That being the case, "the qualities, and so on, increase" is applied to the sixth stage on down. "The coming and going, and so on, ceases" means that the way of abandoning the object to be abandoned in twelve grades of strong, medium, and weak is concepts stop on the six stages on down [to the second stage]. Also, in terms of the twelvefold dependent origination, sensation on down cease in reverse order.[83]

"The inner sign is that the vāyu stops at six finger lengths" refers to the outer six finger lengths, stopping at the measure of the twelve outer and inner finger lengths. Also, the enumeration is that ten thousand eight hundred[84] karma vāyus† cease. As for "The outer sign is the bindu stabilized at the secret place, the navel, and the heart," in each of the three cakras, sixteen knots in the central nāḍī are released two at a time. It is also explained that the refined element will not revert again. "One sees a saṃbhogakāya"‡ means that one sees the face and the empowerment.

The summary is the "six stages on the path of cultivation," explained in conformity with scripture: the second stage is Immaculate, the third stage is Illumination, the fourth stage is Radiating Light, the fifth stage is Difficult to Purify, and the sixth stage is Directly Facing. As such, the six stages are explained through the vase empowerment. {107}

Now, "the empowerments, four by four, are received from the saṃbhogakāya" explains the four stages included in the secret empowerment.

*The four empowerments.

†The six dependent originations on down.

‡The person from whom one on the seventh stage obtains empowerment.

The explanation of the cause, the explanation of the signs, the explanation of the result, and the explanation of the summary are to be understood four by four.

Now, first, in the cause, there is the direct cause and the indirect cause. The indirect cause is the empowerment and the path. When applied with the text itself, it is "the secret empowerment."* On the path, [the indirect cause] is applied to "the path of the self-empowerment." In empowerments, [indirect cause] is applied to "one reaches the culmination of the secret empowerment."

Also, there are two in the direct cause: The outer dependent origination is taking the four empowerments from the saṃbhogakāya† without regard to sessions.[85] The inner dependent origination will be supplied below, applied to "seeing the seed syllables of the six realms in the bhaga maṇḍala and obtaining mastery over the six seed syllables."

The explanation of the result is explained with "the saṃbhogakāya is naturally accomplished without effort."

The three in the explanation of the signs [are as follows]: From the perspective of the nondeceptive sign arising in the mind, it is said, "mastery over the five faculties," and so on. Since the earth vāyu is mastered in the central nāḍī,‡ one cannot be crushed by the harm of the earth element. One should understand that one should swap the [other] three [elements] here.[86] Since one masters the space vāyu in the central nāḍī, one has no fear of abysses that are immeasurable, empty, and so on. The inner dependent origination that produces [such abilities] is explained with "mastery over . . . the vāyus of the five pure essences is obtained." Also, at that time, since the earth vāyu, and so on, become slightly stronger in the central nāḍī from the seventh stage up to the tenth stage, one is able to emanate as one wishes, as earth,§ and so on. "The five abilities" are any of the four abilities, the power to emanate as earth, and so on, and the ability to vanish from one's own and others' sights.[87] {108} "There is no impediment in . . . the gazes" means that since one obtains power over the vāyu and mind that gather in the sense gate of the eye, at that moment one obtains power over the four gazes, the eight gazes, and so on.[88] "Seeing the seed syllables of the six realms in the bhaga

*The empowerment at the time of the cause and at the time of the path.

†From the empowerment.

‡From the ūrṇā on down.

§Slightly tangible.

maṇḍala" is the secret dependent origination of seeing *a*, the seed syllable of the devas, and so on.

Outwardly, "teaching the dharma in the language of sentient beings" refers to teaching the dharma to the six classes of sentient beings in their own language, according to their inclinations. "Generic" characteristics* are shared similarities. "Intrinsic characteristics"† are unshared differences. There are "no impediments" that occur in those. "The eight outer syllables" are the eight syllables, *a ka ca ṭa ta pa ya śa*, on the inner circle of the navel. "The vowels and consonants" are the fifty syllables seen on the outer circle, the secret dependent origination.

Externally, "no impediment in the twelve branches of the discourses of the dharma of the sutras" means at that moment one becomes a great lord of speech. It is the time of awakening from conventions, the time when all supreme words are accomplished, and the time when one obtains power over the four kinds of correct knowledge.‡ "One is able to enjoy the five amṛtas and the six tastes" means that since the refined element arrives at the throat cakra and is stabilized, one can enjoy the six tastes[89] of the outer world.

The transformation into the melody of Brahma means that since the *āḥ* of the heart center arrives in the throat cakra, through secret dependent origination one's voice has twelve or sixty tones, and so on, and it can be heard by oneself and others as melodious, irrespective of distance. Thus it is said, "the transformation into the melody of Brahma."

With respect to "elucidated by the six lines, '*A* is the supreme of all seed syllables' and so on," the *Māyājāla Tantra*[90] states:

> *A* is the supreme of all seed syllables,
> the sublime syllable of great meaning.
> Arising from within without arising,
> free from all verbal expression, {109}
> it is the supreme cause of all expressions
> and totally clarifies all words.

To explain the inner dependent origination that produces such phenom-

*The compounded are impermanent, and so on.
†Earth is hard, and so on.
‡Words, meanings, definitions, and rhetoric.

ena, the meaning is that inwardly there are two stages for each cakra. Further, the refined element* never moves from those cakras, arising through the power of actualizing stability. Elsewhere, the six lower stages appear as the six ornaments on the nirmāṇakāya. Here, the six ornaments appear on the saṃbhogakāya. One should understand that the six ornaments that appear on the saṃbhogakāya are the embodiments of the six buddha families.

Now, the explanation of the nondeceptive signs is the other qualities that arise in the mind, "above the seventh bhūmi, the victors of the four cakras shake a billion saṃbhogakāya buddhafields, and so on." Previously, on the sixth stage on down, the seven sets of qualities are exchanged, such as shaking one hundred buddhafields of the nirmāṇakāya, and so on. Here, one should understand that one exchanges the seven sets of qualities, such as shaking one hundred million saṃbhogakāya buddhafields.

"The inner sign is that the vāyu stops at ten fingerbreadths" refers to twenty inner and outer fingerbreadths. The enumeration is eighteen thousand karma vāyus cease in the central channel. "The outer sign is the bindu stabilized at the throat" means that once the twelve knots of the central nāḍī have been released in the second cakra, the refined element never moves from that cakra and becomes stable. That is the explanation of the three signs.

The summary is "the ten stages on the path of cultivation:" The seventh stage is Gone Far, the eighth stage is Immovable, the ninth stage is Excellent Wisdom, and the tenth stage is Cloud of Dharma. These names correspond with scripture.

Now, in the explanation of the two stages of the gnosis of the wisdom consort empowerment, there are four topics: the explanation of the cause, and so on. In the cause, there is the indirect cause and the direct cause. In the indirect cause, there is both the empowerment and the path. The empowerment† is applied with "the gnosis of the wisdom consort empowerment." The path is applied with "the path of the maṇḍalacakra method." {110}

In the direct cause, there is both inner and outer dependent origination. The outer dependent origination is "the empowerments, four by four." One receives the four empowerments, without regard to sessions, from the victor, in whom the nirmāṇakāya and saṃbhogakāya are undifferentiated.

*Principally the vāyu.

†Both the time of the cause and the time of the path.

The inner dependent origination is supplied below, "once the fundamental maṇḍala of bodhicitta is seen." Those briefly explain the causes.

"The dharmakāya is naturally accomplished without effort" is the result. Since it will be explained at the time of the result, it will not be mentioned here.

Now, in the explanation of the three signs, from the perspective of the nondeceptive sign that arises in the mind, internally, "the five powers" are when the five vāyus of the five refined elements and the five bodhicitta amṛtas merge into one taste and those gain strength in the central nāḍī. Externally,* the arising of the five powers means that since the earth vāyu becomes powerful in the central nāḍī, one is able to emanate as earth. The other three can be substituted there. Since the space vāyu and its [corresponding] bodhicitta become powerful in the central nāḍī, one is able to vanish from one's own and others' sights.

Now, from the perspective of both direct and indirect causes, the calculation of the qualities of the gnosis of the wisdom consort empowerment, "once the empowerment of the three kāyas and the five gnoses is obtained" means that once the totally purified mudra is empowered with the three perceptions,† the fire of passion melts the refined elements of the body through the union of method and wisdom that gather from all the nāḍīs into the *haṃ* of the crown. The bodhicitta descends from the crown to the throat. At that moment there is the gnosis of joy because the experience of bliss is slight. The afflictions to abandon are half-pacified,‡ and the path of the śrāvakas is traversed. The refined element descends to the heart. There is the gnosis of supreme joy because the experience of bliss increases. The afflictions to abandon are three quarters pacified,§ and the path of the pratyekabuddhas is traversed. Since the second bliss is enjoyed, {111} one obtains the empowerment of the saṃbhogakāya. When the refined element descends to the navel, because that bliss is in union with the adornment of nonconceptuality, it is the gnosis of the joy devoid of joy. Since all the afflictions to be abandoned are pacified, one traverses the path of bodhisattvas. Since one realizes nonconceptuality totally free of all proliferation, one obtains the empowerment of the dharmakāya. That refined element descends to the

*Up to the crown cakra.
†Instantly.
‡The imputations.
§The manifestation of connate joy.

secret place. Since that bliss is in union with emptiness, it is the gnosis of the connate joy. Since the pacification of all afflictions to be abandoned is stabilized, one traverses the path of great awakening.* Since the bindu is not stable, one obtains the empowerment from the nirmāṇakāya. As such, there is the empowerment of the three kāyas.

That is also the presentation for the empowerment of the five gnoses.† Since all phenomena manifest as a nonarising essence, there is the empowerment of the mirrorlike gnosis. Since one realizes that samsara and nirvana are the same, there is the empowerment of the gnosis of uniformity. Since one correctly realizes without losing the relative jasmine-like [bodhicitta], there is the empowerment of the individually discerning gnosis. Since truth is accomplished from oneself, there is the empowerment of the successful activity gnosis. The empowerment of the dharmadhātu gnosis is obtained through the meaning of nonconceptuality. Also, that is presented as the empowerment of the five mudras: Since concepts are not touched by the connate, there is the empowerment of the brahmin girl. Since concepts do not touch the innate, there is the empowerment of the ḍombi. Since one's continuum transforms into great bliss, there is the empowerment of the dancing girl. Since great bliss arises in others, there is the empowerment of the dyer. Since signs and concepts are slain violently, there is the empowerment of the caṇḍālī. That‡ is also presented as the empowerment of the eleven herukas: the heruka of form, and so on (one through six); oneself as the commitment heruka (seven);§ others¶ as the gnosis heruka (eight); the heruka of symbolic designation (nine);** the heruka of nominal designation (ten);†† and the meaning gnosis heruka (eleven).‡‡ Those abide within and empower one's body. The ultimate deity is at play in great bliss.{112} There is the empowerment of the twenty-four principles of the deity.[91]

When a practitioner possessing such experience moves their hands in any way, because this becomes a mudra, it is the empowerment of the mudras. Since wherever one steps becomes a maṇḍala, it is the empowerment of

*The thirteenth stage.
†Through special qualities.
‡Through special qualities.
§Generating oneself as the deity.
¶The entry of the gnosis being.
**The rūpakāya.
††Heruka.
‡‡The four liberations.

the maṇḍala. Since whatever one says becomes mantra, it is the empowerment of mantra. Since whatever one thinks becomes concentration, it is the empowerment of the principle of concentration. If one experiences and realizes those four principles, one will obtain the empowerment of gnosis that depends on the wisdom consort. In brief, that empowerment causes the conclusion of both the eleventh and twelfth stages, which one should understand are applied here.

Now, in the explanation of the other nondeceptive qualities of the nondeceptive sign that arises in the mind through the outer and inner dependent origination, which is the nondeceptive dependent origination, "When one sees the five amṛtas gather into the locations" means that when one sees the inseparable five refined element amṛtas and the five vāyus gather into the four palaces,* and so on, it is the inner dependent origination. "One sees the deeds buddhas perform to benefit others" means that one sees the nirmāṇakāyas and the saṃbhogakāyas perform the benefits with body and speech for each of those to be tamed—the meaning of that is totally perfect activity. "When one sees the bindus gather into the nirmāṇacakra and the mahāsukhacakra" means that when the refined elements gather in the nirmāṇacakra of the navel, after that they gather into the mahāsukhacakra of the crown.

When stabilized, as the experiential appearance is nondeceptive, "one sees the buddhas abiding in profundity in the place of Akaniṣṭha." While the saṃbhogakāyas of the victor never move away from the sole bliss and emptiness of the dharmakāya† that is free of proliferation, one should understand that they abide in that state and also perform deeds to benefit those to be tamed. Also, in this case one can also understand that this is called "seeing the dharmakāya buddhafield."‡ At that moment, since one sees the five amṛtas and five vāyus gather§ in the nirmāṇacakra of the navel, it becomes the inner dependent origination. Externally, in the appearances of immaculate samādhi, {113} one sees that the terms and meaning of the supremely secret,¶ profound Vajrayāna vehicle are the specific dharma to be proclaimed to the specific retinue, the fortunate bodhisattvas of the eleventh and twelfth

*The *e vaṃ ma ya* of the four cakras.

†The nondual dhātu and gnosis.

‡On these two stages.

§Gather naturally.

¶The four divisions of tantras.

stages, when the specific place of the five fathers and five mothers of the victor's saṃbhoghakāya transforms into the gnosis appearance of the celestial mansion of the supporting maṇḍala within the dharmodaya.

"The pure essence of mudra" means that since one sees without impediment* the great pure essence in the external locations of the nāḍīs of the mother, the five clairvoyances arise without impediment in the experiential appearance. The shapes of one's† nāḍīs become diverse.[92] If one draws the vāyu, mind, and the pure essence into the nāḍīs, externally, the various magic powers of changing into various forms will be unimpeded.[93] "When shifting to those again" refers to when one shifts and rests [the mind] on locations, such as the *a* that is drawn from the first palace, externally, the memory of the past lives of other sentient beings and oneself arises. Those demonstrate the nondeceptive signs that arise in the mind by means of the four elements in the outer, inner, secret, and nondeceptive dependent origination.

"The inner sign is the vāyu ceasing at twelve finger lengths" refers to the outer twelve finger lengths. There are twenty-four outer and inner finger lengths. The enumeration is that twenty-one thousand six hundred karma vāyus cease in the central channel. Also, the twelve links of dependent origination cease up to ignorance. "The outer sign is the bindu stabilized in the whole crown" means that once the four knots of the central channel are released in the crown cakra, the pure essence becomes irreversibly stable.[94]

The hidden meaning of "the twelfth stage" is the eleventh stage, Gnosis Beyond Comparison, and the twelfth state, Great Gnosis.

Now, in the half stage of the fourth empowerment, there are four topics: the explanation of the cause, the explanation of the signs, the explanation of the result, {114} and the explanation of the summary. In the explanation of the cause, there is both the indirect cause and the direct cause. The indirect cause is both the empowerment and the path. It is the fourth empowerment: as it is said, "the fourth is the . . . empowerment of body, speech, and mind." The path is supplied with "the path of the vajra waves," and "existence is the pure path."

In the direct cause, the outer dependent origination, "further, through . . . the empowerments, four by four," is the appearance that one receives the four empowerments from the undifferentiated three kāyas of the victor in reliance upon an utterly pure knowledge consort of the twelfth stage. The

*Like a mirror.

†As one wishes.

inner dependent origination is the empowerment of the dissolution of the four movements.[95] The scriptural correspondence with that direct cause is "the ultimate path" among the five paths. It is the ultimate dependent origination among the five dependent originations. Also, among that which is to be abandoned, one should understand that the knowledge obscuration is the ultimate purification.

In terms of the meaning of the words, the meaning of "existence is the pure path" is that existence is the three nāḍīs; exhalation, inhalation, and rest; the three poisonous afflictions; body, voice, and mind; and the three realms. The path of purifying those is the three waves.

"Āryas" refers to the five gnoses. "Limb" refers to its cause, the eight consciousnesses. "The attainment of the twofold result" means that from immobilizing the wave of the object on the right, there is the signless liberation; from immobilizing the wave of the subject on the left, there is the liberation lacking aspiration.

Now, in the nondeceptive sign of the ultimate path, the first half of the thirteenth stage, "this great stage gives joy, delights, and satisfies." Our teacher—the victor, the fully perfect Buddha—manifested awakening in two moments. The goddesses of the three realms were joyful in the first moment, delighted in the second moment, and satisfied in the third moment, as if they had seen an infant. The sound of their laughter shook the ground in six ways. Also, "rocked it and pitched it," and so on, can be understood according to the perfection of wisdom sutras. As for "Sound resounds in the place of the māras," since the four māras are conquered, {115} there is a magic display for frightening them, such as the sound of falling meteors, roiling the great oceans, and producing sounds like cymbals to crush their brains. Also, here is supplied, "The time when Māra was tamed in the evening, the time of no obstacles."

"The three realms are seen in the mudra's place" means that all phenomena of samsara and nirvana are one taste, one state, and one mode, without being large or small, wide or narrow, in the single bindu of the utterly refined of the refined elements abiding in the bhaga of the mother of the thirteenth stage, and so on, seeing all phenomena of samsara and nirvana in the manner of seen and seer. This is the same as minor omniscience.

"The eight topics of mastery arise, such as harima,[96] and so on" means that at that time, since the prāṇa and āyāma vāyus enter into the avadhūti, eight signs arise:[97]

> Subtle, light, vanishing into the subtle,
> able to enjoy, a great being,
> causing delight, bringing all under power,
> and engaging in whatever is desired are the eight topics of mastery and wealth.[98]

"The ḍākinīs gather from afar" refers to the moment the inner ḍākinīs gather from afar: the totally refined, refined elements are seen to gather in the palace of the central nāḍī in the form of five fathers and five mothers. Also, the outer ḍākinīs gather from afar. The ḍākinī nirmāṇakāyas, saṃbhogakāyas, and dharmakāyas are seen to empower each pore of oneself, the practitioner, in an undifferentiated manner.

> Just as a flock of geese gathers
> in a lovely pond where lotuses grow,[99]
> from faraway places the ḍākinīs also empower
> one who abides in samaya.[100]

Those passages explain attaining full awakening in the morning and at the time of liberation.

"The inner sign is the prāṇa and āyāma placed in the avadhūti" means the prāṇa and āyāma vāyus of the two nāḍīs enter halfway into the uṣṇīṣa from the outer shape of *a*. {116} "The outer sign is the bindu stabilized in half of the uṣṇīṣa" means the refined element stabilizes halfway in the uṣṇīṣa. At that moment one's genitals withdraw into a sheath, and the conch of dharma, the eternal knot, and the ūrṇā also form.

"The first half of the thirteenth stage" is the summary. The first moment that causes the thirteenth stage is given the name "the four movements of the ultimate path dissolve."

Now, in order to give an extensive explanation from the perspective of the single result, "The fourth is the . . . empowerment of the mind." This means that the fourth is the stage included with the fourth empowerment. Since the right nāḍī is the body, the left nāḍī is voice, and the central nāḍī is the mind, "the empowerment of the mind" means that all the vāyus and the mind belonging to the two nāḍīs first enter the central nāḍī and then cease and dissolve. Also, with respect to the ultimate nondeceptive sign, before there is an outer sign and an inner sign, the nondeceptive sign arises in the mind. Though the saṃbhogakāya is mentioned below, one should understand that it applies to "the ability to shake all the dharmakāya buddhafields."

The result is the emptiness gate of liberation, the subsiding of all dualistic concepts. To explain the meaning of that, "the penetrator" is the penetrator, the totally refined, refined element of the vāyu and mind. The cavity is the central nāḍī. The city where buddhahood manifests, the dharmadhātu, is the ultimate palace of the emptiness gate of liberation. "Penetrates . . . with bodhicitta" means the totally refined, refined element of vāyu and mind penetrate the central nāḍī, and having opened it, the four movements dissolve into the supreme uṣṇīṣa.

From the perspective of the nondeceptive sign arising in the mind because of the half-stage, "the result is the ability to shake all saṃbhogakāya buddhafields, and so on." This was applied to the twelfth stage, {117} but in all that follows, one should understand it is to be applied here. "The inner sign is the prāṇa and āyāma ceasing in the avadhūti" means that they enter first and then cease in the second moment.

Now, in order to give a very extensive explanation of the support for that, "upon the attainment of the thirteenth stage, the consorts of the thirteenth stage, and so on, are summoned with the mind."

[Qualm:] Is one's progress to the thirteenth stage based on the prediction of the padminī in the final gathering of the elements? If there is the path of the swift messenger already, such a support is not required.

[Reply:] That is not so. One should understand that when one is on the first stage, the knowledge consort is on the first stage. Likewise, if one is on the seventh stage, the knowledge consort is on the seventh stage. Likewise, if one is on the tenth stage, the knowledge consort is on the tenth stage.

"Summoned with the mind" means making evident through mere recollection, without depending on outer substances.

Now, in taking the four empowerments of the dissolution of the four movements with the ultimate path, the person from whom the empowerment is taken is "the master . . . the concentrated essence of the sugatas of the three times." "Three times" refers to the three cakras that arise in order as above; the three nāḍīs; inhalation, exhalation, and rest; and the trio of the melting, bliss, and nonconceptuality of the bindu.[101] In brief, since the refined element becomes totally purified, there is just a tip of hair.

"The pledged deity is inseparable from the guru" means that the bindu, and so on, manifest as the ordinary guru, the nirmāṇakāya of the victor guru. The saṃbhogakāya guru, the dharmakāya guru, and the svabhāvakāya guru are realized to be undifferentiated.

The location in which that perfect guru abides is "in the bhaga," those supreme anthers of the mother of the thirteenth stage, and so on. "Receiving siddhi" means that in the two moments of the empowerment of the dissolution of the four movements received from that guru, {118} one receives the siddhi of realizing the five kāyas. "Existence is the pure path" is the empowerment of the dissolution of the four movements. The subsidiary topics are as before. Those explain the direct cause.

"The very pure svabhāvakāya is naturally accomplished without effort" means that since the four kāyas of the transformation of the support are the same thing,[102] the transformation of the supported is called "the accomplishment," which is the result.

Though it is said, "the result is the ability to shake all saṃbhogakāya buddhafields, and so on," one should understand "the result is the ability to shake all svabhāvakāya buddhafields, and so on."[103]

Though "the inner sign is the prāṇa and āyāma ceasing in the avadhūti," the prāṇa and āyāma vāyus of the two nāḍīs [enter the central nāḍī, and] the four movements dissolve into the supreme uṣṇīṣa. "The outer sign is the bindu stabilized in the whole uṣṇīṣa" means that all the support and the supported transform once the supreme uṣṇīṣa of the head is accomplished.

Those correspond with the scriptures concerning the mundane path and the transcendent path. According to paths, there are five. According to factors conducive to awakening, there are thirty-seven. According to stages, there are twelve and a half. This explains all paths.

Now, to explain the result accomplished by those paths, "The elimination of the defects and faults of cultivation through the dissolution of the four movements of outer and inner dependent origination is the thirteenth stage. There is omniscience. The thirteenth stage, Vajradhara, appears to be an arrangement of dependent origination. In buddhahood, the retinue attains buddhahood in a single group."

The meaning of this is that one has completed the accumulations and exhibits the five kāyas according to how the dependent origination is arranged. In particular, the importance of benefiting others is generating the bodhicitta that was not generated before, and so on. The importance for both self and others is attaining buddhahood in a single group.

Among those, the first is the movement of all the nāḍīs gradually dissolves and the central nāḍī becomes supreme. From that, it is said that "all kāyas are the nirmāṇakāya." Beginning from the blazing major and minor marks of Bhagavān Mahāvajradhara, the supreme nirmāṇakāyas such as Śākyamuni, and so on, {119} there is benefit for all those to be tamed through appearing in the form of all migrating beings and as the entire container, such as wish-fulfilling trees, and so on.

The secret empowerment [dissolves] the movement of the syllables. The movement of all syllables gradually dissolve. Because the color dissolves, it is white. Because the shape dissolves, *ahaṃ mithi*[104] is the indestructible syllable of union. Through the power of its dissolution, the four māras are overwhelmed, which is like the strength of *hūṃ*. From that, it is said, "All speech is the saṃbhogakāya," producing the languages of all migrating beings, beginning with Sanskrit, the sounds of all the elements, and the sound of the totally pure voice that arises from space for the benefit of those to be tamed.

The gnosis of the wisdom consort empowerment dissolves the movement of the amṛta. Since the movement of the supreme refined element dissolves from the gradual refinement of the nine elements, the amṛta transforms. It is said, "All minds are the dharmakāya." One knows the nature and the extent of everything, and one realizes how dependent origination is arranged.

The fourth empowerment dissolves the movement of the vāyu. Once the karma vāyu gradually dissolves, it becomes the gnosis vāyu. With respect to that transformation of the vāyu, it is said, "All bodies, speech, and minds are the svabhāvakāya." At the time of all bodies, it is all speech and minds. When it is both [speech and minds], since it is the same, those to be tamed are benefited insofar as [all bodies, speech, and minds] are one substance. Those explain the four kāyas of the support. The transformation of the supported[105] is "the svabhāvakāya, the very pure, effortlessly accomplished kāya." Also, the four kāyas are the one totally pure gnosis, manifesting in appearance, this way and that. As such, the *Māyājāla Tantra* states:

> Buddhahood has the nature of five kāyas.[106]

Since the svabhāvakāya is single:

> The single eye of gnosis is immaculate.[107]

The importance of the benefit of others {120} has inconceivable qualities, such as generating the bodhicitta that was not generated before, ascending from stage to stage, full awakening, giving the blind sight, and so on—more than can be described here. The importance for both oneself and others is buddhahood in a single group—the practitioner himself,[108] a knowledge consort with a totally pure continuum, a guru of the lineage, an empowering ḍākinī,[109] and a disciple who is a totally pure field are all liberated at the same time. In order to understand those words, the meaning is explained: the words and meanings are inseparable.

Now, in the explanation of the summary of the treatise, "Secret Mantra" is secret because it is not the domain of Brahma, Viṣṇu, Maheśvara, or the śrāvakas and pratyekabuddhas who are beyond the world. "Mantra" means empowered internally. "Vajrayāna" means that since the four [maṇḍalas] in one's body and the resultant kāyas—Vajradhara, and so on—are inseparable, [the body] is employed in the path. The cause empowerment is first obtained from the guru. The path empowerment is meditated on in four sessions, and so on, by oneself. The result empowerment is the dissolution of the four movements. "Investigated with concepts" means the path. "Realization lacks concepts" means the view. "The appearance of gnosis" is the result. Alternately, investigating with concepts is the mundane path, nonconceptual realization is the transcendent path, and the appearance of gnosis is the result. Alternately, investigating with concepts is the characteristic, diversity; nonconceptual realization is nature, emptiness; and the appearance of gnosis is the essence, union.

Now, in order to categorize the paths explained in that way into profound, mediocre, and ordinary, "the profound path is the guru." The person of best capacity is complete from the guru; that is, through the person of best capacity's devotion and veneration of the guru, without the guru even explaining a single word or the disciple {121} meditating for a single session, since dependent origination is naturally arranged, the disciple will follow to the conclusion.

"Samaya" is the mediocre path. The mediocre person trains in the three means of training in the twenty samayas. If they are broken, they are also mended with the five means of mending. The [mediocre person] will also complete the path and follow the conclusion.

"Analytical cessation of the body" is the path of the average person. Since it is difficult for them to arouse experience, arrange dependent origination and have confidence. Since they arrange dependent origination in five stages, employ the remedies with the body and abandon what is to be abandoned with the body. [This path] is called "the analytical cessation of the body." Those explain the intimate instruction of the path with its result, without omission or addition.

In order to explain that the treatises are complete with those, "the oral instruction and the intimate instructions of the path with its result are complete." Thus, the path and the result have been explained according to the prior commitment to explain. "Oral instruction" means the mundane path. "Intimate instruction" means the transcendent path. Alternately, oral instruction is the confirmation of the path, and intimate instruction is the confirmation of the result. Alternately, oral instruction is the explanation by the guru, and the intimate instruction is the arising of the authority of recalling one's experience. As such, that is the way they are categorized. "Complete" is a term that explains there is neither too much nor too little, neither omissions nor additions, thus "*samāptamithi*."

samāptamithi

This supreme path of great yoga
ornamented with all qualities,
equally filling all places with its renown,
was composed by the one who bears the name Sakya.

In the great hall of the temple called Sakya,
I, Drakpa Gyaltsen, received this with devotion—
the treasure of the basis and the path to omniscience,
the foundation of developing all qualities.
By the merit of this writing, may all migrating beings
quickly obtain omniscience with this supreme path.

This gift of dharma was composed by the yogin Drakpa Gyaltsen.
sarva maṅgalaṃ[110]

PART TWO

The Ripening Empowerment

9. The Beautiful Ornament of the Six Limbs

The Medium-Length Activity of the Direct Realization of Śrī Hevajra[1]

Ngorchen Könchok Lhundrub

The Path with Its Result tradition is best known today, both within and outside the Tibetan community, through the writings of Ngorchen Könchok Lhundrub (1497–1557), the tenth abbot of Ngor Evaṃ Chöden, who compiled the principal sādhanas and empowerment manuals. His writings are among the most authoritative presentations of the Path with Its Result, forming the basis for the *Explanation for the Assembly*.

According to the biographical text *Ocean That Bestows Wishes*,[2] Könchok Lhundrub's father, Kundrub Dar (Kun grub dar),[3] was an adept in the Bön religion as well as a devotee of Buddhism. Könchok Lhundrub's mother, Lhamo Budren (Lha mo bu 'dren), was reputed to be a gnosis ḍākinī. She was the niece of Könchok Phelwa (dKon mchog 'phel ba, 1445–1514), the seventh abbot of Ngor, who in turn was the son of Sönam Pal, the younger nephew of Ngorchen Kungpa Zangpo.

Könchok Lhundrub was born on an auspicious day in 1497 when the asterism Puṣya fell on a Thursday. He was given the name Lhagö Dar (Lha rgod dar). Displaying precocious abilities, Lhagö Dar began his education at Sakya Monastery in 1510 at the age of seven. Five years later, he was sent to Ngor Evaṃ Chöden, where he was granted the novitiate ordination by his great-uncle Könchok Phelwa and the famed Lowo Khenchen Sönam Lhundrub (kLo bo mkhan chen bSod nams lhun grub, 1456/1441–1532/1525), taking the monastic name Könchok Lhundrub. Muchen Sangye Rinchen (Mus chen Sang rgyas rin chen, 1450–1524), the eighth abbot of Ngor, granted Könchok Lhundrub full ordination in 1517. From then on, he strictly avoided meat, alcohol, and garlic and refrained from eating after the noon meal.

Könchok Lhundrub continued his education until 1522. From 1522 until 1534, the young scholar entered an intensive period of study and retreat on the Ngor Vajrayāna curriculum, focusing principally on Hevajra. His biographers record that he was skilled in explanation, debate, and composition and was a prolific author.

Könchok Lhundrub received the Path with Its Result transmission from the leading masters of his day. During the summer of 1521, he received it from Muchen Sangye Rinchen. The second time was in 1524, when Sakya Lochen (Sa skya lo chen, 1485–1533), the twenty-second Sakya throne holder, was invited to Ngor. In 1525, Könchok Lhundrub received this transmission a third time from Lowo Khenchen. He received it a final time in 1533 from Lhachok Senge (Lha mchog seng ge, 1468–1535), the ninth abbot of Ngor. In addition, he received many teachings on Kālacakra, Cakrasaṃvara, Vajrabhairava, and so on, as well as a plethora of minor cycles and sādhanas.

In 1535, Lhachok Senge passed away after a long illness and Könchok Lhundrub was installed as the tenth abbot of Ngor Monastery at the age of thirty-eight, a position he held for the next twenty-two years, until his own passing in 1557. Könchok Lhundrub's teaching career began in earnest with his installation as the tenth Ngor abbot, a role for which he had trained his entire adult life. He immediately began teaching the year of his ascension, offering all the Hevajra, Vajrapañjara, and Saṃpūṭa tantras, bestowing the Vajramālā empowerments, as well as the Raktayamāri, Vajrabhairava, and the Cakrasaṃvara traditions of Luipa, Kṛṣṇācārya, Ghaṇṭapāda, and so on. He bestowed the Path with Its Result a total of twenty-seven times; the Vajramālā, repeatedly; and empowerments, innumerable times. He repeatedly gave the explanations for the eight ancillary path cycles.

At thirty-two, Könchok Lhundrub composed several polemical works defending the Sakya view and practice. Some of these have survived, such as the *Knowledge Mantra of Brahma*, a detailed refutation of Muse Lodrö Rinchen Senge, a direct disciple of Lama Tsongkhapa and the founder of Sera Je College.

Könchok Lhundrub wrote sādhanas for many practices included in the famed Seven Maṇḍalas of Ngor—specifically, Cakrasaṃvara, Vajrayoginī, Vajrabhairava, Sarvavidyā, and Mahākāla—as well as many others that continue to be practiced today. In addition, he wrote on Sakya history, poetry, and many other subjects.

Könchok Lhundrub's writings on the Path with Its Result amount to more than three western volumes. The first of the four texts presented here is the *Beautiful Ornament of the Six Limbs*, composed in 1537. The second is the undated *Beautiful Ornament of Bali Offerings*. The third is the *Beautiful Ornament of the Great River of the Empowerment of Śrī Hevajra*, composed in 1552. The fourth is the *Condensed Essential Citations and Intimate Instructions of the Empowerment Rite of the Intimate Instruction Tradition of Śrī Hevajra*. The last of these texts is substantially the work of Könchok Lhundrub but is presented here as it was abbreviated by Loter Wangpo (bLo gter dbang po, 1847–1914), in order to make the empowerment easier to bestow.

A highly realized master, Könchok Lhundrub described this realization in his verse autobiography:

> Having abandoned distractions and evil friends
> and tamed my mind in retreat,
> I was blessed by the definitive Mañjuśrī
> to see the meaning of the nonarising nature of all phenomena.

Ngorchen Kunchok Lhundrub passed away in 1557 at age sixty-one, as he had predicted eleven years earlier.

The Six-Limbed Sādhana

Jetsun Drakpa Gyaltsen's *Catalog of Hevajra Dharma Cycles* summarizes the main practice cycles of the Hevajra tradition into three traditions: the cycle of Ḍombi Heruka, the student of Virūpa; the cycle of Saroruhavajra, the student of Anaṅgavajra; and the cycle of Kāṇha Samayavajra, who like Virūpa was a direct disciple of the female guru Nairātmyā. The Ḍombi Heruka and Saroruhavajra cycles were transmitted to Drokmi Lotsāwa by Gayadhara. The Kāṇha Samayavajra cycle was transmitted to Gö Khukpa Lhetse ('Gos khug pa lhas btsas) by Kṛṣṇa Śāntibhadra.

The Saroruhavajra and Ḍombi Heruka cycles are considered the two main Hevajra sādhana systems in the Sakya school, as they both came through Drokmi. The former is an extensive sādhana belonging to the cycle of Saroruhavajra,[4] given the eponymous title, *Saroruha's Sādhana*. The latter is a so-called medium-length sādhana belonging to the cycle of Ḍombhi Heruka, *The Six-Limbed Sādhana*, composed by Durjayacandra. The principal difference between these two sādhanas is their structure. According to Panchen Ngawang Chödrak[5] (Ngag dbang chos grags, 1572–1641), *Saroruha's Sādhana* is structured on a four-limbed model according to the system of the *Hevajra Tantra*. By contrast, *The Six-Limbed Sādhana* is structured around the six buddha families, according to the system of the *Vajrapañjara Tantra*. The six limbs are as follows: the limb of Vairocana, generating the celestial mansion; the limb of Vajrasattva, generating the deity maṇḍala; the limb of Akṣobhya, taking the empowerments; the limb of Amitābha, tasting amṛta; the limb of Amoghasiddhi, presenting offerings; and the limb of Ratnasambhava, giving praise.

The Tibetan antecedents to this specific text are the six-limbed sādhana authored by Drakpa Gyaltsen,[6] the Hevajra abhisamaya arrangement by Sönam Gyaltsen,[7] and the arrangement authored by Könchok Gyaltsen.[8] *The Beautiful Ornament of the Six Limbs* is directly based on the latter. This sādhana is related to the cause empowerment and does not include the body maṇḍala, for which permission is given during the path empowerment, which is not included here in Kongtrul's presentation.

---

namaḥ śrī cakranātharatnavardhāya[9]

Having bowed to Hevajra,
the indivisible skillful means of all-pervading compassion
and the wisdom of luminous emptiness possessing the supreme of all aspects,
listen to this explanation of the method for accomplishing the six families of victors.

During the evening in an agreeable place, a practitioner who has received the empowerment into this maṇḍala and maintained samaya should sleep in the state of luminous emptiness, the inconceivability of all phenomena. In the early morning one rises with the pride of great bliss of a divine body. One washes if it assists one's concentration. Having previously performed the yogas of offering and bali, one adopts the conduct of concentration on a seat marked with a crossed vajra. One faces east and sits. One focuses on the objects of refuge as if they were actually present.

> Beginning from this moment until seated on the seat of awakening, I and all sentient beings, equal with space, go for refuge to the venerable, glorious, and sublime root and lineage gurus, the embodiments of the body, speech, mind, qualities, and activities of all tathāgatas of the ten directions and three times, the sources of the eighty-four thousand sections of the dharma and the sovereigns of the noble sangha. {125} We go for refuge to the perfect buddha bhagavāns. We go for refuge to the sublime dharma. We go for refuge to the noble sangha.

At the conclusion of repeating this as much as possible, one joins one's palms together and recites:

> I prostrate and go for refuge to the guru and the Three Jewels. May you please bless my continuum.

One imagines that the objects of refuge melt into light and dissolve into oneself.
Recite three times:

> I will practice the profound path in order to attain the stage of perfect buddhahood for the benefit of all sentient beings.

[Vajrasattva meditation and recitation:]

> Bhagavān Vajrasattva Śrī Heruka instantly appears on a lotus and moon* disc on one's crown. His body is white in color. He has one face and two hands, which hold a vajra and a bell. He embraces the mother. Adorned with the six bone ornaments, he sits with his feet crossed in vajra posture. Resembling himself, the master of his family{126} adorns his head. Mother Vajragarvi, whose body is white in color, is seated on his lap in union with the father. She holds a curved knife and skull cup and is adorned with the five mudras. In the father's heart, there is a moon disc, upon which there is *hūṃ*. Rays of light shine from this syllable,

*The stem of the lotus is inserted into the brahma aperture.

inviting the essence of the minds of all tathāgatas in the ten directions to dissolve into the *hūṃ* in the form of wisdom amṛta.

Through offering the supplication, "Bhagavān, bless us to cleanse and purify from the root the misdeeds, obscurations, faults, and downfalls that I and all sentient beings have accumulated from time without beginning," amṛta flows from *hūṃ*, filling the body of the father. Amṛta passes through his vajra, filling the body of the mother. As a stream of amṛta descends from the entire bodies of both the father and the mother, entering through one's crown, all illnesses, evil spirits, misdeeds, and obscurations leave through the rectum, urethra, and the soles of the feet, in the form of soot, pus, blood, and creatures. All vacant places are filled with white amṛta.

One recites the mantra twenty-one times, or as much as possible:

oṃ śrī vajraheruka samayam anupālaya[*] *heruka tvenopatiṣṭha*[†] *dṛḍho me bhava*[‡] *sutoṣyo me bhava*[§] *anurakto me bhava*[¶] *supoṣyo me bhava*[**] *sarva siddhiṃ me prayaccha*[††] *sarva karmasu ca me*[‡‡] *cittaṃ śreya kuru hūṃ*[§§] *ha ha ha ha ho bhagavān vajraheruka*[¶¶] *ma me muñca heruko 'bhava*[***] *mahāsamayasatva āḥ*[†††] *hūṃ phaṭ*

At the conclusion, one offers the following supplication:

I am ignorant and confused.
I have transgressed and damaged my samaya. {127}
Guru and protector, please shelter me!

[*]The commitment of the Adamantine Blood Drinker is to protect me.
[†]Blood Drinker, remain nearby.
[‡]Please act as a support for me.
[§]Be pleased with me.
[¶]Please care for me.
[**]Please greatly nourish me.
[††]Please bestow all siddhis upon me.
[‡‡]Also, all my activities.
[§§]Turns into excellent virtue in my mind.
[¶¶]As the transcendently endowed destroyer Adamantine Blood Drinker.
[***]Liberate me and make me a blood drinker.
[†††]The great commitment being, *aḥ*.

To the chief holder of the vajra, who is
endowed with a compassionate nature,
the chief of all migrating beings, I go for refuge.

I reveal and confess all my damaged root and branch samayas of body, speech, and mind. Please bless me to cleanse and purify all accumulations of misdeeds, obscurations, faults, and downfalls.

Having offered the supplication, Vajrasattva father and mother melt into light, dissolving into oneself through one's crown. One's body becomes like a rainbow. Instantly, one appears as Śrī Hevajra. In one's heart a lotus arises from *paṃ*, and a sun maṇḍala arises from *raṃ*, upon which is a blue *hūṃ*, the essence of one's mind free from both subject and object. Light rays shine from that, inviting the nine-deity Hevajra maṇḍala from its natural abode. Guru Akṣobhya adorns the head of the principal.

With the *vajra samājaḥ* mudra, invite the maṇḍala and recite:

oṃ vajra samājaḥ

Joining one's hands together, recite:

namo guru bhyaḥ
namaḥ śrī hevajramaṇḍala bhyaḥ

One imagines that goddesses emanate from the *hūṃ* at one's heart and present offerings:

Gaurī holds the moon,
Caurī holds the vessel of victory over the māras,
Vetālī holds water,
Ghasmarī holds medicine,
Pukkasī holds the vajra,
likewise, Śavarī holds the elixir of life,
and Caṇḍālī beats a drum.
While they make offerings to the principal,
Ḍombinī embraces him with the passion of great desire.[10]

[Recite three times:]

I go for refuge to the Three Jewels
and individually confess each misdeed.
I rejoice in the merit of beings.
I bear in mind the bodhicitta of the buddhas.
I go for refuge until awakening
to the Buddha, the dharma, and the supreme sangha.
I generate bodhicitta
in order to truly accomplish my own and others' benefit. {128}
Having generated supreme bodhicitta,
I invite all sentient beings to practice the pleasing supreme conduct of awakening.
May I accomplish buddhahood
in order to benefit migrating beings.[11]

One recites the promise to uphold the vows three times:

All buddhas and bodhisattvas,
all heroes and yoginīs, please heed me!
From this time forward,
until the seat of awakening is attained,
I, the vidyādhara, will generate
the sublime, unsurpassed bodhicitta
that definitely causes the awakening
of the protectors of the three times.

The training of discipline,
collecting positive dharmas,
and acting for the benefit of sentient beings are the three disciplines,
each of which I will firmly uphold.

From this time forward, I will firmly uphold
the unsurpassed Three Jewels—
the Buddha, the dharma, and the sangha—
and the vows arising from the yoga of the Buddha.

For the great, supreme vajra family,
I shall truly uphold
the vajra, bell, and mudra.
I will also uphold the masters.

For the pleasing samayas
of the great, supreme jewel family,
I shall always present the four kinds of offerings
daily during the six time periods.

For the pure, great lotus family
that arises from great awakening,
I will uphold all sublime dharmas
of the outer, inner, and secret yānas.

For the great, supreme karma family,
as I possess all vows,
I will truly uphold them and
perform whatever activities of offering I can.

Having generated
the sublime, unsurpassed bodhicitta,
I shall maintain all vows
for the benefit of all sentient beings.

I shall free those who are not free.
I shall liberate those who are not liberated. {129}
I shall provide solace to those without solace.
I shall place all sentient beings in nirvana.[12]

Cultivate the four immeasurables:

May all sentient beings have happiness and the causes of happiness. May they be free from suffering and the causes of suffering. May they never be separated from the bliss that is free from sorrow. May they dwell in equanimity, free from attachment and aversion to those near and far.

All phenomena are appearances of one's mind. Further, one's mind is illusory. This should be understood to be nonreferential emptiness by nature.

Recite:

oṃ śūnyatā jñānavajra svabhāvātmako 'haṃ
From the state of emptiness arises *paṃ*, from which a lotus arises. A sun maṇḍala arises from *raṃ*, upon which is *hūṃ*. From *hūṃ* a crossed vajra with twenty tines arises. [Those in] the east are white; the south, yellow; the west, red; the north, green; and the center of the crossed vajra, dark blue and marked with *hūṃ*. Since light rays from the *hūṃ* shine into the ten directions, there is a vajra ground below surrounded by a vajra fence and a vajra tent above. The area outside is filled with blazing fires of gnosis.

[Recite three times:]

oṃ rakṣa rakṣa hūṃ hūṃ hūṃ phaṭ svāhā

A lotus arises from a *paṃ*, and a sun arises from *raṃ*, upon which there is a golden *bhrūṃ*. A spinning yellow cakra with ten sharply tipped spokes and a vast, wide, and hollow center arises from *bhrūṃ*.

Recite three times:

oṃ vajra cakra rakṣa hūṃ hūṃ hūṃ

Within the center of the cakra and in each of the ten directions, there are lotuses and sun maṇḍalas. Upon the sun in the center, there is a golden *bhrūṃ*. Upon the sun in each of the ten directions, there is *hūṃ hūṃ hūṃ hūṃ hūṃ hūṃ hūṃ hūṃ hūṃ hūṃ*. The *hūṃ* in the south is yellow, and the one in the west is red. All others are blue. From the complete transformation of all the syllables in their respective places, oneself arises in the center as yellow Uṣṇīṣa Cakravartin, {130} who holds a yellow wheel. In the east, blue Yamāntaka holds a hammer. In the south, white

Prajñāntaka holds a club. In the west, red Padmāntaka holds a lotus. In the north, blue Vighnāntaka holds a vajra. In the northeast, blue Acala holds a sword. In the southeast, blue Ṭakkirāja holds a goad. In the southwest, blue Nīladaṇḍa holds a club. In the northwest, Mahābala holds a trident. Above, blue Hūṃkara holds a vajra and a bell crossed at his heart, making his own gesture. Below, blue Śumba holds a pestle. Apart from Hūṃkara, all others hold their own hand implements aloft with their right hands and make threatening gestures at their hearts with their left hands.

The deities in the center and cardinal directions are terrifyingly wrathful, with three round, wide, and bloodshot eyes. Their bodies are muscular, short, and large-bellied. They wear tiger-skin skirts and are adorned with snakes. Their yellow beards, eyebrows, and hair sweep upward. The other wrathful deities are beautifully wrathful—slightly graceful and slightly wrathful. Their bodies are slender and erect. Their hair is black, and they wear silk skirts and jewel ornaments.

They all stand with their left leg extended in the midst of a blazing fire of gnosis. For all:

> Mohavajrā is in the eyes,
> Dveṣavajrā is in the ear,
> Mātsaryavajrā is in the nose,
> Rāgavajrā is in the mouth,
> Īrṣyāvajrā is in the body, {131}
> and Nairātmyāyoginī is in the mind.[13]

> Kāyavajrā is in the crown, Vakvajrā is in the throat, and Cittavajrā is in the heart.[14]

Rays of light shine from the *hūṃ* at one's heart, inviting the protection wheel's eleven wrathful ones and their retinues from their natural abode, surrounded by innumerable assemblies of wrathful gnosis beings.

oṃ vajra samājaḥ

If one wishes, one can make the offerings as above. Recite:

jaḥ hūṃ baṃ hoḥ

To elaborate, the mantras that occur below are the extensive absorption.

Once again light rays from the *hūṃ* located at the heart invite the five families of empowerment deities with their retinues.

Recite:

oṃ vajra samājaḥ

If one wishes, one can make the offerings as above.

Offer a supplication:

oṃ abhiṣiñcatumāṃ sarvatathāgata
Reciting *oṃ vajrībhava abhiṣiñca hūṃ*, the water of the vase is conferred upon the crown, filling the body and purifying all taints. The excess water overflows. Vairocana adorns the head of Yamāntaka, Amitābha adorns the head of Padmāntaka, and Akṣobhya adorns the heads of all others.

One imagines that light shines from the *hūṃ* located at one's heart, filling one's pores with innumerable tiny vajras. *Hūṃ* transforms into a single upright blue vajra. The center of the vajra is hollow, inside of which one's mind is imagined as a single *hūṃ*. One imagines the first initial of the name of anyone one wishes to protect, such as superiors, and so on. Furthermore, if one wishes to protect the guru, their initial is imagined above, one's own initial is imagined inside, one's siblings' initials are imagined to the left, one's parents' initials are imagined in front, one's spouse's and children's initials are imagined to the right, the initials of one's employees and retinue are imagined behind, and the initials of one's wealth and properties are imagined below.

In the gaps in the eight directions between the spokes of the cakra, *yaṃ* arises as an air maṇḍala and *raṃ* arises as a fire maṇḍala above it. Above those, one imagines harmful ones with emaciated bodies, disheveled hair, and inverted heads who vomit blood from their mouths.

Since light rays shine from the *hūṃ* at one's heart, imagine that the consciousnesses of the harmful ones are summoned and dissolve into [the visualized harmful ones]. When oneself as Uṣṇīṣa Cakravartin utters *hūṃ*, the faces of the wrathful ones in the eight directions look outward, and the wrathful ones in the middle, zenith, and nadir {132} extend their right legs. Since the cakra spins rapidly to the left, the bodies of the harmful ones are lifted by the air, burned by the fire, and chopped up by the spokes of the cakra. One imagines that once all their misdeeds and obscurations from beginningless lifetimes are purified, their consciousnesses are born in the buddhafield of Akṣobhya. Recite the following mantra as much as possible:

> *namaḥ samanta buddhānāṃ*[*] *namaḥ samanta dharmānāṃ*[†] *namaḥ samanta saṃghānāṃ*[‡] *oṃ sitātapatra*[§] *oṃ vimala*[¶] *oṃ śaṅkara*[**] *oṃ pratyaṃgira*[††] *vajra uṣṇīṣacakravarti*[‡‡] *sarva yantra*[§§] *mantra*[¶¶] *mulakarma*[***] *bhandanaṃ*[†††] *tāḍanaṃ*[‡‡‡] *kīlanāṃvā*[§§§] *mamakrite*[¶¶¶] *yenakenacita*[****] *kritantata*[††††] *sarvāntu*[‡‡‡‡] *cchindha cchindha*[§§§§] *bhindha bhindha*[¶¶¶¶] *ciri ciri*[*****] *giri giri*[†††††] *mara mara*[‡‡‡‡‡] *hūṃ hūṃ hūṃ hūṃ hūṃ hūṃ hūṃ hūṃ hūṃ hūṃ phaṭ phaṭ phaṭ*[15]

[*] Homage to all buddhas.
[†] Homage to all dharmas.
[‡] Homage to all sanghas.
[§] White Umbrella.
[¶] Immaculate.
[**] Giver of bliss.
[††] Repel.
[‡‡] Adamantine Topknot Universal Emperor.
[§§] All machinations.
[¶¶] Mantras.
[***] Fundamental actions.
[†††] Bind.
[‡‡‡] Strike.
[§§§] Stab with a kīla.
[¶¶¶] Do it for me.
[****] In every way.
[††††] Do it.
[‡‡‡‡] All.
[§§§§] Cut, cut.
[¶¶¶¶] Pierce, pierce.
[*****] Powder, powder.
[†††††] Suppress, suppress.
[‡‡‡‡‡] Kill, kill.

If one wishes, recite the following as much as possible:

> *oṃ bhayanāsani*[*] *trāsani*[†] *sarvamārapratyaṃgira*[‡] *vināsani*[§] *yegecita*[¶] *duṣṭanasatva*[**] *mamavirūpakaṃkurvana*[††] *titāni*[‡‡] *sarvamāranipratyaṃkāriṇipatatu*[§§] *hūṃ phāṭ svāhā*[16]

Joining one's vajra palms together, recite:

> The intentions and plans of all enemies and obstructors—whoever possesses thoughts of hostility, thoughts of malice, {133} thoughts of harm, evil intentions, and evil plans toward our sublime, glorious gurus and ourselves—are pacified! If those are not pacified, bind all their bodies [clap]. Bind their voices [clap]. Bind their minds [clap]. Crush their power! Crush their sorcery! Crush their strength! All will be crushed by their own mantra recitations! Their own flesh will be eaten by the gods and demons whom they practice!

One recites this while imagining crossed vajras marked with *hūṃ* on both palms. Each finger is a single-tined vajra. As one claps one's hands, one imagines that the harmful ones are pressed between those tines. From one's heart, one imagines many wrathful ones resembling oneself coming forth, bearing weapons and rendering the bodies and sense organs of all harmful ones into tiny particles. These are burnt by fire and scattered by air. If one wishes, recite:

> The assembly of wrathful deities
> crush the bodies and voices
> of all enemies and obstructors into dust
> and liberate their consciousnesses into the dharmadhātu.

[*] Cause terror and ruin.
[†] Cause fright.
[‡] Repel all māras.
[§] Ruin their form.
[¶] In every way.
[**] Savage sentient beings.
[††] Who act negatively against me.
[‡‡] Those.
[§§] Repel all māras!

Recite three times:

oṃ rakṣa rakṣa hūṃ hūṃ hūṃ phaṭ svāhā

Oneself as Uṣṇīṣa Cakravartin melts, from which arises a dharmodaya tetrahedron. The outside is white, the inside is red, and its mouth is wide and faces upward. The fine tip of the dharmodaya points downward. Within that, a blue maṇḍala of air arises from *yāṃ*, like a drawn bow. Also, the handle is marked with *yām*. The tips are adorned with pennants. Above that, a triangular red fire maṇḍala arises from *raṃ*, which is marked with *raṃ*. Above that, a round white water maṇḍala arises from *vaṃ*, which is marked with a vase. Above that, a square yellow earth maṇḍala arises from *laṃ*, with half-vajras on each corner, which are each marked in the center with *laṃ*. Above that, a yellow ten-spoked cakra arises from *bhrūṃ*, which is marked with *bhrūṃ*.

In the space above those, the intermediate-state consciousness is represented by *oṃ āḥ hūṃ* with a red *hoḥ* on either end. {134} Those syllables dissolve into the elements and the cakra. All merge into one taste, transforming into a square, four-doored celestial mansion made of gems. Inside there are walls composed of five layers: black, green, red, yellow, and white, in that order.* On top of the walls, there is a precious yellow ledge, from which hang decorative strands and tassels. Above, it is adorned with a precious parapet and gutters.

Outside the walls on a red peristyle filled with objects of desire, sixteen goddesses present many offering substances to the Bhagavān. Within the walls, there are eight pillars. Upon those, there are four vajra beams with checker-patterned designs and a beautiful lintel. Narrowing in the center, the celestial mansion is adorned with a vajra and a jeweled finial.

In front of each of the four doors, there are four pillars, which support a four-stepped portico, upon which there is a wheel of dharma, umbrella, and a pair of deer. Moreover, the celestial

*This is according to the intention of the Lopön Rinpoche [Sönam Tsemo, bSod nams rtse mo, 1142–1182]. According to Jetsun Rinpoche [Drakpa Gyaltsen, Grags pa rgyal mtshan, 1147–1216], the sequence is meditated from inside as black, white, yellow, red, and green.

mansion is adorned with many ornaments, such as drapes, streamers, garlands of flowers, moons moved by the wind, yak-tail whisks with jeweled handles, and so on.

Outside, there are eight great charnel grounds: the charnel ground of Caṇḍogra is in the east, Karaṅkabhīsma is in the south, Jvālākula is in the west, Gahvara is in the north, Aṭṭahāsa is in the northeast, Lakṣmīvana is in the southeast, Ghorāndhakāra is in the southwest, and Kilikilārava is in the northwest.[17]

Eight great trees inhabit those charnel grounds: an acacia tree (Skt. *śirīṣa*) is in the east, a mango tree (Skt. *cūta*) is in the south, an aśoka tree (Skt. *kaṅkeli*) is in the west, a bodhi tree (Skt. *aśvattha*) is in the north, a spurge tree (Skt. *mahāvṛkṣa*) is in the northeast, a pongamia tree (Skt. *karañja*) is in the southeast, a banyan tree (Skt. *vaṭa*) is in the southwest, and an arjuna tree is in the northwest.

Eight directional guardians dwell at the roots of those trees: In the east, yellow Śakra rides upon an elephant, holding a skull with a vajra insignia in his left hand. In the south, blue Yama rides a water buffalo, holding a skull and a club in his left hand. In the west, white Varuṇa rides a crocodile, holding a skull and a noose in his left hand. In the north, yellow Kubera rides a horse, holding a skull and a staff in his left hand. In the northeast, white Maheśvara rides a white ox, holding a skull and a spear in his left hand. In the southwest, red Agni rides a man. He has one face and four hands. He holds a time-stick and a skull in his two right hands; he holds a pitcher and a mālā in his two left hands. In the southwest, black Rākṣasa rides a zombie, holding a skull and a sword in his left hand. In the northwest, blue Maruta rides a deer, holding a skull and a pennant in his left hand. All make a gesture of homage to the Bhagavān with their right hand.

There are eight great clouds in the sky above those trees: yellow Garjita is in the east, blue Āvartaka is in the south, white Aghora is in the west, yellow Ghūrṇita is in the north, white Ghana is in the northeast, red Pūraṇa is in the southeast, blue Varṣana is in the southwest, and blue Caṇḍa is in the northwest.

There are eight great nāgas residing in those charnel grounds: yellow Vāsuki is in the east, blue Padma is in the south, black Karkoṭaka is in the west, red Takṣaka is in the north, {136} white

Mahāpadma is in the northeast, blue Hūluṇṭa is in the southeast, green Kulika is in the southwest, and yellow Śaṅkhapāla is in the northwest. All have cobra-headed hoods with seven flares. Their lower bodies are coiled serpent tails. Their upper bodies are bodies of devas with palms clasped together.

There are eight field guardians residing in the branches of the trees: in the east, white *Devasangha[18] has an elephant face; in the south, blue Yama has a water buffalo face; in the west, red Megharāja has a crocodile face; in the north, yellow Yakṣasenāpati has a horse face; in the northeast, smoke-colored *Pretasabha has an ox face; in the southeast, red *Ṛṣisabha has a man's face; in the southwest, black *Rakṣasagaṇa has a zombie face; and in the northwest, green *Vāyurāja has a deer face. Their upper bodies emerge from among the branches, holding curved knives and skulls.

Furthermore, there are bodies that are decapitated, hanging, prostrate, and impaled on wooden stakes. Severed heads, skeletons, jackals, crows, owls, vultures, and zombies make the sound *phaim*. All those charnel grounds were also directly realized by the siddhas of the past.[19] Yakṣas, rākṣasas, pretas, piśācas, unmadas, apasmāras, ḍākas, ḍākinīs, ponds, fires, stupas, and siddhas completely surround the celestial mansion.

Within this, there is a dais for the deities: the east side is white, the south side is yellow, the west side is red, the north side is green, and the center is blue. In the middle, there is a multicolored, eight-petaled lotus, {137} in the center of which is a sun maṇḍala. Upon the sun, there is the essence of the four māras (such as affliction, and so on) in the form of yellow Brahma, white Indra, blue Upendra, and black Rudra. All are stacked one upon the other. Upon the moon maṇḍalas on each of the eight petals, yellow Brahma is in the east; white Indra, in the south; blue Upendra, in the west; black Rudra, in the north; blue Yama, in the northeast; yellow Kubera, in the southeast; black Rākṣasa, in the southwest; and smoke-colored Vemacitra, in the northwest. All lie facing upward, serving as the seats of the [eight] directions.

Recite:

oṃ sarvatathāgata nilayavajra svabhāvātmako 'haṃ

Upon the central seat, there is the essence of the thirty-two marks of the Buddha, like the form of stars: *a ā i ī u ū ri rī li lī e ai o au a aṃ*, recited twice. From those melting, the mirrorlike gnosis arises as a moon maṇḍala. Upon it, there is the nature of the eighty minor marks, like a row of lamps: *ka kha ga gha ṅga, ca cha ja jha ña, ṭa ṭha ḍa ḍha ṇa, ta tha da dha na, pa pha ba bha ma, ya ra la va, śa ṣa sa ha kṣa, ya ra la va ḍa ḍha*, recited twice. From those melting, the gnosis of uniformity arises as a sun maṇḍala.

Between both of those maṇḍalas, a three-sectioned white skull arises from *hūṃ*, which has a crossed vajra insignia marked in the middle with *hūṃ*. To the left of that, a blue curved knife arises from *aṃ*, which is marked with *aṃ* on the handle. These two are the gnosis of individual discernment. The merging of the sun, moon, hand implements, and seed syllables is the gnosis of successful activity.

The complete transformation of the body {138} resulting from all those merging together is the essence of the gnosis of the dharmadhātu: oneself becomes the cause Bhagavān Vajradhara, white in color, with eight faces, sixteen hands, and four feet. The principal face is white, the right face is blue, the left face is red, the upper face is smoke-colored, and the remaining two pairs of faces are black. Each face has three eyes, four bared fangs, and upswept yellow hair. The crown is marked with a crossed vajra. The sixteen hands hold sixteen skull cups. The skull cup in the first right hand contains a white elephant. The skull cup in the first left hand contains yellow Pṛthivī. Those two hands embrace the consort. In the other right hands, the second skull cup contains a blue horse; the third, an ass with a blaze; the fourth, a yellow ox; the fifth, an ash-colored camel; the sixth, a red man; the seventh, a blue śarabha;[20] and the eighth skull cup contains a cat with a blaze.

In the other left hands, the second skull cup contains white Varuṇa; the third, red Agni; the fourth, green Vāyu; the fifth, white Candra; the sixth, red Sūrya; the seventh, blue Yama; and the eighth skull cup contains yellow Kubera. On each head there is a head ornament with five dried human heads. The father has a necklace of fifty fresh heads. He has six bone ornaments. He stands in the ardhaparyaṅka[21] dancing posture, with the toes of the two left legs pointed toward the thighs of the two extended right legs.

He has nine dramatic moods:
graceful, heroic, hideous,
laughing, shouting, terrifying,
compassionate, ferocious, and peaceful.[22]

In his lap is the mother, blue Vajranairātmyā, who has one face, two hands, three eyes, and upswept yellow hair. {139} She holds a curved knife in her right hand and clasps the father with her left hand, while holding a skull cup. She has a head ornament with five dried human heads and a necklace of fifty dried skulls. She has five bone ornaments. Her left leg is extended, and her right leg wraps around the father. The couple stands in the midst of a blazing fire of gnosis.

The space of the mother vanishes. From the state of emptiness arises *aḥ*, from which arises an eight-petaled lotus marked in the center with *aḥ*.

oṃ padmasukhadhara[*] *mahārāgasukhaṃdada*[†] *caturānand-abhagaviśva*[‡] *hūṃ hūṃ hūṃ kāryaṃkuruṣvame*[§]

The secret place of the father vanishes. From the state of emptiness, there is *hūṃ*, from which arises a five-tined vajra marked in the center with *hūṃ*:

oṃ vajramahādveśa[¶] *caturānandadayakaḥ*[**] *khagamukha ekāra-sonātha*[††] *hūṃ hūṃ hūṃ kāryaṃkuruṣvame*

Ha ha si si kundurha vajra dhrik, the sound of great bliss from

[*]The lotus is the bearer of bliss.
[†]Granting the bliss of great passion.
[‡]The various portions of the four joys.
[§]Perform the activity for me!
[¶]Great Adamantine Wrath.
[**]Bestower of the four joys.
[††]The face of the ḍākinī protects one taste.

the couple engaging in union resounds in their secret places, inviting all tathāgatas of the ten directions. They enter the mouth of the father. The compassionate fire of passion within his heart melts the tathāgatas into light, which passes through the form of the father's body, falling from his vajra path into the space of the mother, and subsequently transforming into eight bindus. Those transform into the eight seed syllables: *gaṃ caṃ vaṃ ghaṃ paṃ śaṃ laṃ ḍaṃ*.

After those [seed syllables] melt into light, transform into the eight goddesses, and issue forth from the space of the mother—in the east, black Gaurī holds a curved knife in her right hand and a rohita fish in her left hand; in the south, purple Caurī holds a ḍamaru in her right hand and a pig in her left hand; in the west, yellow Vetālī {140} holds a tortoise in her right hand and a skull cup in her left hand; and in the north, green Ghasmarī holds a snake in her right hand and a skull in her left hand. In the northeast, blue Pukkasī holds a lion in her right hand and an ax in her left hand; in the southeast white Śavarī holds a bhikṣu in her right hand and a mendicant's staff (Skt. *khakkhara*) in her left hand; in the southwest, red Caṇḍālī holds a wheel in her right hand and a plow in her left hand; and in the northwest, multicolored Ḍombinī holds a vajra in her right hand and makes a threatening gesture with her left hand. All have one face, two hands, three eyes, and upswept yellow hair. They are naked and adorned with five bone ornaments. All have head ornaments made of five dried skulls and necklaces made of fifty dried skulls. They stand in the ardhaparyaṅka dancing posture with the left leg extended in the midst of a blazing fire of gnosis.

Because the couple engages in union, once again from the sky, the intermediate-state consciousness—represented by *oṃ āḥ hūṃ* with a red *hoḥ* on either end—enters the mouth of the father. It passes through his body and the vajra path into the space of the mother. Because of the condition of the arrival of the syllables there, the fire of passion melts the couple into light. Upon the four māras, they transform into the essence of great bliss in the form of bindus with the nature of Vajrasattva.

oṃ sarvatathāgata anurāgaṇavajra svabhāvātmako 'haṃ

One's consciousness moves to each of the four goddesses in the intermediate directions. Imagine they invoke one with songs:

> Lord with a compassionate mind, arise!
> Protect me, Pukkasī.
> Abandon the nature of emptiness,
> and unite with me in great bliss.
> Since I shall die without you,
> Hevajra, you must arise!
> Abandon the nature of emptiness,
> and accomplish Śavarī's goals. {141}
> Joyful lord who entertains the world,
> why have you departed into emptiness?
> Without you, I won't know what to do.
> I, Caṇḍālī, implore you.
> Trickster, I know your mind!
> You must arise!
> Since I, Ḍombinī, am weak-minded,
> do not interrupt your compassion![23]

As a consequence of those invocations:

> Those bindus transform into a blue *hūṃ* and a blue *āṃ* with terrifying, blazing light. Those syllables melt, from which one arises as blue result Vajradhara, with eight faces, sixteen hands, and four feet. The principal face is blue, the right face is white, the left face is red, the upper face is smoke-colored, and the remaining two pairs of faces are black. Each face has three eyes, four bared fangs, and upswept yellow hair. The crown is marked with a crossed vajra. The sixteen hands hold sixteen skull cups. The skull cup in the first right hand contains a white elephant. The skull cup in the first left hand contains yellow Prithivī. Those two hands embrace the consort. In the other right hands, the second skull cup contains a blue horse; the third, an ass with a blaze; the fourth, a yellow ox; the fifth, an ash-colored camel; the sixth, a red man; the seventh, a blue śarabha; and the eighth skull cup contains a cat with a blaze.
>
> In the other left hands, the second skull cup contains white

Varuṇa; the third, red Agni; the fourth, green Vāyu; the fifth, white Candra; the sixth, red Sūrya; the seventh, blue Yama; and the eighth skull cup contains yellow Kubera.

On each head, there is a head ornament with five dried human heads. The father has a necklace of fifty fresh heads. He possesses six bone ornaments. He stands in the ardhaparyaṅka dancing posture, with the toes of the two left legs pointed toward the thighs of the two extended right legs.

He has nine dramatic moods:
graceful, heroic, hideous,
laughing, shouting, terrifying,
compassionate, ferocious, peaceful.

In his lap is the mother, blue Vajranairātmyā, who has one face, two hands, three eyes, and upswept yellow hair. She holds a curved knife in her right hand and clasps the father with her left hand, which holds a skull cup. She wears a head ornament with five dried human heads and a necklace of fifty dried skulls. She possesses five bone ornaments. Her left leg is extended, and her right leg wraps around the father. The couple stands in the midst of a blazing fire of gnosis.

Within the heart of all deities, there is each one's respective seed syllable upon lotuses and suns: *hūṃ aṃ gaṃ caṃ vaṃ ghaṃ paṃ śaṃ laṃ daṃ*. Lights shine from those seed syllables, touching the outer universe, which transforms it into the essence of the celestial mansion. The light touches sentient beings, transforming them into the essence of the nine deities.

In all, white Mohavajrā arises from *muṃ* in the eyes, blue Dveśavajrā arises from *daṃ* in the ears, yellow Mātsaryavajrā arises from *paṃ* in the nose, red Rāgavajrā arises from *raṃ* in the mouth, green Īrṣyavajrā arises from *aṃ* at the forehead, black Nairātmyāyoginī arises from *naṃ* in the heart, white Kāyavajrā arises from *oṃ* at the crown, red Vakvajrā arises from *aḥ* at the throat, and blue Cittavajrā arises from *hūṃ*. All have one face, two hands, three eyes, and upswept yellow hair. They are naked and adorned with five bone ornaments. They have head ornaments made of five dried skulls and necklaces made of fifty dried skulls. They stand on corpses in the ardhaparyaṅka dancing posture with the left leg extended, in the midst of a blazing fire of gnosis.

Light shines from the *hūṃ* at one's heart, {142} inviting the nine-deity maṇḍala of Hevajra from its natural abode, surrounded by an inestimable assembly of buddhas and bodhisattvas.

oṃ vajra samājaḥ

Invite with the *vajra samājaḥ* mudra. Place one's palms together and recite:

Gaurī holds the moon,
. . . .
embraces him with the passion of great desire.

If one elaborates, offer the praise that occurs below:

You are surrounded by a troupe of yoginīs . . .

With the pinky finger of the left fist interlaced with the index finger of the right fist, recite:

oṃ vajra gaurī ākarṣaya jaḥ

Black Gaurī wields a goad, with which she invites the deities into the protection wheel.

With the two fists placed back to back, making the eye of a noose, recite:

oṃ vajra caurī praveśaya hūṃ

Red Caurī wields a noose, with which she touches the throats of the gnosis beings, who then dissolve downward from the forehead. With the two pinkies and index fingers interlaced, recite:

oṃ vajra vetālī bandha baṃ

Yellow Vetālī wields a chain, with which she touches the feet of the gnosis beings and commitment beings, causing them to merge.

With the two fists held crossed back to back at both wrists, recite:

oṃ vajra ghasmarī waśaṃ kuru hoḥ

Green Ghasmarī holds a bell, with which she produces the sound of bells everywhere, inside and out. One imagines that the gnosis beings merge with the commitment beings.

> Once again the light rays shine from the *hūṃ* at one's heart center, inviting the empowerment deities: the five families of tathāgatas, the four mothers, the eight bodhisattvas, the six goddesses, and the ten wrathful ones.

Present offerings as above. If one wishes, recite the offering of praise:

> Homage and praise to Dveṣavajrā.[24]
> Homage and praise to Mohavajrā.
> Supplications to Mātsaryavajrā.
> Protect me, Rāgavajrā.
> Be proud, great Īrṣyāvajrā.
> All are the supreme samaya of all vajras.
> Accomplish the activities.
> May I please all vajra holders.[25]

Repeat three times:

> All bhagavān tathāgatas,
> bhagavān great beings,
> those with the nature of compassion,
> may you please confer the empowerment upon me.

> {143} Having transformed into the form of Heruka, those tathāgatas hold up precious vases filled with amṛta:

> The great vajra empowerment
> from the three secrets of all buddhas
> is granted to the one
> to whom all throughout the three realms prostrate.[26]

oṃ vajribhava abhiṣiñca hūṃ

Saying this, the tathāgatas confer the empowerment, the knowledge consorts sing vajra songs, the bodhisattvas recite benedictions, the wrathful ones frighten away obstructors, and the goddesses present offerings. The stream of empowerment water fills one to the brow, one obtains the vase empowerment, and the taints of the body are purified.

> The wheel on the crown is Akṣobhya.
> The nature of the earrings is Amitābha.
> The necklace is Ratnasambhava himself.
> The bracelets are said to be Vairocana.
> The girdle is Amoghasiddhi.
> The protector Vajradhara is located on all the limbs.[27]

The stream of empowerment water fills one to the throat, one obtains the secret empowerment, and the taints of the voice are purified. The *aṃ*[28] of the nirmāṇacakra at the navel is the karma mudra. The *hūṃ* of the dharmacakra at the heart center is the dharma mudra. The *oṃ* of the saṃbhogacakra at the throat is the mahāmudra. The *haṃ* of the mahāsukhacakra at the crown is the samaya mudra.

The steam of empowerment water fills one to the heart center, one obtains the gnosis empowerment of the wisdom consort, and the taints of the mind are purified.

> Mohavajrā is in the eyes,
> Dveṣavajrā is in the ears,
> Mātsaryavajra is in the nose,
> Rāgavajrā is in the mouth,
> Īrṣyāvajrā is in the body,
> and Nairātmyāyoginī is in the mind.

> Kāyavajrā is in the crown, Vakvajrā is in the throat, and Cittavajrā is in the heart.

That stream of empowerment water fills one to the feet; one obtains the fourth empowerment; and the taints of body, voice, and mind are purified. {144} The remaining water overflows; the heads of the father, mother, Gaurī, and Pukkasī are adorned with

Akṣobhya; Caurī and Śāvarī are adorned with Vairocana; Vetālī and Caṇḍālī are adorned with Ratnasambhava; and Ghasmarī and Ḍombinī are adorned with Amitābha.
oṃ sarvatathāgata abhiṣekata vajrasvabhāva atmako 'haṃ

Either prepare actual amṛta or imagine it, and recite:

oṃ vajra amṛta kuṇḍali hana hana hūṃ hūṃ hūṃ phaṭ svāhā
oṃ svabhāva śuddhaḥ sarvadharma svabhāva śuddho 'haṃ
From the state of emptiness arises *yaṃ*, from which arises a blue air maṇḍala in the shape of a bow marked with pennants. Above the air maṇḍala, {145} a red fire maṇḍala arises from *raṃ*, in the shape of a triangle marked with flames. Above the fire maṇḍala, a three-sectioned white skull arises from *a*, with the forehead facing toward oneself. Above the skull, a moon maṇḍala arises from *a*. Above the moon, in the east, cow meat arises from *go*; in the south, dog meat arises from *ku*; in the west, horse meat arises from *ṅga*; in the north, elephant meat arises from *ha*; and in the center, human meat arises from *na*.

Above each of those meats, in the east, excrement arises from *bhrūṃ*; in the south, blood arises from *āṃ*; in the west, bodhicitta arises from *jrīṃ*; in the north, the refined part of great meat arises from *khaṃ*; and in the center, urine arises from *hūṃ*.

Above those, in the east, *bhrūṃ* is the mirrorlike gnosis; in the south, *āṃ* is the gnosis of uniformity; in the west, *jrīṃ* is the gnosis of individual discernment; in the north, *khaṃ* is the gnosis of successful activities; and in the center, *hūṃ* is the gnosis of the dharmadhātu.

On the perimeter of the moon, *a ā i ī u ū ṛi ṛī li lī e ai o au a aṃ* circles to the left, and *ka kha ga gha ṅga*, {146} *ca cha ja jha ña, ṭa ṭha ḍa ḍha ṇa, ta tha da dha ṅga, pa pha ba bha ma, ya ra la va, śa ṣa sa ha kṣa* circles to the right.

In the sky above that, there is an inverted white *oṃ*. Above that, a sun maṇḍala arises from *raṃ*. Above the sun maṇḍala, a five-tined vajra arises from *hūṃ*, which is marked in the center with *hūṃ*.

Rays of light shine downward from *hūṃ* in the center of the vajra. By striking the pennants of the air maṇḍala, the motion of the air ignites the fire, boiling the five meats and five amṛtas. Those melt into light. The rising steam touches both *oṃ* and the vajra, which is marked in the center with *hūṃ*, causing a stream of amṛta to flow.

Once again, from *hūṃ* light shines in the ten directions, causing the true gnosis amṛtas from the heart centers of all tathāgatas to arrive in the form of herukas with two arms. These herukas dissolve into the *hūṃ* in the center of the vajra, causing the vajra to become heavy. The vajra, sun, and *oṃ* fall into the skull. Once melted, those become nondual with the aforementioned amṛta, which transforms into an ocean of amṛta with perfect color, scent, taste, and potency.
oṃ āḥ hūṃ ha ho hrīḥ

Take the amṛta with the left ring finger and taste it. Since the amṛta is consumed by the deities with tongues that are vajra tubes, imagine [the deities] are blissfully satiated.

Oṃ sarvatathāgata amṛta svadana vajrasvabhāva atmako'haṃ

Imagine that goddesses emanate from one's heart center, presenting offerings:

Gaurī holds the moon,
Caurī holds the vessel of victory over the māras,
Vetālī holds water,
Ghasmarī holds medicine,
Pukkasī holds the vajra,
likewise, Śavarī holds the elixir of life
and Caṇḍālī beats a drum.
While they make offerings to the principal,
Ḍombinī embraces him with the passion of great desire.

oṃ sarvatathāgata puja vajrasvabhāva atmako 'haṃ

You are surrounded by a troupe of yoginīs.
You have attained the supreme mind.

You ornament all migrating beings with the animate and
inanimate.*
The one who rouses sentient beings with compassion,
the illusory emanation whose mind has accomplished the vajra—
Śrī Heruka, rejoice with a vajra mind!

oṃ sarvatathāgata stuti vajrasvabhāva atmako 'haṃ

At this juncture one should meditate without being interrupted by extraneous concepts. Focus the mind on the insubstantial, illusory appearance of the celestial mansion and the deities. When that appearance becomes stable, practice the completion stage according to the guru's instructions.

Recall the purities:

His eyes are red due to compassion.
His limbs are black due to his loving mind.
The four means of conversion are
said to be his four feet.
His eight faces are the eight liberations.
His hands are the sixteen emptinesses.
His ornaments are the five buddhas.
In order to tame the savage, he is wrathful.
His flesh is known as Pukkasī.
Likewise, his blood is Śavarī.
Caṇḍālī is described as his semen.
Ḍombinī is his pure marrow and fat.
His skin is the seven limbs of awakening.
His bones are the four truths.[29]

If one wishes, recite:

Lungs, breath, and likewise, insanity,
consumption, leprosy, and smallpox,
and also liver and spleen conditions
are renowned as the ox, and so on.[30]

*The deities and the celestial mansion.

The eight lords who grant benefits
are Prithivī first, up to Kubera, who comes last.[31]

The wheel on the crown is Akṣobhya.
The nature of the earrings is Amitābha.
The necklace is Ratnasambhava himself.
The bracelets are said to be Vairocana.
The girdle is Amoghasiddhi.
The protector Vajradhara is located on the limbs of all.

The Bhagavān is the gnosis of the dharmadhātu.
Gaurī is the mirrorlike gnosis.
Caurī is the gnosis of uniformity.
Vetālī is the gnosis of individual discernment.
Ghasmarī is the gnosis of successful activity.
Pukkasī is limitless love.
Śavarī is limitless compassion.
Caṇḍālī is limitless joy.
Ḍombinī is limitless equanimity.[32]

The celestial mansion is the purity of the thirty-seven adjuncts to awakening. The eight charnel grounds are the purity of the orifices of the body, combining the nostrils together as one orifice.

The aggregate of matter is Vajrā.
Likewise, sensation is Gaurī.
Perception is Vāriyoginī.
Formations is Vajra Ḍākinī.
Nairātmyāyoginī abides {147}
as the principal aggregate of consciousness.[33]

Earth is explained to be Pukkasī.
The element of water is said to be Śavarī.
Fire is understood to be Caṇḍāliṇī.
Air is stated to be Ḍombinī.
Hatred is explained to be Vajrā.
Desire is Vāriyoginī.
Jealousy is Vajra Ḍākinī.

Envy is Guptagaurī.
Likewise, confusion is explained as Vajrā.[34]

Mohavajrā is in the eyes.
Dveṣavajrā is in the ears.
Mātsaryavajra is in the nose.
Rāgavajrā is in the mouth.
Īrṣyāvajrā is in the body.
Nairātmyāyoginī is in the heart.

Form is always explained to be Gaurī.
Sound is stated to be Caurī.
Smell is Vetālī.
Taste is stated to be Ghasmarī.
Touch is explained as Bhucarī.
The dharmadhātu is Khecarī.[35]

Having recited the above, recall the meaning. Following the recollection of the purities, there is no fault if one engages first in the yoga of conduct. As for the yoga of recitation, though it is proper to maintain the pride of the principal father and mother at all times following the dissolution of the maṇḍala, here it is done only in the context of the approach, and so forth.

Now then, the mantra garland arises from *āṃ* in the heart of the mother, leaving her mouth and entering the mouth of the father. The mantra garland then travels through his body, exiting through the path of the vajra and finally entering the lotus of the mother. The mantra garland travels through her body, entering the mouth of the father from her mouth. Imagine that light rays, which correspond to the activities, shine from the mantra garland that spins uninterruptedly, bringing the gods under control.

Pick up the empowered mālā and recite the root mantra, the essential mantra, and the quintessential mantra:

*oṃ aṣṭānanaya** *piṅgalordhākeśavartamane*† *caturviṅṣatinetrāya*‡

*The highest praise, with eight faces.
†Ochre hair sweeps up.
‡With twenty-four eyes.

> *ṣoḍaśabhujāya*[*] *kṛṣṇajīmūtavapuṣe*[†] *kapālamālānikadhārine*[‡] *adhmātakrūracittāya*[§] *ardhendudaṃṣṭrīṇe*[¶][36] *mārayamāraya*[**] *kārayakāraya*[††] *garjayagarjaya*[‡‡] *tarjayatarjaya*[§§] *śoṣayaśoṣaya*[¶¶] *saptasāgarān*[***] *nāgāṣṭakān*[†††] *bandhabandha*[‡‡‡] [§§§] *ghriṇa-ghriṇa*[¶¶¶] *śatrūn*[****] *ha hā hi hī hu hū he hai ho hau haṃ haḥ phaṭ svāhā*[††††]

The essence and near-essence mantras of the father:

> *oṃ devapicuvajra*[‡‡‡‡] *hūṃ hūṃ hūṃ phaṭ svāhā*
> *oṃ vajrakartāri hevajrāya*[§§§§] *hūṃ hūṃ hūṃ phaṭ svāhā*

The mother and the yoginīs:

> *oṃ āḥ a ā i ī u ū ṛi ṛī li lī e ai o au a aṃ hūṃ phaṭ svāhā*
> *oṃ āḥ aṃ hūṃ phaṭ svāhā*
> *oṃ āḥ naṃ vajranairātmāya hūṃ phaṭ svāhā*

Recite the retinue mantras one-tenth the amount of the father's and the mother's mantras.

[*] Sixteen hands.
[†] Whose body exists like [the color] of a rain cloud.
[‡] Wearing a mālā of many skulls.
[§] Whose mind is internally fierce.
[¶] With canines like half-moons.
[**] Kill, kill!
[††] Do it, do it!
[‡‡] Roar, roar!
[§§] Plunder, plunder! [The text here reads *tarjjaya*, corrected to *tarjaya*.]
[¶¶] Drink, drink!
[***] The seven seas.
[†††] The eight nāgas.
[‡‡‡] Bind, bind!
[§§§] The eight nāgas.
[¶¶¶] Seize, seize!
[****] The enemy.
[††††] Split! Bestow excellence.
[‡‡‡‡] Vajra Gentle Deity.
[§§§§] Vajra Flaying Knife. Hevajra.

oṃ āḥ gaṃ hūṃ phaṭ svāhā
oṃ āḥ gaṃ vajragaurī hūṃ phaṭ svāhā
oṃ āḥ caṃ hūṃ phaṭ svāhā
oṃ āḥ caṃ vajracaurī hūṃ phaṭ svāhā
oṃ āḥ vaṃ hūṃ phaṭ svāhā
oṃ āḥ vaṃ vajravetālī hūṃ phaṭ svāhā
oṃ āḥ ghaṃ hūṃ phaṭ svāhā
oṃ āḥ ghaṃ vajraghasmarī hūṃ phaṭ svāhā
oṃ āḥ paṃ hūṃ phaṭ svāhā
oṃ āḥ paṃ vajrapukkasī hūṃ phaṭ svāhā
oṃ āḥ śaṃ hūṃ phaṭ svāhā
oṃ āḥ śaṃ vajraśavarī hūṃ phaṭ svāhā
oṃ āḥ laṃ hūṃ phaṭ svāhā
oṃ āḥ laṃ vajracaṇḍālī hūṃ phaṭ svāhā
oṃ āḥ daṃ hūṃ phaṭ svāhā
oṃ āḥ daṃ vajraḍombinī hūṃ phaṭ svāhā

Place one's palms together and recite:

> Please bless me and all sentient beings with the body, speech, mind, qualities, and activities of all tathāgatas. Please bless me to swiftly obtain the essential, supreme siddhi of mahāmudrā, the stage of Hevajra. {149}

If one has not dissolved the maṇḍala as above, imagine the following:

> Since light rays shine from *hūṃ* in one's heart center, the universe and the inhabitants of the three realms all melt into light and dissolve into the protection wheel. The protection wheel dissolves into the eight charnel grounds. The eight charnel grounds dissolve into the celestial mansion. The celestial mansion dissolves into the eight goddesses. The eight goddesses dissolve into one's eight faces.

With the exception of the predawn session, following the other three sessions, sing the vajra song in connection with the bali offering:

kolla ireṭṭhi abolā[*] *mummuṇire kakkolā*[†] *ghaṇe kripiṭaho vajja i.*[‡]
karune kia i narolā[§] *tahiṃ bharu khājja ī.*[¶]
gādheṃma aṇā bijja i.[**]
hale kāliñjara pani a i.[††]
dundura bājji a i.[‡‡]
causama kacchurī sihlā[§§] *kāppuralā*[¶¶] *i a i.*
māla indhaṇa sāliñja[***] *tahiṃ bharu khā i a i.*[†††]
phreṃ khaṇa khata karante[‡‡‡] *śuddha aśuddhana muṇi a i.*[§§§]
nirasu aṃge cadāvi[¶¶¶] *tahiṃ ja sarāva pani a i.*[****]
mala aje kunduru bāṭa i.[††††]
diṇḍama tahin na bājji a i.[‡‡‡‡]

Thus, recite the vajra song.

Recite the benediction:

The first virtuous fortune of the world
is the Buddha, endowed with eyes that resemble lotus blossoms.
The protector of the three realms who has abandoned the three taints
is endowed with abundance, resembling a mountain of gold.

[*]The vajra resides at Kolla Mountain.
[†]The lotus resides at Mummuni Field.
[‡]Ho, play the drum in the assembly!
[§]Do not talk. Out of compassion . . .
[¶]There, one should eat meat.
[**]The diligent one drinks alcohol.
[††]Ho, the fortunate may enter!
[‡‡]The unfortunate may not enter.
[§§]Catuḥsama, musk, blood.
[¶¶]And camphor should be smeared.
[***]Stew and great meat. [This line is missing in *DNZ*.]
[†††]Should be eaten in quantity.
[‡‡‡]One should come and go.
[§§§]Do not perceive pure or impure.
[¶¶¶]Wear bone ornaments on the body.
[****]Place a man's corpse there.
[††††]Gather, engage in intercourse.
[‡‡‡‡]At that time, do not avoid the untouchable.

The second virtuous fortune of the world
is the Buddha's immovable, supreme doctrine,
the sublime dharma that pacifies all living beings,
renowned throughout the three realms, to which devas and
humans present offerings.

The third virtuous fortune of the world
is the sublime sangha, which is endowed with the dharma,
enriched through hearing,
and an object of offering for humans, devas, and asuras. {150}
The supreme assembly is conscientious and the basis of prestige.
Those are the three virtuous fortunes of the world.[37]

Offer the aspiration:

In birth after birth,
may I be born into a good family
and possess samaya, mental stability,
and devotion to a guru who teaches Hevajra.

In birth after birth,
may I hold the vajra, ring the bell,
recite the profound dharma,
and consume the śukra of the queen with equanimity.

May all sentient beings be happy!
May all sentient beings be liberated
by any flawless path,
and through that may they attain buddhahood.

When entering into daily activities, with the pride of the principal couple, understand that everything, both subject and object, is the maṇḍala of deities, and be free from attachment and aversion.

When eating, touch the food with the thumb and ring finger of the left hand and recite *oṃ aḥ hūṃ*, imagining that one's food and drink become amṛta. With confidence in presenting an offering to the *hūṃ* at the heart, the essence of all the deities, eat without attachment. Recite *oṃ ucchiṣṭa balingta bhakṣasi svāhā*. Snap one's fingers and give the remainder to the powerful elemental spirits. If one is a householder, one should engage in the yoga of passion while possessing the three perceptions. When going to sleep:

> Imagine that the mother dissolves into the father. The extra faces and hands of the father dissolve into the primary face and hands. He dissolves into the *hūṃ* at the heart center. The foot of *hūṃ* dissolves into the body. The body of *hūṃ* dissolves into the head. The head dissolves into the crescent. The crescent dissolves into the bindu. The bindu dissolves into the nāda. Finally, the nāda disappears. Go to sleep in the state of connate luminosity, free of grasping.

When waking from sleep before dawn, rise with the pride of the deity, like a fish jumping from the water. At the conclusion of the evening session, sing the vajra song and offer benedictions and aspirations. When washing, this should be done either according to the time of the empowerments or depending on whether one is doing an extensive or concise yoga. Recite the one-hundred-syllable mantra and then wash.

Having presented the offering and bali as they separately occur, as previously explained, one should enter into the predawn session, and so on.

As such, if one practices the ten yogas without interruption, {151} relatively, one will follow the conclusion and, ultimately, it is certain one will manifest the stage of Vajradhara.

Once the six elements, six objects, six migrations, six sense organs,
six colors, and six aggregates (when including the dharmadhātu) are
purified,
this method of accomplishment causes the attainment
of the six families of victors. This method has six limbs.

This liturgy, the *Beautiful Ornament of Direct Realization*,
was composed according to the intention of my great, kind guru
on behalf of many intelligent disciples,
in dependence upon the discourses of Jetsun's forefathers.

Since most of the mantras were rectified
on the basis of several Sanskrit texts,

having understood them according to the long and short vowels and
the demarcations,
the mantras can be practiced purely by the discerning.

Though I have diligently endeavored to use discernment
to disclose the profound meaning, because my intelligence is meager,
if there are errors, I beg the forbearance of the gurus and yidams.
Please purify all my misdeeds.

Through all the virtue generated from endeavoring in this practice and
whatever other virtue there may be,
may I quickly attain unsurpassed awakening,
in order to fulfill the intention of the supremely kind guru
and accomplish the benefit of all sentient beings throughout space.

Having taken the immaculate feet of several sublime nirmāṇakāya tutors upon my crown, such as the sovereign Vajrasattva in essence, the supremely kind king of dharma Ratnavardha, the possessor of limitless compassion Muchen Sangye Rinchen [Mus chen sang rgyas rin chen, 1450–1524], and the lord of the wise, Lotsāwa Jamyang Khenpo;[38] having attained faith through knowing the words and meanings of the precious discourses of the sovereigns of Jambudvīpa; having taken the text of the sādhana composed by Muchen Sempa Chenpo as my basis; having understood and obtained faith in the words and meanings of the precious discourses of the Jetsun Sakyapa fathers and sons, the masters of the doctrine in Jambudvīpa; {152} having ornamented the text with the advice of learned gurus; and with the aim of making a commemorative offering to the three lord-guru fathers and sons, on the tenth day of the waxing phase of the middle autumn month of the female Iron Sow year (1537), this *Beautiful Ornament of the Six Limbs: The Medium-Length Activity of the Direct Realization of Śrī Hevajra* was composed by the learned monk, Könchok Lhundrub, at the temple of Pal Evaṃ Chöden, for the purpose of an easy introduction for the faithful. May it be supremely virtuous!

As a support for this composition, it is important to examine and investigate in detail the discourses of the glorious Sakyapa fathers and sons.
sarva maṅgalaṃ

10. The Beautiful Ornament of the Bali Rite of Śrī Hevajra[1]

Ngorchen Könchok Lhundrub

The Beautiful Ornament of the Bali Rite of Śrī Hevajra combines several traditions together into one. It has three main sections: the bali offering of Hevajra, the bali offering to the principal dharmapālas of the Sakya school including the eight deities associated with Pañjaranātha Mahākāla and the five deities of Caturmukha Mahākāla (Zhal bzhi pa), and the bali offering to the ḍākinīs.

The eight-deity Mahākāla consists of two subgroups: the three-deity "brother and sisters" group, composed of Pañjaranātha Mahākāla, Śrī Devī Kāmadhātviśvarī, and Ekajati; and the five deities who belong to the Karmanāthas (*las mgon*), the activity protectors. Mahākāla and Śrī Devī are both offspring of Mahādeva and Umadevi. Umadevi's transcendent form is identified as Ekajati in this group of deities, which explains her iconographic position above Śrī Devī and to the left of Mahākāla.

Pañjaranātha (Gur gi mgon po) is so named because this form of Mahākāla is found in the fifteenth chapter of the *Vajrapañjara Tantra*. Amezhab asserts that this form of Mahākāla is the chief or essential form of Mahākāla among all the Mahākāla tantras.[2] However, the sources for the origin story of Mahākāla and Mahākālī, along with the incarnation series and relationships that inform the iconography of these three deities, are found in the prologues of three texts:[3] the *Ḍākinī's Blazing Tongue of Flame Tantra*, the *Śrīdevi Black Butcher Tantra*, and Aśvaghoṣa's *Great Charnel Ground Commentary*.

The Karmanāthas, also known as the Mönbu Putra siblings (Mon bu putra ming sring), are composed of Kālayakṣa and Kālayakṣī, who are emanations of Mahākāla and Mahākālī. They in turn emanate Putra, Bhaṭa, and Rākṣasi Ekajati.[4] The source for this group of deities is said to be chapter 20 of the *Mamo Wheel of Life Tantra*.[5] While this group of deities is considered part of the eight-deity Mahākāla grouping, their bali offering has been traditionally placed after the bali offering of Caturmukha.

The second group is the maṇḍala of Caturmukha Mahākāla, or four-faced Mahākāla, considered the chief protector of the Sakyapa doctrinal view. This protector is exoterically represented in Sakya iconography as so-called brahmin Mahākāla. Tradition maintains that Caturmukha Mahākāla, also known as Kṣetrapāla (Zhing skyong), accompanied the eleventh-century translator Nyan Lotsāwa Darma Drak (Dar ma grags) on his return to Tibet as a servant in the form of an Indian brahmin. Representations of Caturmukha Mahākāla and his four sisters are never displayed in public settings. Thus, the brahmin Mahākāla is used to represent this important Sakya protector in most paintings.

---

namaḥ śrī cakranātharatnavardhāya

Having obtained empowerment and possessing the samayas, a practitioner who wishes to offer bali[6] to the pledged deity and the dharmapālas should ornament their dwelling with canopies, curtains, and so on. If there is an image of the dharmapālas, it should be arranged to face east or south. In front of that image, on a surface covered with any kind of cloth ornamented with various kinds of grain, arrange either two or five balis for the mundane and transcendent deities, pure preliminary-enjoyment water offerings, and so on. In front of the practitioners, arrange the requisite articles, such as a vajra, a bell, the inner offering, and so on.

> *oṃ vajra amṛta kuṇḍali hana hana hūṃ hūṃ hūṃ phaṭ svāhā*
> *oṃ svabhāva śuddhaḥ sarvadharma svabhāva śuddho 'haṃ*

> From the state of emptiness arises *yaṃ*, from which arises a blue air maṇḍala in the shape of a bow marked with pennants. Above the air maṇḍala, {155} a red fire maṇḍala arises from *raṃ* in the shape of a triangle marked with flames. Above the fire maṇḍala, a three-sectioned white skull arises from *a*, with the forehead

facing toward oneself. Above the skull, a moon maṇḍala arises from *a*. Above the moon, in the east, cow meat arises from *go*; in the south, dog meat arises from *ku*; in the west, horse meat arises from *ṅa*; in the north, elephant meat arises from *ha*; and in the center, human meat arises from *na*.

Above each of those meats, in the east, excrement arises from *bhrūṃ*; in the south, blood arises from *āṃ*; in the west, bodhicitta arises from *jrīṃ*; in the north, the refined part of great meat arises from *khaṃ*; and in the center, urine arises from *hūṃ*. Above those, in the east, *bhrūṃ* is the mirrorlike gnosis; in the south, *āṃ* is the gnosis of uniformity; in the west, *jrīṃ* is the gnosis of individual discernment; in the north, *khaṃ* is the gnosis of successful activities; and in the center, *hūṃ* is the gnosis of the dharmadhātu.

On the perimeter of the moon, *a ā i ī u ū ri rī li lī e ai o au a aṃ* circles to the left and *ka kha ga gha ṅa,* {156} *ca cha ja jha ña, ṭa ṭha ḍa ḍha ṇa, ta tha da dha na, pa pha ba bha ma, ya ra la va, śa ṣa sa ha kṣa* circles to the right. In the sky above that, there is an inverted white *oṃ*. Above that, a sun maṇḍala arises from *raṃ*. Above the sun maṇḍala, a five-tined vajra arises from *hūṃ*, which is marked in the center with *hūṃ*.

Rays of light shine downward from *hūṃ* in the center of the vajra. By striking the pennants of the air maṇḍala, the motion of the air ignites the fire, boiling the five meats and the five amṛtas. Those melt into light. The rising steam touches both *oṃ* and the vajra, which is marked in the center with *hūṃ*, causing a stream of amṛta to flow.

Again, from *hūṃ* light shines in the ten directions, causing the true gnosis amṛtas from the heart centers of all tathāgatas to arrive in the form of herukas with two arms. These herukas dissolve into *hūṃ* in the center of the vajra, causing the vajra to become heavy. The vajra, sun, and *oṃ* fall into the skull. Once melted, they become nondual with the aforementioned amṛta, which transforms into an ocean of amṛta with perfect color, scent, taste, and potency.
oṃ āḥ hūṃ ha ho hrīḥ

Empower this by reciting the above mantra three times.

In the space above, three dharmodayas arise one above the other from *e e e*. Inside of each arises an eight-petaled lotus from *paṃ paṃ paṃ*. In the center and on the eight petals of the lotus located in the upper dharmodaya arise nine *oṃ* syllables, which transform into Kāyavajra in the center, Maheśvara in the east, Indra in the south, Brahma in the west, Viṣṇu in the north, Kāmarāja in the southeast, Gaṇapati in the southwest, Bhṛṅgariṭi in the northwest, and Kumara Kārttikeya in the northeast. Each is white in color, with one face and two hands, which hold a vajra and a bell, and each embraces a knowledge consort that resembles themselves. {157}

In the center of the lotus located in the middle dharmodaya, a blue Śrī Hevajra arises from *hūṃ* . . . compassionate, ferocious, and peaceful.[7] The mother, blue Vajranairātmyā, arises in his lap with *āṃ* and . . . stands in the midst of a blazing fire of gnosis.

In the east, black Gaurī arises from *gaṃ* . . . .* Likewise, in the south, red Caurī arises from *caṃ* . . . . In the west, yellow Vetālī arises from *vaṃ* . . . . In the north, green Ghasmarī arises from *ghaṃ* . . . . In the northeast, blue Pukkasī arises from *paṃ* . . . . In the southeast, white Śavarī arises from *śaṃ* . . . . In the southwest, red Caṇḍālī arises from *laṃ* . . . . In the northwest, multicolored Ḍombinī arises from *ḍaṃ* . . . stand in the midst of a blazing fire of gnosis.

The eight *hūṃ*s on the eight petals transform completely into Indra in the east, Yama in the south, Varuna in the west, Kubera in the north, Agni in the southeast, Rākṣasa in the southwest, Vāyu in the northwest, and Maheśvara in the northeast. Each is red in color, with one face and two hands, which hold a vajra and a bell, and each embraces a knowledge consort resembling themselves.

In the center and on the petals of the lotus located in the lower dharmodaya, nine *āḥ* syllables transform into Vakvajra in the center, Karkoṭa in the east, Śaṅkhapāla in the south, Ananta in the west, Vāsuki in the north, Takṣaka in the southeast, Kulika

*Clearly recall the features and hands.

in the southwest, Padma in the northwest, and Mahāpadma in the northeast.

All twenty-four elementals, adorned with bone ornaments, stand on lotus and sun seats with their right legs extended. Since light rays shine from the *hūṃ* in one's heart, all celestial devas dissolve into the eight great devas. All terrestrial sentient beings {158} dissolve into the eight directional guardians. All subterranean sentient beings dissolve into the eight nāgas. In the eyes of all is Mohavajrā . . . in their hearts is Cittavajrā.

Since light rays shine from the *hūṃ* in one's heart, all buddhas and bodhisattvas of the ten directions are summoned in the form of Hevajra's nine-deity maṇḍala with the assembly of deities of body, voice, and mind.

oṃ vajra samājaḥ

Invite with a snap of the fingers accompanied by their respective mudras:

oṃ vajra gaurī ākarṣaya jaḥ
oṃ vajra caurī praveśaya hūṃ
oṃ vajra vetālī bandha baṃ
oṃ vajra ghasmarī waśaṃ kuru hoḥ
Again, since light rays shine from the *hūṃ* in the heart, the five families of empowerment deities are summoned with *oṃ vajra samājaḥ*.

Place one's palms together:

Gaurī holds the moon,
. . . .
embraces him with the passion of great desire.

Offer the supplication:

All bhagavān tathāgatas,
. . . .
may you please confer the empowerment upon me.

They say:

> The great vajra empowerment . . . *abhiṣiñca hūṃ* . . .

> And confer the empowerment with the water from the vase. The taints of their whole bodies are purified. The remaining water overflows, and Kāyavajra and the eight great devas have Vairocana as a head ornament. The heads of the father and mother, Gaurī . . . Ḍombinī are adorned with Amitābha, and the heads of the eight directional guardians are adorned with Akṣobhya. The heads of Vakvajra and the eight great nāgas are adorned with Amitābha.

Present the four water offerings accompanied by their respective mudras:

> *oṃ bhagavān mahākaruṇika hevajra saparivāra oṃ nīrī hūṃ khaṃ svāhā, oṃ vajra niviti hūṃ khaṃ svāhā oṃ sarva śodhani svāhā oṃ jaḥ hūṃ baṃ hoḥ khaṃ raṃ mahā argham praticcha svāhā*

The deities' tongues are vajras that arise from *hūṃ* and are marked with *hūṃ*s, which are the size of a grain of rice. Imagine they sip the bali through proboscises of light that arise from the vajra.

Having performed a preliminary lotus roll, one opens one's vajra palms facing upward and recites: {159}

> *oṃ bhagavān mahākaruṇika hevajra saparivāra oṃ inda jama jala jakṣa bhūta bihni vāyu rakha canda sujja māda pappa talapātāle aṭṭasappa svāhā, idaṃ baliṃ bhuñja jiṃgha phulla dhūppa māṃsa bhiṃgu ambha sappa sādha khantikhuṇi pheḍagāda oṃ a kāromukhaṃ sarvadharmaṇāṃ ādyanutpannatvāta oṃ āḥ hūṃ phaṭ svāhā*[8]

Recite this and snap one's fingers. As such, present the bali offering three times, five times, and so on. Present the offerings accompanied by their respective mudras:

> *oṃ vajra puṣpe āḥ hūṃ* . . . likewise at the beginning and end until . . . *dhūpe, āloke, ghandhe, naividye*, and *śabda*.

> *hūṃ aṃ gaṃ caṃ vaṃ ghaṃ śaṃ laṃ ḍaṃ oṃ āḥ hūṃ*, the sublime offering is presented to the mouths of the Hevajra nine-deity maṇḍala and the assembly of deities of body, speech, and mind.

Present this by scattering the inner offering with the thumb. With the vajra in the palm, ring the bell three times:

> Gaurī holds the moon,
> . . . .
> embraces him with the passion of great desire.

Offer praise:

> Akṣobhyavajra is great gnosis,
> the vajradhātu, the great intellect,
> the supreme one of the three vajras and the three maṇḍalas.
> Homage and praise to Vajraḍāka.
>
> Vairocana is great purity,
> vajra peace, great joy,
> supreme natural luminosity.
> Homage and praise to Buddhaḍāka.
>
> Ratnarāja is very profound,
> immaculate vajra space,
> unsoiled because of natural purity.
> Homage and praise to Ratnaḍāka.
>
> Vajrāmitābha, great king,
> is the holder of the vajra space of nonconceptuality,
> the one who attained the perfection of desire.
> Homage and praise to Padmaḍāka.
>
> Amoghavajra, {160} the perfect buddha,
> is the one who perfects all wishes,
> who arises from the pure nature.
> Homage and praise to Viśvaḍāka.[9]

Hold the vajra at the heart, and ring the bell once [per line]:

> Eight great devas and your retinue,
> eight nāgas and your retinue,
> eight lokapālas and your retinue,
> entire host of yakṣas,
> entire host of rakṣas,
> entire host of bhūtas,
> entire host of pretas,
> entire host of piśācis,
> entire host of unmadas,
> entire host of apasmāras,
> entire host of ḍākas,
> entire host of ḍākinīs,
> that entire host of bhūtas, and so on,
> as many of them as there are—
> come here and please heed me!
> Accept this bali offering.
> May we yogis and our retinue
> all attain health, longevity, power, wealth,
> prestige, fame, good fortune,
> and vast enjoyments.
> Grant me the siddhis of the activities
> of pacifying, increasing, and so on.
> Those with samaya, protect me
> and give me assistance in all siddhis.
> Prevent untimely death, illnesses,
> spirit attacks, and obstructors.
> Prevent bad dreams, bad omens,
> and bad actions.
> Increase happiness in the world, good harvests,
> grain, and increase the dharma.
> Produce all excellent virtue
> and accomplish all that my mind desires!

Though one has already accomplished the blessing of the bali offerings, in order to recall the blessing, show the left hand to the bali offerings, recite *oṃ*, and imagine they are empty. {161} Show the right hand, recite *āḥ*, and imagine there is a white skull cup, vast and white, with the forehead facing toward oneself. Show both hands and recite *hūṃ*, imagining the skull is filled with the five meats and the five amṛtas. Show the garuḍa mudra, and recite *ho*. Imagine all transforms into gnosis amṛta, and recite *oṃ āḥ hūṃ ha ho hrīḥ*. For the purpose of these supplementary words above, refer to the sādhana. For the mudras, refer to the *Beautiful River of Empowerments*. Next:

> Located in the space before one, a lotus arises from a *paṃ* and a sun maṇḍala arises from a *raṃ*, upon which is a dark-blue *hūṃ*. Light shines from this, destroying all savage, obstructing enemies. The light then returns. Vajramahākāla arises with one face and two hands from the complete transformation of *hūṃ*. At his heart, his right hand holds a curved knife and covers his left hand, which holds a skull filled with blood. He bears a *gaṇḍī*[10] of emanation on his forearms. He possesses three eyes and bares his fangs. His ochre hair sweeps upward. He is adorned with a diadem of five dried skulls and a necklace of fifty fresh heads. He is adorned with the six bone ornaments and snakes. He wears a tiger-skin skirt, a crown, and a silk shawl of various colors. He stands on a corpse with the posture of a crouching dwarf. To his right are black birds; to the left, black dogs; behind him, jackals; and in front, black men. Above him is an emanated messenger, a garuḍa. He has Akṣobhya on his crown and stands in the center of the blazing fire of gnosis.
>
> On his right, Ekajati arises from *ṭaṃ*. Her color is blue. She has one face and two hands, holding a vase filled with amṛta to her heart. She wears an upper garment of silk and a tiger-skin skirt. {162} She has a single braid of hair that hangs down on the left. She has a wrathful mood. In the ocean of blood that arises from *trak* in her vast belly is *bhyoḥ*, from which arises Śrī Devī Kāmadhātviśvarī, riding an ass. Her color is blue-black, with one face and four hands. In the first right hand, she holds a sword. In the second right hand, she holds a skull filled with blood. In the first left hand, she holds a javelin. In the second left hand, she holds a trident. She has a tiara of five dried human skulls and a necklace of fifty fresh heads. She is adorned with six bone ornaments. She wears an upper garment of elephant hide,

a lower garment of cowhide, and a skirt of felt tied with a belt of a powerful nāga. She has three eyes and bares her fangs with a human corpse in rigor mortis in her mouth. She is adorned with a poisonous snake as her right earring and a lion as her left earring. There are spots of blood, smears of grease, and piles of great ash arranged on her body. She is extremely emaciated. The sun and moon rise from her navel. She roars *hūṃ* and *bhyoḥ* in the midst of one hundred thousand mātṛkas[11] and flesh-eating ḍākinīs.

Both siblings have *oṃ* at their forehead, *āḥ* at their throat, and *hūṃ* at their heart. Light rays shine from the *hūṃ*s, summoning the protector from the heart of Vairocana in Akaniṣṭha and the goddess from her natural abode, along with their retinues. Recite *oṃ vajra samājaḥ* and snap one's fingers.

Place one's hollow palms together, making the samaya mudra of the protector, cover the index fingers or cover one's vajra, and ring the bell for each individual line:

Protector, arise from the seat of all tathāgatas.
Now is the age of the five degenerations.
Come and remain in this evil place,
and guard the doctrine of Śākyamuni. {163}
In order to benefit us,
please come to this place.[12]

oṃ śrī mahākāla e hye hi

While placing one's vajra palms together, with the fingers slightly interlaced, and either making the mudra of the goddess or holding the vajra and bell, invite her with:

Protector, arise from the seat of all tathāgatas,
. . . .
please come to this place.

oṃ śrī mahākāli devī e hye hi
jaḥ hūṃ baṃ hoḥ

Place the palms together with the three middle fingers spread, and offer a lotus seat:

> *oṃ padmakamalā stāṃ*
> *oṃ śrī mahākāla grihnedaṃ mahākālidevī grihnedaṃ arghaṃ svāhā padyaṃ svāhā, oṃ vajra puṣpe . . . śabda aḥ hūṃ*

Imagine that one places the samaya mudra of the protector at one's heart on his head and with the stable pride of the deity recite:

> *oṃ śrī mahākālā samayasmara samayamātrikama samayarakṣantu*

Imagine that one places the samaya mudra of the protector at one's heart on her head:

> *oṃ mahākālidevī samayasmara samayamātrikama samayarakṣantu*

To elaborate, recite this and clap one's hands:

> Śrī Vajramahākāla, siblings, and your retinue of servants and loyal subordinates, accept this vast bali offering. Do not transgress the commands and samayas of the glorious root and lineage gurus. Protect your samaya. Guard the doctrine. Extol the Three Jewels. In particular, with methods of pacification, please eradicate all evil intentions, plans, and conflicts of the host of misleading obstructing enemies who harm and injure the doctrine of the Buddha, the holders of the doctrine, and us practitioners and our retinue, creating obstacles to our accomplishment of the path. If they cannot be tamed with methods of pacification, {164} please eradicate them with whatever means is appropriate—frighten and oppress them, divide, threaten, and subdue them. In brief, pacify all obstacles to accomplishing the dharma, support the accomplishment of our intentions and desired plans that accord with the dharma, and propagate and increase the doctrine, the doctrine holders, and all worldly people.

With vajra-folded palms facing up and open, recite three or five times:

> *oṃ śrī mahākālā saparivāra namaḥ sarvatathāgate bhyo viśva mukhe bhyaḥ sarva thakaṃ udgate spharaṇa imaṃ gaganakhaṃ grihadaṃ balyadi svāhā*

Recite three or five times for the protector:

> *oṃ śrī mahākālāya śasanaupahariṇi eṣa apaścimakālo amaṃ idaṃ ratnatraya apakariṇi yadi pratijñasmara sitada idaṃ duṣṭa kha khā khāhi khāhi mara mara ghrina ghrina bhandha bhandha hana hana daha daha paca paca dina dinamekana māraya hūṃ phaṭ*

Recite three or five times to present offerings to the goddess:

> *oṃ śrī mahākālīdevī saparivāra namaḥ sarvatathāgate . . .*

Make offerings as before:

> *oṃ śrī mahākāla grihnedaṃ . . . śabda . . .*

Offer the inner offering:

> With *oṃ mahākālāya hūṃ hūṃ phaṭ phaṭ svāhā* and *oṃ roru roru vitiṣṭha badhotsī kāmala rākṣasī*[13] *hūṃ bhyoḥ*, this sublime offering is presented to the mouths of Śrī Vajramahākāla's siblings.

Recite:

> Spread the doctrine of the Buddha. Produce vast, excellent virtue in the world. Pacify all negative conditions and obstacles of our masters and the retinue of disciples. Please accomplish all positive conditions as we wish.

With a vajra in one's palm, ring the bell for each verse and offer the praise:

> I praise the one who arose from the syllable *hūṃ*,
> Mahākāla, with two hands,

one face, {165} blazing blue in color,
holding a copper curved knife and a skull.

I praise the one who wears a necklace of heads,
terrifying with bared fangs,
short in stature, with great brilliance,
and whose red face is contorted.

I praise Mahākāla,
who consumes those who hate the master,
whoever harms the Three Jewels,
and the slayers of sentient beings.[14]

bhyoḥ
I praise you, blazing fire arising from the depths of the ocean,
she who has the power to dry all oceans,
Gaurī Mahākālī,[15]
the daughter of Mahādeva sent forth
in order to pacify all women,
the one to whom devas and asuras pay homage,
you who know the name and are unafraid
of any human illness,
the sister of Yāma, the mother of Māra—
I praise Kāmadhātviśvarī.[16]

Holding one's vajra to one's heart, recite:

Śrīnātha and retinue,
Śrīdevī and retinue,
accept the oceanic cloud of outer, inner, and secret offerings
and this vast bali offering,
empowered by samādhi, mantra, and mudra.
Please increase the doctrine of the sugatas in the ten directions,
extol the Three Jewels,
ensure the longevity of the holders of the doctrine,
and perform vast, positive actions.

In particular, please pacify the negative conditions, illnesses, spirit attacks, and obstacles
of us practitioners and our retinue;
expand our longevity, intelligence, and merit;
and increase our hearing, reflection, and meditation.
The desired activities I request are
the activity of pacifying all obstacles of Yama Māra {166}
and expanding the doctrine of the explanation and accomplishment
of Vajrayāna's four great divisions of tantras.

After that, for Caturmukha, bless the bali just as performed above:

In front of oneself, a lotus arises from *paṃ* and a sun maṇḍala arises from *raṃ*, upon which a curved knife marked with a *hūṃ* arises from a *hūṃ*. This transforms into Śrī Mahākāla with four faces: the two primary faces are stacked one atop the other and are black in color. The right and left face are dark green. He has four hands: the first right hand and first left hand hold a curved knife and a skull full of blood held to the heart, one above the other. The lower right hand holds up a sword, and the lower left hand holds up a mālā made of bone. His ocher hair sweeps upward, and he has three eyes. He bares his fangs, curling his lower lip. He has a diadem of five dry skulls and a necklace of fifty fresh heads. He wears a brahmin's thread and has ornaments of bone and snakes. He stands with his right leg bent and his left leg extended. He has fierce and terrifying accouterments. With his voice, he proclaims *ha ha*, *hūṃ hūṃ*, and *kṣim kṣim*.

To his right is black Ḍombinī; to the left is green Caṇḍālī; in front is red Rākṣasi; and behind is dark-yellow Siṃghalī. All four also have one face and two hands, which hold curved knives and skulls. They are naked, unadorned, very agile, and have wrathful accouterments. There is an *oṃ* at [each] forehead of the principals and retinue, *āḥ* at their throats, and *hūṃ* at their hearts. Light rays shine from the *hūṃ*s, summoning Mahākāla Caturmukha and the four great mother rākṣasīs from the charnel grounds of Mount Kailash, Śītāvana, Potala, and Hāhārava. Recite *oṃ vajra samājaḥ* and snap one's fingers.

Make the five-tined vajra mudra by placing one's palms together, {167} curling the ring fingers inside, and placing the index finger on the back of the middle finger, like a horn, so that the index finger protrudes, or alternately hold the vajra and bell and invite:

> Just as long ago, you, Oh Fierce One,
> made a promise in the presence of Vajradhara
> when you were invited to carry out the four activities,
> please come in order to protect the doctrine of the Buddha.

Invite with:

> *oṃ mahākālā kālā vikāla rātrita ḍombinī caṇḍālī rākṣasi siṃghalī devī saparivāra e hye hi*

Absorb with:

> *jaḥ hūṃ baṃ hoḥ*

As before, offer a lotus seat with:

> *oṃ padmakamalā stāṃ*

Present offerings with:

> *oṃ mahākālā kālā vikāla rātrita ḍombinī caṇḍālī, rākṣasi siṃghalī devī saparivāra arghaṃ . . . śabda*

With the five-tined vajra mudra held at the heart, imagine one places the vajra on their heads and places them in samaya with:

> *oṃ mahākālākālā vikāla rātrita ḍombinī caṇḍālī rākṣasi siṃghalī devī namaḥ saparivāra samayasmara samayamātrikama samayarakṣantu*

To elaborate, give the command with:

> Śrī Mahākāla Caturmukha and your retinue, accept this vast bali offering.

With vajra-folded palms facing up and open, recite three or five times:

> *oṃ mahākālākālā . . . devī namaḥ sarvatathāgate . . .*

If one wishes to elaborate, offer with the long mantra given below and offer as above. The inner offering is recited as before:

> With *oṃ mahākālākālā . . . devī namaḥ oṃ āḥ hūṃ*, the sublime offering is presented to Śrī Mahākāla Caturmukha and your retinue.

Ring the bell once per line and recite:

> *hūṃ*
> Arise as great compassion from the nonconceptual dhātu!
> From the celestial mansion, a storied, great pavilion of elements,
> oath-bound guardian of the sugata's teachings,
> Vajramahākāla, arise from the dhātu!
>
> Powerful glorious one, bring the three realms under control.
> Great powerful one with bared fangs and a curled lip,
> adorned with a garland of resounding bells,{168}
> Caturmukha, you guard the region of Kailash.
> In the presence of the perfect Buddha,
> with four faces for guarding the doctrine,
> Mahākāla Caturmukha
> and the four great mother rākṣasīs
> are offered food of great meat, flowers, incense,
> the first portion of alcohol, and pure flesh and blood.
> Guard the doctrine of the victor,
> and accomplish the activities with which you are entrusted!

Next, bless the bali offering of the Karmanāthas just as before.

> *Ya* emanates from the heart of the protector, and *maṃma* ema-

nates from the heart of the goddess. On a lotus and sun, Kālayakṣa, black, with one face and two hands, arises from *yaṃ*.[17] His right hand holds a curved knife, and his left hand holds a skull filled with blood. He wears a human skin and golden earrings. Kāliyakṣī arises from *maṃma*, with one face and two hands. Her right hand holds a golden razor, and her left hand holds a skull filled with brains and blood. She wears a garment of black silk and a coral hair ribbon.

The two *tri* syllables, which arise from the heart of the father, and the *bhyoḥ* syllable, which arises from the heart of the mother, transform into the Putra brothers and sister. Black Putra arises from *tri*, with one face and two hands. His right hand holds a razor, and his left hand holds a skull filled with blood. He wears shorts and a garment of black silk. Black Bhaṭa[18] arises from *tri*, wearing a fur coat of tiger skin. He holds a samaya stick in his right hand and a human heart in his left hand. Rākṣasi Ekajati arises from *bhyoḥ*. She holds a golden curved knife in her right hand and an intestine in her left hand, with flames blazing from her mouth. Also, all five are dark blue in color and possess three extremely wrathful eyes. They are adorned with garlands of bone and necklaces of fresh human heads. Fearsome and aggressive, they stand in the manner of destroying savage beings. {169}

Furthermore, to their right is a column of one hundred men adorned with battle gear. To their left is a column in form of bhikṣus. One hundred black mantrins follow behind, and one hundred black women lead the way. Furthermore, inconceivable messengers, such as black birds, black dogs, wolves, and so on, with the remains of samaya breakers surround them.

Lights rays shine from their hearts, summoning the Karmanāthas and their retinue of attendant messengers from their natural abode, *oṃ vajra samājaḥ*.

Imagine they are absorbed:

jaḥ hūṃ baṃ hoḥ

Rely on the samaya mudra from the protector section, place it on their heads, and place them in samaya:

ali ali ma ja ja śaṃ śaṃ li śi de a śva ded mo smugs putri a li ma ja ja nag mo sha la rub ja ja oṃ ro ru ro ru ru tri ca pa la a śug me ma hūṃ ma bhyoḥ jaḥ jaḥ samayasmara . . .

To elaborate:

Karmanāthas and your retinue of attendant messengers, accept this vast bali offering.

With vajra-folded palms facing up and open, offer the bali three or five times:

ali ali ma . . . ma hūṃ ma bhyoḥ jaḥ jaḥ idaṃ baliṃ bhuñja kha kha khā hi khā hi

Present the offerings:

oṃ argham . . .

The inner offering is recited as before:

This sublime offering is presented to the mouths of the activity messengers and their retinue, the oath-bound yakṣa father and mother, the attendant putra brothers and sister, the four emanated columns, and the male and female arrogant ones.

Ring the bell once per line and offer the praise:

hūṃ
The terrifying forms of the yakṣa father and mother,
with accouterments of fearsome aggression,
destroy the māras and obstructing enemies.
I praise the great father and mother guardians of the doctrine {170}

Black Mönbu Putra, you[19]
wear a bark[20] sash on your body
and hold a mendicant's staff of gośīrṣa wood in your hand.[21]
I praise you, Black Putra.

Mönbu Bhaṭa, you have a striped, tiger-fur coat,
wear a silk sash on your body,
and hold a sharp samaya stick in your hand.
I praise you, Mönbu Bhaṭa.

Mönmo Golden Razor,
Mahākālī with a flaming mouth,
you hold a golden razor in your hand.
I praise you, Kālī.

A hundred great black women
depart and lead the way.
The column on the right
is the one hundred men adorned with battle gear.
The column on the left
is the one hundred śrāvaka arhat bhikṣus.
The terrifying ones who follow behind
are the one hundred black mantrins wielding kīlas.
I praise the entire retinue.
I also offer praise during the three times.[22]

Making the mudra with the two index fingers, place the tips of the thumbs together, the tips of the index fingers together, and with the remaining fingers like flames, rotate this at the forehead toward the left. Lift one's face, gaze upward, and say:

phaiṃ

Recite:

oṃ vajra aralli hoḥ jaḥ hūṃ baṃ hoḥ vajraḍākīnyaḥ samaya stvaṃ driśya hoḥ[23]

Imagine that light rays shine from the *hūṃ* at the heart, and the eight charnel grounds, which formed in Jambudvīpa at the beginning, arrive in the space in front. Imagine one offers a torma to them. With palms open and facing up, recite this mantra three times and offer:

oṃ kha kha khā hi khā hi sarva yakṣa rākṣasa bhūta preta piśāci unmada apasmara ḍāka ḍākinyādaya imaṃ baliṃ gṛhinantu samaya rakṣantu mama sarva siddhi mame prayacchantu {171} *yathai vaṃ yathe ṣṭvaṃ bhuñjatha jigatha pipatha mātikramatha mama sarvakārtayā satsukhaṃ viśuddhaye sahayikabhavantu hūṃ hūṃ phaṭ phaṭ svā hā*[24]

Offer with:

oṃ arghaṃ svāhā pādyaṃ svāhā oṃ vajra puṣpe . . . śabda

Offer the inner offering as before:

I offer the sublime offering to the mouths of Buddhaḍāka, Vajraḍāka, Ratnaḍāka, Padmaḍāka, and Viśvaḍāka, and to all ḍākas and ḍākinīs of the three abodes.

Ring the bell once per line:

Entire assembly of devas,
entire assembly of nāgas,
entire assembly of yakṣas,
entire assembly of rākṣasas,
entire assembly of of bhūtas,
entire assembly of pretas,
entire assembly of piśācis,
entire assembly of unmadas,
entire assembly of apasmaras,
entire assembly of ḍākas,
entire assembly of ḍākiṇịs,
and entire assembly of bhūtas—
all come here
and please heed me.
In order to guard the doctrine and benefit migrating beings,
those of you who promised to abide by commitments,
loyal subordinates of the great glorious one,
with unbearably savage, ferocious, and terrifying forms,
tame the savages and destroy those of the dark side.

Bestow the fruit of the practitioner's activities.
I pay homage to the eight assemblies of yakṣas, and so on,
who possess inconceivable strength and power.
Eight classes, your queens, children, and servants—
grant the kindness of all siddhis to me.
May this practitioner, [insert name], and retinue
attain health, longevity, wealth, power,
prestige, fame, good fortune,
and vast enjoyments.
Bestow upon me the siddhi of the activities
of pacification, increasing, and so on.
May the guardians always accompany me!
May the ones with samaya guard me
and prevent untimely death, illnesses,
spirit attacks, and obstructors, and
prevent bad dreams, bad omens,
and negative deeds.
Expand happiness in the world, provide good harvests
and grain, increase the dharma,
produce all excellent virtue,
and accomplish all that my mind desires.[25]

If one is going to perform the recitations, burn an incense mixture of white mustard seed, gugul, poison, and great fat. Recite one mālā round of the Devapicu mantra. Imagine that from the heart of one's pledged deity, the mantra shines with rays of light, {172} touching the heart of the protector and retinue and invoking their mental continuums. They hear whatever one commands. Recite the seven-syllable mantra:

oṃ mahākāla hūṃ phaṭ

Recite the twelve-syllable mantra:

oṃ mahākālaya hūṃ hūṃ phaṭ phaṭ svāhā

Recite the Śāsana mantra as much as possible. Also, one can recite the three mantras corresponding to their general order. Next, focus on the goddess, and recite the Roru mantra. To elaborate, recite:

> *oṃ hūṃ śrīya devī kālī kālī hūṃ bhyoḥ*

Similarly, focus on Caturmukha, and recite the principal's mantra:

> *oṃ mahākālakāla vikāla ratrita hūṃ phaṭ svāhā*

Next, recite as much as possible.

> *oṃ mahākālakāla bikaṭṭakārāla lambita oṭha lambākaveka lambakavāli ravighaṇḍi rutramālabihure cchedahakale halenahale pimbijāli bāmeghundhidhariyaṃ ma eṃ dahinakartikakāroṭi bibhiṣaṇadha eṃ bāmeśūlapaṇi haradora narasmīramāla pātālekṣiṃkārakala mahāpoṭale mahākāla Śrīkapila kelasaṃ kṣeṭapāla hā hā kāre hūṃ hūm kare purvabhāṣabhi uṃ jau jantimaṃ sabhata phulla dhupa i ka habali jigha ha daśa dikauttaravari ḍombinī caṇḍālī rakṣasī siṃghalī hana hana bhandha bhandha mara mara daha daha paca paca kṣim kṣim lehi baliṃ dehisiddhi bikālaśatrūṃ māraya hūṃ phaṭ*[26]

Next, focus on the Karmanāthas. Among the worldly beings, females invoke the males. To begin, recite the call of the females found in the second section: *oṃ ro ru ro ru ru tri ca pa la*, and so on. Then the call of the males is recited from the first section: *ali ali ma*, and so on. When one has completed the recitations, offer with:

> *oṃ śrī mahākāla grihnedaṃ mahākālidevī grihnedaṃ arghaṃ svāhā padyaṃ svāhā oṃ vajra puṣpe . . . śabda aḥ hūṃ*

Present the inner offerings. At the end of the mantra, recite as before:

> This sublime offering is presented to the mouths of the Śrī Vajramahākāla siblings and retinue, and to Mahākāla Caturmukha, the lord of great power, and his retinue. {173}

Holding the vajra and bell, praise with any new or ancient traditional verses of praise one knows. Ringing the bell continuously, perform the vajra song and the aspirations, just as in the sādhana. If one wishes to preserve the bali, afterward leave the transcendent bali[27] to prevent obstacles. If the mundane bali is performed at night, take it out with a glorious flame. As it occurs below, give this in the general way. If it is morning, perform the subsequent rites of mending excess and omissions.

If one is performing the amendment and confession connected with this, after one completes the offering that follows the recitation, rise, face the shrine, and as a preliminary, prostrate to the guru, the pledged deity, and the dharmapālas with any verses that one knows. Then with flowers, recite the words of the confession three times.

If one is performing this rite in connection with amendment and restoration, the amendment and restoration of Pañjaranātha should be performed here. The amendment and restoration of Caturmukha, a ceremony performed in connection with the bali offering as above, is done here. To elaborate, after the words of the invitation are performed as above, the amendment bali is blessed and offered. Performing the actual amendment and restoration here is not a flaw. If one uses a melody for the praise, other than the offering of the bali as above, do not perform the words of the praise and the offering. In this section, one just recites the praise and makes the offering to the protector siblings and Caturmukha in order. After that, give the common command of activities:

> May the teaching of the Muni long endure.
> May the ground produce all the abundant prosperity for the world
> and peace.
> May the sublime people who hold his lineage,
> adorned with abundant prosperity, remain firm.
> May all our goals
> and those of our retinue be accomplished,
> such as longevity, health, happiness, and abundance.
> May we have the power to benefit migrating beings.

Holding the vajra and bell, recite the following, followed by the vajra song and the aspiration:

Entire assembly of devas . . .

Next, perform the praise to the Karmanāthas, {174} purifying a clean spot in one's dwelling or on the roof with incense and lifting up the mundane balis in their order, beginning from the end of the row. With music recite:

hūṃ
Glorious protector, Mahākāla,
invincible mistress of the three worlds, Śrīdevī,
lord of the charnel ground, Kṣetrapāla, and retinue,
who never violate the command of the siblings,
eight classes of gods and demons of existence and retinue,
male and female arrogant ones and retinue,
garuḍas, black birds, dogs, jackals, and retinue,
Karmanāthas, Putra, and so on, and their retinues,
the oceanic host of guardians and retinue—
come here and accept this ornamented bali offering!
Accept this bali offering of flesh and blood!
Accept this food of black plums![28]
Accept this offering of the first portion of wine!
Solemn thanks are offered for entrusted deeds performed in the past.
Accept this solemn reminder to perform entrusted deeds in the present!
Protect my retinue and repel negative conditions.
Please pacify all the many
hateful enemies, harmful obstructors,
māras, and obstacles.
Quickly accomplish deeds for spreading the doctrine!

Recite the Śāsana mantra and bring the bali to a clean place. Imagine the guests dissolve into the bali. Rejoicing, they return to their own places. Return inside and mend any excess and omissions with the one-hundred-syllable mantra. Recite:

Whatever I have not prepared, whatever was defective,
whatever I have done with a confused mind
or asked to be done,

I request the forbearance of the protector for all.

If there is an image, scatter flowers on it and recite:

> All buddhas and bodhisattvas dwelling in the ten directions, please heed me! For as long as all sentient beings, equal with limits of space, remain on the paths and stages of nonabiding nirvana, may the victors remain firm without passing into nirvana. Specifically, assembly of deities who were generated in this supporting image, please remain firm for as long as it [the image] has not been destroyed by the four elements. Through remaining firm, please protect, provide refuge, and assist me and all sentient beings.
> *oṃ supratiṣṭha svāhā*

If there is no image:

> *oṃ*
> You who perform all benefits for all sentient beings,
> please grant the corresponding siddhi.
> Even though you have departed for buddhafields,
> please return once again.

Recite *vajramuḥ* and snap one's finger.

> The gnosis beings of the bali guests that do not depend on an image depart, and the samaya beings dissolve nondually into oneself, *jaḥ hūṃ baṃ hoḥ*.
>
> Mohavajrā is in the eyes . . . . Cittavajrā is in the heart.

Say:

> *oṃ sarvatathāgata kāya vākka citta vajra svabhāva ātmako 'haṃ*

Dedicate the root of merit to awakening and pass one's time in conduct that corresponds with the dharma. This is the way one performs the amendment, confession, and so on, in connection with the dedication of the bali. The sādhana activity that depends on the bali is the ritual procedure known as "balisādhana," which is the meaning that one must derive from the *Victory Over the Enemy Bali Rite*[29] and its supplement, *Victory Over Armies*,[30] ornamented with intimate instructions and procedures, but there is no melody or playing of the drum. One should distance oneself from those with misconceptions, who maintain that engaging in those with the bali dedication is the so-called balisādhana. I request practitioners, "Having trained correctly and become expert in the terms and conventions, it is necessary to be diligent in the method of paying respect in every way to the precious doctrine."

In order to make the rite easily accessible for those of inferior
intelligence,
this *Beautiful Ornament of the Bali Rite*
of the Pledged Deity and Dharmapālas{176}
was composed at the monastery of Evaṃ Chöden
by venerable Könchok Lhundrub,
who touched the dirt of the feet
of the unequalled, kind lord of the maṇḍala,
Ratnavardha,[31] and his disciples.
Having compared most of the mantras
with Indian texts and corrected them as needed,
only the short and long vowels and divisions
are used here.
Whoever values this should simultaneously confess
to the protector the misdeeds of their three doors.
Through that merit may oneself and all others
be victorious over the enemy, Māra.
Virtue.

11. The Beautiful Ornament of the Great River of the Empowerment of Śrī Hevajra[1]

Ngorchen Könchok Lhundrub

This text presents the procedure for setting up and blessing the maṇḍala and also the guru's self-admittance rite, which are the preliminaries for the major two-day Hevjara empowerment. Its central focus is the blessing of a painted cloth maṇḍala. These preliminaries may also consist of a multiday creation of a sand maṇḍala. It is necessary for the guru to perform the rite of self-admittance into the maṇḍala before the actual two-day empowerment may be conferred upon disciples.

Of the three main empowerments in the Path with Its Result system, the first is the cause empowerment, which is presented in this volume. It permits the disciple to practice the yogas associated with the vase empowerment, such as the practice of Vajrasattva, maṇḍala offerings, and guru yoga; to meditate on the view of the inseparability of samsara and nirvana; to practice the generation stage sādhana presented here; and to take the abbreviated empowerments. Second, the path empowerment allows the student to add the inner body maṇḍala visualization, take the extensive empowerments daily, and practice the yogas associated with the secret empowerment. Third, the blessing of either Vajranairātmyā or Vajrayoginī permits the student to practice the yogas associated with the third and fourth empowerments. As already noted, Jamgön Kongtrul did not include these last two, the path empowerment and the ḍākinī blessing, or the various ancillary blessings in *The Treasury of Precious Instructions*.

{177} *namaḥ śrī cakranātharatnavardhāya*

Having bowed to the guru,
inseparable from Śrī Hevajra,
listen to the *Beautiful Ornament of the Great River of the Empowerment*,
explained for the benefit of those of inferior intelligence.

There are eight general topics:
(1) accepting followers, (2) the approach, (3) the earth ritual,
(4) the setup, (5) drawing and ornamentation, (6) sādhana and offerings,
(7) admittance and taking empowerment, and (8) the concluding rites.
The first three among these
are to be understood elsewhere.

The Setup

For the setup,
there is the preparation, main subject, and conclusion.

In the place where the maṇḍala is fabricated,
in the center of the layout
of the eight major lines of the maṇḍala,
place a drop of scented water, and in the circles
at the four corners and the eight directions,
place a bunch of flowers.

On top of a tripod, and so on,
carefully arrange a maṇḍala heap
of Pṛthivī.
If one is using a cloth maṇḍala,
also arrange a maṇḍala or heaps
for the nine deities.
If one places Pṛthivī below
and the maṇḍala of nine deities above, it is attractive.
Outside of those, on the eastern boundary,
the boundary is marked with flowers.

In the east, there is washing water for the feet and washing water for the face.
In the southeast, there is water for cleaning the mouth. In the south, there is drinking water.
At the southwest border, there are flowers.
In the west, there is both incense and a lamp.
In the northeast, there is scented water. In the north, there is food.
Those are arranged in a square. Inside of those,
with the extras in both the east and west, {178}
in the four directions and four intermediate directions,
at each there is incense, a lamp, and food
arranged on the four corners circling to the right.
Place a bali in proximity
to the maṇḍala of Pṛthivī, if it can be prepared.
Also arrange separate offerings,
beginning from the northeast to the southwest.
Place any necessary transcendent and mundane balis.
If one places to one side
the preliminary bali,
and, if possible, the offering for all activities,
the five offerings of flowers, and so on,
one will see it as excellent.

In front of the master, place the vajra, bell,
the inner offering, the pair of garments, and so on.
Thoroughly wash two or ten vases.
Thoroughly bind with
good, unfrayed cloth that has five or seven tassels
and attach images of the right hand implements of each deity.
If there are no more than two vases, carefully attach
a skull (which rests on a lotus
and is marked with a crossed vajra)
and a curved knife to the victorious vase,
and attach an image of a crossed vajra to the activity vase.
Recite the Amṛtakuṇḍali mantra, and
carefully fumigate them with gugul.
Whip them with white mustard seeds.

Fill them two-thirds of the way with pure water.
Add the preparation of the thirty-five substances:
the five seeds (barley, wheat, beans, rice, and sesame), {180}
the five precious things
(gold, silver, coral, pearl, and lapis lazuli),
the five medicines (*Tinosporia sinensis*, raspberry,
white calamus root, cuttlebone, and fragrant orchid),[2]
the five essences (salt, jaggery, milk,
butter, and honey),
the five excellent scents (white and red sandalwood, saffron,
camphor, and nutmeg),
the five meats, and the five amṛtas.
Place kuśa grass as ornaments for the mouths of the vases,
and place the vases on seeds. According to the arrangement of the deities,
the activity vase should be placed to the right of Pukkasī's vase.
If there are no more than two vases,
place the victorious vase on the right
and the activity vase on the left, reversing those.
Place the dharma conch filled with scented water
and a vajra with the dhāraṇī cord on the victory vase.
When it is necessary to set up for the disciples,
arrange the outer offerings, tooth sticks,
protection threads, kuśa grass, and so on.

Such an explanation is arranged as a mnemonic for the intention of the great river of empowerment but should be understood in detail from seeing the ceremonial lineage.

In the main topic, after one has generated oneself, recited the mantra, and made offerings,
following the dissolution of the maṇḍala, one should perform in order the preparations
of Pṛthivīdevī, the deity, the vase, and the disciples.

Maintaining the pride of one's deity, scatter the inner offering on the preliminary bali with the tip of the vajra, cleanse with "Amṛtakuṇḍali," and so on, then purify with "svabhāva." Also, one should recall this cleanse and purification as outlined below.

Next, show the left hand to the bali and say *oṃ*. Show the right hand and say *āḥ*. Show both and say *hūṃ*.

Face both palms upward,
wrap the two ring fingers together,
place the tips of the middle finger and thumbs together,
and press with the two wrathful fingers.[3]

Show the garuḍa mudra, say *hoḥ*, and bless it by reciting *oṃ āḥ hūṃ ha ho hrīḥ* three times. Then, with the Hūṃkara mudra, bend the two forefingers and invite the bali guests with *oṃ mahābhūta saparivāra akarṣaya jaḥ*. With a lotus roll, place the vajra palms face up and recite *oṃ indra jama . . .* three times. Make offerings with *oṃ vajra pūṣpe āḥ hūṃ*, and so on, and say:

> *oṃ mahābhūta saparivrāa oṃ āḥ hūṃ*, the sublime offering is offered to the mouths of {181} the three divisions of the twenty-four bhūtas.

Present the inner offering with the thumb and ring finger.

Hold the vajra above the right breast,
ring the bell in front of the heart,
and lower the hand above the breast.
The sound resounds as body, speech, and mind.

As it says, ring one's bell three times. Then, offer with "Gaurī holds the moon . . . ." Praise with "Akṣobhyavajra is great gnosis . . . ." Hold the vajra to one's heart and ring for each line. After "Eight great devas and your retinue . . . ," say:

> For the purpose of completing the intentions of the minds of the sublime gurus and obtaining the stage of the essence Hevajra—the siddhi of supreme mahāmudrā for the benefit of all sentient beings—I request that the great maṇḍala be erected here in this place, that it be accomplished, that the offerings be presented,

and that I may admit myself and take the empowerments. (Or apply this at the right time: may I please admit the disciples and confer the empowerment.) Powerful guardians, may you please prevent all obstacles until the activities of the great maṇḍala are finished, and please prevent all obstacles and be supportive until awakening is obtained.

Recite *muḥ*, and as one touches the ground with the right hand, imagine that the bali guests depart into the ten directions outside the practice building:

Any savage elementals who delight in the dark side are not empowered to see the secret conduct, should not remain here, and should go elsewhere.

Recite the Aṣṭā mantra, wave the vajra, and ring the bell. Imagine that the obstructors among the bali guests are frightened away and carry the bali to a clean place.

Next, purify the place and the offering articles:

The place arises from the state of emptiness: A square celestial mansion of great freedom, made from many precious substances, arises from *bhrūṃ*, {182} decorated with four doors and four porticos, and adorned with all ornaments. The offering substances are inside this palace that possesses complete characteristics. Within a vast and wide kapāla of gnosis that arises from *a*, from *hūṃ* arises pure and unimpeded foot-washing water, face-washing water, mouth-rinsing water, drinking water, flowers, incense, a lamp, supreme scent, food, and music—all made of divine substances, made from the mundane and transcendent virtuous causes, excellent in essence and clean, pervading the limits of space, and uninterrupted until samsara is empty.

With each individual mudra, [recite]:

oṃ nīrī hūṃ khaṃ svāhā oṃ vajra niviti hūṃ khaṃ svāhā oṃ sarva śodhani svāhāoṃ jaḥ hūṃ baṃ hoḥ khaṃ raṃ mahā argham svāhā oṃ vajra puṣpe āḥ hūṃ

Likewise, apply *oṃ vajra . . . āḥ hūṃ* to *dhupe, aloke, gandhe, naividye*, and *śabda*. Finally, hold the vajra to the heart, ring the bell continuously, and play whatever musical instruments one has, reciting three times:

> *oṃ vajra ghande raṇita praraṇita sampraraṇita sarvabuddha kṣetra pracalite prajñāpāramita nādasvabhāve vajradharmahridaya santoṣaṇi hūṃ hūṃ hūṃ ho ho ho akhaṃ svāhā*

> Imagine that the place and the offering articles are empowered by all buddhas and bodhisattvas.

The mudras for the offerings:

Place the faces of the two fists together,
extend the middle fingers, and touch the tips, the mudra of the four waters;
turn the fists up and scatter, the mudra of flowers;
turn them over and pour, the mudra of incense;
raise the thumbs up straight, the mudra of the lamp;
face the palms outward, the mudra of the supreme scent;
turn them over, the mudra of food;
then snap the fingers and make the sound of music.

Next, if a large group is worthy of the master and is happy to make the request, {183} led by the activity disciple,[4] they should offer three prostrations, offer a seven-heap maṇḍala, and recite:

> All this, in which nothing is lacking, is offered to the glorious, sublime guru, the essence of all the buddhas of the three times, and the sangha of vidyādharas, in order to abide in the profound samādhi of the two stages.[5]

Having offered three prostrations in front of the master, place sticks of incense in a vessel filled with flowers. Offer each of the other disciples a flower. Holding the flower in their palms, they then should offer three prostrations by either kneeling or standing and bowing with faith.

Recite the following three times, and at the end of each line scatter flowers:

Abiding in pure nondual samādhi is essential
while presenting offerings to the heroes and yoginīs
with a cloud bank of emanated Samantabhadra offerings,
and for patrons in order to pacify obstacles and perfect the two
accumulations.

Offer three prostrations, and apart from the flowers of the master, collect the flowers from the others. Offer three prostrations, and request that all in unison should make a maṇḍala offering. Having made this request, the whole assembly offers a maṇḍala as a gift to the guru as the vajra master of the assembly. The maṇḍala with its heaps is placed in front of the master. Then, the master again adds a flower to the heap of flowers and offers the maṇḍala while reciting:

This, in which nothing is lacking, is offered to the sublime, glorious root and lineage gurus, the assembly of the deities of the maṇḍala of the pledged deity, and the assembly of buddhas and bodhisattvas.

The activity disciple places the maṇḍala near the shrine, wherever it is proper, prostrates three times, and is seated among the ranks. The summary for that is:

Offer three prostrations and offer a maṇḍala.
Offer three prostrations and distribute flowers.
Offer three prostrations and make the request.
Offer three prostrations and gather the flowers.
Offer three prostrations and perform the requesting maṇḍala.
Offer three prostrations and sit in the row. {184}

Next, after the complete meditation and recitation of the self-creation according to the six-limbed sādhana (beginning from going for refuge up to the completion stage, and recalling the purities and the mantra recitation):

May myself and all sentient beings please be empowered by the body, speech, mind, qualities, and activities of all sugatas. Please bless us to quickly obtain the stage of essence Hevajra, the siddhi of supreme mahāmudrā.

At the end of this recitation, cleanse and purify the limitless, mentally emanated offerings, as above, "Within a vast and wide kapāla of gnosis that arises from *a* . . . music made of divine substances."

With each mudra, recite as above:

oṃ nīrī hūṃ khaṃ svāhā . . . śabda āḥ hūṃ

Here, all empowerment of the offerings should be understood as before. Next, beginning with a lotus roll, recite the following accompanied with the individual mudras:

When chanting *oṃ bhagavān mahakaruṇika hevajra saparivāra*, modify with *oṃ nīrī hūṃ khaṃ svāhā* up to *śabda*. The inner offering is presented with *hūṃ aṃ gaṃ caṃ vaṃ ghaṃ śaṃ laṃ ḍaṃ oṃ āḥ hūṃ*, while a sublime offering is presented to the mouths of the Hevajra nine-deity maṇḍala.

Place one's palms together and present offerings:

Gaurī holds the moon . . .

Offer praise with:

You are surrounded by a troupe of yoginīs.
You have attained the supreme mind . . .

Recite:

Since light rays shine from *hūṃ* in one's heart center, the universe and the inhabitants of the three realms all melt into light and dissolve into the protection wheel . . . the eight goddesses dissolve into one's eight faces. The mother dissolves into the father. The father's extra faces and hands dissolve into the main face and hands. Oneself becomes Heruka with one face and two hands.

Then, dissolve the maṇḍala.

Next, if there is a separate offering for Pṛthivī, light the lamps, and so on. If connected with the earth rite, {185} having imagined that Pṛthivī had previously been placed in the sky, she arrives in the maṇḍala in front. It is sufficient to present her with only the bali offering. If not connected with that rite, cleanse and purify the offerings.

> From the state of emptiness, a lotus arises from *paṃ* and a moon arises from *aḥ*, upon which is *paṃ*, from which Pṛthivī arises. She is yellow in color with a peaceful demeanor. She is adorned with precious ornaments and holds a precious vase with two hands to her heart. Mohavajrā is in the eyes . . . . Cittavajrā is in the heart. Light shines from the *hūṃ* in one's heart, summoning Pṛthivī from below the ground, *oṃ vajra samājaḥ.*

Cross the fists on one's shoulders. From the sound of snapping, one curls the two index fingers like a hook and invites with the *vajra samājāḥ* mantra. One should recall this in the occurrences of the *vajra samājāḥ* mantra below.

oṃ vajra gaurī ākarṣaya jaḥ, and so on.

The mudras for those are:

Make a hook with the little finger of the left fist
and the index finger of the right fist.
Making the eye of a lasso and placing the fists back to back
is the lasso mudra.
Interlocking the index finger and pinky
is the chain mudra.
Crossing both fists at the back of
the wrists is the bell mudra.

One should recall that these are the mudras of Gaurī, and so on, which occur below. Invite with:

> Once again, light rays from the *hūṃ* located at the heart invite the five families of empowerment deities with their retinues, *oṃ vajra samājaḥ.*

Offer the supplication:

May all the tathāgatas please confer the actual empowerment here.
oṃ vajribhava abhiṣiñca hūṃ

Recite this, imagining that while the empowerment is conferred with the water of the vase, her body is filled, taints are purified, and the excess water overflows. Then, imagine that Ratnasambhava adorns her crown.

Apply *oṃ pṛthivī* to the beginning of *nīrī hūṃ khaṃ svāhā*, and so on, up to *śabda*. Present the offering of great music with *ghande raṇita*. Sprinkle the torma with water and recite *oṃ āḥ hūṃ* three times. Then recite:

The bali transforms into a great ocean of amṛta with perfect color, scent, taste, and power.

Making the mudra of supreme generosity with the right hand, recite the following mantra three times and then snap one's fingers:

oṃ pṛthivī oṃ akaro mukhaṃ . . .

Holding the vajra and bell, wave the vajra between every line, and ring the bell between every verse, reciting three times:

Mother who holds various jewels,
goddess, you who are under the power
of the wrathful offering of Hevajra—
the maṇḍala will be drawn in this place.

Just as the protector, Lion of the Śākyas,
conquered the hordes of Māra,
likewise, in order to become victorious over the hordes of Māra,
I will draw the maṇḍala.

To elaborate, hold the vajra to the heart and ring the bell once for each verse.

For the purpose of completing the intentions of the mind of the sublime gurus . . . in this place, I request permission and the siddhis of activity.

Imagine that one hears the permission granted:

> Vidyādhara, you may engage in the activities of maṇḍala as you please.

Touch the ground with the right hand and recite:

> *oṃ vajra muḥ* Pṛthivī dissolves into the maṇḍala and torma.

Pṛthivī dissolves into the maṇḍala heap and the bali offering.

The setup for the deity, if one has not arranged the heaps, is to smear scented water on the maṇḍala base while reciting:

> *oṃ medini vajrabhāva hūṃ hūṃ hūṃ phaṭ*

And recite:

> *oṃ rakṣa rakṣa hūṃ hūṃ hūṃ phaṭ*

In that place, imagine that instantly there is a protection wheel with the eight charnel grounds. Place a single flower inside that, and imagine it instantly becomes the celestial mansion and seat. Corresponding with the placement of each heap, one can also generate the deities as they occur below. The cleansing and purification for the ritual is:

> From the state of emptiness, *paṃ* arises, {187} from which arises a lotus. A sun maṇḍala arises from *raṃ*, upon which is *hūṃ*, from which arises a crossed vajra . . . filled with blazing fires of gnosis.

oṃ rakṣa . . . as in the sādhana.[6]

> As such, within the protection wheel, from *e* arises a dharmodaya. The outside is white, the inside is red, and its mouth is wide and faces upward. The fine tip of the dharmodaya points downward. Within that, a blue maṇḍala of air arises from *yāṃ*, like a drawn bow. Also, the handle is marked with *yāṃ*. The tips are adorned with pennants. Above that, a triangular red fire maṇḍala

> arises from *raṃ*, which is marked with *raṃ*. Above that, a round white water maṇḍala arises from *vaṃ*, which is marked with a vase. Above that, a square yellow earth maṇḍala arises from *laṃ*, with half-vajras on each corner, each marked in the center with *laṃ*. Above that, a yellow ten-spoked cakra arises from *bhrūṃ*, which is marked *bhrūṃ*. From those merging into one taste as appearances of one's own mind, arises a square, four-doored celestial mansion of great liberation made of gems.

Alternately, this is the meaning of the statement that one meditates as far as the protection wheel and celestial mansion according to the medium-length sādhana. Having generated the four elements within the dharmodāya, having recited the medium-length sādhana up to, "There is the intermediate-state consciousness represented by *oṃ āḥ hūṃ* with a red *hoḥ* on either end," it is also excellent if one generates [the celestial mansion]:

> Those syllables dissolve into the elements and the cakra. All merge into one taste . . .

Also, up to and including the above, one should recite according to the sādhana from:

> The celestial mansion of great liberation made of gems . . . yak tail whisks with jeweled handles, and so on. Outside of that, there are eight great charnel grounds, in which there are eight trees, the eight directional guardians who dwell at the root of those trees, the eight clouds that are in the sky above them, the eight great nāgas residing there, the eight field guardians that reside in the branches of the trees, and also the eight ponds, eight fires, eight stupas, eight heroic siddhas, eight yoginīs, eight ghosts, eight ḍākas, and eight ḍākinīs, and which are totally full of corpses, {188} zombies, and so on. Surrounded by the eight charnel grounds, within the celestial mansion there is a dais for the deities: the east side is white . . . smoke-colored Vemacitra is in northwest. They all lie facing upward, serving as seats of the [eight] directions.

The above is recited just as in the sādhana.

> Next, *hūṃ śrī hevajra nāma*, on the central seat is blue essence Hevajra . . . compassionate, ferocious, and peaceful. Likewise, *naṃ nairātma nāma*, in his lap is Vajranairātmyā . . . stands in the midst of a blazing fire of gnosis. *Gaṃ gaurī nāma*, in the east, black Gaurī holds a curved knife in her right hand and a rohita fish in her left hand. Likewise, *caṃ caurī nāma*, in the south, red Caurī . . . *vaṃ vetālī nāma*, in the west, yellow Vetālī . . . *ghaṃ ghasmarī nāma*, in the north, green Ghasmarī . . . *paṃ pukkasī nāma*, in the northeast, blue Pukkasī . . . *śaṃ śavarī nāma*, in the southwest, white Śavarī . . . *laṃ caṇḍālī nāma*, in the southwest, red Caṇḍālī . . . *ḍaṃ ḍombinī nāma*, in the northwest, multicolored Ḍombinī . . . in the midst of a blazing fire of gnosis.

The above is recited just as in the sādhana.

> For all, Mohavajrā is in the eyes . . . . Cittavajrā is in the heart. Light rays shine from one's heart, inviting the Hevajra nine-deity maṇḍala from its natural abode, surrounded by an infinite assembly of buddhas and bodhisattvas.

Invite with the *vajra samājaḥ* mudra.

Append the name mantra, *oṃ bhagavān mahākaruṇika hevajra saparivāra*, to the offerings from *niri hūṃ khaṃ* to *śabda*. Absorb with the mantra and mudra of Gaurī, and so on.

> Once again light rays shine from the *hūṃ* in one's heart, inviting the five empowerment deities and their retinue.

Invite with the Samāja mantra, and make offerings with:

> *oṃ pañcakula saparivāra oṃ nīrī . . . śabda*

With the exception of visualizing gnosis beings and the offerings for the empowerment deities, {189} what comes below should also be understood as it is here. Next, offer the supplication:

All bhagavān tathāgatas,
. . . .
may you please confer the empowerment upon me.

Then:

The great vajra empowerment . . .

Saying *oṃ vajribhava abhiṣiñca hūṃ*, the empowerment is conferred with the water of the vase through the crown. The body is filled, the taints are purified, and the remaining water overflows over the heads of the father and mother, Gaurī . . . Ḍombinī are adorned with Amitābha.

This is just as in the sādhana.

Next, ignite the lamp, and cleanse, purify, and bless the offerings. Imagine that the front-generated principal deity is indistinguishable from one's root guru. To offer the four water offerings, place the two fists to the left side, with the upper one placed face down on the lower one:

Untainted and appealing,
this foot-washing water of sublime, divine substance
is offered to the Bhagavān and his retinue.
Having accepted it, be pleased with me.

Recite *oṃ bhagavān* . . . ; release the mudra and beginning with the fivefold desire roll, make the mudra described before; recite *oṃ nīrī hūṃ khaṃ svāhā*; and finish with a snap of the fingers. Likewise, using the same verses, the same beginning and end of the mantra, and the same mudras:

This face-washing water of sublime, divine substance . . . *oṃ bhagavān* . . . *oṃ vajra niviti hūṃ khaṃ svāhā.* This mouth-rinsing water of sublime, divine substance . . . *oṃ bhagavān* . . . *oṃ sarva śodhani svāhā.* This drinking water of sublime, divine substance . . . *oṃ bhagavān . . . jaḥ hūṃ baṃ hoḥ khaṃ raṃ mahā argham praticcha svāhā.*

Likewise, make the individual mudras for flowers, and so on:

> This flower is good and virtuous,
> arising purely from a pure growing place,
> having accepted my faithful offering,
> be pleased with me.
> *oṃ bhagavān . . . oṃ vajra puṣpe aḥ hūṃ svāhā*

Likewise for the others:

> The supreme incense smell,
> which is the supreme scent that arises from the forest,
> having accepted my faithful offering . . . *dhupe* . . . .
> Subduing and purifying rākṣasas,
> virtuous and removing darkness . . . *āloke* . . . . {190}
> This is the virtuous, excellent scent
> arising purely from a pure growing place . . . *ghandhe* . . . .
> The undefiled essence of medicine stimulates the appetite,
> these curds of mantra food . . . *naividya* . . . .
> Untainted and appealing,
> this music of divine substance
> is offered to the Bhagavān and his retinue . . . *śabda* . . . .
> At the conclusion, play great music and recite *ghande raṇi* . . . .

Cleanse and purify the pair of garments:

> From the state of emptiness arises a *hūṃ*, from which arises a thin, smooth, light, pure, and sheer cloth made of divine substances, and applied as a pair:
>
> > The divine garment, which is thin, smooth, and light,
> > is worn on the indivisible vajrakāya.
> > When it is offered with indivisible faith,
> > may I obtain a vajrakāya.[7]

Recite:

> *oṃ bhagavān . . . oṃ vajra vaṣṭaya āḥ hūṃ svāhā*

Beginning with a lotus roll, take the garment with both fists and first offer the lower garment, then offer the upper garment. Imagine that one has made an offering to each deity.

Next, with the left ring finger, take the inner offering and scatter it with the tip of the thumb, imagining that the skull cups of all the deities are filled with amṛta. Recite:

> Essence of all the bodies, speech, minds, qualities, and activities of the tathāgatas in the ten directions and the three times, possessor of inconceivable activity of deeds of omniscient gnosis and compassionate love, to the mouth of the greatly kind root guru [insert name], *oṃ āḥ hūṃ*.

Next, recite the names of the gurus of the Path with Its Result lineage gurus, from Vajradhara down to one's root guru, and make the offering.

> Further, [the sublime offering is presented] to the mouths of the sublime gurus from whom empowerments have been conferred, explanations of tantra and intimate instructions have been obtained, and with whom I have made a dharma connection, *oṃ āḥ hūṃ*.

Next recite these mantras:

> The *aṣṭa, devapicu, kartari, oṃ āḥ a āḥ i ī,* {191} and *oṃ āḥ gaṃ hūṃ phaṭ svāhā . . . oṃ āḥ daṃ hūṃ phaṭ svāhā* [the sublime offering is presented] to the mouths of the assembly of deities of the Hevajra maṇḍala, *oṃ āḥ hūṃ*.
>
> Further, the deities of the maṇḍalas connected with the four major divisions of tantras—action tantra, conduct tantra, yoga tantra, and unsurpassed mahāyoga tantra—*oṃ āḥ hūṃ*.

Next, place a drop [of amṛta] on one's tongue, brow, and the crown of one's head, and say *oṃ āḥ hūṃ*, imagining one presents an offering to all the deities in one's body. On the day of the setup, here, sprinkle [the inner offering] on the middle portion.

Next:

oṃ śrī mahākālaya oṃ āḥ hūṃ, oṃ śrī dharmapāla caturmukha oṃ āḥ hūṃ

Moreover, [the sublime offering is presented] to the mouths of the oath-bound, glorious protectors who have promised to defend and protect the wheel of dharma, *oṃ āḥ hūṃ.*

[The sublime offering is presented] to the mouths of the nirmāṇakāyas who aid sentient beings, the inconceivable heroes and yoginīs who dwell in the places, the neighboring places, the fields, the neighboring fields, the cchandohas, the neighboring cchandohas,[8] the meeting places, the neighboring meeting places, the pīlavaṃs,[9] the neighboring pīlavaṃs, the charnel ground, and the neighboring charnels grounds, *oṃ āḥ hūṃ.*

[The sublime offering is presented] to the mouths of the assembly of the forty-eight field guardians; the messengers born from places, born from castes, and born from mantra; ḍākinīs born from karma; and the vajra ḍākas and ḍākinīs of the three places, *oṃ āḥ hūṃ.*

Furthermore, [the sublime offering is presented] to the yakṣas, rākṣasas, bhūtas, piśācis, pretas, unmadas, apasmaras, mātṛkas, kṣetrapālas, messengers, yakṣinīs, and siddhas, *oṃ āḥ hūṃ.*

Further, after the twelve tenma[10] and {192} their retinue, the place lords, landlords, regional lords, village lords, those aboriginal beings of Tibet and Kham, all sentient beings included in the six classes of migrating beings, the five destinies,[11] and the four kinds of birth are satisfied and filled with immaculate bliss, may they swiftly attain the stage of unsurpassed buddhahood, *oṃ āḥ hūṃ.*

Oneself tastes [the inner offering] and recites:

oṃ sarvatathāgata amṛta svadana vajrasvabhāva atmako 'haṃ

Ring the bell three times. Imagine the eight goddesses emanate from one's heart and present offerings:

Gaurī holds the moon . . .

Imagine they offer praise:

You are surrounded by a troupe of yoginīs . . .

Recite the *Praise to Hevajra*[12] in twenty-four lines or any praise one knows. Kneel on one knee, holding the vajra and bell. Ring the bell between each verse and recite three times:

I pay homage and praise the king of knowledge,
Śrī Heruka, the great hero.
Protector with a compassionate nature,
permit me to draw the maṇḍala
in order to love the disciples
and present offerings to you.
Bhagavān, I am devoted, and
therefore I am suitable for your kind deeds.
Buddhas who benefit the wheel of migrating beings,
please heed me!
Bodhisattvas who abide in the result,
other mantra deities,
the worldly guardian devas,
any powerful bhūtas,
those who delight in the Buddha's doctrine,
and those with a vajra eye,
please heed me!
For the benefit of migrating beings,
I, the vidyādhara, will correctly draw
the maṇḍala called Hevajra
with whatever articles I can prepare. {193}
Having infinite compassion
for my disciples and myself,
please permit me to [draw] the maṇḍala and everything
through your compassionate intent.

Imagine one is granted permission with:

Vidyādhara, you must greatly benefit others!

The vase setup can either be done here or elsewhere:

> From the stage of emptiness arise two *paṃ*s, from which lotuses arise. From two *a*'s arise moon maṇḍalas, upon which are two *bhrūṃ*s, from which arise two vast and wide vases, with narrow bases, full bellies, thin throats, open mouths, curled lips, and tied with ribbons of divine cloth. The mouths are adorned with sprigs of a wish-fulfilling tree. Inside, they are completely filled with water and various essences. Within the victorious vases, on the center of an eight-petaled lotus is a sun maṇḍala, upon which there is the essence of the four māras, such as affliction and so on, in the form of yellow Brahma . . . stacked one upon the other. Upon the moon maṇḍalas on each of the eight petals, yellow Brahma is in the east . . . smoke-colored Vemacitra is in northwest. They all lie facing upward, serving as seats for the [eight] directions.

If there are ten vases, say, "Upon ten lotuses and moon maṇḍalas . . ." and:

> In the victorious vase, on a lotus and sun, there is the essence of the four māras, such as affliction, and so on, and in the eight vases in the eight directions are a lotus and moon seat, upon which in the east is yellow Brahma . . . . In the vase for all activities, there is a lotus and sun seat.
>
> In the victorious vase, upon the central seat, there is the essence of the thirty-two marks of the buddha, like the form of stars: *a ā* . . . . The complete transformation of the body resulting from all those merging together is {194} the essence of the gnosis of the dharmadhātu, the blue Bhagavān, essence Hevajra . . . stands in the midst of a blazing fire of gnosis. The space of the mother vanishes . . . which passes through the form of the father's body, falls from his vajra path into the space of the mother, and subsequently transforms into eight bindus. Those transform into the eight seed syllables: *gaṃ caṃ vaṃ ghaṃ paṃ śaṃ laṃ ḍaṃ*.
>
> After those [syllables] melt into light, transform into the eight goddesses, and issue forth from the space of the mother, "In the east, black Gaurī holds a curved knife in her right hand and a rohita fish in her left hand . . . in the midst of a blazing fire of gnosis."

Thus, the goddesses [are generated].

> In the vase of all activities is green Amṛtakuṇḍali, with one face and two hands: the right hand holds a crossed vajra, and the left hand holds a bell with a similar handle to his hip. He is adorned with jewels and snakes and wears a tiger-skin skirt. With his left leg extended and his right leg contracted, he is standing in the midst of a blazing fire of gnosis. For all of them, "Mohavajrā is in the eyes . . . Cittavajrā is in the heart."
>
> Light rays shine from the *hūṃ* in one's heart, inviting all buddhas and bodhisattvas in the ten directions in the form of the Hevajra nine-deity maṇḍala and Amṛtakuṇḍali with the *vajra samājaḥ* mantra.

Present offerings and perform the summoning and absorption. Invite the empowerment deities, present offerings, offer the supplication, and confer the empowerment. The deities are sealed with the master of the family as before. After, saying "Ghasmarī and Ḍombinī are adorned with Amitābha," recite:

> Amṛtakuṇḍali is adorned with Amoghasiddhi on his crown.

Next, make offerings{195} by applying *oṃ bhagavān* . . . to the beginning of the four water offerings and the outer offerings. Present the inner offering:

> *hūṃ aṃ gaṃ caṃ vaṃ ghaṃ śaṃ laṃ ḍaṃ oṃ āḥ hūṃ*
>
> The sublime offering is presented to the mouths of the Hevajra nine-deity maṇḍala and Amṛtakuṇḍali. Gaurī holds the moon . . . .

The praise:

> You are surrounded by a troupe of yoginīs . . . .
>
> I pay homage and praise the enemy of the obstructors,
> the deity that proclaims the terrifying sound of *hūṃ*,
> conquers all the obstructors,
> and grants all siddhis.[13]

Beginning with a lotus roll, pick up the *dhāraṇī* thread:

> Imagine that the red mantra garland in one's heart travels along the dhāraṇī thread and touches the heart of the deities. The deities become red and are brought under one's control. Amṛta streams from their pores filling the vase.

Recite the essence mantras of the father and mother, the short mantras of the goddesses, and the Amṛtakuṇḍali mantra of the activity vase one hundred times each. Make the offering and praise as before.

> Bhagavān, please grant me and all sentient beings the supreme and common siddhis.

Recite the one-hundred-syllable mantra three times and roll up the dhāraṇī thread:

> *oṃ śrī vajraheruka* . . .
> Whatever I have not prepared, whatever was defective,
> whatever I have done with a confused mind
> or asked to be done,
> I request the forbearance of the protector for all.

In conclusion, beginning with a lotus roll, take the dharma conch, pour a drop into the vase, and recite:

> *oṃ āḥ hūṃ* Through the condition of the drinking water, the deities melt into light, and the water of the vase becomes the nature of amṛta.

Next, cleanse and purify the bali according to the sādhana and recite:

> From the state of emptiness arises *yaṃ* . . . *oṃ āḥ hūṃ ha ho hrīḥ*.
>
> In the front-created eight charnel grounds, {196} there are eight *hūṃ*s on the eight petals that transform completely into Indra in the east . . . .
>
> In the dharmodaya located in the upper northeastern charnel ground, in the center and on the eight lotus petals are nine *oṃ* syllables, which transform into Kāyavajra in the center, Maheśvara in the east . . . .

> In the dharmodaya located in the lower southwestern charnel ground, in the center and on the eight lotus petals are nine *āḥ* syllables, which transform into Vakvajra in the center, Karkoṭaka in the east . . . in their hearts is Cittavajrā.
>
> Light rays shine from the *hūṃ* in one's heart, summoning all the buddhas and bodhisattvas in the forms of the three classes of the twenty-four bhūtas.

Invite with the *vajra samājaḥ* mantra and mudra, summon, and absorb. Invite the empowerment deities, present offerings, offer a supplication, and confer the empowerment as in the bali offering [*The Beautiful Ornament of the Bali Rite of Śrī Hevajra*]:

> The remaining water overflows and Kāyavajra and the eight great devas have Vairocana as a head ornament . . . the eight directional guardians are adorned with Akṣobhya. The heads of Vakvajra and the eight great nāgas are adorned with Amitābha.

Having presented the bali offering, one should perform the offerings, praise, and entrustment of activities according to the torma rite. One should offer the bali of the separate guardians and the general ḍāka torma as they occur, and one should perform the vajra song, the benediction, dedication, and aspiration.

The setup for the disciples is:

The activities of the body, generate renunciation,
confer the inner empowerment, request the main topic,
generate enthusiasm, perform the daily confession,
perform the protection, present the offerings,
toss the tooth stick, pour water in the palm,
tie the protection cord, give the kuśa grass,
explain the profound dharma, and examine the dream.

The concluding rite is cleaning, purifying, and empowering the offerings. Apply *oṃ bhagavān* . . . to the beginning of the four water offerings, the outer offerings, and the great music offering. Present the inner offering:

> *hūṃ aṃ gaṃ caṃ vaṃ ghaṃ śaṃ laṃ ḍaṃ oṃ āḥ hūṃ*, the

> sublime offering is presented to the mouths of the Hevajra nine-deity maṇḍala.

Play great music and: {197}

> Gaurī holds the moon . . . .

The praise:

> You are surrounded by a troupe of yoginīs . . . .

One should understand "Perform the mentally generated outer and inner offerings and the praise," which will occur below, in just this way.

Next, place one's hands together, recite the one-hundred-syllable mantra three times, and recite:

> Whatever I have not prepared, whatever was defective, . . .

At the end of this, connect the two pinkies of one's fists, straighten the index fingers and touch their tips, and reverse the uṣṇīṣa mudra on the crown, and recite:

> *oṃ vajra uttiṣṭha* Until all the maṇḍalas of the support and supported that exist are invited tomorrow into the space in front, please grant all supreme and common siddhis to myself and all sentient beings.

Once again, perform the mentally produced outer and inner offerings, the praise, and offer a supplication:

> Bhagavān, please grant all supreme and common siddhis to myself and all sentient beings.

If there are images of the torma guests, the dharmapālas and so on, offer a supplication, and scatter flowers:

> All buddhas and bodhisattvas dwelling in the ten directions, please heed me. For as long as all sentient beings dwell on the

> stages and paths without having entered nonabiding nirvana, may all victors please remain firm, without entering nirvana. In particular, may the assembly of deities that has been generated and invited to these images remain firm for as long as they are not destroyed by the four elements. Having remained firm, please protect, provide refuge, and assist me and all sentient beings, *oṃ supratiṣṭha vajraya svāhā.*

If there are no images, the above is unnecessary. Next, for those without an image:

> *oṃ*
> You act on behalf of all sentient beings {198}
> and correspondingly grant siddhis.
> Even though you may have departed for buddhafields,
> please return again.

Snapping one's thumb and ring finger, the gnosis beings depart.

> *oṃ āḥ hūṃ vajra muḥ* The commitment beings nondually dissolve into oneself, *jaṃ hūṃ baṃ hoḥ.* Mohavajrā is in the eyes....

Offer the supplication and gather the used bali offerings. If there is no need to use the chalk line for layout or bless the sand, enter into the daily conduct and perform the yoga of sleep.

According to the section on the colored sand, after accomplishing the drawing and ornamentation of the maṇḍala as it occurs below, then perform the sleeping yoga. In the morning, awaken with the rising yoga and recite the following three times, recalling the three purities:

> *oṃ svabhāvaśuddho sarvadharmā svabhāvaśuddho 'haṃ oṃ vajra śuddho sarvadharmā vajra śuddho 'haṃ oṃ yogaśuddho sarvadharmā yogaśuddho 'haṃ.*

The Drawing and Ornamentation

Drawing and ornamentation is done by setting the chalk line according to custom. In the center of the maṇḍala or in the center of the basis of the family, one should draw a *hūṃ* in blue sand with the vajra. Likewise, draw a *bhrūṃ* in white in the east, an *āṃ* in yellow in the south, a *jriṃ* in red in the west, and a *khaṃ* in green in the north. Also, the chalk line corresponding to each color should be placed above each container of sand.

In front of this maṇḍala, arrange five offerings and one bali. With pride in oneself as Śrī Hevajra, cleanse and purify the sand. Five *pāṃ*s arise from the state of emptiness. Lotuses and five *rāṃ*s arise from those. Sun maṇḍalas arise from those, upon which Akṣobhya, with eight faces and sixteen hands, arises from the blue colored *hūṃ*. In his eight right hands he holds vajras, and in his eight left hands he holds vajra-handled bells. He is in union with the consort, blue Māmakī, who holds a curved knife and a skull. {199} Likewise, from the white *bhrūṃ* arises white Vairocana. In his eight right hands he holds wheels, and in his eight left hands he holds wheel-handled bells. The consort, white Buddhalocanā, holds the same hand implements. Yellow Ratnasambhava arises from the yellow *āṃ*. In his eight right hands he holds jewels, and in his eight left hands he holds jewel-handled bells. The consort is yellow Ratnatārā. Red Amitābha arises from the red *jrīṃ*. In his eight right hands he holds lotuses, and in his eight left hands he holds lotus-handled bells. The consort is red Pāṇḍaravāsinī. Green Amoghasiddhi arises from the green *khaṃ*. In his eight right hands he holds swords, and in his eight left hands he holds sword-handled bells. The consort is green Samayatārā, resembling him in all hand implements. If one wishes to make this more concise, the five families can each be generated with one face and two hands. All have *oṃ* at the forehead, *āḥ* at the throat, and *hūṃ* at the heart.

Imagine a sun arises from the *ma* in one's right eye and a moon arises from the *ṭa* in one's left eye. The two eyeballs transform into blazing *hūṃ*s. Blink one's eyes, and the gnosis being arrives in the form of the five families from the hearts of the setup deities and all the tathāgatas and is nondually absorbed into the commitment being.

Imagine that the deities in the sky say *oṃ vajribhava abhiṣiñca hūṃ*. The empowerment is conferred with the water of the vase, their bodies are filled, taints are purified, the excess water overflows, and their crowns are adorned with the masters of their families.

Offer with:

> *oṃ vajra puśpe . . .*

Praise with:

> Akṣobhyavajra is great gnosis . . .

Empower the bali offering by reciting *oṃ āḥ hūṃ* three times. Present offerings with the mudra of supreme offering with the right hand and *akaro* . . . . Recite *oṃ vajracitrasamaya mātrikrama hūṃ*. Touch the sand with the left thumb and ring finger and erase the syllables. {200} The deities melt into light and transform into the sand made from the dust of the tathāgatas. The master picks up the chalk lines and extends the lines to disciples who maintain the pride of Gaurī, in the order of the chalk lines: blue, white, yellow, red, and green. Recite:

> To emulate:
> all phenomena are emulated,
> all phenomena are extremely vast,
> and all phenomena travel everywhere.[14]

First, twist each line individually and then all together, imagining those become all the tathāgatas. Wrap them around the vajra, and sprinkle amṛta upon them with the thumb and ring finger.

Next, the master should rise and look toward the east from the west side of the maṇḍala. The vajra with chalk line wrapped around it should be held in front of one's navel. Reciting *ja jaḥ* twice, give the end of the line to the disciple facing west from the east. The disciple then recites *ja jaḥ* twice and holds [the vajra] at the level of the navel. The master recites *oṃ vajra sutraṃ samaya mātrikrama hūṃ*.

> Sugatas who fill space,
> it is time to benefit migrating beings.
> May you please come here,
> invoked with the sound of the chalk line.[15]

First, turn the lines from up to down, then pick them up into the sky and let them fall down to the ground. Since they are set on the eight great circles, imagine that the maṇḍala arises immediately. At that time, the sound of the chalk line summons all buddhas. Following their arrival from space, imagine they bless [the maṇḍala] and set the line. The sequence of setting the lines:

West to east, north to south, southeast to northeast,
northwest to southwest, northwest to northeast, and southeast to southwest—
set the straight lines, moving clockwise and counterclockwise. {201}
In the clockwise direction of southeast to northwest and southwest to northeast,[16]
move clockwise, skip the reverse, and set the diagonal lines.
Since it exists from east to west, gather the chalk line.
One should understand that the first two sets
are done by the master, and the last two sets [are done] by the disciple.

Next, reversing the uṣṇīṣa mudra at the crown, recite *oṃ vajra vegākrama hoḥ*. Lifting the gnosis chalk line into space, the master enters inside. Beginning with preparatory lotus rolls, hold the vajra to the heart and the bell to one's hip and recite *hrīḥ hrīḥ*. With a wrathful gaze, look at the four doors in a clockwise direction from the east, imagining the doors are opened. Divide the basic lines in front of the doors with scented water and recite, "All obstructions to freedom and omniscience are excluded."

Next, the master sits facing east in the center of the maṇḍala:

> The dharmadhātu is pure.
> In order to liberate the *dhātu* of sentient beings,
> I shall draw the essential maṇḍala
> of the great king, Hevajra.[17]

Recite *oṃ vajracitra samaya mātrikrama hūṃ*. Then, from within, in order, draw the door area with black, green, red, yellow, and white, and having covered the skull, place a vajra upon it. Make an offering with the five offerings. Filling the drawing cone[18] from the bottom with white, and so on, the disciple draws in order from the center. When one is connecting the walls proportionally, remove the skull and connect them. Investigate the signs. If negative, present the bali offering to the deities in the sky and protect with Amṛtakuṇḍali.

As for the colored sand:

On the red sun in the center
is a lotus with a blue center and green stamens.
The eight petals are either decorated with {202}
the colors of the goddesses or the colors of the directions.
The circular beam is black with gold vajras.
The daises are the colors of the directions, adorned with vases.
Draw the skull marked with a crossed vajra and
the curved knife, and the seat
in the location of the principal.
Draw the right hand implement of each goddess
in their own location.
The desire objects are red, the lintel is yellow,
the base of the nets are blue, the nets are white,
the yak-tail whisks are multicolored, and the outline is blue.
Next to the two black inner archways [of the four doors]
are the eight pillars, the pillar ornaments, and the directionally colored enclosure.
The portico is [colored] in the order of red, blue, green, and yellow,
decorated with the lotus, wheel of dharma, and umbrella, as one wishes.
The [outer] sun maṇḍala is green, the lotus petals
are multicolored, and the outer [rim] is pale red.
The ground of the charnel grounds is black with symbols
in as many colors as possible.
The perimeter is black and the vajras are white.
The volcanoes are drawn multicolored.
After completing the drawing, the remaining sand
should be collected along with the gnosis chalk line,
and one should offer the five offerings.
oṃ āḥ hūṃ vajra muḥ The gnosis beings depart
and the emanations gather into oneself.

Next, the outer perimeter of the maṇḍala is smeared with the ingredients of the cow[19] and scented water. Arrange whatever offerings one can prepare. With incense and music, the master with a vajra in his right hand holds the victorious vase, and the disciples hold the remaining vases in order, circumambulating the maṇḍala. At the end of each deity's mantra, the master adds, "Please grant the actual abhiśeka upon me" and presents each vase to the location of each deity. Finally, place the vases upon their seats in the main and intermediate directions of the maṇḍala. When there are no more than two vases, {203} repeat the presentation of the victorious vase as many times as there are deities, and at the end place them in the east. When presenting the activity vase, recite the Amṛtakuṇḍali mantra, say, "Please defend myself and the maṇḍala against all obstacles," and place it outside near the northeast.

On the day of the main subject,
the general and individual offerings to the maṇḍala
are arranged in a circle if using a sand maṇḍala,
or [arranged] in a square if using a cloth maṇḍala,
along with the offering of preliminary
and outer bali offerings to the transcendent and mundane deities.
If one is conferring the disciple empowerment,
for that one needs the maṇḍala,
blindfolds, flowers, gugul, sesame,
the offerings of the six families, crowns,
vajra, bell, an eye probe,[20] mirror,
conch horn, wheel, book,
bow and arrow, patched robe, amṛta, and so on.
One must gather all of these requisite items.

The Sādhana and Offering

> Later on at a suitable time, the guru takes the seat and performs [the sādhana], beginning with the three preliminaries on up to the supplication following the mantra recitation, as in the setup. When dissolving the maṇḍala, recite, "Since light rays shine from *hūṃ* in one's heart center, the universe and the inhabitants of the three realms all melt into light and dissolve into the protection wheel . . . . The eight goddesses dissolve into one's eight faces."
>
> Next is the accomplishment of the front generation:
>
> The image, merging oneself,
> leaving the womb, setup, merging the commitment with the gnosis being,

the moment of birth, the setup, merging the commitment
with the gnosis being,
inviting the gnosis being there—the six for the support and
the five for the retinue—
the principle is the concise system of merging the six.

For a mere drawing, there is no need to do the rite of generating the image. {204} Merge oneself and the front [generation] as below. If it is performed like the moment of birth, it is the concise system.

Image, generation, merging with oneself,
leaving the womb, setup, samaya and gnosis beings,
and merging the gnosis being.

Because there are seven for the image, it is the extensive system. Thus, the method of accomplishment is cleansing and purifying the drawn maṇḍala. Recite from the generation of the common protection wheel, "From the state of emptiness arises *paṃ*, from which a lotus arises. A sun maṇḍala arises from *raṃ*, upon which is *hūṃ*. A crossed vajra arises from [*hūṃ*]" up to "smoke-colored Vemacitra is in northwest. They all lie facing upward, serving as the seats of the [eight] directions."

Then, one's self-generated protection wheel and the front-generated protection wheel become nondual. One's self-generated eight charnel grounds and the front-generated eight charnel grounds become nondual. One's self-generated celestial mansion and the front-generated celestial mansion become nondual.

In the middle of one's own maṇḍala, the principal couple appears. "The space of the mother vanishes . . . ," and so on, as in the sādhana. A bindu falls from the space of the mother, which splits into two. One part completely transforms into a square, four-doored celestial mansion made of gems, adorned with a four-stepped portico, adorned with all ornaments, and with all characteristics totally complete. Outside of this, there are the eight charnel grounds and the protection wheel.

The other part splits into nine parts, and [those] are placed upon each seat. {205} Visualize that "the central bindu is the

Bhagavān Essence Hevajra . . . . The couple stands in the midst of a blazing fire of gnosis. The bindu in the east is black Gaurī . . . . The bindu in the south is red Caurī . . . . The bindu in the west is yellow Vetālī . . . . The bindu in the north is green Ghasmarī . . . . The bindu in the northeast is blue Pukkasī . . . . The bindu in the southeast is white Śavarī . . . . The bindu in the southwest is red Caṇḍālī . . . . The bindu in the northwest is multicolored Ḍombinī . . . in the midst of a blazing fire of gnosis." If one is unable to do this, then simply recite the names of the deities.

Next, infinite principal fathers and mothers emanate inside the mother's space, pervade all [outer] space, purify all hatred and the aggregate of consciousness of all sentient beings, and establish them in the gnosis of the dharmadhātu. [Those emanations] return and dissolve into oneself. Recite, "The Bhagavān Essence Hevajra is blue . . . stands in the midst of a blazing fire of gnosis."

Likewise, infinite Gaurīs emanate inside the mother's space, purify the ignorance and material aggregate of all sentient beings, and establish them in the mirrorlike gnosis. Those emanations return and are placed on the Brahma seat. In the east, black Gaurī holds a curved knife in her right hand and a rohita fish in her left hand.

Infinite Caurīs emanate inside the mother's space, purify the pride, envy, and sensation aggregate of all sentient beings, and establish them in the gnosis of uniformity. Those emanations return; visualize the faces and hands, and so on, of red Caurī placed on the Indra seat in the south. {206}

Infinite Vetālīs emanate inside the mother's space, purify the desire and perception aggregate of all sentient beings, and establish them in the individually discerning gnosis. Those emanations return; visualize the faces and hands, and so on, of yellow Vetālī placed on the Upendra seat in the west.

Infinite Ghasmarīs emanate inside the mother's space, purify the jealousy and formation aggregate of all sentient beings, and establish them in the successful-activity gnosis. Those emanations return; visualize the faces and hands, and so on, of green Ghasmarī placed on the Rudra seat in the north.

Infinite Pukkasīs emanate inside the mother's space, purify

the earth element of all sentient beings, and establish them in limitless loving kindness. Those emanations return; visualize the faces and hands, and so on, of blue Pukkasī placed on the Yama seat in the northeast.

Infinite Śavarīs emanate inside the mother's space, purify the water element of all sentient beings, and establish them in limitless compassion. Those emanations return; visualize the faces and hands, and so on, of white Śavarī placed on the Kubera seat in the southeast.

Infinite Caṇḍālīs emanate inside the mother's space, purify the fire element of all sentient beings, and establish them in limitless joy. Those emanations return; visualize the faces and hands, and so on, of purple Caṇḍālī placed on the Rākṣasa seat in the southwest.

Infinite Ḍombinīs emanate inside the mother's space, purify the air element of all sentient beings, and establish them in limitless equanimity. Those emanations return; visualize the faces and hands, and so on, of multicolored Ḍombinī placed on the Vemacitra seat in the northwest . . . in the midst of a blazing fire of gnosis. {207}

Infinite celestial mansions emanate inside the mother's space, purify the impure universe of all sentient beings, and establish them in the realization of the thirty-seven factors conducive to awakening. Those emanations return and dissolve into the front-generated celestial mansion.

Infinite eight charnel grounds emanate in the space of the mother, purify the eight worldly dharmas of all sentient beings, and establish them in the eight examples of illusion. Those emanations return and dissolve into the eight front-generated charnel grounds.

Infinite protection wheels emanate inside the space of the mother; purify all the obstacles of body, voice, and mind of all sentient beings; and establish them on the stage of the trio of the body, speech, and mind vajras. Those emanations return and dissolve into the front-generated protection wheel.

The above recitation is for those who prefer pulling a plow. If one prefers to complete the arising, after generating the maṇḍala in the womb, the entire maṇḍala of the support and the supported emanates from the mother's space, pervading all of space and benefiting all sentient beings. When the emanation returns, imagine it becomes nondual with the front-generated maṇḍala. Otherwise, as in the other above:

> One abides at the eastern door
> with the yoga of the principal couple
> and also leaves the womb.
> At that time the five principals merge.

Apart from resembling the rites above and below, when the self and front generation merge—having discarded the visualization of oneself arriving in the middle of the maṇḍala and {208} having empowered the mother's space of the principal couple visualized at the eastern door of the maṇḍala, as explained above and below—after the principal couple leaves the womb and returns, they are established on the central seat, and so on. Below, other than the form of the principal couple, one abandons visualizing the activities of Heruka. Likewise, abiding at the eastern door and engaging in presenting the offerings, and so on, is one system. If the accomplishment and offerings are performed by the activity disciple, they should be performed in this way.

Next, recite, "All those deities have Mohavajrā in the eyes . . . . Cittavajrā in the heart." At the time of the first main subject, wave the vajra with the hand and imagine that light rays from the heart frighten away all the obstructors who follow the setup deities. Recite the Aṣṭa to all the setup deities in the sky, using the beginning, *oṃ bhagavān*, and so on, and presenting the four water offerings with *oṃ nīri*, and so on. Summon and absorb with the Gaurī mantra, mudra, and so on. However, this is not required in the second main subject.

Next, since light rays shine from *hūṃ* in one's heart, the maṇḍala of Bhagavān Hevajra surrounded by all the buddhas and bodhisattvas is invited with the *vajra samājaḥ* mantra and mudra from their natural abode. Present the four water offerings as above and summon. Absorb with the Gaurī mantra and mudra, and so on. Once again, light rays shine from the *hūṃ* in one's heart, inviting the empowerment deities. Present offerings to them, confer the empowerment, and seal with the masters of the family as in the deity setup. {209}

Next, visualize the deities and recite the one-hundred-syllable mantra as much as one likes, *hūṃ śrī hevajra oṃ śrī vajra heruka* . . . . In the same way, recite as much as one likes: *aṃ nairātma oṃ śrī vajra heruka . . . gaṃ gaurī, oṃ śrī vajra heruka . . . caṃ caurī oṃ śrī vajra heruka . . . vaṃ vetālī oṃ śrī vajra heruka . . . ghaṃ ghasmarī oṃ śrī vajra heruka . . . paṃ pukkasī oṃ śrī vajra heruka . . . śaṃ śavarī oṃ śrī vajra heruka . . . laṃ caṇḍālī oṃ śrī vajra heruka . . . ḍaṃ ḍombinī oṃ śrī vajra heruka* . . . . Following this, with vajra-folded palms, recite, "Maṇḍala of support and supported, please remain firm. Through remaining firm, please grant me and all sentient beings supreme and common siddhis." At the conclusion of this, recite, "A heruka in a one-faced and two-handed form separates from the heart of the principal of the maṇḍala and is established in the eastern doorway."

Next, beginning from empowering the offerings, present the water offerings, the outer offerings, the pair of garments, the inner offering, the mentally produced offerings, the short praise, and the long praise as explained in the section on the setup. Then taste the amṛta with one's tongue and recite:

oṃ āḥ hūṃ Imagine one pleases the essence of all the deities. It is very important not to omit this.

Next, an accomplishment assistant recites the Aṣṭa and places the maṇḍala under guard. Oneself and the assistant leave the accomplishment house or go to a place outside and shut the maṇḍala with a curtain, whichever is best. Placing a bali on a shelf, to the right arrange the four water offerings, and to the left arrange the five outer offerings, holding these up, front to back, [when they are being offered].

In front of these, arrange the inner offering. Sprinkle the bali with water, {210} and with the vajra and bell bless the bali with the inner offering.

[Recite the bali offering from] "In the space above the bali, three dharmodayas arise from *e e e*, one above the other. Inside of each arises an eight-petaled lotus from *paṃ paṃ paṃ*. In the center and on the eight petals of the lotus located in the upper dharmodāya, nine *oṃ* syllables arise, transforming into Kāyavajra in the center . . . in the center and on the eight petals of the lotus located in the middle dharmodāya, the nine *hūṃ*s transform. Cittavajra is in the center, Indra in the east . . . . In the center and on the petals of the lotus located in the lower dharmodaya are nine *āḥ* syllables that transform into Vakvajra in the center . . . ," up to the conferral of empowerments as before.

[Recite,] "Kāyavajra and the eight great devas have Vairocana as a head ornament. Cittavajra and the eight guardians are adorned with Akṣobhya, and Vakvajra and the eight great nāgas are adorned with Amitābha." At the conclusion of this, present the four water offerings, *oṃ nīri*, and so on, and present the bali offering with *oṃ inda*, *jama*, and so on, from the offerings onward, in order to prevent obstacles and give assistance. Up to this point, it is like the section of the preliminary bali offering.

Next, ring the bell continuously and perform the vajra song, the benediction, and the aspirations. At that time the accomplishment assistant gathers the offering—beginning with the food offering and up to the mouth-washing water—into the bali container. The master makes the drinking-water mudra and recites, *oṃ hrīḥ viśuddha sarvadharma sarvapapaṃ nicasyasaṃ śodhaya sarva vikalapāna apanaya hūṃ*.

At that time, the disciple circumambulates the drinking-water bali container, and the remainder bali is held up in the direction of departure. {211} Recite the one-hundred-syllable mantra from the *Vajrapañjara Tantra*: *oṃ vajrasatva samayam anupālaya vajrasatva tvenopatiṣṭha dṛḍho me bhava sutoṣyo me bhava supoṣyo me bhava anurakto me bhava śaśva me bhava hridayamme adhiiṣṭha sarva siddhiṃ me prayaccha sarva karmasu ca me cittaṃ śreyaḥ kuru hūṃ ha ha ha ha ho bhagavān vajra ma me muñca vajri bhava mahāsamayasatva āḥ*, with *muḥ* at the end.[21]

Touching the ground with the right hand, imagine that the bali guests depart the accomplishment house in the main and intermediate directions. The day following the accomplishment and offering, the gnosis beings depart and the commitment being dissolves into oneself.

Whichever [system above one uses], say *oṃ āḥ hūṃ* and protect the three places of oneself and the accomplishment assistant. Carry the bali to a clean place with music. Recite the Aṣṭa and play music continuously. After the master presses the bali down with his heel, return inside, recite the one-hundred-syllable mantra, and if there is room, circumambulate the maṇḍala three or seven times. If there is no room, then imagine one circumambulates the peristyle. In conclusion, place one's hands together at the eastern door and recite, "Since I am a beginner, whatever faults there may have been in the accomplishment of the maṇḍala under the power of unclear samādhi, lethargy and agitation, adding and omitting things from the rite, and not preparing the offerings or using damaged offerings, please have forbearance for all of those and please mend my excesses and omissions." {212} Having made a prostration while holding the bell and vajra, sit in the row.

> If it is the basis for a consecration,
> at this occasion one should do the setup for a consecration.
> In the afternoon one should perform the self-admittance.
> Having done the accomplishment and offering
> of the maṇḍala the day before,
> one should do the consecration,
> and, if possible, perform an extensive burnt offering.
> The next day, perform the self-admittance,
> confer the empowerment upon the disciples, and so on.
> If one is not performing the consecration and burnt offering,
> at this time perform the self-admittance,
> confer the empowerment upon the disciples, and so on.
> Regarding the second main subject,
> at this occasion generate the vase as before,
> perform the self-admittance, and so on.

Admittance and Receiving Empowerment

Between the admittance and receiving the empowerment, first is the self-admittance:

> Just as at the time of birth
> he was washed with water by the devas,

likewise, I shall wash
with this pure divine water.

oṃ sarvatathāgata abhiṣekata samaya hūṃ

Rinse one's mouth with the water of the activity vase. Thinking that the front-generated principal is one's root guru, imagine that the requisite deeds of the guru are performed by the principal of the maṇḍala and a progression of empowerment substances separate from his heart. The empowerments are performed by a heruka that separates from his heart, but in reality they are all done by oneself. Offer a maṇḍala requesting the dharma in order to enter into the maṇḍala. Recite three times:

My teacher, great joyous one,
with Nairātmyā embracing your neck,
master, please heed me.
Great protector, please explain to me
the mode of great awakening.
Please grant me those samayas.
Also, please grant bodhicitta to me.
Buddha, dharma, and sangha{213}
are my three refuges; please grant them to me.
Protector, please allow me to enter the city of great freedom.

Since the custom of proclaiming the vows at the occasion the self-admittance also occurs, if one prefers to do it this way, proclaim them once:

I go for refuge to the Triple Gem,
the Buddha, the dharma, and the sangha.
This stabalizes the vows
of the pure buddha family.

Also, the mudra of the vajra and bell
should be held by you of great intelligence.
Whatever bodhicitta may be, it is the vajra.
Wisdom is explained to be the bell.
You should uphold the master;
the guru is equivalent with a buddha.
This is the samaya vow of the
pure vajra family that you should uphold.

For the great supreme jewel family,
always offer the four kinds of generosity—
things, fearlessness, dharma, and loving kindness—
three times during the day and [three times] during the night.

You must uphold the sublime dharma
of the three yānas—outer, inner, and secret.
This is said to be the samaya vow
of the pure lotus family.

For the great supreme karma family,
one must correctly uphold
all vows that one possesses.
Also, one should engage in the activity of offering as much as possible.

The fourteen others are
fully explained as defeats.
What is to be avoided and what is never to be discarded
are explained as the root downfalls
and recited every day,
three times during the day and three times at night.
If there is a violation, the practitioner
possesses a gross fault.

One must never kill creatures,{214}
never take what has not been given,
never engage in sexual misconduct,
and never tell lies.

One must avoid alcohol,
the root of all ruin.
Apart from benefiting sentient beings,
there is nothing to do; avoid everything.

One should rely upon sublime people.
One should venerate all practitioners.
The three actions of the body,
the four of the voice,
and the three of the mind

must be guarded as much as possible.

Do not wish for the Hīnayāna and
do not turn your back on the benefit of sentient beings.
Also, do not abandon samsara
and never have desire for nirvana.

You must not belittle
that which is concealed to devas and asuras.
Do not step over mudras, seats, weapons,
or signs.

These are explained to be the samayas.
You must always guard them.
The vast samayas to be emulated
are explained in the secret tantras.[22]

Here, it is also fine to omit this at the time of the self-admission.

Next, recite the daily confession three times, "I go for refuge to the Three Jewels . . ." and recite the taking of vows of the five families three times, "All buddhas and bodhisattvas . . . ."

Blindfold one's eyes with *ākhaṃ vira hūṃ*. With that mantra, pick up the garland of flowers.

Imagine that from the heart of the principal an infinite host of wrathful Amṛtakuṇḍalis emanate, frightening far away all the obstructors and misleaders who create obstacles to taking the empowerments. Recite the *amṛta* mantra and sprinkle water from the activity vase.

Imagine the first inquiry. [The guru asks:]

"Child, who are you? And what would you like?"

[The disciple answers:]

"I am a fortunate one who would like great bliss." {215}

In the second inquiry, [the guru asks:]

"Child, how is that to be done?"

[and the disciple answers:]

> "With the samaya of supreme buddhahood."
>
> Upon a moon maṇḍala in one's heart, there is a five-tined white vajra shining with light. *oṃ sarvayoga citta utpādayāmi* Place the vajra on one's heart and recite *suratisamaya stvaṃ hoḥ siddhya vajra yathā sukhaṃ*.

For the instruction for [maintaining] secrecy, place the vajra on one's crown and recite:

> Now, you who abide in the family of all tathāgatas and all heroes and yoginīs must not speak of this great secret of all tathāgatas in front of those who have not been admitted into the maṇḍala of all tathāgatas or those who lack faith.

Recite *hūṃ jāḥ hūṃ* or *jāḥ hūṃ baṃ hoḥ*, imagine oneself in the presence of the principal, and slightly bow one's head to the maṇḍala. To place one in samaya through the benefits, place the vajra on the crown and recite:

> If you are going to obtain the siddhis of all tathāgatas through some gnosis, not to mention other siddhis, you who have generated such vajra gnosis must not speak of it in front of those who have not seen the great maṇḍala, or, child, you will violate your samaya.

To place one in samaya through reflecting on faults, place the vajra at the heart and recite:

> Śrī Heruka, now this
> has truly entered your heart.
> If you speak of these methods,
> [your heart] will truly burst and you will die.[23]

Again, place the vajra on the crown and recite:

> This is your samaya vajra. If you speak to anyone about these means, {216} it will split your head.

To place one in samaya through both [benefits and faults], pour some water from the victorious vase into the dharma conch, or, in this context of the self-admittance, taste the inner offering and recite:

> This is your hell water.
> If you violate samaya, it will burn.
> If you guard samaya, siddhis
> will be accomplished with this vajra amṛta.[24]
>
> *oṃ pañca amṛta udaka ṭha ṭha ṭha*

To place one in samaya through the guru's strict command, place the vajra on one's head and recite:

> Henceforth, child, you should say, 'I, Śrī Heruka, shall do this!' It is necessary for you to do that. You must never belittle me. If you do, you will be unable to avoid terror at the time of death, and you will be a sentient being falling into the great hell.

Now you should offer a maṇḍala as a gift for requesting the descent of gnosis and recite:

> This maṇḍala of the four continents, Sumeru . . .

Recite three times:

> Empowered by all tathāgatas, Śrī Heruka, please let this descend upon me!

Oneself appears in the form of Heruka. Below one's feet, there is a *yaṃ*, from which arises a blue air maṇḍala in the shape of a drawn bow, with two handles facing downward and the two tips facing up, marked with waving pennants. Above that, having spread one's legs, on the two soles of the feet, there are green *jhaiṃ* syllables, intense and difficult to bear. From the *raṃ* in between one's legs, there is a red, triangular fire maṇḍala marked with flames. In the heart, arising from *laṃ*, there is a square yellow earth maṇḍala, marked with three-tined vajras on the four corners and a *hūṃ* in the center. At the throat, {217} a round white water maṇḍala marked with a vase and an *a* arises from *vaṃ*. On the crown, an air maṇḍala, like thick smoke, marked with *ha* arises from *yāṃ*.

Light shines from the heart of the principal, striking the air maṇḍala below the feet, stirring the air, and igniting the fire at the groin. The *jhaiṃ* at the soles of the feet ignite, and the fire enters the ankles and meets in the region of the groin. Since that [the fire] blazes intensely, it heats the earth maṇḍala at the heart. The foam of the boiling water maṇḍala of the throat falls on the earth maṇḍala of the heart. Then, lifted up by the air maṇḍala below the feet and pressed down by the air maṇḍala of the crown, imagine one vibrates in space. At that time, the light rays that shine from the heart of the principal and [from] all buddhas and bodhisattvas are absorbed and dissolve into all one's pores, falling like a great snow blizzard.

Imagine this is performed by the principal, ring the vajra bell, and recite this many times:

hūṃ a ha jhaiṃ and *aveśaya stvaṃbhaya stvaṃbhaya ra ra ra ra ca la ya ca la ya hūṃ a ha jhaiṃ*

At the time of self-admittance, do not use a fumigation substance or the incense rite. In order to stabilize this on the crown of one's head, recite:

tiṣṭha vajra

Ring the bell between each verse, and recite this three times:

Admit me, the disciple,
into the essential maṇḍala,
the abode of all tathāgatas,
the supreme city of Śrī Heruka.[25]

May the stage of the family,
and likewise, the stage of merit,

become whichever family is suitable.
However much merit there is here,
likewise, may it be so here in the maṇḍala.

Investigate the color of the sky. {218} If one sees white, yellow, red, black, green, or multiple colors, one should think that one will accomplish the pacifying, increasing, power, and destructive or various activities, respectively, and recall this. Ringing the bell continuously, one should recite the praise:

Homage and praise to Dveṣavajrā . . .

Imagine that a flower is offered to the head of the principal. Recite and offer:

oṃ pratīccha vajra hoḥ

Heruka replies:

oṃ pratigrihna stvaṃ imaṃ satva mahābala

Since one makes a request to the deity that is struck with the flower, that deity places the flower upon one's own head:

oṃ
Vajrasattva, henceforth
you shall endeavor to open your eyes
and see all differences—
the vajra eye is unsurpassed.[26]

Imagine the blindfold is released.

Mahāsattva, look, look
at the supreme city of great freedom.
Wherever the flower falls,
that is you, Heruka.
Look at this excellent maṇḍala;
now generate faith in this.
You have been born into the family of buddhas,

empowered by mantra and mudra.
You have been born into the family of yoginīs.
You must preserve the samayas
and also endeavor in the mantras.

Since one receives the introduction to the deity and the maṇḍala is displayed, imagine that one has seen the entire maṇḍala of the support and the supported made from the appearance of gnosis.

Imagine that one prostrates to the feet of the guru:

oṃ
I have been admitted to the maṇḍala
of the great vajra maṇḍala.

oṃ
I have seen the maṇḍala
of the great yoga maṇḍala.

oṃ
Confer the empowerment upon me in the maṇḍala
of the great secret maṇḍala.

Recite:

samaya hoḥ hoḥ hoḥ

This maṇḍala of the four continents, Sumeru . . . {219} is offered as a gift to request the vajra-disciple empowerment . . . .

Offer the supplication:

Just as a great offering was bestowed
upon the Buddha by Bodhivajra,
please now grant me the vajra of space
for the purpose of protecting me.[27]

In the eastern region of the maṇḍala, there is the maṇḍala of the empowerment platform, which is square, with four doors beautified with four porticos, a peristyle, lintel, strands and tassels,

> whisks, a parapet, and so on, totally complete in all characteristics. In the center, there is a jeweled throne supported on lions. Upon a lotus, sun, and four piled seats, oneself transforms into Bhagavān Essence Hevajra, who is blue with eight faces and sixteen arms and is in union with Vajranairātmyā. Or if one prefers, recall the complete hands and faces.
>
> Imagine that to the right and left of that are the purified articles; above, there is a canopy; on the right, an umbrella; on the left, a victory banner; and surrounding all of this are inconceivable kinds of offerings, conches, streamers, flower garlands, and so on. Purify with the three, *oṃ nīri*, and so on, and *oṃ arghaṃ praticcha hūṃ.*
>
> All my misdeeds and obscurations gathered throughout beginningless lifetimes are expelled through my nostrils in the form of the seed syllable of misdeeds, *kaṃ*, and dissolve into the sesame seeds in front. Imagine that Heruka burns them and throws them into the water.

Alternately, one can imagine the purification with mustard seeds. Recite:

> *oṃ sarvapāpaṃ dahana vajrāya vajrasatvya sarvapāpaṃ dahana svāhā*

Imagine that one rotates the right fist over the left, the left fist over the right, and both fists to the left. Imagine that the seeds are tossed into the fire and water.

Likewise, recite *oṃ hūṃ ḍa ḍi ta phaṭ*, rotate the fists, and sweep. Also, after both of those procedures are repeated three times, imagine that the seeds are placed in the water and thrown away. Recite:

> May all my bad luck, misfortune, and inauspicious signs be pacified! {220}

Imagining that the maṇḍala deities recite benedictions to you, ring the bell and scatter flowers while reciting the three verses:

> The first virtuous fortune of the world . . .

If one prefers, one also can recite the benediction to the twelve deeds,[28] which occurs separately. Finally, recite:

> May there be the highest benefit of our own and our retinue's victory over all negativities to be abandoned!

There are two in the actual empowerment. First, the vajra-disciple empowerment:

> *oṃ svabhāva* . . . My aggregate of consciousness and the empowerment substance (the water of the victorious vase) vanish, becoming emptiness. Both arise from the state of emptiness as *hūṃ* upon a lotus and sun, which transform into vajras marked with *hūṃ*. Light rays shine from those vajras and return, transforming into blue Akṣobhya Hevajra, with eight faces, sixteen arms, and four feet. The eight right hands hold vajras, and the eight left hands hold vajra-handled bells. They are in union with their consort, blue Māmakī, who holds a curved knife and a skull. The couples are adorned with bone ornaments. Mohavajrā is in their eyes . . . Cittavajrā is at their hearts.
>
> Light rays shine from *hūṃ* in their hearts, invoking all tathāgatas of the ten directions in the form of the Akṣobhya couple.

Invite with the mudra:

> *oṃ vajra samājaḥ*

Repeat twice:

> *jaḥ hūṃ baṃ hoḥ*

If one wishes, one can absorb with the individual mantras.

> Again, light rays shine from *hūṃ* in their hearts, inviting the empowerment deities—the five tathāgatas, {221} the four mothers, the eight bodhisattvas, the six goddesses, and the ten wrathful ones—with the *vajra samājaḥ* mantra and mudra.

Offer a supplication, "All tathāgatas, please confer the actual empowerment here."

They reply, *oṃ vajribhāva abhiṣiñca hūṃ*. Their bodies fill with water, purifying taints. The excess water overflows, transforming into Akṣobhya, who adorns their heads. The empowerment substance, the Akṣobhya couple, enter into union and melt, transforming into the empowerment substance, the water of the victorious vase.

[Offer the supplication:]

All bhagavān tathāgatas . . .

Since the supplication was offered:

The great vajra empowerment
from the three secrets of all buddhas
is granted to the one
to whom all in the three realms prostrate.[29]

oṃ vajribhava abhiṣiñca hūṃ

The tathāgatas confer the empowerment, the knowledge consorts sing vajra songs, the bodhisattvas recite benedictions, the wrathful ones frighten away obstructors, and the goddesses present offerings. The stream of empowerment water fills one to the brow, one obtains the vase empowerment, and the taints of the body are purified. Filling down to the level of the throat, one obtains the secret empowerment; filling down to the heart center, one obtains the gnosis empowerment of the wisdom consort; and filling the whole body, one obtains the fourth empowerment of supreme great bliss. The taints of body, voice, and mind and their traces are purified. The remaining water overflows, adorning one's head with Akṣobhya.

Present offerings:

oṃ vajra puṣpe āḥ hūṃ . . . naivīdye āḥ hūṃ As such, {222} one has

> received the empowerment of water through Akṣobhya . . . and the seed of Akṣobhya is planted in one's continuum.

Recite this according to the *Time of the Path.*[30] Apart from discarding the invitation of the empowerment deities and the special features of Akṣobhya, one should understand that the following is adapted to the family:

> *svabhāva* . . . My aggregate of sensation and the empowerment substance (the crown) vanish, becoming emptiness. Both arise from the state of emptiness as *āṃ* upon a lotus and sun, which transform into jewels marked with *āṃ*. Light rays shine from those jewels and return, transforming into yellow Ratnasambhava, with eight faces, sixteen hands, and four legs. The eight right hands hold jewels, and the eight left hands hold jewel-handled bells. They are in union with their consorts, yellow Ratnatārā, who holds a curved knife and a skull. Both couples are adorned with bone ornaments. Mohavajrā is in their eyes . . . . Light rays shine from *āṃ* in their hearts, invoking all tathāgatas of the ten directions in the form of the Ratnasambhava-Hevajra couple.

Invite as before and absorb each. After this point, to simplify the rite, one does not need to invite the empowerment deities other than the invitation above.

[Offer a supplication:]

> "All tathāgatas, please confer the actual empowerment here."

Saying, *oṃ vajribhāva abhiṣiñca hūṃ*, the empowerment is conferred upon the deities of the empowerment substances through their crown, filling their body and purifying taints. The excess water overflows, transforming into Ratnasambhava, who adorns their heads. The empowerment substance, the Ratnasambhava couple, enter into union and melt, transforming into the empowerment substance, the crown.

Offer a supplication:

> "All tathāgatas, please confer the actual empowerment upon me."

The great empowerment of the great jewel
from the three secrets of all buddhas . . .

oṃ vajrī ratnakumuṭa . . .

The crown is tied onto one's head. Imagine the empowerment has been conferred.

Saying, *oṃ vajribhāva abhiṣiñca hūṃ* . . . adorning one's head with Ratnasambhava, present the five offerings:

puṣpe . . .

As such, one has received the empowerment of water through Ratnasambhava . . . and the seed of Ratnasambhava is planted in one's continuum.

svabhāva . . . My aggregate of perception and the empowerment substance (the vajra) vanish, becoming emptiness. Both arise from the state of emptiness as *jrīṃ* upon a lotus and sun, which transform into red lotuses marked with *jrīṃ*. Rays of light shine from those red lotuses and return, transforming into red Amitābha-Hevajra with eight faces and sixteen hands, holding red lotuses in the right hands and lotus-handled bells in the left hands. They are in union with their consort, red Pāṇḍaravāsinī, who holds a curved knife and a skull. Both couples are adorned with bone ornaments. Mohavajrā is in their eyes . . . . Light rays shine from *jrīṃ* in their hearts, invoking all tathāgatas of the ten directions in the form of the Amitābha couple, who are absorbed.

As before:

All tathāgatas . . . *vajribhāva*, the empowerment is conferred through the crown of the empowerment deities . . . adorning their heads with Amitābha. The empowerment substance, the Amitābha couple, enter into union and melt, transforming into the empowerment substance, the vajra.

All tathāgatas . . .

The vajra empowerment of all buddhas

is conferred upon you today.
You must take this vajra
in order to accomplish all buddhas.

oṃ mahāvajra hūṃ {224}

Imagine that the vajra is placed in your right hand.

> *vajrībhava* . . . the water of the vase . . . adorning one's head with Amitābha.

Present the five offerings:

> *puṣpe* . . . As such, one obtains the vajra empowerment through Amitābha . . . the seed of Amitābha is planted in one's continuum.
>
> *svabhāva* . . . My aggregate of formations and the empowerment substance (the bell) vanish, becoming emptiness. Both arise from the state of emptiness as *khaṃ* upon a lotus and sun, transforming into swords marked with *khaṃ*. Rays of light shine from those swords and return, transforming into green Amoghasiddhi-Hevajra, with eight faces and sixteen hands, holding swords in the right hands and sword-handled bells in the left hands. They are in union with their consort, green Samayatārā, who holds a curved knife and a skull. Both couples are adorned with bone ornaments. Mohavajrā is in their eyes . . . . Light rays shine from *khaṃ* in their hearts, invoking all tathāgatas of the ten directions in the form of the Amoghasiddhi couple, who are absorbed.
>
> All tathāgatas . . . vajribhāva, the empowerment is conferred through the crown of the empowerment deities . . . Amoghasiddhi, who adorns their heads. The empowerment substance, the Amoghasiddhi couple, enter into union and melt, transforming into the empowerment substance, the bell.

Offer a supplication:

> All tathāgatas . . .

Imagine the bell is given into one's left hand:

oṃ vajra adhipatitvaṃ, abhiṣiñcami tiṣṭha vajrasamāya stvāṃ

The empowerment water is conferred with:

vajrībhava . . . adorning one's head with Amoghasiddhi.

As such, one obtains the bell empowerment through Amoghasiddhi . . . {225}the seed of Amoghasiddhi is planted in one's continuum.

svabhāva . . . My aggregate of matter vanishes, becoming emptiness. It arises from the state of emptiness as *bhrūṃ* upon a lotus and sun, transforming into a wheel marked with *bhrūṃ*. Rays of light shine from that wheel and return, transforming into white Vairocana-Hevajra with eight faces and sixteen hands, holding wheels in the right hands and wheel-handled bells in the left hands. He is in union with his consort, white Buddhalocanā, who holds a curved knife and a skull. The couple is adorned with bone ornaments. Mohavajrā is in their eyes . . . . Rays of light shine from *bhrūṃ* in his heart, invoking all tathāgatas of the ten directions in the form of the Vairocana couple, who are absorbed.

Offer the following supplication, and imagine the empowerment is conferred:

All tathāgatas, please confer the actual empowerment upon me.

Saying, *oṃ vajrasattva stvaṃ abhiṣiñcami vajranāma abhiṣekata*, one is granted the name:

Oh, tathāgata called Śrī [insert name] Vajra.

Ring the bell over one's head.

The water of the vase is conferred, filling the body and purifying taints. The excess water overflows, adorning one's head with Vairocana.

Present the five offerings:

> *puṣpe* . . .
> As such, one obtains the name empowerment through Vairocana . . . the seed of Vairocana is planted in one's continuum.

One can also recall the hand implements of the five families according to how they occur in the *Vajrapañjara Tantra*.

> Everything that appears
> is the principal, one's excellent deity.
> The nature of all phenomena is unclouded and pure.
> It must be seen as the wisdom of the Buddha.[31] {226}

> One must reflect that the appearance of any and all apparent phenomena is not ordinary but rather is the excellent deity that has the nature of the five families of tathāgatas and the five gnoses.
>
> *svabhāva* . . . My conceptual grasping to the dharmatā of the five aggregates as ordinary vanishes, becoming emptiness. It arises from the state of emptiness as *hūṃ* upon a lotus and sun, which transforms into a vajra marked with *hūṃ*. Rays of light shine from that vajra and return, transforming the dharmatā of the five aggregates into white Vajrasattva, with eight faces and sixteen hands. The hand implements generated resemble Akṣobhya's [implements]. [Vajrasattva] is in union with his consort, white Vajragarvi, who holds a curved knife and a skull. The couple is adorned with bone ornaments. Mohavajrā is in their eyes . . . .
>
> Rays of light shine from *hūṃ* in his heart, invoking all tathāgatas of the ten directions in the form of the Vajrasattva couple, who are absorbed.

Offer a supplication:

> All tathāgatas . . . *vajrībhava* . . . the empowerment water is conferred, filling the body and purifying taints. The excess water overflows, adorning one's heads with Akṣobhya.
>
> Next, a vajra arises from *hūṃ*, which possesses the nature of the twenty-eight deities. Imagine the vajra is placed in one's hand, and recite the following mantra:

This is the nature of all buddhas . . . .[32]

Wave the vajra, hold it to one's heart, and exclaim:

Henceforth, I will enter into the nature of the body, speech, and mind of Mahāvajradhara in order to subdue ordinary conduct!

Offer a maṇḍala as a gift for requesting the vajra master empowerment.

Recite the supplication three times:

Once the protector confers the empowerment . . . [33]{227}

Imagine that oneself is placed upon the empowerment platform in the form of Mahāvajradhara.

A vajra is placed in one's hand and held to one's heart, and adding the mantra, recite:

This is the nature of all buddhas . . . [34]

Recite:

The being who has no beginning or end . . .[35]

This vajra illustrates the dharmadhātu free from all proliferation, the essence of inseparable cognizance and emptiness. Think that one's mind is bodhicitta without beginning or end, free from all extremes of proliferation, the vajra of definitive meaning.

Next, the bell that arises from *āṃ* has the nature of the twenty-three deities.

This bell is said to emulate all the sounds . . .[36]

The bell is placed in one's left hand, rung, and then held to one's left hip, facing up. Recite:

aḥ
Existence is pure by nature . . .[37]

This bell illustrates the dharmadhātu free from all proliferation, empty of arising, cessation, and duration. Think that one's voice is the definitive bell, illustrating all existence is pure by nature.

Next, either meditating on Vajrasattva as was just explained, or with two hands, without completing all four limbs, recite:

Holding the vajra and bell . . .[38]

One becomes white Mahāvajradhara with one face and two hands, holding a vajra in the right hand and a vajra-handled bell in the left hand. He is in union with his consort, white Vajragarvi, who holds a curved knife and a skull and is sixteen years old. Mohavajrā is in their eyes . . .

Rays of light shine from *hūṃ* in his heart, invoking all tathāgatas of the ten directions in the form of the Vajradhara couple, who are invited with mantra and mudra, and absorbed.

Recite:

Holding the vajra and bell,
. . . .
Holding the great vajra and the great bell,[39]
. . . .
The bliss of existence is very weak . . .[40]{228}

Imagine this is said:

Ordinary bliss is impure. In order to exhaust the suffering of existence, one must engage in the yoga of the excellent deity and enjoy all desired enjoyments. Everything must be turned into an offering! There is nothing beyond the attainment of the body of Mahāvajradhara's union. That being so, you must dwell in this samādhi.

In order to stabilize that, imagine that various articles are offered by the tathāgatas who fill the sky, and that they confer the empowerment with vases filled with the water of gnosis. Raise the victorious vase:

> The great vajra empowerment . . . . The taints upon one's body, voice, and mind and their traces are purified.

Recite as in the section on the Akṣobhya water empowerment.

> The excess water overflows adorning one's crown with the essence of all tathāgatas, Vajrasattva.

If one prefers, at the conclusion of "The great vajra empowerment . . . ," extensively confer the empowerment water with each vase, and at the end, seal with the master of the family. Whichever choice one makes, recite and scatter flowers to consecrate:

> *oṃ supratiṣṭha vajraya svāhā*

Present the five offerings:

> *puṣpe . . .*

Put down the vajra and bell, the crown, and so on . . .

> As such, you have obtained the empowerment of Mahāvajradhara. Since all taints of your aggregates, sense elements, and sense bases have been purified, all of those are included in your mind. Since that mind is Vajrasattva, the nature of Akṣobhya, one's mind is a pure maṇḍala.

Recite:

> The explanation of the maṇḍala
> is that the intellect is the sublime maṇḍala.
> The explanation of the celestial mansion
> is that the mind is the storied celestial mansion.
> Its square outside

is the nature of uniformity.
Anyone's mind of love, and so on,
is explained as the four chalk lines.
Mindfulness of dharma
is explained to be the vajra line.
Liberation from all views {229}
is explained to be the gnosis line.
The correct explanation of the ornaments
is the vows of discipline, and so on.
Whatever is the mind of the five faculties
arises as the fivefold wall.
The explanation of the doors
is that there are four kinds of liberation.
The four porticos
are called the four correct renunciations.
The four foundations of mindfulness
are the four levels [of the portico roof].
The four door bracings[41]
are the four bases of magic power.
Likewise, the ornamental garlands of flowers
are the seven limbs of awakening.
The eight-limbed path of the noble ones
is said to be the eight pillars.
The special gnosis of the path
is renowned as the yak-tail whisks.
The explanation of the [decorative] strands
is that they eliminate all afflictions,
the essence of eliminating them all.
Because the afflictions are thieves, be mindful.
The union of the two pure accumulations
is turning the wheel.
Since half the afflictions are eliminated,
there are the tassels.[42]

That being the case, the mind is the celestial mansion. Its essence is the thirty-seven factors conducive to awakening. The appearances of the aggregates, sense elements, and sense bases to the mind are the deities of the complete three seats. The five

> aggregates are the seat of the tathāgatas; the four elements are the seat of the knowledge consorts; the inner sense bases are the seat of the bodhisattvas; the outer sense bases are the seat of the goddesses; and the agent exhausting the afflictive obscuration, and so on, is the male and female wrathful ones.

If one is condensing this, after the verse "turning the wheel," "the mind is the celestial mansion, its essence is the thirty-seven factors conducive to awakening" is sufficient. If one prefers the extensive version, then recite the purities of the aggregates, sense elements, and sense bases.

> There are three kinds of permission:
> concise, slightly extensive, and very extensive.

The concise permission is:

> Henceforth, you are a vajra master,
> you must gather disciples! {230}

Since this is said, "Benefit sentient beings through various methods!" If one is doing the slightly extensive permission, in addition to the foregoing, it is only the explanation of the emanations of the five families that occurs below. There are three sections in the extensive permission. The permission of the offering deities is beginning with a dance roll and placing both fists at the hips:

> Beginning from today, I offer
> a blissful celebration that manifests to
> the perfect buddhas and bodhisattvas
> through the yoga of Vajragarvi.
> *āḥ*

Likewise, place the two fists beside one's mouth:

> Gracefully toss a garland
> to be offered to all buddhas.
> One also will never be separate from the tathāgata.

That is the garland ornament.
oṃ

The two fists are like words uttered from one's mouth:

You offer this song of sublime dharma
to all embodied beings.
Through that, the siddhi of the sugata
is the swift experience of bliss.
gī

The vajra palms dance in a circle around one's crown:

That dance of palms
is offered to all buddhas.
The buddhas move in the manner of dancers
through the activity of gathering.
hoḥ

Make the mudra of incense with the two fists:

Since incense was offered to the perfect buddha,
he is well-sated with excellent strict discipline.
May embodied beings be satisfied with gnosis
as an accouterment of the sugata.
hūṃ

Make the flower mudra:

Flowers are scattered over the buddhas,
completing the limbs of awakening.
May the major and minor marks
of the body of the sugata be obtained!
bhrūṃ

Make the lamp mudra:

Since the lamp of dharma is well ignited,
similar to Vajradharma,
may the blind ignorance of sentient beings
be removed with the lamp of gnosis.
pra

With the right hand hold the dharma conch, and with the left hand make the motion of anointing:

By offering this scent to the victors,
embodied beings will meditate upon
discipline, samādhi, wisdom,
and the gnosis of liberation.
gā

The permission to benefit sentient beings is the actual praise through the mantra, opening one's eyes with the probe {231} or, if that is not available, with the vajra.

Just as the sighted victor
removed the cataracts of the world,
child, the victors shall remove the cataract
of your ignorance.

oṃ vajra netra avaharapaṭalaṃ hrīḥ praṃ[43]

Pick up the mirror and recite:

All phenomena are like reflections,
clear, pure, and unclouded,
ungraspable, inexpressible,
arising from causes and karma,
natureless, and nonabiding.
Born as a child of the protector,
one must understand phenomena in that way,
yet engage in benefiting sentient beings impartially.

Pick up the bell that arises from *āḥ*. Ring the bell and recite:

Space is the characteristic of everything.
There is no characteristic for space.
By unifying with space,
the uniform, supreme of all [aspects] manifests.

hoḥ One is given the bow and arrow. Imagine the following is said, and point the bow and arrow toward the four directions, above, and below:

May all tathāgatas be loving!

Pick up the mirror and vajra and say:

oṃ vajrasattva
Like Vajrasattva [reflected] in a mirror,
clear, pure, and unclouded,
child, the lord, the nature of Vajrasattva,
abides in your heart.

One must understand that bodhicitta, the master of all the buddhas, is just like this.

The permission to explain the dharma is:

Say *oṃ vajra hetu maṃ* and roll the wheel under foot, *oṃ vajra bhaṣa raṃ* and take the conch in the right hand, *oṃ vajra ghaṇḍe aḥ* and take the bell in the left hand, and *a* and take the volume on the forearms:

Henceforth, I shall turn the wheel of dharma
merely by generating bodhicitta.
In order for you to have no doubt,
with an undivided mind,
you must fill the dharma conch
with all immaculate things. {232}
Always give explanations to people
through the ritual means of mantra conduct.
Having done so, one must be grateful
and helpful to the buddhas.

Vajra holder, all of that
you must always guard.[44]

Beginning with a dance roll, one must make the great mudras of each of the individual five families. First is Vairocana:

To benefit all sentient beings
and to tame all sentient beings
everywhere in many various ways,
turn the dharma wheel.

Likewise, other than the first three lines, substitute the vajra wheel and the mudra of Akṣobhya, the jewel wheel and the mudra of Ratnasambhava, the lotus wheel and the mudra of Amitābha, and the multicolored wheel and the mudra of Amoghasiddhi.[45] Imagine that you are given permission, "As such, you must turn the dharma wheel, vajra wheel, jewel wheel, lotus wheel, and the multicolored wheel for all sentient beings. You must blow the dharma conch and proclaim and explain [the dharma]!"

As such, whether you have a sand maṇḍala or a cloth-generated maṇḍala, generate the understanding that you have principally obtained the vase empowerment into the maṇḍala. The taints of the body are purified; you have been empowered to guard the twenty-two samayas; the symbol is gathering the five and pressing the tip;[46] you are empowered to meditate on the path, the creation stage; and the seed of the result, the nirmāṇakāya, is planted in your continuum.

Offer a maṇḍala as a gift for requesting the secret empowerment.

Offer praise:

You are surrounded by a troupe of yoginīs . . .

Recite three times:

Oh Bhagavān of great peace . . .[47]

Saying, *oṃ āḥ hūṃ*, the eyes are covered with a blindfold. {233}

> Imagine that the sound of joy of the guru couple's union invites all tathāgatas, who enter into the father's mouth and at his heart melt into light through the fire of passion. The bodhicitta, the bindu that is like a pearl, which falls into the space of the mother from the path of the vajra jewel, is placed on one's tongue. Taste the amṛta.

Recite:

> Just as the buddhas of the past . . .

> Say *oṃ āḥ hūṃ hoḥ*, and because the amṛta was tasted, the bindu spreads from the throat, filling the entire body; all eighty natural concepts[48] cease. The samādhi of clarity and emptiness arises in one's continuum and is protected by saying *oṃ āḥ hūṃ*. Imagine one removes the blindfold.

After the guru transforms into the form of Śākyamuni, while holding the corners of the dharma robe like the ears of a deer and holding the vajra and bell with the right hand, which makes the mudra of conferring protection, imagine that he makes a prediction through one's secret name. A prediction is made for oneself in just that way. Recite:

> Here, I will give you a prediction:
> Vajrasattva Tathāgata,
> since the world is pure,
> you are released from bad migrations in the world.

> Oh, Tathāgata Śrī [insert name] Vajra, my prediction to all those below, on, and above the ground, *bhūr bhūvaḥ svaḥ*,[49] is the prediction that all buddhas and bodhisattvas and all maṇḍalacakras make in one voice, which is the power of this mantra and mudra.

To generate understanding:

> As such, one obtains the secret empowerment in the maṇḍala of relative bodhicitta; the taints of the voice are purified; the

samaya is being authorized to rely on the pill of five meats and five amṛtas; the symbol is touching the thumb and ring finger; one is empowered to meditate the path, the stage of the self-empowerment; and the seed of the result, the saṃbhogakāya, is planted in one's continuum. {234}

Offer a maṇḍala as a gift to request the gnosis of the wisdom consort empowerment. The praise and supplication are the same as before [in the secret empowerment]. With *oṃ āḥ hūṃ*, the eyes are covered with a blindfold. Imagine that the guru confers a consort[50] upon oneself. Recite, "Great being, take the goddess . . . ."[51]

Imagine the consort inquires:

Child, can you consume feces and urine,
. . . .
kissing the lotus of the bhaga?[52]

One replies:

I will consume feces and urine . . .

Having pleased the consort, she removes the clothes from her body; having scented her lotus with saffron, and so on, while showing her blossoming lotus as the supreme nāḍī, [she says,] amazing! This bhaga of mine . . . *stvaṃ padmabhañja mokṣa hoḥ* and imagine she arrives on one's lap. One appearing as Hevajra and Vajranairātmyā is the perception of the deity. Recalling the empowerments of the space and the secret with the mantra is the perception of mantra. The thought "The connate is realized on the basis of this method" is the perception of dharma. Entering into union through being inseparable with the three perceptions is the method of employing the nirmāṇakāya, saṃbhogakāya, and dharmakāya as the path, respectively. One should imagine one has generated the realization of the four joys, which descend from above and are stabilized in ascending order. With *oṃ āḥ hūṃ*, imagine the blindfold is removed.

Next, to summarize the solace of the path, recite:

Do not abandon bodhicitta.
One who merely generates
the mudra of the so-called vajra

will undoubtedly become a buddha.
Never criticize the sublime dharma,
and never discard it;
the ignorant or the confused
do not rely upon it.
Never abandon the vajra and bell.
Never criticize the master,
who is equal to all the buddhas.
Having abandoned oneself, {235}
never engage in the torment of asceticism.
Just as bliss is found in bliss,
here, in the future, you will be a perfect
buddha.[53]

To elaborate:

Never criticize the master.
Never transgress the word of the sugata.
Never criticize siblings.
Never abandon love and bodhicitta
for sentient beings.
Never criticize one's own or another's dharma.
Never teach the unfortunate.
Never abuse one's body.
Abandon doubts about the dharma.
Do not be friendly toward hostile beings.
Never measure dharmatā.
Never abandon fortunate sentient beings.
Always guard samaya.
Never criticize women.

Until one is on the seat of awakening,
never abandon the Three Jewels.
One should always protect samaya.
One must carry the vajra and bell.
Always keep the crown.[54]
Always ladle the burnt offerings.[55]
Always construct the maṇḍala.

> Always perform the consecration of sugatas.[56]
> Give the bali to the great bhūtas.[57]
>
> Never abandon the embrace of the mudra,
> and do not engage in the activities of stupas;
> the three supreme vajras should not prostrate.
> The activities of the body, such as maṇḍalas, and so on,
> should not be done, even in dreams.
> Never prostrate to worldly masters,
> but always prostrate to venerable gurus.
> Continuously recite mantras,
> and also practice concentration.
> Always gather disciples,
> and always give explanations.
> Always defend sentient beings.
> Always greatly please the buddhas.
> Make water offerings to Jambhala,
> and always correctly engage in all activities.
> Even building stupas of sand
> should be done by the wise according to the rites.[58]

One should recall the meaning of this.

The solace of the result is: {236}

> There are no misdeeds in the triple realm,
> such as being free from desire.
> Therefore, you must never be
> free from desire.
> *mahāsamaya hana hūṃ phaṭ*[59]

The meaning of that is that one must have attachment to the deity and the guru with great faith, one must have attachment to sentient beings with great compassion, and one must have attachment to the truth of the dharma with great wisdom. Since separation from these three is a great misdeed, training is not being separated from these three.

Next, at the conclusion of making three full-length prostrations to the maṇḍala, imagine that one offers one's body to the maṇḍala:

The disciple who holds the mantras
and the tantras offers this.[60]

Since that offering is presented, imagine that the solace of the result arises.

To the one who holds the mantras and the tantras,
the buddhas, bodhisattvas,
and the devas speak in accord:
"Be compassionate to sentient beings.
Draw the maṇḍala according to the rites.
Through the generation of your diligence,
practitioners will be joined to mantra.[61]
That being so, be grateful and
helpful to the buddhas."[62]
Enter the supreme city,
the vast kingdom of the three realms,
the source of all glorious qualities,
victorious over the hordes of Māra.[63]

As such, one has obtained the empowerment of the gnosis of the wisdom consort in the bhaga maṇḍala of the mudra; the taints of the mind are purified; the samaya is to never criticize women; the symbol is the mudra of supreme awakening; one is empowered to meditate on the path, the maṇḍalacakra; and the seed of the result, the dharmakāya, is planted in one's continuum.

Offer a maṇḍala as a gift for requesting the fourth empowerment.

Recite three times:

Compassionate protector . . .

Saying, *oṃ āḥ hūṃ*, imagine that the eyes are covered with a blindfold. {237}

This gnosis is extremely subtle . . .[64]

The body adopts the characteristics of concentration. The movement of the breath is settled. The mind has eliminated all other discursive concepts of the three times. Generate the understanding that the entire inanimate universe and animate inhabitants are one's mind. The mind's characteristic is clarity, its nature is emptiness, and its essence is union. The three [the characteristic, nature, and essence] are inseparable. Generate the definitive understanding that the four naturally pure kāyas that exist as innate attributes are essentially inseparable with the four kāyas of the result. Since the other methods for actualizing that are incapable of generating realization—because they are expressed in words, and so on—the example is introduced on the basis of the gnosis of the third empowerment.

To realize that, at the occasion of the third empowerment, the appearance of the form of the deity's body, faces, and hands is natureless; appearing as the illusory body is the nirmāṇakāya. The deity's mental continuum that arises in the form of the gnosis of great bliss that is produced from union with the mudra is the saṃbhogakāya. The mere appearance of the great bliss of the deity's body—free from the trio of arising, abiding, and ceasing—is the dharmakāya. Even though those three kāyas seem to be distinct, their intrinsic inseparability is the svabhāvakāya.

In brief, the natural state (*gshis*) of the mind is nothing whatever. Its radiance (*gdangs*) is unceasing as great bliss. Its potential (*rtsal*) arises as a diversity. One should understand it is beyond all objects of meditation and meditating agents, like space. Just as [this] space and [that] space have the same taste, remain relaxed without grasping in the state of the same taste of mind, bliss, and emptiness, and remain in equipoise. In conclusion, remove the blindfold with *oṃ āḥ hūṃ*.

Recite:

Having been admitted into and seen
the maṇḍala of the supreme secret, {238}
today you all are liberated from all misdeeds.
Today you all abide in bliss.
In this, the vehicle of great bliss,
henceforth there is no death.

Be joyful, fearing nothing at all.
Since existence is utterly pure,
you are released from bad migrations in existence.[65]

Raise enthusiasm through recalling the meaning of this.

Generate realization: As such, you have obtained the empowerment into the maṇḍala of ultimate bodhicitta; the taints and all traces of body, voice, and mind are purified; the samaya is the intention to guard the samayas that were mentioned; the symbol is indicating space with the index finger; one is empowered to meditate on the path, the vajra waves; and the result, the svabhāvakāya, is planted in one's continuum.

Thinking that one vows to protect the samayas obtained at the occasion of those [empowerments], recite three times:

Whatever the principal commands . . .

Offer a maṇḍala in appreciation for receiving the empowerments in their entirety. When one has offered one's body and all enjoyments, think, "please enjoy them."

Henceforth, I offer . . .

Next, sing the song of the three samayas, and think, "By the power of the maṇḍala in which one is empowered, the master by whom the empowerment is conferred, and the disciple upon whom the empowerment is conferred, who are not beyond the nature of natureless, nonarising great bliss, also I will become realized!"

Between each verse, wave the vajra and ring the bell:

oṃ
Because space has the characteristic of birth,
it is the supreme one without beginning and end,
the nature of great Vajrasattva.[66]
May I accomplish Hevajra![67]

The great siddhi is the supreme of all,
the great lord is the excellent deity,

the holder of the vajra is the king of all.
May I accomplish the unchanging supreme one! {239}

You have never possessed flaws,
with affection for all those with desire,
greatly delighted with great desire.
May the Bhagavān be accomplished through that!

The supreme of all the utterly pure,[68]
the tathāgata liberated from the beginning,
Samantabhadra is the nature of all.
May I be accomplished as a bodhisattva!

The supreme of all great siddhis,
the supreme mudra of the great lord is
praised as the great vajra of accomplishment.
May I accomplish the lord of Vajragarvi![69]

Pervading the mind of all sentient beings,
entering the mind of all sentient beings,
the father of all sentient beings,
the supreme samaya is uniform desire![70]

Think that though the maṇḍalacakra appears in the manner of a reflection, through the power that arises from the nondual emptiness and compassion of the dharmakāya and the power of the master who has realized that, may the disciple perceive the form of a natureless reflection in an appearance that lacks characteristics. Recite the power of truth:

Whatever is the power of the truth
of the maṇḍala whose nature is method and wisdom,
by that truth, may I accomplish the
wishes of the protector.

All phenomena are like reflections—
clear, pure, and unclouded,
ungraspable, inexpressible,

arising from causes and karma,
and, likewise, arising from reality.
By that truth, may the maṇḍala
be perceived by all the disciples
as a stainless, clear reflection.[71]

At this occasion sprinkle the inner offering, water, and alcohol on the bali offerings, and offer the mundane and transcendent bali offerings, like at the occasion of the setup.

As for admitting the disciples and conferring the empowerment:
The disciples who have been prepared
are to wash and be seated in the row.{240}
Offer a maṇḍala and supplication.
The vows should be done according to the sequence of proclaiming and taking them,
tie the blindfold and distribute the garland of flowers,
purify with Amṛtakuṇḍali, question and reply,
generate inner bodhicitta, the instruction of secrecy,
admit into the maṇḍala and place in samaya,
offer the maṇḍala and a supplication,
descent and stabilization of the gnosis being,
supplicate, inquire about color, praise,
offer the flower, loosen the blindfold,
begin to explain the maṇḍala,
offer a gift for the empowerment and a supplication,
generate the deity, dispel misfortune, recite the benediction,
confer the empowerments of
the water, crown, vajra,
bell, name, strict discipline, and
master, explain the purities,
grant permission, the secret empowerment, the prediction,
the gnosis of the wisdom consort empowerment, give solace,
the fourth, the praise for raising enthusiasm, and so on,
the connection, and the introduction of symbols.
[All] should be understood through the previous reasons.

The Concluding Rites

Refresh the offerings and cleanse, bless, and empower them. Perform the outer, inner, and mentally produced offerings, and the praise. Recite the one-hundred-syllable mantra three times, "Whatever I have not prepared . . . ," and so on, and request forbearance. If one is using a cloth maṇḍala, at the conclusion of "All buddhas and bodhisattvas dwelling in the ten directions . . . ," say, "In particular, may the assembly of deities that have been generated and invited to these images remain firm for as long as they are not destroyed by the four elements." If one is using a sand maṇḍala, on a day other than the day the maṇḍala deities are requested to depart, as above, after saying "in particular," say, "assembly of deities that have been generated and invited into the sand maṇḍala for as long as the rite of requesting your departure is not performed . . . ." Request the gnosis beings of the torma guests that do not have images to depart {241} and gather the commitment beings, as in the setup.

On the day of requesting the departure of the sand maṇḍala, when performing the concluding rite, place the vases on the border, and like the other rites, after "Whatever I have not prepared . . . ," and so on, request forbearance for errors with, "Since I am a beginner . . . ," in order for the bali guests to remain firm.

At the conclusion of "*oṃ* You perform all benefits for all sentient beings . . . ," snap the thumb and ring finger with *vajra muḥ*. The gnosis beings of the bali guests who lack a support, the gnosis beings of the sand maṇḍala, and the gnosis beings of the vase deities depart into the dharmadhātu. The commitment beings dissolve nondually into oneself with *jaḥ hūṃ baṃ hoḥ*. Recite *oṃ āḥ hūṃ*.

Then play music, recite *oṃ a kāromukhaṃ sarvadharmaṇāṃ ādyanutpannatvāta oṃ āḥ hūṃ phaṭ svāhā* and *oṃ gili gili hūṃ jaḥ*, and recall reality. With the tip of the vajra, first break the northeast wall, in a clockwise sequence. Say, "Please depart to wherever you wish." If there is a wish for sand, take it from the signs of the deities and give it. The rest should be gathered from the border and poured into a container. Perform the rite of inviting the sand into the ocean, or, if unable to do this, one should request the departure with great reverence in a river that flows into an ocean or a spring. Wash away the layout marks from the border with scented water, so that no marks remain. If one can, at this occasion one should perform a burnt offering, scatter flowers in all directions, sing benedictions, play various instruments, perform a group feast or have a celebration, and so on. Having held a great celebration, one should abide in the conduct that corresponds with the dharma. {242}

As such, this method of
the accomplishing, offering,
and employing empowerment as the path
in the maṇḍala of Hevajra
is this *Beautiful Ornament of the River of Empowerment.*
In order to benefit those of low intelligence,
and while prioritizing the self-admittance,
if closely examined,
it will be understood to be easy.
With few words, easy to use, and requisites complete,
it is divided into extensive, medium, and concise,
an earring for all confused scholars.
The one who can understand something like this is a scholar.
Though based upon the excellent explanations of the forefathers
and witnessing many sublime traditions,
if there are faults, I confess with all three doors simultaneously
to the noble ones.
By the merit of excellent diligence,
after all infinite migrating beings
reach the conclusion of the excellent path of the great secret,
may they accomplish all the activities of the victor.

This practice of the *Great River of Empowerment*, divided into stages, was composed on the twenty-fifth day of the month of Jyeṣṭhā, in the male Water Tiger year (1542) called Śubhakṛt,[72] at the urging of many intelligent and dilgent ones, by the venerable Könchok Lhundrub, who obtained faith from understanding the words and meanings of the precious oral instruction of the second Vajradhara, the Jestun Sakyapa, and his son, in dependence upon taking the untarnished garland of dust of the feet of the many tutors whose behavior corresponds with dharma, but principally from the instruction of the greatly kind Ratnavardha, who is inseparable from the sovereign protector of the maṇḍala. It was faithfully committed to writing in the retreat center of Pal Evaṃ Chöden by Gönpo Rinchen Palzang, a scholar of scripture and reasoning.

One must look at the supporting text, the *Great River of Empowerment*, again and again![73] Moreover, the difficult portions of the words and meanings were mended and edited by that author.

sarva maṅgalaṃ

Virtue, virtue.

12. The Condensed Essential Citations and Intimate Instructions of the Empowerment Rite of the Intimate Instruction Tradition of Śrī Hevajra[1]

Jamyang Loter Wangpo

This text presents Loter Wangpo's abbreviation of Könchok Lhundrub's *Condensed Essential Citations and Intimate Instructions of the Empowerment Rite of the Intimate Instruction Tradition of Śrī Hevajra*, which lays out the second part of the two-day empowerment, the empowerment for the disciples. This part of the empowerment also has two parts: the preliminary part of the empowerment, performed on the first day, prepares the students for receiving the main part of the empowerment on the second day.

namaḥ śrī cakranātha ratnavardhāya

I bow to Guru Hevajra,
the one who engages in ripening infinite disciples
with amazing, emanated rūpakāyas,
while never moving from great bliss and emptiness.

Listen to this explanation of the concise distinctions
between the connections and significance of
the admittance of disciples into his great maṇḍala
and the rite of conferring the empowerment.

The summary is:

The benefits, the faults,
the knowledgeable qualified master, the disciple,
the time, the place, the maṇḍala,
the definition, and the commencement of the rite.

The disciples who aspire to receive empowerment into the maṇḍala of Śrī Hevajra, having washed, prostrated, and presented gifts, should be seated in order of seniority. The activity disciple distributes and gathers flowers. The master states:

> You must generate the mind of supreme bodhicitta with the thought, "In order to attain the stage of a perfect buddha for the benefit of sentient beings equal with space, for that purpose, I will receive the profound empowerment that is the true foundation of Vajrayāna, and I promise to guard the vows and samayas."
>
> Having recalled how the practice of the dharma to be received arose from the immaculate treatise systems of Mahayana, listen! {245} Among the inconceivable amṛta of the sublime dharma taught by the truly perfect Buddha, corresponding with the inclination of disciples, here, it is the Mantrayāna that is superior to the Mahayana vehicle of the perfections through the four features. Among the four major divisions of tantras, this is unsurpassed yoga tantra. Also, among the trio of method tantra, wisdom tantra, and nondual tantra, this is nondual tantra. Among [the various systems] that follow the root and explanatory tantras of Śrī Hevajra, the empowerment of the great maṇḍala of Essence Hevajra as explicated by Virūpa, the great lord of yogins, will be accomplished.
>
> The benefits of obtaining the empowerment are as follows: People of highest faculties will attain liberation immediately after the empowerment. It is said that if people of lesser capacity always maintain familiarity with the empowerment itself, they will accomplish supreme siddhi {246} within seven lifetimes, even though they do not meditate on other paths. It is said that if people of lesser capacity are not tarnished by root downfalls after obtaining the empowerment, they will become accomplished within sixteen lifetimes. It is said that for people who cannot be liberated by the empowerment, the method that renders them

suitable to be shown the liberating path is the empowerment itself. Therefore, you should be very enthused to receive this empowerment, the source of all qualities.

Having ascertained the benefits of obtaining the empowerment, the faults of not obtaining that beneficial empowerment are as follows: If one thinks that one can accomplish the result when one makes effort on the [Vajrayāna] path without obtaining empowerment, the Buddha has said it is not so. It is said that without obtaining the empowerment, the lineage is broken; even though one meditates on the topics of creation and completion, siddhi will not be obtained; and even if one obtains mundane minor siddhis, one will go to lower realms in one's next life. Those intelligent ones who wish to accomplish their own and others' benefit by relying on the Vajrayāna path must have exceptional faith in empowerment.

Who may confer such an empowerment that is beneficial to obtain and faulty when not obtained? When the qualifications of the master are summarized:

The supreme master who confers the empowerment
understands the mantras, tantras, and intimate instructions,
is very adept in the activities of rites,
and bears compassion for the disciple.[2]

As stated, {247} it is necessary for the master to be fully qualified.

The qualifications of the disciple upon whom the empowerment is conferred are:

Faithful, compassionate, with a very disciplined mind,
few concepts, intelligent,
aspires to the supreme path of mantra,
and keeps harmony within the group.[3]

Each qualified disciple, from one to twenty-five, should behave appropriately during the ceremony.

As such, having ascertained the qualifications of the master and disciple, the time when the empowerment is conferred is when there is a positive conjunction of planets and stars during the waxing moon. If there is a special conjunction during the waning moon, it is explained that there is no fault.

The place where the empowerment is conferred is a region ruled by a dharma king that lacks internal and external dangers. In particular, the empowerment should be conferred where the earth rites have been correctly performed by either oneself or previous gurus. It is essential that the place be isolated from unsuitable people.

With respect to the maṇḍala upon which the empowerment depends, the definitive ultimate maṇḍala to be illustrated is explained to be attaining and maintaining the essence, great bliss. Though there are many explications by each mahāsiddha for the provisional relative maṇḍala that illustrates that [ultimate maṇḍala], when summarized, there are three types of maṇḍalas: sand, cloth, and body maṇḍalas (or, when adding samādhi maṇḍalas, there are four). Among these, nowadays, the principal maṇḍalas most appropriate for the ripening of the majority of people are the sand and cloth maṇḍalas.

The definition of the empowerment (*dbang*) that is to be conferred (*skur*) upon someone is "to distribute" (*gtor ba*, Skt. *kṣepa*) and "to place" (*blugs pa*, Skt. *prakṣip*). The four empowerments respectively produce the shoots of the four kāyas in dependence upon being distributed and placed upon the crown, tongue, {248} genitals, and vāyu and mind; hence they are called "empowerments" (*dbang*).

In the rite of conferring the empowerment, there is the cause empowerment for preparing one for the path, the path empowerment for total familiarity, and the result empowerment for preparing for the inalienable[4] result. Though described as three through context, many become one through the person. Apart from this, here it is explained in accordance with the rite of ripening. That being the case, in the stages of practice that gradually arise from the lineage of gurus who have accomplished the intention of the tantra divisions, there is both the method of conferring the empowerments into the sand maṇḍala through seven or eight direct realizations of the empowerment and conferring the empowerment into the cloth maṇḍala through the setup and main part.

Among these two, in the rite of the place during the fourth part—either according to the sand maṇḍala empowerment or according to the cloth maṇḍala—the time of the setup falls upon the first evening. Within that, there is the setup of Pṛthivī, the consecration of the deity and the vase. I have already finished the first three consecrations.

Now, the setup for the disciples is:

The activities of the body, to generate renunciation,
confer the inner empowerment, request the main topic,
generate enthusiasm, perform the daily confession,
perform the protection, present the offerings,
toss the tooth stick, pour water in the palm,
tie the protection cord, give the kuśa grass,
explain the profound dharma, and examine the dream.

Among these fourteen, first, the activities of the body include washing, prostrations, presenting an entry gift, and (since each person in the row has a handful of flowers) entering with devotion. With the thought that the master is no different than the essence of all buddhas, {249} the devoted disciples should present a maṇḍala as a gift for requesting the subjects of the setup.

Having presented such a maṇḍala, engage in the generation of the stable wish for nirvana:

Whoever aspires to mantra siddhi
must enter into this maṇḍala,
but the ones who wish for merit are different.
Aspiring for self and others in the next world,
those with great faith
and intelligence should enter the maṇḍala
without aspiring for the result in this life.
Those who aspire for the result in this life
will not accomplish it in the next.
If one focuses upon the next life,
this result will be accomplished without effort.[5]

Those who aspire for the gnosis of a vajra holder, the siddhi of mantra, should enter into the great maṇḍala, but those who wish for either happiness in this life, the state of humans and devas in the next life, or to become śrāvakas[6] or pratyekabuddhas for their own benefit should not enter, because their accomplishments rest upon inferior methods, without depending on entering into the maṇḍala. That being so, those faithful, intelligent ones who aspire for the nonabiding nirvana that goes beyond existence and peace for the benefit of themselves and all others should enter this great maṇḍala, but those who aspire for the result of happiness in this life will not accomplish their benefit in the next life. Those who focus on omniscient buddhahood's nonabiding nirvana for the benefit of others will easily accomplish their own and others' benefit by entering the maṇḍala. Having ascertained that is the case, one should act according to this wish.

No matter where one stays in samsara's three realms, one in samsara will never transcend its suffering, defects, and flaws. If it is wondered what are the aspects of suffering in those three realms, {250} hell beings suffer from heat and cold; pretas suffer from hunger and thirst; animals suffer from eating one another, being slain, and servitude; humans suffer from never attaining desires and the visitation of the undesirable; for asuras there is the suffering of fighting, wounds, amputations of the body, and so on; and for devas there is the suffering of death, falling from higher states to lower states, and a mental suffering even greater than the suffering of the body of a hell being, when it is understood that in the end, one will be born in lower realms. Nevertheless, if it is thought that one should obtain the awakening of a śrāvaka or a pratyekabuddha, the awakening of a śrāvaka or a pratyekabuddha does not possess complete qualities of abandonment and realization and cannot produce the great activities that benefit others. Since in the end they are engaged for a long while in attaining buddhahood, it is not the result for which the intelligent aspire.

If it is asked [for what result] one should aspire, the suffering of the three realms is transcended without abiding in the extreme of samsara due to great wisdom. One does not abide in the extreme of nirvana, but one necessarily obtains the stage of omniscient buddhahood's nonabiding nirvana, which produces the benefit of sentient beings without interruption due to great compassion.

That aspiration is not only for one's personal benefit. Just as there is no limit to space, there is no limit to sentient beings. Each and every sentient being without limit has been one's father and mother. Each one of them has protected one from harm and has only kindly bestowed immeasurable benefits. All of them wish for {251} the desideratum, happiness, but because they lack skill in means, some experience actual suffering; others experience great, fearful nonvirtue, the cause of suffering. Blinded by the cataract of ignorance, they are missing a cane that supports freedom. They have no leader, a virtuous mentor. One must feel compassion for such beings who have slipped from the path of higher realms and freedom and wander in the abyss of the three lower realms.

However, having generated compassion, there is no benefit in leaving it there, as beings must be liberated from suffering and placed in happiness. At present one is incapable of doing that, and even those more powerful than oneself (such as Brahma, Śakra, śrāvakas, and pratyekabuddhas) are likewise incapable. If it is asked who is capable, only a perfect buddha is capable. Thus, one must attain the stage of perfect buddhahood by every means for the benefit of our grandmothers, all sentient beings.

Since nothing is attained in absence of a cause or in absence of a condition, the principal cause and condition are correctly receiving empowerment, the basis of the Vajrayāna path. Please generate true bodhicitta with the thought that one must promise to guard the samayas and vows and make effort on the path. All virtue of the three doors motivated by such wishes is the cause of buddhahood and the implicit means by which one obtains the result of happiness in this life, as well as the states of a human or deva in the next life. For example, when there is an excellent harvest of white rice, similarly there is stalk and chaff.

For the purpose of the inner empowerment, you should visualize in the following way: Light rays shine from the heart of the master, who appears as the Śrī Hevajra couple. Since those light rays strike your bodies, {252} they burn and purify all your misdeeds and obscurations gathered during beginningless lifetimes, transforming your bodies into balls of light. While you visualize that, through the condition of the master uttering *hūṃ*, you all enter into the master's mouth. After being purified again by the *hūṃ* in his heart, you travel through the master's body, fall into the lotus of the goddess, and immediately transform into the form of Śrī Heruka, with one face and two arms.

Once again light shines from the heart of the master, inviting the tathāgatas of the ten directions, who enter into the father's mouth, travel through his body, fall into the lotus of the goddess, and dissolve into your crown as you appear in the form of Heruka. You should imagine that you have simultaneously received the empowerment and the descent of gnosis. Light rays shine again and through the condition of the master uttering *hūṃ*, with the pride of Heruka, you emerge from the mother's left side. Imagine that you each are placed in your row. The purpose of this activity is to render you a suitable recipient for hearing secrets until you actually receive the main empowerment. This is accomplished at this time in order that the master not commit the fault of proclaiming secrets.

To request the main topic, in the presence of the master who is nondual with the Hevajra couple, with the uncommon refuge and generation of bodhicitta, and with the thought to request the Vajrayāna samayas and vows, place one's palms together and repeat this supplication after the master three times:

Embraced by Nairātmyā about the neck,
Great Joy, please teach me!
Master, please head me! {253}
Great protector, please explain to me
the method of great awakening.
Please grant me the samayas,
also please grant me bodhicitta,
and please grant me the three refuges:
the Buddha, the dharma, and the sangha.
Protector, please grant me entry
into the supreme city of great freedom.[7]

The meaning of this is, having addressed the master as "Great Joy," for the purpose of requesting that stage of the buddhas that demonstrates the method of great awakening for oneself, one supplicates entry into the supreme city of great freedom through the bestowal of samaya: the samayas of mantra, the bodhisattva vow of the uncommon daily confession that serves as the basis for those samayas, and the vows of individual liberation, together with refuge in the Vajrayāna Three Jewels that serves as the basis for those bodhisattva vows.

As such, here, since enthusiasm is generated because it is understood that "It is very excellent that the mind that aspires for Vajrayāna, the special path, has been aroused," it is very special.

Here, child of Mahayana,
you are the recipient of the great means.
The supreme means of Secret Mantra conduct
shall be correctly explained to you.
The perfect buddhas of the past,
the perfect buddhas of the future,
and the perfect buddhas of the present
all remain in order to benefit migrating beings.
Since they all know the profound rites
of Secret Mantra,
the hero gained omniscience
in front of the Bodhi tree.
With that unexcelled yoga of Secret Mantra,
the protector, Lion of the Śākyas,
whose great power conquered
the hordes of very fierce māras,
arrived in accordance with the world,
turned the wheel, and so on, and passed into nirvana,
in order to obtain omniscience.
Child, this is done by the intelligent![8] {254}

The meaning of this is as follows: You have all become my children through this rite, thus you are called by the endearment "child"; that is, you are recipients of the Mahayana dharma.

Also, in Mahayana there are the perfection and mantra vehicles. Among these two, the supreme Secret Mantra Vajrayāna will be explained to you. In general, Vajrayāna is the sole path traversed by all tathāgatas of the three times. In particular, our unparalleled teacher, this king of the Śākyas, tamed Māra and attained buddhahood through relying upon the path of Mantra inestimable eons ago, showing once again the method of attaining buddhahood in Jambudvīpa: the twelve deeds, from the turning of the wheel of dharma up to demonstrating nirvana in order to lead the beings of the world and counteract clinging to permanence. That being the case, since it very good fortune to encounter Vajrayāna, the sole path traversed by all tathāgatas of the three times, you children of dharma must have no other thought than the Mantrayāna in order to obtain the state of omniscient Mahāvajradhara.

For generating bodhicitta through the preliminary daily confession, visualize in the following way: One should imagine the Bhagavān Hevajra nine-deity maṇḍala as inseparable with the guru, who is surrounded by all buddhas and bodhisattvas and resides in the space in front of oneself, like a thick bank of clouds. Oneself and all sentient beings are seated before them. One should think that all misdeeds and obscurations gathered in beginningless lifetimes {256} are entirely confessed in the presence of the uncommon object, the Three Jewels of Vajrayāna, by means of the four powers. Furthermore, one should think that all the virtue of samsara and nirvana gathered in the three times is delightful and rejoice in it. One should mentally commit that one will meditate on the characteristic of emptiness, the ultimate bodhicitta that all buddhas have relied upon. One should think that one goes for refuge to the uncommon object, the Three Jewels of Vajrayāna. One should possess the aspirational bodhicitta, thinking that one will obtain the stage of Mahāvajradhara's unsurpassed buddhahood in order to benefit oneself and all sentient beings. One should possess engaged bodhicitta, thinking that for that latter purpose, one will gradually train in the methods of Vajrayāna. One should dedicate merit, thinking, "With the root of such virtue as that, may I attain unsurpassed, perfect buddhahood for the benefit of all sentient beings." Recalling those topics, place one's palms together and repeat the seven-branch prayer three times:

> I go for refuge to the Three Jewels
> and individually confess each misdeed.
> I rejoice in the merit of beings.
> I bear in mind the bodhicitta of the buddhas.
> I go for refuge until awakening
> to the Buddha, the dharma, and the supreme sangha.
> I generate bodhicitta
> in order to truly accomplish my own and others' benefit.
> Having generated supreme bodhicitta,
> I invite all sentient beings to practice the pleasing, supreme conduct of awakening. {257}
> May I accomplish buddhahood
> in order to benefit migrating beings.[9]

Based on the three recitations of the daily confession, those who have not obtained the uncommon personal liberation and bodhisattva vows receive them; those who have received them refresh them, and having received them, increase them; and [the vows that] are damaged are also restored.

As such, the vows should be guarded in order to prevent obstacles to the generation of bodhicitta. Since light rays shine from the *hūṃ* in the heart of the master and strike your bodies, imagine that they burn up and purify your misdeeds, spirits, and obstructors.

Wave one's vajra and recite:

oṃ aṣṭānanaya piṅgalordhākeśavartamane caturviṅgṣatine-trāya ṣoḍaśabhujāya kṛṣṇajīmūtavapuṣe kapālamālānikadhārine adhmātakrūracittāya ardhendudaṃṣṭrīṇe mārayamāraya kāray-akāraya garjayagarjaya tarjayatarjaya śoṣayaśoṣaya saptasāgarān nāgāṣṭakān bandhabandha ghriṇaghriṇa śatrūn ha hā hi hī hu hū he hai ho hau haṃ haḥ phaṭ svāhā

By reciting this, one is protected from obstacles. The master touches the three places of the disciples with the scented water and the vajra and utters, *oṃ āḥ hūṃ*. Appearing as Heruka, on your foreheads is *oṃ*, from which arises a wheel marked with *oṃ*, from which arises Kāyavajrā; at your throats is an *āḥ*, from which arises a lotus marked with āḥ, from which arises Vakvajrā; and at your hearts is *hūṃ*, from which arises a vajra marked with *hūṃ*, from which arises Cittavajrā. Next, the three places are touched in ascending order and *hūṃ āḥ oṃ* is uttered. The three places are then touched in descending order and *oṃ āḥ hūṃ* is uttered. Imagine they are stabilized. {257}

Having done so, while your body, voice, and mind have existed as the three vajras from the beginning, this rite introduces and clarifies this fact. As such, as soon as one has generated bodhicitta and the three doors have been transformed into deities, there is the excellent object of offering. Having presented a flower to the head, one should imagine the offering is made with *oṃ vajrapuṣpe āḥ hūṃ*. There is incense for the nose, *dhupe*; a lamp for the eyes, *aloke*; scent for the mind, *gandhe*; and food for the tongue, *naividye*. The offerings are enjoyed without attachment to objects of desire through understanding the three doors to be deities.

As such, after having been protected from the obstacles of negative conditions, generated [the three doors] as deities, and [established] positive conditions through offerings, as an indication of the prediction of siddhi, there is the indication based on the tooth stick.

For reciting the actual tooth stick mantra, purify with the *svabhāva* mantra:

From the state of emptiness arises *hūṃ*, from which arise the tooth sticks, twelve fingerbreadths in length and topped with a flower, which have the power to indicate the prediction of siddhi for the vajra disciples.

By empowering them, you should imagine that the tooth stick held between your palms has been empowered for the purpose of indicating the prediction of your siddhi. With *oṃ āḥ jihva vajra saṃvartani svāhā*, imagine that your empowered toothstick is made of gold or silver, and as if you are scraping your teeth, light rays arise from the flower on top and travel through your mouth. Because they go inside, like an emetic administered by a skilled physician, imagine that you have vomited up all misdeeds and obscurations gathered since beginningless lifetimes to the arising of the gnosis of the empowerment. {258} Say *oṃ vajra hasa haṃ*, open your palms, and toss the tooth stick without looking at the enclosure.

Toss the tooth stick in an enclosure that is one square cubit, smeared with scent, and arranged with nine heaps.

If the flower of the tooth stick points to oneself, this represents excellent siddhi; if it points above, it represents the siddhi of flying in space; if it points below, it represents traveling beneath the ground; it if points east, pacifying siddhi; south, destructive siddhi; west, power siddhi; and if north, increasing siddhi.[10] If the tooth stick falls on an intermediate direction, it indicates the accomplishment of minor siddhis, such as the excellent vase, and so on. That is the method of rendering the disciple a suitable recipient of the vase empowerment. Just as the tooth stick purifies the taints of the body, such as those of one's mouth, teeth, and so on, one should also understand that the vase empowerment principally purifies the body.

Pour a handful of water to produce clear dreams and purify the taints of speech while reciting three times, *oṃ hrīḥ viśuddhaḥ sarvadharmāḥ sarvapāpaṃ nicasya saṃśoddhaya sarva vikalpāna apana hūṃ*.

That is the method of making the disciples suitable for receiving the secret empowerment. Just as the handful of water purifies your speech, also the secret empowerment purifies the taints of the voice.

The protection cord is given in order to prevent obstacles during dreams.

Recite *hūṃ* and, as above, cleanse and purify the yarn in which three vajra knots have been tied.

From the state of emptiness arises *hūṃ*, from which arises red yarn (equal in length to the bodies of the vajra disciples, coiled three times, and tied with three vajra knots), which has the ability

> to prevent obstacles to the vajra disciples' three doors. Light rays shine from the heart of the master, inviting the assembly of gnosis yarn from the hearts of the setup deities. They dissolve into the commitment yarn.

Pick up the protection cords between one's palms and recite the root mantra. {259}

> Having thus empowered them, tie the cords around the left upper arm of the men and the right upper arm of the women.

Having recited this, tie the cords according to the custom. Sprinkle them with a little vase water and stabilize this by reciting the one-hundred-syllable mantra that is found in the *Vajrapañjara Tantra*.

> That is the method of making disciples suitable for receiving the gnosis of the wisdom consort empowerment. While tying the protection cord is for preventing obstacles to the element, the basis of purification of the gnosis of the wisdom consort, the gnosis of the wisdom consort empowerment is also conferred upon the amṛta element.
>
> The kuśa grass is given in order that one's dreams be undisturbed and to consecrate one's mattress.

As above, cleanse and purify the long and short stalks of kuśa grass.

> From the state of emptiness arises a *dhiḥ*, from which arises a long and short stalk of kuśa grass, the base and tip of which are unequal, that are able to prevent disturbing dreams. Having thus empowered by reciting *dhiḥ*, the short kuśa-grass stalk is given to the right hand, and the long kuśa-grass stalk is given to the left. The meaning is that kuśa grass is the unsurpassed purificatory substance, and since the fourth empowerment removes all signs and concepts, giving the kuśa grass is the preliminary for the fourth empowerment. Just as the Bhagavān sat on a seat of undisturbed kuśa grass, one should lie on a mattress of kuśa. Having realized that dreams are illusory, the interdependent origination of the Buddha is employed as the path.

The explanation of the profound dharma in order to generate enthusiasm is:

In the world, the omniscient ones
are like uḍumbara flowers,
arising but rarely
or not at all.
Also, the means of Secret Mantra conduct
is rare—
the ability to perform the unsurpassed,
unequaled benefit of beings. {260}
Whoever has engaged in misdeeds
for many past tens of millions of eons
will exhaust those the moment this maṇḍala is seen—
what need is there to mention one who dwells
in the means of mantra conduct of infinite renown?
If one recites the protector's secret mantra,
one will attain the unsurpassed stage.
Those whose minds never waver concerning
this supreme conduct
will expel all suffering
and eliminate the lower realms.
Your unequalled attainment,
great beings, is a distant attainment.
Why? It is the doctrine the victors and their children,
all great beings, uphold.
While you are born,
you all will be born
into the Mahayana.
Greater than Mahayana,
this supreme path is glorious.
Since you are traversing this,
you will have the great, self-originated fortune
of a tathāgata:
omniscience about the world.[11]

The meaning of that is as follows: Just like uḍumbara flowers are rare in the world, buddhas are rare. When a buddha demonstrates the manner of attaining buddhahood in the world, in a region nearby an uḍumbara flower grows. If that buddha is born into a kshatriya family, the flower is white, and if born into a brahmin family, the flower is yellow. When that buddha is conceived, the flower buds out. When that buddha is born, it opens. When that buddha engages in youthful sports, it blossoms. When that buddha engages in ascetic practices, it becomes slightly faded. When the buddha shows the means of attaining buddhahood, it blossoms. When the buddha turns the wheel of dharma, it fully blossoms. When the buddha shows the means of nirvana, it falls off after drying out. Therefore, since both of those are equivalent in terms of rarity, a buddha's {262} advent into the world is rare. After such an advent, [there is] the teaching of the dharma. Within the dharma, the teaching of Mahāyāna is rare. Within Mahayana, the teaching of Secret Mantra Vajrayāna is most rare.

If it is wondered, "If it is so rare, of what benefit is it? Horns on a hare and sky flowers are also rare," they are not the same; the rare possess great beneficial qualities. If those who have gathered misdeeds for many tens of millions of eons indeed see the great maṇḍala, become purified, receive empowerment, are diligent in the samayas and vows, practice the conduct of mantra that protects the mind from signs and concepts, endeavor in the recitation of the secret mantras, and stabilize the mind in this path, through all of that, they will eliminate the stream of suffering of the three lower realms and existence. That being the case, the attainment of the omniscient is the supreme attainment, upheld through the wisdom, love, and power of all the victors and their children. Since you will be born into their family, there is no doubt that you will quickly become a tathāgata of wisdom who directly perceives the reality of the world, based upon the supreme path of Mahayana. Thus, you should be especially joyous.

Having generated such enthusiasm, in order to examine the dream and, if it is bad, to protect against it:

Listen, child! Sleep, for tomorrow
you will see the maṇḍala.
All that you see in your dream
should be related to me honestly.

In one's practice house one should have a comfortable mattress. Place the short stalk of kuśa given to you by the master under your pillow and place the long stalk under your mattress. Don clean clothes and lay down on your right side, {262} lying in the pose of the sleeping lion and putting at a distance from your mind all concepts of the three poisons. While recalling the deity and the guru, one should think, "Tomorrow I will see the maṇḍala of the pledged deity!" While one recalls such heartfelt joyful enthusiasm, go to sleep and a prophetic dream will arise. The signs of good dreams are said to be:

If one sees a buddha in one's dream,
it is like a direct perception of an ocean of qualities.
If one sees a stupa or a statue,
or is building a stupa,
or listening to the dharma from a pure bhikṣu,
or listening to anyone
practicing the dharma
or, likewise, reading sutras . . .[12]

If while dreaming you see a statue of the tathāgata or a stupa; hold a book of sublime dharma; are seated in an assembly of the sangha; listen to dharma from your guru; or if the sun and moon rise; if you are anointed a king; ride horses and elephants; are warmed during the day in a cave; are given a dharma talk by a pure bhikṣu; obtain excellent food of one hundred tastes; find treasures, such as a cache of rice, and so on; if many people bow to you; if you explain dharma to many people; meet your parents, guru or spouse; are adorned with clothes and jewels; and so on, it is a good dream. Having understood that you will attain excellent, medium, and average grades of mantra siddhi, you should joyfully meditate without attachment and celebrate.

If bad dreams occur, the signs are that you climb a red-lacquer mountain; gather oleander[13] blossoms; {263} climb on a tomb or a pile of sand or ash; ride backward on either a monkey or an ass; ride a pig, camel, or water buffalo; engage in intercourse with a women wearing black clothing; enter abysses and gorges; fall from mountains and trees; are eaten by dogs, crows, or cannibals;

are threatened by black men with iron cudgels, who shave one's hair, smear sesame oil on one's body, and bind one's skull with a red garland, and so on. If these occur, since it is somewhat negative, it is necessary to be diligent in the methods of preventing the results of such bad dreams—such as understanding that all phenomena are no different than appearances in dreams; soon after waking, thinking that in reality [dreams] are not even slightly established and sealing the dream by training in its falsity; receiving the reading transmission according to the intimate instructions of the lineage gurus of the yoga of the Buddha's eye and practicing that; and offering the fire puja of pacification, and so on.

After those activities of the setup of the disciples are carefully accomplished, tomorrow is the main subject, conferring the empowerment.

The significance of the main subject, conferring the empowerment, is:

You should generate supreme bodhicitta, thinking, "Mahāvajradhara's unsurpassed, perfect, complete buddhahood must be obtained in order to benefit all sentient beings. For that purpose, I will receive the empowerment that is more profound than the profound and practice its topics properly."

In order to continually practice the dharma that is received, one must request to hear it, having recalled how to do so in the precious tantras of Vajrayāna.

We have obtained a human body of freedom and endowments difficult to attain. We have met the doctrine of the Buddha difficult to meet. {264} At this occasion of practicing the path of Vajrayāna, the essence of the doctrine, it is necessary for us to engage in a pure, sublime dharma. The reason for that is while ultimately all sentient beings are endowed with naturally pure buddha nature, now, until the two temporary obscurations and their traces are abandoned, we are continually born in samsara, suffering without interruption. We can never transcend unbearable suffering, no matter where we are born in samsara. In order to place all those suffering sentient beings who have been our fathers and mothers on the stage of buddhahood, we must abandon all the pointless activities of this life and obtain the stage of Śrī Hevajra, whose nature is the union of nonreferential great compassion and great wisdom. Therefore, we should sincerely think, "For that purpose, having purified our continuums with the view that realizes twofold selflessness, we must receive the vase empowerment, which empowers us to meditate on the creation stage, and we must receive the three higher empowerments and their attendant teachings, which empower us to meditate on the completion stage."

Having finished everything up to the purification of the place in the setup rites, there are four types of rites in the main subject: drawing and ornamentation, accomplishment and offering, admittance and receiving the empowerment, and the concluding rites.

In drawing, there is drawing with the chalk lines, drawing with colored sand, arranging the hand symbols, and decorations. In the offering and accomplishment, there is accomplishment by means of actualizing the commitment maṇḍala through the preliminary self-generation; {265} the accomplishment by means of empowering the sense bases and body, speech, and mind; the accomplishment by means of inviting the gnosis maṇḍala; and the accomplishment by means of conferring the empowerment and sealing with the master of the family. Having accomplished these four types, inwardly there is pleasing the maṇḍala with offerings and outwardly there is satisfying the host of bhūtas with offerings. I have carefully accomplished these beforehand.

If the empowerment is being given into a cloth maṇḍala, prior to "In the rites of the main subject" above, [say,] "In the offering and accomplishment . . . I have carefully accomplished these beforehand."

For the admittance and conferral of empowerment, there are two subjects: the master's self-admittance and taking empowerment, and the disciple's self-admittance and conferral of the empowerment. First, with respect to the self-admittance and taking empowerment, all empowerments conferred upon the student are taken [by the master] in the manner of self-admittance. Those have also been carefully accomplished. Following those, the mundane and transcendent bali offerings to please the outer and inner ḍākinīs, singing the song of the three samayas in order to admit the disciples, and proclaiming the truth of suchness have already been accomplished.

Now, for your portion, in the admittance and conferral of empowerment upon the disciples, there are two topics: being admitted to the maṇḍala for the purpose of matching the fortune of the deity and, having been admitted, the actual rite of conferring the empowerment.

As it says:

Offer a maṇḍala and supplication,
the vows should be done according to the sequence of proclaiming and taking them,
tie the blindfold and distribute the garland of flowers,
purify with Amṛtakuṇḍali, question and reply,
generate inner bodhicitta, the instruction of secrecy, {266}
admit into the maṇḍala and place in samaya,
offer a maṇḍala and supplication,
descent and stabilization of the gnosis being,
supplicate, inquire about color, praise,
offer the flower, loosen the blindfold,
begin to explain the maṇḍala, ...[14]

To begin, possessing the conviction that the master is truly Śrī Hevajra, the essence of all tathāgatas of the three times, you should offer a maṇḍala as a gift for requesting admittance into the maṇḍala. Having offered such a maṇḍala, recite this supplication after me three times:

Embraced by Nairātmyā about the neck,
Great Joy, please teach me.
Master, please head me!
Great protector, please explain to me
the method of great awakening.
Please grant me the samayas.
Also please grant me bodhicitta.
Please grant me the three refuges:

the Buddha, dharma, and sangha.
Protector, please grant me entry
into the supreme city of great freedom.

To obtain the samaya called "the true samaya of the principal aspiration through offering supplication," there is both obtaining samaya through a promise and through a rite.
In order to obtain samaya through a promise, listen to this proclamation, which discloses those samayas:

> I go for refuge to the Triple Gem:
> the Buddha, the dharma, and the sangha.
> This is to stabilize the vows
> of the pure buddha family.

Also, the mudra of the vajra and bell
should be held by you of great intelligence.
Whatever bodhicitta is, it is the vajra. {267}
Wisdom is explained to be the bell.
You should uphold the master;
the guru is equivalent with a buddha.
This is the samaya vow of the
pure vajra family that you should uphold.

For the great supreme jewel family,
constantly offer the four kinds of generosity—
things, fearlessness, dharma, and loving kindness—
three times during the day and three times at night.

You must uphold the sublime dharma
of the three yānas: outer, inner, and secret.
This is said to be the samaya vow
of the pure lotus family.

For the great, supreme karma family,
one must correctly uphold
all vows that one possesses.
Also, one should engage in the activity of offering as much as possible.

The fourteen others are
fully explained as defeats.
What is to be avoided and what is never to be discarded
are explained as "the root downfalls,"
recited every day,
three times during the day and at night.
If there is a violation, the practitioner
has a gross fault.

You must never kill creatures,
never take what has not been given,
never engage in sexual misconduct,
and never tell lies.
One must avoid alcohol,
the root of all ruin.
Apart from benefiting sentient beings,
there is nothing to do—avoid everything.

One should rely upon sublime people.
One should venerate all practitioners.
The three actions of the body,
the four of the voice,
and the three of the mind
must be guarded as much as possible.

Do not wish for the Hīnayāna,
do not turn your back on the benefit of sentient beings,
also do not abandon samsara,
and never have desire for nirvana.

You must not belittle
that which is concealed to devas and asuras.
Do not step over mudras, seats, weapons, {268}
or signs.

These are explained to be the samayas.
You must always guard them.

The vast samayas to emulate
are explained in the secret tantras.

The meaning of that is as follows: The samaya of Vairocana is upholding the outer, inner, and secret Three Jewels as places of refuge. Just as Vairocana is the support for all qualities because he is the body of all buddhas, he is also the support for all vows because of the vow of holding the three refuges.

The samaya of Vajrākṣobhya is upholding the outer, inner, and secret; the bell and vajra; and the masters. Just as Akṣobhya is the essence of bodhicitta, the three samayas and the master are also held with bodhicitta.

The samaya of Ratnasambhava is giving things, fearlessness, dharma, and loving kindness, three times during the day and three times during the night, and the six acts of generosity. If unable to do so in actuality, you must never be separate from the aspiration to do so. Just as Ratnasambhava, the essence of generosity, purifies greed, generosity is the antidote to abandoning the poor and greed.

The samayas of the lotus family, Amitābha, are promising to uphold the sublime dharma of action tantra and conduct tantra outwardly; yoga tantra inwardly; unsurpassed yoga secretly; and the three vehicles, śrāvakayāna, pratyekabuddhayāna, and bodhisattvayāna. Just as Amitābha, the essence of wisdom, purifies speech, also the dharma is upheld by wisdom and taught with speech.

The samaya of the karma family, Amoghasiddhi, is keeping all the samayas and making effort in the activities of offerings. Just as Amoghasiddhi, the essence of diligence, is the nature of activity, {269} also, both keeping the vows of diligence in the practice of virtue and making offerings to the buddhas preserve the activities of the buddhas.

Having proclaimed the samayas of the individual five families, in the proclamation of the general samayas of the five families, there are two topics: the general explanation of the three disciplines and the individual explanations. First, the two verses, "The fourteen others are . . . ," refer to the explanation in the

> *Ākāśagarbha Sutra* that there is one downfall for a bodhisattva king, one for a bodhisattva minister, four shared downfalls for the king and minister, and eight for novice bodhisattvas. Those show that there are fourteen vows that require protection.
>
> In the individual explanations, there is the discipline of refraining from faulty conduct, gathering virtuous dharmas, and acting on behalf of sentient beings. The first is covered by the two verses, "You must never kill creatures . . . ." The discipline of refraining from faulty conduct is any of the seven kinds of bodhisattva individual liberation vows[15] obtained according to their respective rites. If someone has not obtained those, then at the time of the setup and the admittance, the individual liberation vows that are obtained are equivalent to the vows of a full upāsaka. It is taught that those four bases of training and the fifth concerning alcohol should not be forsaken, other than to benefit others. Gathering virtuous dharmas is the six lines, "One should rely upon sublime people . . . ," practicing the ten virtues through relying on sublime people and practitioners who practice virtue, because those ten include all practices of the perfections. {270}
>
> Acting on behalf of sentient beings is the single verse, "Do not wish for the Hīnayāna . . . ," which demonstrates that it is necessary to accomplish the benefit of sentient beings through abandoning all negative factors for acting on behalf of sentient beings.
>
> The proclamation of the summary of those is the single verse, "You must not belittle . . . ," which demonstrates abandoning conduct harmful to others, causing others to lose faith, and needing to protect not only the individual liberation and bodhisattva vows but also the samayas explained in the lower tantras, such as the *Secret Tantra of General Rites*, and so on, since the vows of the lower tantras are also included in the higher tantras. Focus upon this while keeping the meaning of those in mind.

Thus, for the disclosure, recite the daily confession, as in the setup: "I go for refuge to the Three Jewels . . . to benefit migrating beings."

> After you have purified your continuum, thinking that you will uphold the general and specific vows of the five families, recite the following after me three times:

All buddhas and bodhisattvas,
all heroes and yoginīs, please heed me!
From this time forward
until the seat of awakening is attained,
I, the vidyādhara, will generate
the sublime, unsurpassed bodhicitta
that definitely causes the awakening
of the protectors of the three times.

The training of discipline,
collecting positive dharmas,
and acting for the benefit of sentient beings are the three
disciplines,
each of which I will firmly uphold.

From this time forward, I will firmly uphold
the unsurpassed Three Jewels—
the Buddha, dharma, and sangha—
and the vows arising from the yoga of the Buddha.

For the great, supreme vajra family,
I shall truly uphold
the vajra, bell, and mudra.
I will also uphold the masters. {271}

For the pleasing samayas
of the great, supreme jewel family,
I shall always present the four kinds of offerings
daily during the six time periods.

For the pure, great lotus family
that arises from great awakening,
I will uphold all sublime dharmas
of the outer, inner, and secret yānas.

For the great, supreme karma family,
as I possess all vows,
I will truly uphold them,

performing whatever activities of offering I can.

Having generated
the sublime, unsurpassed bodhicitta,
I shall maintain all vows
for the benefit of all sentient beings.

I shall free those who are not free.
I shall liberate those who are not liberated.
I shall provide solace to those without solace.
I shall place all sentient beings in nirvana.

Having promised to uphold the samayas and vows, the samayas and vows that should be upheld arise primarily from the empowerment. Since you must be admitted to the maṇḍala prior to the conferral of the empowerment, whether or not you have been admitted to the maṇḍala of Śrī Hevajra and have received the empowerment previously, the symbol of admittance is that one should imagine that one has been blindfolded.

Tie the blindfolds and utter:

ākhaṃ vīra hūṃ

When you meet the deity of the maṇḍala, it is improper to meet the deity empty-handed. You should imagine that you have a string of flowers of the five families held in your hands, which is given with the mantra, *ākhaṃ vīra hūṃ*.

An inconceivable host of Amṛtakuṇḍalis leaves from the heart of the master. Imagine that they frighten all the obstructors and misleaders who cause obstacles for those receiving the empowerment far away.

Sprinkle water from the activity vase and recite:

oṃ vajra amṛtakuṇḍali hana hana hūṃ hūṃ hūṃ phaṭ {272}

Having prevented obstacles, ask the disciples:

For the purpose of ascertaining your family,
child, who are you and what would you like?

Recite after the master with the conviction that you are giving the reply, "I am a fortunate one who would like great bliss."

"Child, how is that to be done?"

Recite after the master with the conviction that you are giving a reply, "With the samaya of supreme buddhahood."

With that desire for the samaya of supreme buddhahood's supreme, unchanging great bliss, the visualization for the purpose of generating the bodhicitta of inner Secret Mantra is done in the following way: You should develop intense relative bodhicitta by thinking that you will accomplish unsurpassed benefits for all sentient beings. Imagine that its form arises as a complete moon maṇḍala, like the full moon. Think that the reality of all phenomena is bliss and emptiness free from all extremes of proliferation, like space. Imagine that its form arises as a white, five-tined vajra radiating light on top of that moon maṇḍala. Repeat the following recitation: *oṃ sarvayoga citta utpādayāmi.*

Imagine that the bodhicitta generated in all yogas is stabilized by placing the vajra on the heart. *oṃ surati samayastvaṃ siddhyavajra yathā sukhaṃ*

Since the generation of the bodhicittas is the outer admittance, it is extremely important to introduce its significance, "It is improper to speak of the generation of bodhicitta and the continual practice of Secret Mantra below in the presence of those who are not suitable recipients." {273} The instruction for secrecy is, "Henceforth, you have been fully admitted into the family of all tathāgatas and all heroes and yoginīs, and you should not speak of the sublime, great secret of all tathāgatas in the presence of those who have not been admitted into the maṇḍala of all tathāgatas, nor to those who lack faith." Thus, this is the outer admittance for those who have been instructed in secrecy.

For the purposes of inner admittance, you must imagine that you take hold of the vajra in the master's hand and you are admitted through the eastern door of the maṇḍala. Bow your head in the direction of the maṇḍala, and repeat *hūṃ jaḥ hūṃ* or *jaḥ hūṃ baṃ hoḥ*. Reciting this mantra with the above conviction, one should imagine one has been placed in the eastern door of the maṇḍala.

The preliminary for the inner admittance is the four placements in samaya. The first is placement in samaya through its benefits. If you are going to obtain the siddhis of all tathāgatas through some gnosis, not to mention other siddhis, you who have generated such vajra gnosis must not speak of it in front of those who have not seen the great maṇḍala, or, child, you will violate your samaya.

Placement in samaya through reflecting on faults is:

Śrī Heruka, now this
has truly entered your heart.
If you speak of these methods,
it will truly burst and you will die.

Also, this is placement in samaya through reflecting on faults: This is your samaya vajra. If you speak to anyone about these means, it will split your head. For the placement in samaya through the oath water, give the water of the victorious vase poured in the dharma conch:

This is your hell water.
If you violate samaya, it will burn.
If you guard samaya, siddhis
will be accomplished with this vajra amṛta.

oṃ pañca amṛta udaka ṭha ṭha ṭha

The placement in samaya through the guru's command is "Henceforth, child, you should say, 'I, Śrī Heruka, shall do this!' It is necessary for you to do that. You must never belittle me. If you do, being unable to avoid terror at the time of death, you will be a sentient being falling into the great hell." Thus, these are the preliminary placements in samaya.

Now, for the main part of the inner admittance, offer a maṇḍala as a gift for requesting the descent of gnosis. Having offered the maṇḍala, recite this supplication after me three times, "Empowered by all the tathāgatas, Śrī Heruka, please let this descend upon me!"

Having offered the supplication, your bodies should be in a position with your knees drawn up, without leaning on anything. Placing your palms together while holding a flower, your minds should not be distracted while performing the following visualization: One should understand that all phenomena are natureless, like reflections or illusions. From that state, you appear in the form of Heruka. Below your feet there is a *yaṃ*, from which arises a blue air maṇḍala in the shape of a drawn bow, with the two handles facing downward and the two tips facing up, marked with waving pennants. Above that, having spread your legs, on the two soles of the feet, there is a green syllable *jhaiṃ*, intense and difficult to bear. From the *raṃ* in between your legs, there is a red, triangular red maṇḍala marked with flames. In the heart, arising from *laṃ*, {275} there is a square yellow earth maṇḍala, marked with three-tined vajras on the four corners and a *hūṃ* in the center. At your throat, from *vaṃ* arises a round white water maṇḍala, marked with a vase and an *a*. On your crown, an air maṇḍala marked with *ha* arises from *yāṃ*, like thick smoke.

With the conviction that the master is the real Vajrasattva, light shines from the heart of the master, striking the air maṇḍala below your feet, stirring the air, igniting the fire at your groin, and igniting the *jhaiṃ* at the soles of the feet, with the fire entering the ankles and meeting in the region of the groin. Since that blazes intensely, it heats the earth maṇḍala at your heart. The foam of the boiling water maṇḍala of the throat falls on the earth maṇḍala at your heart. Then, lifted up by the air maṇḍala below the feet and pressed down by the air maṇḍala of the crown, imagine you vibrate in space. At that time, light rays shine from the heart of the master, and all buddhas and bodhisattvas are absorbed, dissolving into all of your pores, falling like a great snow blizzard.

Wave the vajra and ring the bell, recite the following mantra, and use incense and play music:

hūṃ a ha jhaiṃ and *aveśaya stvaṃbhaya stvaṃbhaya ra ra ra ra ca la ya ca la ya hūṃ a ha jhaiṃ*

At the time of the cause empowerment, perform this visualization for the purpose of gain: Upon your heads is the sublime guru, in adult form, with both hands in the mudra of equipoise, and seated with both legs in vajra posture. Through the condition of strong conviction in that, since the guru dissolves into one's crown, imagine your continuum has been empowered.

Recite the root mantra many times, use incense, and play music.

As such, imagine that the stream of the empowering descent of gnosis is stabilized by placing the crossed vajra on one's crown.
tiṣṭha vajra

Having stabilized the descent of gnosis, the signs are that if it descends into your body, you can dance in the sky. If it falls on your speech, you can speak in Sanskrit. If it falls on your mind, you can know the three times, and so on. Having recognized those, they should be brought onto the path.

As such, for the purpose of introducing that descent of gnosis with the excellent deity, the master should offer a supplication to the maṇḍala:

Admit my disciples
into the essential maṇḍala,
the abode of all tathāgatas,
the supreme city of Śrī Heruka.

May the stage of the family
and, likewise, the stage of merit
become whichever family is suitable.
However much merit there is here,

likewise, may it be so here in the maṇḍala.

Having offered this supplication, you must look with your blindfolds into the sky in front of the maṇḍala for the purpose of investigating the signs of siddhi and tell me which color you see.

The master asks, "Oh, what appears to your sight? If it is white, then you will accomplish pacifying; yellow, increasing; red, power; blue or black, destroying; green, multicolored, or banded, various activities."

After having investigated the signs of siddhi, the praise through understanding that all deities of the master are the complete three seats is:

Homage and praise to Dveṣavajrā.
Homage and praise to Mohavajrā.
Supplications to Mātsaryavajrā.
Protect me, Rāgavajrā.
Be proud, great Īrṣyāvajrā.
All are the supreme samaya of all vajras.
Accomplish the activities. {277}
May I please all vajra holders.

Next, presenting a flower to the maṇḍala is as follows: The maṇḍala of Bhagavān Śrī Hevajra exists here, other than displaying the form of the principal and retinue in order for the singular gnosis of perfect, complete buddhahood to tame those to be tamed, in its essence there exists neither good nor evil. Nevertheless, thinking, "May the flower fall on the deity for which I have gathered karma," say *oṃ praticcha vajra hoḥ* and present the flower.

Meditate on that and present the flower. The deity upon which [the flower] falls is ascertained to be the one with whom one's karma is closest. That flower is then taken by the master:

oṃ pratigrihṇa stvāṃ imaṃ satva mahābala

Having addressed the deity, imagine that they once again return the flower garland.

The flower is placed on the head of the disciple, and the blindfold is removed.

oṃ
Vajrasattva, henceforth
you shall endeavor to open your eye
and see all differences—
the vajra eye is unsurpassed.

Hevajra pāśya means "Hevajra, look!" It is the command to look carefully at the maṇḍala. Once again, the encouragement to look at the maṇḍala is:

Mahāsattva, look, look
at the supreme city of great freedom.
Wherever the flower falls,
that is you, Heruka.
Look at this excellent maṇḍala;
now generate faith in this.
You have been born into the family of the buddhas,
empowered by mantra and mudra.
You have been born into the family of yoginīs;
you must preserve the samayas
and also endeavor in the mantras.

Further, the maṇḍala of Śrī Hevajra exists here. Outside of it is the vajra fence, {278} a pavilion, and volcanoes. Within the protection wheel are the eight charnel grounds (totally full with corpses, zombies, and so on), in which there are eight trees; the eight directional guardians who dwell at the root of those trees; the eight clouds that are in the sky above them; the eight great nāgas residing there; the eight field guardians that reside in the branches of the trees; and also the eight ponds, eight fires, eight stupas, eight heroic siddhas, eight yoginīs, eight ghosts, eight ḍākas, and eight ḍākinīs. Surrounded by the eight charnel grounds, there is a thirty-two-petaled lotus inside of a dharmodaya. In the center, there is sun disc, upon which there is a square celestial mansion of great freedom with four doors. Inside there are walls composed of five layers: black, green, red, yellow, and white. On top of the walls, there is a precious yellow ledge, from which hang decorative strands and tassels. Above, it is adorned with a parapet and gutters. Outside the walls on a red peristyle filled with desired objects, sixteen goddesses present many offering substances to the Bhagavān. Within the walls, there are eight pillars. Upon those, there are four vajra beams with checker-pattern designs and a beautiful lintel. Narrowing in the center, the celestial mansion is adorned with a vajra and a jeweled finial.

In front of each of the four doors, there are four pillars, which support a four-stepped portico, upon which there is a wheel of dharma, an umbrella, and a pair of deer.

Moreover, the celestial mansion is adorned with many ornaments, such as drapes, streamers, garlands of flowers, {279} moons moved by the wind, yak-tail whisks with jeweled handles, and so on.

Within this, there is a dais for the deities: the east side is white, the south side is yellow, the west side is red, the north side is green, and the center is blue. In the middle, there is a multicolored, eight-petaled lotus, in the center of which is a sun maṇḍala. Upon the sun is the essence of the four māras (such as affliction, and so on) in the form of yellow Brahma, white Indra, blue Upendra, and black Rudra. All are stacked one upon the other. Upon the moon maṇḍalas on each of the eight petals, yellow Brahma is in the east, white Indra is in the south, blue Upendra is in the west, black Rudra is in the north, blue Yama is in the northeast, yellow Kubera is in the southeast, black Rākṣasa is in the southwest, and smoke-colored Vemacitra is in the northwest. They all lie facing upward, serving as the seats of the [eight] directions. This is the supporting celestial mansion.

The supported deities are as follows: In the east, black Gaurī holds a curved knife in her right hand and a rohita fish in her left hand. In the south, purple Caurī holds a ḍamaru in her right hand and a pig in her left hand. In the west, yellow Vetālī holds a tortoise in her right hand and a skull cup in her left hand. In the north, green Ghasmarī holds a snake in her right hand and a skull in her left hand. In the northeast, blue Pukkasī holds a lion in her right hand and an ax in her left hand. In the southeast, white Śavarī holds a bhikṣu in her right hand and a mendicant's staff in her left hand. In the southwest, red Caṇḍālī holds a wheel in her right hand and a plow in her left hand. In the northwest, multicolored Ḍombinī holds a vajra in her right hand and makes a threatening gesture with her left hand. Surrounded by these eight goddesses, in the center is Bhagavān Essence Hevajra, who is blue, with eight faces, sixteen hands, and four feet. {280} The principal face is blue, the right face is white, the left face is red, the upper face is smoke-colored, and the remaining two pairs of faces are black. Each face has three eyes, four bared fangs, and upswept yellow hair. The crown is marked with a crossed vajra. The sixteen hands hold sixteen skull cups. The skull cup in the first right hand contains a white elephant. The skull cup in the first left hand contains yellow Pṛthvī. Those two hands embrace the consort. In the other right hands, the second skull cup contains a blue horse; the third, an ass with a blaze; the fourth, a yellow ox; the fifth, an ash-colored camel; the sixth, a red man; the seventh, a blue śarabha; and the eighth skull cup contains a cat with a blaze.

In the other left hands, the second skull cup contains white Varuṇa; the third, red Agni; the fourth, green Vāyu; the fifth, white Candra; the sixth, red Sūrya; the seventh, blue Yama; and the eighth skull cup contains yellow Kubera.

On each head, there is a head ornament with five dried human heads. The father has a necklace of fifty fresh heads. He possesses six bone ornaments. He stands in the ardhaparyaṅka dancing posture, with the toes of the two left legs pointed toward the thighs of the two extended right legs.

He has nine dramatic moods:
graceful, heroic, hideous,
laughing, shouting, terrifying,
compassionate, ferocious, and peaceful.

In his lap is the mother, blue Vajranairātmyā, who has one face, two hands, three eyes, and upswept yellow hair. She holds a curved knife in her right hand and clasps the father with her left hand, which holds a skull cup. She wears a head ornament with five dried human heads and a necklace of fifty dried skulls. She possesses five bone ornaments. {281} Her left leg is extended and her right leg wraps around the father. The couple stand in the midst of a blazing fire of gnosis.

As such, with a mind joyful at the thought, "I have seen the whole maṇḍala of the supported deities and their support," imagine one prostrates at the feet of the master. Repeat the following:

oṃ
I have been admitted to the maṇḍala
of the great vajra maṇḍala.

oṃ
I have seen the maṇḍala
of the great yoga maṇḍala.

oṃ
Confer the empowerment upon me in the maṇḍala
of the great secret maṇḍala.

samaya hoḥ hoḥ hoḥ

This is the dharma of admittance into the maṇḍala for the purpose of having fortune equal with the deity.

Having been admitted, for the actual empowerment—the first of the two empowerments, the vajra-disciple empowerment and the vajra master empowerment—as it is said:

Offer a maṇḍala and a supplication,
generate the deity, dispel misfortune, recite the benediction,
confer the empowerments of
the water, crown, vajra,
bell, name, strict vow,
and if one wishes, give the reading transmission for the mantras.[16]

First, present a maṇḍala as a gift for requesting the vajra disciple empowerment. Having offered such a maṇḍala, recite this supplication after me three times:

Just as a great offering was bestowed
upon the Buddha by Bodhivajra,
please grant me now the vajra of space
for the purpose of protecting me.

Having offered this supplication, perform this visualization to dispel misfortune: In the eastern region of the maṇḍala, there is the maṇḍala of the empowerment platform, which is square, with four doors beautified by four porticos, and with a peristyle, lintel, strands and tassels, whisks, a parapet, and so on, {282} totally complete in all characteristics. In the center of a jeweled throne supported on lions, a lotus, a sun, and the four seats piled up, you are Bhagavān Essence Hevajra, who is blue, with eight faces and sixteen arms, and in union with Vajranairātmyā. If one prefers, recall the complete hands and faces. Imagine that to the right and left of that are purified articles; above, there is a canopy; on the right, an umbrella; on the left, a victory banner; and surrounding all of this are inconceivable kinds of offerings of conches, streamers, flower garlands, and so on. Imagine one purifies with the four water offerings: *oṃ nīri hūṃ khaṃ svāhā oṃ vajra nivite hūṃ khaṃ svāhā oṃ sarvasaṃśodhani svāhā, oṃ arghaṃ praticcha hūṃ.*

All your misdeeds and obscurations gathered throughout beginningless lifetimes are expelled through your nostrils in the form of the seed syllable of misdeeds, *kaṃ*, and dissolve into the sesame seeds in front. Imagine that a heruka, inseparable from the *karma vajra,*[17] separates from the heart of the master; burns the sesame seeds on the right, the essence of your misdeeds and obscurations; and throws them into the ocean of dharmatā on the left, *oṃ sarvapāpaṃ dahana vajrāya vajrasatvya sarvapāpaṃ dahana svāhā*. Thus, you should imagine that you have been purified with water, *oṃ hūṃ ḍa ḍi ta phaṭ*. May all bad luck, misfortune, and inauspicious signs of the vajra disciples be pacified! Having dispelled misfortune, imagine that the master and the retinue lift the victorious vase and recite the rite of benediction:

The first virtuous fortune of the world
is the Buddha, endowed with eyes that resemble lotus blossoms. {283}
The protector of the three realms who has abandoned the three taints
is endowed with abundance, resembling a mountain of gold.

The second virtuous fortune of the world
is the Buddha's immovable, supreme doctrine,
the sublime dharma that pacifies all living beings, which is
renowned throughout the three realms, and to which devas and humans present offerings.

The third virtuous fortune of the world
is the sublime sangha, endowed with the dharma, enriched through hearing,
an object of offering for humans, devas, and asuras.
The supreme assembly is conscientious and the basis of prestige.
Those are the three virtuous fortunes of the world.

Whatever may be the good fortune of the tathāgata,
coming here from the center of the celestial mansion of Tuṣitā
in order to benefit beings, followed by Indra and the devas,
by that good fortune, henceforth, here may you have peace.

Whatever may be the good fortune that in his last existence
the protector was born in the Lumbini grove
amid shining leaves and a rain of flowers and attended by many devas,
by that good fortune, henceforth, here may you have peace.

Whatever may be the good fortune of abandoning home
at midnight to pursue asceticism with delight
in order to conquer those with various faults, followed by Indra and the devas,

by that good fortune, henceforth, here may you have peace.

Whatever may be the good fortune of being encircled with a
garland of offerings on the banks of a river,
causing astonishment in order to pacify, purify existence,
and be highly praised by the king of nāgās,
by that good fortune, henceforth, here may you have peace.

Whatever may be the good fortune of the tathāgata's
accomplishment of inconceivable virtue,
having been praised by a deva of great, amazing renown
in that supreme city called Kapilavastu, {284}
by that good fortune, henceforth, here may you have peace.

Whatever may be the good fortune of diligently accomplishing
the extensive benefit of sentient beings,
the collection of precious, sublime dharma arose from the Muni,
the one who awakened in order to benefit sentient beings.
By that good fortune, henceforth, here may you have peace.

Whatever may be the good fortune of possessing a body that
blazes with light like the color of gold,
being seated on a grass seat like the color of sapphire
and being seated cross-legged with an immovable body,
by that good fortune, henceforth, here may you have peace.

Whatever may be the good fortune of the Bhagavān conquering
the hordes of māras with loving kindness at the base of the king of
trees
and the various amazing forms in heaven and earth,
by that good fortune, henceforth, here may you have peace.

Whatever may be the good fortune of the tathāgata giving
teachings,
having entered Vārāṇasī with amazing signs filling the earth and
heavens
and turning the sublime dharma wheel,

by that good fortune, henceforth, here may you have peace.

In order to offer and uphold the sublime benefit of whatever good fortune there is,
the meritorious deeds praised by the noble ones
are the virtues taught by the Bhagavān, the Lion of the Śākyas.
By that good fortune, henceforth, here may you have peace.[18]

After the vajra disciples are victorious over all negative conditions to be abandoned, may they have the best good fortune!

Having accomplished those preliminaries for conferring the empowerment, in the main subject, conferring the empowerment, one should ascertain the following: The ultimate, connate, great, natural luminosity pervades all migrating beings. {285} But for as long as they unceasingly appear as aggregates, sense bases, and sense elements, which arise based on grasping "I" and "mine," through the power of the deluded traces of the relative, they experience only suffering. Therefore, it is necessary to purify the mind itself, which is the basis for samsara and nirvana. Thus, the introduction to the object of purification and the purifier in the topics of the empowerment through stabilizing the certain knowledge of the connate nature of the mind as the ultimate vow is very important. Sakya Paṇḍita states:

> Empowerment is not merely a gateway for dharma.
> Since Secret Mantra employs dependent origination as the path,
> it is the instruction for arranging dependent origination.
> Having planted the seed of buddhahood
> in the aggregates, sense bases, and sense elements,
> the method of causing buddhahood in this lifetime
> is given the name "empowerment."[19]

Hence, it is said to be necessary to arrange all outer and inner dependent originations of buddhahood through the four empowerments. Further, the impure appearances in the relative are purified by the purities of the individual deities through possession of the wisdom that understands purity in the basis of purification, natural purity.

If it is asked if there is liberation through that, one's mind appears as impure as a deluded entity. Having purified that [impurity] through mantra and understood [one's mind] in a personally intuited gnosis, there is liberation through meditating on the deity. Purification is valid because of natural purity, and purification is necessary because of temporary, impure taints. Since that naturally pure aspect is engaged through clinging to freedom from temporary taints, that method is liberating because it is nondeceptive by being engaged and connected with clinging. Further, the coarse basis of purification is the thirty-two phenomena that appear as the aggregates, sense bases, and sense elements. {286} There are thirty-two coarse concepts that apprehend those objects of purification as ordinary. The purifier is the thirty-two deities of the complete three seats. Since the mode of purification is "changing the color" of that which appears as the phenomena of the basis of purification into the deity or gnosis, the result of purification is transforming [the phenomena of the basis of the purification] into the thirty-two deities of the complete three seats.

Since it is necessary to understand the three seats forward and backward, the three seats are the seat of the male and female tathāgatas, the seat of the male and female bodhisattvas, and the seat of the male and female wrathful ones.

The three seats actually complete in the maṇḍala in the sky will be invited below. The three seats are complete in the front-created maṇḍala, the master and empowerment substances generated as deities, and in those who have been generated [in the form of the deity] though the purities. Also, among those four, the aggregates, sense bases, and sense elements of the disciples are empowered as the complete three seats, complete through the activities of the three seats. The three seats in disciples that have been generated as deities are understood as complete through the purities. Since they receive the empowerment through meditation, it is very important to understand these. In the actual rite, in the first of the two—the empowerment of the five families conferred based on oneself as the excellent deity and the empowerment that empowers body, speech, and mind based on Mahāvajradhara—for each of the empowerments of the five families, the purity of the three spheres is empowered through the four [limbs]. For instance, through empowering the three spheres with these four limbs in the Akṣobhya empowerment, prior to the crown empowerment, only the disciples and the empowerment substance change. Though only the yoga of Akṣobhya is relevant, since the normal custom is done here, it should be visualized in this way.

The master recites:

oṃ svabhāva śuddha sarvadharma svabhāva śuddho'haṃ
My aggregate of consciousness, the empowerment substance (the water of the victorious vase), and the vajra master vanish, becoming emptiness. All three arise from the state of emptiness as *hūṃ* upon a lotus and sun, which transform into vajras marked with *hūṃ*. Light rays shine from those vajras and return, each transforming into a blue Akṣobhya-Hevajra, with eight faces, sixteen arms, and four feet. Of the sixteen hands, the right hands hold an elephant, horse, ass, ox, camel, man, śarabha, and cat; the left hands hold Pṛthivī, Varuṇa, Agni, Vāyu, Candra, Sūrya, Yama, and Kubera. His crown is marked with a black vajra. He is in union with his consort, blue Māmakī, who holds a curved knife and a skull. The couple is adorned with bone ornaments.

Mohavajrā is in the eyes,
Dveṣavajrā is in the ears,
Mātsaryavajra is in the nose,
Rāgavajrā is in the mouth,
Īrṣyāvajrā is in the body,
and Nairātmyāyoginī is in the mind.

Kāyavajrā is in the crown, Vakvajrā is in the throat, and Cittavajrā is in the heart.
Light rays shine from *hūṃ* in their hearts, invoking all tathāgatas of the ten directions in the form of the Akṣobhya couple.

Invite with the mudra:

> *oṃ vajra samājaḥ*
>
> *Jaḥ hūṃ baṃ hoḥ*, they dissolve into you; *jaḥ hūṃ baṃ hoḥ*, they dissolve into the empowerment substances generated as deities; and *jaḥ hūṃ baṃ hoḥ*, they dissolve into the master. Again, light rays shine from *hūṃ* in their hearts, inviting the empowerment deities: the five tathāgatas, the four mothers, the eight bodhisattvas, the six goddesses, and the ten wrathful ones, *oṃ vajra samājaḥ*.

Invite with the *vajra samājaḥ* mantra and mudra. {288}

> Offer a supplication: "All tathāgatas, please confer the actual empowerment here."
>
> They reply, *oṃ vajribhāva abhiṣiñca hūṃ*, conferring empowerment upon the deities of the master and empowerment substances. Their bodies fill with water, purifying taints. The excess water overflows, transforming into Akṣobhya, who adorns their heads. The empowerment substance, the Akṣobhya couple, enter into union and melt, transforming into the empowerment substance, the water of the victorious vase.
>
> In order for you to completely accomplish the four limbs, recite this supplication after me:
>
> All bhagavān tathāgatas,
> the great bhagavāns,
> and those with a compassionate nature—
> please confer the empowerment upon me.
>
> Having offered this supplication, imagine that the embodied maṇḍala in the sky and the master simultaneously raise the vase filled with the gnosis amṛta, in which the three seats are complete and which has the nature of Akṣobhya, and confer the empowerment upon you, appearing as Akṣobhya, through your crown:
>
> The great vajra empowerment
> from the three secrets of all buddhas

is granted to the one
to whom all in the three realms prostrate.[20]

oṃ vajribhava abhiṣiñca hūṃ

The tathāgatas confer the empowerment, the knowledge consorts sing vajra songs, the bodhisattvas recite benedictions, the wrathful ones frighten away obstructors, and the goddesses present offerings. The stream of empowerment water fills you to the brow, you obtain the vase empowerment, and the taints of your body are purified. It fills down to the level of the throat, and you obtain the secret empowerment. It fills down to the heart center, {289} and you obtain the gnosis empowerment of the wisdom consort. It fills your whole body, and you obtain the fourth empowerment of supreme great bliss. The taints of your body, voice, and mind and their traces are purified. The remaining water overflows, adorning your head with Akṣobhya. Imagine offerings are presented by the goddesses who reside in the sky: *oṃ vajra puṣpe āḥ hūṃ oṃ vajra dhupe āḥ hūṃ oṃ vajra āloke āḥ hūṃ oṃ vajra gandhe āḥ hūṃ oṃ vajra naividye āḥ hūṃ.*

As such, one has received the empowerment of water through Akṣobhya, hatred is purified, the aggregate of consciousness is transformed, the mirrorlike gnosis is actualized, and the seed of Akṣobhya is planted in one's continuum.

In what follows, having skipped generating the master as the deity and the invitation of the empowerment deities, apart from changing the deity and the empowerment substance, the sequence of the rite is the same. Recite the visualization for the purpose of the crown empowerment of Ratnasambhava in this way:

svabhāva . . .
Your aggregate of sensation and the empowerment substance (the crown) vanish, becoming emptiness. Both arise from the state of emptiness as *āṃ* upon a lotus and sun, which transform into jewels marked with *āṃ*. Rays of light shine from those jewels and return, each transforming into a yellow Ratnasambhava-Hevajra, with eight faces, sixteen arms, and four legs. Of the sixteen hands,

the eight right hands hold a kāraṇḍa bird,[21] a ruddy shelduck, an owl, a chukar partridge,[22] a cuckoo,[23] a marsh harrier, a kite, and an osprey. In his left hands he holds [the eight nāgā kings:] Karkoṭaka, Śankhapālo, Kulika, Padma, Mahāpadma, Takṣaka, Vāsuki, and Ananta. His crown is marked with an eight-faceted jewel. He is in union with his consort, yellow Ratnatārā, who holds a curved knife and a skull. {290} The couple is adorned with bone ornaments. Mohavajrā is in the eyes . . . . Rays of light shine from *āṃ* in their hearts, invoking all tathāgatas of the ten directions in the form of the Ratnasambhava couple, *oṃ vajra samājaḥ jaḥ hūṃ baṃ hoḥ*, and dissolve into you; and *jaḥ hūṃ baṃ hoḥ*, and dissolve into the empowerment substance generated as the deity.

Offer the supplication, "All tathāgatas, please confer the actual empowerment here."

Sprinkle water from the victorious vase and apply this in all cases.

They reply, "*oṃ vajribhāva abhiṣiñca hūṃ*," conferring empowerment upon the deities of the empowerment substance, filling the body and purifying taints. The excess water overflows, transforming into Ratnasambhava, who adorns their heads. The empowerment substance, the Ratnasambhava couple, enter into union and melt, transforming into the empowerment substance, the crown.

In order for you to completely accomplish the four limbs, recite after me this supplication to the empowerment deities residing in the sky: "All tathāgatas, please confer the actual empowerment upon me."

Having offered this supplication, imagine that the embodied maṇḍala in the sky and the master simultaneously raise the crown, in which the three seats are complete and which have the nature of Ratnasambhava, conferring the empowerment upon you through your crown, while appearing as Ratnasambhava:

The great empowerment of the great jewel
from the three secrets of all buddhas

is granted to the one
to whom all in the three realms prostrate.

oṃ vajrī ratnakumuṭa abhiṣiñcmi vajra rāgata vajraśali hoḥ For the limb of stabilizing that empowerment, imagine that the empowerment is conferred through the crown of one's head with the water of the vase.

Sprinkle the water of the victorious vase on the crown and apply this in all cases. {291}

Saying *oṃ vajrībhava abhiṣiñca hūṃ*, the water of the vase is conferred through the crown, filling the body and purifying taints. The excess water overflows, transforming into Ratnasambhava, who adorns one's head.

Imagine that offerings are presented by the goddesses who reside in the sky: *oṃ vajra puṣpe āḥ hūṃ . . . naividye āḥ hūṃ.*

As such, one obtains the crown empowerment through Ratnasambhava, pride and envy are purified, the aggregate of sensation is transformed, the gnosis of uniformity is actualized, and the seed of Ratnasambhava is planted in one's continuum.

Recite the visualization for the purpose of the vajra empowerment of Amitābha in this way:

svabhāva . . . Your aggregate of perception and the empowerment substance (the vajra) vanish, becoming emptiness. Both arise from the state of emptiness as *jrīm* upon a lotus and sun, which transform into red lotuses marked with *jrīm*. Rays of light shine from those red lotuses and return, each transforming into a red Amitābha-Hevajra with eight faces, sixteen arms, and four legs. Of the sixteen hands, the eight right hands hold a bear, vulture, rhinoceros, an Indian bison, a tiger, a monkey, a sea crocodile,[24] and a fox.[25] The eight left hands hold a crow, owl,[26] a white bird, a parrot, a lion, a sarus crane,[27] a blackbuck, and a pig. His crown is marked with a red lotus. He is in union with his consort, red Pāṇḍaravāsinī, who holds a curved knife and a skull.

> The couple is adorned with bone ornaments. Mohavajrā is in their eyes . . . . Rays of light shine from *jrīṃ* in their hearts, invoking all tathāgatas of the ten directions in the form of the Amitābha couple, *oṃ vajra samājaḥ jaḥ hūṃ baṃ hoḥ*; dissolving into you, *jaḥ hūṃ baṃ hoḥ*; {292} and dissolving into the empowerment substance generated as the deity.

Offer the supplication, "All tathāgatas, please confer the actual empowerment here."

They reply *oṃ vajribhāva abhiṣiñca hūṃ*, conferring empowerment upon the deities of the empowerment substance, filling the body and purifying taints. The excess water overflows, transforming into Amitābha, who adorns their heads. The empowerment substance, the Amitābha couple, enter into union and melt, transforming into the empowerment substance, the vajra. In order for you to completely accomplish the four limbs, recite after me this supplication to the empowerment deities residing in the sky: "All tathāgatas, please confer the actual empowerment upon me."

Having offered this supplication, imagine that the embodied maṇḍala in the sky and the master simultaneously raise the vajra, in which the three seats are complete and which have the nature of Amitābha. After giving the vajra to you, appearing as Amitābha, in your right hand the empowerment is conferred.

The vajra empowerment of all buddhas
is conferred upon you today.
You must take this vajra
in order to accomplish all buddhas.

Saying *oṃ mahāvajra hūṃ*, they present the vajra to one's right hand. For the limb of stabilizing that empowerment, imagine that the empowerment is conferred through the crown of one's head with the water of the vase.

Saying *oṃ vajrībhava abhiṣiñca hūṃ*, the water of the vase is conferred through the crown, filling the body and purifying taints. The excess water overflows, transforming into Amitābha, who adorns one's head. Imagine offerings are presented by the goddesses who reside in the sky: *puṣpe* . . . .

As such, one obtains the vajra empowerment through Amitābha, desire is purified, the aggregate of perception {293} is transformed, the gnosis of individual discernment is actualized, and the seed of Amitābha is planted in one's continuum. Recite the visualization for the purpose of the bell empowerment of Amoghasiddhi in this way:

> *svabhāva* . . .
> Your aggregate of formations and the empowerment substance (the bell) vanish, becoming emptiness. Both arise from the state of emptiness as *khaṃ* upon a lotus and sun, transforming into swords marked with *khaṃ*. Rays of light shine from those swords and return, each transforming into a green Amoghasiddhi-Hevajra, with eight faces, sixteen arms, and four legs. Of the sixteen hands, the eight right hands hold Budha, Bṛhaspati, Ketu, Rāhu, Maṅgala, Śukra, Śanina, and Viṣṇurāja.[28] The eight left hands hold Brahma, Rudra, wicked Kamadeva, Viṣṇu's daughter, Iśādhāra, Mahāvira,[29] Vemacitrin, and the asura, Balī. His crown is marked with a white sword. He is in union with his consort, green Samayatārā, who holds a curved knife and a skull. The couple is adorned with bone ornaments. Mohavajrā is in their eyes . . . . Rays of light shine from *khaṃ* in their hearts, invoking all tathāgatas of the ten directions in the form of the Amoghasiddhi couple, *oṃ vajra samājaḥ jaḥ hūṃ baṃ hoḥ*, dissolving into you; and *jaḥ hūṃ baṃ hoḥ*, dissolving into the empowerment substance generated as the deity.

Offer the supplication, "All tathāgatas, please confer the actual empowerment here."

They reply, *oṃ vajribhāva abhiṣiñca hūṃ*, conferring empowerment upon the deities of the empowerment substance, filling the body and purifying taints. The excess water overflows, {294} transforming into Amoghasiddhi, who adorns their heads. The empowerment substance, the Amoghasiddhi couple, enter into union and melt, transforming into the empowerment substance, the bell.

In order for you to completely accomplish the four limbs, recite after me this supplication to the empowerment deities residing in the sky: "All tathāgatas, please confer the actual empowerment upon me." Having offered this supplication, imagine that the embodied maṇḍala in the sky and the master simultaneously raise the bell, in which the three seats are complete and which has the nature of Amoghasiddhi. After giving the bell to you, appearing as Amoghasiddhi, in your left hand, the empowerment is conferred.

oṃ vajra adhipatitvaṃ, abhiṣiñcami tiṣṭha vajrasamāya stvāṃ

The bell is given into your left hand.

For the limb of stabilizing that empowerment, imagine that the empowerment is conferred through the crown of one's head with the water of the vase.

Saying *oṃ vajrībhava abhiṣiñca hūṃ*, the water of the vase is conferred through the crown, filling the body and purifying taints. The excess water overflows, transforming into Amoghasiddhi, who adorns one's head. Imagine offerings are presented by the goddesses who reside in the sky: *puṣpe* . . . . As such, one obtains the bell empowerment through Amoghasiddhi, jealousy is purified, the aggregate of formations is transformed, the wisdom of successful activity is actualized, and the seed of Amoghasiddhi is planted in one's continuum.

Recite the visualization for the purpose of the name empowerment of Vairocana in this way:

svabhāva . . .

Your aggregate of matter vanishes, becoming emptiness. It arises from the state of emptiness as *bhrūṃ* upon a lotus and sun, transforming into a wheel marked with *bhrūṃ*. Rays of light shine from that wheel and return, transforming into white Vairocana-Hevajra {295} with eight faces, sixteen arms, and four legs. Of the sixteen hands, the eight right hands hold a peacock, a water buffalo, a crocodile,[30] a rohita fish,[31] a tortoise, a nāga,[32] a grey goose, and a hare.

> The eight left hands hold an alpine salamander,[33] a green horse,[34] a poisonous snake, a black Tsang pig,[35] a mouse, a yak, a musk deer, and a white bird with a red head.[36] Their crown is marked with a white wheel. You are in union with your consort, white Buddhalocanā, who holds a curved knife and a skull. Both couples are adorned with bone ornaments. Mohavajrā is in their eyes . . . . Rays of light shine from *bhrūṃ* in their hearts, invoking all tathāgatas of the ten directions in the form of the Amoghasiddhi couple: *oṃ vajra samājaḥ jaḥ hūṃ baṃ hoḥ*, and dissolve into you. Since there is no empowerment substance generated as a deity, in order for you to completely accomplish the four limbs, recite after me this supplication to the empowerment deities residing in the sky: "All tathāgatas, please confer the actual empowerment upon me."

Having offered this supplication, imagine that the embodied maṇḍala in the sky and the master simultaneously raise the name in which the three seats are complete, which has the nature of Vairocana, and is taken from the deity upon which your flower fell and was given to you.

oṃ vajrasatva stvaṃ abhiṣiñcami vajranāma abhiṣekata "Oh . . . ." If someone does not have a secret name, give them a new one. For men: Laughing Vajra, Playful Vajra, Sporting Vajra, Alalavajra, Shoot of Extreme Joy Vajra, Dveṣavajra, Vajrasattva, Mahāvairocanavajra, Hevajra, and so on. For women: Vajragarvi, Vajra Weapon, {296}Vajranairātmyā, Astonishing Bliss, Vajra Dancer, and so on. These are given according to the family [to which you belong].

For the limb of stabilizing that empowerment, imagine that the empowerment is conferred through the crown of one's head with the water of the vase. Saying *oṃ vajrībhava abhiṣiñca hūṃ*, the water of the vase is conferred through the crown, filling the body and purifying taints. The excess water overflows, transforming into Vairocana, who adorns one's head. Imagine offerings are presented by the goddesses who reside in the sky: *puṣpe* . . . .

As such, one obtains the name empowerment through

Vairocana, ignorance is purified, the aggregate of matter is transformed, the gnosis of the dharmadhātu is actualized, and the seed of Vairocana is planted in one's continuum.

The meaning of that empowerment is:

Everything that appears
is the principal, one's excellent deity.
The nature of all phenomena is unclouded and pure;
it must be seen as the gnosis of the Buddha.

"Everything" means that the appearance of any and all apparent phenomena (*chos can*, Skt. *dharmin*) is the principal, the excellent deity. That deity is not temporary, but because all phenomena are unclouded by nature, they have been pure as the deity since the beginning. Since such temporary taints have been removed by this rite, henceforth, having abandoned all concepts that grasp those phenomena as ordinary, you must see all of those as the gnosis of buddhahood. Since those five afflictions (such as ignorance [Skt. *avidyā*], and so on) are transformed into the five gnoses of knowledge (Skt. *vidyā*), this is called the knowledge empowerment. Alternately, since the five knowledge mothers (*rig ma*), such as Buddhalocanā, are the activity of the five knowledge fathers (*rig pa*), this is called the knowledge empowerment.

Having empowered all apparent phenomena as the deity, dharmatā (*chos nyid*) is introduced as the sixth buddha, Vajrasattva. For the purpose of conferring the empowerment of the strict vow that empowers body, speech, and mind, visualize in the following way: *svabhāva* .... Your conceptual grasping to the dharmatā of the five aggregates as ordinary vanishes, becoming emptiness. It arises from the state of emptiness as *hūṃ* upon a lotus and sun, which transforms into a vajra marked with *hūṃ*. Rays of light shine from that vajra and return, transforming the dharmatā of the five aggregates into white Vajrasattva with eight faces and sixteen hands. Of the sixteen hands, the eight right hands hold an elephant, horse, ass, ox, camel, man, śarabha, and cat. The eight left hands hold Pṛthivī, Varuṇa, Agni, Vāyu, Candra, Sūrya, Yama, and Kubera. His crown is marked with a black vajra. You are in union with your consort, white Vajragarvi, who holds a curved knife and a skull. The couple is adorned with bone ornaments. Mohavajrā is in their eyes . . .

Rays of light shine from *hūṃ* in your heart, invoking all tathāgatas of the ten directions in the form of the Vajrasattva couple, *oṃ vajra samājaḥ jaḥ hūṃ baṃ hoḥ*, and dissolving into you. The master offers a supplication, "All tathāgatas, please confer the actual empowerment here." Saying *oṃ vajrībhava abhiṣiñca hūṃ*, the water of the vase is conferred through the crown, filling the body and purifying taints. The excess water overflows, transforming into Akṣobhya, who adorns one's head.

A vajra arises there from *hūṃ*, with its size and all qualifications complete, having the nature of twenty-eight deities. In its center is the Vajrasattva couple. {298} On the five upper tines are the five families, such as Vairocana, and so on. Below them, the eight bodhisattvas (such as Avalokiteśvara, and so on) are on the lotus petals. The lower tines are the five ḍākinīs, such as the gnosis ḍākinī, and so on. Below them, the eight goddesses (such as Aṅkuśa, and so on) are on the eight lotus petals. Imagine that the vajra is given into your right hand for the purpose of the empowerment of the strict vow:

This is the nature of all buddhas,
resting in Vajrasattva's hand.
You must always take this
and stabilize the strict vow of a vajra holder.

oṃ sarvatathāgatasiddhi vajrasamaya tiṣṭhaiṣa stvāṃ dhārayāmi vajrasattva hīḥ hi hi hi hi hūṃ

Through reciting this, wave the vajra that has been bestowed and hold it to your heart. Henceforth, you must overcome ordinary behavior and abide in the nature of Mahāvajradhara's body, speech, and mind.

As such, since you have received the special vows of the five families through the act of obtaining the water, crown, vajra, bell, and name empowerments of the action and conduct tantras and attaining the five knowledge empowerments, you are authorized to explain and hear the action and conduct tantras. On the basis of that, having overcome ordinary body, voice, and mind, because you have obtained the empowerment of the strict vow that empowers the body, speech, and mind of Mahāvajradhara, you are authorized to guard the individual and specific samayas of the five families by obtaining the special, unsurpassed vajra-disciple empowerment through obtaining the empowerment of the disciple empowerment of yoga tantra. Though you are not authorized to explain the yoga tantras, you are authorized to hear them. You are empowered into the collection of activities and accomplishment of siddhis that are explained in the unsurpassed yoga tantras.

That being the case, you must {299} endeavor in the meditation and recitation of the deity upon whom your flower fell. Since all buddhas are pleased by that recitation, you will accomplish all inferior and mediocre siddhis.

If one wishes, meditate and give the transmission for the recitation of the root mantra.

As such, after your coarse aggregates, sense bases, and sense elements have been empowered as deities by the six common empowerments, there is the irreversible wheel empowerment, which is the first empowerment of the four uncommon empowerments that empower the four subtle maṇḍalas as the four kāyas.

Offer a gift and a supplication, place the empowerment platform,
give the three samayas, confer the water empowerment,
consecration, offerings, explaining the presentation,
the dance, and so on, the eye probe, mirror,
bell, bow, arrow, and the second mirror,
explaining the dharma, and explaining the emanation in order to generate realization.

First, offer a maṇḍala as a gift for requesting the irreversible master empowerment. After offering that maṇḍala, offer this supplication by reciting after me three times:

Once the protector confers the empowerment
of the irreversible wheel upon me,
teach me the reality of the deities of the maṇḍala
and all the activities of a master.
Grant me the samayas and vows
of all buddhas.

Having offered the supplication, the disciples are placed on the empowerment platform. If there is no empowerment platform, say, "Imagine that as soon as you disciples were created as the deity on the empowerment platform explained before, you are seated with the pride of Vajrasattva. Above you is a canopy; on your right, an umbrella; and on your left, a victory banner. Around the platform, you are surrounded by inconceivable kinds of offerings, {300} such as conches, streamers, flower garlands, and so on.

It is necessary to give the three samayas in order to the disciples. First, for the purpose of the samaya of vajra mind, imagine that the vajra that was explained to arise from *hūṃ* and possesses the nature of twenty-eight deities is given into your right hand.

This is the nature of all buddhas,
resting in Vajrasattva's hand.
You must always take this
and stabilize the strict vow of a vajra holder.

oṃ sarvatathāgatasiddhi vajrasamaya tiṣṭhaiṣa tvāṃ dhārayāmi vajrasattva hi hi hi hi hūṃ, wave the vajra you have been given, hold it to your hearts, and request the entrustment of mind from the principal of the vajra.

The being who has no beginning or end—
very joyful Vajrasattva,
Samantabhadra, the lord of all,
the supreme lord of Vajragarvi—
is the Bhagavān, the glorious, preeminent person.

oṃ mahāvajra hūṃ
The meaning of this is as follows: Listen, this vajra represents the essence of inseparable cognizance and emptiness, the dharmadhātu free from all extremes of proliferation. Imagine that one's mind is the definitive vajra, bodhicitta without beginning or end, free from all extremes of proliferation.

For the purpose of the bell, the samaya of speech, from *a* arises a bell complete with all characteristics, with the nature of twenty-three deities: inside the vase is Prajñāpāramitā with her male consort; above the five tines are the five families; on the eight petals below are the eight bodhisattvas; and on the top of the bowl [of the bell], on blue poppies, are Tārā, and so on. {301} Imagine this is given into your left hand.

This bell is said to emulate the sound of all bells
of all yoginīs.
You also must always hold this bell.
The victor asserts it as supreme awakening.

The bell that has been given to you should be held at your left side with the mouth facing up. Request the entrustment of the mind from the principal of the bell.

aḥ
Existence is pure by nature
and by nature is free from existence.
The mind that knows natural purity
transforms existence into sublime nirvana.

oṃ vajraghaṇḍe aḥ
The meaning of that is as follows: Listen, this bell represents the dharmadhātu, free of all extremes of proliferation, empty of arising, abiding, and ceasing. Imagine that your speech is the definitive bell that explicates the natural purity of all existence. For the purpose of the consort, imagine you become white Bhagavān Vajradhara, with one face and two hands, holding a vajra and a bell. You are in union with the consort, white Vajragarvi, who holds a curved knife and a skull. She is sixteen years old. Mohava-

jrā is in their eyes. . . . Rays of light shine from *hūṃ* in the master's heart, invoking all tathāgatas of the ten directions in the form of the Vajradhara couple, who are invited with *oṃ vajra* samājaḥ, and with *jaḥ hūṃ baṃ hoḥ*, they nondually dissolve into you. Imagine that the main section of the vajra master empowerment is given.

Holding the vajra and bell
while in union with the sixteen-year-old Prajñā,
fully embraced in one's arms,
is said to be the empowerment of the master. {302}

Imagine she has been given through the concise permission.

Holding the great vajra and the great bell
is the vajra empowerment.
From now onward, you have become a vajra master,
gathering a group of disciples.

The extensive description of the principal of the consort is as follows: You should hold your vajra and bell crossed at your hearts, as if you are holding the sixteen-year-old wisdom consort. Based on the experience of bliss at the touch of her breasts, and so on, imagine that bodhicitta permeates your whole body.

The bliss of existence is very weak.
In order to purify great suffering,
the method of the sublime, highest bliss
is the samaya you have accepted.

While making use of any
sensual enjoyments you desire,
with the yoga of one's excellent deity,
present offerings to oneself and others.

In order to stabilize the mental body,
all tathāgatas have proclaimed:
"The samaya of the consort

must never be transgressed."

The meaning of that is as follows: Ordinary bliss is impure. In order to exhaust the suffering of existence, engage in the yoga of one's deity and enjoy all desired enjoyments. Offerings must be made to all! Through this, one will never go beyond the attainment of the Mahāvajradhara's kāya of union. Thus, you must dwell in this samādhi. Since the extensive offering follows below, until the offerings, one must not leave the samādhi with the consort.

In order to stabilize that, imagine that the tathāgatas and their retinue fill space, {303} lift various offering articles and vases filled with gnosis amṛta, and confer the empowerment.

The great vajra empowerment
from the three secrets of all buddhas
is granted to the one
to whom all throughout the three realms prostrate.

Saying *oṃ vajribhāva abhiṣiñca hūṃ*, the tathāgatas confer the empowerment through the crown, the knowledge consorts sing vajra songs, the bodhisattvas utter benedictions, the wrathful ones drive away obstructers, and the goddesses make offerings. Since the empowerment is conferred, the stream of empowerment water fills your body down to the brow and you obtain the vase empowerment. It fills your body down to the throat and you obtain the secret empowerment. It fills your body down to the heart and you obtain the empowerment of the gnosis of the wisdom consort. It fills your whole body and you obtain the fourth empowerment of supreme great bliss. The taints upon your body, voice, and mind, as well as their traces, are purified. The excess water overflows, transforming into Vajrasattva, the essence of all tathāgatas, who adorns one's head.

Imagine that the embodied maṇḍala in the sky and the master simultaneously consecrate the disciples as dharma kings of the three realms, *oṃ supratiṣṭha vajraya svāhā.*

Having performed the consecration, for the purpose of the

investiture, imagine that goddesses residing in the sky offer extensive offerings, *oṃ vajra puṣpe . . . naividye āḥ hūṃ.*

As such, you have obtained the empowerment of Mahāvajradhara. Since all the taints of your aggregates, {304} sense elements, and sense bases have been purified, all of those are included in your mind. Since that mind is Vajrasattva, the nature of Akṣobhya, one's mind is a pure maṇḍala.

The explanation of the maṇḍala
is that the intellect is the sublime maṇḍala.
The explanation of the celestial mansion
is that the mind is the storied celestial mansion.
Its square outside
is the nature of uniformity.
Anyone's mind of love, and so on,
is explained as the four chalk lines.
Mindfulness of dharma
is what is explained to be the vajra line.
Liberation from all views
is explained to be the gnosis line.
The correct explanation of the ornaments
is the vows of discipline, and so on.
Whatever is the mind of the five faculties
arises as the fivefold wall.
The explanation of the doors
is that there are four kinds of liberation.
The four porticos
are called the four correct renunciations.
The four foundations of mindfulness
are the four levels [of the portico roof].
The four door bracings[37]
are the four bases of magic power.
Likewise, the ornamental garlands of flowers
are the seven limbs of awakening.
The eight-limbed path of the noble ones
is said to be the eight pillars.
The special gnosis of the path
is renowned as the yak-tail whisks.

The explanation of the strands
is that they eliminate all afflictions,
the essence of eliminating them all.
Because the afflictions are thieves, be mindful.
The union of the pure two accumulations
is turning the wheel. {305}
Since half the afflictions are eliminated,
there are the tassels.

That being the case, the mind is the celestial mansion, the essence of which is the thirty-seven factors conducive to awakening. The appearances of the aggregates, sense elements, and sense bases to the mind are the deities of the complete three seats. The five aggregates are the seat of tathāgatas; the four elements are the seat of the knowledge consorts; the inner sense bases are the seat of the bodhisattvas; the outer sense bases are the seat of the goddesses; and the agent exhausting the afflictive obscuration, and so on, is the male and female wrathful ones.

Having thus explained the presentation of the maṇḍala and the deities, it is necessary to accomplish the permissions so that the disciples will understand the presentation [above]. First, the permission of the offering deities is requesting the performance of the eight mudras of dancing, and so on.

Beginning with a dance roll, place both fists at the hips:

Beginning from today, I offer
a blissful celebration that manifests to
the perfect buddhas and bodhisattvas
through the yoga of Vajragarvi.
āḥ

Likewise, place the two fists beside one's mouth.

Gracefully toss a garland
to be offered to all buddhas.
One also will never be separate from the tathāgata.

That is the garland ornament.
oṃ

The two fists are like words uttered from one's mouth.

You offer this song of sublime dharma
to all embodied beings.
Through that, the siddhi of the sugata
is the swift experience of bliss.
gī

The vajra palms dance in a circle around one's crown.

That dance of palms
is offered to all buddhas.
The buddhas move in the manner of dancers
through the activity of gathering.
hoḥ

Make the mudra of incense with the two fists.

Since incense was offered to the perfect Buddha,
he is well sated with excellent strict discipline.
May embodied beings be satisfied with gnosis
as an accouterment of the sugata.
hūṃ

Make the flower mudra.

Flowers are scattered over the buddhas,
completing the limbs of awakening.
May the major and minor marks
of the body of the sugata be obtained!
bhrūṃ

Make the lamp mudra.

Since the lamp of dharma is well ignited,
similar to Vajradharma,
may the blind ignorance of sentient beings
be removed with the lamp of gnosis.
pra

With the right hand holding the dharma conch and with the left hand making the motion of anointing, [say]:

By offering this scent to the victors,
embodied beings will meditate upon
discipline, samādhi, wisdom,
and the gnosis of liberation.
gā

Henceforth, all one's activities, whether dancing with the body, singing a song with the voice, and so on, are neither unvirtuous nor neutral and are imagined to be divine offerings.

The permission for benefiting sentient beings is as follows:

Using the eye probe or the vajra, [recite]:

oṃ aṣṭānanaya piṅgalordhākeśavartamane caturviṅgṣatinetrāya ṣoḍaśabhujāya kṛṣṇajīmūtavapuṣe kapālamālānikadhārine adhmātakrūracittāya ardhendudaṃṣṭrīṇe mārayamāraya kārayakāraya garjayagarjaya tarjayatarjaya śoṣayaśoṣaya saptasāgarān bandhabandha nāgāṣṭakān ghriṇaghriṇa śatrūn ha hā hi hī hu hū he hai ho hau haṃ haḥ phaṭ svāhā

Praise with the root mantra. Imagine that from *praṃ* arises {307} the eye probe that has the nature of the perfection of wisdom or that from *hūṃ* arises the vajra of gnosis, which removes the cataract of ignorance by poking directly into the eye, endowing one with the power to engage in the benefit of sentient beings.

Just as the sighted victor
removed the cataracts of the world,
child, the victors shall remove the cataract

of your ignorance.

oṃ vajra netra avaharapaṭalaṃ hrīḥ praṃ
One has been endowed with the power to engage in the benefit of sentient beings.
For the purpose of recognizing, "I must benefit sentient beings through knowing that all apparent phenomena are like reflections in a mirror," display the mirror.

All phenomena are like reflections:
clear, pure, and unclouded,
ungraspable, inexpressible,
arising from causes and karma,
natureless and nonabiding.
Born as a child of the protector,
one must understand phenomena in that way,
yet engage in benefiting sentient beings impartially.

As such, the permission of the first mirror has been given.

For the purpose of recognizing that you must benefit sentient beings through knowing that though all relative phenomena appear as a multitude from the assemblage of dependently originated causes and conditions, the sound of the bell cannot be found if one investigates from where the sound arises—the bowl, the clapper, and the effort of the person [to ring it]—being empty by nature. Likewise, dharmatā (which has the characteristic of space) is empty of arising, abiding, and cessation. Give the bell that arises from the ordinary vowel.

Space is the characteristic of everything.
There is no characteristic for space. {308}
Manifest as the uniform supreme of all [aspects]
by unifying with space.

[After you] have recognized that the nature of all phenomena is emptiness, for the purpose of recognizing that it is necessary to conquer the thoughts of personal benefit, since one will fall to the stage of a śrāvaka or pratyekabuddha if one in particular lacks skillful means even if one possesses the wisdom of realizing suchness, it is said "Ho, may all tathāgatas be loving!"

Give the bow and arrow that arise from *ho.* Imagine the six arrows of method that fill the bow of wisdom are shot in the four directions, above and below, and conquer the thought of personal benefit, saying, "May all tathāgatas be loving!"

Further, that wisdom that realizes reality is not just an understanding through the general meaning, such as the wisdom that arises through hearing and reflection. However, for the purpose of recognizing that the gnosis of empowerment enters one's heart—apparent yet natureless, like Vajrasattva reflected in a mirror—there is the permission of the mirror and vajra.

vajrasatva
Like Vajrasattva [reflected] in a mirror—
clear, pure, and unclouded—
child, the lord, the nature of Vajrasattva,
abides in your heart.

Recognize that bodhicitta, the lord of all buddhas, is this! These are the permissions for benefiting sentient beings.

The permission to explain the dharma is as follows: Say *oṃ vajra hetu maṃ* and roll the wheel under one's foot. The meaning is "I will guide sentient beings from samsara." If it is asked what the way is, [say,]{309} *oṃ vajra bhaṣa raṃ*, and the conch is given into one's right hand. Blowing the conch means, "Gather the sentient beings into a retinue!" If it is asked by which means, with *oṃ vajra ghaṇḍe aḥ*, take the bell given into one's left hand and say, "Proclaim the sound of dharma." If it is asked with what dharma, with *a*. The volume of tantra is placed on one's forearms, meaning, "Proclaim this dharma." Through such certainty, blow the conch, ring the bell, and read the volume.

Henceforth, I shall turn the wheel of dharma
merely by generating bodhicitta.
In order for you to have no doubt,
with an undivided mind,

you must fill the dharma conch
with all immaculate things.
Always give explanations to people
through the ritual means of mantra conduct.
Having done so, one must be grateful
and helpful to the buddhas.
Vajra holder, all of that
you must always guard.

Once the permission to explain the dharma has been given in general, for the purpose of recognizing the dharma that is to be explained, there is the teaching of the Vajrayāna dharma (which is connected with the five families of tathāgatas), the permission that explains the emanations of the five families. With the pride of each family, please make the mudras by observing the master.

For Vairocana:

To benefit all sentient beings
and to tame all sentient beings
everywhere, in every different way,
turn the dharma wheel.

Likewise, for the following, the first three lines are the same. For Akṣobhya, "turn the vajra wheel." For Ratnasambhava, {310} "turn the jewel wheel." For Amitābha, "turn the lotus wheel." For Amoghasiddhi, "turn the multicolored wheel."

As such, you must turn the dharma wheel, vajra wheel, jewel wheel, lotus wheel, and the multicolored wheel for all sentient beings. You must blow the dharma conch to proclaim and explain [the dharma]!

As such, whether you have a sand maṇḍala or a cloth-generated maṇḍala, generate the understanding, "You have principally obtained the vase empowerment into the maṇḍala: the taints of the body are purified; you have been empowered to guard the twenty-two samayas; the symbol is gathering the five and pressing the tip;[38] you are empowered to meditate on the path, the creation stage; and the seed of the result, the nirmāṇakāya, is planted in your continuum."

The summary for the secret empowerment is:

Offer a maṇḍala, praise, and supplication.
Confer the empowerment, make the prediction, and generate
understanding.

First, offer a maṇḍala as a gift for the secret empowerment. Having offered a maṇḍala, imagine that the master is offered a qualified consort and recite after me this praise:

You are surrounded by a troupe of yoginīs,
you have attained the supreme mind,
you ornament all migrating beings with the animate and
inanimate,
the one who rouses sentient beings with compassion,
the illusory emanation whose mind has accomplished the vajra—
Śrī Heruka, rejoice with a vajra mind!

Having given praise, recite after me this supplication three times:

Oh Bhagavān of great peace,
who is solely engaged in the vajrayoga, {311}
the one who accomplished the indivisible mudra
that arises from the vajrayoga—
lord, just as you have a great nature,
make me just like you.
Save me, the one who has no savior,
who is sunk in the morass of samsara.

Having offered the supplication, in order to represent having not seen the bodhicitta maṇḍala beforehand, say *oṃ āḥ hūṃ* and please tie one's blindfold, visualizing the following: Imagine that the sound of joy of the guru couple's union invites all tathāgatas, who enter into the father's mouth and in his heart melt into light through the fire of passion. The bodhicitta, like a pearly bindu, which falls into the space of the mother from the path of the vajra jewel, is taken by the thumb and ring finger of the master and placed on your tongue.

Just as the buddhas of the past
conferred empowerment upon bodhisattvas,
I will confer the secret empowerment
with the empowerment of the stream of bodhicitta.

Imagine that the amṛta that was received is the essence that unifies all buddhas, say *oṃ āḥ hūṃ ho*, and please taste it. Since the amṛta was tasted, bodhicitta fills the syllables, *ya ra la va*, which are the support in the throat, existing in the manner of a commitment being. That bodhicitta with the complete three seats, which is given by the master, merges in the manner of the gnosis being. After the eighty coarse concepts (arising as the companions of the trio of illumination, spreading illumination, and imminent illumination) cease, the empty, very empty, and totally empty experiences arise. {312} The nature of the three illuminations and the three emptinesses become one taste, and the samādhi of supremely clear and empty self-originated gnosis (clear, vast, and nonconceptual) arises in one's continuum. This is the main part of the secret empowerment. As the symbol of receiving that empowerment, say *oṃ āḥ hūṃ* and remove your blindfold.

The prediction as a support for that is as follows: Predictions are normally declared by the nirmāṇakāya, but on this occasion, once the master has taken up the pride of Śākyamuni, taking the corners of the dharma robe with the left hand, folded in the shape of deer's ears, and making the mudra of granting perfection while holding the vajra and bell in the right hand, the master and retinue declare the prediction, stating "You will all become tathāgatas named according to your secret name."

oṃ
Here I will give you a prediction:
Vajrasattva tathāgatas,
since the world is pure,
you are released from bad migrations in the world.

Oh, Tathāgata Śrī [insert name] Vajra, my prediction to all those below, on, and above the ground, *bhūr bhūvaḥ svaḥ*, is the prediction that all buddhas, bodhisattvas, and all maṇḍalacakras make in one voice, which is the power of this mantra and mudra.

Generate the joy of thinking that since there is a prediction, you will definitely become a tathāgata.

To generate realization:

As such, one obtains the secret empowerment in the maṇḍala of relative bodhicitta; the taints of the voice are purified; the samaya is being empowered to rely on the pill of five meats and five amṛtas; {313} the symbol is touching the thumb and ring finger; one is empowered to meditate on the path, the stage of the self-empowerment; and the seed of the result, the saṃbhogakāya, is planted in one's continuum.

The summary of the empowerment of the gnosis of the wisdom consort is:

The maṇḍala, praise, supplication, bestowing the knowledge consort,
question and reply, and so on, conferring the actual empowerment,
providing solace, and generating understanding.

To begin, offer a maṇḍala as a gift for requesting the gnosis of the wisdom consort. Having offered such a maṇḍala, repeat after me the praise and supplication, just as in the secret empowerment:

You are surrounded by a troupe of yoginīs
. . . .
and are sunk in the morass of samsara.

To represent that you have not seen the bhaga maṇḍala beforehand, say *oṃ āḥ hūṃ* and tie on your blindfold. The visualization is to imagine that from the heart of the master, a qualified knowledge consort emanates, comely, youthful, and adorned with all ornaments, and she is given to you.

Great being, take the goddess,
the comely one possessing diverse forms,
who grants the four joys in the four places.
Accept her! Accept her and present offerings.

Imagine that the consort that has been given to you asks you a question in order to investigate whether you are a suitable recipient for the secret continuous practice:

Child, can you consume feces and urine
and, likewise, menses and semen,
and happily delight in great meat?
Child, will you always delight
in devotion to women,
kissing the lotus of the bhaga?

As inquired, imagine that you reply with enthusiasm {314} and recite after me:

I will consume feces and urine
and, likewise, menses and semen,
and happily delight in great meat.
I will always delight
in devotion to women,
kissing the lotus of the bhaga.

Having replied, the consort replies:

> Amazing! This bhaga of mine
> is the source of all bliss.
> If one relies upon it, according to the proper rites,
> I will remain before him.
> All activities, such as serving the buddhas, and so on,
> are performed within the lotus.
> The king of great bliss himself
> always resides within this lotus.[39]
> Those fools who avoid this
> lack supreme siddhi.[40]

stvaṃ padmabhañja mokṣa hoḥ Imagine that she arrives on your lap. Your manifestation as Bhagavān Hevajra and the consort Vajranairātmyā is employing the nirmāṇakāya as the path, the perception of the deity. The space of the mother vanishes, and from the state of emptiness arises an *āḥ*, from which arises a red lotus with eight petals with stamens marked with *āḥ*s: *oṃ padmasukhadhara mahārāga sukhaṃdada caturānanda bhagaviśva hūṃ hūṃ hūṃ kāryaṃ kuruṣvame.*

The place of your secret vanishes. From the state of emptiness, there is *hūṃ*, which transforms into a five-tined vajra marked in the center with *hūṃ*: *oṃ vajramahādveśa caturānandadayaka khagamukha e kārasonātha hūṃ hūṃ hūṃ kāryaṃ kuruṣvame.*

Empowering the space and the secret is employing the saṃbhogakāya as the path, the perception of mantra. The thought "The connate is realized on the basis of this method" is employing the dharmakāya as the path, the perception of dharma.

Without being separate from employing the three kāyas as the path and the perceptions, imagine the four joys of the outer sequence. {315} To begin, the first moment, looking at the form of the consort, listening to her voice, smelling her scent, tasting her honeyed lips, kissing her, embracing her, caressing[41] her, and so on, is the gnosis of joy. The second moment, the union of the bola and the kakkola, is the gnosis of supreme joy. The third moment, the activity of intercourse, is the gnosis of the joy of separation from joy. The fourth moment, seeking the nāḍī of Vajradhatviśvari, is the experience of the connate gnosis.

The joy that depends on the inner places is as follows: Imagine that the fire of the passion of such union melts all the pure elements, which gather in the *hūṃ* of the crown. The bodhicitta arrives at the throat from the crown, the gnosis of joy is actualized, the imputed afflictions to be abandoned are pacified, and the path of the śrāvakas is traversed. The bodhicitta arrives at the heart from the throat, the gnosis of supreme joy is actualized, the connate afflictions to be abandoned are pacified, and the path of pratyekabuddhas is traversed. The bodhicitta arrives at the navel from the heart, the gnosis of joy of separation is actualized, all afflictions to be abandoned are pacified, and the path of bodhisattvas is traversed. The bodhicitta arrives at the place of the secret from the navel; the white and red bodhicitta meet at the top of the tip of the method, the lord of the family and the beautiful nāḍī of the wisdom consort; the pacification of all the afflictions to be abandoned is stabilized; and the path of great awakening is traversed. In brief, the illustration that is able to illustrate the gnosis of buddhahood is called "the example gnosis." {316} Those are the descending four joys.

In order to accomplish the four joys that are stabilized in ascending order, the bodhicitta is held at the tip of the secret and the space through the power of the unmoving vāyu. Since that is drawn up with the vāyu with the tone of *hūṃ*, the bodhicitta travels up the central nāḍi. Since it becomes stable in the center of the navel cakra, which bears the name Sthavira, one experiences the four joys included in joy, and one has the fortune of accomplishing the result of the corresponding cause, the nirmāṇakāya. Moving up from the navel, since the bodhicitta becomes stable in the middle of the heart cakra, which bears the name Sarvāstivāda, one experiences the four joys included in supreme joy, and one has the fortune of accomplishing the ripened result, the dharmakāya. Moving up from the heart, since the bodhicitta becomes stable in the middle of the throat cakra, which bears the name Saṃmītya, one experiences the four joys included in the joy of separation, and one has the fortune of the result generated by a person, the saṃbhogakāya. Moving up from the throat, since the bodhicitta becomes stable in the middle of the crown cakra, which bears the name Mahāsaṃghika, one experiences the four joys included in the connate joy, and one has the fortune of realizing the immaculate result, the svabhāvakāya. At that time, imagine that the bodhicitta permeates the entire body, the bodhicitta is totally permeated with bliss, the bliss is permeated with nonconceptuality, and the samādhi of inseparable bliss and emptiness arises in your continuums.

If one wishes to condense this, give the introduction according to the *Time of the Path*.

That concludes the main section of the empowerment of the gnosis of the wisdom consort. As a symbol that one has received that empowerment, remove the blindfold.

To provide solace in order to support that empowerment, [say]:

Never criticize the master. {317}
Never transgress the word of the sugata.
Never criticize siblings.
Never abandon love and bodhicitta
for sentient beings.
Never criticize one's own or another's dharma.
Never teach the unfortunate.
Never abuse one's body.
Abandon doubts about the dharma.
Do not be friendly toward hostile beings.
Never measure dharmatā.
Never abandon fortunate sentient beings.
Always guard samaya.
Never criticize women.

Until one is upon the seat of awakening,
never abandon the Three Jewels.
One should always protect samaya.
One must carry the vajra and bell.
Always keep the crown.
Always ladle the burnt offerings.
Always construct the maṇḍala.
Always perform the consecration of sugatas.
Give the bali to the great bhūtas.

Never abandon the embrace of the mudra,
and do not engage in the activities of stupas—
the three supreme vajras should not prostrate.
The activities of the body, such as maṇḍalas, and so on,
should not be done even in dreams.
Never prostrate to worldly masters,
but always prostrate to venerable gurus.
Continuously recite mantras,

and also practice concentration.
Always gather disciples
and always give explanations.
Always defend sentient beings.
Always greatly please the buddhas.
Make water offerings to Jambhala
and always correctly engage in all activities.
Even building stupas of sand
should be done by the wise according to the rites.

The meaning of that, from the perspective of abandoning that which is to be abandoned, is the fourteen root downfalls. From the perspective of relying upon that which is to be relied upon, it is the seven things to be accomplished by beginners. For those whose minds are slightly more stable, {318} there are the five things in which to train. By implication, once great stability is attained, it is necessary to behave free of accepting and rejecting the means of so-called liberation from samayas and vows. Since this is explained, after recognizing those, one must reject and accept appropriately.

For providing the solace of the result, to begin, there is the training in the secret gnosis of the maṇḍala:

There are no misdeeds in the triple realm,
such as being free from desire.
Therefore, you must never be
free from desire.
mahāsamaya hana hūṃ phaṭ

The meaning of that is that one must have attachment to the deity and the guru with great faith, one must have attachment to sentient beings with great compassion, and one must have attachment to the truth of the dharma with great wisdom. Since separation from these three is a great misdeed, train in not being separated from these three.

Next, imagine that one circles the maṇḍala three times with the pride of Heruka, holding umbrellas with golden handles. After placing the umbrellas to the side at the eastern door of the maṇḍala, at the conclusion of the mudra of touching the earth, you must offer all your bodies to the maṇḍala of the master. You must bow your head in the direction of the maṇḍala.

The disciple who holds the mantras
and the tantras offers this.

Since the offering was made, imagine that all the maṇḍalas in one voice provide the solace of the result.

To the one who holds the mantras and the tantras,
the buddhas, bodhisattvas, {319}
and the devas speak in accord:
"Be compassionate to sentient beings.
Draw the maṇḍala according to the rites.
Through the generation of your diligence,
practitioners will be joined to mantra.
That being so, be grateful and
helpful to the buddhas."
Enter into the supreme city,
the vast kingdom of the three realms,
the source of all glorious qualities,
victorious over the hordes of Māra.

The meaning of that is that the buddhas and bodhisattvas speak in accord to you as great vajra masters who hold the mantras, tantras, and intimate instructions, and think of you as a dear child. Henceforth you must properly accomplish the activities of the vajra master through your love for sentient beings and perform the great benefit of sentient beings. The great kingdom of the three realms is equivalent to living in the city of buddhas.

Generate understanding:

As such, you have obtained the empowerment of the gnosis of the wisdom consort in the bhaga maṇḍala of the consort; the taints of the mind are purified; the samaya is to never criticize women; the symbol is the mudra of supreme awakening; one is empowered to meditate on the path, the maṇḍalacakra; and the seed of the result, the dharmakāya, is planted in one's continuum.

The summary for the fourth empowerment is:

Offer the maṇḍala and a supplication, confer the word
empowerment,
praise, generate realization, and so on.

To begin, offer a maṇḍala as a gift for requesting the empowerment. {320} After offering the maṇḍala, repeat after me the supplication three times:

Compassionate protector,
having conferred the three empowerments upon me,
empower me with the fourth empowerment
that possesses the supreme of all aspects.

After offering the supplication, to represent that you have not seen the maṇḍala of ultimate bodhicitta beforehand, say *oṃ āḥ hūṃ* and tie on your blindfold.

The enumeration of the empowerment is the fourth empowerment of the word, the fourth empowerment's words, the fourth empowerment's meaning, the fourth empowerment's support, the fourth empowerment employed as the path, and the fourth empowerment's actualized result. Among those, the first is to whom the fourth empowerment of the word is explained. The *Saṃpūṭa Tantra* states:

> Bestow the fourth [empowerment] of the precious word
> upon those devoted to the profound and vast.[42]

This should be given to no one other than the disciple who is devoted to the guru, the experience of the gnosis of the wisdom consort, profound emptiness, and extensive methods. If devotion toward the guru is absent, certainty in the words of the guru will not arise. If devotion to the experience of the empowerment is absent, it will not be different than the view of hearing and reflection. If devotion toward freedom from proliferation is lacking, [the experience of the third] will be no different than ordinary desire. If devotion toward the inconceivable method is lacking, one will not have the ability to care for others. Thus, it is said that the fourth empowerment should be given to the disciple who has obtained the qualified vase empowerment, and so on.

The way that [experience of the third empowerment] is introduced with words is stated in the *Hevajra Tantra*:

> This gnosis is extremely subtle.
> It is like a vajra, space,
> free of taints, grants liberation, and is peace itself.
> You are its father.

The meaning of that is as follows: Since this gnosis that was experienced at the occasion of the third empowerment {321} is difficult to realize through examples, proofs, and so on, it is extremely subtle. Since it cannot be analyzed with signs and concepts, it is like a vajra. Since it is free from a center or periphery, it is like space. Since it is free from the taint of affliction, it is free of taints. Since it grants the stage of Mahāvajradhara, who exhausted existence, it grants liberation. Since it never arose from the beginning, it is peace. Since in the world one increases one's own family, also the gnosis generated in one's continuum depends on one's meditation; thus, you yourself are its father.

For the purpose of practicing the meaning of that, your body should adopt the characteristics of concentration. The movement of the breath is settled. The mind has eliminated all other discursive concepts of the three times. Generate the definitive understanding that the entire inanimate universe and animate inhabitants are one's mind. The mind's characteristic is clarity, its nature is emptiness, and its essence is union—the three [the characteristic, nature, and essence] are inseparable. Generate the definitive understanding that the four naturally pure kāyas, which exist as innate attributes, are essentially inseparable with the four kāyas of the result. Since the other methods for actualizing that are incapable of generating realization because they are expressed in words, and so on, the example is introduced on the basis of the gnosis of the third empowerment.

To realize that, at the occasion of the third empowerment, the appearance of the form of the deity's body, faces, and hands are natureless. Appearing as the illusory body is the nirmāṇakāya. The deity's mental continuum that arises in the form of the gnosis of great bliss produced from the union with the mudra is the saṃbhogakāya. The mere appearance of the great bliss of the deity's body, {322} free from the trio of arising, abiding, and ceasing, is the dharmakāya. Even though those three kāyas seem to be distinct, their intrinsic inseparability is the svabhāvakāya.

In brief, the natural state (*gshis*) of the mind is nothing whatsoever. Its radiance (*gdangs*) is unceasing as great bliss. Its potential (*rtsal*) arises as a diversity. One should understand it is beyond all objects of meditation and meditating agents, like space. Just as [this] space and [that] space have the same taste, remain relaxed without grasping in the state of the same taste of mind, bliss, and emptiness, and remain in equipoise.

That is the conclusion of the fourth empowerment. In conclusion, remove the blindfold with *oṃ āḥ hūṃ*.

The praise to support that is:

Having been admitted into and seen
the maṇḍala of the supreme secret, {323}
today you all are liberated from all misdeeds;
today you all abide in bliss.
In this, the vehicle of great bliss,
henceforth, there is no death.
Be joyful, fearing nothing at all.
Since existence is utterly pure,
you are released from the bad migrations in existence.

The meaning of that is as follows: Having received and upheld the essence, great bliss, based upon having been admitted into and seen this maṇḍala of the sublime supreme secret, henceforth, you are liberated from misdeeds and suffering. Since you have been admitted to this result vehicle of great bliss, you should especially rejoice in this path. As such, since you have obtained the wealth of the utterly pure existence, the four kāyas, there will be the accomplishment of the vast benefit of sentient beings.

Generate realization:

> As such, you have obtained the empowerment into the maṇḍala of ultimate bodhicitta; the taints and all traces of body, voice, and mind are purified; the samaya is the intention to guard the samayas that were mentioned; the symbol is indicating space with the index finger; one is empowered to meditate on the path, the vajra waves; and the result, the svabhāvakāya, is planted in one's continuum.
>
> Having obtained the complete empowerment by means of the foregoing, thinking that one will keep and guard all the samayas that one received at those occasions, repeat after me three times:
>
> Whatever the principal commands,
> I will do all that.
>
> Having summarized and promised to hold the samayas, offer a maṇḍala in order to give thanks for obtaining the complete empowerment. Having offered such a maṇḍala, when making an offering to repay the kindness of the master, thinking that they should enjoy a portion, repeat after me three times:
>
> Henceforth, I offer
> myself to you as a servant.
> Accept me as a disciple,
> and please employ me in any way.
>
> Since with those you have correctly received the empowerment into the great maṇḍala of Bhagavān Śrī Hevajra as explained by Śrī Virūpa, the lord of yogins, and as practiced by the glorious Sakyapa, the second Vajradhara, and his disciples, please perform the benefit of yourself and others through effort on the path, keeping and guarding the samayas, and so on.

Say this and perform the concluding rites.

> As such, by the merit of composing
> this condensed essence that explains

the empowerment of Hevajra,
may all migrating beings attain the empowerment of Vajradhara.

This *Condensed Essential Empowerment Rite of Hevajra* is abbreviated from the *Great Explanation of Empowerment* by venerable Könchok Lhundrub on behalf of many diligent disciples, composed as an amplification of *The Beautiful Ornament of the Great River of the Empowerment of Śrī Hevajra,* {324} set down in writing by Nātharatna. If one wishes to understand this in more detail, it can be understood from [Könchok Lhundrub's] *Treasury of Citations and Intimate Instructions: The Excellent Explanation of the Words and Meanings of the Empowerment of Śrī Hevajra.* As such, having abbreviated the omniscient Ngorchen Könchok Lhundrub's *Condensed Essential Citations* and named it an empowerment rite for convenience, this was written by Loter Wangpo while making a compilation[43] of the infinite tantra division according to the intention of Thartse Vajradhara.[44] The scribe was Bhikṣu Dharmabhadra, the one who has obtained faith in the tantric texts.

May this be a cause for myself and all migrating beings to reach the stage of Hevajra.

sarvadākalyānaṃ bhavantu

Virtue, virtue, virtue.

13. The Lineage Supplication of the Path with Its Result, the Precious Oral Instruction[1]

Ngorchen Kunga Zangpo

This lineage prayer is the first text in Ngorchen Kunga Zangpo's collected works and the final text in the ripening empowerment section here. The actual title of this text is *String of Pearls*, though this was excluded in Jamgön Kongtrul's collection. Like all lineage prayers, it has been supplemented over time. The additions to the prayer illustrate how the Sakya Path with Its Result transmission split into three mains branches—the Sakya, Ngor, and Tshar—which were reunified by Jampa Namkha Chime (Byams pa nam mkha' 'chi med, 1765–1820), the forty-fourth abbot of Ngor, through whom all modern lineages of the Sakya Path with Its Result have passed.

From the rain of the four virtuous empowerments
of the four pure maṇḍalas
grows the harvest of the four liberated kāyas.
I offer a supplication to the four omniscient gurus.

I offer a supplication to sovereign Vajradhara,
powerful Nairātmyā, the powerful lord [Virūpa],
mahasiddha Kāṇha, Ḍāmarupa,
Avadhūtīpa, and Gayadhara.

I offer a supplication to Drokmi, the great guru,
Setön Kunrik, Zhangtön Chöbar, glorious Sakyapa,

the Jetsun brothers, the paṇḍita lord of dharma,
and Chögyal Phakpa.

I offer a supplication to Könchok Pal,
the lord of dharma Sönam Pal, Sönam Gyaltsen,
and venerable Palden Tsultrim.

According to the supplemental lineage from the regent of the Evaṃ Monasteries found in the *Explanation for the Assembly*:

> Buddhaśrī, Ngorchen Dorjechang,
> and Sönam Gyaltsen.
>
> I offer a supplication to the regent Kunga Wangchuk,
> the tutor Könchok Pal, Lhachok Senge,
> Könchok Lhundrub, Sangye Senge,
> Namkha Palzang, and Sönam Lhundrub.
>
> I offer a supplication to Palchok Gyaltsan,
> Sangye Phuntsok, Sönam Palden,
> Palden Chökyong, {327} Chökyong Zangpo,
> Namkhai Chime,
> and to my root gurus.

According to the Sakya family lineage, after "Lhachok Senge, Könchok Lhundrub," in the interval is:

> Mantradhara dharma lord Kunga Rinchen
> and Sönam Wangpo.
>
> I offer a supplication to Kunga Sönam,
> Kunga Tashi, Sönam Rinchen, Kunga Lodrö,
> Namkha Chime, the true embodiment of all refuges,
> and the root gurus.

Having ascertained the names, one should understand each one in connection with their sphere of attainment.

According to the lineage found in the *Explanation for Disciples*, in the interval after Sempa Chenpo:

I offer a supplication to the union of the lineages, Dakchen
Vajradhara,
lord of dharma Kunpang, Losal Gyatso,
Khyentse Wangchuk, Labsum Gyaltsen,
and Wangchuk Rabten.

I offer a supplication to Sönam Chokden,
Sobnam Chokdrub, Khyenrab Jampa,
Morchen, Nesar Je,
Kunga Lodrö, Namkha Chime Pal,
and the root gurus.

Through the power of those supplications,
may renunciation and the two bodhicittas arise in my heart.
May my mind be encouraged though hearing the qualities of the
result,
and may I be empowered to embark upon the path of the great
secret.

Having received the vase empowerment into the sand maṇḍala
of the externally generated shapes, once the obscurations of the
body
are purified through the process of the nāḍīs by meditating on the
creation stage,
may I be empowered to obtain the stage of the nirmāṇakāya.

Having received the secret empowerment into the inner maṇḍala
of the bodhicitta of the bhaga, once the obscurations of the voice
are purified through the process of the syllables by meditating on
the path of caṇḍālī,
may I be empowered to obtain the stage of the saṃbhogakāya.

Having received the third empowerment in the secret maṇḍala
of relative bodhicitta, once the obscurations of the mind

are purified through the process of the amṛta by meditating on the path of the messenger,
may I be empowered to obtain the stage of the dharmakāya.

Having received the fourth empowerment in the ultimate maṇḍala
of ultimate bodhicitta, once the obscurations of the three doors
are purified through the process of vāyu by meditating on the path of the waves,
may I be empowered to obtain the stage of the svabhāvakāya.

At all times until that is attained,
having all positive conditions extolled by the victor,
may desired goals be well accomplished in accord with the dharma,
and may there be the good fortune of vast abundance of existence and peace.

This supplement to the composition of Ngorchen Mahāvajradhara was edited by Chatral Khyentse Wangpo. May its virtue be excellent.
sarva maṅgalaṃ

PART THREE

The Liberating Instructions

14. The Complete Clarification of the Hidden Meaning

The Instructional Manual on How to Give Instructions According to the Treatise of the Path with Its Result[1]

Lama Dampa Sönam Gyaltsen

Lama Dampa Sönam Gyaltsen (1312–1375), the fourteenth Sakya throne holder, was born into the Khön family in 1312, the female Water Mouse year. He was the youngest of nine children. His father was Dakchen Zangpo Pal (bDag chen bzang po dpal, 1262–1324), the eleventh Sakya throne holder. His mother was Machik Zhönu Bum (Ma gcig gzhon nu 'bum). His elder half-brother Namkha Lekpe (Nam mkha' legs pa'i rgyal mtshan, 1305–1343) was the twelfth Sakya throne holder, and his elder brother Jamyang Donyö Gyaltsen ('Jam dbyangs don yod rgyal mtshan, 1310–1344) was the thirteenth Sakya throne holder.

When Sönam Gyaltsen was conceived, his mother dreamt that the sun entered her abdomen and that she drank in one gulp the Tsangpo River in Yeru. Because of these dreams, at birth Sönam Gyaltsen was initially named Nyima Dewe Lodrö, meaning "wisdom of the blissful sun." By every account he was an extraordinary child and considered a rebirth of a bodhisattva dwelling on the stages.

To recount a few highlights of his education and training, at the age of three, Nyima Dewe Lodrö was given the empowerment of the five-deity Raktayamāri by Rongpa Sherab Senge (Rong pa shes rab seng ge, 1251–1315). He received the reading transmission of the *a ra pa ca na* mantra from Lama Zangpo (bLa ma bZang po, dates unknown). He was assisted by his tutor in a three-month retreat on the Sakya tradition of Mañjuśrī. At that time he also began studying the Hevajra tantra.

When Nyima Dewe Lodrö was eight, he started to give explanations of dharma, which were very favorably received. He also began to seek permission to ordain from his parents, but they refused to grant him permission for fear that he might not be able to maintain the ordination vows. Instead, at the age of eleven, he received lay vows, empowerments, and other teachings from his elder half-brother Lhachen Kunga Lodrö (bLa chen ti śrī Kun dga' Blo gros, dates unknown).

Until the age of sixteen, Nyima Dewe Lodrö received empowerments and instructions on the main tantric curriculum of Sakya from Lama Zangpo and Lama Zhönu Pal (gZhon nu dpal, dates unknown). At the time of requesting the six-limbed yoga of Kālacakra and the pith instructions of Avalokiteśvara from Lama Zangpo, Nyima Dewe Lodrö beheld the face of Mañjuśrī. He also received many Vajrayāna teachings from his father, Dakchen Zangpo Pal. He first received Path with Its Result and other Vajrayāna teachings from Lama Palden Senge (dPal ldan seng ge, dates unknown).

At seventeen, Nyima Dewe Lodrö was granted novice ordination from the Jonang abbot, Sönam Drakpa (bSod nams grags pa, dates unknown), receiving the name Sönam Gyaltsen, by which he would be known for the rest of his life. At twenty, he received full ordination from Sönam Drakpa, together with his elder brother, Jamyang Donyö Gyaltsen. It is said that Sönam Gyaltsen was impeccable in observing his monastic vows—giving up meat, alcohol, and abstaining from eating after the noon meal.

At the age of twenty-four, Sönam Gyaltsen met the mahasiddha Naza Trakphukpa Sönam Pal (Na bza' brag phug pa bsod nams dpa1, 1277–1350). Though the Path with Its Result teachings were certainly transmitted by many masters during the late thirteenth and early fourteenth century, Ngorchen Kunga Zangpo records a brief hiatus of Khön family masters in the primary lineage, with the main line of transmission passing from the seventh Sakya throne holder, Chögyal Phakpa Lodrö Gyaltsen Palzangpo (Chos rgyal 'phags pa bLo gros rgyal mtshan dpal bzang po, 1235–1280), to Zhangtön Könchok Pal (Zhang ston dkon mchog dpal, d. 1317), and from him to Trakphukpa.

Under Trakphukpa's guidance, Sönam Gyaltsen progressed very quickly in his meditative experience, greatly impressing his teacher. Thus, Trakphukpa proceeded to grant a whole collection of teachings to Sönam Gyaltsen, many of which he had already received. In particular, Sönam Gyaltsen had a very good experience of caṇḍālī yoga in the practice of the Vajrayoginī of the Sakya school. He understood that Trakphukpa was an extraordinary guru, and he became the principal lineage holder of Trakphukpa's teaching. Nevertheless, Sönam Gyaltsen continued to study under the leading masters of his day, including Butön Rinchen Drub and many others.

In the traditional histories of Sönam Gyaltsen's life, not much is recorded of his activities on a yearly basis from his twenty-seventh year until his sixty-second year. Notable among his activities, however, are the restoration of Samye Monastery, where he spent considerable time, and the replacement of the throne of the Jowo statue in Lhasa. He composed many texts, attained high levels of experience and realization through practicing Vajrayāna teachings, and taught extensively all over Tibet until passing away in 1375 at the age of sixty-three. Realizing that he was shortly going to pass away, as part of his last testament given on the twentieth day of the sixth Tibetan month, he extolled the virtues of monastic discipline, declaring "From the time I was seventeen, I have been pure in my discipline. All my activities as a novice and as a fully ordained monastic have served to stabilize my mind." He passed into his final samādhi, known in Tibetan as thukdam (*thugs dam*), and remained in that state until the evening of the twenty-fifth day.[2]

Sönam Gyaltsen's writings had an enduring impact on the Sakya school. The text translated here in the first portion of this volume, *Clarification of the Hidden Meaning*, is a commentary on Jetsun Drakpa Gyaltsen's *How to Give Instructions According to the Treatise*. His other major Path with Its Result text is his commentary on *The Vajra Verses* known under the sobriquet, *The Black Volume*. In addition, Sönam Gyaltsen composed a highly regarded text on the royal dynasties of Tibet called the *Clear Mirror*.

Relying on Jetsun Rinpoche's grand outline as a basis, which is part of a collection in the *Yellow Volume* called *Four Great Trees of the Treatise*, Sönam Gyaltsen begins his explanation with an outline of the Vajrayāna preliminary practices, which are used as the foundation for the sequential contemplations described in this manual. At that time the presentations of the three appearances and the three tantras had not been formally separated. Thus, quite early in the text, one is instructed to engage in yoga practices in order to prevent the pain in one's body that can arise from practicing meditation for extended periods, and so on. On the basis of these instructions, one enters into the contemplations of the three appearances and the three tantras. This text forms the basis for all later presentations of the Path with Its Result in both the tradition of *Explanation for the Assembly* and the tradition of *Explanation for the Disciples*. As such, it represents one of the most seminal texts of the entire Sakya tradition.

Homage to the guru and the vajra ḍākinīs.

Having bowed to the guru, with the excellent deity,
who correctly teaches others the clarification[3]
of *The Vajra Verses*, the lineage passed from one ear to the next,
the speech of Virūpa, the lord of magic power,
and having offered a supplication with loving thoughts for others,
in order that this supreme instruction never decline,
and to remove the taints affecting my speech,
I shall clarify the sequence of instructions according to the tradition of the lineage.

Now then, a faithful, compassionate disciple who has properly obtained empowerment, wishes to be free from the suffering of samsara, and wishes to obtain omniscience through Secret Mantra Vajrayāna, should offer a gift for instruction with a preliminary feast and bali offerings and offer a maṇḍala prior to offering this supplication, reciting these words one time:

> Omniscient one, endowed with a body of gnosis,
> who has purified the wheel of existence,
> may the lord kindly protect me today
> with the precious explanation.
> May the lord protect others
> with your stainless lotus feet.
> May the great Muni, the hero of migrating beings,
> bestow the supreme thought upon me. {331}

Flowers are distributed into the hands [of the disciples]. [They should] offer three prostrations. Offer a prostration to the guru and recite the supplication once. That is one cycle; repeat this three times. Afterward, in the presence of the guru say, "We disciples have gathered here. Please accept us for the stages of the extremely profound instruction, and kindly please bestow them."

Having offered a maṇḍala and prostrations, be seated in the row. The guru says, "These supplications, and so on, are not done for the pride of the master or for intellectual understanding. These come from the intimate instructions of the master and the lineage who have obtained the goal taught by the buddhas in the tantras. *The Five Stages* states:

> Whatever is very dear
> or very special
> because of [one's] inexhaustible desire—
> that should be offered to the guru.[4]

And:

> Having abandoned all [other] offerings,
> it is proper to begin offering to the guru.
> By pleasing them, the supreme gnosis of
> omniscience will be obtained.[5]

Likewise:

> Whoever does not supplicate the guru
> will not be born in this family.[6]

Fifty Verses on the Guru states:

> Holding a flower maṇḍala in hand, {332}
> . . . .
> the one who wishes to listen [to the teaching] should offer three supplications.[7]

At that time the guru should investigate the signs. If the intimate instruction is explained when the breath of both master and disciple move through the right nostril, even though experience may arise, it will not be stable and obstacles will arise. When the breath moves through both nostrils, it is called the "neutral vāyu." Since it is switching sides and at that time samādhi will be very weak, [the samādhi] will be unstable. If the intimate instruction is explained when the breath moves through the left nostril, though experience will arise slowly, since it will arise stably and there will be few obstacles, that is the time [the instruction] is to be explained. Furthermore, if the breath is moving through the right nostril for a long while, one meditates on it moving through the left nostril and it is possible [the breath] will switch sides. If it does not switch, then "nourish the breast." The breath will switch sides by strongly massaging the breast with the elbow of the right arm and massaging the right cheek with the palm. If the breath refuses to switch, one should lie down on the right side for one or two days, and so on, and apply nourishing the breast; the breath will then switch. At that time one should explain the stages of instruction.

Here there are (1) the preliminaries and (2) the main subject, meditating on the path.

I. The Preliminaries

In the first topic, there are (1) the preliminaries for instruction and (2) the common preliminaries.

A. The Preliminaries for Instruction

Meditate on (1) accumulation and purification and (2) practicing the three trainings.

1. Accumulation and Purification

In the first of these, there are two topics.

a. Maṇḍala Offerings

The offering maṇḍala, for the purpose of gathering merit, is practiced according to the *Guhyasamāja Tantra*:

> The wise fill this buddhafield
> with the seven precious articles,
> offered daily by the intelligent
> for siddhis by those wishing siddhis.[8]

Having gone for refuge three times to the guru and the Three Jewels beforehand, one should meditate on bodhicitta for a long while, thinking that one should obtain buddhahood and, for that purpose, one should gather the accumulation of merit.

Then, the place where one resides should be meditated on as empty with the *svabhāva* mantra. {333} Imagine that from the state of emptiness arises a *bhrūṃ*, from which arises a precious celestial mansion, inside of which is a precious throne, on top of which is a lotus, sun, and moon seat, on which sits the sublime guru, the embodiment of all buddhas of the three times in the form of Heruka. Around him are seated the lineage gurus, buddhas, and bodhisattvas.

Imagine that in the center of seven heaps composed of pure substances and clean flowers, there is Sumeru, the king of mountains, decorated with eight great peaks. The eastern face is composed of crystal; the southern face, sapphire; the western face, ruby; and the northern face, gold. Furthermore, in the east is Purvavideha, in the south is Jambudvīpa, in the west is Godānīya, and in the north is Kurava. Between the east and the center is the sun; between the center and the west is the moon. Above are the enjoyments of devas and humans, filled with inconceivably excellent and superior things, such as the seven precious royal emblems, the wish-granting cow, the uncultivated harvest, the wish-fulfilling tree, gold, silver, grain, food, clothes, and so on. Imagine those things are offered to the guests in front, who are not concerned with those offerings.

Offer this supplication three times: "May [offerings to] the sublime guru, the embodiment of the body, speech, mind, qualities, and activities of all buddhas of the three times, complete the accumulation of merit and gnosis in my continuum." As such, repeat that many times and begin counting the offerings. One should have strong devotion to the guru.

b. Vajrasattva

The purification for removing negative conditions is beginning the approach of the one-hundred-syllable mantra. Further, on the crown of one's head is Vajrasattva holding a vajra and a bell and Vajragarvi holding a curved knife and a skull cup. {334} Both are white, adorned with precious ornaments, and seated in equipoise with crossed legs. Meditate on a white syllable *hūṃ* on a moon disc in Vajrasattva's heart. A stream of amṛta arises from it, filling the Bhagavān couple. The amṛta falls through the crown of one's head, like a rain shower. That stream of amṛta expels all of one's misdeeds as a black substance from one's two paths of excretion and the two soles of the feet.

Imagine that the vacated space becomes filled with amṛta and recite the one-hundred-syllable mantra.

The confession through the four powers is the power of the witness and firm refuge; the power of overcoming [faults], regretting past misdeeds and confessing them; the power of avoiding recommitting faults, thinking that henceforth one will never commit them again even at the cost of one's life; and the power of the continuous antidote, reciting the mantra dhāraṇī, meditating on emptiness and compassion, and so on.[9]

As such, when practicing both the accumulation and purification in three or four sessions daily, with one hundred or one thousand repetitions each session, it is best if practiced for one year. It is mediocre if practiced for one month. It is average if practiced for three, five, or seven days or if there are signs of purifying misdeeds (dreaming of washing, pus and blood, unclean things, or sentient beings expelled from the body), wearing white clothes and being adorned with white ornaments and flowers, and flying in the sky. In actuality, also the body feels light, health is good, one's mind is lucid, and samādhi is clear.

The signs of increasing merit are that one has many dreams, such as sitting on a great throne, putting on fine, new clothes, eating fine food, wearing fine ornaments, the sun and moon rising, climbing great mountains, beating a drum, blowing a conch horn, being praised by everyone, and so on. When there is an ample quantity of both accumulation and purification, samādhi arises with ease and obstructions are few.

As such, having counted the number of both accumulation and purification, offer flowers to the guru. The guru investigates the signs. If there remain great obstacles and samādhi is poor when reaching the agreed upon number, {335} begin effort in accumulation and purification again. If [the number] is reached, obstacles are few, and samādhi is good, change the [teaching] session.

2. The Three Trainings

There are three in practicing the three trainings.

a. Training the Body

Wash the entire body with chang or urine, and massage; stay in an isolated dwelling; and perform circumambulations, walking carefully without raising dust. Practice according to:

> One should roll the head on the neck,
> wave the two arms separately,
> and shake the legs strongly
> to train the five limbs.[10]

Roll the head both right and left. Nod in the four directions, and nod right and left twice. Further, with vajra fists crossed at the heart, do not close one's eyes. If the eyes are closed, faults will occur in the eyes. Wave the two arms individually. Having circled them around the head, shake them. Without circling the head, shake them in front above the shoulder one time and pull the bow. Shake the legs in the four directions, one by one. Using such a method until the body is tired causes all nāḍīs to become pliable, preventing strong pain of the nāḍīs and vāyus. Next, relax the body and voice and naturally sustain clarity. One should naturally sustain relaxation. First, having identified the characteristic of the mind [clarity], rest on that. Second, since one understands union on the basis of the essence of mind [emptiness], rest freely.

b. Training the Voice

Having discarded activities of the voice, such as recitations of text, repetitions of mantra, conversations, and so on, remain silent. That will cause the breath to be gentle and easy.

c. Training the Mind

Relax, having renounced mental distractions, such as view, meditation, and so on. {336} Reflecting on the dharma, devotion, compassion, and so on, relax. Through that, one should engage the mind on the object. In brief, the body is trained with yantras of the body, speech is trained with the isolation of speech, and the mind is trained by the mind remaining relaxed. Those three resemble breaking and training a horse before a race. Since one engages in those for months and years, it is possible that samādhi will arise by itself.

> By training the ordinary body, voice, and mind,
> gnosis will arise.[11]

By engaging in those, the signs of the purification of the body are that the body is comfortable, floats, and feels light and that one is able to remain in a posture for a long while. The signs of training the voice are that one does not sense the movements of the breath, it does not move in and out, and one breathes without difficulty. The signs of training the mind are clarity and lucidity, absence of distraction, and so on. Until those signs arise, one should make effort.

B. The Common Preliminaries

The common preliminaries has two topics.

1. The Three Crucial Points

The three crucial points have three topics.

a. Body

The critical point of the body is being seated cross-legged or with the knees drawn to the chest. If one is cross-legged, one should be sitting either in the bodhisattva posture or the vajra posture, with the hands in the mudra of equipoise. If one is seated with the knees drawn up to the chest, sitting evenly on the two legs and the buttocks, like a tripod, there will be no pain if one places a load on one leg. One's hands make the meditation belt mudra or the fighting hearth mudra.[12] For both of those positions, the head is slightly bent, the eyes fall on the tip of the nose, the tongue rests on the palate, and the teeth and lips are evenly closed. One should primarily sit cross-legged at all times when one is young, during the fall and spring, when one has blood and pitta illnesses, and when it is warm {337}or mostly hot. One primarily uses the position of the knees drawn to chest at all times when one is old,[13] during the winter season, when one has excess kapha, and when it is cold. Further, because of the critical point of the body, the nāḍīs will not be disturbed. Since the mind is stabilized by that, samādhi arises naturally, similar to the foundation of the walls of a house.

b. Voice

The critical point of the voice is that until the discomfort of the throat is removed, one should forcefully expel the breath through the nostrils, similar to sweeping a dirty house.

c. Mind

The critical point of the mind is equipoise through relaxing the mind for a little while, similar to a horse breathing before a race.

2. Meditation

There are three topics in the meditation.

a. Bodhicitta

The meditation of bodhicitta is as follows: In order to transform all activities of accumulation into others' benefit and in order to accomplish the Mahayana path, think, "I must obtain buddhahood in order to benefit all sentient beings. For that purpose, I shall mediate on samādhi."

b. Guru Yoga

Meditating on the guru as a branch of perfecting the accumulations is meditating on the guru on a lotus, sun, and moon seat on the crown of one's head, and offering the supplication from the depth of one's heart, "Please empower me so that the special samādhi arises in my continuum." At the end, through the power of devotion, the guru dissolves into one's crown.

c. Deity Yoga

The meditation on the deity for the purpose of abandoning ordinary concepts is uttering *hūṃ* and meditating on the protection wheel; uttering *hūṃ* and meditating on divine pride or a two-armed heruka. In order to prevent obstacles afflicting the body, imagine a white *oṃ* on a moon on the crown. In order to prevent obstacles afflicting the voice, {338} imagine an *āḥ* on a red lotus in the throat. In order to prevent obstacles afflicting the mind, imagine a black *hūṃ* on a sun in the heart center and utter *oṃ āḥ hūṃ* three times; through that visualization, obstacles will be prevented.

The three trainings, the three crucial points, and the three meditations are the nine limbs of concentration, which are the preliminaries for all concentrations.

II. The Main Subject, the Path

In the main subject matter of the path, there are two topics: (1) the instruction on the three appearances and (2) the instruction on the three tantras, which summarize the whole treatise[14] into three tantras.

A. Three Appearances

The instruction on (1) impure appearances, (2) experiential appearances, and (3) pure appearances.

1. Impure Appearances

In *The Vajra Verses* it is said "for a sentient being." Since one understands the faults of samsara through investigating the realms of sentient beings, to begin, reflect on the faults of samsara. "In affliction" refers to being led into the three lower realms because of experiencing the three poisonous afflictions in three grades: strong, medium, and weak. Since the freedoms and endowments that free one from those lower realms are difficult to acquire, next one meditates on the difficulties of acquiring such freedoms and endowments. Because "impure appearances" refers to gathering karma based on impure deluded appearances, next there is the meditation on confidence in the causes and results of karma.

a. Faults of Samsara

Though the forms of suffering of samsara are inconceivable, when summarized into categories, there are three sufferings: the meditations on (1) the suffering of suffering, (2) the suffering of change, and (3) the suffering of formations.

i. Suffering of Suffering

The first of these three is reflecting on (1) the suffering of hell beings, (2) the suffering of pretas, and (3) the suffering of animals.

I) Hell Beings

The first of these three is reflecting on (1) the hot hells, (2) the cold hells, and (3) the temporary, peripheral hells.

A) Hot Hells

For the first of these three, *Letter to a Friend* states:

> Those sentient beings who engage in negative conduct
> will always suffer in the hells, such as
> Saṃjiva, Kālasūtra, Pratapana, {339}
> Saṃghata, Raurava, Avīci, and so on.[15]

The sufferings of Saṃjiva ("live again"), Kālasūtra ("black line"), Saṃghata ("crushing"), Raurava ("wailing"), Mahāraurava ("great wailing"), Tapana ("inferno"), Pratapana ("great inferno"), and Avīci ("unbearable") are unbearable.

In Saṃjiva, the beings perceive each other as mortal enemies. Whatever they pick up becomes a weapon, with which they strike and murder one another. When a cold wind rises up or the sound "live again" comes from the sky, they are revived in their former bodies, and once again they strike one another as before and suffer.

In Kālasūtra, four or eight lines are made on the body. One is sawed and chopped with an axe from head to foot. At that time, when the lower body is severed, the wounds on the upper body heal; when the upper body is cut, the lower body heals. One experiences nothing other than such suffering.

In Saṃghata, the hell guardians drive sentient beings between mountains with goat, sheep, and horse heads. When the two mountains collide, they are crushed like sesame and pulverized. After the two mountains separate and their bodies are just as they were before, they again experience the suffering of being pulverized.

In Raurava, when sentient beings arrive at a house, through the power of karma it becomes an iron house with no doors. Since the interior burns with flames, there is the experience of the suffering of wailing and weeping because of the extreme danger.

In Mahāraurava, the iron house has two stories. Since the interior burns with flames, there is the experience of the suffering of even more wailing and weeping.

In Tapana, {340} after sentient beings are impaled with flaming iron stakes from anus to crown, they experience the suffering of smoke and tongues of flames pouring out of their orifices.

In Pratapana, after sentient beings are impaled with flaming iron tridents through their shoulders and crown, they experience the suffering of flames within their bodies; billows of flames and smoke pour out of their throats and mouths; and after their bellies split open, their guts spill out.

In Avīci, since there are flames in the four directions, above, and below, they become indistinguishable from the bodies of the sentient beings in hell. When they experience the suffering of burning, even though there are sentient beings, other than inferring their presence through their sounds of remorse, one cannot directly indicate them. Moreover, they experience incalculable suffering, such as stepping[16] on iron embers that are burning simultaneously, being cooked in an iron pot in flaming oil, being stabbed by kīlas through long tongues of flame on an iron plain, being fed liquid metal, traversing a ground of burning sand, and so on.

On the basis of the suffering arising in each subsequent hell becoming greater than the last, the experience of suffering in each one increases.

If it is wondered how long one must experience those sufferings, the *Treasury of Abhidharma* states:

> A single day of the lower devas
> of the desire realm
> equals fifty human years.
> . . . .
> In the six hells, Saṃjiva and so on, in order,
> a single day equals the life span of the desire realm devas.
> Therefore, they resemble the desire realm devas.
> Life in Pratapana is half a minor eon; in Avīci,
> one minor eon.[17]

Since a single day for the four great kings is fifty human years, {341} their life span is five hundred years. Since a single day for the Trāyastriṃśa devas is one hundred human years, they live for one thousand deva years. Since one day for the Yāmā devas is two hundred years, they live for two thousand deva years. Since a single day for the Tuṣitā devas is four hundred human years, they live for four thousand deva years. Since a single day for the Nirmāṇarataya devas is eight hundred human years, they live for eight thousand deva years. Since a single day for the Paranirmitavaśavartin devas is one thousand six hundred human years, they live for sixteen thousand deva years. Counting the life span of those deities as a single day, they can be applied to six of them, Saṃjiva and so on, respectively. The Pratapana hell beings live for half a minor kalpa. The Avīci hell beings live for a whole minor kalpa.

B) Cold Hells

The eight cold hells are Ārbuda ("blister"), Nirārbuda ("cracked blister"), Huhuva, Hahava, Aṭaṭa ("chattering teeth"),[18] Utpala ("blue poppy"), Padma ("lotus"), and Mahāpadma ("great lotus"). These are directly above the hot hells, and the suffering is very specific.

First, conditions for warmth—houses, clothes, sun, and so on—are absent, like living on a face of a Himalayan mountain. [Sentient beings there] are struck by cold winds and blizzards and tormented. They experience the suffering of the body filled with blisters. Second, the blisters also crack open, their skin is split open by iron bugs with sharp beaks, and they experience the suffering of blood and lymph seeping out. Third, since they are tormented by the intense cold, it is unbearable, and they howl with the sound "hu hu." Fourth, since they are tormented by the cold, it is as if their bodies and minds are parted; lymph seeps from their eyes and nose; their throats are dry; and they experience suffering, moaning "ha ha" in a whimper. Fifth, because of the intense cold, {342} they suffer, exhausted, with teeth clenched from being extremely tormented without even being able to speak. Sixth, since they are tormented in that way, their bodies become blue through the force of the wind and they experience the suffering of splitting into five or six pieces. Seventh, since they are tormented even more than that by the wind, their skin becomes red in color, the blood is exhausted and coagulated, and there is suffering of the skin breaking into eight or ten pieces. Since the eighth [cold hell] is even colder than the last, the skin blisters, splitting into one hundred or one thousand wounds. One experiences the suffering of lymph and marrow seeping out. *Letter to a Disciple* states:

> An indescribably cold wind penetrates to the bone.
> Their frozen bodies shiver and contract into a fetal position.
> One hundred blisters arise and erupt, from which creatures emerge
> that tear [the body] with their beaks, leaking fat, lymph, and marrow.
> Exhausted, teeth clenched, hair and pores standing on end,
> with eyes, nose, and throat completely tormented with pain,
> body and mind separate—they are overwhelmed,
> dwelling in the cold hells, crying out in extreme distress.[19]

The life span in those hells as stated in the *Treasury of Abhidharma*:

> The life span of Arbuda is
> exhausted when once every one hundred years a sesame seed
> is removed from a bushel of sesame.
> The life span of the others is multiplied by twenty.[20]

The commentary cites a sutra. The Bhagavān only used examples for the life span in those [hells]:

> "Bhikṣus, for example, a Magadha bin of sesame is filled with eighty bushels of sesame. If one were to remove from that one sesame seed every passing one hundred years, bhikṣus, that entire Magadha bin of sesame seeds would be completely emptied much faster than a life span of a sentient being born in Arbuda, which I cannot describe."[21] {343}

[The Bhagavān] further explains that each subsequent hell multiplies this by twenty.

C) Temporary Peripheral Hells

Reflect on the temporary peripheral hells. In the four directions of the eight hot hells are Kukūla ("pit of embers"), Kuṇapa ("putrid swamp"),

Kṣuramārga ("plain of razors"), Asipattravana ("forest of swords"), Ayaḥśalmalīvana ("thorn grass mountain"), and Vaitaraṇī ("river"). In these, the beings of the hot hells experience countless sufferings. The *Treasury of Abhidharma* states:

> For all eight, there are sixteen more.
> Those are on the four sides—
> Kukūla, Kuṇapa,
> Kṣuramārga, and so on, and the river.[22]

If it is asked what kind of suffering is experienced, once the beings of the hot hells are freed from actual hot hells, they depart for another direction. After they fall into Kukūla, when stepping with their feet, those become bone, as all the flesh is burnt away. When they lift their feet, those are restored. Also, when they walk, their feet burn. They remain like that for a long time. When freed from that hell, they arrive at Kuṇapa, which is filled with a rotting swamp of excrement, and they suffer being eaten by bugs with iron beaks. When freed from that hell, they arrive on a plain filled with sharp-edged razors. When they step with their feet, they are cut into pieces; when they lift their feet, they are restored. When freed from that hell, they run across the plain, arriving in front of an appearance of beautiful trees, but the leaves turn into weapons. When they fall into those, they experience the suffering of their bodies being cut up. When freed from that hell, they are chased by iron dogs, donkeys, and wolves. When they see the peak of Ayaḥśalmalīvana, they climb it quickly, suffering while their bodies struggle with eight-inch, downward-facing thorns that strike the surface of their bodies. When they arrive at the peak, since the iron beaks of crows, white birds, and vultures dig out their eyes and peck their skin, they utter cries of torment. {344} When they descend, the upward-facing thorns pierce their bodies and they experience the suffering of losing consciousness, and so on. When freed from that, they are beaten by hell guardians on the banks of the Vaitaraṇī River and suffer there for a long time.

In brief, one should think that since those born there are helpless, one should make effort in methods to avoid being born there. The method is practicing the path. Supreme among those different paths is this instruction of the Path with Its Result. Exhaust one's body and mind by meditating in that way, and then relax and rest.

II) Pretas

Reflect on the suffering of pretas. After being freed from the hells, if one is born in the realm of Yama, the suffering is incalculable. Here, there are pretas with (1) outer obstructions, (2) inner obstructions, and (3) obstructions to eating and drinking.

A) Outer Obstructions

Since whatever food and drink one sees all becomes pus, blood, and so on, glacial water, the groves of Mount Malaya, and forests burned by fire all become distorted appearances. *Letter to a Disciple* states:

> Because of the ripening of utterly unbearable karma,
> all this diversity appears distorted to these confused ones.[23]

B) Inner Obstructions

[*Letter to a Disciple* states:]

> With a mouth the size of the eye of a needle and tormented
> with a huge, terrifying belly, even if an ocean were imbibed,
> it could not pass through their narrow throats.
> Even a drop of water burns its mouth, causing thirst.[24]

That is how [the preta with an inner obstruction] suffers.

C) Obstructions to Eating and Drinking

Letter to a Friend states:

> At night some have flaming mouths,
> eating sand as food, which makes their mouths blaze.[25]

As it says, all of whatever food they eat becomes flames and they experience many sufferings, such as burning in their belly, and so on. They can live for five hundred years, with a preta day equaling one human month. The *Treasury of Abhidharma* states: {345}

> Pretas live for five hundred years, a day equaling one month.[26]

That is how [the preta with an obstruction to food and drink] suffers. Since those born there are helpless, reflect on that just as before.

III) Animals

Reflect on the suffering of animals. The two topics for animals are the animals that live in the depths, such as the ocean and the darkness between continents, and those that are scattered about, living in the places of devas and humans. *Letter to a Friend* states:

> Furthermore, in the birthplace of animals, there are various sufferings,
> such as killing, bondage, beatings, and so on.
> Without the virtue that brings peace,
> they eat one another, which is very unbearable.
> Some die for their pearls, wool, bone, blood,
> flesh, and hide.
> Powerless, others are kicked, struck,
> whipped, goaded, and enslaved.[27]

Their life span is addressed in the *Treasury of Abhidharma*:

> The supreme length of an animal's life is an eon.[28]

Since those born there are helpless, reflect just as before.

ii. Suffering of Change

There are two topics in reflecting on the suffering of change.

I) Shared Suffering of Change

Reflect on the shared, general suffering of change. Even if one attains the happiness of samsara, it is not stable. After one parts with [such happiness], one must experience much suffering. Thus, the happiness of samsara has no substance. For example, having been born as Indra, he can fall down to earth and suffer. There are incalculable sufferings: Just as after Māndhāta[29] was born a cakravartin king, he was born as the lowest of all. After obtaining the happiness of a desire realm deva, one can be born in hell. After being born as the sun and moon [devas], one might be conceived in darkness, and so on. *Letter to a Friend* states:

> After Indra becomes an object of worldly veneration,
> he falls to the earth through the power of karma.
> Having become a cakravartin,
> the cakravartin also becomes a subject.[30]

And:

> Having obtained the extremely great bliss of desire of the deva realm
> and having obtained the passionless bliss of Brahma, {346}
> one experiences the uninterrupted suffering
> of becoming the fuel of Avīci Hell.
> Obtaining [birth] as the sun and moon, the light
> of one's body illuminates the entire world,
> but, once again, after one arrives in the pitch darkness,
> one cannot even see one's outstretched hand.[31]

Since those born there are helpless, and so on, reflect just as before.

II) Specific Suffering of Change

Reflect on the specific suffering of change of human beings. In general, though the suffering of change exists in samsara, if one is not convinced [of the suffering of change] because it is not obvious when one primarily examines human beings, the wealthy become paupers, the powerful become weak, enemies become friends and friends become enemies, and so on. When one looks at one's neighbors, relatives, and the population of one's nation, all are never where they were before. In brief, as it is said:

> In the end all accumulations are exhausted.
> In the end the high become low.

In the end meetings disperse.
In the end the living die.[32]

Since those born there are helpless, reflect just as before.

iii. Suffering of Formations

Reflect on the suffering of formations. If it is thought that one must make effort in achieving enjoyments and a retinue in order to abandon suffering and accomplish happiness in samsara, desire is never satisfied. After a desire is achieved, one will strive for the next desire and the next desire after that, getting older and older, slowly dying. No matter what work is done, it is never satisfactory; even the work finished in formers lives is dissatisfactory to the mind.[33] The *Madhyamaka Four Hundred* states:

Work done with effort
perishes effortlessly when it is finished.
Even though that is so,
you still are not free of attachment to work.[34]

As such, since those born there are helpless, reflect just as before. Through reflecting {347} on and determining that despite anything one does, there is no happiness no matter in what realm one is born, one turns to the dharma.

b. Freedoms and Endowments

There are three topics in reflecting on freedoms and endowments: (1) the difficulty of acquiring them, (2) the benefit of acquiring them, and (3) their impermanence.

i. The Difficulty of Acquiring Them

It is necessary to make effort in the methods of not being born into samsaric suffering. Also, the support of accomplishing that goal is this lifetime's body with freedoms and endowments. The freedoms and endowments are these things to be avoided. *Letter to a Friend* states:

> Birth as one holding wrong view, an animal,
> a preta, or a hell being,
> birth in a country lacking the teachings, or a borderland,
> birth as a barbarian, or birth as an idiot or mute,
> or as a long-lived deva—[these] are the eight births whose fault is the lack of freedom.[35]

There are ten endowments: The five personal endowments are birth as a human, in a central land, with complete faculties, with devotion to the object (that is, devotion to Vinaya), and not engaging in wrong actions (that is, not engaging in the five heinous deeds or asking others to do so). The five external endowments are that the Buddha came to the world, that he taught the dharma, that his doctrine remains, that others have also entered the doctrine, and that there is the affection of patrons, and so on, for the sake of others.

These endowments are difficult to acquire. As the *Introduction to the Conduct of Awakening* states:

> For that reason the Bhagavān has said,
> "Just like a turtle putting its neck
> in the ring of a wooden yoke [floating] in the great ocean,
> a human birth is very difficult to acquire."[36]

The reason freedoms and endowments are difficult to acquire is that when one observes the realm of sentient beings, there are inconceivable sentient beings who do not obtain a body. Even if they obtain a body, there are inconceivable sentient beings who do not obtain a human body. Even if a human body is obtained, obtaining the freedoms and endowments {348} is a mere possibility. Therefore, when one has obtained endowment in this life that is difficult to obtain, it is necessary to take this to heart and also practice the path. Reflect on the fact that the supreme path is the one-pointed practice of this intimate instruction of the Path with Its Result.

ii. The Benefit of Acquiring the Freedoms and Endowments

Reflect on the great benefit of acquiring the freedoms and endowments. If it is wondered why the freedoms and endowments difficult to acquire must be obtained, the benefit is very great. Since this body with freedoms and endowments is able to achieve higher realms in the next life, the nirvana of the lower vehicles, and even omniscient buddhahood, it is extremely beneficial. As *Letter to a Disciple* states:

> The path that is acquired by humans of mental fortitude,
> which becomes an aspect of guiding migrating beings who rely on
> the path of the sugata,
> is neither acquired by devas and nāgas nor by asuras,
> garuḍas, vidyādharas, kinnaras, or mahoragas.
> After acquiring the actual human birth so difficult to acquire,
> whoever in reality bears that in mind and is diligent in that [path]
> will become accomplished.[37]

iii. Impermanence of the Freedoms and Endowments

Reflect on the impermanence of the freedoms and endowments. Reflect on (1) the certainty of death, (2) the uncertainty of the time of the death, and (3) that nothing is of benefit at the time of death.

I) The Certainty of Death

If it is wondered, "Since those freedoms and endowments difficult to acquire are permanent because they endure for a long while, what is the need to make haste in accomplishing the path?" There is not even a slightly permanent entity in the freedoms and endowments. As the *Introduction to the Conduct of Awakening* states:

> Without pausing day and night,
> life always gets shorter.
> Having been shortened, it cannot be extended.
> How can someone like me not die?[38]

Thus, the subject is the certainty of death. Some die because of the disturbance of outer and inner disturbances of the elements, others die because of disturbances of obstructive misleaders, and still others die because of the negative conditions of disturbances of protective gods, and so on. There is not even a single kind of sentient being who does not die in the end.

II) The Uncertainty of the Time of Death

If it is wondered, "Though in the end there is death, for the time being when one has not died, why is it necessary to take the freedoms and endowments to heart at present?" {349} the *Introduction to the Conduct of Awakening* states:

> It is not rational to remain content
> saying, "I shall not die today."[39]

Since the time of death is uncertain, it is necessary to practice the path right now. The reasons for that are that life spans in Jambudvīpa are not fixed, there are many unfavorable conditions, and favorable conditions are rare. Thus, the time of death is uncertain. The *Treasury of Abhidharma* states:

> Here [in Jambudvīpa, life spans] are undefined. The least is
> ten years; at the beginning, incalculable.[40]

Ācarya Nāgārjuna states in *Necklace of Gems*:

> The conditions of death are many;
> the conditions of life are few.
> Those are the conditions of death;
> therefore, always practice the dharma.[41]

III) Nothing is of Benefit at the Time of Death

If it is thought, "The food and wealth gathered in this life, as well as the servants, relatives, friends, and so on, that one has sustained are beneficial when one dies," when the time of certain death arrives, it cannot be averted by substances such as food, wealth, and so on, it cannot be averted with mantras, and it cannot be averted with dependent origination. The *Sutra of Advice to the King* states:

> Great King, old age conquers youth, illness conquers health, decline conquers all abundance, and death conquers life. Since their action is swift, those cannot be averted by strength[42] or

averted by wealth. It is not easy to pacify those with substances, mantras, and medicine.[43]

c. Causes and Results of Karma

Meditating on the confidence in causes and results of karma is reflecting on the cause and result of (1) unvirtuous actions, (2) virtuous actions, and (3) neutral actions.

i. Nonvirtue

Reflect on nonvirtue.

I) Cause

[The ten unvirtuous deeds are as follows]: Taking life, taking what has not been given, and sexual misconduct are the three unvirtuous actions of the body. Lying, calumny, harsh words, and idle speech are the four unvirtuous actions of the voice. Envy, malice, and wrong view are the three unvirtuous actions of the mind. The ten unvirtuous actions and all the actions of body and voice are motivated by the three poisons, which lead them to nonvirtue. As [the *Necklace of Gems*] states: {350}

> The actions generated from these three—
> desire, hatred and ignorance—are unvirtuous.[44]

II) Result

Reflect on the result of unvirtuous actions. The *Treasury of Abhidharma* states:

> Because of suffering, because of death,
> and because of absence of vitality, there are three results.[45]

Thus, since the deed of killing through taking life generates suffering and causes death and loss of vitality,[46] the ripened result is suffering in the three lower realms. The result that corresponds with the cause [of taking life] is that wherever one is born, corresponding to the causal deed, taking life will be enjoyed. The experience that corresponds with the cause [of taking life] is a shortened life. The dominant result is that external medicines have reduced effectiveness. Likewise, for taking what is not given, and so on, each produce three results. Accordingly, suffering in the three lower realms is the ripened result. Enjoying this and that nonvirtue wherever one is born, corresponding with the causal action, arises from the result that corresponds with the cause. The *Necklace of Gems* states:

> Because of killing, one's life is short.
> ....
> Because of stealing, one is impoverished.
> Because of sexual misconduct, one has enemies.
> Because of lying, one is much slandered.
> Because of calumny, one is friendless.
> Because of harsh words, one hears unpleasant speech.
> Because of idle speech, one's words are not respected.
> Envy destroys hope in the mind.
> It is explained that malice bestows fear.
> Because of wrong view, one's view is inferior.[47]

The dominant result, in respective order, is:

> The outer world lacks vitality; hail is frequent;
> the dust is thick; the smell is bad; the terrain is uneven,
> contaminated with salt, and so on; the seasons are untimely;
> and grain is either scant or nonexistent.[48]

III) Avoiding Nonvirtue

Reflect on avoiding those [unvirtuous actions]. As such, think, "Since the result of unvirtuous actions is the production of suffering, henceforth, until attaining buddhahood, for as long as I have not died, or for a short period such as a year, I will not engage in unvirtuous actions of the three doors even for a moment."

ii. Virtue

Reflect on virtue.

I) Cause

Though killing through slander is explicitly stated, {351} the ten virtues are non-killing through non-slander. Principal among those are the absence of desire, the absence of malice, and the absence of envy. Thus, all actions motivated by the three roots of virtue are virtuous. As [the *Necklace of Gems*] says:

> The actions generated from these three—
> absence of desire, hatred, and ignorance—are
> virtuous.[49]

II) Result

Reflect on the result. The ripened result of virtuous conduct is birth in good places and obtaining the three awakenings.[50] The result that corresponds with the cause is enjoying virtuous conduct wherever one is born, corresponding to the causal deed. The experience that corresponds to the cause is the ten, such as long life, and so on. The dominant result is also tenfold: the world is vital, and so on.

III) Accomplishing Virtue

Reflect on accomplishing virtue. Think, "Since the benefits of virtue exist in that way, in general, henceforth until awakening is obtained, and in particular, for as long as I am alive, and also necessarily, for a year from now, my three doors will never be separate from virtuous deeds."

iii. Neutral Action

Reflect on neutral action.

I) Cause

Also, there are [actions] that are not connected with any virtuous or unvirtuous motive. The neutral actions that are neither virtuous nor unvirtuous are eating food, walking, and so on.

II) Result

Reflect on the result of those [neutral actions]. Even though one engages in those actions, those are unable to produce the virtuous and unvirtuous results above.

III) Transformation

Transforming [neutral actions] into favorable and virtuous actions is to think, "Even though one engages in that action, since it does not produce a ripened result, it will not produce a cause of freedom from samsara. Therefore, I must transform it into virtue by all means." Thus, all actions performed with the three doors must be connected with bodhicitta. The *Four Hundred Verses* states:

> Through reflection a bodhisattva
> transforms everything, either virtuous or unvirtuous,
> into wholesome virtues.
> If it is asked why, it is because they are transformed by the power
> of the mind.[51]

2. Experiential Appearances

Since the experiential appearance is "Experiential appearances are for a practitioner in samādhi," {352} meditate on the experiential appearance. The common practitioner meditates on the common experiential appearances that arise repeatedly in their continuum. The uncommon practitioner meditates again and again with conviction on the experience that arises.

a. Common Experiential Appearance

There are three topics in the common experiential appearance: (1) love, (2) compassion, and (3) bodhicitta.

i. Love

The *Introduction to Madhyamaka* states:

> Imparting benefit to migrating beings
> is called "great love."[52]

In the corresponding reflection, meditate on love for (1) friends, (2) enemies, and (3) ordinary beings.

I) Relatives

As such, having visualized one's birth mother, one should think, "this mother conceived me in the womb and placed me in leisure and endowment, which cannot be attained even with one hundred austerities. Then, having held me in her belly for nine or ten months, she abandoned harmful conduct and relied on conducive practices. When I was born from her womb, she cared for me with a loving mind, and having picked me up, she nursed me and gave me food and drink. She cleaned my poop with her hands, and having gathered many misdeeds, misery, and negative speech on my behalf, my mother gave to me all that she has. In brief, she nourished this cherished body, kept me alive, and impoverished herself. This mother is extremely kind." When that is understood, it is necessary to repay her kindness in this life with kindness. If one does not repay her, no one should be more ashamed than oneself. *Letter to a Disciple* states:

> What vile person could happily abandon those
> who held them in their lap as a helpless child,
> who lovingly nursed them with mother's milk,
> endured much fatigue, and upon whom they depended for love?
> What vile person could happily go and
> abandon those afflicted ones without protection from suffering,

in whose womb an opportunity to dwell was found,
who cared for them with affection, holding them in mind?[53] {353}

Think, "If I am to repay their kindness for such activities, if I were to provide abundant happiness for them, their kindness to me would be repaid. Therefore, if my mother in this life were to have the temporary happiness of devas and humans or the ultimate happiness of buddhahood, I would rejoice." Further, one should think, "Such happiness will not be obtained if the cause, virtue, is not accumulated. How wonderful it would be if she encountered virtuous actions, the cause of such happiness," and concentrating one's three doors into one point, repeat one hundred or one thousand times, "May my mother meet with happiness and the causes of happiness." Further, reflecting on her kindness and counting just as before, one should continue until the hairs of the body stand on end and one weeps uncontrollably.

Next, visualize all your relatives, such as your parents, and so on, in front of you. Reflect on the fact that these [relatives] are also close to you in this life. They are very kind because of all the benefits they have bestowed upon you. That is not all—they have acted as your mother in many previous lives, and each one who has been a mother benefited you as much as your own mother. Having reflected in this way, count as before.

II) Enemies

Having the perception that these are mothers just like one's own mother, when one gives rise to unfabricated love, visualize before yourself all those who are enemies who have caused harm to you directly or indirectly. Meditate on love for them as before, thinking, "Though these enemies harm me at present, not having recognized me as their child through insanity or inability, they were my mothers in past lives," and so on.

III) Ordinary Beings

Having given rise to love for enemies, visualize the sentient beings throughout space who are neither enemies nor friends. *Letter to a Friend* states:

The pile of bones of each and every being
equals Sumeru and surpasses it.

> The extent of mothers
> exceeds even the number of
> juniper berries that can be gathered.[54]

By such means, there is no end to repaying the kindness of every sentient being who has been our mother. {354} Thus, reflect on the reasons that each mother has benefited you, as before.

ii. Compassion

The *Introduction to Madhyamaka* states:

> Protecting those who suffer
> is the meditation called "great compassion."[55]

There is meditating with reference to (1) sentient beings, (2) phenomena, and (3) nonreferential compassion.

I) Sentient Beings

Think from the bottom of your heart, "Other than being joyful when mother sentient beings meet happiness and the causes of happiness, in reality those sentient beings are tormented by the three kinds of suffering through wrong action. How sad that these beings engage in unvirtuous actions that are the cause of suffering." You should count one hundred or one thousand times, with sadness for these mother sentient beings that are tormented with suffering.

II) Phenomena

Think, "These mothers of mine are not established in terms of sentient beings or the self of a person but are designated as self and sentient beings through ignorance and suffer. How sad." Meditate on compassion as before.

III) Nonreferential Compassion

Think, "Though these sentient beings are not established as truly existent by nature, because of strong clinging to true existence in persons and phenomena, they wander in samsara. How sad that they suffer," and meditate on compassion, as before.

iii. Bodhicitta

In the meditation on bodhicitta, there is (1) aspirational bodhicitta, (2) engaged bodhicitta, and (3) ultimate bodhicitta.

I) Aspirational Bodhicitta

The *Ornament of Direct Realization* states:

> Bodhicitta is generated out of the wish
> to attain perfect, full awakening to benefit others.[56]

[Think,] "As such, the time has come for me, the child, to free all mother sentient beings from suffering and its causes. {355} If I were to become free without freeing my mothers, it would be beyond shameful." *Letter to a Disciple* states:

> If one liberates oneself alone, there is no one more shameful,
> ignoring and leaving their relatives to be born, die, and
> transmigrate,
> trapped in the ocean of samsara,
> appearing as if fallen into a maelstrom.[57]

Think, "The power to liberate those mother sentient beings does not exist in Brahma, Indra, śrāvakas, or pratyekabuddhas—what need to mention myself? On the other hand, if it is asked in whom does such power exist, since it exists in buddhas alone, I must attain the stage of buddhahood in order to benefit all sentient beings." Think, "Having attained buddhahood, I will place all sentient beings on the stage of nirvana through the three vehicles." Think, "Having gradually trained those in the three families,[58] I will place them on the stage of buddhahood" until the yearning wish for buddhahood arises, like a thirsty person who wants water.

II) Engaged Bodhicitta

There are three: (1) equalizing self and other, (2) exchanging self and other, and (3) training in difficult conduct.

A) Equalizing Self and Other

The *Introduction to the Conduct of Awakening* states:

> Endeavor and meditate first on
> equalizing oneself and others.[59]

If it is asked for whom this is done, reflect [as indicated in the *Introduction to the Conduct of Awakening*]:

> When both myself and others
> are the same in wanting happiness,
> if there is no difference between myself [and others],
> for what reason shall I alone be happy?
> When both myself and others
> are the same in not wanting suffering,
> if there is no difference between myself [and others],
> for what reason do I protect myself and not others?[60]

From the bottom of one's heart think, "Since sentient beings are my mothers, whatever they want should be accomplished by me. Since sentient beings are the same as me, wanting happiness and not wanting suffering, henceforth, just as I would do for myself, I will take on the suffering of all sentient beings and I will accomplish all aims of their happiness." Recite, "May all sentient beings have happiness and the causes of happiness. May all sentient beings be free from suffering and the causes of suffering," {356} and meditate again and again until an uncontrived mind arises again and again.

B) Exchanging Self and Other

The *Introduction to the Conduct of Awakening* states:

> Someone who wishes to swiftly protect
> themselves and others
> should engage in the secret, sublime conduct of
> exchanging self with other.[61]

If it is asked how, [the *Introduction to the Conduct of Awakening* states]:

> I shall send to others,
> and, likewise, I will take from others.[62]

In order to abandon self-cherishing, visualize sentient beings before oneself. Having abandoned self-cherishing and the thought of self-cherishing, one should think, "May all the suffering and negative karma of the continuums of sentient beings ripen in my continuum, and may all my enjoyments of my body, merit, and happiness be continually sent to sentient beings." Then count one hundred times, one thousand times, and so on, "May the suffering of all sentient beings ripen upon me. May my happiness and virtue ripen in the continuums of sentient beings." Meditate until an unfabricated mind arises repeatedly.

C) Training in Difficult Conduct

The *Introduction to the Conduct of Awakening* states:

> This detracts from [their] happiness,
> and I shall always inflict harm.

If it is asked how, think, "Since all of my body, enjoyments, and merit should be fully sent to sentient beings, after each sentient being fully obtains it, they will be happy and content." After all unwanted death, beatings, injuries, hot and cold, hunger and thirst, fatigue, and so on, of sentient beings ripen upon oneself, reflect on the suffering of incalculable illness, death, pain, and hunger and thirst, seeing whichever suffering is primary. One should first take on the suffering of those sentient beings. After such reflection, one should train in the difficult conduct of taking up the burdens of others.

III) Ultimate Bodhicitta

Meditate according to the *Guhyasamāja Tantra*, which states:

> Free from all entities, {357}
> devoid of aggregates, sense elements, sense bases,
> and subject and object,
> since phenomena are uniformly without a self,
> one's mind never arose from the beginning,
> naturally empty.[63]

If it is asked how, one must determine that all outer and inner phenomena—beginning with the sentient beings who are the object of exchanging self and other, oneself who makes the exchange, and the exchanged happiness and suffering—are appearances of one's mind. That mind is not established. Since the mind did not cease in the past, will not arise in the future, and does not abide in the present, it is empty by nature. Rest through relaxing the mind for a time in that state.

b. Uncommon Experiential Appearance

The meditation for repeatedly giving rise to a conviction about the arising of the experience of the uncommon yoga is mentioned in the *Vajrapañjara Tantra*:

> First, there is the aspect of clouds;
> second, a semblance of smoke;
> third, the aspect of fire flies;
> fourth, blazing butter lamps;
> and fifth, a constant appearance
> resembling immaculate space.
> These are all causes of omniscience
> and bring about siddhis.[64]

The Vajra Verses states:

> The visions, dreams, and experience of undistracted meditation,

> three by three, appear as all three realms, seemingly prior to concepts.

After the practitioner starts out on the path of Vajrayāna, though inconceivable experiences will arise, when those are summarized, there are fifteen: the three paths (clearing the entryway, severing desire, and the great path of awakening), the three experiences (physical, mental, and dreams), the three dependent originations (the dependent origination of reversing the vāyu, visions, and dreams experiences), the three heats (prior to concepts, gathering the nine elements, the blazing bindu, and stabilizing heat), and the three samādhis (the characteristic, diversity; the nature, emptiness; and the essence, union). Further, these fifteen {358} are included in samādhi alone.

These experiences are produced in dependence upon the dependent origination of the nāḍīs of the body, the syllables of the nāḍīs, the element amṛtas, and the essential gnosis vāyus, which are all dominated by the mind. Think, "Though there is no reason to rejoice in the conducive conditions for those experiences, there is also no reason to be disappointed in negative conditions," and meditate on cutting proliferation repeatedly. When an experience arises one time, having understood that "this is a physical experience; this is a mental experience," one should remain natural.

3. Pure Appearance

The instruction on pure appearance is as follows: If it is wondered what the benefit is of maintaining these various experiential appearances on the path, it is replied that since one maintains them on the path and meditates, one traverses the path of the three gatherings of the elements, and having followed the conclusion, one progresses gradually through the stages and realizes the continuous wheel of inexhaustible body, speech, and mind. Further, the inexhaustible body is the inconceivable secrets (such as the invisible uṣṇīṣa, and so on) and all bodies appear in forms to tame whomever is to be tamed. Inexhaustible speech is being able to hear inconceivable speech whether near or far. All speech teaches dharma to each one to be tamed in their own language simultaneously, which is understood by all. Inexhaustible mind is the knowledge of all inconceivable minds. The continuous wheel is the uninterrupted wheel of activities in the deeds that beautify both self and other. Meditate on the thought, "There are many incalculable qualities in buddhahood, such as liberating those to be tamed, and so on." After that, think, "Because I practice, I will obtain such a result as this," and meditate until a special enthusiasm repeatedly arises.

B. The Three Tantras

In the instruction on the three tantras, there is (1) the subject,[65] the cause, the composition of samsara; (2) the path, the method of meditating; and (3) the result, the stage of buddhahood. {359}

1. The Subject, the Cause, the Composition of Samsara

One must generate confidence in the extensive or concise explanation at the time of the impure appearances.

2. The Path, the Method of Meditating

There is (1) the basis, abiding in samaya; (2) the means of instructing a person; and (3) for generating special conviction, there is recognizing samādhi and presenting the divisions of the path.

a. The Basis, Abiding in Samaya

The root of all paths and the principal path of the intermediate person is empowerment and abiding in samaya. Since one abides in samaya, it is valid for instructing everyone. Therefore, if one breaks samaya, it is restored after it has been purified by taking empowerment and confessing all breaches of the subsidiary samayas. It should then be properly maintained.

b. The Means of Instructing a Person

There are three topics: (1) meditating on the inseparability of samsara and nirvana in the all-basis cause tantra in order to eliminate proliferation with the view, (2) meditating on the path method tantra to generate experiences on the path, and (3) realizing the result, the five kāyas.

i. The All-Basis Cause Tantra

There is (1) the concise explanation of the inseparability of samsara and nirvana through the three connate phenomena, (2) the extensive explanation through the three points of practice, and (3) the very extensive explanation through the three tantras.

I) The Concise Explanation through the Three Connate Phenomena

A) The Three Connate Phenomena

The first of these two is the actual method of practicing through the three connate phenomena, which are similar to the three meditations: spend some days on devotion to the guru; in the middle, enter into recognition through resting one's mind; and then, include all inner and outer phenomena with one's mind. There is not a single external phenomenon apart from the mind. Having established the intrinsic nature of the mind, do not dismiss clarity; identify clarity to be the characteristic of the mind. When that clarity is investigated, one cannot find any type, color, or shape, and so on. Because it is empty by nature, it is clear. Since it cannot be found, it is called "empty." {360}

As such, at the time of clarity, it is empty; at the time of emptiness, it is clear. Since both clarity and emptiness individually cannot be separated by anyone, they are nondual, in union, inexpressible, and unfabricated, called "the essence of the mind." Having mentally ascertained this, rest in that state without distraction. At that time, when concepts stir, they are continuous. Whatever concepts arise through memory, it is recalled that the essence of those is the union of clarity and emptiness. Remain in equipoise. Apart from that, since this is not a mere generic object, when [clarity and emptiness] are experienced in union by one's mind, this is called "experience in the view." One should recognize whichever of the three arise: the apparent side, the empty side, or the essence of union.

B) The Twenty-Seven Connate Phenomena

Next is the practice through the twenty-seven connate phenomena. One wanders in samsara under the power of not recognizing those three phenomena. Since one erred about true existence in the characteristic,[66] clarity, there is desire; the vāyu, inhalation; the syllable, *oṃ*; the nāḍī, the lalanā;

the element, semen; the illness, blood and pitta; the spirit, female class; and the arising of the coarse body. Because of erroneously imputing the nature, emptiness, as not empty, there is hatred; the vāyu, exhalation; the syllable, *hūṃ*; the nāḍī, the rasanā; the element, blood; the illness, vata; the spirit, male class; and the arising of coarse speech. Since one erroneously imputed union as differentiated clarity and emptiness, there is ignorance; the vāyu, abiding; the syllable, *āḥ*; the nāḍī, the central one; the element, merged semen and blood; the illness, kapha; the spirit, nāga class; and the generation of the nāḍīs of the whole coarse [body]. Eliminate proliferation by thinking about the way they are, and rest in that state in equipoise. To elaborate, in the imputation of grasping to true existence in either non-clarity, non-emptiness, or differentiated clarity and emptiness, as before, recall that since these are the root of this and that samsaric phenomena, because one is striving to be free, do not permit proliferation concerning these. Remove discursiveness and remain in one-pointed equipoise on any of the three characteristics. {361}

II) The Extensive Explanation through the Three Points of Practice

In the extensive explanation, (1) all phenomena are mind, (2) the mind is illusory, and (3) illusions are established as natureless.

A) All Phenomena Are Mind

There are four primary examples and four subsidiary examples for establishing [all phenomena] to be mind.

1) The Four Primary Examples

Establishing all phenomena as mind with the example of being influenced by sleep is as follows: Of the three topics here, since the preparation, the meditations, has already been described, in the main subject, one begins to recall the example. Make a very clear dream that one has had an object of the mind and reflect in the following way: "These various appearances of a past dream are like daytime appearances when one is dreaming. Though they appeared as if they were true, when one's wakes from sleep, since objects in a dream are not established at all, there were also no outer objects. On the other hand, since one clearly experienced it, the dream was not nothing.

Develop the conviction that such appearances are the mind itself under the power of delusion.

Merging appearances with that is as follows: What is the difference between the appearances of a dream and present appearances? Experientially, I experienced the dream. In terms of truth, [appearances] also are not true. If they were true, it would be necessary for the mode of appearance to appear the same. Also, a single appearance can become many appearances in the mind through different conditions, because of appearing in a single day. Having generated such a conviction, resting in that state means relaxing the mind in that state of conviction. To elaborate, maintain mindfulness in thinking, "What is the difference between this and a dream?" Rest without concepts.

In the three parts to the conclusion, the dedication is offering the aspiration, "Based on those vast roots of merit, may I attain buddhahood in order to benefit all migrating beings."

Compassion for those who do not realize this is meditating on the thought, "How sad it is that sentient beings cause their own suffering in samsara through being firmly caught by grasping to 'I' and 'mine,' not realizing that all phenomena are like a dream."

In order to always recall the meaning of the example, {362} one continually thinks, "If whatever exists during the day, such as companions, enjoyments, and so on, is a mere appearance, it is the appearance of a dream." As such, one should meditate again and again. Having gained conviction in the first example through the preparation, main subject, and conclusion, even if one does not gain conviction in the first example after a long while, do not switch the focus to the second example. The preparation, main subject, and conclusion should be applied to the following and practiced. When the essentials of the examples are explained in order, the second primary example is the example of intoxication. If one is intoxicated with alcohol, one has no fear of anything, or it causes laughing and crying.

The third primary example is the example of illness: Appearances are yellow because of jaundice, and oneself appears as many.

The fourth primary example is the example of spirits. When oneself or others are oppressed by spirits, various fears seem vivid even while they are nonexistent.

2) The Four Subsidiary Examples

Among the four subsidiary examples, the first is double vision. If one presses one's eyes, a single entity, such as a pillar, vase, and so on, is seen as two. If one closes either eye, [the second object] will vanish. It cannot exist externally, but it is not nothing, since one saw it. Therefore, one's mind appeared as that [second object] through the power of error.

The second subsidiary example is ophthalmia. When the eye is influenced by ophthalmia, when one looks at the sky, one sees hairs or a mass of bees, which are seen but do not exist.

The third subsidiary example is the fire wheel: When one lights the end of a small stick and quickly whirls it, it appears to be a wheel. When that fire is in one place, it is not seen elsewhere.

The fourth subsidiary example is spinning. Extend one's arms and spin the body in all directions, so that the ground appears to be the sky and the sky appears to be the ground. Based on those, {363} sever proliferation with "outer appearances are not created by fate, a creator, subtle atoms, and so on. They are the magic display of one's mind." This is the meaning indicated by the *Vajrapañjara Tantra*:

> There is neither a buddha nor a person
> outside the precious mind.
> Objects abide in consciousness
> and do not exist externally at all.

The *Sutra on Entering Lanka* states:

> The mind disturbed by traces
> appears as objects.
> The mind that lacks existent objects
> falsely perceives external objects.[67]

And *The Vajra Verses* states:

> Phenomena are appearances of the mind.

B) The Mind Is Illusory

There are two topics in establishing the mind as illusory.

1) The Four Primary Examples

Among the four primary examples, if one wonders, "Are illusions true?" they are not. For example, when a mantra is applied to the materials for an illusion, such as a potsherd, a monkey tail, and so on, many nonexistent things appear, such as horses, elephants, houses, and so on. Likewise, through the cause of traces, the mind is deluded about the diversity. At present, one's mind arises as an apparent diversity, but without traces it would not arise [as an apparent diversity], because nothing at all is established ultimately or arises independently.

The second primary example is a mirage: when the moisture of the ground is struck by the wind, from a distance one sees a valley filled with water.

The third primary example is the water moon: when three conditions meet—the sky is cloudless, the moon has arisen, and there is pure water—a reflection of the moon appears in the water. However, if these conditions do not assemble, a reflection of the moon does not appear.

The fourth primary example is lightning: when the conditions of moisture in the sky and wind meet, lightning appears as a flash of a very clear ray of light.

2) The Four Subsidiary Examples

The first of the four subsidiary examples is Haricandra's city: {364} In the southeast, in Harikela, on the morning following a night rain when the clouds have vanished, a real city appears but does not exist. Alternately, the features of the city of King Haricandra are very vivid, and one wonders if the reflections of houses, humans, horse, elephants, and so on, arose.

The second subsidiary example is a city of gandharvas: a city that appears when a string of clouds nears a specific place.

The third subsidiary example is clouds: When a cloud bank appears in the sky, when it first arises, where does it come from? When it vanishes, where did it go? Though it cannot be found, a cloud appears because vapor from the earth forms in the sky.

The fourth subsidiary example is a rainbow: diverse colors appear for a long while in the distance from the meeting of sunrays and obscuring clouds, but those will not appear at all when one arrives in front of them.

Sever proliferation by means of those examples, recalling, "There is no true nature in the mind itself. Through the power of the various transformations of the mind, various results arise based on various causes and conditions."

The *Hevajra Tantra* states:

> A nature does arise from the beginning.
> Not false and not true, likewise,
> it is asserted that everything is like a moon in the water.
> The yoginī must know this.[68]

The *Saṃpūṭa Tantra* states:

> Like a city of gandharvas,
> similar to an illusion or a mirage,
> equivalent to Haricandra's city,
> like seeing a lover in a dream.[69]

Also, the perfection of wisdom sutras state that everything, from matter up to omniscience, is like an illusion, and Ācārya Virūpa states, "[Phenomena] are reflections."

C) Illusions Are Established as Natureless

[This has two topics:] (1) establishing appearances as dependently originated and (2) establishing dependent origination as inexpressible.

1) Dependent Origination

In the first of the two, there are four primary examples of both [primary and subsidiary examples].

a) The Four Primary Examples

The first primary example is recitation. If one wonders whether productions from an assembly of causes and conditions are true, they are not. When the recitation of a disciple arises from the recitation of the guru, the recitation of the disciple will not arise without being dependent on the recitation of the guru. Likewise, nothing is transferred to the disciple, the earlier and later utterance, {365} birth and death, the previous and later moment, and so on, because in all instances, without depending on the former, the latter will not arise; it is called "unceasing." Since the former does not transform into the latter, it is called "nonarising." Therefore, since nothing remains in the middle, one is freed from all reifications, because there is no arising or perishing, coming or going, or center and periphery. One must generate this conviction.

The second primary example is a lamp. Light is produced when the conditions of a dry wick, oil, and a flame meet.

The third primary example is a mirror. When a highly polished mirror encounters a form, a reflection arises.

The fourth primary example is a seal. When a seal is made from a horn, and so on, and it is impressed in wax or clay, there is an image that resembles the design in the seal.

b) The Four Subsidiary Examples

In the four subsidiary examples, the first is the lens. When three conditions meet—a cloudless sky, a very clean lens, and very clear sunrays—a fire will quickly arise in dry tinder.

The second subsidiary example is a seed. This is also the meaning of the *Rice Seedling Sutra.* Since fertile soil, a warm month, moisture, and a viable seed meet, a sprout grows into a stalk of grain.

The third subsidiary example is sourness. Since a trace of having eaten a sour fruit exists in one's continuum, when others eat a sour fruit of the same type, because that trace is activated, one's jaw clenches and one salivates.

The fourth subsidiary example is an echo. When one is in front of a high house or cliff and utters a single clear sound, sounds resembling that arise. All those sounds would arise without being based on an individual cause, but since the prior cause does not transfer to the subsequent result, {366} it is called "nonarising." Thus, apply the first example to all later seven examples.

Not even one of those causes and conditions of so-called illusions are established as truly existent. Since the cause does not become the result and the result will not arise without depending on the cause, this is the meaning of establishing "neither coming nor going, arising nor ceasing." The *Hevajra Tantra* states:

> In this way, from a fire stick, fire board, and the effort of a man's hands, fire [suddenly] arises. The fire is not in the stick. It is also neither in the fire board nor in the hands of the man. Since the fire is not [present] in even one of those when one searches thoroughly in every way, while that fire is not true, it also is not false. That is how the yoginī should think about all phenomena.[70]

The *Verses on the Rice Seedling Sutra* states:

> Just as the moon is reflected in the water,
> in the same way, there is death and transmigration from this life,
> but no one at all appears to be born a living being.[71]

Ārya Nāgārjuna states:

> Through [the examples of] recitation, a lamp, a mirror, a seal,
> a lens, a seed, sourness, and an echo,
> while the aggregates are connected in a series,
> the learned understand that nothing transfers.[72]

And Ācārya Virūpa states, "The path arises as outer and inner dependent origination."

2) Inexpressibility

There are two topics in establishing illusions to be inexpressible.

a) The Four Primary Examples

The first primary example is the laughter of an infant. When an infant laughs, they cannot say why. Even though there is a reason for the laugh, they do not know how to describe the nature of that cause.

The second primary example is the dream of a mute. When a mute dreams, they are unable to say, "It was like this."

The third primary example is itching. When someone else scratches an itch under the arm, and so on, even though the itch is experienced, they cannot say, "Here it is."

The fourth primary example is sexual pleasure. When the pleasure of intercourse is experienced, it cannot be described. {367}

b) The Four Subsidiary Examples

In first of the four subsidiary examples, the gnosis of the third of the four empowerments is the experience of the gnosis at the time of empowerment.

The second subsidiary example is secret union. At the occasion of the lower maṇḍalacakra, there is the gnosis of relying on the hand consort.[73]

The third subsidiary example is the wave of enjoyment, the gnosis that arises from pressing the passage of the vāyu, having avoided the passage through which the bindu moves and the passage through which blood moves, among the three nāḍīs in the throat.

The fourth subsidiary example is the maṇḍalacakra, the gnosis that arises based on an actual or a gnosis mudra as [will be described] later. Those experiences also cannot be described by "This is it." In the same way, when there is conviction about all phenomena [being in the state of] union or arising from causes and conditions while lacking inherent existence, since one is unable to say, "This is it," generate a conviction in the thought that they are inexpressible and remain in equipoise. With respect to those, the *Hevajra Tantra* states:

> The connate cannot be expressed by another;
> it cannot be found at all.[74]

And the *Sutra That Explains the Two Truths* says:

> Deva child, the ultimate truth is totally beyond all conventions, undifferentiated, unborn, unceasing, and free from an object to express or an expression, a knower, or a knowable object.[75]

Koṭalipa states:

> Nonduality is merely a name;
> that name does not exist.

....

Practitioners upholding "the nondual,"
be patient toward me.[76]

And *The Vajra Verses* states, "Never being separate from the meaning of the ocean of suchness."

There are four methods for those. Having confirmed the thirty-two examples, since this is clearly asserted, extract the four primary examples. When practicing in the manner of confirming each of those four characteristics[77] with each of those examples, {368}[the example of the dream] is among the examples establishing appearances as mind. Confirm the four characteristics with the example of a dream. Recall a clear dream. Since that is not established externally apart from the mind, it is mind. Since concepts during the day arise from diverse causes, they are illusory. When awaking from a dream and sleep, nothing arises later that is not based on something earlier. Since nothing transfers from something earlier to something later, because there is no coming or going, it is dependent origination. Though appearances seem to contradict those three [mind, illusion, and dependent origination], experience does not contradict those.[78] Since one cannot describe the experience, "It is like this," it is inexpressible.

Likewise, among the examples of illusion, there is the moon in the water; among the examples of dependent origination, there is the seed; and among the examples of inexpressibility, there is recalling the bliss of scratching an itch. For each of those, develop conviction through confirming mind, illusion, dependent origination, and inexpressibility. As before, merge those with appearances, and practice.

To generate conviction by reducing those primary examples into one: generate the connate gnosis on the basis of the wave of enjoyment and for that confirm mind, and so on, and practice, as before. As such, since one meditates on appearances as mind, the mind that clings to outer objects is reversed. Since one meditates on mind as an illusion, the mind that clings to the true existence of the mind is reversed. Since one meditates on illusions as dependently originated, the mind that clings to coming and going and permanence and annihilation is reversed. Since one meditates on dependent origination as inexpressible, also the mind is comprehended to be free from extremes, like space.

III) The Very Extensive Explanation through the Three Tantras

In the very extensive explanation through the three tantras, there is (1) the all-basis cause tantra, (2) the body method tantra, and (3) the mahāmudrā result tantra.

A) The All-Basis Cause Tantra

As such, all phenomena—inclusive of the causes and results of samsara and nirvana—are complete in the form of a trace or a seed in this all-basis mind, which is supported on the four maṇḍalas in the same manner as the scent of a flower depends on the flower. {369} Further, when those [traces or seeds] meet with an activating condition, they appear as a variety of characteristics. Likewise, since those appearances are not established as truly existent, they are empty by nature. Generate the conviction that since they are apparent while empty and empty while apparent, they are unified by nature. Rest in that state one-pointedly. The *Hevajra Tantra* states:

> This so-called "samsara,"
> this is nirvana.[79]

Nāgārjuna states:

> You have not asserted a nirvana
> by abandoning samsara.
> Lord, you have explained the nonperception
> of samsara to be peace.[80]

The Vajra Verses states, "Because samsara and nirvana are complete in the all-basis tantra."

B) Empowerment, Path, and Experience

Generate conviction in (1) the empowerment, (2) the path, and (3) experience.

1) The Empowerment

a) Maṇḍala

First, samsara and nirvana are merged in the maṇḍala. From the perspective of the extensive vase empowerment, the five aggregates are purified by the five buddhas; the five elements are purified by the five knowledge consorts; the inner sense bases are purified by the bodhisattvas; the outer sense bases are purified by the goddesses; and the eight major joints, the crown, and the soles of the feet are purified by the male and female wrathful ones. The bases of purification is samsara; the purifier is nirvana. Having recalled the essence of this and that purifier of the bases of purification and meditated, samsara and nirvana are inseparable.

From the perspective of the higher empowerments, with respect to the bhaga maṇḍala of syllables, the *bhrūṃ āṃ jrīṃ lāṃ hūṃ* of the heart are the five buddhas; *lāṃ māṃ pāṃ tāṃ* are the four mothers; the syllables *pu ja*, and so on, are the twenty-four places; the fifty vowels and consonants are the bodhisattvas and goddesses; and the ten *hūṃ*s of the eight joints, the crown, and the soles of the feet are the ten male and female wrathful ones.

With respect to the bodhicitta maṇḍala, the five pure amṛtas are the buddhas; the four elements and bliss, which have the nature of space, are the five knowledge consorts; the sense organs such as the eyes, and the teeth, nails and so on, the pure essence of the twenty-four countries, are the bodhisattvas; the objects of one's body, such as form, and so on, {370} are the goddesses; and all of the pure essence of the primary and secondary limbs of the body is the male and female wrathful ones.

From the perspective of the essential gnosis vāyus, the nine hundred vāyus that become each of the five fundamental vāyus are the buddhas; since for each of those, there are an even two hundred twenty-five vāyus, when nine hundred vāyus are divided by four elements, those are the knowledge consorts, the vāyus moving through the eyes, and so on. The nine hundred twenty-four subsidiary vāyus are the bodhisattvas and the goddesses. The subsidiary pervading vāyus that exist in the skin, pores, and so on, are the male and female wrathful ones.

b) The Empowerment

Samsara and nirvana are merged in the empowerment: From the perspective of the vase empowerment, the empowerment substances (such as the vase, and so on) and also the disciples upon whom the empowerment is conferred are generated as the couples of the five families, and the sense bases, and so on, are empowered. Since the empowerment is conferred by the deities of the complete three seats, the five elements, the five aggregates, and the five afflictions are empowered as the five mothers, the five buddhas, and the five gnoses, respectively.

In the secret empowerment, the bindu is accomplished by the guru in whom the three seats are complete. When the empowerment is conferred with the bodhicitta on the disciple in whom the three seats are complete, the aggregates and the pure essence of the amṛta are the seat of the five buddhas; the pure essence of the sense bases are the seat of the bodhisattvas; the pure essence of the elements are the seat of the goddesses; and the pure essence of the eight joints, the crown, and soles of the feet are the seat of the ten male and female wrathful ones.

In the empowerment of the gnosis of the wisdom consort, the three seats are complete in the disciple's body, the bhaga [of the consort], and the bodhicitta. The consort in whom all three seats are complete is given to him. Because they enter into union with the three perceptions, the empowerment is conferred by means of maintaining the experience of the descent, retention, reversal, and spreading of the support, the relative bodhicitta in which the three seats are complete.

In the fourth empowerment, the master in whom the three seats are complete introduces samsara and nirvana as inseparable through bestowing the fourth empowerment with any of the five [types of consorts] on the disciples in whom the three seats are complete.

Also, the basis of purification of those is samsara, the purifier is nirvana, and the realization that both of those have the same flavor is the inseparability of samsara and nirvana. {371}

c) Gnosis

Merging samsara and nirvana in the gnosis of empowerment is as follows: The gnosis that arises from the vase empowerment is the union of apparent objects and emptiness. The gnosis that arises from the secret empowerment is the union of clear consciousness and emptiness. The gnosis that arises from the third empowerment is the samādhi of the union of physical bliss and emptiness. The extremely pure view that arises from the fourth empowerment is the supreme samādhi of bliss and emptiness.

Also, the bases of purification of those empowerments are the five aggregates and elements to be purified, which are the seat of the buddhas and knowledge consorts arising from arresting the pure essence of those and the ten vāyus. The purified six sense bases and their objects are the seat of bodhisattvas and goddesses that arises from arresting the pure essence of those and the nine hundred twenty subsidiary vāyus. The pure essence of the joints, the crown, and the soles and the pervading vāyu that exists in the skin and pores are the seat of the male and female wrathful ones.

As such, the three gnoses of the three seats, appearances, clarity, and the first three joys are samsara. Emptiness and the connate joy are nirvana. The one taste of those in the essence of a single consciousness is inseparability. The *Guhyasamāja Tantra* states:

> In brief, the five aggregates
> are explained to be the five buddhas.
> The vajra sense bases
> are the supreme maṇḍala of bodhisattvas.[81]
> . . . .
> Earth is Buddhalocanā.
> The element of water is Māmakī.
> Pāṇḍarā and Tārā
> are known as fire and air.[82]

And *The Vajra Verses* states, "Explain . . . the empowerment of the cause with the four threes: the seats, and so on."

2) The Path

There are three topics[83] for generating conviction in the path.

a) Creation Stage

The merging of samsara and nirvana and generation of conviction in the creation stage is as follows: The object of purification in the preliminary gathering of the accumulations is past karma. The purifier is the two accumulations, the cause of samsara and nirvana. Since those two are included in the single mental continuum of the practitioner, [samsara and nirvana] are inseparable. The dharmodaya illustrates the three liberations. Both samsara and nirvana arise from liberation. The universe is purified by the celestial mansion. {372} Both [the universe and celestial mansion] arise from the four elements and appear as appearances of samsara and nirvana. Because they both are meditated on by the practitioner as one taste, [samsara and nirvana] are inseparable.

Also, in the rite of creation, arising from the five direct realizations is warmth-and-moisture birth; arising from a bindu is egg birth; emerging from the womb is womb birth; and arising from just the essential word is apparitional birth. Also, with respect to the color and hand implements of the deity, the object to purify is the five afflictions and the purifiers are the nature of the five gnoses. Since one meditates on the color and hand implements of the five buddhas, they are a purifier. Also, the right and left hands and feet are samsara and nirvana. The half-crossed and fully cross-legged positions are union. Equipoise is nirvana. The off-session yogas are practices consistent with samsara. Since those are inseparable in the continuum of a single practitioner, samsara and nirvana are inseparable.

b) The Self-Empowerment

To generate conviction in the merging of samsara and nirvana in the self-empowerment, the vāyu is inhalation, the syllable is *oṃ*, the object to purify is desire, the experience is clarity, and the result is the nirmāṇakāya. The vāyu is paused, the syllable is *āḥ*, the object to purify is ignorance, the experience is union, and the result is the sambogakaya. The vāyu is exhalation, the syllable is *hūṃ*, the object to purify is hatred, the experience is emptiness, and the result is dharmakāya. Since those are realized to be one taste, samsara and nirvana are inseparable.

c) Maṇḍalacakra

To generate conviction in the merging of samsara and nirvana in the maṇḍalacakra, the five aggregates and the five afflictions of oneself and the consort, the sense bases and their objects, and concepts, and so on, are samsara. The gnosis of the four joys that arises from union empowered by the three perceptions is nirvana. Since those are practiced as inseparable in the continuum of a single practitioner, samsara and nirvana are inseparable.

d) The Path of Waves

To generate conviction in the merging of samsara and nirvana in the path of the waves, {373} the four supporting maṇḍalas of oneself and the padminī consort are samsara. The supported, supreme bliss and emptiness, is nirvana. Since they are in union, samsara and nirvana are inseparable.

3) Experience

Generate conviction in experience.

a) Impure Experience

Generate a special conviction in cause and result on the basis of the impure experiential appearances. When many experiences arise, including the three realms of samsara and the six birthplaces in the universe and inhabitants, through the dependent origination of the four maṇḍalas that support one's continuum, while consciousness does not move from one's body in this life, the various experiential appearances of the six realms arise in the following way: After death, having appropriated bodies of each of the six realms through the power of karma, how would the various experiences of the six realms not arise? It is certain they will arise. However, they are all appearances of one's mind, which is contaminated by karma. One should generate the conviction that they arise as different appearances of the six realms while one is seated on one seat. Based upon that, one will have confidence in the causes and results of karma and abandon wrong views.

b) Path Experience

Accomplishing all paths as one vehicle based on the experience of the path is as follows: When many experiences arise based on the supporting four maṇḍalas—such as the view of permanence and annihilation; the view of the insentient self; the view that Brahma, Iśvara, and so on, are creators of the world; the view that subtle atoms and the elements are a cause; the inexpressible self; and the views of Vaibhāṣikas, Sautrāntikas, Yogācārins, and so on—since these all only arise in one's experience on the basis of the modes of the four maṇḍalas, one should generate the conviction that they are appearances of delusion that cannot be established as true and that there is not the slightest difference between all vehicles, and meditate. One realizes there is only one vehicle based on that. {374}

c) Result

Generating a special devotion to buddhahood on the basis of the experiential appearance of the seed syllables is as follows: Since the vāyu and mind gather in the *a* of the heart, the experiences of the dharmakāya arise, and since the vāyu and mind gather in the syllables of the five families at the heart, the experiences of the saṃbhogkāya and nirmāṇakāya arise. However, when it is perceived that "this is the nature of the three kāyas," this is not actual buddhahood but rather an experiential appearance. One should think that if one attains buddhahood, it is much superior to this, a source of inconceivable qualities, and generate enthusiasm repeatedly, thinking how wonderful it would be to obtain it.

C) Result Mahāmudrā Tantra

Generate conviction in the inseparability of samsara and nirvana through the noncontradiction between transformation (*gnas 'gyur*) and effortless accomplishment (*lhun gyis grub*) and meditate. The seeds of the four kāyas naturally abide within the four supporting maṇḍalas. When they are realized, the result is effortlessly accomplished because the four kāyas are effortlessly accomplished. Since that cause is equivalent with the dharmatā of samsara, it is samsara. While the nature is like that, the manifestation of the inconceivable qualities of the four kāyas is the qualities transforming into the four kāyas by means of the path of the supporting four maṇḍalas in which [the qualities] abide. Transformation is called nirvana. When from the perspective of dharmatā, [the result is] effortlessly accomplished, when seen from the perspective of qualities, [the result] is a transformation. Thus, there is no contradiction. Generate conviction in inseparability through the dharmatā and the transformability of the result. Having gained such conviction, one has reached the conclusion of hearing and reflecting upon the view, and slight gnosis produced by meditation has arisen.

This concludes the explanation of the instruction in the all-basis cause tantra.

ii. Body Method Tantra

In the meditation on the body method tantra, in order to generate conviction in the path, there is meditating on the paths of the vase empowerment, the secret empowerment, the gnosis of the wisdom consort empowerment, and the fourth empowerment.

I) The Vase Empowerment

In the [path of the vase empowerment], there are the activities of the creation stage and focusing the mind on the creation stage.

A) The Activities of the Creation Stage

Prior to entering into the practice, one must receive the empowerment of the time of the path and refresh one's samaya. If one's guru is not present, then one must draw the accomplishment maṇḍala and perform the extensive self-admittance. {375} Having avoided negative conditions, enter into the practice when one has arranged the positive conditions. Further, one should recite the approach of four hundred thousand through the outer and inner creation stage, or as much as possible, and perform a peaceful fire puja with ten percent of that number.

B) Focusing the Mind

The outer and inner creation stages remove concepts of ordinariness, and at the conclusion of complete immersion in meditating intensely for a long time, through the preliminary three crucial points, all the deities [of the maṇḍala] are visualized as apparent yet natureless, like reflections. In particular, visualize the central eye and focus the mind on that one-pointedly. If it is clear, eliminate distraction and fully engage the mind on another entity. Visualize again and meditate. If the visualization is unclear, stop for a while and relax. Meditate again. If it is still unclear, then look at a drawing of an eye and visualize that. If that does not make it clear, then having drawn an eye in the middle of one's forehead, place a very clear mirror in front of oneself—not too close, not too far, not too high, and not too low—and look at it. Close the eyes and meditate. Again look at the image in the mirror, and again meditate. By repeating this again and again, the object will become clear.

By meditating in that way, when clarity is desired in something and that clarity arises, one is approaching the individual purity of each deity. If one wishes to overcome distraction in clarity and one is able to overcome this, one is approaching the purity of suchness. The special experience of śamatha that arises based on those is approaching the purity of one's own cognizance.

By such means train on the path and sustain the view that arises based on that [training] with the three essences: If one focuses the mind on the object, such as the eye, and so on, it is the aspect of appearance. If only an experience of emptiness arises, since the visualization does not appear, this is the empty aspect. If one focuses the mind on the arising of signs from smoke, and so on, it is the essence of union. {376} Among those is the way of practicing the essence of post-equipoise. If [experience] does not arise, one must practice the means of sustaining the view according to how it is described in the treatise.

Next, focus on the three eyes as before and meditate. After that, focus on the whole head, then the whole body, then the seats, then the deities of the maṇḍala, and then the celestial mansion and protection wheel, and meditate as before. One must train until one is familiar, in the same way one familiarized oneself with the samādhi of the central eye.

As such, clearly focusing on the deities of self-generation, one should meditate on any external entities as the deity. Familiarize oneself and gradually increase its size; meditate and become familiar with appearances within one's range of vision as the deity. Next, increase the size of the deity and maṇḍala one meditates, and in the end, meditate that the deity and maṇḍala fill the world. Next, having reduced the deity and maṇḍala even smaller in size, meditate and visualize the deity and the maṇḍala inside, the size of a mustard seed. The stages of those visualizations should be meditated until one becomes familiar with them, just like the visualization of the central eye.

One should be familiar with those, meditating and familiarizing oneself such that though the deities and maṇḍala are the size of mustard seeds, they are meditated as filling the world, without the vast world becoming smaller and without the bodies of the deities becoming larger.

Also, all those deities should be meditated as the essence of the union of appearance and naturelessness.

II) The Secret Empowerment

In the path of the secret empowerment, there is (1) the intimate instruction of the pervading [vāyus] and (2) the intimate instruction of the pervaded [nāḍīs].[84]

A) The Intimate Instruction of the Pervading [Vāyus]
1) The Preliminaries of Concentration

The preliminaries of concentration: If one's guru is present, then receive empowerment. If he is not present, then perform the self-admittance. Also, if he is not present, offer maṇḍalas, recite the one hundred syllables, {377} gather accumulations [to create] positive conditions, and purify obscurations [to remove] negative conditions. Practice the extensive physical training[85] and the thirty-two activities,[86] or practice the concise training of the five limbs as much as one can, engaging in the physical training again and again. The extent of the training is that it is no longer difficult or painful, and the body is comfortable and light. For some, it is possible that samādhi may arise indirectly at this occasion. Whatever the case may be, if one practices the physical training for a long time, samādhi will arise for a long time and obstacles will not occur.

2) The Seven Intimate Instructions of Vāyu

Though there are many systems of visualization for the main section of concentration, since this is the lord of yogins' path instruction through the signs of heat in the caṇḍālī and vāyu in the first gathering of the elements, he asserts the vāyuyoga as the main one. Also, though the perfect, complete buddha taught inconceivable intimate instructions for that, when those are summarized, they are summarized into exhaling, inhaling, and holding the vāyu. When employing that as the path, there is prāṇāyāma[87] or vajra recitation; the three intimate instructions for full exhalation; two intimate instructions for full inhalation; and uniting [the upper and lower vāyus] for employing the pause as the path, for a total of seven.

a) Prāṇāyāma and Vajra Recitation

First, [for prāṇāyāma,] there is the method of practice.

i) Method of Practice

After the nine limbs of concentration, there is one cycle and two nostrils; having blocked the right nostril, [the breath] moves in the left nostril. Next, as above, it should move easily. Further, since it resembles expelling faults, begin with the *āyāma*: focus the mind on the right nostril and when exhaling the vāyu, be mindful it is moving out; when inhaling, be mindful that it is moving in. When it pauses briefly, be mindful that it paused. Through focusing one's mind on that one-pointedly, if no other concepts move, it is called *the path of clearing the entry*; if one abides one-pointedly in an objectless state, {378} it is called *the path of eliminating attachment*; and if the mind is focused on signs, such as smoke, and so on, it is called *the path of great awakening.*

Whichever of those samādhis arise, one should give a "reward" to the *āyāma* for the purpose of enhancement: extend the exhalation, shorten the inhalation and the pause, and with the mind recall, "Long exhalation, short inhalation, and short pause inside." At that time, if the breath does not move through the left nostril but moves through the right, block the right nostril with a ball of cotton, and so on, and train in the breath moving through the left nostril. If the breath does not change even though the right nostril is blocked, train in imagining that it moves through the left nostril. Because that is the key point of the arising of samādhi and reversing [the flow of the breath from the right nostril to the left], begin from the prāṇa, mindful of inhalation, resting, and exhalation.

If one wishes to perform vajra recitation, when inhaling, recall *oṃ*; when pausing, *āḥ*; and when exhaling, *hūṃ*. When samādhi arises from that, as a limb for stabilizing that, gradually reward the prāṇa: extend the inhalation, shorten the exhalation, and in correlation with that, keep in mind to extend the inhalation and the pause, and shorten the exhalation. Here, pausing for a long while inside gives rise to inconceivable samādhis. Afterward, by relaxing the effort of both the vāyu and the mind, as in the instruction on the view, a supreme experience will arise by sustaining the view with three characteristics.

ii) Culmination

There are two in the culmination of prāṇāyāma.

(I) Clear Movement

"Clear movement" means that when the five vāyus move through either of the nostrils, the location, color, shape, and length of the vāyus of the four elements moving through the front, and so on, in the right, left, upper, and lower passageways, become visible to the eyes.

(II) Ascertaining the Aspect

"Ascertaining the aspect" refers to the ability to shift the vāyu to the right and left and send it through other sense organs. {379}

iii) Qualities of Meditation

The qualities of meditation are accomplishing the four activities: When the movement of the earth vāyu is clear, one can accomplish the activity of increasing with a mere mantra, or a mere thought or aspiration. In the same way, the activity of pacification is accomplished by the water vāyu; power is accomplished by the fire vāyu; and the activity of destruction is performed by the air vāyu.

Further, having entered into the prāṇa vāyu of another, when one looks thoroughly into another, the clairvoyance of knowing the minds of others arises.

iv) The Faults Removed

When the faults are removed, the obstacles of any condition of sudden death, such as falling into an abyss or falling down a mountain or being struck by lightning, and so on, are prevented. One also attains slight power over longevity. Since this is the basis of all qualities, it is important to meditate on this until signs arise.

b) Full Exhalation

Next are the three limbs of full exhalation for stabilizing and enhancing the vāyu.

i) Exhaling Through the Prāṇa

The four sections in blocking the āyāma and exhaling through prāṇa.

(I) Method of Practice

Having performed the preliminary nine limbs, the method of practice is while seated with knees drawn to the chest, the head is slightly bent[88] down and the mind is directed to the tip of the nose or the left nostril.

Placing the index finger on the middle finger, block the right nostril, inhale and expel by blowing through the left. Until the exhalation is complete, do not inhale, and clear the breath out until there is no remaining exhalation. Afterward, resting in a relaxed manner without visualization or effort is the third intimate instruction. In the branches of exhalation, a very important point is to not allow the vāyu to come inside. Since this expels faults, a nonconceptual samādhi may naturally arise. When leaving the sessions, one should rest in a state without any concepts at all.

(II) The Culmination

The culmination {380} is that since there is no movement of exhalation, after leaving the breath out for as long as one wishes, it stops and does not return inside.

(III) The Qualities

The qualities are that the body becomes filled with bliss and nonconceptuality arises swiftly.

(IV) The Faults

The faults that can be removed are upper body pain and discomfort in the heart. Also, when meditating on this path, when one goes to a frightening place or crosses a river, blocking the āyāma and exhaling through the prāṇa in seven rounds will definitely remove obstacles.

ii) Through Both Nostrils

Exhale through both nostrils for increasing strength. The method of practice is performing the complete limbs of concentration, as before. Focus one's mind on the ūrṇā. The key point of vāyu is increasing strength and blowing out intensely through both nostrils. The measure of being able to hold the breath out is resting for a single day. It is a very important point not to allow inhalation after exhalation. When one inhales, rest without focus or effort.

Further, exhale as before. The key point of vāyu is the same as before. Meditate upon that for three days. Next, focus the mind in the space a cubit in front of oneself, then four cubits, then the length of a bow shot, then the size of a wide valley, then the length of circling the continent, then the size of the four continents, then the size of the billion-world universe, and finally focus the mind on all the space of the whole universe. Alternately, meditate and focus the mind on total nonconceptuality. Afterward, identify the view—the samādhi of clarity and emptiness—and remain in equipoise. The culmination is the same. The qualities are the arising of the ultimate experience of clarity. The faults this can remove are all headaches, bloodshot eyes, and so on.

iii) Exhaling through the Mouth with Sound

Perform the nine limbs of awakening, as before. Having clenched one's teeth, the key point of the mind is focusing the mind on the space that surrounds one, four cubits in diameter, {381} or focusing the mind on the sound "si." The key point of the vāyu is exhaling by blowing through the teeth with the sound "si." The measure of being able to hold the breath out is suppression. A very important point is to not allow inhalation after exhalation. When one inhales, rest without focus or effort. If blood or pitta predominate, exhale with sound. If cold vata predominates, exhale without sound. The culmination is the same as before. The qualities are the body floats, is light, and has a good complexion. The fault it is capable of removing is all hot diseases, such as stale blood (*khrag ro*), sudden epidemics, and the rest.

The enhancement practice for those three is to make the fighting hearth mudra and alternately raise the shoulders. In order to increase the strength of the upper vāyu, exhale and strongly pull up the lower vāyu and [then] strongly contract the lower abdomen. The enhancement is that behavior will cause the vāyu to emerge through the crown, like incense smoke. Expel the vāyu through the rectum. Focus one's mind on the maṇḍala one cubit below and press the upper vāyu down as long as one can. Contract the lower vāyu slightly and do not allow the belly to expand at that time.

c) The Two Intimate Instructions for Full Inhalation

i) Inhaling Through the Prāṇa

Blocking the āyāma and inhaling through the prāṇa is as follows: The body is seated cross-legged. Perform the nine limbs of concentration. Imagine that the vāyu is slowly absorbed at the navel in a shape like an eggshell, white outside and yellow inside. Tilt the head slightly forward, place the right index finger over the middle finger, block the right nostril, gradually inhale fully, and roll the head once to the right and throw it back. Soundlessly swallow saliva, the mount of the wind, and press the vāyu down for as long as one can. Repeat once and inhale the breath again and again until one cannot inhale. When one cannot hold it anymore, it is important to exhale without a focus and relax.

The culmination of this {382} is being able to hold this for as long as one wishes without pain. The qualities are the arising of inconceivable warmth and bliss. It is said that the experience of the Lord of Yogins arose from this. The faults removed are diseases of cold, tumors, and indigestion.

ii) Inhaling through the Mouth with No Sound

Inhale fully through the mouth with no sound. The method of practice is performing the nine limbs of concentration, as before. Imagine that all the vāyu is slowly absorbed down into a blue dharmodaya at the navel. Fully inhale the vāyu slowly through the mouth into its open surface and swallow saliva without making sound. Press the larynx with the chin and hold for as long as one can. When one exhales, exhale slowly without a focus. Afterward, maintain the view.

The culmination of this is that if one can press down for a day and a night, one is without pain. The qualities are the arising of bliss and clarity because of being accompanied with heat. The faults this can remove are illnesses of the abdomen, such as ascites, and so on. In particular, if one presses down on the vāyu, like a drill, into a painful site, the pain will be removed and all disturbances of the body will be removed.

Directly following the previous two visualizations, a visualization to meditate upon in common with both is as follows: Inside of a white light in the navel is a vermillion *a*, which is like a stroke. Visualize that the vāyu seeps into it. As the white light disappears, it seeps into the red *a*. Visualize that there is a flame one or two inches in length. Otherwise, visualize a red dharmodaya at the navel, wide like the ground. Again, the method is that as one presses down on the vāyu, that dharmodaya becomes bigger, and in the end covers the whole earth. The inside of it becomes empty, and vāyu is introduced inside. Again, meditate that it becomes as deep as the ocean. Since one again presses down the vāyu, the base of the dharmodaya, like the mouth of a copper horn, is inside the rectum, {383} is vivid red, and there is no evident bottom. Imagine that all the vāyu enters this and hold the vāyu. Again, imagine [the dharmodaya] is as high as the sky. Again, the method is that one visualizes all the vāyu entering [the dharmodaya] again and once one merges one's mind with space, they become one taste and a supreme samādhi of emptiness without periphery or center will arise. Occasionally, one should engage in the behavior of a cat.

The enhancement practice for both of those is to be seated cross-legged. Both hands should hold the legs where they are crossed. Shake the body, and without constraining the lower vāyu, press down on the upper vāyu. Expand the lower belly as much as possible and meditate. This causes wrinkles to vanish and removes indigestion. The enhancement for this is as follows: Just as before, the vāyu seeps down about four cubits from the nāḍī of the secret place, like incense smoke, and also emerges from the top of the head about one cubit, is bluish, and rises a good distance. Focus the mind on that, and then contract the lower vāyu as much as possible, pressing down the upper vāyu, and meditate. At that time, it is said one should not allow the belly to contract inward. That will spread warmth throughout the whole body. One should sustain that warmth naturally.

As such, other than cultivating the vāyu and focusing on the tip of the nose, rest for a short while. The mind should remain relaxed. That is cognizance maintaining control of the mind.

d) Unification

Now, since uniting [the vāyu] is the root of all paths and the cause that generates all qualities, there are four in this method of meditating. The method of practice is as follows: The legs are crossed. The hands are in the posture of equipoise; that is, the lower hand is covered or the hands cover the knees. Perform the complete nine limbs of concentration. In the navel, there is the fire of caṇḍālī, an *a* that is like the shape of a stroke. Imagine it is thin, hot, sharp, and intense.

Next, contract the lower vāyu slightly, then {384} draw the upper vāyu in with the effort of soundlessly touching the head to the ground, and meditate that all the vāyu dissolves into the fire at the navel (or meditate without focusing on the visualization at all). Finish with the upper vāyu and swallow saliva. Strongly draw the lower vāyu up and unite [the upper and lower vāyus] in the navel, pressing the belly into the spine. Expand the lower belly and slightly bend the neck. Press the larynx with the chin and hold the vāyu as long as one can. At that time, since the lower vāyu is contracted, the upper vāyu automatically ceases. Since the upper vāyu is pressed down, the lower vāyu is drawn up automatically. If one does not wish to exhale, this is the supreme arising of the precious jewel. The extent of pressing down the vāyu:

> For the most diligent, uninterrupted;
> for the more diligent, sixty-four;
> and for the medium, thirty-two.
> There is no specified number for the average.

When applied in a session, it is said that for those of best diligence, the unification is uninterrupted; for those of more diligence, in every session the unification is held for a count of sixty-four; for those of medium diligence, the count is thirty-two in every session; and for those of average diligence, it is meditated on without a specified number, but this is not the main activity. When measurement is applied to each unification, tap each knee and snap one's fingers, and increase in each session. A person of good health and diet and great faith and diligence will do this day and night without interruption. A person of weaker health and diligence will practice sixty-four rounds from the perspective that a whole day is divided into sixty-four twenty-four-minute periods. The medium person, less healthy and with weaker diligence than that, will practice thirty-two rounds[89] per session from the perspective of thirty-two twenty-four-minute periods. A person of average faith and diligence will not have a specified number, practicing seven, ten, or twenty-one rounds per session. Also, increasing the rounds in every session every day {385} will cause the average to become the best.

As such, one should train [maintaining union] through daily conduct to be able to remain in the cross-legged posture for as long as one wishes. Then train with the knees drawn up. Having trained in that way, train in standing. After that, train in all activities. Afterward, train in the view: naturally maintaining clarity and naturally maintaining relaxation. The culmination of each unification is that one is able to unify [the upper and lower vāyus] many times during the day and night, and through this—along with yantra yoga—samādhi will arise. By merely drawing up the lower vāyu, all vāyus will automatically cease.

The faults removed are disturbances of the body, and so on. The qualities of meditation are that the samādhi of bliss and emptiness arises without regard to equipoise or post-equipoise, and one accomplishes all mundane and transcendent siddhis. Those can be understood in the manuals for removing obstructions.

B) The Intimate Instructions of the Pervaded

The key points of the intimate instructions of the pervaded are as follows: Clear visualization is crucial for the practitioner meditating on caṇḍālī. Even if the vāyu is pressed down only slightly, if the visualization is clear, a good experience will arise. If the visualization is unclear, even if the vāyu is pressed down strongly, the experience will be slow to arise, just as the visualization is unclear. Here, if one visualizes the blazing and dripping above the heart, an experience of clarity will arise. If the vāyu is pressed down weakly with the focus below the navel, heat and bliss principally arise. Thus press down strongly. It is important to master one visualization, rather than switching through all the visualizations again and again. Also, it is necessary to apply those vāyu yogas and caṇḍālī with respect to season, age, and illness. Cultivate vāyu yoga in the summer and caṇḍālī in the winter. If one desires the experience of nonconceptuality, cultivate it in the spring. For the experience of bliss, cultivate it in the fall. When a youth, cultivate vāyu yoga; when an adult, cultivate caṇḍālī; when old, cultivate nonconceptuality. Also, when blood and pitta predominate, cultivate vāyu yoga; if vata predominates, {386} cultivate caṇḍālī.

When those intimate instructions on those practices are condensed, there are nine: five that do not depend on cakras, three that depend on cakras, and the rapid one that depends on the key point of intimate instructions.

1) Not Dependent on Cakras

There are five in the first set.

a) Nourishing the Lamp

There are eight in nourishing the lamp.

i) Train in the Path

The crucial point of the body is being seated with the knees drawn to the chest and the arms in the mudra of the meditation belt. Having completed the nine limbs of concentration beforehand, seek the path of concentration with the vāyu of either the prāṇa or the āyāma. Four fingerbreadths below the navel, visualize an inverted, dark-red *kṣa* syllable that has the nature of fire. In the navel there is an upright red *aṃ*. Open and close the lower door three times. Since the vāyu touches the lower tip, the fire maṇḍala of the groin blazes. Since it touches the *kṣa*, the fire blazes more. That fire touches the *aṃ* at the navel, and since a very fine stream of amṛta element falls, imagine that it nourishes the fire of the *kṣa*, like pouring oil into a fire pit. When one meditates on those visualizations, if they are not clear, closing the eyes and meditating should be sufficient. Train as described:

> Clear, intense, and short—
> train in the caṇḍālī yogas.[90]

While holding the visualization, do not inhale. On the basis of a clear visualization, inhale the vāyu and also silently swallow saliva, the horse of the vāyu, and press on the larynx with the chin. Intensely visualize the blazing and dripping in a form that resembles struggling to comb hair. Unite the vāyus moderately by constricting the lower door.

ii) Maintaining the View

Maintaining the view is the actual samādhi. By investigating any experiences that arise in the body and mind from that previous visualization, after any of the fifteen experiences arise, when the mind remains one-pointedly [on whichever experience arises], relax any effort of vāyu and mind. In a state of deep relaxation of body and mind, maintain clarity or relaxation and rest without moving. {387} Further, when the mind is distracted, meditate intensely on the training of the path, the effort of vāyu and mind. As such, the training on the path and sustaining the view will increase. Alternately, having engaged in the main training of the path, at the end of the session maintain the view, whichever is thought most convenient.

iii) Naturally Sustain Heat

No matter what experience of the various characteristics (high, low, happiness, or suffering) arises, it is recognized as samādhi arising from inner dependent origination. Without regarding faults and qualities, abandon concepts of joy and sadness and keep on the path.

iv) Number of Sessions

There is no specific number of sessions. In a single day, meditate without a specific number of sessions, four, six, and so on.

v) Length of Sessions

There is no length of session. In a session, there is no length of the meditation, such as dividing that session into twenty-four divisions, and so on.

vi) Mental Engagement

Investigating the object of mental engagement is as follows: If one is happy but not happy to meditate, there will be no meditation. If one does not mediate while happy, there will be no progress. If one meditates while unhappy, there will be obstacles. If one meditates once, like a skittish horse, one will not like it, and later after this becomes a bad habit, one will not be able to meditate at all.

vii) Evaluating Health

If health is good, meditate; if bad, restore one's health and relax for a while. If one meditates when one is not in good health, disturbances in the body will occur.

viii) Urging with the Quirt of Diet and Behavior

Eat a diet that is light and very nutritious. One's behavior must not be excessive but carefree. Do not stay in the sun, near fires, or in the wind. Do not stay in dusty places. Train in sitting cross-legged or with the knees drawn up.

b) Thunderbolt of Brahma

The training in the path is as the guru has said:

> The arrow of fire on the bow of air
> strikes the target, the *haṃ* of bodhicitta, {388}
> swiftly causing gnosis to blaze.
> There is no repeated application.

The body is cross-legged, with the two hands covering the knees. The other key points of the body are as before. Perform the complete nine limbs of concentration, as before.

The key point of mind is visualizing a fire arrow, which is hot, violent, and very sharp, on the bow of air at the sphincter, with its notch facing toward the rectum. Meditate that the central nāḍī runs straight from the secret place to the crown. At the upper tip of this is an inverted *haṃ* filled with bodhicitta.

The key point of vāyu is fiercely contracting the vāyu at the lower door. By joining the lower belly to the vertebrae, the bow and arrow change position from behind, above, and below, and the arrowhead enters the central nāḍī. By drawing the upper body upward, the bow is drawn and the lower belly and lower vāyu are drawn up strongly. Since the eyes stare upward, that fire arrow enters the path of the central nāḍī. Since it strikes the *haṃ* in the crown, there are two ways: the stream of amṛta drips steadily, like an elongated thread, or white like the color of pearls. Meditate until the samādhi of bliss occurs, relaxing the lower and upper vāyus simultaneously. Forcefully expand the lower belly, and then press the belly to the spine. Because of that, the upper vāyu will automatically cease. Thus there is no need to hold and no need to exhale either. This is called "the key point of pacifying vāyu." At that time, if the mind is distracted, do not meditate on the visualization of the bow and arrow but focus the mind on the dripping bindu above the heart or at the navel. If one faints due to the power of the samādhi, one should hit the seventh vertebrae[91] with one's fists or a slap. If that does not help, one should splash cold water, and so on, and practice the intimate instruction with eight key points, as before. Also, in subsequent sessions one should meditate on the visualization in each session. Maintaining the view, and so on, are as before. {389}

c) Nāḍī Yoga

The training on the path is whichever crucial point is easiest, such as the body being cross-legged, and so on. Also, the other preliminaries should be completed beforehand. In conjunction with the exhalation, visualize the red rasanā on the right, which has the nature of fire, running from the secret place to the right nostril. In conjunction with inhalation, visualize the white lalanā on the left, which has the nature of lunar water, running from the secret place to the left nostril. Both those nāḍīs are thick and thin, like a medium-sized bamboo stalk. In conjunction with the breath pausing inside, visualize the central nāḍī running from the secret place to the brahma aperture. It possesses four characteristics: it is thin, like the stalk of a lotus flower; it is straight, like the trunk of plantain tree; it is clear, like sesame oil; and it is red, like a parrot tree flower. To begin, train in a short exhalation and long exhalation and subsequently, a long pause. As such, since one trains again and again and the mind remains where it is placed without a definite place to remain, countless experiences arise through meditation. Allow all experiences of heat to be sustained naturally. There is no definite length of session, and so on, as before. Nonconceptuality is primarily what arises from this intimate instruction.

d) The Wheel of the Churning Stick

The path of training is as follows: The hands make the meditation belt mudra. Having fully completed the other preliminaries as before, the key point of the mind is visualizing the red central nāḍī that runs from the navel to the crown in the center of the body. It is either thick or thin. The two nāḍīs to the right and left are visualized as either thick or thin. For the vāyu, pressing the upper vāyu down fills both the right and left nāḍīs. Then, like rolling a churning stick with the hands, {390} meditate that the central nāḍī is pressed by the knot of the two nāḍīs, churning and turning it. Alternately, the two nāḍīs wrap around the central nāḍī three times, turning it like a churning rope. Imagine that the lower tip of the central nāḍī churns the short *a* at the navel, which is below in the manner of the base of the churn,[92] causing sparks [that fill the body].[93] Contract the lower vāyu and then strongly unite the upper and lower vāyu. Here, urge with the quirt of diet and behavior. Train on the path without a [specified] number and length of sessions. Maintain the view. Whatever experiences arise should be sustained naturally, as before. Heat and bliss primarily arise from this.

e) The Bindu Yogas

Among the four in the bindu yogas, if one wishes for [an experience] of clarity, train in the union of the sun and moon in the heart; if one wishes for stability, train in the single warrior in the navel; if one wishes to increase bliss, train in the bindu of bliss in the secret place; and if one wishes to increase physical strength, train in the seed of white hair at the ūrṇā.

i) The Union of the Sun and Moon

The first, the union of the sun and moon, is the intention of the *Great Illusion Tantra*. The crucial point of the posture is sitting cross-legged with the hands covering the knees or in the position of equipoise. Having completed the nine limbs of concentration, inside of the heart, which is like an empty egg, below there is a moon and above there is a sun. Both are the size of a bean. In between those is a bindu the size of a mustard seed. Imagine that it has these three characteristics: its color is pink, its aspect is clear, and its essence is bliss and emptiness. Since one focuses the mind on that, on the basis of the sound of "sing" arising from the bindu, a tiny hole arises in the sun, the width of a single horsehair. Mentally look down and inhale vāyu silently through the mouth. It absorbs through the hole into the bindu. Based on that, when the vāyu pauses, a very fine thread of light ray arises from that bindu, emerging from the hole. Imagine it wraps around the sun, moon, and bindu six and a half times, and press the wind down for as long as one can. When one can no longer press the vāyu down, exhale slowly and soundlessly through the nostrils. That thread retracts and dissolves into the bindu. In this case, the sun and moon are method and wisdom. The bindu is the all-basis. {391} The half-wrapping from that bindu is the afflicted mind. The six complete wrappings are the group of six consciousnesses. Since one meditates in that way, the ultimate, very clearly visualized samādhi arises and clairvoyance will also arise quickly. The key points of the intimate instruction are the same as before.

ii) The Solitary Warrior

Second, for the solitary warrior, the preliminaries are the same as before, except the body is cross-legged. Imagine a bindu the size of a chickpea. It has three characteristics: it is white in color, its aspect is clear, and its essence is the union of bliss and emptiness. For the upper vāyu, block the āyāma. Since one inhales through the prāṇa or soundlessly through the mouth and then presses down, imagine that [the vāyu] dissolves into the bindu. A special, nonconceptual samādhi arises swiftly, like deep sleep. The key points of the intimate instruction are the same as before.

iii) The Bindu of Bliss

Third, for the bindu of bliss, the preliminaries are the same as before. The key point of the mind is as follows: A bindu is imagined inside the "vase" of the vajra of method or in the bhaga of wisdom. It has three characteristics: its color is ruby and its form is bliss and clarity, its essence is union, and its size is that of a mustard seed. Through the application of opening and closing the sphincter, the lower vāyu dissolves into the bindu. Further, contract the sphincter, contract the lower vāyu even more, and meditate. When releasing [the hold], relax slowly. If one relaxes too strongly, it is said that one might lose the bindu. By meditating that way, a blissful feeling that the jewel is going to split will arise. If the bindu leaks or desire arises, prevent it with a wide-open stare, and focus the mind on the ūrṇā. That will pacify it. At that moment, by moving the belly, the bliss that arises will spread throughout the body. Through meditating in such a way, feelings of nausea can be eliminated and, if it is mastered, diseases can be removed. This is a product of supreme bliss. The key points of the intimate instruction are the same as before. Here, primarily, only the lower vāyu is employed, causing a samādhi of bliss {392} to arise swiftly.

iv) The Seed of White Hair at the Ūrṇā

Fourth, for the seed of white hair at the ūrṇā, the preliminaries are the same as before. The key point of the mind is imagining the crooked body of the inverted *haṃ* located in the crown inside of the ūrṇā; it resembles a silk thread, is shiny white, and possesses the experience of bliss. At the nāḍī of the uvula, there is an inverted white *suṃ*. In the heart, there is an upright blue *hūṃ*. When the vāyu of āyāma is exhaled, after it moves from the back of the uvula, it touches the *haṃ* and heats the *haṃ*. A stream of amṛta flows from that and falls on the *suṃ* of the uvula. After that is filled, the amṛta falls from it and is imagined to dissolve into the *hūṃ*. Focus one's mind on it. When one inhales again, meditate on the descent, as before; the two drippings are applied to mental experience. On occasion, to slightly move the nāḍī of the uvula,[94] press the larynx with the chin, place the tongue on the palate, and meditate. Initially, the saliva will be thick. Then it will be like curd. After that, a lot of saliva will emerge. One will become free of desire for solid food. A key point is not losing the saliva. If it is lost, it is said one's health will be poor and one's enjoyments will become meager. This corresponds only with the prāṇāyāma vāyu. The qualities are that the tissues of the body (*lus zungs*) will increase greatly, the body will be as fast as a horse, one will be free of white hair and wrinkles, and the mind will be clear and straight. The key points of the intimate instruction are the same as before.

Those demonstrate the five intimate instructions that do not depend on cakras.

2) Based on Cakras

a) The Sharp One Based on a Single Cakra

For the sharp one based on one cakra, the crucial point of the body is that the knees are drawn up to the chest. Having completed the nine limbs of samādhi, visualize the karma vāyu naturally located at the anus and the gnosis fire naturally located at the groin. The outer circle of the navel cakra is devoid of the array of syllables on the sixty-four outer petals. On the eight inner petals {393} are the heads of the series: *a ka ca ṭa ta pa ya śa*, circling to the right. Imagine an extremely fine *aṃ* syllable in the center of a triangular knot of nāḍīs in the navel. All syllables are visualized to be red in color. Through the application of opening and closing the sphincter, the lower vāyu touches the tip of the fire, igniting the fire of the groin. That strikes the *aṃ* at the navel. Focus on the fire arising from *aṃ*—red, very hot, about two inches or so [in height], and so on—and unite the vāyus gradually. Press the larynx with the chin and hold the vāyu as long as one can. That will cause sudden warmth and heat below the navel. If one faints from bliss, one should either walk or walk in a cold breeze. Since it is possible that pain will arise in the forehead, allow it to be natural. The keys points are maintaining the view, and so on, as before. Since this is a visualization for quickly giving rise to experience, it is called the "sharp one."

(b) The Quick One Based on Two Cakras

The quick one based on two cakras is as follows: Having performed the preliminaries, the key point of the mind is as before, above the navel cakra, the eight petals of the cakra at the heart are free from an array of syllables. In the center [of the heart cakra], imagine that an inverted, pale-blue *hūṃ*, which resembles mercury, is on the verge of dripping. Next, imagine that the *āṃ* [of the navel cakra] and the *hūṃ* are both connected within the very fine central nāḍī. Then, the vāyu meets the tip of the fire. Open and close [the sphincter] three times, and on the last time, since it is kept closed, the fire of the groin blazes and supplements the *āṃ* at the navel. Since a very fine thread of fire blazes from the *āṃ* in the central nāḍī up to the *hūṃ*, and a fine [stream] of bodhicitta drips down to the *āṃ*, focus the mind on the blazing and dripping and the white and red aspects, and meditate.

While maintaining the visualization, inhale the upper vāyu and do not exhale, like a merchant who has nothing left to sell. Repeat the visualization and press down on the vāyu gently. If one presses the vāyu down strongly, it is possible the visualization will become unclear. If the visualization is unclear, even if one presses down on the wind, the qualities will not arise, so one must do it properly. When one cannot hold the vāyu, slowly exhale. The key points of the intimate instruction are the same as before.

With respect to that, the visions that will arise, which are gathered by heat, are the five signs and the five subsidiary signs. First, from the perspective of the forward order of movements of the vāyus of the five elements that arise from the right nostril being arrested, the signs of smoke, mirages, fireflies, blazing lamps, and a cloudless sky arise. From the perspective of the reverse order of movements of the vāyus of the five elements that arise from the left nostril being arrested, the signs of darkness, rainbows, lightning, moonbeams, and sunbeams arise. Since these can arise either in equipoise or post-equipoise as visions or as dreams respectively, recognize them and sustain all experiences naturally.

c) The Stable One Based on Four Cakras

The stable one[95] based on four cakras is as follows: The preliminaries are performed as before. Also visualize the two active cakras. On the outer circle of the sixty-four petals of the navel cakra, the sixteen vowels (repeated twice) and the consonants (omitting *ha* and *kṣa*) are counterclockwise. The eight petals of the inner circle are as before [*a ka ca ṭa ta pa ya śa*], clockwise. All syllables are red in color and stand upright.

Next, in the four directions on the eight petals of the heart are *bhrūṃ āṃ jriṃ khaṃ*. In the four intermediate directions are *lāṃ māṃ pāṃ tāṃ*. *Hūṃ* is in the center. All syllables are black and inverted. On the sixteen petals of the throat cakra, there are the sixteen vowels, clockwise. *Aṃ* is in the center. All syllables are red and stand upright. On the thirty petals of the crown cakra, there are the vowels (counterclockwise) and the consonants from *ka* to *ta* (clockwise). *Haṃ* is in the center. {394} All syllables are white and inverted. Likewise, visualize the three nāḍīs: the right nāḍī is the red rasanā; the left nāḍī is the lalanā; and in the middle is the central nāḍī, which has four characteristics, running from the navel to the brahma aperture.

Next, through the application of opening and closing the sphincter, the mother of fire (*me ma*) and mother of sleep (*gnyid ma*) vāyus meet at the tip, igniting the fire at the groin. Since the fire strikes the *aṃ* at the navel, that warm vāyu moves through the rasanā on the right, burns the seed syllables in the heart, continues through the rasanā, destroys the seeds syllables of the throat, and continues through the rasanā, striking the *haṃ* in the crown. The *haṃ* melts into light and descends through the lalanā, expanding the seeds syllables in the throat, which were visualized before. [The light] continues through the lalanā, expanding the seed syllables in the heart that were visualized before. It then continues further through the lalanā, striking the *aṃ* of the navel, causing the *aṃ* to blaze more. Through the slightly opened central nāḍī, [the fire] moves like a tongue of lightning through the central nāḍī, destroying the *hūṃ* of the heart and the *āṃ* of the throat without hesitation or impediment. Merely by touching the *hāṃ*, a fine stream of amṛta flows and falls through the central nāḍī. Focus the mind on the blazing and dripping in the throat from that fire[96] being driven down [by the amṛta]. If it is held too long, it is difficult to press down on the vāyu and there is a risk of the uvula dropping. Next, focus on the heart cakra and meditate. If it is held too long, there is risk of heart palpitations and disturbances. Finally, focus the mind on the blazing and dripping at the place four fingerbreadths above the navel, and sustain the vāyu in union for a proper time. The rest is the same as before.

3) The Seven Based on the Key Points of Intimate Instructions

a) The Pale-Red Fire

The visualization of the pale-red fire is as follows: Draw the knees up to the chest and cross the feet. The two hands cross and cover the shoulders. Outwardly, this is the double tripod of the body (with six feet). {396} Inwardly, this is the double tripod of the nāḍīs. Secretly, this is the double tripod of bodhicitta. Thus, there are eighteen [feet]. One should complete the other limbs of concentration.

Next, visualize one's body as hollow and empty, like an inflated balloon.[97] Without a specific source, a pale-red fire is imagined to fill the inside of the body. Focus the mind on the fire. Having blocked the vāyu of the āyāma, inhale through the prāṇa and press it down for as long as one can. Counting the number mentally, unite the vāyu twelve times and press down, until one can no longer hold the count, and then increase by uniting the vāyu twelve times without counting. When all are combined, one should hold as long as one can for twenty-four unifications of the vāyu, both counted and uncounted. Making effort during the counted unifications destroys; relaxing during the uncounted unifications gives benefit. Further, counting is entering the path; not counting is sustaining the view. Do not investigate mental objects of engagement; meditate diligently without engagement until one has completed the length of the session and the numbers in the session. After completing [both the length and numbers of the session], also do not meditate while mentally distracted.

One should not evaluate one's health. Also, if one's health is bad, one should rest properly. After that, even if one's health is good, do not meditate. Urge with the quirt of diet and behavior. All experiences should be sustained naturally. Maintain the view. Meditate in four sessions. The best will do so for three days and then change the visualization; the medium, five days; and the average, nine days. The very best will give rise to the experience of heat either quickly or slowly. Afterward, change the points of the mind for stability.

b) Blazing Fire

The visualization of the blazing fire is as follows: The preliminaries and the main subject are as before. Imagine a red *raṃ* syllable on both soles of the feet. Then, since one flexes the tendons of the legs, the blazing fire travels through the nāḍī of the ankles and enters the major nāḍī of the thighs. Since [the fires] meet at the secret place, focus on the fire's sharpness, swiftness, intensity, and violence:{397} it is as sharp as a needle, as quick as a lamp disturbed by the wind, as intense as something hot to the touch, and as violent as billowing sparks. The others are the same as before.

c) Fighting Bindus

When that visualization is clear, there are the fighting bindus. Imagine a white bindu the size of a bean at the tip of the previous fire. Two inches above that, visualize a red bindu the size of a pill. When one unites the vāyu, those two strike each other repeatedly, like two fighting eggs. Focus the mind on the entire body filled with billowing sparks and stabilize that.

d) The Wheel

That fire in the secret place moves straight up, like the central pillar of a stupa, upon which is that bindu, upon which is a wheel of fire with four or eight spokes. On each spoke there are both long and short vowels, head to head. The front, back, right, and left of that wheel do not touch the navel, the spine, or the two kidneys. The wheels turn right or left, whichever way is easiest. Imagine that the whole interior of the body is filled with sparks, tightly constrict the lower vāyu, and unite it with the upper vāyu. Here, the inner key point of the central pillar, the intermediate key point of the wheel, and the outer key point of the seed syllables are important.

e) Intensely Blazing Fire

The visualization of the intensely blazing fire is as follows: On the basis of the previous visualizations, a dark-red fire rises from the wheel of fire. Its essence is hot and its nature is supple. It fills up to the throat. Imagine there are small flames, like a fire consuming juniper leaves. Stabilize that.

f) Greatly Blazing Fire

The visualization of the greatly blazing fire is as follows: Since the fire becomes greater, the entire inside and outside of the body is imagined as a blazing fire, like a burning ball of iron.

g) Total Burning Fire

The visualization for the totally blazing fire is as follows: That fire becomes larger and larger. Focus the mind on all appearing things burning the fire. Afterward, maintaining the view is relaxing the effort of holding the mental visualization {398} at the end of the session. Since one leaves one's eyes in a wide-open stare, an experience of nonconceptuality without center or periphery arises. Having collected one's mind, a samādhi of union will arise because of equipoise.

The other key points are as before. Explain the later visualizations on the basis of the earlier visualizations and meditate. Here, since the best meditate on this for twenty-one days, the medium for thirty-five days, and the average for sixty-three days, they will reach the culmination.

The method of removing the obstacle for this should be understood in the treatise. In these situations, there is enhancement through the eight enhancements and the six instructions in these situations. As such, train on the path with the intimate instructions of caṇḍālī, and meditate until the view, self-originated gnosis, is attained. These bring on the first gathering of the elements. Therefore, in these situations, it is necessary here to evaluate the importance of the thirty protections and the removal of obstacles.

III) Gnosis of the Wisdom Consort Empowerment

In meditating on the path of the gnosis of the wisdom consort empowerment, there is (1) the extensive path and (2) the condensed path.

A) The Extensive Path

[The extensive path has three topics:] (1) the preparation is empowering the three perceptions, (2) the main subject is the recognition of the descent and hold, and (3) the conclusion is reversal and spreading.

1) The Preparation

Since one is relying upon a gnosis knowledge consort, oneself and the gnosis knowledge consort are visualized either through the four limbs or instantly, imagining that both are reciting the root mantra, and so on, as much as possible. Then, to empower the space and the secret, the ordinary space of the mother vanishes and from emptiness *āḥ* arises, from which a red lotus with eight petals arises, empowered with an *āḥ* marking the anthers. The ordinary secret place of the father vanishes and from a state of emptiness arises a *hūṃ*, from which arises a blue five-tined vajra, marked with a *hūṃ* at the navel. {399} In the passageway, there is an upright, dark-red *phaṭ*, and the jewel is empowered with a string of *oṃ*s, which substitutes for the string of pearls. Imagine that the jewel tip arises from *svā*.

Next, one abandons concepts of ordinariness by relying on the gnosis knowledge consort. Having actualized the connate gnosis, for a moment one thinks that one has obtained the dharmakāya.

2) The Main Part

Look at the form of that gnosis consort, since the fire of passion is ignited, the bindu descends. Recognize where the bliss arises, and wherever it arises, place the mind one-pointedly on that. If it seems that one is going to lose the bindu, prevent this with a wide-open stare. Cross the two vajra fists at the chest, press the stomach into the spine, and roll back the eyes into the sky. One will be able to maintain the secret, but do not actually engage in union. In all of those, naturally maintain the experience. Also, one should use passionate words, scent the body of the consort, taste her honeyed lower lip, and so on. One should touch her with various kinds of touch, touch her upper and lower body, bite and scratch her, embrace and kiss her, massage her nipples, and so on. Those will ignite the fire of passion, as before.

Then, imagine the uniting of the bola and kakkola.[98] The bindu descends. Meditate on bliss. Prevent the loss of the bindu with a wide-open stare and maintain the secret. Do not engage in the visualization of intercourse.

Next, using the motion of a tortoise, since one slowly engages in intercourse, the bindu descends. If there is a similar experience of bliss, shoot it into the sky above, then to the Brahmaloka, to Akaniṣṭha, and so on. Prevent the loss of the bindu with a wide-open stare. If the bindu is difficult to hold, then draw it up with the unification [of the upper and lower vāyus] that arrests the upper vāyu; block the right nostril with the left finger, inhale through the *prāṇa*, and rotate the head and entire body to the right; shake the upper torso; and shake the head. {400} If the bindu is arrested, from now on the signs should arise as they are explained in the treatise. At that time, having unified bliss and emptiness, since a samādhi of unidentifiable bliss arises, this should be recognized and sustained for a long while.

3) Conclusion

There are three sections.

a) Reversing the Bindu Upward

In reversing the bindu upward, there are four movements of the body and two movements of voice and speech: drying the ocean of Sumeru, bringing the four continents under control, putting the tongue in its own place, opening the supreme sense organ upward, guiding the power of the voice with a loud and long *hūṃ*, and shooting the bow and arrow of the *hūṃ* and *phaṭ* of samādhi.

Expand the belly and then press the stomach to the spine. After strongly clenching the toes and fingers, cross the two vajra fists at the heart and tighten the biceps and calves. After placing the tongue on the palate, curl it back. After opening the eyes widely, look at the space above the crown. After inhaling the vāyu, with a loud and long sound of *hūṃ*, the vāyu is drawn up inside, and one gradually contracts the lower belly. At the time of empowering the secret beforehand, that *phaṭ* is pulled up by the *hūṃ*, and the *hūṃ* is pushed up by the *phaṭ*. Imagine that they are gradually drawn from the secret to the crown. All of those are done simultaneously.

b) Spreading the Bindu around the Body

To spread the bindu around the body, tie the belt of the vāyu, throw the noose, turn the body like a grinding wheel, and employ childish behavior as the path. Sit cross-legged, inhale the vāyu, and press it down for as long as possible. Make very tight vajra fists and cross them facing up, placing them in front of the waist, like tying a belt. Lie on one's back, and wave and stretch one's feet and arms in turn. {401} Sitting cross-legged, cover the knees with one's hands and rotate the abdomen. Among those key points of the body, bend one's head forward, right, and left, three times each, and shake it. Roll backward and forward in the four directions. Exhale the breath forcefully between the teeth with a hissing sound. The bodhicitta will spread throughout the whole body through those means, and an experience of supreme bliss and emptiness will arise.

c) Preventing Loss

To prevent loss, practice according to the six preventions of leaking.

B) The Condensed Path

In the condensed path, there are three parts.

1) Preparation

The preparation, bringing the downward-voiding vāyu under control, is as follows:

> There is a sun on the right hand and a moon on the left hand,
> which are crossed, covering the two knees.
> Make nine long *hūs* and short *hus* in front,
> three on the right and three on the left,
> exhaling three times and inhaling three times.
> One should train in this cycle.
> In three days, the genitalia recedes into a sheath.

In this way, train the downward-voiding vāyu. The method is to sit on the roof of one's house with the knees drawn up to the chest, recalling that the right hand is the sun and the left hand is the moon. Place the hollow of the elbows on the knees, cross the hands, cover the lower part of the legs, and straighten the waist. Bend the throat forward, simultaneous inhaling the vāyu. The inhaled vāyu is drawn in once, at length in the beginning, with the sound of *hūṃ*. As soon as that is complete, repeat it once. At the end, inhale a very short breath once. Those three are to be done in conjunction. Also, the lower vāyu should be drawn up without interruption during the period of three repetitions, corresponding with the previous three [inhalations]. At that time, one should pull up the sphincter at the same time as the three repetitions.

At the end of the third repetition, tilt the head up three times, and then hold the vāyu for as long as one is able. Open the eyes wide. Twist to the right once, {402} then twist to the center once, then twist to the left once, and then twist to the center again. After that, rapidly exhale the vāyu through one's nostrils three times in succession. Then inhale three times in succession. In the same way, repeat on the right and then the left.

Since one trains by rotating one based on another, the vāyu will be under control for half a day. For the average practitioner, if the secret place withdraws into the sheath within three days, one has obtained control over the downward-voiding vāyu. Even if it is does not withdraw, the secret place becomes very short and one will not lose bindu.

If one cannot manage such methods because of health, repeat three times in the middle and three times each on the right and left. At that time, if headaches and nausea occur, relax the sphincter. If there is heat in the heart or constipation, one is unable to urinate. The ascending vāyu has moved into the downward-voiding vāyu, so it is important to break this up.

2) Main Part

In the main part, there is the explanation of descending and holding:

> Having performed the empowerment, and so on,
> slightly constrict the anal sphincter,
> suck strongly on both middle fingers,
> and stare upward with both eyes.
> This will retain the bindu.
> Also, strongly utter "ha ha."
> Also, one should perform the other physical yantras.
> These two will retain the bindu.

The way to practice this method is as follows: The key point of the body is the knees drawn up to the chest. Empower the gnosis mudra with the three perceptions. Unite the bola and kakkola. The bindu will descend by the mere back-and-forth motion. In order for one overwhelmed by bliss to hold the bindu, alternate slightly constricting and pushing out the sphincter. Do not shut the eyes; stare upward. Alternately, suck on the right and left index and middle fingers. Inhale, without allowing any [of the breath] to leave the mouth, and suck intensely at the same time. When sucking on the right fingers, open the left eye widely. When sucking on the left fingers, open the right eye widely. Doing those three movements at the same time will definitely arrest the bindu. Further, leading with the voice alone,{403} at the end of strongly inhaling with *ha*, strongly expel [the vāyu] with many repetitions of *ha*. At the end, hold the vāyu for as long as possible. The other yantras of the body applied while the upper vāyu is stopped are straight forward.

3) Conclusion

The conclusion, reversing and spreading, is as follows:

> *Hi hi* like an elephant, growl *hūṃ hūṃ* like a tigress,
> retch like a predator, and sniff like a fox.
> Drawing up in stages through the navel, heart,
> throat, and crown,
> distribute the bindu through the body with the mudra of
> liberation.

The meaning of this is as follows: The posture is to be seated cross-legged, with the weight of the body either distributed on the toes planted on the ground or the heels. The hands are tightly clenched into vajra fists and crossed over the heart. The key point of the mind is imagining that bodhicitta arrives at the navel from the tip of the jewel of the vajra. The key point of the voice is expelling the sound of *hi* at the same time while exhaling the vāyu. Draw the bindu up at the same time one draws up the vāyu from inside the *hing*. Repeat that many times in close succession, and then hold the vāyu as long as one can. Likewise, imagine that the bindu is drawn up to the navel, expel the vāyu with *hu*, inhale with *hūṃ*, and repeat many times in succession. Imagine that the bindu is drawn to the throat; it is drawn up within by the sounds of *hak hak* many times in succession. Imagine that the bindu is drawn to the crown. After inhaling through the nostrils, utter *hik* and tilt the occiput back. Stare upward, and then hold the vāyu as long as one can. Also, in the interval between the earlier and later utterances, hold the vāyu as long as one can.

Next, to spread the bindu with the mudra of the liberated lion, the two thumbs are placed in the ears, the two index fingers are placed on the eyes, the two middle fingers are placed on the nostrils, and the two pinkies and ring fingers close the lips. The elbows are straight out in front. Then rotate right, rotate left, and then spin like a drill. After that, squeeze the nostrils with the thumb and forefinger, and inhale the vāyu strongly, shaking the head and shaking the body. At the beginning of each session of this path, {404} one should complete the nine limbs of concentration. At the conclusion, maintain the view, dedicate merit, and, likewise, meditate on compassion for all unrealized sentient beings, as before.

Since the view of this path is the samādhi of bliss and emptiness, after recognizing this, remain in equipoise after relaxing the body and mind. This is the second gathering of the elements, the bindu called "the path instruction of bliss and emptiness."

IV) The Fourth Empowerment

In the path of the fourth empowerment, there are two topics.

A) The Preliminaries

The preliminaries are as follows: One should perform the three preliminaries on a very large and soft cushion in a solitary place without excess sunlight. Then perform the thirty-two activities. First do them in ascending order, then do them in descending order, then pair the first with the last, and so on. Repeated once, this makes ninety-six movements in each session. One should accomplish either three, two, or one session. If one cannot accomplish that, then one should practice the purification of the five limbs for four or three sessions and also practice the nine limbs of concentration for a long time.

B) The Main Subject

1) The Wave of the Body

The wave of the body, stirring the lower vāyu, is preceded by prāṇāyāma, and so on. First, the preliminaries and conclusion are the same as before. Meditate on the seven vāyu yogas until there are repeated signs. Next, meditate on the actual wave of the body. Sit cross-legged with the hands covering and pressing on the knees. Straighten the waist, press the stomach to the spine, and press down on the upper vāyu by exhaling the vāyu three times and inhaling three times. Alternate pressing down on the right and left pelvic bone. Gently contract and then strongly pull up. If one strongly contracts, one will lose strength. When one releases, the lower vāyu is released beforehand. Since one trains without a specific number of sessions or length of sessions, the body is blissful and a samādhi of clarity arises in the mind. If one's health seems questionable, move the belly, twist the upper body, and prevent [the loss of bindu] with a stare. Project the mind into space. On occasion, enhance with the eight enhancements. At that time, releasing the lower vāyu without exhaling the upper vāyu is a key point.

2) Wave of the Voice

For the voice, there is forceful and gentle.

a) The Wave of the Peaceful and Forceful Voiced Inhalations

Go to an isolated place, sit cross-legged, with crossed-vajra fists at the heart. Bow the head forward without touching the ground, and with the tone of *a*, the vāyu flows through the teeth soundlessly. At the same time as the vāyu is inhaled, rise up, slowly inhaling through the mouth until full. In conjunction with that, the lower belly and the lower vāyu are gradually constricted. At the end, tilt the head back, stare with the eyes, and press the vāyu down as long as one can. When one can no longer hold, slowly exhale. As soon as one is finished exhaling, draw the breath in again. Do this three times in front, three times to the right, and three times to the left. Having done seven rounds each during each session, practice in four sessions. Afterward, maintain the view of supreme bliss and emptiness. If this is cultivated, a sound like a flute will arise.

b) The Forceful Voiced Inhalation

The body and voice are as before. The difference is that there is inhalation with the sound of *hūṃ*. Since emitted sound becomes increasingly loud, when finished it can be heard from far away, like a great horn. The others—the length of the session, and so on—are the same as before.

3) The Wave of the Mind, Samādhi

The meditation of samādhi is based on the gnosis consort. Here, there are three parts.

a) The Purification of the Method's Continuum

After being empowered with the perception of the father and mother, the couple instantly enter into union. The purified elements of the father and mother arrive at the tip of the central channel, transforming into light rays, which arrive at the navel. The navel cakra vanishes like dawn, becoming clearer and clearer, like sunrise, and more and more inflated, like an inflated lung. Then, the light rays travel up the rasanā, arriving at the heart. Recall the three features [as in the navel cakra]. {406} Again, the light rays travel through the rasanā, arriving at the throat. Recall the three features. Again, the light rays travel through the rasanā, leaving the right nostril in the form of light rays. The maṇḍala of the excellent deities emanates from the door of the light rays, conferring the four empowerments on sentient beings and transforming the universe into a celestial mansion and the inhabiting sentient beings into the excellent deity. The universe and inhabitants transform into the form of light rays, merging with the emitted light rays, becoming the essence of amṛta, entering the brahma aperture, and arriving at the crown. Recall the three features. When the light rays arrive at the throat, they possess the radiance of one thousand suns. When they arrive at the heart, as a sign of one's continuum transforming into the five kāyas, the light transforms into the five colors. Imagine that they abide like before in the space of the mother after emerging from the navel through the path of the pure nāḍī. That causes the concepts of the apprehender to subside and brings the rasanā under control. One gains control over the āyāma vāyu and imagines that one has realized the signless gate of liberation. Likewise, when performed on the left, the concept of the apprehender subsides, one brings the lalanā under control, obtains power over the prāṇa vāyu, and imagines that one realizes the wishless gate of liberation. In the same way, when performed on the central nāḍī, the subtle concepts of subject and object subside, the central nāḍī is purified, one obtains control over the resting vāyu, and one imagines that one realizes the emptiness gate of liberation.

b) The Purification of the Wisdom's Continuum

Visualize the purification of the mother's three nāḍīs. [The light rays] arrive at the doors of the right and left nostril through the right and left nāḍīs, but there is no emission of light rays. However, it is explained that one can either perform the radiating and gathering from the brahma aperture or not.

c) Purifying Each Continuum

After the pure element travels through the central nāḍī of the father in the form of light rays, those dissolve into the supreme uṣṇīṣa. Similarly, those [light rays dissolve into the supreme uṣṇīṣa] of the mother. Recall that the five kāyas are effortlessly accomplished in both the father and mother. These visualizations are done in concert with the inhalation and exhalation of the vāyu. {407} Since [the breath] is held, there is no need for four sessions. At that time there is no definite experience that arises. Since any experience that arises should be sustained naturally, the experience of the four joys, which are stabilized by the extremely pure reality of all phenomena, arises in their continuums. Consequently, there is the final gathering of the elements, the path instruction of the faultless, fundamental gnosis.

These are gradated instructions intended for average people, an instruction performed in one hundred twenty sessions. Someone claims that since the instruction on the three visions was set aside, there is also a fault through the view. [It is replied,] there is instruction on all three visions: the all-basis cause tantra, the four method tantras of the path, and an instruction through each of the four paths. Apart from the cause tantra, having done both preliminaries and ascertained the view beforehand, both extensively and concisely, next there is the practice. The position that the lord of yogins, Virūpa, himself emphasized was solely the physical training and vāyu, after having practiced a small amount of the creation stage and stabilized it. The visualizations of the vāyu yoga and caṇḍālī are called the cause of samādhi or the path. The view, self-originated gnosis, is called samādhi. If those do not arise, then there is a fault. The view that is confirmed beforehand through hearing and reflection is faulty. This is called the faultless view, the example gnosis, or mahāmudrā. Since a result will not arise without a cause (the visualizations of vāyu yoga or caṇḍālī), the view (self-originated gnosis) will arise based on a cause. Therefore, be diligent in the cause.

Furthermore, having trained for an entire year on the entire treatise that has already been demonstrated, some classes of people train for a single year on the peaceful inhalation of the voice, then spend another year on the forceful inhalation of the voice, and after that, meditate solely on the wave of the mind, samādhi. This is the entryway for those of supreme diligence.

c. Generating a Special Conviction

There are three topics: generating a special conviction, {408} recognizing samādhi, and presenting the divisions of the path. Certainty is generated by the four authorities and the eight aural instructions. Samādhi is recognized, and the divisions of the path are presented, as well as the signs of accomplishing the maṇḍalacakra. The first is demonstrated in the treatise, the second is demonstrated in the three gatherings of the elements, and the third is demonstrated in the four conclusions. Because of those, since someone arrives at some stage through realization, it is necessary to give the instructions appropriate to the path at that time.

3. The Result, the Stage of Buddhahood

The result, the five kāyas that are naturally accomplished without effort, will be explained at the time of the result.

The instruction manual, *Clarifying the Hidden Meaning,*
was composed according to deep and extensive beams and pillars
in the treatise and manuals
on the essential instruction of the Path with Its Result.
Because I fear decline in this degenerate age,
may the gurus and ḍākinīs have forbearance
for this clear disclosure of the hidden meaning.
Through this merit, may I and all migrating beings
in every birth never be separate from this profound path.

Though this instruction manual on the Path with Its Result, called the *Clarification of the Hidden Meaning,* was intended to clarify the instructional manuals of the Jetsun founders, for a long while I lacked courage due to the fierceness of the guardians and laziness. In the beginning, the meditator known as Śākya Zangpo, possessing great devotion to this path, offered a supplication and a gift of gold; in the middle, the vajra holder, Drakpa

Zangpo, who possessed the capacity of speaking knowledgeably and freely because he had trained his continuum in the outer and inner oral instructions, and also the virtuous mentor, the practitioner Palzang, and so on, greatly implored me with a flower-studded bali offering; finally, the nephew of the sublime virtuous mentor, Kunga Yeshe, and so on, made many supplications. On their behalf, I, the vajra-holding bhikṣu, Sönam Gyaltsen Palzangpo, completed this text during the constellation of Aśvini, on the morning of the twenty-ninth day, the time when the ḍākinīs gather, during the special time, the month the Buddha bestowed empowerment, during the year Sarvajit (1347). The transcription was nicely done by the virtuous mentors, Sherab Dorje and Mañjuśrī.

May obstacles to accomplishing the path be pacified at all times.[99] May this be very auspicious and meritorious.

15. The Threefold Instruction

The Instruction through Eleven Key Points,
The Instruction through Six Key Points, and The Instruction through the Trio of Best, Medium, and Average Capacity[1]

THE *THREEFOLD INSTRUCTION*, omitted from Kongtrul's table of contents, is composed of three short texts: *The Instruction Through Eleven Key Points, The Instruction Through Six Key Points*, and *The Instruction Through the Trio of Best, Medium, and Average Capacity*. These three texts are commentaries on the remaining three texts in the *Four Great Trees of the Treatise.*

Opening the Door of the Key Points

The Clarification of the Manual of the Instruction of the Eleven Key Points[2]

oṃ svasti siddhi
Homage to the gurus.

All paths that are the cause of giving rise to samādhi are traversed through eleven key points.

I. The Mundane Path

There are three for the mundane path.

A. The Gathering of the Elements

For the first, the gathering of the elements, there are four.

1. Training on the Path

The special key point of training on the path.

2. The Wave of the Body

The key point of the wave of the body is stirring the lower vāyu, having done prāṇāyāma, and so on, beforehand.

3. The Peaceful Inhalation of the Voice

The key point of the peaceful inhalation of the voice.

4. The Strong Inhalation of the Voice

The key point of the strong inhalation of the voice.

B. The Middle Gathering of the Elements

For the middle gathering of the elements, there are three.

1. Mahāmudrā

The key point of mahāmudrā, nourishing the view.

2. The Eight Enhancements

The key point of the eight enhancements.

3. The Four Close Mindfulnesses

The key point of the four close mindfulnesses.

C. The Final Gathering of the Elements

For the final gathering of the elements, there are two.

1. The Four Correct Renunciations

The key point of the four correct renunciations.

2. The Wave of the Mind

The key point of the wave of the mind, samādhi.

II. The Four Empowerments and the Three Maṇḍalas

For the twelfth stage of the transcendent path, there is the key point of the four empowerments and the three maṇḍalas.

III. The Four Movements Dissolving on the Half Stage

For the ultimate path, there is the key point of the four movements dissolving on the half stage. Thus, the path is traversed through eleven key points.

For practice, the first four key points (A.1–4), the first key point of the middle, and the last key point of the third (B.1, C.3) are the practice through the six key points. For this, there are the preliminaries and the main part.

I. The Preliminaries

First, there is the preliminary accumulation and purification and the key point of the session preliminaries: the three crucial points, the three meditations, and the three activities of wisdom, which constitute the extensive path, {410} and the practice according to the instruction for those of best, medium, and average capabilities.

II. The Main Part

Second, in the main part, there are three in the key point of special training.

A. The Physical Training

The physical training is having completed the nine preliminaries beforehand. On a comfortable seat in an isolated place where there is not excessive sun, one does one series of the thirty activities in the forward progression; then a series in reverse progression; finally, an alternating series. After completing all of those once in every session, there are ninety-six activities. As such, those should be accomplished for three, two, or even one session. If one wishes to attain siddhi in this lifetime, it is said that physical training is a major key point. Next, engage in the training of voice and mind as in the extensive path.

B. The Seven Vāyu Yogas and the Eighteen Caṇḍālī Visualizations

After having trained in prāṇāyāma beforehand, the key point of the wave of the body by stirring the lower vāyu is meditating on the seven vāyu yogas and the eighteen caṇḍālī visualizations, as in the extensive path. On those occasions, enhance with the key points of the eight enhancements: decrease or increase the duration of the sessions, tighten or loosen the mind, alternate eating and fasting, and use care or be free in terms of conduct. The key point of the mind should change according to circumstances. Rely on the amṛta of various objects. The eight path cycles[3] should be applied, such as *The Stages of the Inconceivable*, but one should not meditate after the session has ended.

C. The Path of the Third Empowerment

Then, engage in the actual wave of the body by stirring the lower vāyu. After that, there is the key point of the peaceful voiced inhalation, followed by the key point of the forceful voiced inhalation. Then, there is the key point of nourishing the view, mahāmudrā. The path of the third empowerment is as presented in the treatise. Next, for the wave of the mind, the samādhi is according to the text.

For those, there are three sessions for the three purifications; seven sessions for the vāyu yoga; twenty-five sessions for the eighteen caṇḍālī visualizations; one session each for the wave of the body, the peaceful voiced inhalation, and the forceful voiced inhalation; eight sessions for the path of the third empowerment; and three sessions for the wave of the mind. {411} Thus the path is taught in forty-two sessions. The preparation for all of those is the nine limbs of concentration. The three concluding practices should be applied in all sessions.

The instruction for direct realization of the extensive path
is arranged by summarizing the method of practice
for the six key points
from the eleven instructions on the key points.

The clarification of the *Manual of the Instruction of the Eleven Key Points*, called *Opening the Door of the Key Points*, was composed by the monk, Sönam Gyaltsen. Virtuous.
This is not a tradition of instruction on the words. It is only an instruction on practice.
śubhaṃ

The Key to the Key Points

The Clarification of the Six Key Points[4]

Homage to the guru and the vajra ḍākinī.

Śrī Virūpa's position is that though the path is summarized into extensive, medium, and brief and explained for those who are the best, medium, and average, the topics are held to be included in six key points, which in turn are held to be included in six topics. These six topics are abiding in the cause, from whom the empowerment is obtained, cultivation on the path, experience arising in the view, the signs arising in the conclusion, and manifesting all the topics in the result. There are two topics in the practice of this.

I. The Preliminaries

The instruction on the preliminaries are the preliminary accumulations and purification: the three crucial points of the common preliminaries, the three meditations, and the three for the activities of wisdom, totaling nine, which are practiced according to the extensive path and the instructions for those of best, medium, average capabilities. These are the dharmas that are necessary for the preliminaries in the five stages of instruction.

II. Main Subject

In the main subject, there is (1) the instruction according to the stages of the four paths and (2) the instruction according to the vase, secret, gnosis of the wisdom consort, and the fourth empowerment.

A. The Four Paths
1. The Vase Empowerment

There are six topics in the path of the vase empowerment.

a. Abiding in the Cause

Abiding in the cause is the three preliminaries. After the three preliminaries, in the supporting body, there are four cakras and three principal nāḍīs; that is, the seven palaces of the precious nāḍīs. The fundamental all-basis, the supported, exists in those in the manner of a flower and its scent.[5] {412} Also, generate certainty in the idea that all phenomena of samsara and nirvana are complete in the form of seeds and traces in both the support and the supported, and rest one-pointedly in that state. If there is movement of concepts, one should understand that whatever appearances of samsara and nirvana arise are the inner dependent origination of the concurrent assembly of the support and the supported, body and mind. Maintain the view. At the conclusion, dedicate the merit, seal with the similes of dreams and illusions, and meditate on compassion for sentient beings who have not realized that [view].

b. From Whom the Empowerment Is Obtained

The vase empowerment is received from the guru, or if the guru is not present, the extensive vase empowerment is received from the maṇḍala visualized as inseparable from the guru. Generate certainty in the maṇḍala, the empowerment, the master, the purification of taints, the path, the view, the conclusion, the time of death, the bardo, the symbol, the example, the samayas, and the result.

c. Cultivation on the Path

Cultivation on the path is visualizing the support of the body maṇḍala and its one hundred fifty-seven deities. Having received the complete four empowerments through the four verses of receiving the medium empowerment, focus on Cittavajra, then the navel, then the place of the secret, then the throat, and then the crown. After that, focus on the twelve goddesses of subject and object, all the way through the universe and inhabitants appearing as the deity. Meditate repeatedly on the experience of the three essences.

d. The Experience Arising in the View

Stabilizing previous experience and sustaining the view according to the section in the treatise on the six oral instructions and the ultimate nature arise simultaneously.

e. The Conclusion Arising as the Signs

The path with signs is cultivated through merely recalling the qualities explained in the treatise, "The qualities included within the trio of signs—outer, inner, and ultimate—arise like this on the six stages of the vase empowerment from meditating on the creation stage." {413}

f. Manifesting All Topics in the Result

The nirmāṇakāya is naturally accomplished without effort; that is, understanding the union of apparent objects and emptiness. The one-pointed equipoise on that state arises at the same time as the ultimate nature. Further, since that includes four topics—the path,[6] the view, the conclusion, and the ultimate result—there are four [topics] for the effortlessly accomplished four kāyas.

2. The Secret Empowerment

There are six topics in the path of the secret empowerment.

a. Abiding in the Cause

Abiding in the cause refers to the support (the syllables that are the basis of speech: the fourteen syllables of the maṇḍala of the bhaga, the eight outer syllables, and the fifty vowels and consonants in the navel) and the supported (the all-basis that exists in the manner of a flower and its scent, and so on, just as before).

b. From Whom the Empowerment is Obtained

The secret empowerment is obtained from the guru, and so on, just as before.

c. Cultivation on the Path

Cultivation on the path is the three purifications, the seven vāyu yogas, and the eighteen caṇḍālī visualizations, as in the extensive path, meditated on in twenty-five sessions and practiced until an experience of self-originated gnosis repeatedly arises.

d. The Experience Arising in the View

The stabilization of previous experience, sustaining the view according to the section in the treatise on the six oral instructions, and ultimate intrinsic cognizance arise simultaneously. At that time, if the clarity and emptiness of the mind are not unified, engage in the crucial points of the body. In a house that is set in a high location, open and close one's eyes appropriately. One should recognize that method and wisdom are nondual; that is, "the characteristic of the mind is clarity, the nature of the mind is emptiness, and the essence of the mind is unfabricated." Sustain this naturally.

e. The Conclusion Arising as the Signs

Since one meditates on the path of the secret empowerment, the trio of signs—outer, inner, and ultimate—arise like this in the four stages of the secret empowerment, and so on, as before.

f. Manifesting All Topics in the Result

The saṃbhogakāya is naturally accomplished without effort; that is, {414} the realization of clarity and emptiness in union arises simultaneously as an ultimate intrinsic cognizance. When divided, there are four topics, as before.

3. The Third Empowerment

There are six topics in the path of the third empowerment.

a. Abiding in the Cause

Abiding in the cause means abiding in the support, the amṛta elements. Generate certainty that the all-basis, and so on, are supported upon the maṇḍalas of the four fundamental pure essences of the nine elements of bodhicitta, as before.

b. From Whom the Empowerment is Obtained

The third empowerment is obtained from the guru, and so on, as before.

c. Cultivation on the Path

The path of the third empowerment is divided into eight sessions and practiced according to the extensive path; that is, meditated until the experience of bliss and emptiness repeatedly arises.

d. Experience Arising in the View

The stabilization of previous experience, sustaining the view according to the section in the treatise on the six oral instructions, and the ultimate melting bliss arise simultaneously. At that time, having united physical bliss with emptiness, [the view] arises based either on the wave of enjoyment or the union of the secret.

e. The Conclusion Arising as the Signs

Apply the inner, outer, and ultimate signs in the two stages of the gnosis of the wisdom consort in the path of the third empowerment, and practice as before.

f. Manifesting All Topics in the Result

The dharmakāya is naturally accomplished without effort. The realization of the union of bliss and emptiness arises at the same time as the bliss of melting. When divided, there are four topics, as before.

4. The Path of the Fourth Empowerment

There are six topics in the path of the fourth empowerment.

a. Abiding in the Cause

Generate certainty that the support, the gnosis vāyus that pervade and dominate the three supporting maṇḍalas, support the all-basis, and so on, as before.

b. From Whom the Empowerment is Obtained

The fourth empowerment is obtained from the guru, and so on, as before.

c. Cultivation on the Path

Having divided up the path of the fourth empowerment into eight sessions, it is practiced according to the extensive path {415} and meditated until the experience of supreme emptiness repeatedly arises.

d. Experience Arising in the View

The stabilization of previous experience and sustaining the view according to the section in the treatise on the six oral instructions arise at the same time as the ultimately supreme of all aspects.

e. The Conclusion Arising as the Signs

Repeatedly generate the one-pointed, fervent meditation on the signs, having recalled the qualities: "The qualities included within the trio of signs, outer, inner, and ultimate, arise like this on the half-stage of the fourth empowerment [from meditating on] the path of the fourth empowerment."

f. Manifesting All Topics in the Result

The svabhāvakāya is naturally perfected by nature; that is, the realization that all phenomena included in objects, mind, and so on, are empty, arising at the same time as the supreme of all aspects, becoming four topics, as before.

As such, there are sixty-nine topics in the path instruction: twelve topics in the vase empowerment, thirty-one topics in the secret empowerment, and thirteen topics apiece for the third and fourth empowerments.

B. The Instruction for the Path of the Vase Empowerment

For the instruction of the path of the vase empowerment, there is a preliminary, main subject, and as before, a conclusion, cultivation on the path. Then, since one can reach the culmination of all other paths solely through the vase empowerment, the other three arise naturally; that is, realizing the view as [the union of] clarity and emptiness is the path of the secret empowerment. Since [the view] is realized to be [the union of] bliss and emptiness, it is the path of the third empowerment. Since [the view] is realized to be the union of either appearances, clarity, or bliss [with emptiness], it is introduced as the path of the fourth empowerment. At the time of the result, the effortlessly accomplished four kāyas (the understanding that objects are appearance and emptiness, mind is clarity and emptiness, the body is bliss and emptiness, and all phenomena of samsara and nirvana are intrinsically empty), the nirmāṇakāya, saṃbhogkāya, dharmakāya, and svabhāvakāya, arise simultaneously as the nature, intrinsic cognizance, the bliss of melting, and the supreme of all aspects. Each of those four is explained because of the division of the four kāyas into four, including a path,[7] a view, a conclusion, and a culmination.

C. The Instruction for the Path of the Secret Empowerment

For the instruction on the path of secret empowerment, {416} the preliminaries and main subject are divided into thirty-one sessions, as before. The experience at the conclusion of the path, the diversity being empty while apparent, is the path of the vase empowerment. Being empty while blissful is the path of the third empowerment. Union is introduced as the path of the fourth empowerment.

D. The Instruction for the Path of the Third Empowerment

For the instruction on the path of the third empowerment, there are two preliminaries, and the seven vāyu yogas are added to the beginning of the path in the main section. In the conclusion, the gnosis in the path of the four joys is introduced as the path of the fourth empowerment. Since the others are applied as before, having divided the main part into twenty sessions, there is the instruction.

E. The Instruction for the Path of the Fourth Empowerment

In the path of the fourth empowerment, there are two preliminaries, and in the section of the main subject, during each session, there are the practices of the three trainings: the seven vāyu yogas for the wave of the body and the peaceful and forceful voiced inhalations in three moments in every session. That being the case, since the culmination of the path can be reached solely by the path of the fourth empowerment, the other three arise naturally. The experience of appearance and emptiness as empty while appearing is the path of the vase empowerment. Empty while clear is the path of the secret empowerment; there is not an iota of grasping to generate because both appearances and clarity, empty of their own essence, are bliss. Emptiness while blissful is the path of the third empowerment. As such, that emptiness of each one's own essence is not temporary, but since it has been engaged with as pure since the beginning, it is introduced as the path of the fourth empowerment. Otherwise, the path of the fourth empowerment is the instruction through twenty-one sessions, as before. The explanation of the five dharmas of the preliminaries and conclusion are to be applied in every session.

Among those, though the gradual instruction is practiced as a verbal instruction, these four step-by-step instructions are only a meaning instruction. However, these four are not done as a single stage of instruction, but because there are four complete instructions, there is no person for whom the path is not complete.

Without error, a brief clarification has been set forth
of the six oral instructions that are the key points for guiding
the three kinds of persons, best, medium and average,
with the two kinds of instruction:
extensive, medium, and condensed, and profound, mediocre, and
shallow. {417}

The Clarification of the Six Key Points called *The Key to the Key Points* was composed by the monk, Sönam.
śubhaṃ

The Brief Clarification of the Stages of Instruction for Guiding Those of the Three Capabilities: Best, Medium, and Average[8]

oṃ svasti siddhaṃ

Homage to the greatly compassionate, venerable gurus.

The position of Mahācārya Virūpa is that when all people who have entered the path are categorized, there are held to be seven: three kinds of practitioners biased toward method, three kinds of practitioners biased toward wisdom, and practitioners who unify method and wisdom.

For the first category, the average wish merely to gather accumulations, the medium wish to receive the four empowerments in four sessions, and the best wish to accomplish everything in dependence upon the recitations and burnt offerings. For the second category, those of average diligence wish to meditate only on the emptiness of phenomena, the medium wish to focus the mind on the creation stage, and the best wish to focus the mind on the vāyu yogas.

Having arrived before the guru in possession of the empowerment and samayas and having engaged in the generation stage of any deity and its essence mantra, if any of them wish to be sustained by that instruction, there are the preliminaries and a main subject in the method of guiding them.

I. The Preliminaries

Though there are fifteen dharmas, when condensed, those are condensed into twelve.

A. The Preliminaries of the Instruction

The three in the preliminaries of the instruction are the one-hundred-syllable mantra for purifying negative conditions; maṇḍala offerings for gathering the accumulation of positive conditions; and reflecting upon the faults of samsara, the method of generating renunciation.

B. The Three Crucial Points of the Session

There are three crucial points of the session preliminaries: the three preliminaries, the three activities of wisdom, and the three activities of the method, but since these are included in the middle three, there is no [separate] practice, and so on. The first of the second {418} is meditating on love, compassion, and bodhicitta, according to the treatise.

3. The Three Preliminaries

(1) All phenomena are determined to be mind, (2) mind is determined to be illusory, and (3) illusion is determined to lack inherent existence.

a. All Phenomena Are Determined to be Mind

Having performed the six-session preliminaries beforehand, in this way everything, outer, inner, and secret, is one's mind and is not created by chance or God or formed from coarse and subtle particles or emanated by the tathāgatas. Everything is one's mind, the aspect of which has been influenced by karma and negative traces without beginning, just like the example of a dream of one under the influence of sleep, and so on. Reflect on the thought that nothing inside or outside is established. Having put that thought aside, now rest in the sheer clarity of the mind. One should cultivate this for three, five, or seven days.

b. Mind Is Determined to be Illusory

Train in the four examples: dreams, illusions, reflections, and double vision. The first among those is training in double vision. In the two appearances of double vision, since one is false and one is true, it cannot become one. However, in the same way, if one is true, since one side is false, it will vanish into one. Neither appearance is true. In the same way, one should meditate on the thought that this mind also is not true.

There are two in reflections: the inside of the mirror and the moon in water. Also train in these two as follows: If that reflection exists, it is reasonable that it would substantially exist, but it does not. If that reflection does not exist, it would be reasonable that it would not appear, but it is appearing. In the same way, reflect on the thought that the mind is like an illusion. If the appearances of an illusion exist as substantial entities—the tail of a cow, monkey, or, more commonly, horse, elephant, and so on—it is reasonable that they would be true. But if they do not exist, it is reasonable that they would not appear. From this fact, reflect on the mind that seems to appear like an illusion. Since one reflects on dreams like that, one should eliminate doubts concerning the mind being illusory. Those examples reverse grasping true existence in the mind. As such, one should train in each of those four examples {419} for a minimum period of three days, as it is said that one should train in those four for twelve days.

c. Illusion Is Determined to Lack Inherent Existence

To say "lack inherent existence" is to determine that there is no entity and no reference point. Therefore, determine that illusions lack inherent existence and rest for a little while in that state. Those are the three determinations.

II. The Main Subject

As such, having performed those preliminaries beforehand, there are two topics in the main subject.

A. Practitioners Biased toward Method

There are three grades of practitioners biased toward method.

1. Practitioners of Average Diligence

There are two kinds among those of average diligence. Those who have not obtained more than the vajra-disciple[9] initiation meditate on the single hero deity, having performed the preliminaries beforehand. Having visualized the universe as the maṇḍala and the inhabitants as deities through the spreading and return of light rays of compassion, they engage in recitation. After that, having recalled the three essentials as below, they pass time on the yogas of conduct, such as bali offerings, and so on. As such, they accomplish whatever they can, one, two, or three sessions, and so on. Also, meditating on the body maṇḍala is excellent, but if it is not meditated on, there is no contradiction. Then seal with the view, as below.

If the vajra master empowerment has been obtained, meditate on the maṇḍalacakra. Otherwise, it is the same as before.

2. Practitioners of Medium Diligence

Having performed the preliminaries beforehand, the practitioner of medium diligence meditates on eliminating extraneous concepts, starting from inviting the refuge field up to absorbing the gnosis beings. Then, having clearly visualized the body maṇḍala, the mind is placed in equipoise for a period. The conclusion is the same as before. Having taken either the extensive, medium, or concise [empowerments], after that, meditate on the three essentials. The deceptive appearance is the essence of the apparent side, lack of inherent existence is the essence of the emptiness side, and their inseparability is the essence of union. Rest the mind on the essence of union. Then, depending on one's inclination, either recite mantras or not. When arising [from the session], {420} one should go with the recollection of the three essentials: red and white appearances are the side of appearances, their lack of inherent existence is the side of emptiness, and the union of those two is the essence of union. With such a recollection, enter the conduct. In that way, there is definitely only four sessions. Meditate by sustaining the view by all means. Even if one does not apply the bali offering in all sessions, it should not be absent from every final session [of the day].

3. Practitioners of Best Diligence

From the three in those of the best diligence, the way of meditating on the deity and sustaining the view are the same as before, but at the end of the four sessions, the main point is sustaining the view.

Accomplishing the collection of activities is as follows: Having accomplished the four-hundred-thousand mantra approach and the forty-thousand mantra supplement burnt offering, one can accomplish the collection of activities taught in the tantras. If one is not able to accomplish as much as that, later one should try to accomplish that. If one cannot accomplish more than that, then accomplish that much at a minimum. In brief, having accomplished the one-million-two-hundred-thousand mantra approach, one should do the one-hundred-twenty-thousand mantra burnt offering, and afterward accomplish the activities.

B. Practitioners Biased toward Wisdom

There are three grades of practitioners biased toward wisdom.

1. Practitioners of Average Diligence

Having performed the preliminaries beforehand, the practitioner of average diligence engages in the three topics of the main subject.

a. The Characteristic of the Mind

To identify the characteristic of the mind, clarity, look at anything internal or external. Having looked intently at that essence of clarity, maintain nonconceptual equipoise in the state. Since there is no specific number of sessions, meditate in equipoise. In conclusion, dedicate the root of virtue, seal with the simile of dreams and illusions, and meditate on compassion for sentient beings who have not realized that.

b. The Nature of the Mind

To identify the nature of the mind, emptiness, look at anything external or internal. It is empty by nature. It does not exist inside the body, and it also does not exist outside. If one looks into the sky, there is nothing in the sky. Therefore, having looked intently into that state of empty nature, maintain nonconceptual equipoise. The conclusion is as before.

c. The Mind as Unfabricated

To identify the mind as unfabricated, when one is in such equipoise, since at the time of clarity it is empty and at the time of emptiness it is clear, that clear and empty essence is unfabricated.{421} The mind should rest like it is the middle of space. The conclusion is as before.

2. The Practitioner of Medium Diligence

Having performed the preliminaries beforehand, the practitioner of medium diligence engages in the three topics of the main subject.

a. The Meditation of the View

The practitioner of medium diligence, practicing in four sessions, and so on, starting from inviting the refuge field up to sealing the master of the family, rests the mind on that clearly, intensely, and for a short while. For the conclusion, maintain the three essentials, as before.

b. Taking the Empowerment

The empowerments are taken in their extensive, medium, or concise form in the *Time of the Path* sādhana.

c. Focusing the Mind

When focusing the mind, there is focusing the mind on general features and focusing the mind on specific features.

i. Focusing the Mind on General Features

There are four. The visualization for meditation is as follows: Having visualized the maṇḍalacakra, once it is clear, then it is clear, so stop. If it is unclear, it is unclear, and so stop. One should meditate in that manner as indicated.

Having done so, if the visualization remains unclear, one should visualize with a recitation, saying, "The central eye is wrathful and bloodshot," and as before, one should extract the poison of concentration and meditate.

If that is still not clear, the so-called "recitation recited by another" is another person saying [to you], "The central eye . . . ." Extract the poison of concentration and meditate.

If that is still not clear, "visualizing by looking" means to draw a very attractive central eye, and having gazed at it, extract the poison of concentration and meditate.

ii. Focusing the Mind on Specific Features

The way of focusing the mind on specific features has two approaches: focusing from the outside and focusing from the inside. According to the first approach, one begins from the central eye, as in the extensive path, and focuses the mind on the universe and inhabitants appearing as the deity. According to the second approach, beginning from the visualization of the crown cakra, and so on, one focuses the mind step by step beginning from the six palaces up to the universe and inhabitants appearing as the deity. The method of focusing is the same as before. These two ways of focusing should be meditated on according to what is suitable for one's mind, {422} but it is not necessary to meditate both ways. The conclusion is just as before. The supreme among practitioners do not engage in mantra recitation, bali offerings, reciting sutras, and so on, but instead engage in focusing the mind on the creation stage equipoise and, having cultivated that, are said to merge with the deity by meditating on the three essentials and practicing in four sessions.

3. The Practitioner of Best Diligence

Having performed the preliminaries beforehand, among the forty-five different practices for the practitioner of best diligence, in the main subject, the clear characteristic of the mind, the empty nature of the mind, and the unfabricated essence of the mind are the same as before.

Next, in the key points of the specific training, it is necessary to engage in six months of physical training beforehand. Even before that, it is necessary to engage in the two preliminaries of accumulating positive conditions and purifying negative conditions. Afterward, in an isolated place without excess sun, one should engage in the three preliminaries on a large, soft, comfortable seat and perform the forward sequence of the thirty-two activities, followed by the reverse sequence, and then complete it with the paired sequence, performing ninety-two actions in each session. One should practice for six months in three, two, or one session [per day]. It is said that if one wishes to obtain siddhi in this life, the physical training is a very important key point.

Next, one should train the voice and mind according to the extensive path. Having engaged in prāṇāyāma, and so on, beforehand, the key point of the wave of the body, which stirs the lower vāyu, is the seven vāyu yogas and the eighteen caṇḍālī visualizations that are meditated on according to the extensive path. In those contexts, the progress through the eight enhancements occurs. Next, there is the actual wave of the body, followed by the key point of the wave of the peaceful voiced inhalation, then the key point of the forceful voiced inhalation, and finally the key point of mahāmudrā, nourishing the view. The path of the third empowerment is the same as the text of the extensive path. After that, there is the key point of the wave of the mind, samādhi, as in the treatise.

Now, to write about the definition of the sessions: from the two preliminaries that all people need, for the preliminaries of the instruction, there is both accumulation and purification. {423} There are three in reflecting on the faults of samsara. In the session preliminaries, there are the three critical points of body, voice, and mind. In the three preliminaries, there are three in the meditation on love, three in the meditation on compassion, and three in the meditation on bodhicitta. There are three in determining the activities of wisdom, for a total of twenty.

In the main subject, for average practitioners biased toward the method, there are two: meditating on the deity and sealing with the view. For the medium, there are three: generating the deity, receiving empowerment, and sealing. For the best, there are three: meditating on the deity, maintaining the view, and accomplishing the collection of activities. For the average practitioner biased toward wisdom, there are three sessions: the clear characteristic of the mind, the empty nature of the mind, and the unfabricated essence of the mind. For the medium, there are five sessions: meditating on the deity, receiving empowerment, focusing the mind on general features, [focusing the mind on] one subject, and focusing the mind on the specific features. For the best, there are thirty-seven sessions: the clear characteristic of the mind, the empty nature of the mind, and the unfabricated essence of the mind; the key point of the specific training; the seven vāyu yogas; the eighteen caṇḍālī visualizations; the wave of the body; the peaceful voiced inhalation; the forceful voiced inhalation; the preliminaries for the path of the third empowerment, done according to the condensed path and the five trainings in the main part; and the way of training uniformly. The conclusion is implied. There are three in the wave of the mind. Thus, there are a total of forty-five sessions.

Since this instruction on the trio of people of best, medium, and average capability
does not contradict the speech of the venerable gurus,

in order to bring clarity, please pardon errors,
and by this virtue, may the connate gnosis be reached.

The Brief Clarification of the Stages of Instruction for Guiding Those of the Three Capabilities: Best, Medium, and Average was composed by the monk Sönam Gyaltsen at the repeated urging of the meditator Śākya Zangpo. *sarvadā maṅgalaṃ bhavatu*[10]

16. Notes on the Intimate Instruction, the Explanation of the Concealed Path[1]

Dakchen Lodrö Gyaltsen

Lodrö Gyaltsen (bDag chen bLo gros rgyal mtshan, 1444–1495) is one of the most important masters of the Path with Its Result tradition, as the emergence of the separate *Explanation for Disciples* begins with him, though it was not explicitly codified until it was written down during the latter half of the sixteenth century by disciples of Tsharchen Losal Gyatso (Tshar chen blo gsal rgya mtsho, 1502–1567), to supplement Ngorchen Könchok Lhundrub's magisterial presentation of the Path with Its Result in his *Beautiful Ornament of the Three Appearances* (1549) and *Beautiful Ornament of the Three Tantras* (1552).

Lodrö Gyaltsen, commonly referred to as Dakchen Dorje Chang, was the twenty-first Sakya throne holder. His father, Jamyang Namkha Gyaltsen ('Jam dbyangs nam mkha' rgyal mtshan, 1398–1472), the eighteenth Sakya throne holder, was regarded as an emanation of Padmasambhava. His mother, Machik Paljung Gyalmo (dates unknown), was considered an emanational ḍākinī. His elder brother, Sherab Gyaltsen (Shes rab rgyal mtshan, 1436–1494), was the twentieth Sakya throne holder.

Lodrö Gyaltsen's highly descriptive biography composed by Tsharchen, *Necklace of Enchanting Blue Poppies*,[2] recounts that he was born in 1444 in Shab Geding (*shab dge sdings*), near Shigatse. He remained with his parents until he was six years old. During that period he received many Sakya ancestral teachings from his father, including the Path with Its Result, and was the sole recipient of special instructions about the Sakya dharmapālas.

When Lodrö Gyaltsen reached six years of age, Jamyang Könchok Zangpo ('Jam dbyangs dkon mchog bzang po, dates unknown), regarded as an emanation of the Shambhāla king Rudra Cakravartin, was invited to Geding. Jamyang Könchok Zangpo bestowed the preliminary vows of a novice and gave the boy the name Lodrö Gyaltsen Palzangpo.

Having received a great number of transmissions from Jamyang Könchok Zangpo between the ages of eight and twelve, Lodrö Gyaltsen then traveled to upper Nyang to study with Lopön Palchok (sLob dpon dpal mchog, dates unknown), where he delved into a standard scholastic curriculum, including epistemology, madhyamaka, the three vows, the stages of the path, and so on. During this time Lodrö Gyaltsen again received the Path with Its Result, additional supporting texts such as *The Black Volume*, the eight ancillary path cycles, and so on, as well as other Vajrayāna cycles.

During Lodrö Gyaltsen's thirteenth year, he was summoned to Sakya by Dakchen Kunga Wangchuk of the Sakya Zhithok palace, who bestowed upon him all four transmission lineages of Hevajra, Naropa's Vajrayoginī system, and many other important transmissions. When he was fifteen, Lodrö Gyaltsen received novice ordination from both Könchok Gyaltsen, the second abbot of Ngor Monastery, and Dakchen Kunga Wangchuk. It is recorded that from this time forward he maintained his novice vows perfectly.

When Lodrö Gyaltsen was fifteen, he faced some health issues, so he and Dakchen Kunga Wangchuk went into retreat together on the deity Hevajra, thus restoring his health. Following this retreat, he received further empowerments from Nider Ngawang Drakpa, a direct disciple of Ngorchen Kunga Zangpo.

Kunga Wangchuk passed away when Lodrö Gyaltsen was eighteen. For the next two years he engaged in intensive study and practice. When Lodrö Gyaltsen reached age twenty in 1464, in accordance with Kunga Wangchuk's last wishes, he took full ordination from Ngorchen Könchok Gyaltsen.

Lodrö Gyaltsen also received a wide variety of teachings at this time from Ngorchen Könchok Gyaltsen, including *The Explanation of the Path with Its Result for the Assembly* and the single transmission lineage (*chig brgyud*) of *The Explanation of the Path with Its Result for Disciples*, as well as other single transmission lineages associated with the Path with Its Result teachings. In 1465 the young master bestowed Path with Its Result for the first time in Tsang Rinchen Gang. From 1484 to 1488, he bestowed it twice yearly. He would bestow it twenty-five times during his lifetime.

Between 1465 and 1469, Lodrö Gyaltsen toured the region of Kham, where the young Sakya master was required to display his power in apotropaic rites against the jealous imprecations of rivals. As a result, his reputation grew considerably and the people of Kham made extremely generous donations.

Lodrö Gyaltsen returned to Central Tibet in 1469, arriving back in Sakya in 1470 and installed as the Sakya throne holder by his father and elder brother. In 1472, Lodrö Gyaltsen's father passed away and his brother Sherab Gyaltsen was installed as the head of the family. Lodrö Gyaltsen returned to visit Jamyang Könchok Zangpo, receiving the profound six-limbed yoga of Kālacakra. Within him was born the realization of mahāmudrā, the nonconceptual gnosis, free from all concepts and meditation, the emptiness supreme in all aspects beyond all phenomena of coarse and subtle particles.

During the seven-year period between 1473 and 1479, Lodrö Gyaltsen deepened his realization through several retreats. He engaged in the main daily practice of the Sakya school known as the four unbreakables: *The Profound Path Guru Yoga*,[3] *The Time of the Path*[4] *Hevajra Sādhana*, *Naropa's Khecari*,[5] and the *Virūpa Protection*[6] practice. He also maintained a daily practice of the mother tantra Cakrasaṃvara systems of Luipa, Ghaṇṭapāda, and Kṛṣṇācārya, as well as the father tantra systems of Raktayamāri and Vajrabhairava. Lodrö Gyaltsen also maintained other various practices, never wavering from the experiential state of the view, the inseparability of samsara and nirvana.

Lodrö Gyaltsen made an extraordinary impression on people. When he gave teachings, some people easily experienced samādhi. When he gave empowerments, many people experienced shuddering, spontaneously spoke in Sanskrit, or experienced the gnosis free of proliferation. He was constantly attended by amazing incidents witnessed by many people, such as bali offerings spontaneously bursting into flames, and so on. People saw him walking without touching the ground. Lodrö Gyaltsen himself had many visionary experiences, such as seeing the dharma protectors Mahākāla and Śrīdevī in person.

In 1494 his elder brother, Sherab Gyaltsen, passed away. In the final year of Lodrö Gyaltsen's life, he bestowed Path with Its Result one final time as well as a vast array of other teachings. While Lodrö Gyaltsen had many important students, foremost was Doringpa Kunzang Chökyi Nyima (rDo ring pa kun bzang chos kyi nyi ma, 1449–1524), who in turn became the teacher of Tsharchen Losal Gyatso, the founder of the Tsharpa tradition.

In late spring of 1495, Lodrö Gyaltsen spent two months in strict retreat at the Sakya retreat site, Khau Kyelha, a place he often frequented. At the conclusion of his retreat, he showed signs of declining health, which manifested externally as earthquakes, gales, and strange portents. While people became nervous and upset, Lodrö Gyaltsen never demonstrated any discomfit. Doctors were invited to give their diagnosis, administer medicines, and so on. In the late summer Lodrö Gyaltsen began to show signs of serious decline, and though many rituals were performed on his behalf, Lodrö Gyaltsen declared, "These won't benefit me, but they will be beneficial for the community."

Lodrö Gyaltsen passed away at dawn on the fourth day of the ninth Tibetan month during the late summer of 1495 at the age of fifty-one, amid many auspicious signs such as rainbows, divine scents, showers of divine flowers, earth rumblings, and so on.

Among the many texts composed by Lodrö Gyaltsen, his thirty-five principal compositions focused on various aspects of Vajrayāna and praises and hagiographies of important masters of the lineage. Among those, two texts by Lodrö Gyaltsen are presented here: *Notes on the Intimate Instruction: The Explanation of the Concealed Path* and *The Manual That Clarifies Symbols and Meanings*. The first is a brief text outlining yogic techniques in conjunction with an abbreviated version of the Hevajra practice for advanced practitioners. These instructions had been passed down orally from the time of Sachen. There is a text by Sakya Paṇḍita called *The Concealed Path*,[7] but it merely outlines the stages of the path based on nāḍīs, bindus, and vāyus.

Having bowed to the feet of the one who bears the name Könchok—
inseparable from the glorious lord of magic power
and the sublime Jetsun Kunga Nyingpo—
I shall write a summary of the instruction.

The *Explanation of the Concealed Path* is among the four profound dharmas that were never to leave the Iron Mountain Temple of Palden Sakya and [the one] that the lord of yogins, Virūpa, conferred as a personal instruction on the venerable Sakyapa.

There exist methods of accomplishing both the supreme siddhi and common siddhis.

I. Supreme Siddhi

Here is the method of realizing supreme siddhi, the stage of Mahāvajradhara, in this lifetime: In the method of practicing the four empowerments all at once based on the yantras of the body, the qualified vajra master has either given or not given the complete instruction of the extensive path to the disciple. To properly instruct and explain the instruction to one who possesses the empowerments and samayas, there are two: the preliminaries and the main subject.

A. The Preliminaries

There are both (1) common preliminaries and (2) uncommon preliminaries.

1. The Common Preliminaries

The practitioner should practice going for refuge, generating bodhicitta, accumulating, and purifying for as many days as they can.

2. The Uncommon Preliminaries

They should practice guru yoga to instill empowerment and the creation stage as the basis for the completion stage. Also, in every session they should meditate [on the two stages] in tandem. Possessing the key points of the body [while seated] on a meditation seat and having gone for refuge and generated bodhicitta beforehand, [one imagines that] upon a jeweled throne above the crown of one's head, on a sun and moon seat, is the guru, the embodiment of all the buddhas, appearing in the form of either the sixteen-handed heruka or Mahāvajradhara. His three places are meditated on with the three syllables. {427} Light shines from the seed syllable in the heart, inviting all lineage gurus, deities, buddhas, bodhisattvas, ḍākinīs, and dharmapālas, who dissolve [into him]. He becomes the embodiment of all places of refuge. Supplicate the guru with intense devotion, the embodiment of all buddhas of the three times. At the conclusion of supplicating him by saying, "Please empower my continuum . . . ," the guru melts into the form of greatly blissful bodhicitta, which dissolves into one's crown. Imagine that one's body, voice, and mind become inseparable with his body, speech, and mind. Remain in equipoise. Whatever experience arises should be sustained naturally.

The creation stage is meditated on next. Since this is the path for those of sharpest capabilities, it is not necessary to meditate on the extensive sādhana. My guru said, "At the time one is admitted to the maṇḍala, when the gnosis being is admitted, the empowerment is bestowed. Hence one should think, 'I am Hevajra.' Thus, instantly visualize Hevajra with eight faces and sixteen arms. Focus on the complete body and meditate. It is unnecessary to meditate according to the many instructions of visualization in the extensive path."

Those are the preliminaries.

B. The Main Subject

In the main subject, there are (1) primary and (2) secondary visualizations.

1. Primary Visualizations

[This has three topics:] (1) the key point of preparing the body, (2) the key point of the meditative visualization, and (3) the key point of holding the vāyu.

a. Preparing the Body

Since one has practiced based on the yantras of the body, assemble a wheel made of clay or wood, which is approximately three inches in height, with the diameter of the circle made by the tip of the thumb meeting the tip of the index finger, with thin and very flexible spokes. {428} When engaging in the main part of the concentration, while seated on a comfortable seat, which is thick, and so on, meditate beforehand on refuge, generating bodhicitta, and the deity. Then, adopt the wide posture that is like an elephant's trunk, place the wheel in front of the rectum, and alternately raise each thigh. In concert with drawing up the lower vāyu, having constricted the sphincter, be seated on the wheel. If it is slightly uncomfortable because it is a little high, make it a little lower by placing it at the border, at the edge of the buttocks. Place the hands on both knees. Straighten the spine. These are the key points of preparing the body.

b. The Visualization

The natural condition of the body is as follows: The mouth of the lungs faces down and the liver is stuck to the sides. When meditating on both of those, after the first and second [practices], the lungs are an upward-facing white lotus with eight petals and the liver is a downward-facing maroon lotus with eight petals. The tips of both [the lung and the liver lotuses] slightly cross, and they are imagined to be in the form of the celestial mansion. With respect to the anatomy of the vajra body, though the heart exists facing down, it can be raised up with the mind and should be imagined to exist between the two lotuses. The knot of the conjunction of the three channels in the center of the heart forms the shape of a *hūṃ*. Focus on that. Then meditate on the vajra ḍāka. That *hūṃ* in the center of the heart is a blue heruka with three red, round eyes. His fangs are bared. His two hands hold a vajra and a bell. His right leg is extended above a sun and his left leg is contracted above a moon. {429} His head has an uṣṇīṣa and five locks that hang to the left. He is meditated on standing in the middle of a blazing fire of gnosis. His consort appears by mere recollection, without the need to extensively visualize her faces and hands. Furthermore, that *hūṃ* is visualized in the form of a heruka, but there is no meditation through transformation of a seed syllable. That is the key point of the visualization meditation.

c. Holding the Vāyu

The key point of holding the vāyu is as follows: Expel the stale vāyu three times and expand the belly slightly. Place the tongue on the palate, open the eyes a little widely, and touch the crown to the floor. Draw in the vāyu with the tone of *ha*, and having inhaled, gradually press down inside the hollow upper body, uniting the upper and lower vāyus.

The visualization for the mind is that one should imagine the petals vibrating in the heart of the seat of Cittavajra. When one can no longer hold the vāyu, release it slowly. Again touch the crown to the floor. Inhaling is said to be "inhaling the vāyu like picking something up from the ground."[8] As such, when it is said that "the white and red radiances will arrive by maintaining the seven basic yantras and meditating," if the path of white radiance occurs, it is a good sign. If the path of red radiance occurs, it is not a good sign. Thus, one should administer nutritious food and meditate.

As such, if one meditates on the first visualization,[9] one might feel that consciousness is transferring. If there is intense heat in the heart region, one should protect this forcefully and call for help. It will definitely be removed.

2. The Secondary Visualizations

The secondary visualizations are the practices described as "blazing, shifting, stable, and . . . ."[10] The body is cross-legged, with the hands crossed at the heart in vajra fists with the thumbs pressing down on the base of the ring fingers.

The visualization for the mind is as follows: From the crown of the body down to the place of the secret, {430} the central nāḍī is the size of a wheat stalk, and so on. It is red in color and straight—neither crooked nor curved like a piece of twine. At the base of the vajra, imagine an upright, blazing *hūṃ* that cannot be overcome by the four māras. At the crown, imagine an inverted *haṃ* filled with bodhicitta. Bow the head to the ground and inhale the vāyu through both nostrils, unifying [the upper and lower vāyus]. Many *hūṃ*s separate from the blazing *hūṃ*. Since those shine up and down the central nāḍī, melting the bodhicitta of the *haṃ*, meditate that the thirty-two nāḍī petals at the crown are filled [with bodhicitta]. Then, imagine that [the bodhicitta] is obstructed by the *hūṃ* and does not drip down. On occasion, sound a long *ha*, as in the intimate instructions. Imagine this visualization clearly. The throat and heart cakras are also filled. Finally, the whole body is filled. Imagine emptiness while blissful, blissfulness while empty, and nondual bliss and emptiness. Focus upon the body of the deity that is like a rainbow. Whatever experiences arise should be naturally sustained. If a lot of sweat arises at those occasions, dry it with the hands and rub. If there is a nosebleed because of pressing too strongly on the upper [vāyu], lay on one's back, and it will stop by placing the two vajra fists on the eyes while extending the neck. If that does not stop it, use the technique of "elevating the bag." If dripping occurs, use the technique of the fourth empowerment.

As such, alternately meditating on the primary and secondary visualizations is the main subject. The others are clear in the instructions. In the instruction manual it is said that the lungs are above and the liver is below. Here, reversing the upper and lower is the intimate instruction of the guru, and since they are connected to the nāḍī of the heart, {431} visualizing the heart upright is said to be easier for beginners. Since the thirty-two yantras are not explained in the root text, they are not necessary. However, if one does them, it is said there is no contradiction.

Based on what I can remember, this was written down by the idle one named Mati according to the essentials of the intimate instruction of the concealed path as explained by the sublime, venerable one, Könchok Gyaltsen.[11] Having requested the forbearance of the assembly of ḍākinīs who own the dharma and their empowerment, may we practitioners who practice the profound path pacify obstacles and having reached the culmination of the two stages, benefit limitless sentient beings.
sarva maṅgalaṃ

17. The Manual That Clarifies Symbols and Meanings[1]

Dakchen Lodrö Gyaltsen

The *Manual That Clarifies Symbols and Meanings* should be regarded as the first formal text in the *Explanation for Disciples* system. The fundamental difference between the *Explanation for the Assembly* and the *Explanation for Disciples* is that the latter includes instructions on luminosity, dream yoga, and illusory body for each of the four empowerments.

Homage to the venerable treasure of omniscience.

Here, there are two topics in the stages of the instructional manual that confirm the meaning of the path and result, illustrated though the maṇḍala of illustrative symbols that descends from the extremely close lineage and is practiced by practitioners who have obtained the extensive instruction on the treatise and obtained the empowerment for this text.

I. The Preliminaries

A. The Common Preliminaries

The common preliminaries are accumulation, purification, and the extensive trio of purification.

B. The Session Preliminaries

The session preliminaries meditated on beforehand are the meditation on the three meditations and the three crucial points.

II. The Main Subject

A. Ascertaining Wisdom with the View

Ascertaining wisdom with the view is extensively confirming (on the basis of a moon in the water) that appearances are mind, mind is an illusion, and illusions are dependently originated and inexpressible.

B. Practicing the Method

There are four in practicing the method.

1. The Vase Empowerment

In the path of the vase empowerment, there are six topics.

a. The Creation Stage Path

i. The Outer Creation Stage

Through the *svabhāva* mantra, from the state of emptiness arises a *bhrūṃ*, from which arises a celestial mansion, in the center of which is oneself instantly created as the father and mother. Since the light that shines from the *hūṃ* in the heart strikes the universe and all inhabitants, they transform into the celestial mansion and deities. Again, light shines from *hūṃ* and the empowerment deities are invited. Present offerings, praises, and take [the empowerment] according to the medium empowerment, but do not seal [with the master of the family]. Next, focus the mind on the appearances of the universe and inhabitants as the celestial mansion and deities or focus the mind on one's central eye.

ii. The Inner Creation Stage

Having visualized the outer creation stage beforehand, light rays again radiate from *hūṃ*, inviting the guru, inseparable from the excellent deity, who dissolves into oneself. Visualize and focus the mind on Cittavajra or focus the mind on the central eye of Cittavajra.

The three essentials of the view (b.) and the conclusion, the inseparability of samsara and nirvana, (c.) are like the extensive explanation. {436}

d. The Time of Death and Transference

i. Signs of Death and Cheating Death

Explaining the signs of death and cheating death is as follows: When the negative condition of death arrives, death can be averted with rites and careful behavior. If longevity is exhausted, it can be extended. If merit is exhausted, merit can be accumulated. If karma is exhausted, it is similar to a lamp that has run out of oil. Because one does not depend on any ripened karma, though it is said that in general there are many signs of death, death is certain when the trio of outer, inner, and secret signs of death converge.

A) The Outer Signs

Since the power of the inner nāḍīs, bindus, and vāyus are impaired, when three things converge—no haze[2] rising from the crown of the head,[3] no light when pressing the eyes, and no roaring sound when blocking the ears—it is certain one will die. If these three [signs] are merely unclear, this indicates a strong illness.

B) The Inner Signs

Through the dispersal of the vāyu in a single direction, the upward [moving vāyu] slightly reverses and moves only with effort. The bindu of the crown moves slightly, and the concluding sign of death is either the nāḍī openings are flaccid and the power of the downward-voiding vāyu is impaired or there is no condition since that vāyu is not impaired but the semen changes such that there are black specks in the white [semen].

C) The Secret Signs

At the time of death, since merit has dwindled and become exhausted, the pure practices of virtue diminish, one is unable to remain in equipoise, without reason the mind becomes difficult, one has aversion to one's region and town, the eyes become more bloodshot than before, and one takes on the behavior of a dying person.

As such, if all signs are complete, the practitioner begins to die. If there are only one or two signs at a time that are out of order, since there is no better way to cheat death than vāyu yoga, one should hold one hundred vase breaths. Count fifteen thousand prāṇāyāmas in a single day and night. Consume space. {437} Engage in the concentration of milking a cow. One-pointedly place the mind in the view of the inseparability of samsara and nirvana. In between sessions, one should renounce everything with the total purity of the three spheres. Because one has damaged samaya, it should be restored. One generates bodhicitta, requests empowerment or takes it by oneself, erects statues of the tathāgatas, and so on. If it is determined on examination that the signs of death can be averted, then cheat death.

ii. Death and Transference

If death cannot be cheated, then one should transfer.

I) Dissolution of the Elements and Sense Organs

Externally, the way the elements and the sense organs dissolve is as follows: Since these signs exist in stages for a person, then, that being the case, when the vajra body was first formed, the nirmāṇacakra formed at the beginning. Based on it, the five cakras and the five pure essences that exist in the form of syllables formed completely, the power of which increases until age twenty-five. They remain unchanged until age forty-five and decline thereafter. At the time of death, since the upward-moving vāyu reverses, it dominates all the vāyus, the knots of the nāḍīs in the five cakras disintegrate, the five vāyus disperse, and the pure essence of the elements gather. Since the fire-accompanying vāyu disperses, one cannot digest food. Since the life-sustaining vāyu disperses, the mind becomes unclear and disturbed. Since the downward-voiding vāyu disperses, one involuntarily urinates and defecates. Since the upward-moving vāyu disperses, one is unable to swallow food and the breath becomes short. Since the pervading vāyu disperses, the functions of the arms and legs are impaired and the veins protrude.

Also, at the time of disintegration, the form of the syllable of the knot of nāḍīs at the navel, which formed at the beginning, disintegrates. Earth and water disperse, moving slightly into the central nāḍī. The outer signs is that {438} after the earth disintegrates into space, one feels as if one is being crushed. One can neither lift one's head nor lift the body with the legs. One is unable to lift a plate of food with one's hand. The body becomes weak. A dark coating forms on the nails, and mucous and spittle flow. The inner signs are that the body is heavy and the mind becomes cloudy and unclear.

Because one feels as if they were sinking under the ground, one [attempts] to get up, crying "lift me, dress me," the hands withdraw, and one tries to look up. The secret signs include the appearance of hazy smoke.

When the knots of the naḍīs of the heart cakra disintegrate, water and air disperse and the pure essences gather inside. The external signs are a dry mouth and nose. The tongue becomes rough. One cannot see the tip of the tongue. The nostrils are hot. The nostrils become depressed. The inner sign is the disturbance and irritation of the mind. The secret sign is visual impairment, like double vision.

When the knots of the naḍīs of the throat cakra disintegrate, the upward-moving vāyu disperses, and since the pure essences gather, the outer signs are the gathering of all warmth from the extremities. The inner heat suddenly produces moistness in reaction to the dampness on the outside. Since fire dissolves into water, the breath of the mouth and nostrils becomes cold. The inner signs are that appearances are alternately clear and unclear, and one is unable to recognize those appearances. The secret sign is flashing red light, like fireflies.

When the knots of the naḍīs of the secret cakra disintegrate, the air vāyu dissipates and the pure essences gather. The outer signs are the extension of the exhalation and the inability to inhale, one pants audibly,[4] there is a wheezing sound when inhaling, and the eyes roll up. The inner signs are that the mind changes. The disintegration of the nāḍīs produces many visions. In particular, the messengers of Yama—with gaping mouths and bared fangs, displaying terrifying forms and performing many harmful activities—come for those who have committed misdeeds, {439} but practitioners will be met by heroes and ḍākinīs. The secret sign is the arising of an indistinct appearance, like a blazing lamp.

At the same time that those [elements] dissolve, the sense organs also dissolve. Further, when the five subsidiary vāyus disperse, the power of the nāḍīs and elements is impaired. The sense organ of sight cannot recognize people and cannot see subtle forms. Since the organ of hearing dissolves, one cannot hear faint sounds. Since the organ of smell dissolves, one cannot smell. Since the sense organ of taste dissolves, one cannot taste. Since the sense organ of touch dissolves, one cannot feel whether the bed is comfortable or uncomfortable. As such, since the ten vāyus disperse, the four elements and the sense organs dissolve. Since the vāyus of the four elements cease, the space vāyu disperses through the crown. The vāyus do not arrive at their place, as all leave the body at once.

Those are the common signs of death. It is said that because [the signs of death] are the activity of a spirit illness for some, it is possible to come back after this point.

II) The Cessation of the Three Illuminations and Concepts

Inwardly, the cessation of the three illuminations and concepts are as follows: Through the dispersal of the support and the supported, the conceptual appearances dissolve. Since this is the point of no return, those are the uncommon signs of death. The *Concise Explanation of Empowerment* states:

> When embodied beings die,
> the lunar amṛta flows down
> and the solar particle ascends.[5]

At the upper tip of the central nāḍī, there is the pure essence of jasmine obtained from the father that exists in the form of *haṃ*. Since the power of the lalanā is impaired from all the upper vāyus dispersing and moving downward, all appearances become brilliant white, known as "the white radiance." That dissolves into illumination. At that time the thirty-three concepts that arise from anger cease. {440}

At the lower tip of the central nāḍī in the navel, there is the essence of blood obtained from the mother that exists in the form of the *a* stroke. Since the power of the rasanā has been impaired from all the lower vāyus dispersing and ascending, all appearances become brilliant red, known as "the red radiance." Consequently, everything dissolves into the spreading illumination. At that time the forty concepts that arise from desire cease.

After that, the pervading vāyu in the crown disperses, and one's cognizance, the king of the mind, is gathered by the pervading karma vāyu. As it disperses, all appearances become black, known as "the black radiance." That is the dissolution into the imminent illumination. At that time the seven concepts that arise from ignorance cease. Thus, since the space vāyu ceases, the outer breath stops. At that time there is the intense suffering of the separation of the body and mind.

III) How the Escort of the Dharmakāya Arises in Luminosity

Secretly, how the escort of the dharmakāya arises in luminosity is as follows:

While the inner breath has not stopped, the sun moves up and the moon moves down, meeting within the central nāḍī. Next, the vāyu and mind enter [the central nāḍī] and those three [the unified sun and moon, the vāyu, and mind] enter the central nāḍī. While those three dwell within the central nāḍī, there is an experience of the connate gnosis. This is the arising of the sheer-naked, ultimate, natural luminosity of death, which is like the depths of pure space. Some sentient beings of remarkable merit remain in this state for a long while. Some with less merit remain in this state for a short time; that is, [the luminosity of death] arises for the length of time it takes to extend and withdraw one's arm, arising even for a bug on a blade of grass. Though it does arise, since those [of less merit] have never encountered it before, they do not recognize it. Since they have little familiarity with this state, they cannot remain in it. {441} At that time, the clear rasanā fades away, the great bliss cakra of the crown collapses, the saṃbhogacakra in the throat is exhausted, the dharmacakra in the heart bursts, the vāyu moves between the *a* and the *haṃ* within the nirmāṇacakra in the navel, and the inner breath stops. The *haṃ* descends and arises as a bindu in the secret place. Since the *a* ascends, blood or lymph emerges from the nostril and mouth. Indistinguishable from the vāyu, consciousness can leave through any of the nine orifices.

IV) The Actual Transference

A) The Transference of the Ball of Light

1) Familiarization with the Basis of Purification

First, the familiarization with the basis of purification is as follows: Having invited the guru and the deity, who are inseparable, before oneself and engaging in the daily confession and supplication with intense devotion, one sits with one's knees drawn toward the chest, blocking the rectum and urethra with the heels, and with the palms crossed, blocking the sides of the occipitals. One is either in the form of the deity or in ordinary form. Imagine a bindu the size of one's thumb at the heart of the body, which resembles a hollow egg. From that bindu, imagine that other similar bindus split off, blocking the anus and urethra, the navel, the mouth, the nose, the two eyes, and the crown. Next, directly in front of the navel, there is a vāyu maṇḍala shaped like a bow, above which is a moon, on top of which is the mind itself imagined as a black *hūṃ*. With the eyes looking upward, inhale and exhale, drawing up the lower vāyu. With twenty-one strong *hūṃ*s or *hik*s, draw up the vāyu maṇḍala, the moon, and the *hūṃ* into the throat. Again, with *ka hi* these descend to the navel. If hindrances arise in the preparations for transference, then those three descend to the soles of the feet. Alternately, focus the mind on a black sphere the size of a bean.

2) Application of the Practice

When it is time to die, {441} eliminate all proliferation about the three times in isolation. When one has no attachment to wealth, home, retinue, master, disciple, deity, or one's body, and so on, even for an instant, there is not a moment of clinging to the appearances of this life.

Do not remain in the presence of those with broken samaya, corrupt discipline, contaminations, or householders, and so on. If one's guru is present, request empowerment. If they are not present, then one can also request this from friends or experienced disciples. Begin virtuous practice, offering supplications, presenting vast offerings in the presence of the guru and deity, and offering tormas to the dharmapālas with supplications to prevent obstacles on the path.

Next, other than being similar to the section of the training on inviting the guru, and so on, the crown is not blocked. By reciting *hūṃ* twenty-one times, one's consciousness flies up, like a pigeon leaving through a skylight, dissolving into the guru's heart. Part the hands and tilt the head back. Further, if one wishes to be reborn a king of humans, do not block the right eye and think of a womb. If one wishes to be reborn in Sukhāvatī, think of a lotus.

B) The Transference of Changing Appearances

1) Transforming into the Deity

The body is cross-legged, and so on, doing what is comfortable. The supplication to the guru in front is the same. After that, recall the many harms that one's body and Yama inflict upon oneself as well as the signs of the dissolution of the four elements. Then, having sealed all that appears with the view of their falsity, one transforms into the deity, merging one's mind with it. Rest in one-pointed equipoise.

2) Preventing Degeneration

As before, in order to prevent harm, having connected all the many deluded appearances, such as the four terrifying sounds, with practice in order to prevent harm, {442} it is important to prevent degeneration.

C) The Transference with Sound

The transference with sound will not be explained here.

e. Merging the Pledged Deity with the Appearances of the Mind
i. The Bardo of Birth and Death

The practitioner should think that the present daytime is a bardo, the body is a mental body, and all that appears are bardo appearances. Moreover, recall that the four terrifying sounds, the three fearsome abysses,[6] and so on, are signs of birth in the six realms. The presentation of the five things to carry, and so on, are explained below. Connect everything with the view and transform great bliss into the essence of the deity. Then, remain in equipoise one-pointedly with one's mind. To eliminate outer reification, recall the guru. Recall the deity they explained. Recall the secret name received from the deity.

ii. The Bardo of Dreams

The bardo of dreams [requires] three abilities: recognizing the dream, training in the dream, and increasing the dream. Think that the bardo of the present is a dream. Also, think that all places, bodies, and so on, are the places, bodies, and so on, of a dream. Recall all appearances of the bardo, such as the terrifying sounds, and so on. Having transformed into the deity within the state of the view, merge this with one's mind, and recall the three recollections one-pointedly.

iii. The Bardo of Existence
I) The Explanation of the Nature of the Bardo of Existence

The bardo consciousness is unstable but sharp. Without being able to direct the mind, it arises as a variety and traces manifest easily. As it is said, [a ghandharva][7] arises in the form of wherever it will be born:

> [The ghandharva] possesses the shape of its previous existence,
> . . . .
> perceives those of the same class with the pure divine eye,
> is endowed with the power of the magic force of karma,
> and moves without impediment supported by whole sense
> organs.[8] {444}

Here, the duration of its life span is seven days. For three and a half weeks, the appearance of its body is connected with its traces. For the next three and a half weeks, the appearance of its body is connected with ripening, arising in the form of wherever it will be born.

Further, since at first one does not know that one has died, though one speaks to one's relatives, they do not reply. They divide one's share of food and drink. Since they take one's residence, and so on, attachment and aversion toward one's wealth arises and one feels sadness about one's relatives. Then, having understood that one has died, at first there is the initial suffering of being parted from relatives. Next, there is the suffering of being chased and pursued by those who inflict much harm, such as Yama, and so on, which is unbearable. At that time, having left one's relatives and seen them change their clothes and tear out their hair, darkness arises. The shedding of their tears appears as an intense hail and a rain of blood falls. Their wails of grief appear as the sounds of Yama, and so on, saying "Strike, slay!" as well as resembling the sounds of disintegrating mountains, roiling oceans, the blazing fire at the end of the eon, and the wind at the end of time. Those occur due to the traces of the dissolution of the four elements. Having seen the three lower realms, one experiences the three fearsome abysses as the suffering of the fear of being born in them.

The signs of birth in any of the six realms and the five objects of smell[9] that arise are as follows: If one is to be born in a hell realm, the mind fixates on the color black. That birthplace appears as a heap of rotten dung or charcoal. If one is going to be born as a preta, one fixates on yellow. That birthplace appears as a hut made of rotten wood or grass. {445} If one is going to be born as an animal, one fixates on blue. That birthplace appears as a rotten carcass or a hole in the ground. If one is going to be born as an asura, one fixates on green. That birthplace appears as a pleasant grove of trees. If one is going to be born as a deva, one fixates on white or red. That birthplace appears as a precious celestial mansion or a white tent. If one is going to be born as a human being, one fixates on a variety of colors. That birthplace appears as the palace of a deva.

Among those births in the five continents or in the center, if one is going to be born in the center, that birthplace will appear as a mating lion and lioness or as a lake adorned with lions. If one is going to be born on the eastern continent, that birthplace will appear as mating elephants or as a lake adorned with them. If one is going to be born on the southern continent, that birthplace will appear as mating horses or as a lake adorned with them. If one is going to be born in the western continent, that birthplace will appear as mating peafowls or as a lake adorned with them. If one is going to be born in the northern continent, that birthplace will appear as mating *shang shang* birds or as a lake adorned with them. Also, one's mind grasps the color of the scent of one's future birthplace. If one is going to be apparitionally born, the mind fixates on flowers. If one is going to have a warmth-and-moisture birth, one has extreme craving for odors and flavors.

Other than being impeded by Mount Meru, Buddha statues, Vajrāsana, and the mother's womb, gandharvas are completely unimpeded and have the magic power of powerful karma and slight clairvoyance. They can see one another in the bardo with the pure divine eye. Their destination is uncertain, but since they do not know on what to rely, they rely on stupas, trees, and so on. Their place is uncertain, so they rely on ravines, brambles, temples, and so on. Their companions are uncertain, so they associate with all beneficial companions and harmful companions. Their food is uncertain. Among gandharavas, some eat good smells, but most eat bad smells. Their behavior is uncertain, and they engage in various behavior without support. {446} Their life span is uncertain. Though their life is exhausted in seven days, they can also die in one or two days.

Furthermore, there is a soft light within the body of a gandharva. Since they lack white and red bodhicitta and subtle ṇāḍīs, the sun, moon, and stars are not visible to them. They do not have a shadow and do not leave footprints. Both the connate gods and demons lead one to the presence of Yama Dharmarāja. After he sets out white and black pebbles, when examining the proportion of virtue and misdeeds, there is the suffering of fear that the black pebbles will exceed the number of white ones.

II) Employing the Bardo of Existence as the Path

Do not cling to the signs of birth in the six realms and the five smells, do not be attached to the signs of birth in the five places, and do not be frightened by the four sounds and four abysses. If Yama displays the infliction of much harm, and so forth, on the physical body that does not exist in the bardo, he cannot harm this empty mental body. One should think that even if all worlds arose as one's enemy, those could not inflict harm. One should recall these three recollections.

No matter what kind of pleasant or unpleasant things arise, one should understand that the appearance of outer suffering arises from the activity of the vāyu and mind. It can be arrested with the elixir of the view. Having transformed into the maṇḍala of the supremely blissful deity who merged with one's mind, rest one-pointedly. Further, one blocks the womb with the three antidotes: the view, the deity, and abandoning the womb through recognizing the nature of suffering.

The instruction for the womb when it is not blocked is as follows: If there are signs that one will be born in the three lower realms, take birth in a royal family. Since one strongly aspires to go to Sukhāvatī, and so on, it is the dependent origination for being born there. Further, it is necessary to cultivate and become familiar with the view now. {447} If one does not cultivate the view now, it will not arise later on. Therefore, now, during the day, train on the bardos of life and death; at night, train on the bardo of dreams. Constantly engage in the strong recollection of the mindfulness of death. It is said that even if these words and their meaning of the bardo were followed by a dog that kept this in mind, after practicing whatever arose in the bardo, it would follow the conclusion.

f. Dreams

i. Recognizing Dreams

There are three topics in recognizing dreams. There are two topics in the actual recognition.

I) The Preliminaries

The preliminaries are that, in a solitary place, one's diet should be balanced, one's behaviors should be relaxed, and one should minimize conversation.

II) The Main Subject
A) The Visualization

From morning until afternoon, one should have the strong aspiration, "This evening I shall be in the grip of a dream and I will recognize it as a dream." From the afternoon onward, do not hold this strong aspiration, but when one is going to sleep, have a strong aspiration.

When going to sleep, visualize a four-petaled lotus in the center of the throat. At the center is a white *oṃ*. In the four directions, there are white or red syllables, *a nu ta ra*, circling left from the front. At the conclusion of focusing one's mind, beginning from *a*, focus one's mind on the *oṃ*, and go to sleep. The sign of recognizing the dream is the arising of various terrors, such as dwelling in a ravine or on a mountain, and so on.

B) Eliminating Dispersion

If one has not recognized the dream, make a strong aspiration and when going to sleep, visualize a chickpea-sized black bindu on the eyebrows. If that does not help one recognize the dream, then visualize a white bindu on the brow, as before.

C) Abandoning Deviations

If the above does not help one recognize the dream and the dispersion increases, one should abandon deviations. Strip naked in an empty valley, and so on, and run, yell, sing, stay on elevated places over terrifying ravines, and {448} tear at one's hair. Then, recite as before, transforming one's body, and go to sleep. Visualize a mustard-seed-sized white bindu at the forehead. As one goes to sleep, one will recognize one's dream. If one is never able to recognize one's dream, request empowerment from the guru, have a hero's celebration, and so on. If one is distracted from recognizing the dream, or if one does not recognize the dream, then one should recite the one-hundred-syllable mantra and rely on the instruction for removing obscurations.

ii. Purifying the Dream
I) The Preliminaries

During the day, strongly aspire to recognize the dream and train in it. Think that right now one is in a dream. Aspire to see the four continents after arriving at the summit of Mt. Meru; to be seated higher than the sun and moon; to see the divine mansion once one arrives in the Trāyastriṃśa heaven; to listen to the dharma once one reaches Oḍḍiyāna, Tuṣita, Sukhāvatī, and so on; and to eliminate doubts.

II) The Main Subject

Since one goes to sleep, just as in recognizing the dream, if one recognizes the dream, go to Oḍḍiyāna, and so on, as before.

iii. Increasing the Dream

I) The Preliminaries

During the day, one should have a strong aspiration to recognize, train, and increase the dream. Other than resting, as before, whatever the dreamer dreams is multiplied, and one should request dharma teachings in those dreams, and so on. All of whatever appears, such as ravines, and so on, including oneself, should be transformed into the dog-faced ḍākinī or the yidam and multiplied by one hundred.

II) The Main Subject

Since one goes to sleep in that state, one should increase the dream however one wishes.

iv. Abandoning the Dream

As such, if one has a slight ability to recognize, purify, and increase the dream, then abandon it. If discomfort arises in the body, perfect one's realization by meditating on reality. {449}

I) Generating Bliss

Imagine a mustard-seed-sized white bindu at the upper top of the central nāḍī, in the middle of one's brow, and go to bed. Through union with the consort, one generates bliss. Furthermore, after sealing the bliss with emptiness, practice.

II) Meditating on Reality

Having done so, if there is clinging to the aspect of physical bliss, then in order to abandon the taste of afflicted unions, meditate on reality, the real state of all phenomena, and in particular, remain in equipoise on the meaning of the inexpressibility of dreams.

III) Training in the Illusory Body

As such, even if the mind and the body are realized to be illusory, the explanation for interrupting the time of returning to samsara is the necessity of training in the illusory body.

A) Training in the Impure Illusory Body as an Illusion

This impure body of this life is apparent and insubstantial, like reflections in a mirror. Although one may evaluate one's reflection in a mirror as better or worse, one does not think of it as pure or impure. Likewise, evaluating oneself as better or worse is the same. One should understand the eight worldly dharmas as being similar to the example of illusion. Having understood unpleasant speech to be like an echo, one should practice without becoming displeased. That is how one trains in the impure illusory body.

B) Training in the Pure Illusory Body as an Illusion

Practice that all tathāgatas, such as the saṃbhogakāya, and so on, are like reflections in a mirror, apparent and insubstantial. Practice that the universe and beings are like the illusory forms of the deity. When that arises, one is skilled in the pure illusory body.

C) Training in Both Kinds of Illusory Body as an Illusion

These various appearances, from sentient beings to buddhas, are not truly established, because when they appear, they are empty by nature. {450} When the illusionist utters the mantra *aṃgu saṃgu* over substances such as a horn drum, a monkey tail, and so on, those things appear as horses, elephants, men, women, and so on. When those [illusory horses and elephants] appear, they are not established in any way. They did not exist before and do not become nonexistent. While the nonexistent is realized to be nonexistent, the [illusory] horses and elephants never existed at all—before they emanated, when they were emanated, and when they vanish. They are devoid of arising in the beginning, abiding in the middle, and ceasing in the end. Though such false appearances are not truly established, they are established as mere appearances. Likewise, with respect to the appearances of a deluded mind, though the diverse appearances of samsara and nirvana arise, when they appear, they are not established and are empty by nature.

Now then, if it is asked what appears, there is no appearance from an existent. Appearances arise from the collective dependent origination of karma and traces. Those false appearances do not become nonexistent while the concept has not arisen. When the concept arises, the false appearance returns to the initial state of having never existed. It did not exist before and then become nonexistent later. Recognizing the nonexistent as nonexistent is the realization. Therefore, since the time of the nonarising, arising, and liberation of these diverse appearances of the present never arose, it is the same as being devoid of arising, abiding, and ceasing.

As such, being nonexistent while appearing and arising in every way while being nonexistent, an illusion is a mere appearance that cannot be denied, because there is nothing to reify in reality. The experience of the view beyond all extremes of denial or reification, existence or nonexistence, permanence or annihilation, truth or falsity, and so on, is the ultimate skill in the illusory body.

Even though one trains in transforming the external body of this life, it remains a condition for dreams. {451} No matter what terrifying appearances may arise, such as the five scents, the four sounds, the three abysses, Yama, and so on, they are dreams. There is not anything to fear. Jump into [those appearances], overcome all hesitation, and recall the three recollections. After transforming everything into the pledged deity and merging it with one's mind, rest one-pointedly.

After waking up, the dream of the three lower realms[10] and the present appearances of the daytime are no different at all. Having understood that both are illusory, one should have no clinging to the dream. As such, train in daytime appearances as a dream. If one practices after merging the dream with daytime, it is said that the clairvoyance of knowing the three times and predictions by ḍākinīs becomes possible.

2. The Secret Empowerment

a. The Self-Empowerment

i. The Visualization of the Pervading Vāyu

The key points of the visualization for the pervader are that the session preliminaries are the same as those for the vase empowerment. Visualize the central nāḍī that runs from the crown to the navel in the center of the body. Also, the vāyu is exhaled through the āyāma and inhaled through the prāṇa, remaining inside. Mentally recite *hūṃ oṃ āḥ* and visualize the three nāḍīs. In correspondence with the movement of the vāyu, think that vāyu is moving out, moving in, or abiding. Further, that vāyu is meditated as a blue *hūṃ*, white *oṃ*, and red *āḥ*. To progress, it is very important for the mind to follow exhalation, inhalation, and the pause of the vāyu.

Giving a reward corresponds with the vāyu: When exhaling through the āyāma, it is long; when inhaling through the prāṇa, it is short; and when pausing inside, it is short. {452} After training in that for several days, one should think that the exhalation through the āyāma is short and the inhalation through the prāṇa and the pause inside are long. One should train until one has certainty in the aspect and the movement is evident.

ii. The Visualization of the Pervaded

The visualization of the pervaded is visualizing either the extensive one, with the three nāḍīs and the four cakras, or the solitary nāḍī petals. Since one inhales the upper vāyu evenly through the two nostrils, the vāyu enters both the rasanā and lalanā. Since they meet at the lower tip of the central nāḍī, slightly draw up the lower vāyu. Since [the lower vāyu] touches the *āṃ* of the navel, the fire that blazes from the navel enters the central nāḍī. Having burned the *hūṃ* of the heart and the *oṃ* of the throat, [the vāyu] touches the *haṃ* of the crown, from which bodhicitta falls. After [the bodhicitta] restores the *oṃ* and *hūṃ*, there is blazing and dripping four fingerbreadths above the navel. Draw up the lower vāyu between the two upper vāyus and press down. When one can no longer hold, exhale slowly. Then repeat as before.

Both (b.) the view and (c.) the conclusion are like the extensive explanation.

d. The Time of Death

i. The Preliminaries

The first of the two, the preliminaries for the application of activities, is inviting the guru, offering supplications, and abandoning clinging, as before. Here, one should recall the outer, inner, and secret signs of the dissolution of the four elements. Those also should be understood as empty luminosity. Merge this with one's mind and rest one-pointedly.

ii. The Application of the Activity

Since all signs and indications of the dissolution of the four elements arise in actuality, all are directed to change into empty luminosity. By doing so, {453} after all vāyus and mind are brought into the central nāḍī, the mother and child luminosities meet, and one will follow the conclusion.

e. The Bardo

i. The Preliminaries

The preliminaries are recalling the whole of the presentation of the bardo in the section on the vase empowerment. After transforming everything into empty luminosity, merge it with one's mind and rest in equipoise. Further, recall the view taught by one's guru; caṇḍālī, the path taught by that guru; and the actual self-originated gnosis.

ii. The Main Subject

Since all appearances [described] in the section of the bardo arise in actuality, at that time one needs to practice in the following way: the way that is done is, following all appearances arising in the form of the vowels and syllables, self-originated gnosis arises and one will follow the conclusion.

f. Dream Yoga

Train in recognizing dreams, and so on, as before. After all those are transformed into empty luminosity, multiply them, and recall the three recollections.

3. The Gnosis of the Wisdom Consort Empowerment

a. The Maṇḍalacakra

The path of the gnosis of the wisdom consort, the maṇḍalacakra is: Having performed the session preliminaries, and so on, since one engages in union with the mudra, the red and white bodhicitta is produced from the *haṃ* in the crowns of the couple and descends to the secret place through the stages of the four joys. The connate gnosis arises because the red and white bodhicitta unites, like the sun and moon. Again, one practices the four joys stabilized by the consort, and if there is too much dripping, behave like the four animals.

Both (b.) the view and (c.) the conclusion are like the extensive explanation.

d. The Time of Death

Invite the guru, and so on, as before.

Since these signs of the disintegration of the knots of the nāḍīs of the five cakras, the gathering of the pure essences, and the dissolution of the vāyus that were placed in their seats {454} arise in actuality, those should be practiced as bliss and emptiness. That causes the vāyu and mind to enter into the central nāḍī. *Vajra* is emptiness, and *sattva* is bliss. After Vajrasattva arrives in person, one will follow the conclusion.

e. The Bardo

i. The Preliminaries

The preliminaries are recalling the presentation of the bardo. Having transformed all of those into bliss and emptiness, merge those with one's mind and rest one-pointedly. Here, recall the guru who teaches the connate gnosis, the path of messengers, and the actual connate gnosis.

ii. The Main Subject

Since all appearances [described] in the section of the bardo arise in actuality, at that time one needs to practice in the following way: the way that is done is that once phenomena arise like a string of pearls of bodhicitta, the connate wisdom arises, and one will follow the conclusion.

f. Dreams

As before, train in form, and so on. Multiply all those dream appearances. Having transformed them into bliss and emptiness, one should recall the three recollections.

4. The Path of the Fourth Empowerment
a. The Vajra Waves
i. Purifying the Continuum of the Method

The preliminaries are the same as before. Visualize the three nāḍīs from the crown to the secret place. Since one engages in union with the consort, bodhicitta is produced from the *haṃ* in crowns of both. Since it falls to the secret place through the stages of the four joys, once both bodhicittas merge at the lower end of the central nāḍī, they transform into rays of light. Those enter into the rasanā of the method. The three cakras—the navel, heart, and throat—are imagined to vanish like daybreak, becoming more and more clear like sunrise and becoming more and more inflated like an inflated lung, {455} endowed with three characteristics.

Those rays of light leave from the left ear and fill all worlds with five-colored rays of light. Countless maṇḍalas of Hevajra emanate on the tips of the light rays. After that, transform all worlds into celestial mansions and all inhabitants into the deity. The benefit of beings is performed by conferring the four empowerments. After all of those [mansions and deities] are transformed into the form of five-colored rays of light, [the light] enters through the crown. As before, visualize from the crown cakra on down and the [lights rays] descending to the secret place through the rasanā. When those light rays arrive at the throat from the crown, they possess the brilliance of one thousand suns. Since they arrive in the heart, as a sign that one's continuum has been empowered as the five gnoses, the light rays become five colors. That purifies the path of the rasanā and arrests the concept of apprehended objects. Since the rasanā is brought under control, one obtains power over the vāyu of the āyāma. Imagine that one has realized the signless gate of liberation and rest in equipoise in that state.

Once again, the light rays enter the path of the lalanā, leaving through the left ear, and so on, and since the light rays come and go in every way just as before, the concept of the apprehending subject is arrested. Since the lalanā is brought under control, one obtains power over the prāṇa. Imagine that one realizes the aspirationless gate of liberation and rest in equipoise in that state.

Once again the light rays come and go through the central nāḍī. As they ascend, visualize the crown cakra, and do everything else as before. The concepts of both subject and object are arrested, and since the central nāḍī is brought under control, one obtains power over the paused vāyu. Imagine that one realizes the emptiness gate of liberation and rest in equipoise in that state. {456}

ii. Purifying the Continuum of the Wisdom

The difference from the above visualizations is that at the time of the rasanā and lalanā, the light rays do not leave the ears. They can either leave or not leave the central nāḍī.

iii. Purifying the Continuum of Both

When the respective white and red elements of the method and the wisdom enter the lower tip of the central nāḍī, one imagines that after entering, and likewise, returning through all three nāḍīs, [the white and red] elements dissolve into the uṣṇīṣa.

Both (b.) the view and (c.) the conclusion are like the extensive explanation.

d. The Time of Death
i. Cultivating the Basis of Training
I) Cultivating Sound

Cultivating sound is to perform the vāyu yoga for forty-two days, as explained in the treatise. Since the key point of the body is the same as in the section on the vase empowerment, draw [the vāyu maṇḍala, moon, and *hūṃ*] up into the throat with twenty *hiks*. Since here there is no twenty-first, one refreshes those with twenty *ka his*.

II) Cultivating the External Syllables

If one transfers through the rectum, urethra, stomach, mouth, eyes, ears, or crown, one will be born as a hell being, animal, desire realm god, preta, yakṣa, human, kinnara, deva, or in the form or formless realms. Block the nine orifices, as in the treatise.

III) Cultivating the Inner Syllables

The visualization is like the section that explained the four cakra caṇḍālī yoga, with the three nāḍīs and four cakras. Imagine that in the rasanā and lalanā, there are sixteen upright red vowels, and in between those are the forty inverted white consonants. When exhaling through the āyāma, the three nāḍīs, the four cakras, and the syllables are visualized ascending from the navel. When inhaling through the prāṇa, beginning from the crown, one visualizes the same in descending order. {457}

ii. Applying the Activity

At the time of death, make oneself comfortable, either drawing the knees up to the chest or sitting cross-legged. Visualize in the same way as when cultivating the three nāḍīs, the four cakras, and the syllables.

When exhaling, imagine that the vāyus of the rasanā and lalanā enter the central nāḍī through the *a*. Similarly, when inhaling, imagine [that the vāyu of the rasanā and lalanā enter the central nāḍī] through the *haṃ*. Having done so, at the time of the luminosity of death when all vāyus and the mind have entered the central nāḍī, after the experience of true reality dawns, one will follow the conclusion.

e. The Bardo
i. The Preliminaries

Train in the preliminaries by recalling the presentation of the bardo, as before. Practice all appearances as true reality, merge them with one's mind, and rest in one-pointed equipoise. At that time, recall the guru who shows reality; recall the path, the vajra waves; and recall the view, reality.

ii. The Main Subject

The main subject is the four terrifying sounds, and so on, that arise in actuality [described] in the section of the bardo of existence. Seal them all with the view, reality. Here, one should recall the three recollections. Since one practices in that way, all that appears arises as the essence of the view. Once the three nāḍīs, the four cakras, and the syllables are completely clear, one will follow the conclusion. That being so, the section on the bardo of the fourth empowerment, the presentation of the bardos of birth and death, and the bardo of dreams during the day and during the night should be practiced in their respective contexts.

f. Dreams

Dreams are recognizing, purifying, and so on, as before. At that time, all of whatever arises is recognized as the view, reality, and one multiplies oneself. Also, at this occasion one recalls the three recollections. {458}

18. Dewar Shekpa Pal Taklung Chenpo's Notes

The Oral Teaching of Pal Phakmo Dru on The Medium-Length Instruction on the Path with Its Result and Advice on the Intimate Instructions of the Four Experiences[1]

Tashi Pal

According to the *Red Annals*, Tashi Pal (1142–1209/1210) was born in Bong Rateng in the Naksho region of Dokham. His parents were Banlön Barpo (Ban blon 'bar po, dates unknown) and Drabzhi Za Gesum Tromo (Brab zhi bza' dge gsum khro mo, dates unknown). According to the biography composed by Ngawang Namgyal (Ngag dbang rnam rgyal, 1571–1626), Tashi Pal learned to read and write between the ages of seven and eight. When he was eleven, he trained in the practice of Vajrakīlaya under a local mantra practitioner. At Thangkya Temple, he trained in medicine with a monk named Khuwo Bandhe, who also encouraged him to ordain. Tashi Pal's father opposed this and refused him permission.

When Tashi Pal was seventeen, he disobeyed his father and ran away to Thangkya Temple, where he received novice ordination and studied there for a while. When he was twenty-four, he left for central Tibet. According to the *Garland of Jewels*, Tashi Pal received many teachings in Kham, U, and Tsang from more than one hundred teachers on subjects such as Mahāmudrā, the Six Dharmas of Naropa, Cakrasaṃvara, Kālacakra, and so on.

One day while in meditation, a feeling of great remorse and renunciation arose in Tashi Pal, giving rise to a special realization. On meeting Phakmo Drupa (Phag mo gru pa rDo rje rgyal po, 1110–1170), the nature of that experience was revealed to him. Phakmo Drupa explained, "All that arises and appears is the movement of the dharmakāya and the arising of great luminosity. When all taints of a mind directed toward an object of meditation and a meditator vanish automatically, it is the realization of the victorious stage of the dharmakāya's continuous meditation of nonmeditation." Tashi Pal would remain with Phakmo Drupa until the latter's death in 1170. Tashi Pal acted as Phakmo Drupa's scribe, writing down all instructions, including the corpus of Phakmo Drupa's writings on the Path with Its Result. Ngawang Namgyal reports that when Tashi Pal attended the funerary rites for Phakmo Drupa, a flash of light from the vajra in the heart of Phakmo Drupa's body shone out, dissolving into the heart of Tashi Pal. At the same time, Phakmo Drupa's body emitted the scent of sandalwood and lignum aloes.

Tashi Pal spent time during his thirties in various places, putting into practice the teachings he received. In 1180, at age thirty-eight, Tashi Pal took full ordination and established his eponymous hermitage, Taklung Gompa (*stag lung dgon pa*). Only a single volume of personal writings exists. It is recorded that his students came from central Tibet and eastern Tibet, as well as China, India, Kashmir, Oḍḍiyāna, Śrī Lanka, and so on. Tashi Pal passed away in 1209, having gained considerable fame as one of the principal disciples of Phakmo Drupa Dorje Gyalpo.

The pair of texts presented here are *Dewar Shekpa Pal Taklung Chenpo's Notes: The Oral Teaching of Pal Phakmo Dru on The Medium-Length Instruction on the Path with Its Result* and *Advice on the Intimate Instructions of the Four Experiences*, which is excluded from Kongtrul's catalog. Kongtrul selected these texts to represent the Phakdru Path with Its Result lineage. Another representative copy was not found.

The first text in this chapter presents a somewhat different version of preliminary practices than the standardized version found in the common Sakya curriculum. In general, however, the Path with Its Result practices, such as prāṇāyama, caṇḍālī yoga, and so on, are presented in a manner consistent with the general Sakyapa approach. As such, apart from Phakmo Drupa's own writings on the Path with Its Result system,[2] this text presents a rare picture of the system as it was practiced outside the Sakya tradition during the twelfth century.

The second text, *Advice on the Intimate Instructions of the Four Experiences*, describes in great detail the dream experiences, physical experiences, mental experiences, and visionary experiences one might have as a practitioner during the completion stage of the system.

Having bowed with true, supreme devotion to
the lotus feet of the precious, venerable Virūpa,
who completed the four empowerments, effortlessly accomplished the
three kāyas,
and gained mastery over the outer and inner ḍākinīs,
this instruction on the four experiences in the three gatherings
will be clearly written according to his precious words.

In the system of the Path with Its Result, without the arising of inner experience, outer doubts will not be eliminated. In order to eliminate doubts, one does not use citations when applying the oral instructions of the treatise. When applying the treatise systems, one does not use the oral instructions.

In order to cause inner experience to arise, the two preliminaries are first to gather the accumulations based on maṇḍala offerings and [second] to purify obscurations relying on the one-hundred-syllable mantra. In order to generate indestructible, unsurpassed awakening, it is necessary to gather accumulations and purify obscurations, similar to preparing wool by boiling it in dye and rinsing it in a clean drain in order to dye it brightly.

At the time of maṇḍala offerings, meditate on one's yidam. It is said that [visualizing] the guru above the crown of one's head is sufficient. Whichever instruction one uses, whether extensive or concise, the teaching should start on the third, fifth, or an odd-numbered day. One should offer balis with three or five pellet ornaments and three maṇḍalas. Also, recite the one-hundred-syllable mantra three times. {461} It is said reliance on this system is nothing other than the guru creating dependent origination.

Imagine that the fifteen-deity maṇḍala of Nairātmyā, Lord Virūpa, Kāṇha, Ḍāmarupa, Avadhūtīpa, Gayadhara, Drokmi, Setön Kunrik, Zhang Gon, and Lama Sakyapa are seated in the sky in front. Imagine that the seven heaps on the maṇḍala are filled with jewels, Sumeru, the four continents, the sun, and the moon.

Next, purifying misdeeds by relying on the one-hundred-syllable mantra is as follows: Upon a lotus and moon seat on one's crown is Vajrasattva, [seated] with the left leg drawn in and the toe of the right leg touching one's brahma aperture. He is as white as a swan or jasmine and endowed with bone ornaments. He has one face and three eyes and is seated in a wrathful mood. His two hands hold a vajra and bell, while embracing Vajragarvi. The mother's color, face, hands, and ornaments are the same as the father. In a mountain of fire, she embraces the father with both her arms and legs. They are seated, kissing. As such, imagine that in the heart of Vajrasattva is a white *hūṃ*, the color of silver on a moon. Since light shines from that [syllable], {462} it summons gnosis amṛta from the hearts of the heroes, ḍākinīs, buddhas, and bodhisattvas in their natural abodes, which arrives at Vajrasattva's brahma aperture and fills the interior of his body with white. It arrives to one's brahma aperture from the space between the toenail and flesh of his foot. Imagine that the misdeeds and obscurations are black like liquid soot and are expelled through the rectum, urethra, and the spaces between the ten toenails. For the voice, calculate the number and recite the amount of *oṃ vajrasatva hūṃ* one is able to do.

Next, having completed the instructions above, examine the vāyu for whether or not obstacles will arise. In a single day, the vāyu changes from the right nostril to the left nostril five times.

The time to examine the vāyu is when one is examined by the guru, when one lays down in the evening, when one wakes in the morning, when one arrives in the presence of the guru from the road or one's bed, and after arriving in the presence of the guru (being examined prior to the inquiry by the guru).

When the guru examining the [vāyu] makes an inquiry, the guru can determine three of those [five] without error. At that time the guru sees whether or not obstacles to life and practice exist. Since there will be obstacles if one has not completed the one-hundred-syllable mantras or the maṇḍala offerings, request empowerment from the guru. If one has completed those, there will be no obstacles. If the vāyu moves mostly through the right nostril, there will be obstacles. Since there will be [both] obstacles to longevity and obstacles to the practice:

> When the essence of the breast is thrown away by the crow,
> this is a suddenly arising bad sign.[3]

The method of tricking is to grasp the right elbow with the left hand, pressing down on the right breast. Otherwise, either push it with the heel of the palm or rub[4] it with the palm of the hand. Observe whether the vāyu switches to the left [nostril]. If it switches, because it has been tricked, later on it is sufficient just to press down the vāyu in each session. If it does not switch, since the vāyu has not been tricked, use other methods. If the vāyu predominantly moves through the left, obstacles to longevity and life will not arise. In that case, {463} gather accumulations through presenting maṇḍalas to the guru and purify obscurations in dependence on reciting the one-hundred-syllable mantra.

That examination of whether or not there will be obstacles to longevity, life, and practice with the foregoing examination of the movement of the vāyu into the left and right nostrils is accomplished on behalf of the person.

There are nine parts in the preliminaries for meditation: the three isolations, the three preliminaries, and the three crucial points. The three isolations [are the isolations of body, voice, and mind]. The isolation of the body is the avoidance of walking, sitting, distraction, and fatigue. The isolation of the voice is refraining from talking and recitations. The isolation of the mind is avoiding concepts and generating regret.

The three crucial points are as follows: First, for the crucial point of the body, the seat should have a full moon. The back should be four fingerbreadths high and the front four fingerbreadths lower. If one is a person with a blood or a pitta condition, one should be seated evenly upon this. One should remain [seated] with the five limbs of samādhi. If one has a cold condition, then the body should be seated with the knees drawn up to the chest, with the feet crossed and the arms like a meditation belt, as in the posture for meditating on caṇḍālī. That [posture] resembles the foundation of a house.

The three preliminaries are meditating on bodhicitta, meditating on the pledged deity, and meditating on the guru. First, meditating on bodhicitta is thinking, "I will meditate on the instruction of the path and result in order that all mother sentient beings equal with space have happiness, be free from suffering, and attain buddhahood."

Meditation on the pledged deity is as follows: If one has control, visualize the deity of the five [illegible].[5] If one does not have control, meditate on the five families. Also, if one does not have that under control, meditate on the pledged deity. If lacking a pledged deity, then substitute the meditation of Mind-Akṣobhya or any wrathful deity who possesses the six bone ornaments and stands on the corpse seat with the head directed toward the left. {464}

The meditation of the guru is as follows: Buddhajñānapāda's teaching is that Amitābha* is the essence of the guru's speech. Lord Virūpa says Mind-Akṣobhya is the essence of the guru. The meditation on Mind-Akṣobhya is

*It is sometimes said that the essence is one's guru. The form is solitary Akṣobhya in the sky in front.

as follows: Imagine that on a sun or a moon in one's heart, there is a *hūṃ*, from which light rays shine, inviting the essence of one's guru from their natural abode in the form of the Akṣobhya couple. The father has one face and two hands, which hold a vajra and a bell while embracing the mother Māmakī. He has six bone ornaments and three eyes. The mother also has three eyes and two hands. [She] holds a curved knife in the right hand and a skull full of blood in the left hand while embracing the father. She is adorned with five bone ornaments.

After the couple have been invited in that way, they are imagined to be in the sky* and presented with outer, inner, and ultimate offerings. The outer offerings, lamps, and so on, are imagined to issue forth from the seed syllable in the heart. After the ḍākinīs—Lāma, Khaṇḍaroha, and Rūpinī—issue forth, having emanated the five meats and five amṛtas, imagine they offer those. The offering of reality is imagining the father and mother enter into union and offering bliss.

Next, having mentally dissolved the guru in the form of Akṣobhya into one's crown, imagine that oneself appears as the deity, like a lamp lighting the dark. {465}

With the voice recite:

> The guru is the Buddha.
> The guru is the dharma.
> The guru is also the sangha.

Think and repeat this three times. Those are the three preliminaries.

Among the three crucial points, the crucial point of the body was addressed above. Second, the crucial point of the voice is as follows: Look over the right and left shoulders while turning the neck and then strongly expel through the nostrils three times. Removing the faults of the nāḍīs is like sweeping the house. Third, the crucial point of the mind is pausing at ease in peace, like taking the power from a horse. This is the crucial point of the mind. Those are the nine kinds of preliminaries.

Now, the meditation is as follows: In the initial gathering of the elements, there is the path instruction on the signs of heat of the vāyu and caṇḍālī

*It is sometimes said that one imagines solitary Akṣobhya. Having offered one's body, enjoyments, and so on, he dissolves into oneself. Think that the guru is the embodiment of the Three Jewels. This is sufficient.

yogas. In the middle gathering of the elements, there is the path instruction of bliss and emptiness. In the final gathering of the elements, there is the path instruction of fundamental gnosis.

The path instruction of concentration through the prāṇa and āyāma of the initial gathering of the element is as follows: After pausing naturally, while exhaling tilt the head forward. After exhaling, think that one is inhaling, and meditate on both [inhalation and exhalation] without counted sessions or session breaks. At the end of inhaling, pause. It is said that one should think of the movement of the vaȳu and give it a reward. After the nine preliminaries, since one does not count the inhalation and exhalation of the vāyu, when [the breath] is long, one should think, "long exhalation" ten times. Think, "Inhalation," in the same way. Mentally imagine this for each nostril. When meditating, one begins with exhalation. When pausing, one inhales and rests. As such, there are neither counted sessions nor session breaks. That is for expelling faults.

Now, for concealing the faults inside, since these nine preliminaries are absolutely necessary, {466} after those preliminaries, begin inhaling with the thought, "Inhalation," and while inhaling think, "Inhalation." Repeat ten times. Also, for each [inhalation] think, "The exhalation is short."* When pausing, pause after a long inhalation. When practicing in this way, the name of this prāṇāyāma is called "gradually giving a reward." Elsewhere it is called "the yoga of prāṇa."

There are four sections in the concentration of prāṇa and āyāma: the instruction of mental placement, the faults that can arise, the samādhi that can arise, and the measure of culmination. There can be three topics in the visualizations above, but there can also be four for each one. When included in three, there is the instruction for mental placement. There is focusing the mind merely by thinking of the movement of the vāyu, the path of clearing the entry. When that place becomes completely empty, it is the path of eliminating obstacles. If one sees smoke, mirages, and so on, in that state, it is the path of the union of great awakening. If one is removing a fault, death will be cheated by meditation on the prāṇa and the āyāma.

If it is asked what are prāṇa and āyāma, the movement through the right nostril is called āyāma and the movement through the left [nostril] is called

*Sometimes, if the mind is not focused, it is said that one should apply the five colors of the vāyu to the color of fire. The white color of fire should be apprehended as the water vāyu. This should be applied to the other vāyus. This method is not spoken of.

prāṇa. The exhalation is called āyāma and the inhalation is called prāṇa. If samādhis arise, they will arise as any of the fifteen experiences. The measure of culmination is ascertaining both movement and the clarity of the aspect. Having cultivated the prāṇa and the āyāma, thinking that the earth vāyu moves when the earth vāyu [actually] moves is ascertaining movement. If at that time one sees the color of vāyu as yellow, [the color] is the clarity of the aspect. Apply this to the fire vāyu, and so on. At that time, {467} one can also accomplish any activity to pacify, increase, overpower, or destroy. If one wishes to accomplish an activity of increase, then the earth vāyu moves if one engages as before.* If one wishes to pacify, it is done when the water vāyu moves. If one wishes to overpower someone or something, it is done when the fire vāyu moves, as before. If one wishes to accomplish any destructive activity, it is done when the air vāyu moves. When the space vāyu moves, one should do as before, and one will accomplish any kind of wrathful activity.

After performing the nine preliminaries, press the right nostril with the right finger and exhale through the left nostril; while blocking it out, focus on the interior of the left nostril. When one cannot hold out anymore, allow the vāyu to return completely inside. The name of this is "blocking the āyāma and exhaling through the prāṇa." There are also four parts to this. The instruction for the pause of the vāyu is to block the āyāma and exhale through the prāṇa. If there is a problem to remove, one will remove sudden accidents, such as the destruction of a fort, house, and so on. If any samādhi arises, bliss and heat arise. The measure of culmination is that if after blocking the vāyu out, it does not return inside, then the vāyu is resting in its own place. That is the measure of culmination.

After performing the nine preliminaries, exhale and send the vāyu out through both nostrils. It is said that one focuses on the brow while focusing on the absence of movement. When one cannot hold the vāyu out any longer, allow the vāyu to return completely inside through both nostrils. As such, meditate without sessions or session breaks. Further, for each of these, the guru has said they are to be done in groups of four; this is named the fifth. The name of this one is "developing power"; that is, exhaling through both nostrils. Here, there are also four. {468} This is the instruction for placing the mind. If there is any fault, it will remove all contagious illnesses. If any samādhi arises, it is the arising of any of the five experiences. The

*It is said that without the need for any other mantra or method, having imagined that whatever one wishes to increase will increase, it is enough to emphasize the vāyu.

measure of the culmination is that after endeavoring in holding the vāyu out, when it does not return, the vāyu is resting in its own place. That is the measure of culmination.

After performing the nine preliminaries, exhale through the mouth with sound. Make a gap between the teeth, like horsehair, and expel the vāyu making the sound "si." Focus the mind on conceptuality. When one can no longer hold the vāyu out, allow it to return completely through the mouth. Also, here the instruction for placing the mind is exhaling through the mouth with sound. If any fault arises, this will remove the pain and fevers of bile and blood. [The guru said,] "Since I also experienced that, when one's health is poor and a fever arises, when [this prāṇa yoga] is meditated in each session, a refreshing coolness arises. When any sort of quality or samādhi arises, that is said to be any of the fifteen experiences. As soon as I meditated in this way, my health clearly returned." The measure of culmination is the vāyu resting in its own place, as before. The types of movement for the prāṇa and āyāma are the same. Consequently, there are three kinds of exhalations.

Now, the first of the two inhalations is blocking the āyāma and inhaling through the prāṇa. After performing the nine preliminaries, press the right nostril with the index finger and inhale through the left nostril. Focus on the nostril and meditate. Also, the instruction for placing the mind is to block the āyāma and inhale through the prāṇa. If one performs the four activities, one can remove sudden accidents, such as lightning, the collapse of one's fort or house, and so on. If samādhi arises, it will be both blissful and warm. The measure of culmination is the vāyu resting in its own place, as before.

The second is {469} inhaling through the mouth without sound. After performing the nine preliminaries, in the center of the nāḍī petals of the navel, there is a red triangle of nāḍīs, which is empty in the center. Within that is a nāḍī, imagined to be like half an egg, with the outside white and the inside red. The interior of the egg is empty space. Within the egg, without touching the bottom, there is a short *a*, imagined as a yellow *a* stroke. Make a gap between one's teeth, the size of a horsehair, and inhale through the mouth. Imagine the vāyu dissolving into the *a* stroke, but it is said that one does not imagine the color of the vāyu. At the conclusion of an inhalation, focus on the *a* stroke, and when one can no longer hold in the vāyu, rather than exhaling through the nostrils, exhale through the mouth. That is meditated on without counting sessions or session breaks. Here, there are also four: The instruction for placing the vāyu is inhaling through the mouth without sound. If it is asked which fault is removed, it removes swelling and maldigestion. If it is asked what kind of qualities and samādhis arise, any of the fifteen experiences are generated. The measure of culmination is the vāyu resting in its own place, as above.

The first of the three waves, meditating on the wave of the body by stirring [the vāyu] of the lower door, is as follows: The body adopts vajrāsana, the hands are in [the mudra] of equipoise, the back is straight, and the gaze falls on the tip of the nose. Here, one does not draw the knees up to the chest. The preliminaries are the same as for the others. Since one moves the right thigh over the left and then moves the left thigh over the right, this expels the stale vāyu through the lower door. This is called "the lower vāyu takes its seat." Furthermore, the lower vāyu is also arrested in its own place without being drawn up, becoming tightly controlled.

Next, when inhaling through the nostrils, one imagines a dark-blue aperture in the center of the triangle of nāḍīs and focuses on that. {470} Join the upper and lower vāyus. This is meditated on without counting sessions or sessions breaks. When the vāyu is exhaled, it is exhaled through the nostrils. Also, it is said that it is unnecessary for the vāyu to travel to the brahma aperture. The name of this in Sanskrit is *zhiwa śāntika*;[6] in Tibetan, this is called "union" (*kha sbyor*) or "holding a vase" (*bum pa can*).

Here, there are also four in the instruction for holding the vāyu, which is zhiwa śāntika. If it is asked what fault is removed, if one meditates on the fundamental state, the four kinds of pathological humors are like clouds vanishing in the sky. If it is asked which kind of qualities and samādhis arise, all fifteen experiences are generated. The measure of culmination is that since the vāyu is pacified in its own place, by closing the lower door and meditating, [the vāyu] does not leave through the lower door. If one is to be instructed in this for many days, the first instruction is to be seated cross-legged for three days. The next instruction is to lie on one's back and meditate for three days.

It is very important not to confuse these three key points. The three key points [concern inhaling and exhaling through the mouth, inhaling and exhaling through the nostrils, and inhaling and exhaling through the prāṇa]. When inhaling through the mouth, it is an error to inhale through the nostrils or block them. When exhaling through the mouth, it is an error to exhale through the nostrils.* When exhaling through the nose, it is an

*It is said that sometimes the mind should rest peacefully. The feet are cross-legged, the right arm is extended in front, and the left arm reaches behind. One should twist a little and

error to exhale through the mouth. When inhaling through the prāṇa, it is an error to inhale through the āyāma. When exhaling through the prāṇa, it is also an error to exhale through the āyāma. Thus, it is said that it is important not to err.

Further, there is the key point of error, the key point of non-error, {471} and the key point of special qualities. First, the key point of error is as follows: If one draws up the vāyu, but it is not held, or one presses down the upper vāyu, but it is not held, these are the key points of error. Drawing the lower vāyu up, holding it, and pressing the upper vāyu down and holding is the key point of non-error. Slightly drawing up the lower vāyu and holding the upper vāyu, and slightly pressing down the upper vāyu and holding the lower vāyu is the key point of special qualities. If it is wondered what is implied up to this point, when the three movements of the prāṇa and the āyāma are considered together, it is the first yoga [prāṇāyāma]. Blocking the āyāma and exhaling through the prāṇa, developing strength and exhaling through both, and exhaling with sound through the mouth are the next three exhalation yogas. Inhaling soundlessly through the mouth and blocking the āyāma while inhaling through the prāṇa are the next two inhalation yogas. The branch of holding the vāyu through union, or zhiwa śāntika, is the seventh yoga. From the point of view of the path, there are four: [inhalation, exhalation, pausing, and union]. From the point of view of [vāyu] yoga, there are seven: [prāṇāyāma, the three exhalations, the two inhalations, and union]. The path instruction of the signs of heat of the vāyu and the caṇḍālī of the first gathering is the seven vāyu yogas. From the three waves, there is the wave of the body, stirring the lower door. The wave of the mind, samādhi, is not found here, but [it can be found] in the section on the third empowerment.

Meditating on the wave of the voice, the gentle and rough inhalations, is as follows: After performing the nine preliminaries,* do not adopt a cross-legged posture. Sit with the knees drawn up to the chest and bow one's head

extend. In the same way, alternate with the left in front with right reaching behind. Next, perform with the left leg in front and the right leg behind. Then, one should wave and stretch both legs. Since this reverses blockages in the nāḍīs, it is said to be the same type of *zhiwa śāntika*.

*Sometimes it is said that because the instruction is step by step, the instruction for generating experience by meditating for a long while on union, or zhiwa śāntika, is imagining a blue *hūṃ* in the heart of one's pledged deity. The syllable transforms into an Akṣobhya couple. Focus on the central eye of the father and meditate again and again, without meditating on down in between the knees. Inhale gently, making the sound *hūṃ* with the voice. Lift the head and exhale. Also inhale gently on the right and the left. Next, inhale roughly, making the sound *hūṃ*, with the head between the two knees. Also inhale roughly to the right and the left. If one's balanced elements become unbalanced, purify the elements by stopping the rough inhalation and inhaling gently. As such, meditate without counting sessions or session breaks. Up to this point there is no explanation of the faults and qualities.

After performing the nine preliminaries, imagine that within one's empty heart, there is a dark-blue Mind-Akṣobhya with one face. He has three eyes, which are red like the eyes of a pigeon. He has four bared fangs, and his hair is bound up in a topknot. He has two hands. His right hand holds a vajra, and his left hand holds a vajra-handled bell, while he embraces his consort. His right leg is extended, and his left leg is contracted. The rays inside the empty heart form an eight-petaled lotus upon which he stands. He is adorned with bone ornaments. Likewise, the consort Māmakī, the purified element of water, is similar in terms of color, faces, hands, and fangs. She holds a curved knife in her right hand and a skull full of blood with the left hand, while she embraces the father. She has five bone ornaments. Imagine Vajrasattva is in union with such a consort. Imagine and focus on the heart of Akṣobhya, and meditate by uniting the upper and lower vāyus, as before.

After performing the nine preliminaries, in one's throat imagine red Speech-Amitābha, holding a lotus in his right hand and a lotus-handled bell in his left hand. He embraces his consort Pāṇḍāravāsinī, the purified element of fire. They are similar in face, hands, and all ornaments with the other couple. In the crown, imagine white Body-Vairocana holding a white wheel in his right hand and a wheel-handled bell in his left hand, {473} while embracing his consort Dharmadhatviśvarī. Here also, the accouterments of all the couples are the same as the faces, hands, and method of the previous meditation. At the navel, imagine pure gold Ratnasambhava holding a jewel in his right hand and a jewel-handled bell in his left hand, while embracing his consort Buddhalocanā, the purified element of earth. Also, here, all methods of meditating on the vāyu are the same as before. In the place of the genitalia, imagine green Amoghasiddhi holding a crossed vajra in his right hand and a crossed vajra-handled bell in his left hand, while

---

the vāyu. Sometimes it is said that at the end of meditating on the central eye of Akṣobhya, one should meditate on a pink flame inside of the empty body.

embracing his consort Samayatārā, the purified element of air. Their faces, hands, and accouterments are the same as the other couples. All methods of meditating on the vāyu are the same as before. All the consorts' colors are the same as the fathers' colors. Also, they all hold curved knives in their right hands and skulls filled with blood in their left hands. If the instruction is going to take a long time, then one should spend* three days on each. Medium is five, and average is nine days.

The meditation upon the pale-red fire in the middle of the empty body is as follows: After performing the preliminaries, imagine that inside of one's empty body, a pale-red fire fills the entire body, shedding it like the outer coat of a cow or a horse. {474} Unify the upper and lower vāyus and meditate in counted sessions and without breaks.†

The meditation of the third empowerment is as follows: After performing the preliminaries, in front of oneself meditated on as Heruka, imagine an attractive and youthful human maiden, who in essence is either Nairātmyā or Lady Vajrayoginī or Māmakī. The flesh of her upper body is very firm, her breasts are prominent, the flesh of her lower body is very ample and round, and her waist and wrists are narrow. Her hair is yellow and hangs down. Imagine that one enters into union with her. If the bindu seems to be in danger of being lost, draw it up with *hūṃ* and meditate. Otherwise, it is said that one should protect it with a wide-open stare. As such, after the seven vāyu yogas (for following the path of the prāṇa and āyāma), generate the four experiences with the meditation of the four paths: First, following the meditation on shape in the generation stage, meditate on caṇḍālī. Following that, also meditate on the path method of the maṇḍalacakra.

Following that, meditate on the path of arresting the three vajra waves:

*Sometimes, if those are not clear, since there is an obstacle to remove, it is done as follows: Since the guru dissolves into the crown of the pledged deity that one visualizes, at the navel there is a yellow *sva*; at the heart, a blue *hūṃ*; at the throat, a red *āḥ*; at the crown, a white *oṃ*; and at the secret place, a green *hāṃ*. These syllables transform and are visualized in this respective order as Ratnasambhava, Akṣobhya, Amitābha, Vairocana, and Amoghasiddhi couples. The qualities are the generation of the ultimate samādhi of appearance and emptiness. The fault [to be removed] is: if there is an ugly mark on the body, it will be removed. The ultimate measure is that the signs of cognizance and appearance arise, for example, Meditator of Nag, Sönam Gyaltsen [Nag bsgoms bSod nams rgyal mtshan, direct disciple of Sachen Kunga Nyingpo].

†If one is performing the medium instruction, begin with the seven vāyu visualizations and the caṇḍālī. When this instruction is performed, also here, there is the instruction for the fire blazing up and coming out from the secret place.

After performing the preliminaries, in front of oneself as any Heruka-pledged deity, whichever one finds pleasing, meditate on the mudra in the form of Lady Vajrayoginī or Nairātmyā, who is either like a padminī or a deer. Her flesh and veins are reddish yellow, her feet and hands are red, her yellow hair hangs down, the flesh of her upper body is firm, her breasts are prominent, and the flesh of her lower body {475} is ample and round. Her waist is no more than the size of her wrists. Her voice is like the song of a cuckoo. Imagine entering into union with one such as her.* After one's bindu arrives in the vast space of the mother, both the white and red bindus dissolve separately into the *haṃ* through each one's central nāḍī. Think that the dependent origination of the four movements is complete. Unite the upper and lower vāyus and meditate.

After performing the preliminaries, in front of oneself is a qualified knowledge consort.† Imagine the consort as explained above. Focus on her brow and meditate by uniting the upper and lower vāyus. Focus on the throat, heart, navel, and also the secret place, and meditate, uniting the upper and lower vāyus. One can also draw a picture of those [deities in the five places] and meditate on them.

Following the path instruction on the concentration of the prāṇa and āyāma, generate the four experiences through meditating on the four paths. Following that, in the first gathering of the elements, though there is the path instruction on the signs of heat of the vāyu and caṇḍālī, as above, since it is said to begin with those here, after performing the preliminaries, draw the knees up to the chest, interlaced like a checker pattern. The buttocks should be elevated about four fingerbreadths in this system. The arms should be like a meditation belt, and within the enclosure of the soles of the feet, there is a secondary hollow or a double-stacked triangle. {476} Having imagined this either way, the fire licks up inside the major nāḍī of the thighs. The fire is visualized to reach four fingerbreadths above the secret place. Draw the lower door up, push down, draw up again,‡ push down

*Sometimes, if there is a risk of losing the bindu, it should be prevented with the method of a wide-open stare. Among one's three nāḍīs, the right nāḍī is red, the left nāḍī is white, and the central nāḍī is white outside and red inside. The lower tip of the three nāḍīs pierces the secret vajra. The upper tip is imagined to enter the *hūṃ*. Both the red and the white bindus are imagined dissolving into the *haṃ*s inside of one's three nāḍīs. It is also said that there is no way to measure the loss of the bindu.

†Sometimes this is not mentioned.

‡Sometimes it is said that first one pushes down on the upper vāyu, and then one pulls the

again, and [finally] push the stale vāyu out, drawing it up from the ground and constricting the lower door. Push down the upper vāyu, focus on the fire, and meditate without counted sessions or session breaks. The name of this is "the fire blazing from the secret place."

After performing the preliminaries, above the fire in the secret place,* imagine a ball of flame the size of a sheep dung pellet. Also imagine a ball of flame the size of a sheep dung pellet in front of the navel. By merely uniting the upper and lower vāyus, the two balls of fire meet. Imagine the entire interior of the body filled with twilight-red fire. When exhaling, imagine the two balls of fire arrive separately at their sites; meditate without either counted sessions or session breaks. The name of this is "the struggle of the two bindus." {477} Since after this point it is said that there are neither counted sessions nor session breaks, it is also said that up to this point there are neither counted sessions nor session breaks.

After performing all the preliminaries, there are eight fingerbreadths in general between the two bindus, one on top of the other, above the fire of the secret place. When arriving in front of the navel, a fire wheel is imagined to arrive within three fingerbreadths of the kidneys, without touching them. By simply uniting the upper and lower vāyus, visualize that fire wheel spinning rapidly to the left and press down on the vāyu. Further, imagine in front† a consort who is attractive and youthful, as explained above. But it is not said one should focus on her here in particular. Visualize the general form and press down the vāyu for one session. In the same way, in the twelve visualizations for the fire wheel, there are twelve visualizations for the consort, thus, one can meditate twenty-four visualizations in one session, meditating in four sessions. The name of this is the "fire wheel."

---

lower vāyu up. At this time there is no counting. If one is practicing the long instruction, it is necessary to count the fire blazing up from the secret place from here. Without counting the vāyu in one session, then count twelve, and so on, in pairs. Without exceeding that and without visualization, hold the vāyu for one session without counting. Without counting in the same way, hold the vāyu twelve times. Sometimes count up to twelve and in a session of vāyu, the held vāyu is pressed down twelve times. The session of uncounted [vāyus] is held twelve times. Thus in a single session, there are twenty-four holds [uncounted or] counted in a single session and meditated in four sessions.

*Sometimes it is said that all these are counted yantras, uncounted yantras, and so on, as above. The visualization is the fighting bindus. At the end of an exhalation, two bindus are stacked on top of each other in the secret place.

†Sometimes it is said that at the hub of both wheels, there are two *hūṃ*s, but one does not visualize an external consort. One meditates as above, with and without counting.

After performing the preliminaries, as explained above, below the navel on the four tips of a fire wheel, there are four *hūṃ*s, one fingerbreadth in size, which are the nature of fire. Sometimes, imagine that the fire twists around the *hūṃ*s, blazing even more. Whether there are *hūṃ*s or not, on the spokes of the wheel, there is no difference from the [prior description] without them. After performing the preliminaries, imagine two *hūṃ*s each on the four spokes of the fire wheel, for a total of eight. Visualize the wheel spinning to the left and the consort. The number and length of sessions is the same as above.

After performing all the preliminaries, on each tip of the wheel imagine four vertical red *hūṃ*s, {478} which meet at the head, facing inward toward the wheel.* Imagine five flames, four fingerbreadths high, in the center of the wheel, and meditate. Otherwise, the number of sessions and everything else is the same as before. The name of this is the "blazing fire." When the four *hūṃ*s are applied to the consort, the four joys are indicated. When the eight *hūṃ*s are applied to the joys, the eight joys are indicated. When the sixteen *hūṃ*s are applied to the bindus, the sixteen joys are indicated.

After performing the preliminaries, the five flames, which are four fingerbreadths above the wheel at the navel, do not rise higher than that.† After the spokes spread out, there are six edges, like the shape of a discus weapon. On each edge is a *hūṃ*, one fingerbreadth in size, {479} for a total of six. By merely uniting the upper and lower vāyus, the lower wheel will not spin. That upper wheel of fire with six edges is imagined to move toward the right and move toward the left during the same session. Further, after visualizing

*Sometimes it is said to imagine four *hūṃ*s and a tine on each tip of the fire wheel. One does not imagine the fire at the center of the wheel. Counting or not is the same as before. If the portion of bliss is too small, since bliss is the path of Secret Mantra, it is said that one must enhance the bliss from time to time. If bliss is small, one should imagine a consort of one's preference, who is attractive and youthful. When meditating, whether counting or not, focus the mind on her from time to time.

†Sometimes the tip of the wheel is four fingerbreadths. For the fifth, the fire is the size of the index finger, imagined as five blazing fingers. Everything else is as before. This is said to be the wheel of fire. Also, sometimes at the end of this, after the fire blazes, it blazes up to the heart. If the fiery nature of *hūṃ* is weak, imagine it fills the interior of the body like rainfall and meditate, but do not imagine your retinue. All the other methods are the same as before. Sometimes, those five flames grow upward, reaching the throat. Imagine there is a rainfall from the *āḥ* that is the nature of fire. Once the tips [of the wheel] spread out, it has six edges like the shape of discus weapon. All the other visualizations being the same as before, sometimes that fire at the throat is imagined to be a fire that leaves from one's brahma aperture, and all existents of the universe and beings blaze with fire. The name of this is the "blazing fire."

the consort as explained above, press the wind down for one session. Further, after the inner fire wheel arises, visualize that it fills the entire body. Thus, there are twelve inside, as above, and those are alternated with the twelve visualizations of the consort, as above.

After performing all the preliminaries, above one's navel a fire wheel arises and blazes four fingerbreadths above the heart. Also, there are sparks that issue forth, sparks of fire in the form of vowels and consonants. Moreover, imagine the sparks are created in the form of the vowels and consonants. Hold the vāyu for one session. Further, visualize the entire body filled with fire and hold the vāyu for one session. As such, each of twelve sessions are performed in the same way as the twenty-four sessions, as above. However, it is said there is no reason to visualize the external consort here.

After performing all the preliminaries, above the fire in one's throat, which resembles a sixteen-petaled lotus, there are five flaming tongues of red fire. Imagine they blaze up, nearing the *haṃ*. Suppress the vāyu and meditate in counted sessions, as above. After performing the preliminaries, hold the vāyu for one session. Focus on the body filled with fire for one session, and also suppress the vāyu for one session. As already explained, focus on the external consort. As such, this is the method of meditation with counted sessions, as above. {480}

After performing the preliminaries, visualize the blazing fire to be the size of the billion-world universe, and perform the vāyu yogas, as before. The fire blazes and blazes more. It is then called "a blaze the size of the billion-world universe."

As such, "to gradually give a reward to the vāyu," if those seven visualizations of the vāyu for finding the path of concentration of prāṇa and āyāma are performed concisely, it is the third gathering of the elements. Here, since it is the extensive instruction, they are not included in any of the three gatherings of the elements, because the path of the concentration of prāṇa and āyāma is a preliminary practice.

By meditating on the vāyu and caṇḍālī with the path instruction of the first gathering of the elements, the signs of the vāyu and caṇḍālī are that the nāḍīs unravel, because the vāyu is reversed. Because of that, the blazing fire of caṇḍālī melts the bodhicitta element, and the experience of connate bliss is generated.

If that does not arouse bliss, then in the middle gathering of the elements, the method of arousing bliss at that time is the path instruction of the experience of bliss and emptiness of the bindu in the middle gathering of the elements. Having seen beforehand one or ten human maidens who are attractive, youthful, and passionate, imagine that a drape is placed in front of oneself. Recall the wrathful yoginī, and after that ignite the fire of passion. The bindu descends. Its loss is prevented with an open gaze, and this is kept secret. Among these four, first, to ignite the fire of passion is as follows: Listen to the sound of her falsetto singing and her play, look at her form, and arouse whatever connate bliss one can. If that does not arouse bliss, there is the descent of the bindu: Place one's two thumbs on each palm, make fists, and cross them at the chest. Stare into space with both eyes and shake all parts of the body. Then, if a portion of the bindu is lost, the method for preventing that with a wide-open stare is {481} performed as before with the eyes and hands. The navel is pressed to the spine. Shake the upper body. To "keep the secret," if one is a mantrin, then do not abide in the innate [bliss]. If one is an ascetic, do not imagine the mudra behind the curtain.

As such, until bliss arises, one should meditate without counted sessions or session breaks. There is no need to suppress the vāyu. If one practices like that, if the sixteen joys arise, that is sufficient. If they do not arise, one must practice in the following way: After performing the preliminaries, a blue vāyu leaves from both nostrils. Imagine the consort behind the curtain, as above. When the vāyu leaves the two nostrils, it returns to the secret place. Again the vāyu leaves through one's nostrils. As such, repeat[7] without counted sessions or session breaks.

After performing the preliminaries, imagine the consort behind a curtain in front. Without touching her body, imagine that one speaks words of passion to her about horses, donkeys, and so on, and gazes at her erogenous zones, such as her brow, throat, breasts, navel, and pudenda. Frolic, jest, speak passionate words, and look at her form. Listen to her voice. Since the fire of passion is ignited in that way, if a measure of bindu is lost after bliss arises, protect with the method of the wide-open gaze, as above.

Next, to keep the secret, do not imagine that one enters into union with the consort. It is not necessary to hold the vāyu. Meditate without session breaks.* {482} One should train on [hearing] her voice without seeing her and, following that, train on seeing her form.

*It is said that from the perspective of the consort, among the four, the training on the karma mudra is the physical consort upon whom the mantrin relies. The secret training of the dharma mudra is focusing on the nāḍī when meditating. The gnosis mudra, training on the self-appearing knowledge consort, is imagining that the consort is actually present, as in this

Next, having performed the preliminaries, one should imagine the attractive and youthful consort as the queen, and imagine rubbing her breasts, hearing her laughter, and so on, igniting the fire of passion. If bliss arises through that, and if there is a significant loss after the bindu descends, prevent it with the wide-open gaze, as before. Keeping the secret is that one should at present engage in union.

After performing the preliminaries, one should imagine that the space of the consort and one's own secret place[8] barely touch. However, at this time do not engage in insertion and copulation. Since the fire of passion is ignited, if there is a measurable loss after the bindu descends, prevent it with the wide-open gaze, as before. Keeping the secret is not allowing the loss of bindu.

If the connate gnosis does not arise after rousing joy and the joy of separation, having performed the preliminaries, since it is necessary to possess the four topics above, first, since passion is ignited and one engages in insertion and copulation, if there is a measurable loss of bindu once it descends,[*] one should prevent loss with the wide-open stare. Keeping the secret is not allowing any loss of bindu.

The method of arousing the connate gnosis if it does not arise is as follows: After performing the preliminaries, since the four topics above are necessary, after one has first ignited the fire of passion and engaged in union, the method of causing the bindu to descend is to engage in insertion and copulation. After the bindu descends, when both partners either lose it or do not lose it, both prevent loss with the method of prevention of the wide-open gaze.[†] {483} At that time, if any signs occur, the rectum will spasm or the hairs of the skin will stand up.

When both bindus of the bodies are lost, since the sensation of the bindu is unbearable, there is a sound of moaning. When such bliss occurs, there is the method of unifying it with emptiness. If one presses the external carotid artery with the fingers, because one becomes nonconceptual, that is called "arousing connate gnosis." Both partners not losing the bindu is called "keeping the secret." Consequently, the path instruction of the experience

---

instruction. Mahāmudrā is training in nonduality. In this system, it is the time of accomplishing the first half of the thirteenth stage. Also, here, the guru said that this is held to be so only for the knowledge consort.

[*] This is the Path with Its Result's own approach.

[†] This is said to be the system of the Hevajra tradition.

of bliss and emptiness of the bindu in the middle gathering of the elements is complete.

Now, if the samādhi of the union of appearance and emptiness does not arise, now, for the final gathering of the elements, the path instruction of the faultless, fundamental gnosis is traveling the bank of a lake or a pond and performing the preliminaries. A shadow of a tree or a rock will arise on the lake or pond. Look at the shadow that arises in the morning and disappears in the afternoon. Further, rest the mind in peaceful relaxation. Again, look at the rock or the tree and meditate. Again rest the mind in peaceful relaxation. Repeat[9] those three. It is said that if one engages in this instruction for a long time (one should meditate on each of those for one day) that will arouse the samādhi of the union of bliss and emptiness.

If the samādhi of the union of a clear consciousness and emptiness does not arise, the method of arousing it is that one should visualize a cairn on the ground, which is an arm span in height in front of oneself, and meditate with the eyes closed. Rest the mind in peaceful relaxation. That will arouse the samādhi of the union of a clear consciousness and emptiness.

If the prior instructions do not arouse the samādhi of the union of physical bliss and emptiness, to make it arise if one is ordained, one should imagine a gnosis consort. If there is an actual consort (the karma mudra) then she should disrobe and one should focus one's mind on her brow and meditate. Rest one's mind in peaceful relaxation. If [the samādhi of the union of physical bliss and emptiness] is not aroused by that, then, in the same way, {484} focus on her breasts, navel, and genitalia, and rest one's mind in peaceful relaxation. Repeatedly alternate those. That will arouse the samādhi of the union of physical bliss and emptiness. That is the natural entryway of the fundamental mind, the essence of the unmodified mind, and the samādhi of the final gathering of the elements, in which the experience of bliss and emptiness arises without [a distinction between] equipoise and post-equipoise.

If there is no clairvoyance at that time, the method of generating it is following the bindu's descent through the three nāḍīs into the space of the mother (that one has looked at as above) and drawing the bindu upward in the three nāḍīs. If one wishes for clairvoyant sight, also draw the bindu in to the two nāḍīs of the eyes. If one wishes for clairvoyant smell, again and again draw the bindu in to the two nāḍīs of the nose. If one wishes for clairvoyant hearing, again and again draw the bindu in to the two nāḍīs of the ears. If one wishes for clairvoyant taste, again and again draw the bindu in to the two nāḍīs of the uvula. If one wishes for mental clairvoyance, imagine the bindu spreads all over the body. That will definitely generate clairvoyance.

After the path instruction of concentration through prāṇa and āyāma, one meditates on the four paths and arouses the four experiences. Following that, there is the path instruction of meditating on the signs of heat of the vāyus and caṇḍālī in the first gathering of the elements. Following that, there is the path instruction of the experience of the bliss and emptiness of the bindu in the middle gathering of the elements. Following that, there is the path instruction of the faultless, fundamental gnosis in the final gathering of the elements. If one is performing the concise instruction, one engages only in the seven vāyu yogas. The system of that instruction is following the path of concentration through prāṇa and āyāma in the first gathering of the elements. Follow the five middle vāyu yogas—the three exhalations, and so on—in the middle gathering of the elements. The yoga in the final gathering of the elements is following the path of zhiwa śāntika. At that time, though the three faultless experiences arise in one of best capacity, the following instructions are enough for all training. There is no need for [more] instructions.

If those of medium capacity practice the medium instruction, they follow the path of concentration through prāṇa and āyāma in the first gathering of the elements. {485} In the middle gathering of the elements, they follow the path of concentration with the six vāyu yogas, including zhiwa śāntika union. In the final gathering of the elements, they follow the path of concentration with the caṇḍālī based on the key points of intimate instructions. At that time, though the three faultless experiences arise, the following instructions are sufficient for all training. There is no need for [additional] instructions.

If one is performing the extensive instruction, the general opinion is to do everything in the following way: After the seven vāyu yogas, there is no preliminary other than the instruction beforehand not included in the three gatherings of the elements. No matter which path instruction is performed, extensive or concise, after any of the three faultless experiences arises, it is unnecessary to give instructions, as there are no other trainings. The guru has said, "The three movements of the seven vāyu yogas above condensed into one are called 'prāṇāyāma.'" After tricking prāṇāyāma by gradually giving it a reward, if one wishes for the vāyu to rest, since all adjustments to the vāyu are methods of causing the vayu to rest, it is said that one should "understand that one should give a reward during all seven vāyu yogas."

Not understanding [why] sometimes it occurs that the lower vāyu [is automatically held], I asked about the definite approach of the system of the Path with Its Result. Rinpoche said, "The explanations of those differences are methods of instances of instructions. Those will certainly be shown to you now. Practice them sincerely. If this causes any qualities to arise, merely holding the upper vāyu binds the lower vāyu. When this occurs, the lower vāyu becomes balanced. For as long as it is not balanced, if the merchant of the lower vāyu has not sold all their wares beforehand, the qualities will not arise, problems in the sides [of the body] will arise, and so on.

Advice on the Intimate Instructions of the Four Experiences

Tashi Pal {485}

oṃ svasti

Homage to the sublime gurus. Among the four experiences at the time of practicing the instructions of the Path with Its Result, there are dream experiences, physical experiences, mental experiences, and visionary experiences.

First, at the time of prāṇāyāma, if one dreams of a raven pecking the head of a magpie, the vāyu and mind are gathered evenly in the smoke-colored *duḥ* syllable of the animals. This is an experience of a dream of one being empowered by the all-basis. If one dreams of wearing white felt with a black spot, this is a sign of the arising of a contamination. Further, because it is a dream indicating lack of faith or devotion for one's own guru, {486} the method of removing that is to imagine that the guru in whom one lacks devotion is laughing in the sky in front of oneself. Also, focusing on one's brow repeatedly will remove that [contamination].

If one has a dream in which one thinks that one is seated in the middle of an empty plain and one is afraid of an enemy, it is a dream experience of the vāyu and mind gathering evenly in the yellow *muḥ* syllable of the asuras. If one dreams of traveling on a red river, it is a dream experience of the vāyu arrested in its own place. If one dreams of one's father, mother, or relatives, it is a dream experience of the vāyu and mind gathering at the lower tip of the right nāḍī. This is called "the warmth of past concepts." If one dreams of bugs, it is a dream experience of the vāyu and mind gathering at the lower tip of the central nāḍī. This is called the "face of the ḍākinī."

In the four experiences in the section on the three exhalations, if in one's dream experience one dreams of traveling through a great fire, having a fever, and so on, this is a dream experience of the fire vāyu in the throat arrested in its own place. If one dreams that one is the warden of a jail, this is a dream experience of the vāyu and mind evenly gathering in the blue *nri* syllable. Also, when one rests on one's side, if one has a dream such as the advent of a great emanation, this is a dream experience of the vāyu and mind gathering evenly inside the right nāḍī and does not [indicate] a ghost.

In physical experience, if there is [a sensation] of blazing up on the right side, this is called the "increase of the male vāyu." Since this is based on the right channel and since the male vāyu moves in the thumb, this is that [physical] experience. If one dreams of dying alone, this is a dream experience of the vāyu and mind gathering in the nāḍī of the thumb. This is called "the nāḍī of the ghost of suffering and misery." If one dreams that one rides a blue horse, this is a dream experience of the air vāyu being arrested.

In the four experiences at the occasion of the two inhalations (inhaling through the mouth, and so on), if in one's dream experience one dreams that a building arises on the crown of one's head, this is a dream experience of the blood obtained from the mother gathering upward in one's crown. If one dreams, thinking that a building is pure white at midnight, this is a dream experience of a small portion of the white bodhicitta from the father gathering inside the central nāḍī.

Among the four experiences in the section on union, or zhiwa śāntika, {487} if one dreams of frogs and daikon,[10] the vāyu and mind have gathered evenly in the smoke-colored *duḥ* syllable, which resembles a frog leg and a daikon; that is, it is a dream experience through the power of the all-basis. If one dreams of sinking in a swamp and being unable to get free or being composed from soil, and so on, this is a dream experience through the power of the all-basis, because the earth vāyu has taken its place in the navel. If one dreams of roping an ox, the vāyu and mind have gathered slightly inside the *ni* syllable, which is in the upper body pervaded by all the nāḍīs of samsara and nirvana, like a rope of many fine threads resembling the form of roots, with which one binds an ox. This is a dream experience through the power of the all-basis. If one dreams of scowling human heads appearing before oneself, the vāyu and mind have gathered slightly in countless syllables, other than the fourteen syllables. This is a dream experience through the power of the all-basis. If one dreams of one's lost bindu filling the pleats of one's clothes, and if it is the left side of one's clothes, this indicates the left nāḍī. If one dreams the right side of the clothes are filled, then it is a dream experience of the white bodhicitta located in the right nāḍī. If one dreams that one's body is enveloped by a snake, this is a dream experience of the vāyu and mind gathering slightly in the knots of the right and left nāḍīs after they are slightly freed, like being unbound by a snake. If one dreams that one races very quickly to the moon, like a horse, this is a dream experience of the air vāyu arrested in its own place. At this time, if a dream has not already arisen, this is a dream experience of the vāyu and mind gathering in the wisdom *a* of the mother.

Meditating on the shape [of the body] gradually generates the four experiences through meditating on the four paths. The first of those is the four dream experiences in the section focusing on the eye of Akṣobhya. If one dreams of entering hot water, {488} this is a dream experience of the water vāyu arrested in its own place, the heart. This is the dream experience among the four experiences [described] in the section of the blazing pale-red fire inside the empty body. If it does not arise, the so-called Path with Its Result system extols "the experience of the four dependent originations."

For the dream experiences, among the four experiences in the section on the meditation of the third empowerment's path of method, if one dreams of distributing water in a field, reciting a verse, or seeing a field, the earth vāyu and the water vāyu are slightly arrested in their own place. If one dreams that one acts passionately in a group of women and some are pleased and some are not pleased, this is the arising of an impurity or contamination of samaya in oneself from past lives. Therefore, it is said that every day one must recite the one-hundred-syllable mantra twenty-one times. If a pure white color arises in the evening, this is not an experience of the bindu.

For the dream experiences among the four experiences in the section on immobilization in the three vajra waves, if one dreams of luminous relics, stupas, or parasols arising in one's feces, this is a dream experience of the slight mixing of both the pure part of one's feces and the white bodhicitta. If one dreams of flying, this is a dream experience of the air vāyu being slightly arrested in its own place. If one has dreams of terror and fear of being carried away by an enemy, this is a dream experience of being terrified and frightened even though one is surrounded by one hundred gurus at the time when the vāyu and mind gather slightly in the two nāḍīs above one's kidneys, which resemble a ram's horns. These are called "the nāḍīs of terror and fear."

The four experiences in the section on the fire blazing in the secret place arise as dream experiences. If one dreams that a red rock arises and one hides or flees, this is a dream experience of the slight gathering of the red bodhicitta. If one dreams of assisting a half-clothed woman, this is a dream experience of the vāyu and mind slightly abiding in the lower tip of the central nāḍī. This is called the "face of the ḍākinī." {489}

Among the four experiences of the struggle of the two bindus, the air vāyu being arrested in its own place, which is located behind the line of hair below the navel, is a physical experience. If one dreams of many grandchildren in space surrounding a guru engaged in a consecration, some will call them devaputras and others will say they are dharmapālas, but they are neither. In this tradition, Akṣobhya and the guru are inseparable. The seed syllable in the heart is a dark-blue *hūṃ*. After the bodhicitta descends slightly, because it arrives below and it gathers inside the blue *ni* syllable of the navel, this is a dream experience through the power of the all-basis.

Among the four experiences in the section on the two *hūṃ*s that are on each spoke of a fire wheel, if one thinks one's body has become larger, this is a physical experience of the air vāyu being arrested in its own place. If one dreams of sitting among many beggars, this is an experience of the gathering of vāyu and the impure part of bodhicitta, rather than the gathering of the pure part.

For the dream experience among the four experiences in the section on the four *hūṃ*s that are on each spoke of the fire wheel, if one dreams of eating human flesh or brains, though it is a sign of purifying misdeeds, this is also an experience of the vāyu and mind gathering in the *a* of the wisdom mother through the power of the all-basis. If one dreams of a man shooting an arrow, this is a dream experience of the vāyu and mind gathering in the yellow *suḥ* syllable of the asuras.

For the dreams among the four experiences in the section of the five blazing flames, if one dreams of mounting one's horse, then traveling inside a dog, goat, or sheep, and the dog is stopped by a girl, and also one goes to that girl, this is a dream experience of the blood obtained from the mother gathering slightly in the smoke-colored *duḥ* syllable of animals through the power of the all-basis. When one rides that horse, the air vāyu is arrested in its own place.

For the dream experience among the four experiences in the section on the blazing fire of the blazing *hūṃ* that issues from the five flames, if one dreams of dusk, this is a dream experience through the power of the all-basis, signifying that the white and red bodhicitta have gathered slightly in the central nāḍī. {490} That is said to be like dusk, an outer sign in the section of obtaining butter elsewhere.[11]

For dreams among the four experiences in the section on imagining the so-called blazing great fire reaching the throat and descending on the *a* syllable, if one dreams one rides a horse or that one goes to a tall castle, this is an experience of the air vāyu and the earth vāyu being slightly arrested in their own places.

For the dream experience among the four experiences in the section on everything blazing with fire, if one dreams of making heroes' offerings following donning the dharma robes, the accouterments of an ascetic, this is an experience of the dependent origination of the central nāḍī, the white bodhicitta slightly abiding in the nāḍī of *hūṃ*, which is the palace of the *ya tha da* of the six cakras. Since this is the nāḍī of *hūṃ*, it is a hero. Since the central nāḍī is sitting under the Bodhi tree, this indicates asceticism.

That advice on the intimate instructions of the four experiences
was set down in writing by Tashi Pal
in order to benefit the fortunate.
I request the forbearance of the guru and the ḍākinīs.

The Manual of the Path with Its Result instructions of the lineage from the precious guru [Dorje Gyalpo] are complete.
Ithi. Virtue. *Śubhaṃ.*

19. The Manual of the Three Purities

The Intention of the Vajrapañjara Tantra[1]

Chögyal Phakpa Lodrö Gyaltsen {492}

The last text presented in this volume was composed by Drogön Chögyal Phakpa ('Gro dgon chos rgyal 'phags pa, 1235–1280), the seventh Sakya throne holder, the fifth of the Sakya founders, and notably the nephew of Sakya Paṇḍita (Sa skya paṇḍita Kun dga rgyal mtshan, 1182–1251), one of the most well-known figures in the political history of Tibet due to his relationship with the founder of the Yuan Dynasty of China, Kublai Khan (1216–1294).[2]

Although *The Manual of the Three Purities* does not form part of the usual curriculum of the Path with Its Result, the practices described in its pages are drawn from that system. The three purities, which are also described in texts such as Amezhab's *Opening the Eye to the Concealed*, and so on, include the purity of suchness, which examines the view described in the Hevajra cycle of tantras; the individual purity of the deities, which is related to the creation stage; and the purity of intrinsic cognizance, which is based on completion stage practices.

oṃ svasti siddhaṃ

Homage to the feet of the sublime guru.

From the two topics in the preliminaries of the path, gathering merit is as follows: Be seated on a comfortable cushion in an isolated place. Go for refuge to the guru and the Three Jewels three times, thinking, "I should attain buddhahood for the benefit of all sentient beings. For that purpose I will gather the accumulation of merit," and cultivate bodhicitta for a long while.

Next, with the *svabhāva* mantra, meditate that the place where one is seated is empty. From the state of emptiness arises *bhrūṃ*, from which arises a precious celestial mansion, in which there is a great, precious throne, upon which is piled a seat of a lotus, sun, and moon. On this seat is seated the sublime guru, the embodiment of all buddhas of the three times. Imagine that all lineage gurus and all buddhas and bodhisattvas of the ten directions surround the sublime guru.

Next, imagining that countless emanations of one's body and all sentient beings together prostrate, say *namo guru bhyaḥ, namo buddhāya, namo dharmāya, namas saṃgāya* and prostrate. Then, recite *oṃ arghaṃ pādyaṃ vajra puṣpe āḥ hūṃ vajra dhūppe āḥ hūṃ vajra āloke āḥ hūṃ vajra gandhe āḥ hūṃ vajra naividye āḥ hūṃ*, and imagine the outer offerings are presented.

Next, after arranging a seven-heap maṇḍala, recite, "In the center is Sumeru, the king of mountains. {493} Videha is in the east. Jambudvīpa is in the south. Godaniya is in the west. Kurava is in the north. There is a sun, a moon, and the abundant wealth of devas and humans." Imagine that is presented with devotion to the sublime guru.

Next, in order to purify misdeeds, on top of one's head is a *hūṃ*, which melts into a white vajra marked with a *hūṃ*, from which arises white Vajrasattva, with one face and two hands, which hold a vajra and a bell and embrace the mother. The mother, white Vajragarvi, embraces the father, while holding a curved knife and a skull cup. Both are adorned with bone ornaments and jewels. Imagine *oṃ* at their foreheads, *āḥ* at their throats, and *hūṃ* at their hearts. With *jaḥ hūṃ baṃ hoḥ*, all buddhas dissolve nondually [into those syllables]. Since one offers the supplication, "Please purify all my misdeeds and obscurations," there is a stream of gnosis amṛta. Imagine that all one's outer and inner misdeeds and taints are purified. Recite: *oṃ śrī vajraheruka samayam anupālaya heruka tvenopatiṣṭha dṛḍho me bhava sutoṣyo me bhava anurakto me bhava supoṣyo me bhava sarva* {494} *siddhiṃ me prayaccha sarva karmasu ca me cittaṃ śreya kuru hūṃ ha ha ha ha ho bhagavān vajraheruka ma me muñca heruko 'bhava mahāsamayasatva āḥ hūṃ phaṭ*.

At the conclusion, however many times this is recited, Vajrasattva dissolves into oneself. Dedicate saying, "With that root of virtue, may all sentient beings obtain buddhahood." By saying *oṃ vajra muḥ*, the guru and retinue disperse to their natural abodes. One should engage in this until the misdeeds are purified and there are signs of increasing merit. These are the preliminary activities.

Next is the main section. When the purities are included in three, to begin, the principle of the view and the meditation on the purity of suchness is that when one first examines all inner and outer phenomena, directions and time do not exist; when directions and time are distinguished, singleness is not established; and when singleness does not exist, multiplicity does not arise. Since singleness and multiplicity do not exist, existence is not established. When there is no existence, a nonexistence dependent on that cannot be established. Since the nature of all phenomena is not established as entities that either exist or do not exist and are free from proliferation, the nature of one's mind is termed "free from proliferation." Having eliminated doubt through hearing and reflection, when one meditates, sit on a comfortable seat with the legs crossed.

The first limb is going for refuge to the guru and the Three Jewels. The second limb is the cultivation of bodhicitta with the thought, "I should attain buddhahood for the benefit of all sentient beings. For that purpose, I will remain in equipoise on reality." The third limb is instantly visualizing one's body in the appearance of the pledged deity, natureless like a reflection in a mirror, and remaining in equipoise upon that for a while. The fourth limb is that after one meditates on the sublime guru upon one's head, one cultivates intense devotion by thinking that the guru is the embodiment of all buddhas. {495}

Next is the fifth limb, the main subject: Having eliminated proliferation concerning all phenomena, which lack inherent existence, once all concepts vanish on their own, like clouds dispersing in the sky or ice melting on the water, remain in equipoise in a state of nonconceptuality. Focus on the mind and meditate without grasping; there is nothing to meditate on apart from that. The sixth limb is the first limb of the conclusion: Cultivate intense compassion by thinking, "How sad it is that all sentient beings who are lost in the ocean of the suffering of samsara have not realized the absence of inherent existence of all phenomena." The seventh limb is the second limb of the conclusion: Dedicate by saying, "With this root of virtue, may I and all sentient beings obtain the stage of perfect buddhahood!"

As such, these seven limbs are [the section on] equipoise. When entering into various activities after rising from equipoise, think that all apparent, audible, and sensible phenomena appear while lacking inherent existence, resembling dreams and illusions. Whatever appearances are encountered should be experienced without attachment or clinging to anything, without being pleased or displeased by good and bad or happiness and suffering. As such, through cultivating the purity of suchness, one's view will not become distorted. Having given rise to nonconceptual gnosis devoid of characteristics and concepts, transcendent gnosis will arise. This is the practice of the purity of suchness.

Next, the culmination of meditating on the creation stage of the purity of the individual deities is to meditate on either the complete maṇḍala or any deity, such as the solitary hero. {496} The body is cross-legged, the hands are in the gesture of equipoise, and the spine is straightened. Clearly visualize all the aspects of the deity as apparent and natureless, like reflections in a mirror. Focus solely on the specific appearance of the middle eye. If this is not clear, then gaze at a drawing and visualize it. If it does not become clearer, then draw the central eye on one's own forehead, and place a mirror in front of oneself that is not too close or too far, not too high or too low, and gaze at it. Close the eyes again and meditate. Look again. Meditate again. Through such repetitions, the visualization will become clear.

Next, think that one has a central eye, and remain in equipoise for as long as one wishes, meditating for as long as one is not distracted. Then focus on the three eyes, meditating as before. Then, after one meditates on the whole head, the whole body, the seat, and the maṇḍala, meditate on the deities of the maṇḍala, the celestial mansion, and the protection wheel, as before. Train until there are no distractions while cultivating the samādhi of the central eye. As such, clearly visualize oneself generated as the deity. Also meditate on all external entities as one's excellent deity and remain in equipoise. Through cultivating and developing that, one should meditate on and cultivate all that one can see as the deity.

Next, increase the size of one's meditation deity and maṇḍala and in the end meditate that they fill all worlds. Then gradually reduce the size of the maṇḍala, making it smaller and smaller, and in the end meditate on the deity or the full maṇḍala as extremely tiny, the size of a mustard seed. The stages of visualization for that {497} are also the meditations, such as the visualization of the central eye until one becomes more and more familiar. Cultivate those. Meditate that a mustard-seed-sized deity and maṇḍala fill the vast universe without the universe becoming larger or the form of the deity becoming smaller. Meditate until the cultivation of that samādhi comes to a conclusion. In the same way, meditate that an extremely vast maṇḍala is found inside something as small as a mustard seed, without the deity and maṇḍala becoming smaller or the mustard seed becoming larger. Also, those aspects of the deity are apparent aspects, empty by nature, meditated on as the union [of appearance and emptiness]. The visualization is accomplished in that way and that is the culmination of the creation stage. This is the culmination of meditating on the creation stage of the purity of the individual deities.

Next, to meditate on intrinsic cognizance, to begin, train with the nine limbs of concentration. Be seated on a comfortable seat in an isolated place. Prior to all [the following physical purifications], inhale the vāyu and unify it. Then, as it is said:

> Rotate the head and neck.
> Wave the two arms.
> Strongly shake the two legs.
> This is the training of the five limbs.

As such, perform this until the signs of training arise, such as the body becoming comfortable and light, diseases of the limbs becoming totally purified, and so on. This is the physical training. The training of the voice is remaining silent without performing any activities, such as chanting, mantra recitations, discussions, and so on.

The training of the mind is relaxing the mind while engaging in mental activities with the mind, such as thinking of worldly activities, thinking of dharma, thinking of love and compassion, and so on. Since one meditates on those three trainings for a month or a year, it is possible that [various] types of samādhi will arise based on them. {498}

There are three crucial points. First is the crucial point of the body: The body should adopt a cross-legged position at all times. The hands should be in the gesture of equipoise. The spine should be straight. The head should be slightly tilted. The teeth and lips should be together. The eyes should fall on the tip of the nose. The body should be relaxed. Next, since the support of the voice is the vāyu, the crucial point of the voice is, having forcefully exhaled through the nostrils three times, meditate to remove all faults of the vāyu. Next, the crucial point of the mind is that one should relax the mind without distraction and place the intellect in a state without thoughts. Since one meditates on that for a month, the mind is calmed and there is a samādhi of a mind at ease.

Though the samādhi, which is to be explained below, is to be meditated on, there are three preliminaries: First, meditate for a long while on bodhicitta, thinking, "I should attain buddhahood for the benefit of all sentient beings. For that purpose, I will cultivate samādhi." Second, recite *hūṃ* and appear as one's pledged deity. Meditate on this deity as similar to a reflection in the mirror. Third, generate intense devotion for the guru, who is on the crown of one's head. The three preliminaries are the nine limbs of concentration.

Next, in the main subject of concentration, when one is training in the vāyu, since [vāyu] dominates everything else, the seven vāyu yogas are meditating on prāṇāyāma. There are three exhalations: exhaling through the āyāma and inhaling through the prāṇa; exhaling through both to increase strength; and exhaling through the mouth with sound. There are two inhalations: blocking the āyāma and inhaling through the prāṇa and inhaling through the mouth without sound. In order to employ the pause as the path, unify the vāyu. As such, there are seven.

Next, the stage of meditating on prāṇāyāma is the first vāyu yoga. The way one meditates on prāṇāyāma is that first, having performed the nine limbs, when one exhales through the nostrils, meditate thinking "Exhalation." Likewise, when inhaling, meditate thinking "Inhalation." {499} When resting, meditate thinking "Resting." Since one meditates in that way for a month, and so on, samādhi arises. In order to supplement the exhalation, meditate thinking, "The exhalation is long. The inhalation is short. [The vāyu] rests inside," and train for a month, and so on.

Next, train in the meditation for a month, and so on, thinking "After inhalation, the vāyu is exhaled." Next, supplement the inhalation, recalling, "The inhalation is long, rest inside, the exhalation is short," and train for a month, and so on. Those correspond with the principle of meditating according to inhalation and exhalation. The measure of culmination is called "clear movement," which means that one is able to directly perceive the flow of the earth vāyu as yellow, the water vāyu as white, the fire vāyu as red, and the air vāyu as blue-green. "Ascertaining the aspect" is the ability to switch the vāyu that moves through the right [nostril] to the left. Both of those are the measure of culmination. In dependence on the vāyu, the qualities are accomplishing the four activities; any degree of clairvoyance such as knowing the minds of others; and the elimination of the fault of fearing untimely death from strokes, lightning, and so on. Since the vāyu is the basis of all these qualities, it is important to meditate upon this until the signs are produced. The qualities are that the body floats, is light, and has a good complexion. This [inhalation] removes blood diseases, sudden contagious diseases, fevers, and so on.

Next, in the limbs of exhalation, for the first limb of exhalation, block the āyāma and exhale through the prāṇa. Having already performed the nine limbs of concentration, focus the mind on the left nostril. Close the right nostril with the right index finger, gradually exhale through the left nostril, and rest for as long as one can hold out. When one inhales, inhale gradually, without visualization or effort. Again, exhale as before. Meditate until the signs are produced. The sign is that once the vāyu is exhaled, even though the vāyu is depleted, {500} it can be left outside for as long as one wishes without discomfort. The qualities are that nonconceptual samādhi arises in one's continuum, and all faults, such as pain in the upper body, cold diseases, and so on, are removed.

The second limb of exhalation is exhaling through both nostrils to increase strength: Meditate on the nine limbs of concentration, as before. After focusing one's mind on the brow, strongly exhale through both nostrils. Rest for as long as one can hold out. When one inhales, inhale gradually, without visualization or effort. Again, exhale as before. Meditate that way for several days. Next, focus one's mind on a spot one fathom in front. Then, focus on a spot ten fathoms in front, then one hundred, one thousand, ten thousand, one hundred thousand, and finally on the limits of space. Then exhale, meditating as before. The measure of cultivation is [performed] as before. The qualities are that all head diseases, eye diseases, and diseases of the breath will be removed.

The third limb of exhalation, exhaling soundlessly through the mouth: Having performed the full nine limbs of concentration beforehand, focus the mind directly on the front teeth. After placing the teeth together, exhale through the teeth with the sound of *si*. When inhaling, inhale gradually, without visualization or effort. Meditate until signs arise. The measure of culmination is the same as before. The qualities are the body floats, is light, and has a good complexion. Blood diseases, sudden contagions, and fevers are removed.

The two limbs of inhalation are as follows: [The first limb of inhalation] is blocking the āyāma and inhaling through the prāṇa. Having performed the nine limbs of concentration beforehand, meditate that inside one's navel, there is a ball of light, resembling a hollow egg, empty and vivid, with its outside white and its inside yellow. {501} Focus the mind on all the [inhaled] vāyu becoming slowly absorbed into that egg. Block the right nostril with the right index finger, and gradually inhale until the inhalation is complete, swallowing one's saliva silently, holding the vāyu as long as possible, and pressing down. When one can no longer hold, exhale slowly without a mental visualization. Repeat as before and meditate until the signs arise. The measure of culmination is that one can press [the vāyu] down for as long as one wishes. Even though one presses it down, one experiences no discomfort. The qualities are the arising of heat and bliss. This removes the faults of colds, tumors, and maldigestion.

Next, the second limb of inhalation is inhaling soundlessly through the mouth: Having performed the nine limbs of concentration beforehand, meditate that in the navel there is a dharmodaya, with a blue outside and red inside. Slowly inhale soundlessly through the mouth, inhaling completely, swallowing the saliva silently, and pressing down. When exhaling, exhale slowly without a visualization. Train until the signs arise. The measure of culmination is the vāyu resting inside for as long as desired without discomfort. The qualities are that heat and bliss arise and the elements increase. All faults of ascites and the abdomen are removed.

The method of meditating the union [of the vāyus] is the seventh vāyu yoga. The meditation of union for employing the resting [vāyu] as the path is as follows: Having performed the nine limbs of concentration beforehand, the hands make the mudra of equipoise and one presses below the navel. Meditate that in the navel there is the fire of caṇḍālī in the form of an *a* stroke, which is thin, hot, and vibrating. After that, draw up the lower vāyu slightly. Having gradually inhaled the upper vāyu, imagine that all the [inhaled] vāyu dissolves into the *a* at the navel. After completing the inhalation and swallowing saliva, strongly draw the lower vāyu up with the upper vāyu, {502} and unify the two vāyus in the place of the navel. Imagine that the power of caṇḍālī increases and hold as long as one can. As such, meditate in four sessions until the signs are produced. First apply this in a cross-legged position, then with the knees drawn up to the chest, then standing, then while walking, and so on, training and becoming familiar with this in all activities. The measure of culmination is that whatever activity one does, [the vāyu] can rest and one is able to unify [the two vāyus] as long as one wishes. The qualities are the arising of the many doors of samādhi, and all faults of disturbances of the body are removed.

Next is caṇḍālī yoga. The body has the knees drawn up to the chest in the stove[3] mudra. The four limbs of concentration are as before. Four fingers below the navel, meditate that the fire of caṇḍālī is as fine as a horsehair split into a hundred pieces, one-half a fingerbreadth in size, hot, and sharp. Pressing down on the upper vāyu, constrict the lower vāyu. Having meditated on the method of unifying [the upper and lower vāyus] as before, meditate that the upper vāyu dissolves into the fire of caṇḍālī at the navel. When one is no longer able to hold [the vāyu], exhale slowly. Since one always meditates in that way, to begin, heat arises in the region of the navel. After that, the entire body becomes hot.

Next, to increase the fire of caṇḍālī, meditate by focusing on the region of the abdomen. Then meditate that the fire gradually fills the whole interior of the body. Then visualize that fire outside the body. It fills the perimeter of a fathom, then a furlong, a league, a region, a continent, a world, and finally the fire fills all of space. Unify the vāyus, as before. The measure of culmination is that heat arises continuously without effort. The qualities are that while heat is predominant, {503} the whole body is filled with bliss.

Next is the bindu yoga: After adopting a cross-legged posture, imagine in one's heart a moon disc the size of a round fingernail. On top of that, there is a round white bindu of bodhicitta, the size of a chickpea. After focusing the mind on it, inhale as much as is comfortable. Meditate upon that continually without measuring the duration or frequency of sessions. Cultivate that. Meditate on a bindu of bodhicitta at the brow, as before. Focus on that and meditate, as before. Cultivate that. Meditate that there is a red bindu at the secret place, focus the mind on that, and meditate as before. Cultivate that. Having meditated on all three bindus simultaneously, they become connected by a fine strand. When one exhales, the power of the bindu in the secret place dissolves into the bindu in the heart. When inhaling, the power of the bindu at the brow dissolves into the bindu in the heart. When resting, the power of the bindu of the heart is meditated as increasing the power of the nāḍīs of the body and all elements that exist in the syllable passageways. Without counting sessions, meditate according to how the mind is engaged. The measure of familiarity is that samādhi becomes continuous day and night in that state, and the elements [of the body] increase, despite not eating and drinking. The quality is the arising of the samādhi of great bliss. All faults of the decline of the body and the sense organs, as well as mental suffering, will be removed.

Next, among the teachings on the multiple options for the various meditations on vāyu, caṇḍālī, and bindu yogas, there is the [caṇḍālī] yoga that depends on the four cakras. Having performed the nine limbs of concentration beforehand, imagine the avadhūti nāḍī in the central part of the body as very fine and straight. To the right of that is the rasanā,[4] which has the nature of fire, is red, and faces upward. On the left side, the lalanā, which has the nature of water, is imagined facing down. {504}

In the center of the sixty-four petals of the nirmāṇacakra at the navel, which depends on the central nāḍī, is an upright, multicolored *a*. On the eight petals of the inner circle, imagine the eight syllables *a ka ca ṭa ta pa ya śa*. On the sixty-four petals of the outer circle, imagine the syllables *a ā, i ī, u ū, ri rī, li lī, e ai, o au, aṃ aḥ*, repeated twice, and *ka kha ga gha nga, ca cha ja jha nya, ṭa ṭha ḍa ḍha ṇa, ta tha da dha na, ya ra la va, śa ṣa sa*. In the center of the eight-petaled dharmacakra of the heart, imagine an inverted black *hūṃ bhrūṃ āṃ jrīṃ khaṃ* in the four directions and *laṃ maṃ paṃ taṃ* in the four intermediate directions. In the center of the sixteen-petaled saṃbhogacakra based at the throat, imagine an upright red *aḥ* and a single[5] set of vowels on the petals. In the center of the thirty-two-petaled mahāsukhacakra based at the crown, imagine an inverted white *haṃ* and two sets of vowels on the petals.

Next, the yoga of stirring the lower vāyu ignites the fire of caṇḍālī at the navel. Having been combined with the fire of the rasanā, it burns the heart cakra, then burns the throat cakra, and, once that fire reaches one's crown, it enters the ankles of all buddhas, igniting the fire of caṇḍālī at the navel of the buddhas. Then, the bindu of white bodhicitta descends from the crowns of the buddhas and, having been drawn down by the power of the fire of caṇḍālī, it descends through one's own crown. Combined with the bindu of the lalanā on the left, it descends and revivifies the crown cakra. Combined with the bindu of the lalanā on the left, it descends and revivifies the throat cakra. Having fallen down further, it revivifies the navel cakra.

Then, a fine drop of the bindu touches the *a* at the navel. A very fine light ray of fire arises from the *a*, entering the inside the avadhūti.[6] {505} Since it touches the *haṃ* in the crown, a stream of very fine bindus of bodhicitta descends from the *haṃ* into the central avadhūti. From the location of the bindu, all the syllables and nāḍīs of the body are pervaded by the stream. Also, a very fine fire of caṇḍālī blazes up into the avadhūti. Its power fills the entire body with heat. Focusing upon that, meditate while unifying the vāyu as before. Meditate on that continuously as much as possible. The signs of culmination and the qualities are that the power of the vāyu can remains inside and one can send it out as one wishes. It can [remove] the upper and lower diseases that arise above and below. The power of the bindu prevents the degeneration of the bindu, increases the element, and produces samādhi and clairvoyance. The power of caṇḍālī warms the body, produces a good complexion, and removes all outer and inner illnesses. The power of the nāḍīs removes all disturbances of the elements and produces the ability to demonstrate miraculous powers. As such, having gained control over the vāyu and the mind, and since it is a practice that corresponds with the yoga of passion, which is the path of the third empowerment, this gives rise to transcendent gnosis.

Once one hears the profound and extensive intimate instruction from the buddhas and bodhisattvas and meditates upon it, since one will be able to traverse to the stage of buddhahood, the transcendent path will not be written here. As such, the practice of yoga through the three purities is the method of achieving the transcendent stage.

Having been written by the vajra holder Phakpa in accordance with the intimate instructions of the dharma lord Sakyapa and his disciples, this was presented to the great Khan and his queen.[7]
sarvadā maṅgalaṃ
Virtue.

ABBREVIATIONS

BDRC	Buddhist Digital Resource Center (formerly Tibetan Buddhist Resource Center), www.bdrc.org
Dg.K.	Derge Kangyur (sDe dge bka' 'gyur): Derge edition of the Tibetan canonical collection of sutras and tantras.
Dg.T.	Derge Tengyur (sDe dge bstan 'gyur): Derge edition of the Tibetan canonical collection of commentarial treatises.
DNZ	Jamgön Kongtrul Lodrö Taye, *The Treasury of Precious Instructions. gDams ngag rin po che'i mdzod.* 18 vols. Delhi: Shechen Publications, 1999.
G	*The Collection of All Tantras. Rgyud sde kun btus.* 30 vols. Delhi: N. Lungtok & N. Gyaltsan, 1971–1972. BDRC W21295.
HT	*Hevajra Tantra. Kye'i rdo rje zhes bya ba rgyud kyi rgyal po.* Dg.K. rgyud, *nga* (Toh. 417).
L	*The Explanation of the Path With Its Result for Disciples. Lam 'bras slob bshad.* 21 vols. Dehra Dun: Sakya Centre, 1983–1985. BDRC W23649.
LT	*The Explanation of the Path With Its Result for the Assembly. Lam 'bras tshogs bshad.* 6 vols. Dehra Dun: Sakya Centre, 1985. BDRC W23648.
M	*Chanting the True Names of Mañjuśrī. Mañjuśrījñānasattvasyaparamārthanāmasaṃgīti. 'Jam dpal ye shes sems dpa'i don dam pa'i mtshan yang dag par brjod pa.* Dg.K. rgyud, *ka* (Toh. 360).
Nar.T	Narthang Tengyur (sNar thang bstan 'gyur): Narthang edition of the Tibetan canonical collection of commentarial treatises.
P	*Yellow Volume. Pod gser ma.* In *Lam 'bras Slob bshad.* Dehra Dun: Sakya Centre, 1983–1985. BDRC W23649.
Q	Peking Tengyur: Peking edition of the Tibetan canonical collection of commentarial treatises.
S	*For the Sons. Sras don ma.* In *Lam 'bras slob bshad.* Dehra Dun: Sakya Centre, 1983–1985. BDRC W23649.
SP	*The Red Book. Lam 'bras po ti dmar ma.* Dehra Dun: Sakya Centre, 1985. BDRC W30149.
SKB	*Sa skya bka' 'bum.* 15 vols. Dehra Dun: Sakya Centre, 1992–1993. BDRC W22271.

ST	*Saṃpūṭa Tantra. Saṃpūṭanāmamahātantra. Yang dag par sbyor ba zhes bya ba'i rgyud chen po.* Dg.K. rgyud, *ga* (Toh. 381).
Toh.	A Complete Catalog of the Tibetan Buddhist Canons, edited by Hakuju Ui et al. Sendai, Japan: Tohoku University, 1934.
VT	*Vajrapañjara Tantra. Āryaḍākinīvajrapañjaramahātantrarājakalpanāma. 'Phags pa mkha' 'gro ma rdo rje gur zhes bya ba'i rgyud kyi rgyal po chen po'i brtag pa.* Dg.K. rgyud, *nga* (Toh. 419).
ZDNG	*Lamp of the Key Points of the Profound Meaning. gSung ngag lam 'bras don bsdus ma'i rnam bshad zab don gnad kyi sgon me.* In *The Collected Works of Sönam Senge. gSung 'bum bSod nams seng ge.* Dkar mdzes bod rigs rang skyong khul, sde dge rdzong, rdzong sar khams bye'i slob gling: Rdzong sar khams bye'i slob gling, 2004–2014. BDRC W1PD1725.
ch., chs.	chapter, chapters
f., ff.	folio, folios
p., pp.	page, pages
v., vv.	verse, verses
vol., vols.	volume, volumes

Notes

Series Introduction

1. 'Jam dbyangs mkhyen brtse dbang po (1820–1892), mChog 'gyur bDe chen gling pa (1829–1870), Mi pham rgya mtsho (1846–1912), and many more masters were involved in this movement, including Kongtrul's guru Si tu Pad ma nyin byed (1774–1853). See Smith, *Among Tibetan Texts*, 247–50; Jamgön Kongtrul, *Treasury of Knowledge, Book 8, Part 4: Esoteric Instructions*, 25–48; Ringu Tulku, *Ri-me Philosophy*; etc.
2. The specific text by Shes rab 'od zer that expounds the eight chariots is *Meditation's Ambrosia of Immortality* (*sGom pa 'chi med kyi bdud rtsi*). A study of this has been done by Marc-Henri Deroche: "'Phreng po gter ston Shes rab 'od zer (1518–1584) on the Eight Lineages of Attainment." According to Deroche, "This text may be considered as an (if not the) original source of the '*ris med* paradigm' of the eight lineages of attainment" (p. 17). It is interesting to note that the eight lineages are arranged in a different sequence in that text—Nyingma, Kadampa, Shangpa Kagyu, Lamdre, Marpa Kagyu, Zhije, Jordruk, Dorje Sumgyi Nyendrup—which may have been more chronological than Kongtrul's preferred order.
3. One finds this idea developed in the volume on esoteric instructions in *The Treasury of Knowledge*, where Kongtrul describes in incredibly condensed detail the basic principles and sources of these eight lineages. It is expounded in the catalog of *The Treasury of Precious Instructions* (*DNZ*, vol. 18), published in English as *The Catalog of The Treasury of Precious Instructions*, trans. Richard Barron (Chökyi Nyima). Also see Stearns, *Luminous Lives*, 3–8.
4. Jamgön Kongtrul, *Catalog*, 21.
5. *The Treasury of Precious Instructions. gDams ngag rin po che'i mdzod* (*DNZ*), 12 vols. (Delhi: N. Lungtok and N. Gyaltsan, 1971–1972). Known as the Kundeling printing.
6. *The Treasury of Precious Instructions. gDams ngag rin po che'i mdzod* (*DNZ*), 18 vols. (Delhi: Shechen Publications, 1998). Known as the Shechen printing.

Translator's Introduction

1. See Sharrock, *Hevajra at Bantéay Chmàr.*
2. See Reichle, *Violence and Serenity*, 139.
3. See Davidson, *Tibetan Renaissance*, 41.
4. *Tantra of the Vajra Array*, Dg.K. rnying, *ka* (Toh. 829), f. 202b, lines 5–7. The Tibetan title that is usually given is *bDe mchog sdom 'byung phyi ma'i rgyud*, but this tantra does not actually exist.
5. Amezhab, *Ocean That Gathers*, Collected Works, vol. 21, 425.
6. The account here is given in contrast to the general Nyingma account of the origin of tantras involving King Dza, which the Sakya tradition considers mistaken.
7. Here, Ngorchen cites Kāmadhenupa's explanation that "bhaga" is a reference to the fact that the celestial mansion of Hevajra is not inert matter but in fact composed of gnosis. Kāmadhenupa also gives other interpretations of the term "bhaga." See Kāmadhenupa, *Gathering the Vajra Stanzas*, Dg.T. rgyud, *ca* (Toh. 1192).
8. *rtog pa*, Skt. *kalpa*.
9. Prior to teaching the Hevajra tantras, Alaṃkakalaśa relates that the Bhagavān taught the action tantras in the Thirty-Three Heavens for brahmins. The Bhagavān taught the conduct tantras in the pure abode of Akaniṣṭha for the merchant class, and he taught many yoga tantras on the peak of Sumeru in the form of Śvetaketu, such as the *Sarvatathāgatatattvasamgraha*, then the *Vajraśikhara*, and so on, for the royal class. Following this, the Bhagavān taught the four empowerments principally to the Tuṣitā devas, teaching them the two stages and the *Guhyasamāja*. Following this, in the form of Vajrasattva on a western mountain in Oḍḍiyāna, the Bhagavān taught the *Vajramālā Tantra* for the military class to tame the ten-direction guardians by means of the ten wrathful ones, as well as other father tantras on Kailash, the Vindya mountains, the banks of the Ganges, and so on. For the outcastes, the Bhagavān taught the long and abbreviated *Cakrasaṃvara Tantra* in the pure abodes of the form realm. The Bhagavān then taught Hevajra in Magadhā.
10. *Ornament of Gnosis*, Dg.K. rgyud, *nga* (Toh. 422), f. 134b.
11. *Lamp of Principles*, Dg.K. rgyud, *nga* (Toh. 423), f. 142a.
12. *Vajrapañjara Tantra*, Dg.K. rgyud, *nga* (Toh. 419), f. 35b.
13. Śrī Dharmapāla has been traditionally identified with the famed Yogācāra scholar active in the mid-sixth century.
14. This is identified in the *Collection of All Sādhanas*, vol. 11, 497.
15. The daughter of King Indrabhūti II and the sister of King Indrabhūti III.
16. rNam par rgyal ba'i lha, also known as rNam par rgyal ba'i sde (Vijayasena). See Amezhab, *Ocean That Gathers*, Collected Works, vol. 21, 440.
17. This is a mispelling of *Trai'ura* in Abhayadatta, *Chronicle*, Nar.T. rgyud, *lu* (N

3095), f. 4a. Modern day Tripura lies in Eastern Bangladesh, east of the capital city, Dhaka.

18. This is located in Parharpur, Bangladesh.
19. Ngawang Chödrak, *Laughing Lotus Patch*, in *G*, f. 3b.
20. This is not to be confused with Āryadeva the brahmin, the uncle of Padampa Sangye. See Kongtrul, *Chöd*, 3.
21 Avalokitavrata, *Lamp of Wisdom*, Dg.T. dbu ma, *wa–za* (Toh. 3859), f. 48a, lines 2–3.
22. Loter Wangpo, *Great Ganges River*, in *Collection of All Sādhanas*, vol. 11.
23. To gain insight into the Sakya tradition's perception of Śrī Dharmapāla Virūpa's position in Indian Buddhist history we have to understand when the Sakya tradition understands the parinirvāṇa of the Buddha to have taken place in 2133 B.C.E. This is useful for understanding the Sakya school's tradition that Śrī Dharmapāla Virūpa's life span was either fifteen hundred years or sixteen hundred years.
24. Ācārya Vilasavajra, not to be confused with Līlāvajra, is named eleven times (along with several mentions of Indrabhūtī III, Kāṇha, Ḍombhi Heruka, and other masters of the Hevajra tantra) by Gambhīravajra in the *Marvelous Clear Profound Meaning*.
25. Padmavajra, *Hevajra Sādhana*, Dg.T. rgyud, *nya* (Toh. 1218).
26. Saroruha, *Padminī Commentary*, Dg.T. rgyud, *ka* (Toh. 1181).
27. Samayavajra, *Jeweled Garland*, Q, rgyud 'grel, *phu* (Q 4687). An alternate translation of the same text exists in the Derge Tengyur (Toh. 1183). They appear to be substantially the same text, though Jan-Ulrich Sobisch raises some question as to whether the two texts are translations of the same Sanskrit text. Jetsun Drakpa Gyaltsen clearly identifies the Lhetse translation with Samayavajra. It is described in the colophon as an oral composition.
28. For an exhaustive presentation of the sources and lineages of Path with Its Result literature, see Sobisch, *Hevajra and Lam 'Bras Literature*.
29. A great deal has been written about Virūpa, Drokmi Lotsāwa, and the Sakya school's role in promulgating the Path with Its Result. See Davidson, *Indian Esoteric Buddhism*; Davidson, *Tibetan Renaissance*; and Stearns, *Luminous Lives*.
30. For more information about these lineages, see Stearns, *Taking the Result as the Path*.
31. This deity is commonly referred to as Yangdak Heruka. The name Yangdak is a nickname derived from the title of the sādhana composed by Huṃkāra.

Technical Note

1. *The Treasury of Precious Instructions. gDams ngag rin po che'i mdzod* (*DNZ*), 18 vols. (Delhi: Shechen Publications, 1998).

1. The Vajra Verses

1. *Vāgupadeśaratnasamārgaphalasyagranthavajragathanāmaviharatisma. gSung ngag rin po che lam 'bras bu dang bcas pa'i gzhung rdo rje'i tshig rkang, DNZ*, pp. 1–12. *P*, no title, pp. 10–19.
2. See Stearns, *Illuminating Lives* for more information on the role of Phakmo Drupa in the formation of the earliest corpus of Path with Its Result literature.
3. See Davidson, *Tibetan Renaissance*; Stearns, *Taking the Result as the Path*; and Lama Dampa Sönam Gyaltsen and Virupa, *Treasury of Esoteric Instructions.*
4. This sentence is the start of the actual text, Virūpa's *Vajra Verses.*
5. *P* reads *bzhi* for *DNZ, gzhi.*
6. *P* reads *dgun kyi rlung po*. In *DNZ, dgun* is missing.
7. What is translated here as "movement" and "speech" is literally "dance" (*gar*) and "mantra" (*sngags*).
8. Following *P* and *S, shes pa*; *DNZ, ges pa.*
9. Following *P* and *S, mgyes*; *DNZ, rjes.*
10. Literally, ten times two (*bcu gnyis*).
11. This is the name of the ideal female consort.
12. Following *P, rigs pa*; *S* and *DNZ, rig pa.*
13. *S* reads *rtog pa* for *DNZ* and *P, rtogs pa.*
14. *P* and *S* read *lus bde myos*; *DNZ, lus sems bde myos.*
15. *P* and *S* read *myos*; *DNZ, myon.*
16. *P* and *S* read *las*; *DNZ, la.*
17. *M*, ff. 3a, line 3.
18. While *DNZ* and *P* read *rgya*, "seal," *S* clarifies that *rgya* is to be read as *rgyal ba*, "victor." *S* (ff. 201a.2–202b.2) provides a detailed explanation of different kinds of buddhafields from the point of view of impure appearances, path appearances, and pure appearances. It may be the case that when this treatise was converted from a handwritten manuscript to block print, a shorthand convention in the Tibetan cursive script of linking the final consonant of a word to the same initial consonant in the following word was overlooked. Thus the term was rendered *rgya longs* rather than the correct reading, *rgyal longs.*
19. *S* reads *byang chub kyi sems kyi rlung lnga skyod pa'am*; *DNZ* reads *byang chub kyi sems kyi rlung lnga skyod pa'i*; *P* reads *byang chub kyi sems kyi rlung lnga spyod pa'.* Here the reading found in *S* is followed.
20. *S* and *DNZ* read *longs sku*; *P, chos sku.*
21. *S* reads *sa bcu gsum ma*; *DNZ* and *P, sa bcu ma*, eliding *gsum.*
22. *S* and *P* read *rtog pa*; *DNZ, rtogs pa.*

2. The Summarized Topics of the Vajra Verses

1. *rDo rje tshigs rkang gi bsdus don* in *DNZ*, pp. 11–12. *P*, pp. 19–21, no title.

2. Kunga Gyaltsen, *Hagiography of the Lord Guru*, in *SKB*, vol. 10.
3. *P* reads *samāptaṃithi*; *DNZ*, *samāstamiṣī*.

3. The Verse Summary

1. *gSung ngag rin po che'i rnam 'grel don bsdus tshigs bcad ma*, *DNZ*, pp. 12–15. *G*, pp. 104–6; *P*, pp. 188–91, titled *Thams cad gyi don bsdus pa'i tshigs su bcad pa*. According to *ZDNG*, this text is the first of the eleven commentaries on *The Vajra Verses* authored by Sachen Kunga Nyingpo.
2. *rnam 'grel bcu gcig*. For more information on the eleven commentaries, see Stearns, *Luminous Lives*, 16–25.
3. *G* and *ZDNG* read *virṇani*; *DNZ*, *virvāpa*. *ZDNG* explains that here *virṇa* refers to qualities (*yon tan*).
4. *ZDNG* notes that these are the provisional meaning, definitive meaning, literal meaning, figurative meaning, and so on.
5. *DNZ* and *G* read *gdams ngag*; *ZDNG* reads *man ngag*.
6. *DNZ* and *G* place this heading after these two lines. *ZDNG* places this heading prior to these two lines.
7. *G* reads *snyogs pa*; *DNZ*, *rnyogs pa*.
8. Dome (*mDo smad*) is part of the Qinghai region of Western China, near Lake Kokonor.
9. *ZDNG* identifies this person as the chief (*spon po*) of Lama Kyura Akyab (bLa ma skyu ra a skyabs).

4. The Root Verses of the Illuminating Jewel

1. *lTa ba 'khor 'das dbyer med kyi gzhung rin chen snang ba'i rtsa ba*, *DNZ*, pp. 15–17. *P*, pp. 191–94, titled *Kun gzhi rgyu rgyud las 'phros nas 'khor 'das byer med kyi lta ba'i rtsa ba*.
2. *P*, *'khor 'das dbyer med lta ba'i 'grel*, pp. 194–243.
3. The homage given in *P* is *guru virūpa la namo*.

5. How to Give Instructions According to the Treatise

1. *gSung ngag rin po che lam 'bras dang bcas pa'i khrid yig gzhung ji lta ba bzhin du dkri ba*, *DNZ*, pp. 17–28. *P*, 300–14. This text is part of a quartet of texts called the *Four Great Trees of the Treatise*.
2. Könchok Lhundrub, *Beautiful Ornament of the Three Appearances*, in *LT*, vol. 4.
3. Könchok Lhundrub, *Beautiful Ornament of the Three Tantras*, in *LT*, vol. 4.
4. Here and below, quoted root text is from *The Vajra Verses*.
5. *DNZ* and *G* add *snang ba*.
6. *P* and *G* read *der mi skye ba*; *DNZ*, *der skye ba*.

7. This passage found in *P*, *yi dwags dud 'gro gnyis kyang 'grel*, is missing in *DNZ* and *G*.
8. The male god (*pho lha*) is one of the five deities that always accompany a person's body throughout their lifetime (*'go ba'i lha*). The others are the country god (*yul lha*), female god (*mo lha*), war god (*dgra lha*), and life god (*srog lha*). It is said that when these gods are disturbed, it can result in illness and even death.
9. *G* and *P* read *bsam*; *DNZ*, *sgom*.
10. *P* reads *gnyen* (relative); *DNZ* and *G*, *dgra* (enemy).
11. *G* and *P* read *sems can thams cad la 'bul*; *DNZ*, *sems la 'bul*.
12. *P* reads *cis kyang*; *DNZ* and *G*, *ngas*.
13. These seven topics are defined in Drakpa Gyaltsen's *Seven Topics in the All-Basis Cause Continuum* found in the *Twenty-Two Ancillary Short Texts* (*P*, pp. 128–31). They are the support, the supported, how the supported relies on the support, the relationship between the support and the supported, the way the supported is defined as the cause tantra, the way the cause tantra is defined as the root tantra, and the way samsara and nirvana are complete in the root tantra.
14. *P* and *G* read *med pa*; *DNZ*, *mi dbang*.
15. This passage is missing from *DNZ* and *G*, but is present in *P*.
16. Lhodrak (Lho brag) is a region in southern Tibet.

6. The Versified Instructional Manual

1. *Lam 'bras kyi gzhung ji lta ba bzhin du bkri ba'i khrid yig tshigs bcad ma*, *DNZ*, pp. 28–31. *G*, 121–24. *SKB*, vol. 6, pp. 390–94.
2. For an extensive exploration of these controversies, see Jackson, *Enlightenment by a Single Means*.
3. *G* and *SKB* read *dang po*; *DNZ*, *dad pa*.
4. This refers to meditating on Hevajra or another deity with one face and two hands, as opposed to the Hevajra with eight heads, and so on.

7. The Summarized Topics of the Stages of the Path

1. *Lam 'bras kyi gzhung ji lta ba bzhin du bkri ba'i khrid yig tshigs bcad ma rgyud gsum lam gyi rim pa'i bsdus don bzhugs so*. *DNZ*, pp. 31–33. *G*, pp. 124–26. *The Collected Works of Kunga Zangpo*, vol. 3, pp. 791–94, titled, *rGyud gsum lam gyi rim pa'i bsdus don*.
2. For a comprehensive account of his life and times, see Heimbel, *Vajradhara in Human Form*.
3. Evaṃ Chöden (*e vaṃ chos ldan*) was founded in 1429 in the Ngor valley, in Tsang, Tibet. The Ngor tradition is the dominant Sakya subschool in eastern Tibet, to which both Jamyang Khyentse Wangpo and Loter Wangpo belonged.

8. The Nyakma Commentary

1. *gSung ngag rin po chen lam 'bras bu dang bcas pa'i gzhung rdo rje'i tshig rkang gi 'grel pa*, *DNZ*, pp. 35–121. *G*, pp. 127–221. In *P*, titled *gZhung bshad gnyag ma*, pp. 21–128.
2. For more information, see Stearns, *Illuminating* Lives, 16–24.
3. This refers to Nairātmyā, the female guru from whom Virūpa received these instructions.
4. The lines for the instruction for removing obstacles to concentration and māra are present in *P*, missing in *DNZ* and *G*.
5. *P* reads *bsrel* for *D*, *bsal*.
6. This is a pun on the Tibetan for sugata, deshek (*bde gshegs*), "gone to bliss."
7. *rang rig*, "intrinsic cognizance." We must distinguish the rang rig (*svasaṃvedana*) in Path with Its Result literature from its usage in the Yogācāra school and Buddhist epistemology. Kunga Nyingpo's *Commentary on the Difficult Points*, when discussing the third empowerment, says, "The explanation of the characteristic of the third empowerment is 'intrinsic cognizance (*rang rig*) transforms into gnosis,' and so on. Here, *intrinsic* is a simple rejection of being extrinsic. *Cognizance* arises as the essence of clarity. *Gnosis* is realization, which is the gnosis that is omniscient in all aspects." Sachen further mentions that in the system of Padmavajra, this gnosis is regarded as the meaning gnosis, like the sun between the clouds, whereas in the Ḍombhi Heruka system, this gnosis is regarded as an example gnosis experienced at the time of the third empowerment" (in *SKB*, vol. 1, p. 408). Sachen reconciles the conflict by invoking the Kadampa principle of the three capacities by stating that persons of medium capacity and average capacity will experience this as an example wisdom, while those of highest capacity will be liberated during the third empowerment. By contrast, in the system of Yogācāra school—as well as the Buddhist epistemology of Dharmakīrti—rang rig is taken to be a reflexive cognition or a self-awareness, a cognition or an awareness that necessarily takes consciousness itself as an object of direct perception.
8. Sapan's commentary on this says, "If happy with the object of mental engagement, meditate; if unhappy, do not meditate" (*SP*, p. 77).
9. Sapan's commentary on this says, "If one meditates while one's health is poor, no progress will be made; if one does not meditate while one's health is good, it is also the same." (*SP*, p. 77)
10. The Latin name for this is *Butea monosperma*.
11. The eight sets are *a*, *ka*, *ca*, *ṭa*, *ta*, *pa*, *ya*, and *śa*.
12. The sixteen consonants are *ka*, *kha*, *ga*, *gha*, *ṅa*, *ca*, *cha*, *ja*, *jha*, *ña*, *ṭa*, *ṭha*, *ḍa*, *ḍha*, *ṇa*, and *ta*.
13. *The Concealed Explanation of the Vajra Body* states, "At the lower extremity of the three nāḍīs, four fingerbreadths below the navel, at the lower end of the rasanā, there is the mother of fire, and the *oṃ* of concentration at the split of

the nāḍī knot. At the lower end of the lalanā there is the mother of sleep and the *hūṃ* of union at the split of the nāḍī knot. At the lower end of the central nāḍī, there is the *a* of the center. At the tip of the central nāḍī where the knot splits into two, there is an inverted *kṣa*. In women, it is a *bhrūṃ*" (in *Sakya Lamdre*, vol. 42, p. 805).

14. "'Self-originated gnosis' is self-originated because it does not depend on the condition of external objects" (*S*, p. 105).
15. *S* clarifies that the first two samādhis are included in agitation, and the third is included in lethargy (p. 106).
16. "Clear and light mean faultless" (*S*, p. 106).
17. *HT*, f. 15a, lines 1–2.
18. *S* clarifies that this means to listen to the sound of erotic conversation.
19. Refers to not allowing the loss of the bindu.
20. This refers to relying on an anabolic diet.
21. Some manuscripts present *hūṃ*.
22. *S* describes this as being seated cross-legged, blocking the ears with the thumbs, the eyes with the forefingers, the nostrils with the middle fingers, and the lips with the ring fingers and pinkies (p. 128).
23. Vajragarbha, *Extensive Commentary*, Dg.T. rgyud, *ka* (Toh. 1180), f. 39a, lines 5–6.
24. *S* indicates this is the time of exhalation.
25. *S* indicates this is the time of inhalation.
26. *DNZ* and *P* add a heading: "The explanation of the group of samayas of equipoise."
27. *S* specifies all contradictions with nāḍī and vāyu.
28. *S* defines these as follows: "Vajra means the emptiness of all phenomena. Since nondual gnosis travels in the space of emptiness, it is the vajra ḍākinī. That is the guru, who is not different than the supreme deity, Mahāvajradhara. One should recall the qualities of the five classes of vajra ḍākinī. 'And so on' is an inclusion. The gnosis ḍākinī is immaculate gnosis. Since it travels through space to benefit those to be tamed after being motivated by great compassion, it is a ḍākinī. The mother ḍākinīs travel through space to benefit migrating beings. Since they adopt a female form, they enjoy space and travel to the twenty-four places, and so on, benefiting sentient beings. The flesh-eating ḍākinīs enjoy oblations of flesh and blood, and since they possess magic powers, they benefit sentient beings. That is, they are the lords of the charnel ground, such as Yama, Sakra, and so on—the directional guardians and field guardians—who eliminate the obstacles to the awakening of the practitioner, grant powers, and engage in beneficial activities. The samaya ḍākinī is the one that moves higher and higher on the path through the experience of the gnosis of one's own realization, from not violating the samaya one has obtained and through the empowerment of samaya. Therefore, one's vajra siblings give rise to mantra benefits" (pp. 157–58).
29. The term *khandro* (*mkha' 'gro*) is genderless in Tibetan. In Sanskrit, there is a

male form, *ḍāka*, and a female form, *ḍākinī*. Here, the female form of the Sanskrit term is being used by default out of convenience.

30. *S* lists these five as the five inner ḍākinīs.
31. *S* reads *la*; *P*, *las*.
32. *S* defines "released" (*la dor ba*) with respect to the view as "Nowhere to go apart from that and final" (p. 186).
33. *SP* reads *tsha*; *P*, *tshwa*.
34. *ri sgog*. The latin name for this is *Allium atrosanguineum*.
35. Chang is a kind of Tibetan beer made out of barley, which is boiled, drained, mixed with yeast, and left to ferment in a cloth bundle. Hot water is poured through the fermented lees after three days or so. It is then served either hot or cold.
36. The three fruits are *Terminalia chebula*, *Emblica officinalis*, and *Terminalia bellerica*. These are common ingredients in formulas used in Ayurveda and Tibetan medicine.
37. This term (*srog rtsol*, Skt. *prāṇāyāma*) is used in two ways in the Path with Its Result: it refers to inhalation (*prāṇa*) and exhalation (*āyāma*) and to the left (*prāṇa*) and right (*āyāma*) nostrils.
38. *SP* reads *mi bde ba* for *P*, *bde ba*.
39. *S* clarifies that one imagines one propels the refined element of the whole body into any place where there is discomfort of the sense organs, into which it is absorbed (p. 190).
40. *si hla*. This is a euphemism for blood.
41. *ga bur*. This is a euphemism for semen.
42. *gla rtsi*. This is a euphemism for urine.
43. *bzhi mnyam*, also spelled *gzhi mnyam* (Skt. *catuḥsama*), a euphemism for feces. Catuḥsama is a fragrant unguent composed of equal parts of sandalwood, aloes wood, saffron, and musk.
44. *S* says, "In brief, when both the vāyu and the mind ascend [through the central nāḍī], the faults to be abandoned are abandoned, and the qualities to be obtained are obtained, which is given the designation "freeing knots." However, it is said that in actuality it is not like freeing real knots. Beginning at the tenth stage is the initial preparation; the main subject is enjoyment; and the conclusion is total completion and has the manner of dissolution, in which the knots are released three at a time. *Initial preparation* means the one obtains that first portion of qualities, such as the three signs and so on. *Enjoyment* means one enjoys the expansion and increase of the qualities of the three signs. *Conclusion* means that as soon as there is dissolution, once those individual qualities on each stage are complete, nothing develops further" (p. 197).
45. The devaputra māra is a name for Kamadeva, chief of the devas of the highest position in the desire realm, the Paranirmitavaśavartins.
46. *Supremacy of Vajravārāhi*, Dg.K. rgyud, *ga* (Toh. 378), f. 65a, lines 2–3. The first three lines are sourced from this tantra. The source of the last line is unknown.

47. *S* describes this as gripping the left index finger in a fist made with the five fingers of the right hand (p. 219).
48. *S* describes this as placing the tips of the ring finger and thumb together and making the shape of a source of phenomena (*dharmakara*), which is represented by the Sanskrit syllable *e* (p. 219).
49. *S* states that this is the mudra of Vairocana, where the right hand holds the index finger of the left (p. 219).
50. *S* states this is the right index finger pointing into space (pp. 219–20).
51. The source of the subsidiary symbols of the body has not been located.
52. *S* states this refers to meeting an ignorant person with broken samaya or breaking one's own samayas (p. 224).
53. The detailed procedures for the vase rite can be found in *S* (pp. 227–30).
54. These are the small clay votive stupas made from molds, often composed from the ashes of the deceased.
55. The latin names for these are *Piper nigrum*, *Piper longum*, and *Alpinia officinarum*.
56. *S* specifies the skin of a lynx, wolf, or if those are not available, a dog (p. 235).
57. *S* says, "Though 'In general, the path instruction . . .' is understood, it is said that the so-called gnosis that realizes the knowing mind gradually abandons those things that are to be abandoned and increases qualities exponentially" (p. 241).
58. These five stages correspond to the bodhisattva and buddha stages mentioned in the previous section.
59. The five offerings are flowers, incense, light, scent, and food.
60. These four results are based on the four results found in the *Treasury of Abhidharma* (Dg.T. mngon pa, *ku*, Toh. 4089, ch. 2, p. 56).
61. *snying 'phyo ba*. This is one of the seven heart diseases identified in chapter 34 of the *Intimate Instruction Tantra* from the *Four Medicine Tantras*. The symptoms include headaches, loss of memory, mental instability, depression, logorrhea, withdrawal, easy upset, blisters, shortness of breath, and that the heart feels empty.
62. Nying lung (*snying rlung*) is one of the sixty-three lung (*rlung*), or vāta, illnesses identified in chapter 2 of the *Intimate Instruction Tantra* from the *Four Medicine Tantras* (*rGyud bzhi*). The symptoms include that the body shakes, upper body tension, mental delusion, nonsensical speech, dizziness, light sleep, and that one is afflicted by wheezing.
63. The source of this list of five secondary vāyus is the *First Section Tantra*. Further, these five secondary vāyus take their name from the seven classes of the forty-nine Indian storm gods known as the Maruts. The *Lamp of the Compendium of Practices* (Dg.T. rgyud, *ngi*, Toh. 1803) lists them in a different order and sense organ attribution than what is listed here. See Wedemeyer, *Āryadeva's Lamp that Integrates the Practices*, 180–81.
64. *S* says, "The element gathers impartially, the body coils or the body shakes, causing bliss to arise . . . ." (pp. 299–300).

65. *S* describes these as the four great palaces, the twelve major joints, and both the rasanā and the lalanā (pp. 319–20).
66. *S* says, "One feels one has become a great rock, or one feels that one has absorbed a great rock into one's body. In visions and dream experiences, one climbs up rocks or mountains or falls down from them" (p. 320).
67. *S* says, "The nāḍīs are the thirty-two, or the one hundred and twenty, and so on" (p. 320).
68. *S* says, "The physical experiences are that one thinks one's body becomes a tree trunk; many of the other two experiences arise, such as climbing trees, going into a dense jungle, cutting wood in the forest, and so on" (p. 320).
69. *P* reads *hūṃ*; *S*, *bhrūṃ*.
70. While the text clearly states there are three visionary experiences, it actually lists four.
71. Reading *P*, *nang tshigs kyi rten 'grel*. This is misspelled in *S* as *nang sems kyi rten 'grel* (p. 337).
72. *Akṣara*, meaning "inalterable," is the Sanskrit term translated into Tibetan as *yi ge*.
73. Coconut Island, misspelled as *Na ri ke ri*. *S* misspells this as *Na ri gi ri*, identifying it as a border land of India, in which inhabitants eat only fruit and do not know of other food (p. 350).
74. *S* says, "'Arises from oneself' means that since the vāyu, mind, the five ḍākinīs, and the five ḍākas exist as innate attributes within oneself, they are empowered when the dependent origination is arranged" (p. 353).
75. *S* says, "Just as one is unable to read syllables without the vowels, here also if the six ornaments are absent, one will not be able to recall the purities, because the mnemonic device is absent. If one does not recall the purities, one will not be able to place appearance and emptiness in union. Therefore, the purities are extremely important" (p. 362).
76. These two lines are inverted here and also in S (p. 362), where the full citation is given. (*HT*, f. 26a, lines 3–4.)
77. *S* says, "The empowerment master is the nirmāṇakāya" (p. 368).
78. This procedure is fully described only in the *Gathengma* commentary (p. 423, lines 3–6).
79. The name of our billion-world system.
80. The vajra goddess of form.
81. When 21,600 is divided by 24, there are an average of 900 respirations per hour, which means there are an average of 15 karma vāyus per minute: 1 vāyu every 4 seconds.
82. *S* says, "In general, when one is healthy, the body is without pain, and so on. In a body that remains balanced without engaging in activities that are too intense or relaxed, the vāyu moves in twelve fingerbreadths and moves out twelve fingerbreadths. Apart from the inward and outward movement of the twenty-four karma vāyus, in general, the twenty-four fingerbreadths of inward and outward

[movements] of the controlled vāyu stop when one obtains the twelfth stage. At each stage, each fingerbreadth of the controlled vāyu stops. Here, the portion for the first stage—the vāyu stopping at one fingerbreadth—is one fingerbreadth out and one fingerbreadth in, thus stopping at two fingerbreadths when the outer and inner movement are controlled" (p. 394–95).

83. *S* says, "From the twelve links of dependent origination, one obtains power over birth; on the third stage, one does not gather karma; on the fourth stage, addiction does not arise; on the fifth stage, becoming does not arise; and on the sixth stage, contaminated sensation does not arise (p. 396).
84. This is 6 times 1800.
85. *S* clarifies that on the mundane path, the empowerments are received in four regular sessions; on the transcendent path, there are no specified sessions (p. 398).
86. That is, one cannot be burned by fire, drowned in water, or harmed by wind if one gains control over the respective elemental vāyus.
87. *S* mentions this is a result of gaining control over the space vāyu (p. 399).
88. *S* indicates that these gazes are the gaze that causes falling, the one that causes paralysis, the one that destroys, the one that captures, and so on (p. 399–400).
89. The six tastes are sweet, salty, sour, hot, bitter, and astringent.
90. *M*, f. 3a, lines 2–3. The specific version of this verse reflects an alternate translation found in the *Lamp of the Compendium of Practices*, Dg.T. rgyud, *ngi* (Toh. 1803), f. 72a, lines 1–2.
91. The empowerments of the three kāyas, five gnoses, five mudras, and the eleven herukas.
92. The verse corresponding to this passage is missing.
93. *S* mentions that one can manifest such forms as tigers, lions, and even the form of the Buddha, because the shape of the nāḍīs are transformed (p. 416).
94. *S* says, "Once all the refined elements move up, the three knots are released in the central nāḍī and half the crown cakra is filled with bindu. Since that [bindu] becomes irreversibly stable, one proceeds to the eleventh stage. When the whole crown cakra is filled with the refined element, since it becomes irreversibly stable, once the three knots in the central nāḍī are released, one proceeds to the twelfth bhūmi" (p. 417).
95. *S* describes the four movements as the movement of nāḍīs, the movement of syllables, the movement of the five amṛtas, and the movement of the vāyu (p. 419).
96. Tsang Jampa Dorje Gyaltsen, *Dismissing Attacks against Nyakma*, p. 597, equates *Ha ri ma* with a great being (*bdag nyid chen po*) in its explanation of the following citation.
97. *First Section of The Supreme Great Glorious Uniform Nondual King Tantra*, Dg.K. rgyud, *cha* (Toh. 453), f. 179a, lines 4–5.
98. *S* says, "Since the prāṇa and āyāma vāyus move into the central nāḍī, all the appearances of the three realms, samsara, and nirvana are seen only as the cen-

tral nāḍī; this is "subtle." As it is said, "The black pattern is a mental object" means that the reality of the central nāḍī is seen just as it is. "Lightness" means through the power of that gnosis vāyu, one is able to see all the buddhafields of the worlds in the three realms and ten directions in an instant by virtue of magic power. "Vanishing into the subtle" means that through the power of all the totally refined elements entering into the central nāḍī, inwardly, all samsara and nirvana are able to vanish and both self and other dissolve into emptiness in one's experiential appearances. "Able to enjoy" means at that moment (internally) since it is explained that the central nāḍī's dependent origination of having seen the central nāḍī just as it exists in the mother; (externally) one is able to enjoy consorts, such as Nairātmyā, and so on; connate consorts, such as Rupavajrā, and so on; or field-born consorts, such as the queens of the gathering, and all immaculate sense enjoyments without clinging. "Ha ri ma" is seeing the kāya of blazing major and minor marks while lacking substance and being victorious over the four māras. "Causing delight" means that while one does not transform into a nirmāṇakāya, having shown peaceful and wrathful forms to tame those with attachment and aversion, one is able to satisfy the wishes of those to be tamed. In brief, it means that one is able to emanate as boats, bridges, and so on, if it will benefit sentient beings. "Bringing all under control" means that since one has completed the accumulations, one can bring all migrating beings under control, such as māras, non-Buddhists, and so on. There is not even a single moment when one is not benefiting sentient beings. "Engaging in whatever is desired" means at that moment, for the benefit of oneself and others, one is able to demonstrate whatever various magic powers are desired without impediment, such as placing the billion worlds in a mustard seed, causing the sound of falling meteors and the roiling of the great ocean, making many from one, making less from many, and so on. These are qualities appearing to oneself and others. Further, since it occurs right now if one wishes, this is [the ability] to bring under control. "Mastery" (*dbang*) refers to gaining mastery over all immaculate, desired qualities. Since they are inexhaustible, it is "wealth" (*phyug po*) (pp. 429–30).

99. This citation is found only in Kambala, *The Prolegomena of the Sādhana*, Dg.T. rgyud, *ma* (Toh. 1401), f. 73b, lines 5–6. The first two lines are taken from the *Ancillary Exposition Tantra*, Dg.K. rgyud, *ka* (Toh. 369), f. 369b, line 2. The second two lines are taken from the *Cakrasamvara Root Tantra*, Dg.K, rgyud, *ka* (Toh. 368), f. 239b, lines 6–7. Also, the final line of the verse in Tibetan reads "also will see from afar" (*ring po nas kyang gzigs pa 'gyur*), rather than *P* above (*ring na gnas kyang byin gyis rlo*).

100. *S* says, "One who abides in samaya is a person who has trained on the path, in whose continuum realization has arisen and who has totally completed the accumulations. The ḍākinīs empower the appearance of gnosis gathered by the three kāyas to manifest. "Faraway places" means that though they live in other worlds, when practitioners arrange all the dependent originations

simultaneously, [the ḍākinīs] merely empower the person whose continuum is totally purified" (pp. 428–29).

101. *S* says, "The three times are as follows: the rasanā is the past, the lalanā is the future, and the central nāḍī is the present. Alternately, all upper cakras are the past, all lower cakras are the future, and whatever manifests and is experienced on the basis of those is the present. Alternately, the melting of the bindu that comes from the mother is the past, the bliss obtained from the father is the future, and the exhalation, inhalation, and rest, or the inseparability of both, is nonconceptuality, the present" (p. 434).
102. Here, the support refers to the nāḍīs, syllables, vāyus, and bindus.
103. *S* says, "The treatise is out of order to cause reliance on the guru" (p. 435).
104. Meaning, "I am union."
105. *S* says, "The transformation of the supported, the totally pure mind itself, is the svabhāvakāya, the very pure, effortlessly accomplished kāya. As such, there are five kāyas" (p. 440).
106. *M*, f. 4a, line 6.
107. *M*, f. 6a, line 2.
108. The commentary assumes at the outset that the practitioner is male.
109. *S* says, "A ḍākinī, protector, or goddess that guards one one-pointedly and removes obstacles at the time of the path" (p. 441).
110. The above memorial verse was composed by Drakpa Gyaltsen and concludes the treatise.

9. The Beautiful Ornament of the Six Limbs

1. *dPal kye rdo rje'i mngon par rtogs pa 'bring du yan lag drug pa'i mdzes rgyan*, *DNZ*, pp. 123–52. *L*, vol. 18, pp. 243–74.
2. Köchok Palden, *Hagiography of Könchok Lhundrub*. This is a commentary on Könchok Lhundrub's verse autobiography, *Glorious Source of All Wishes*.
3. Amezhab gives the name Kunga Döndrub (Kun dga' don grub) in *Marvelous Beautiful Waves* (Collected Works, vol. 4, p. 571).
4. Padmavajra. The *Śrīhevajra Sādhana* represents one translation of this text. According to the *Catalog of Hevajra Dharma Cycles*, it was also translated by Drokmi Śākya Yeshe with Gāyadhara. This translation seems to be no longer extant.
5. Ngawang Chödrak, *Essence of Excellent Explanations*, in *LT* 5.
6. Drakpa Gyaltsen, *Six-Limb Direct Realization*, in *SKB* 7.
7. Sönam Gyaltsen, *Direct Realization of Hevajra*, Collected Works, vol. 2.
8. Könchok Gyaltsen, *Six Limbs*, in *Evaṃ Kabum*, 10.
9. This is an homage to Könchok Phel (dKon mchog 'phel ba, 1445–1514), the seventh abbot of Ngor and Könchok Lhundrub's root guru.
10. *HT*, f. 5a, lines 3–5.
11. *VT*, f. 53a, line 4–6.

12. *ST*, ff. 96a–96b.
13. *HT*, f. 18b, lines 6–7.
14. The meaning of the names of these vajra offering goddesses are ignorance, hatred, envy, desire, jealousy, not-self yoginī, body, speech, and mind, respectively.
15. This uncommon protection wheel and the repelling practice are derived from chapters 2, 4, 12, and 14 of the *Vajrapañjara Tantra*. It is based on Sachen Kunga Nyingpo's *Protection Cakra of the Ten Wrathful Ones* (in *SKB*, vol. 2).
16. The *Bhayanāsa Protection Cakra* says, "This bhayanāsa emerges from *The Great Illusion Tantra in Eighty Thousand Lines*. When non-Buddhists cursed the scholarly guru Bari Lotsāwa (Ba ri lo tsā wa Rin chen grags, 1040–1110), Guru Vajrāsana the Younger said, 'Since the non-Buddhists cursed you, destroy them with this repelling [mantra]'" (in *SKB*, vol. 2, p. 284).
17. The names of the charnel grounds, and so on, are taken from Gerloff, "Saroruhavajra's Hevajra Lineage." However, the actual order of the names precisely follows Kṛṣṇa Paṇḍita's *Clarifying the Principles*, Dg.T. rgyud, *nya* (Toh. 1253).
18. The names of the field guardians are only found in Kṛṣṇa Paṇḍita's *Clarifying the Principles* and in Dārika's *Compendium of Principles*, but they do not have any representation in any currently known Sanskrit manuscript. These have been given asterisks to denote that they are tentative reconstructions.
19. Following the reading found in Ngorchen Kunga Zangpo's *Moon Rays*, in *L* 14.
20. This is a mythical eight-legged deer. According to *The Milk Cow*, "A śarabha has eight legs, eyes on top, and can even overpower a lion" (f. 309b, line 5). In one of the Bodhisattva's past lives, he was born as a śarabha, who rescued a king who had tried to shoot him with an arrow.
21. This is a dancing posture, with one foot lifted up to the thigh, as in lotus posture, and the other leg standing firmly on the ground.
22. *HT*, f. 24a, line 7.
23. *HT*, f. 24a, lines 4–6.
24. These five vajras are the buddhas of the five families—hatred, ignorance, envy, desire, and jealousy, respectively.
25. *VT*, f. 50a, lines 4–5. This verse is translated on the basis of the interlinear commentary of chapter 8 of *VT*, according to Drakpa Gyaltsen's *Annotated Vajrapañjara Tantra* (in *SKB*, vol. 7).
26. *Vajra Garland Tantra*, Dg.K. rgyud, *ca* (Toh. 445), f. 260b, line 5.
27. *HT*, f. 7a, lines 4–5.
28. Reading *e* as *aṃ*, following *L*.
29. *HT*, ff. 29b–30a.
30. *VT*, f. 42b, line 4.
31. These two lines are attributed to Durjayacandra by Amezhab in the *Clarification That is Joyful to Behold* (Collected Works, vol. 22.) They are also found in Saroruha's *Padminī* commentary.
32. This is a traditional verse unique to the Sakya school.
33. *HT*, f. 11a, lines 3–4.

34. *HT*, ff. 11a–11b.
35. *HT*, f. 11a, lines 6–7.
36. Ngorchen notes in *Moon Rays*, "Here, *oṃ* is absent in both this sādhana and the *Kaumudī* commentary, but it is present in some Indian copies of the root tantra, the *Saroruha Sādhana*, the *Ratnajvālanāma Sādhana*, and the explanations of former gurus. According to these sources, *oṃ* means 'commitment'" (in *L*, vol. 14, p. 394).
37. Nāgārjuna, *Benedictory Verses*, Dg.T. bstan bcos sna tshogs, *nyo* (Toh. 4410), f. 347a, lines 6–7.
38. Sa skya lotsāwa 'Jam byangs kun dga' bsod nams grags pa rgyal mtshan dpal bzang po (1485–1533), the twenty-second Sakya throne holder.

10. The Beautiful Ornament of the Bali Rite

1. *dPal skye rdo rje'i gtor chog mdzes rgyan*. *DNZ*, pp. 153–75. *L*, vol. 18, pp. 375–97.
2. Amezhab, *The Sun That Illuminates*, Collected Works, vol. 25.
3. Amezhab blends the accounts found in these three tantras to create a cohesive narrative of their subjugation and liberation. Two main narrative tropes are employed in these texts. The first, a narrative of Mahākāla, relates a variation of the tale of the destruction of Tripura, the threefold city of the asuras built by the asura architect Mayāsura. Mahākāla is eventually tamed by Vajrapāṇi and commanded to protect the dharma. The second narrative is a variation on Ravana Daśagriva's abduction of Sita in the *Rāmāyaṇa*. In this retelling, under the influence of Remati, the niece of Daśagriva, Sita Saṅkhapāla (Lha mo dkar mo dung skyong ma), elopes with Daśagriva to Lanka, inspiring the wrath of her mother, Umadevi. Cursed by her mother, Sita turns into a rākṣasī, and after a series of episodes, meets Śākyamuni Buddha under the Bodhi tree, offers her heart to him, and is appointed a guardian of the dharma based on her past aspirations. It is crucial to note that the other name of Saṅkhapāla is Parṇaśavari (Ri khrod lo gyun ma). Parṇaśavari and Śrīdevi are the peaceful and wrathful aspects of the same goddess. Notable as well in the second narrative is the appearance in the *Ḍākinī's Blazing Tongue Tantra* of the famed brahmin Vararuci (mChog sred) who is the source of the lineage of the eight-deity Mahākāla transmission.
4. Amezhab tells us that these three siblings were two brothers and one sister, who aroused the jealousy of the local Buddhist clergy, both ordained and lay, because of the veneration they were receiving. The Buddhist clergy incited a mob of their followers to murder the siblings. The siblings reacted with understandable dismay to their fate, vowing revenge on all who participated in the mob. The elder brother was born as the yama called Killer (gSod byed), the younger brother was reborn as a māra called Hair Bound in a Topknot (Ral pa spyi phyings), and the sister was reborn as a rākṣasī named Golden Razor (gSer gyi spu tri). The members of the mob who slew them were reborn as their ret-

inue: one hundred tsan demons in the form of wild men, one hundred gyalpo spirits in the form of monks, one hundred mantrins wielding kīlas, and one hundred mamos armed with razors.

5. *Ma mo srog gi 'khor lo rgyud.* This tantra no longer seems to be extant.
6. *Bali* is the Sanskrit term translated into Tibetan as *torma* (*gtor ma*). It refers to ritual food offerings.
7. The text here is abbreviated. The practitioner should refer to the *Beautiful Ornament of the Six Limbs* for details regarding the nine-deity maṇḍala, deities, ornaments, and so on.
8. The translation of this offering mantra (*HT*, f. 23a, line 1–2) is taken from Drakpa Gyaltsen's interlinear commentary on the *Hevajra Tantra*. It is as follows: *Inda* is "Indra." *Jama* is "Yama." *Jala* is "Varuṇa." *Jakkha* is "Yakṣa (Kubera)". *Bhūta* is the same. *Bihni* is "Agni." *Vāyu* is the god of wind. *Rakha* is "Rakṣa." *Canda* is Candra, "the moon." *Sujja* is Sūrya, "the sun." *Pappa* is Brahma. *Talapātāle* means "the subterranean regions." *Attasappa* means "eight nāgas." *Idam* means "this." *Baliṃ* refers to the bali or the oblation. *Bhuñja* means "eat." *Jigha* means "smell." *Phulla* means "flowers." *Dhūppa* means "incense." *Māṃsa* means "great meat." *Piṃgha* means "fish." *Ambha* means "I." *Sappa* means "all." *Kajja* means "goals." *Sādha* means "accomplish." *Khantikhuṇi* means "please be patient." *Pheḍagada* means "remove the harmful ones!" *Oṃ* means "the syllable *a* is." *Kāromukhaṃ* means "the door." *Sarvadharmanaṃ* means "all phenomena." *Ṇāṃ* means "from the beginning." *Ādyanutpannatvāta* means "because of having never arisen." Thus, "Indra, Yama, Varuṇa, Yakṣa, Bhūta, Agni, Vāyu, Rakṣa, Candra, Sūrya, Brahma, and the eight nāgas under the ground eat this oblation and smell it. [I offer] flowers, incense, great meat, and fish. Accomplish all of my goals. Please be patient and remove all harmful ones. The syllable *a* is the gate of all phenomena never having arisen from the beginning" (*Annotated Hevajra King Tantra*, in *SKB*, vol. 18, p. 666).
9. The indirect source of this verse is the *Guhyasamāja Tantra*, Dg.K. rgyud, *ca* (Toh. 442), ff. 139a–139b. However, the last line in each verse has been modified in Kambala's *Commentary on Difficult Points*, the direct source of this citation.
10. *Gaṇḍī* refers to the section of single tree trunk between the root and the first branches. It is also the name of the monastic log drum used to summon the monastic community to the bimonthly confessional rite. The *Gaṇḍīsūtra* indicates what material this log drum should be composed of, and so on: "The Bhagavān replied, 'The desirable trees should be examined with great care: Sandalwood (*Santalum alba*), Bilva (*Aegle marmelos*), Rosewood (*Dalbergia* sp.), Aśvattha (*Ficus religiosa*), Red Sandalwood (*Pterocarpus santalinus*), Jujube (*Ziziphus jujuba*), Palmyra (*Borassus* sp.), Parrot Tree (*Butea monosperma*), Agarwood (*Aquilaria malaccensis*), Indian Bay Leaf (*Cinnamomum tamala*), Mango (*Mangifera indica*), Sea Buckthorn (*Hippophae rhamnoides*), Amalaki (*Embellica* sp.), Ting ti sa ra (unidentified), and Aśoka (*Saraca asoca*). Even

if all of these are unavailable, the diligent can make it from Mulberry (*Morus indica*). Diligent king, if none of these exist, it cannot be made" (f. 302b, lines 2–3). The significance of this instrument is described as follows: "King, in that region where the gaṇḍī resounds, there will be prestige, fame, wants, and good harvests. There will be no fear of defeat by enemies. Also, the grain will not spoil. Because of the Buddha's abundant power, the māras will be tamed," and so on (f. 133a, lines 4–5).

11. *Ma mo* in Tibetan.
12. The source of this verse is Śraddhākaravarman's *Medium Rite*, Dg.T. rgyud, *tshu* (Toh. 3774).
13. Reading *rākṣasī* following the anonymous *Sādhana Method of Śrīdevīkālī*.
14. The source of this set of verses is Devakulamahāmati's *Expansion of Principles*, Dg.T. rgyud, *ca* (Toh. 1196). The original source, with slightly different translation, is *VT*, f. 63b, lines 3–5.
15. Reading *dka' zlog* for *bka' zlog*, following *Praise of the Black Śrīdevī King Tantra*, Dg.K. rgyud, *ba* (Toh. 671), f. 208b, line 4. Further, Vararuci's *Praise to Śrīmahākālī* gives *rdzongs dang dka' zlog nag mo che* for *DNZ*, *rdzong dang bka' zlog nag mo ste* (Dg.T. rgyud, *sha*, Toh. 1777, f. 272a).
16. The source of this praise is Vararuci's *Praise to Śrīmahākālī*, Dg.T. rgyud, *sha*, (Toh. 1777). Amezhab states in the *Sun That Illuminates* that the peaceful aspect of this form of Palden Lhamo is the goddesses Parṇaśavari, whose practice is employed to protect against epidemics (Collected Works, vol. 25, p. 33).
17. Corrected to *yaṃ* from *ya*.
18. An alternate spelling is *Bhatra*, probably for *Bhadra*.
19. Reading *khyed* for *skyong* following Padmakāra, *Sādhana of the Monbu Putra Siblings* in *Rin chen gter mdzod chen mo*, vol. 61.
20. Reading *Mon tri*, also known as *Mon dar*, following the *Sādhana of the Monbu Putra Siblings* (*Rin chen gter mdzod chen mo*, vol. 61) above.
21. *sher/shir shing*, Skt. *gośīrṣa*. This is a very expensive kind of sandalwood, reputed for its bronze color and deep scent.
22. This praise is taken from the *Sādhana of the Monbu Putra Siblings*, in *Rin chen gter mdzod chen mo*, vol. 61.
23. The source of this mantra is *Ancillary Exposition Tantra*, Dg.K. rgyud, *ka* (Toh. 369), f. 270b, lines 6–7.
24. The source of this mantra is *Ancillary Exposition Tantra*, Dg.K. rgyud, *ka* (Toh. 369), f. 270b–272a.
25. The version presented in the text is abbreviated. It has been provided in full for ease of reading. The original source for this request for activities is Sönam Tsemo, *Garland of Offerings*, in *SKB*, vol. 5.
26. This mantra has been corrected on the basis of the recension found in *L*.
27. This refers to the one dedicated to Hevajra.
28. *dzam bu ti ka*. This is *Eugenia jambolana*, black plum.
29. Kunga Zangpo, *Victory over the Armies*, Collected Works, vol. 2.

30. Ibid.
31. This refers to Könchok Phelwa (dKon mchog 'phel ba, 1445–1514), the seventh abbot of Ngor.

11. The Beautiful Ornament of the Great River

1. *dPal kye rdo rje dbang gi chu bo chen mo mdzes par byed pa'i rgyan*. In *DNZ*, vol. 5, 177–242. *L*, vol. 18, 293–359.
2. This is *Gymnadenia conopsea*.
3. *Four Places*, Dg.K. mdo, *sha* (Toh. 298), f. 190a, line 2. In this tantra, this mudra is referred as the *vaḍabāmukha* (*rgod ma kha*) mudra, the wild mare's mouth mudra, a reference to a subterranean fire in the southern ocean. For more information on its mythological context, see Wendy O'Flaherty, *The Submarine Mare.*
4. The person appointed to carry out activities on behalf of the assembly.
5. This is an insert one adds to the maṇḍala offering.
6. One skips the uncommon protection wheel and proceeds directly to the generation of the celestial mansion and charnel grounds.
7. Sönam Tsemo, *Great River of Empowerment*, in *SKB* vol. 5, f. 12a, line 4.
8. In his *Origin of Śrī Heruka*, Jetsun Drakpa Gyaltsen identifies *cchandoha* and *upacchandoha* as belonging to the language of rākṣasas. He further identifies the term *pitha* as Sanskrit, *upapitha* as gandharva language, *kṣetra* and *upakṣetra* as yakṣa language, *melāpaka* and *upamelāpaka* as nāga language, and *śmāśana* and *upaśmāśana* as Asura language. In "Sacred Origins of the Svayambhūcaitya," Rospatt states that *cchandoha* corresponds to *saṃdoha* in Śaiva texts but provides no meaningful translation of the term. *Monier-Williams* defines *saṃdoha*'s primary meaning as "milking place."
9. *'thung gcod*, Skt. *pīlavaṃ*. Kongtrul's *Buddhist Ethics* defines this term as "abstinence from drinking" (510, n. 331). A definition cannot be found for *pīlavaṃ*. However, it is possible the term derives from *pīluvana*, a grove of *Salvadora persica* trees.
10. *brtan ma bcu gnyis*. These are the twelve autochthonic Tibetan goddesses tamed by Padmasambhava.
11. These are the hell realm, preta realm, animal realm, human realm, and the deva realm.
12. Saroruha, *Praise to Hevajra*, Dg.T. rgyud, *nya* (Toh. 1222).
13. This verse has been supplied in full, as found in Drakpa Gyaltsen, *Light Rays* (*SKB*, vol. 9, p. 27).
14. Kṛṣṇa Paṇḍitā, *Maṇḍala Rite Textual Commentary*, Dg.T. rgyud, *nya* (Toh. 1254), f. 256ab, line 7. The first line is not actually part of the verse but is treated as such because it also has seven syllables.
15. Sönyompa, *Maṇḍala Rite*, Dg.T. rgyud, *pi*, (Toh. 1882), f. 120, lines 4–5.
16. In this verse, the southeast is called Agni (*me*), the northeast is called Indra

(*dbang ldan*), the northwest is called Vāyu (*rlung*), and the southwest is called Rākṣasa (*srin po*)

17. Kṛṣṇa Paṇḍitā, *Maṇḍala Rite Textual Commentary*, Dg.T. rgyud, *nya* (Toh. 1254), f. 257a, line 4.
18. This is a metal device used to trace the outlines, and so on, of the maṇḍala in colored sand.
19. Traditionally, this is the urine, dung, butter, curd, and milk of a red cow.
20. *mig thur*, Skt. *śalākā*. This term is often rendered as "eye spoon." A *thur ma* is a class of surgical instrument in Ayurveda and Tibetan medicine. These pointed instruments resemble scalpels, cannulas, and so on. Specifically, the *śalākā* is about six inches long and is used for removing cataracts. The general procedure is to make a small hole in the eye, and the instrument is pushed into the pupil, which is then used to scrape the cataract material and break it up. That cataract material is then expelled through the incision, assisted with the instrument, by having the patient sneeze through the nostril opposite to the eye. For a classical description of this procedure, see Murti, *Vagbhaṭa's Aṣṭāṅgahṛdayam*, vol. 3, 133. See also www.himalayanart.org/items/1163/images/primary. See the third row, the set of instruments from the right, second one down, referred to as the "easy to use *śalākā*" (*bya sla'i mig thur*).
21. *V*, f. 34a–34b.
22. Prajñendraruci, *Blazing Jewel Sādhana*, Dg.T. rgyud, *nya* (Toh. 1251), ff. 221a–b.
23. Saroruha, *Ritual Procedure for the Hevajra Maṇḍala*, Dg.T. rgyud, *ta* (Toh. 1263), 9a, line 6.
24. *Glorious First One's Section of the Mantra Divisions*, Dg.K. rgyud, *ta* (Toh. 488), f. 228b, lines 2–3.
25. Saroruha, *Ritual Procedure for the Hevajra Maṇḍala*, Dg.T. rgyud, *ta* (Toh. 1263), f. 9a, line 1.
26. Ibid., 9b, line 5.
27. *VT*, f. 54a, lines 6–7.
28. Nāgārjuna, *Benedictory Verses*, Dg.T. bstan bcos sna tshogs, *nyo* (Toh. 4410), f. 347a, lines 6–7.
29. Since the first line of these verses is in fact the last line of the Tibetan, in the following sections, only the first line will be given where it is indicated that one should switch the last line.
30. This title generally refers to the six-limbed sādhana combined with the body maṇḍala section, *The Beautiful Ornament of the Body Maṇḍala*. According to the Sakya school, it is the body maṇḍala that permits one to take the four empowerments in elaborate form in daily practice. The cause empowerment sādhana by itself does not allow one to take the empowerments in elaborate form, unless one is doing so in the presence of a fully constructed sand or cloth maṇḍala. Therefore, in that sādhana, the empowerment section only provides the brief empowerment.
31. Durjayacandra, *Sādhana of the Maṇḍala Rite*, Dg.T. rgyud, *nya* (Toh. 1240), f.

146b, line 2. The entire verse was added for the purpose of giving sense to the following explanation.

32. *VT*, f. 38a, line 1.
33. Kṛṣṇa Paṇḍitā, *Maṇḍala Rite Textual Commentary*, Dg.T. rgyud, *nya* (Toh. 1254), f. 259a, line 6.
34. *Secret Jewel Ornament Sutra*, Dg.K. rgyud, *tha* (Toh. 493), f. 126a, line 3.
35. *Glorious First One's Section of the Mantra Divisions*, Dg.K. rgyud, *ta* (Toh. 488), f. 264b, line 4–5.
36. Vajraghanta, *Concise Activities*, Dg.T. rgyud, *wa* (Toh. 1431), f. 220b, line 5.
37. *Glorious First One's Section of the Mantra Divisions*, Dg.K. rgyud, *ta* (Toh. 488), f. 192a, line 6.
38. *HT*, f. 17a, line 4.
39. This four-line verse is found in Durjayacandra's *Sādhana of the Maṇḍala Rite* (Dg.T. rgyud, *nya*, Toh. 1240), Prajñendraruci's *Blazing Jewel Sādhana* (Dg.T. rgyud, *nya*, Toh. 1251), and Kṛṣṇa Paṇḍitā's *Maṇḍala Rite Textual Commentary* (Dg.T. rgyud, *nya*, Toh. 1254).
40 *Glorious First One's Section of the Mantra Divisions*, Dg.K. rgyud, *ta* (Toh. 488), f. 207, line 1.
41. *sgo khyud*. These are four strips of metal attached to the outside of doors in order to reinforce them.
42. Sönam Tsemo, *Great River of Empowerment*, in *SKB*, vol. 5, pp. 165–66. This verse is also found in a slightly different translation in Sönyompa, *Maṇḍala Rite*, Dg.T. rgyud, *pi*, (Toh. 1882), ff. 126b–127a.
43. In Kṛṣṇa Paṇḍitā's *Maṇḍala Rite Textual Commentary*, this series of offerings is found in on f. 265a, line 7 and continues to f. 256b, line 6. On f. 265b, line 6, this syllable is is given as *tra(ṃ)*.
44. Kṛṣṇa Paṇḍitā, *Maṇḍala Rite Textual Commentary*, Dg.T. rgyud, *nya* (Toh. 1254), f. 266a, lines 4–5.
45. This part of the rite follows Kṛṣṇa Paṇḍitā, *Maṇḍala Rite Textual Commentary*, Dg.T. rgyud, *nya* (Toh. 1254), ff. 265a–266a.
46. See ch. 8, p. 000 [[x-ref to ms. page 163]] for the meaning of this phrase.
47. *HT*, f. 17a, lines 6–7.
48. The eighty natural concepts refer to to the three classes of concepts related to hatred (33), desire (40), and ignorance (7). See Kongtrul, *Systems of Buddhist Tantra* for a full account and description of these concepts (pp. 260–65).
49. This mantra is clearly related to the first line of the Vedic Gayatri mantra: *oṃ bhūr bhuvaḥ suvaḥ*. *Bhūr* means subterranean, *bhūvaḥ* means terrestrial, and *sva* means celestial, which is reflected in the translation of "below, on, and above the ground" (*sa 'og sa steng sa bla*.) This specific passage is adapted from a text translated by Sakya Paṇḍitā, Rāhulaśrīmitra's *Activity of Empowerment*, Dg.T. rgyud, *ngi* (Toh. 1818), f. 243b, lines 1–3. It appears in this form in Chögyal Phakpa, *Entry into the Empowerment*, in *SKB*, vol. 13, p. 469, lines 2–4.
50. *phyag rgya*, Skt. *mudra*. This is a symbolic name for a female consort.

51. *HT*, f. 29b, line 7.
52 Kṛṣṇa Paṇḍitā, *Maṇḍala Rite Textual Commentary*, Dg.T. rgyud, *nya* (Toh. 1254), f. 267b, lines 5–6.
53. Ibid., ff. 266b–267a.
54. Drakpa Gyaltsen's *Ornament of the Vajrapañjara* says, "Externally this refers to a crown, internally, to the master of the family, and secretly the *haṃ* syllable" (p. 140).
55. Drakpa Gyaltsen's *Ornament of the Vajrapañjara* says that the outer burnt offering is the hearth, the inner is food, and the secret is mantra and dharma (p. 140).
56. The *Ornament of the Vajrapañjara* says that the outer consecration is statues, the inner is the gnosis being in the samādhi maṇḍala, and the secret is bodhicitta of mantra and dharma (pp. 140–41).
57. The *Ornament of the Vajrapañjara* says that the outer is offered to the bhūtas, the inner is food, and the secret is mantra and dharma (p. 141).
58. *VT*, ff. 64b–65a.
59. Kṛṣṇa Paṇḍitā, *Maṇḍala Rite Textual Commentary*, Dg.T. rgyud, *nya* (Toh. 1254), f. 266b, lines 2–3. This passage is referred to here as "the proclamation of the secret."
60. Ibid., f. 266b, line 3–4.
61. Ibid., f. 266b, line 4.
62. Ibid., f. 266a, line 5.
63. Vajraghaṇṭa, *Concise Activities*, Dg.T. rgyud, *wa* (Toh. 1431), f. 221a, lines 3–4.
64. *HT*, ff. 29b–30a.
65. Kṛṣṇa Paṇḍitā, *Maṇḍala Rite Textual Commentary*, Dg.T. rgyud, *nya* (Toh. 1254), f. 266b, lines 5–6.
66. Ānandagarbha's *Extensive Explanation* (Collected Works, vol. 21) explains these two lines as follows: "Just as space has the nature of being free from all substance, because substances such as walls, and so on, are perishable, it is designated as "birth." In the same way, because the nature of the vajra of suchness, Vajrasattva, is free from all taints of all false conceptions, he is designated as "birth" in the continuum of all sentient beings. Therefore, the space endowed with the characteristic of birth is the Bhagavān. That one who is space endowed with the characteristic of birth is without beginning or end. The 'without beginning or end' known to the world is the 'without beginning or end' by means of imputation, but it is not ultimate. Therefore, in order to demonstrate that [this 'without beginning and end'] is superior to [the world's], it is said to be 'supreme,' it is 'the supreme one without beginning and end' in the ultimate. If it is asked what is like that, it is said, 'The nature of great Vajrasattva,' the being possessing the nature of the vajra of suchness is the nature of great Vajrasattva, demonstrating 'the nature of the mind and its mental factors are the same taste as suchness'" (ff. 25a–25b).

67. This passage is commonly used in many initiation rituals where the name of the deity is substituted for Vajrasattva.
68. This line refers to all śrāvaka arhats, pratyekabuddhas, and bodhisattvas.
69. This section of the prayer is taken from *Glorious First One's Section of the Mantra Divisions*, Dg.K. rgyud, *ta* (Toh. 488), f. 226b, lines 2–4.
70. Prajñendraruci, *Blazing Jewel Sādhana*, Dg.T. rgyud, *nya* (Toh. 1251), f. 220, lines 3–6.
71. Kṛṣṇa Paṇḍitā, *Maṇḍala Rite Textual Commentary*, Dg.T. rgyud, *nya* (Toh. 1254), f. 261, lines 6–7.
72. Śubhakṛt (*dge byed*) is the thirty-sixth year of the sixty-year cycle of the Tibetan calendar.
73. Sönam Tsemo, *Great River of Empowerment*, in *SKB*, vol. 5.

12. The Condensed Essential Citations and Intimate Instructions

1. *dPal skye rdo rje man ngag lugs kyi dbang chog lung dang man ngag gi snying po bsdus pa*. DNZ, pp. 243–324. *L*, vol. 18, pp. 399–475.
2. Lodrö Gyaltsen, *Illuminating the Empowerment*, in *SKB*, vol. 14, f. 2a, line 2.
3. Ibid., f. 2a, lines 2–3.
4. The term *inalienable* (*mi 'phrogs pa*, Skt. *asaṃhārya*) comes from the well-known passage of the *Guhyasamāja Uttaratantra*: "Divided by basis, likewise, nature, and inalienability; the nature aspect is cause; inalienability is the result; and the basis is known as the method" (f. 150a, line 2).
5. Kṛṣṇa Paṇḍitā, *Maṇḍala Rite Textual Commentary*, Dg.T. rgyud, *nya* (Toh. 1254), f. 258a, lines 2–3.
6. Here and in what follows, "śrāvaka" refers primarily to śrāvaka arhats.
7. Durjayacandra, *Sādhana of the Maṇḍala Rite*, Dg.T. rgyud, *nya* (Toh. 1240), f. 137a, lines 2–4.
8. Sönam Tsemo, *Great River of Empowerment*, in *SKB*, vol. 5, p. 97, lines 2–5. This passage appears to an amalgam of passages taken from the maṇḍala rites of Padmavajra's *Stages of the Activity* (Dg.T. rgyud, *nya*, Toh. 1219), Durjayacandra's *Sādhana of the Maṇḍala Rite* (Dg.T. rgyud, *nya*, Toh. 1240), and Kṛṣṇa Paṇḍitā's *Maṇḍala Rite Textual Commentary* (Dg.T. rgyud, *nya*, Toh. 1254).
9. *VT*, f. 53a, lines 4–6.
10. Here, the usual directions for increasing (south) and destructive (north) siddhis have been reversed.
11. Sönam Tsemo, *Great River of Empowerment*, in *SKB*, vol. 5, p. 102, lines 1–5. This passage, like the passage mentioned in the endnotes before, appears to be an amalgam of passages taken from the maṇḍala rites of Durjayacandra's *Sādhana of the Maṇḍala Rite* (Dg.T. rgyud, *nya*, Toh. 1240) and Kṛṣṇa Paṇḍitā's *Maṇḍala Rite Textual Commentary* (Dg.T. rgyud, *nya*, Toh. 1254). The original

source from which these passages appear to be adapted is *Āvalokiteśvara's Network*, Dg.K. rgyud, *ba* (Toh. 681), f. 251b, lines 3–6.

12. *Secret Tantra of General Rites*, Dg.K. rgyud, *wa* (Toh. 806), f. 146b–147a. This long passage describes the various kinds of positive dreams one will have the night prior to being admitted into the maṇḍala.
13. Skt. *karavīra*.
14. Könchok Lhundrub, *Great River of the Empowerment*, *DNZ*, vol. 5 (*ca*), p. 240, lines 1–2.
15. These are the individual liberation vows of a bodhisattva upāsaka, upāsikā, śramaṇera, śikṣamāṇā, śramaṇerika, bhikṣu, or bhikṣuni.
16. Könchok Lhundrub, *Great River of the Empowerment*, *DNZ*, vol. 5 (*ca*), p. 240, line 3. The first and final lines of these summary verses are not precisely represented in the quoted source.
17. This is the name for the person who conducts ritual procedures on behalf of the master.
18. While the first three verses are taken from Nāgārjuna, *Benedictory Verses*, Dg.T. bstan bcos sna tshogs, *nyo* (Toh. 4410), f. 347a, lines 6–7. These three verses and the remaining verses are found in Durjayacandra, *Sādhana of the Maṇḍala Rite*, Dg.T. rgyud, *nya* (Toh. 1240), ff. 145a–146a.
19. Sakya Paṇḍita, *Differentiation of the Three Vows*, in SKB, vol. 12, p. 43, line 3–4.
20. Since the first line of these verses is in fact the last line of the Tibetan, in the following sections only the first line will be given where it is indicated that one should switch the last line.
21. This is a species of waterfowl.
22. *bye'u tsa ko ra*, Skt. *cakora*. The latin name for this is *Alectorus chukar*.
23. *bye'u khra*. Ngawang Lekpa's *Commentary on Recalling the Purities and Miscellany* identifies this as the cuckoo (Collected Works, p. 94, line 2).
24. Skt. *nakra*.
25. *ce spyang*. Ngawang Lekpa's *Commentary on Recalling the Purities and Miscellany* identifies this as a fox (*wa skyes*) (Collected Works, p. 94, line 6).
26. Reading *lug pa* as a misspelling of *'ug pa*.
27. *sa ra sa*, Skt. *sārasa*. The latin name for this is *Antigone antigone*.
28. These are, in order, Mercury, Jupiter, Mars, the south lunar node, the north lunar node, Venus, Saturn, and the invisible planet called khyabjuk (*khyab 'jug*) in Tibetan. Ketu, Rāhu, and Viṣṇurāja are all aspects of Rāhula.
29. *lha rgyal ba 'dam pa*. This is identified as the teacher of the Jains in Drakpa Gyaltsen's *Annotated Hevajra King Tantra* (in *SKB*, vol. 18, p. 559, line 4).
30. Skt. *makara*.
31. The latin name for this is *Labeo rohita*.
32. *'og gi klu*. Ngawang Lekpa's *Commentary on Recalling the Purities and Miscellany* identifies as a being with a human upper body with a spread cobra hood, and the lower body of a snake (p. 95, line 6).

33. *sbal pa thu'u*, Ngawang Lekpa's *Commentary on Recalling the Purities and Miscellany* identifies this as a gangbal (*gangs sbal*) or daji (*da byid*), the Latin being *Batrachuperis pinchonii* (p. 96, line 1).
34. *sprin shugs*. Ngawang Lekpa's identifies this, literally "power cloud," as a green horse (p. 96, line 1).
35. *rtsang phag nag po*. Ngawang Lekpa's *Miscellany* identifies this as the Indian goat living in central Tibet (p. 96, line 2).
36. *bya bshad*, species unidentified. Ngawang Lekpa's *Miscellany* identifies this as a white bird with a red head (p. 96, line 2).
37. *sgo khyud*. These are four strips of metal attached to the outside of the doors in order to reinforce them.
38. See ch. 8, endnotes 47 and 48, for the meaning of this phrase.
39. Kṛṣṇa Paṇḍitā, *Maṇḍala Rite Textual Commentary*, Dg.T. rgyud, *nya* (Toh. 1254), ff. 267b–268a.
40. Ibid., f. 267b, line 5.
41. *tsum ba*, Skt. *cumba*. While this word generally means to kiss, it also carries the meaning of intimate touch.
42. This passage does not appear to exist in any text in the canon and appears in only late Sakya sources, such as Könchok Lhundrub's *Condensed Essential Citations* (in *Evaṃ Kabum*, vol. 14, p. 394).
43. This refers to *The Collection of All Tantras* (*G*).
44. Kun dga' bstan pa'i rgyal mtshan, 1829–1870, fifty-fourth abbot of Ngor.

13. The Lineage Supplication

1. *gSung ngag rin po chen lam 'bras bu dang bcas pa'i brgyud 'debs, DNZ*, vol. 5, pp. 325–26.

14. The Complete Clarification of the Hidden Meaning

1. *Lam 'bras bu dang bcas pa'i gzhung ji lta ba bzhin dkri ba'i khrid yig sbas don kun gsal, DNZ*, vol. 5, pp 329–408. *L*, vol. 16, pp. 451–543.
2. This short biography is based on Amezhab, *Source of All Needs and Wants* (Collected Works, vol. 3) and Palden Tsultrim's *Hagiography* (in *Sakya Lamdre*, vol. 1).
3. Reading *L*, *gsal mdzad*; *DNZ*, *gsang mdzod*.
4. Nāgārjuna, *Five Stages*, Dg.T. rgyud, *ngi* (Toh. 1802) f. 53b, line 5.
5. Ibid., f. 53b, line 4.
6. *V*, f. 49b, line 3.
7. Aśvaghoṣa, *Fifty Verses on the Guru*, Dg.T. rgyud, *tshu* (Toh. 3721), f. 10a, line 4 and f. 11b, line 3.
8. *Guhyasamāja Tantra*, Dg.K. rgyud, *ca* (Toh. 442), f. 102b, line 3. This version

is not found in the canon but comes from a work by Sakya Paṇḍita Kunga Gyaltsen's *Trio of Outer, Inner, and Secret Maṇḍala Offerings* (in *SKB*, vol. 12). It may represent his preferred reading of the Sanskrit.

9. This passage is missing from *DNZ* but is found in *L*, pp. 456–57, line 1.
10. *P*, p. 175, line 3.
11. The source text for this citation is unidentified.
12. This means clasping the knees in the arms and covering the [opposite] kneecaps with both hands.
13. Reading *L*, *rgan pa*; *DNZ*, *gzhon pa*.
14. This refers to *The Vajra Verses*.
15. Nāgārjuna, *Letter to a Friend*, Dg.T. spring yig, *ge* (Toh. 4182), f. 44a, lines 5–6.
16. Reading *L*, *bkrab*; *DNZ*, *bskrab*.
17. Vasubandhu, *Treasury of Abhidharma*, Dg.T. mngon pa, *ku* (Toh. 4089), f. 9b, lines 7–10 and f. 10, line 3.
18. Huhuva, Hahava, and Aṭaṭa are onomatopoeia, but only the last one is translatable. The first two are sounds one makes when extremely cold.
19. Candragomin, *Letter to a Disciple*, Dg.T. spring yig, *nge* (Toh. 4183), ff. 49a–b. Both *L* and *DNZ* have lexical issues, so this rendering follows the Dege edition.
20. Vasubandhu, *Treasury of Abhidharma*, Dg.T. mngon pa, *ku* (Toh. 4089), f. 10a, line 3.
21. Vasubandhu, *Commentary on the Treasury of Abhidharma*, Dg.T. mngon pa, *ku* (Toh. 4090), f. 154b, lines 1–3.
22. Vasubandhu, *Treasury of Abhidharma*, Dg.T. mngon pa, *ku* (Toh. 4089), f. 9a, lines 4–5
23. Candragomin, *Letter to a Disciple*, Dg.T. spring yig, *nge* (Toh. 4183), f. 48b, line 4.
24. Ibid., f. 48b, line 4.
25. Nāgārjuna, *Letter to a Friend*, Dg.T. spring yig, *ge* (Toh. 4182), f. 45a, lines 1–2.
26. Vasubandhu, *Treasury of Abhidharma*, Dg.T. mngon pa, *ku* (Toh. 4089), f. 10a, line 3.
27. Nāgārjuna, *Letter to a Friend*, Dg.T. spring yig, *ge* (Toh. 4182), f. 44b, lines 6–7.
28. Vasubandhu, *Treasury of Abhidharma*, Dg.T. mngon pa, *ku* (Toh. 4089), f. 10a, line 3.
29. *nga las nu*. The story of the cakravartin king Māndhāta is well known in Tibetan Buddhism and is recounted in several sutras as well as in the Vinaya. The most extensive versions of his tale are found in the *Basis of Discipline* (Dg.K. 'dul, *ka*, Toh. 1.) and the *Meeting of the Father and Son Sutra* (Dg.K. dkon, *nga*, Toh. 60).
30. Nāgārjuna, *Letter to a Friend*, Dg.T. spring yig, *ge* (Toh. 4182), ff. 43b–44a.
31. Ibid., f. 44a, lines 3–5.
32. Vasubandhu, *Meaningful Compendium of Stanzas*, Dg.T. mngon pa, *thu* (Toh. 4103), f. 260a, line 3. The last line of this citation is missing in *DNZ*.
33. *sems*, missing from *DNZ*.

34. Āryadeva, *Madhyamaka Four Hundred Verses*, Dg.T. dbu ma, *tsha* (Toh. 3846), f. 8b. lines 3–4.
35. Nāgārjuna, *Letter to a Friend*, Dg.T. spring yig, *ge* (Toh. 4182), f. 43b, line 4–5.
36. Śāntideva, *Introduction to the Conduct of Awakening*, Dg.T. mdo, *la* (Toh. 3871), f. 8b, lines 6–7.
37. Candragomin, *Letter to a Disciple*, Dg.T. spring yig, *nge* (Toh. 4183), f. 50a, lines 2–4.
38. *Introduction to the Conduct of Awakening*, Dg.T. mdo, *la* (Toh. 3871), f. 5b, line 2.
39. Ibid., f. 6a, line 6.
40. Vasubandhu, *Treasury of Abhidharma*, Dg.T. mngon pa, *ku* (Toh. 4089), f. 9b, line 7.
41. Nāgārjuna, *Necklace of Gems*, Dg.T. spring yig, *ge* (Toh. 4158), f. 117b, line 1.
42. Reading *stobs*, for *DNZ*, *sbros*, following *Sutra of Advice to the King*, Dg.K. mdo, *dza* (Toh. 221), f. 80b, line 3.
43. Ibid., f. 80b, lines 3–4.
44. Nāgārjuna, *Necklace of Gems*, Dg.T. spring yig, *ge* (Toh. 4158), f. 107b, line 5.
45. Vasubandhu, *Treasury of Abhidharma*, Dg.T. mngon pa, *ku* (Toh. 4089), f. 14a, line 4.
46. *gzi byin*, Skt, *ojas*. Ojas is a vital principle in living beings, which Ayurveda and Tibetan medicine describe as the final pure product of a seven-fold process of separating the tissues of the body such as blood, flesh, adipose tissue, and so on, and the waste products of the body such as urine, sweat, and so on.
47. Nāgārjuna, *Necklace of Gems*, Dg.T. spring yig, *ge* (Toh. 4158), f. 107b, lines 2–3.
48. The *Necklace of Gems* is commonly cited as the source for this verse, but it not attested there.
49. Nāgārjuna, *Necklace of Gems*, Dg.T. spring yig, *ge* (Toh. 4158), f. 107b, line 5.
50. The three awakenings are those of a śrāvaka arhat, a pratyekabuddha, and a full, perfect buddha.
51. Āryadeva, *Madhyamaka Four Hundred Verses*, Dg.T. dbu ma, *tsha* (Toh. 3846), f. 6a, lines 5–6.
52. Candrakīrti, *Introduction to Madhyamaka*, Dg.T. dbu ma, *'a* (Toh. 3861), f. 214b, line 3.
53. Candragomin, *Letter to a Disciple*, Dg.T. spring yig, *nge* (Toh. 4183), f. 52a, lines 2–3.
54. Nāgārjuna, *Letter to a Friend*, Dg.T. spring yig, *ge* (Toh. 4182), f. 43b, line 7.
55. Candrakīrti, *Introduction to Madhyamaka*, Dg.T. dbu ma, *'a* (Toh. 3861), f. 214b, line 3.
56. Maitreyanātha, *Ornament of Direct Realization*, Dg.T. shes phyin, *ka* (Toh. 3786), f. 2b, line 5.
57. Candragomin, *Letter to a Disciple*, Dg.T. spring yig, *nge* (Toh. 4183), f. 52a, line 1.

58. This refers to those who are inclined toward the result of śrāvakas, pratyekabuddhas, or bodhisattvas.
59. Śāntideva, *Introduction to the Conduct of Awakening*, Dg.T. mdo, *la* (Toh. 3871), f. 27a, line 2.
60. Ibid., f.27a, lines 5–6.
61. Ibid., f.28a, line 5.
62. Ibid., f.28b, line 7.
63. *Guhyasamāja Tantra*, Dg.K. rgyud, *ca* (Toh. 442), f. 94b, lines 2–3.
64. *VT*, f. 39a, lines 2–3.
65. Reading *L*, *chos can*; *DNZ*, *rkyen*.
66. Both *DNZ* and *L* read *rang bshin*, "nature," but given context it has been corrected to *mtshan nyid*, "characteristic," in line with the previous section on the three connate phenomena.
67. *Sutra on Entering Lanka*, Dg.K. mdo, *ca* (Toh. 107), f. 165a, line 6. The second two lines come from lines 5–6 and are inverted here.
68. *HT*, f.18a, line 3–4.
69. *ST*, f. 86a.
70. *HT*, f. 18a, lines 4–5.
71. Nāgārjuna, *Verses on the Rice Seedling Sutra*, Dg.T. mdo 'grel, *ngi* (Toh. 3985), f. 20a, line 7.
72. Nāgārjuna, *Verses on the Heart of Dependent Origination*, Dg.T. dbu ma, *tsa* (Toh. 3836), f. 146b, line 4.
73. *lag pa'i phyag rgya*.
74. *HT*, f. 10a, line 2.
75. *Sutra That Explains the Two Truths*, Dg.K. mdo, *ma* (Toh. 179), f. 247a, line 5.
76. The first two lines of this passage from the *Stages of the Inconceivable* are found at DNZ, vol. 6, p. 84, and *P*, p. 351, line 1. The second two lines, however, are found at, *DNZ*, vol. 6, p. 88, line 4 and *P*, p. 355, line 2. These two half verses are traditionally cited together. The version consulted, that of the nine path cycles, was translated by Ratnavajra and Drokmi Lotsāwa. The version found in the Tengyur (D 2228) was translated by Dewa Nyugu (bDe ba myu gu) and Gö Lotsāwa.
77. The four characteristics are appearances are established as mind, mind is established as illusory illusions are established to be dependently originated, and dependent origination is established to be inexpressible.
78. *P*, p. 495, line 3. *de dag 'ga' ba ltar snang yang mi gal bar myong zhing*, truncated in *DNZ*.
79. *HT*, f. 20b, line 4.
80. Nāgārjuna, *Praise to the Incomparable*, Dg.T. bstod, *ka* (Toh. 1119), f. 67b, line 6.
81. *Guhyasamāja Tantra*, Dg.K. rgyud, *ca* (Toh. 442), f. 142b, lines 5–6.
82. Ibid., f. 142b, line 7.
83. There are four topics mentioned in the following section.

84. The second item is misplaced on p. 376, line 7.
85. Loter Wangpo, *Digest of the Stages of Accomplishing Awakening*, in *L*, vol. 20.
86. The original manual for the thirty-two activities can be found in Drakpa Gyaltsen, *Yantras of the Thirty-Two Activities*, in *P*.
87. In Path with Its Result terminology, *prāṇa* (*srog*) refers to the left nostril. *Āyāma* (*rtsol*) refers to the right nostril, as well as the inhalation and the exhalation.
88. Reading *L*, *btud*; *DNZ*, *bstod*.
89. The word used here is *union*, but a margin note indicates this is to be understood as a finger-snap round, as described above.
90. This passage is unidentified.
91. Since Tibetan medicine counts the first vertebrae to be the seventh cervical vertebrae (C7), this refers to the sixth thoracic vertebrae (T6).
92. *srub gtan*.
93. *phra phra har har song ba*. Amezhab's *Opening the Eye to the Concealed* explains that this phrase means "Meditate that the body is filled with sparks that issue forth" (*me stag 'phro 'phro 'phros pas lus gang bar sgom*) (Collected Works, vol. 22, p. 104).
94. Amezhab, *Opening the Eye to the Concealed*, notes that this means curling the tongue back and pressing it to the palate (Collected Works, vol. 22, p. 104).
95. *brtan*, missing from *DNZ*.
96. Reading *P*, *me*; *DNZ*, *oṃ*.
97. *rgyu ma bus*, "an inflated small intestine."
98. These are special terms for male and female genitals that are found in the *HT*.
99. *L* gives instead, "Because of this, may the abundant goals of myself and others be accomplished with ease! *maṅgalaṃ bhāvantu*" (p. 543).

15. The Threefold Instruction

1. *gNad bcu gcig gis dkri ba gnad drug gis kri ba dbang po rab 'bring gsum gyis dkri ba gsum gyi khrid*, *DNZ*, pp. 409–23. *L*, vol. 16, pp. 432–49.
2. *gNad bcu gcig gis dkri ba'i 'khrid kyi gsal byed gnas kyi sgo 'byed ces bya ba*; *DNZ*, 409–11. *L*, vol. 16, pp. 432–35.
3. This is a reference to the eight ancillary path cycles, which form the bulk of DNZ, vol. 6.
4. *gNad drug gis dkri ba'i khrid kyi gsal byed gnad kyi lde'u mig*, *DNZ*, pp. 411–17. *L*, vol. 16, pp. 435–41.
5. This metaphor of the relationship between the mind and body likened to a flower and its scent is originally found in Drakpa Gyaltsen's *Seven Topics in the All-Basis Cause Continuum* (in *P*).
6. *DNZ* excludes the path.
7. This is omitted in *DNZ*.
8. *Dbang po ran 'bring gsum gyis dkri ba'i khrid rim gyi gsal byed nyung du rnam gsal*, *DNZ*, 417–23. *L*, vol. 16, pp. 441–49.

9. Reading *L*, *slob ma*; *DNZ*, *slob dpon*.
10. *Bhavatu* is added in *P*.

16. Notes on the Intimate Instruction

1. *Lam sbas te bshad pa man ngag gi zin bris*, *DNZ*, vol. 5, pp. 425–31. *L*, vol. 18, pp. 27–32.
2. Lösal Gyatso, *Necklace of Gorgeous Blue Poppies*, in *Sakya Lamdre*, vol. 2.
3. *lam zab mo bla ma'i rnal 'byor*. There are a number of texts in this class, which all involve visualizing the guru as Hevajra.
4. *lam dus*. This is a generic name for the *Hevajra Sādhana*, which includes the body maṇḍala and a full set of initiations.
5. *na ro mkha' spyod*. This is the principal Vajrayoginī practice of the Sakya school, for which there are many sādhanas.
6. *bir bsrung*. This is a special practice that involves visualizing oneself as Mahāsiddha Virūpa controlling the sun, which comes from the vision of Sachen Kunga Nyingpo. There are many versions of this practice.
7. Kunga Gyaltsen, *The Explanation of the Concealed Path*, in *SKB*, vol. 12.
8. *rlung sa len ma*. This is explained as "inhaling soundlessly with the nose just touching the ground" in Ameshab, *Ocean of Intimate Instructions* (Collected Works, vol. 22, p. 394).
9. Reading *de ltar dmigs pa dang po sgoms pas*, following Amezhab, *Ocean of Intimate Instructions* (Collected Works, vol. 22, p. 390). *P* and *DNZ* read *lte bar dmigs mang po sgoms pas*.
10. This refers to the three gatherings of the elements: blazing, shifting, and stable.
11. Mus chen dkon mchog rgyal mtshan (1388–1469), second abbot of Ngor.

17. The Manual That Clarifies Symbols and Meanings

1. *brDa don gsal ba'i khrid yig bdag chen rdo rje chang gis mdzad pa*, *DNZ*, vol. 5, pp. 433–58. *L*, vol. 18, pp. 1–27.
2. Reading *L*, *spyi gtsug*; *DNZ*, *spyan gzigs*.
3. Here, "haze" refers to the heat waves one can see over someone's head. When this vanishes, it is a sign of impending death.
4. The texts gives an onomatopoeia for this: *shang shang*.
5. *Concise Explanation of Empowerments*, Dg.K. rgyud, *ka* (Toh. 361), f. 17b, line 1.
6. "The four terrifying sounds are as follows: Since earth dissolves into water, there is the sound of Mount Meru disintegrating. Since water dissolves into fire, there is the sound of the disturbance of the ocean that destroys the eon. Since fire dissolves into air, there is the sound of the fire at the end of the eon. Since air dissolves into consciousness, there is the sound of the wind at the end of the eon. The three fearsome abysses indicate the downward path leading to the

three lower realms." Chögyal Phakpa, *Drogön Phakpa's Explanation*, in *Sakya Lamdre*, vol. 43, pp. 64–65.

7. *dri za*, "smell eater." This is the name for a being in the bardo.
8. Vasubandhu, *Treasury of Abhidharma*, Dg.T. mngon pa, *ku* (Toh. 4089), ff. 7a–b.
9. The gandharva is so-called because it feeds on smells.
10. Reading *ngan song gsum* (*L*, *mdang song*; *DNZ*, *mdangs gsum*).

18. Dewar Shekpa Pal Taklung Chenpo's Notes

1. *Lam 'bras bu dang bcas pa'i khrid yig 'bring po dpal phag mo gru ba'i gsung la bde bar gshegs pa dpal stag lung pa chen po zin bris*, DNZ. vol. 5, pp. 459–90.
2. See *Collected Works of Dorje Gyalpo.*
3. *kva tas nu ma bcud la 'bor/ 'phral du 'byung ba ngo mtshan tshe*. This passage is unidentified
4. Reading *'gum* as a misspelling of *bku mnye.*
5. *bred lnga.*
6. The text renders this as *zhiwa śāntika*, combining the Tibetan term with the intended Sanskrit equivalent, both meaning "pacified" or "at rest."
7. *sga ra ra.*
8. *Bola* and *kakkola* are terms for the male and female genitals found in *HT*.
9. *sga ra ra.*
10. *la phug*. The Latin for this is *Raphanus sativus var. longipinnatus.*
11. *pha ki na mar*?

19. The Manual of the Three Purities

1. *'Phags pa mkha' 'gro ma rdo rje gur gyi rgyud kyi dgongs pa dag pa gsum gyi khrid yig. DNZ*, vol. 5, pp. 491–505. *SKB*, vol. 13, pp. 577–92.
2. For a more detailed account of the relationship between Phakpa and Kublai Khan, see Shakapa, *One Hundred Thousand Moons* (vol. 1, pp. 199–242).
3. *thab mgal gyi phyag rgya.*
4. Here, the Sanskrit term *rasanā* is used instead of the usual Tibetan term *ro ma.*
5. The text states two sets, but this is at odds with all other presentations.
6. *kun 'dar ma.*
7. This refers to Kublai Khan and Chabi.

Bibliography

1. The Present Texts

The Source Volume

Jamgön Kongtrul Lodrö Taye, comp. *The Treasury of Precious Instructions. gDams ngag rin po che'i mdzod.* vol. 5 (*ca*). Delhi: Shechen Publications, 1999. dnz.tsadra.org. BDRC W23605.

The Translated Texts

Chögyal Phakpa Lodrö Gyaltsen (Chos rgyal 'phag pa blo dros rgyal msthan). *The Manual of the Three Purities: The Intention of the Āryaḍākinīvajrapañjaratantra. 'Phags pa mkha' 'gro ma rdo rje gur gyi rgyud kyi dgongs pa dag pa gsum gyi khrid yig.* In *DNZ.* vol. 5 (*ca*), pp. 491–505; Second source: *SKB*, Vol. 13, pp. 577–92.

Dakchen Lodrö Gyaltsen (bDag chen blo dros rgyal msthan). *Notes on the Intimate Instruction: The Explanation of the Concealed Path. Lam sbas te bshad pa man ngag gi zin bris.* In *DNZ.* vol. 5 (*ca*), pp. 425–31; Second source: *L*, Vol. 18, pp. 27–32.

———. *The Manual That Clarifies Symbols and Meanings. brDa don gsal ba'i khrid yig bdag chen rdo rje chang gis mdzad pa.* In *DNZ.* vol. 5 (*ca*), pp. 433–58; Second source: *L*, Vol. 18, pp. 1–27.

Drakpa Gyaltsen (Grags pa rgyal mtshan). *How to Give Instructions According to the Treatise: The Instructional Manual of the Path with Its Result, the Precious Oral Instruction. gSung ngag rin po che lam 'bras dang bcas pa'i khrid yig gzhung ji lta ba bzhin du dkri ba.* In *DNZ.* vol. 5 (*ca*), pp. 17–28. Second source: *L*, vol. 11, pp. 300–14.

———. *The Root Verses of the Illuminating Jewel: The View of the Inseparability of Samsara and Nirvana. lTa ba 'khor 'das dbyer med kyi gzhung rin chen snang ba'i rtsa ba.* In *DNZ.* vol. 5 (*ca*), pp. 15–17; Second source: *L*, pp. 191–94, titled *The View of the Inseparability of Samsara and Nirvana That Are Elaborated from the All-Basis Cause Tantra. Kun gzhi rgyu rgyud las 'phros nas 'khor 'das byer med kyi lta ba'i rtsa ba.*

———. *The Summarized Topics of the Vajra Verses. rDo rje tshigs rkang gi bsdus don.* In *DNZ.* vol. 5 (*ca*), pp. 11–12. Second source: *L*, vol. 11, pp. 19–21, no title.

———. *The Versified Instructional Manual on How to Give the Instruction of the Path with Its Result in Accordance with the Treatise. Lam 'bras kyi gzhung ji lta ba bzhin du bkri ba'i khrid yig tshigs bcad ma.* In *DNZ.* vol. 5 (*ca*), pp. 28–31. Second source: *G*, pp. 121–24. Third Source: *SKB*, Vol. 6, pp. 390–94.

Könchok Lhundrub (dKon mchog lhun grub). *The Beautiful Ornament of the Bali Rite of Śrī Hevajra. dPal skye rdo rje'i gtor chog mdzes rgyan.* In *DNZ.* vol. 5 (*ca*), pp. 153–75, Second source: *L*, Vol. 18, pp. 375–97.

———. *The Beautiful Ornament of the Great River of the Empowerment of Śrī Hevajra. dPal kye rdo rje dbang gi chu bo chen mo mdzes par byed pa'i rgyan.* In *DNZ.* vol. 5 (*ca*), pp. 177–242; Second source: *L*, vol. 18, pp. 293–359.

———. *The Beautiful Ornament of the Six Limbs: The Medium-Length Activity of the Direct Realization of Śrī Hevajra. dPal kye rdo rje'i mngon par rtogs pa 'bring du yan lag drug pa'i mdzes rgyan.* In *DNZ.* vol. 5 (*ca*), pp. 123–52. Second source: *L*, Vol. 18, pp. 243–74.

Kunga Nyingpo (Kun dga' snying po). *A Commentary on the Vajra Verses, the Treatise of the Path with Its Result, the Precious Oral Instruction. gSung ngag rin po chen lam 'bras bu dang bcas pa'i gzhung rdo rje'i tshig rkang gi 'grel pa.* In *DNZ.* vol. 5 (*ca*), pp. 35–121; Second source: *G*, pp. 127–221; Third source: *L*, vol. 11, pp. 21–128, titled *gZhung bshad gnyag ma.*

———. *The Verse Summary of the Topics of the Commentary of the Precious Oral Intimate Instruction. gSung ngag rin po che'i rnam 'grel don bsdus tshigs bcad ma.* In *DNZ.* vol. 5 (*ca*), pp. 12–15; Second source: *L*, vol. 11, pp. 104–6; *L*, pp. 188–91, titled *The Verse Summary of All Topics. Thams cad gyi don bsdus pa'i tshigs su bcad pa gzhung bshad gnyag ma.*

Kunga Zangpo (Kun dga' bzang po). *The Summarized Topics of the Stages of the Path of the Three Tantras of the Versified Manual on How to Give the Instruction of the Path with Its Result in Accordance with the Treatise. Lam 'bras kyi gzhung ji lta ba bzhin du bkri ba'i khrid yig tshigs bcad ma rgyud gsum lam gyi rim pa'i bsdus don.* In *DNZ.* vol. 5 (*ca*), pp. 31–33; Second source: *G*, pp. 124–26, Third source: *Collected Works of Kunga Zangpo. gSung 'bum kun dga' bzang po.* vol. 3, pp. 791–94, titled *rGyud gsum lam gyi rim pa'i bsdus don.* Dehra Dun: Sakya Centre, 1997. BDRC W11577.

———. *The Lineage Supplication of the Path with Its Result, the Precious Oral Instruction. gSung ngag rin po chen lam 'bras bu dang bcas pa'i brgyud 'debs.* In *DNZ.* vol. 5 (*ca*), pp. 325–26.

Loter Wangpo (Blo gter dbang po). *The Condensed Essential Citations and Intimate Instructions of the Empowerment Rite of the Intimate Instruction Tradition of Śrī Hevajra. dPal skye rdo rje man ngag lugs kyi dbang chog lung dang man ngag gi snying po bsdus pa.* In *DNZ.* vol. 5 (*ca*), pp. 243–324; Second source: *L*, Vol. 18, pp. 399–475.

Sönam Gyaltsen (Bsod nams Rgyal mtshan). *The Complete Clarification of the Hid-*

den Meaning: The Instruction Manual on How to Give Instructions According to the Treatise of the Path with Its Result. Lam 'bras bu dang bcas pa'i gzhung ji lta ba bzhin dkri ba'i khrid yig sbas don kun gsal. In *DNZ.* vol. 5 (*ca*), pp 329–408; Second source: L, Vol. 16, pp. 451–543.

———. *The Threefold Instruction: The Instruction Through Eleven Key Points, The Instruction Through Six Key Points, and The Instruction Through the Trio of Best, Medium, and Average Capacity. gNad bcu gcig gis dkri ba gnad drug gis kri ba dbang po rab 'bring gsum gyis dkri ba gsum gyi khrid.* In *DNZ.* vol. 5 (*ca*), pp. 409–23; Second source: *L*, Vol. 16, pp. 432–49.

Tashi Pal (Bkra shis dpal). *Dewar Shekpa Pal Taklung Chenpo's Notes: The Oral Teaching of Pal Phakmo Dru on The Medium-Length Instruction on the Path with Its Result. Lam 'bras bu dang bcas pa'i khrid yig 'bring po dpal phag mo gru ba'i gsung la bde bar gshegs pa dpal stag lung pa chen po zin bris.* In *DNZ.* vol. 5 (*ca*), pp. 459–90.

Virūpa. *The Vajra Verses: The Treatise of the Precious Oral Intimate Instructions of the Path with Its Result. Vāgupadeśaratnasamārgaphalasyagranthavajragathanāmaviharatisma. gSung ngag rin po che lam 'bras bu dang bcas pa'i gzhung rdo rje'i tshig rkang.* In *DNZ.* vol. 5 (*ca*), pp. 1–12. Second Source: *P*, pp. 10–19, titled *The Explanation of the Treatise Headed by the Root Vajra Verses. Rtsa ba rdo rje tshig rkang gtsos pod ser gzhung bshad.* Third source: *L*, vol. 11, pp. 10–19.

2. Works Cited in the Texts

Kangyur (Scriptures)

Ākāśagarbha Sutra. Āryākāśagarbhanāmamahāyānasūtra. 'Phags pa nam mkha'i snying po zhes bya ba theg pa chen po'i mdo. Dg.K. mdo, *za* (Toh. 260).

Ancillary Exposition Tantra. Abhidhānottaratantra. mNgon par brjod pa'i rgyud bla ma. Dg.K. rgyud, *ka* (Toh. 369).

Āvalokiteśvara's Network of Lotuses Root Tantra. Āryāvalokiteśvarapadmajālamūlatantrarāja. 'Phags pa spyan ras gzigs dbang phyug gi rtsa ba'i rgyud kyi rgyal po padma dra ba. Dg.K. rgyud, *ba* (Toh. 681).

Basis of Discipline. Vinayavastu. 'Dul ba gzhi. Dg.K. 'dul, *ka* (Toh. 1).

Cakrasamvara Root Tantra. Tantrarājaśrilaghusaṃvara. rGyud kyi rgyal po dpal bde mchog nyung ngu zhes bya ba, Dg.K, rgyud, *ka* (Toh. 368).

Chanting the True Names of Mañjuśrī. Mañjuśrījñānasattvasyaparamārthanāmasaṃgīti. 'Jam dpal ye shes sems dpa'i don dam pa'i mtshan yang dag par brjod pa. Dg.K. rgyud, *ka* (Toh. 360).

Compendium of the Principles of All Tathāgatas. Sarvatathāgatatattvasaṃgraha. De bzhin gshegs pa thams cad kyi de kho na nyid bsdus pa zhes bya ba theg pa chen po'i mdo. Dg.K. rgyud, *nya* (Toh. 479).

Concise Explanation of Empowerments. Sekoddeśa. Dbang mdor bstan pa. Dg.K. rgyud, *ka* (Toh. 361).

Ḍākinī's Blazing Tongue of Flame Tantra. Ḍākiniāgnijihvajvalātantra. mKha' 'gro ma me lce 'bar ba'i rgyud. Dg.K. rnying, *kha* (Toh. 842).

Dhāraṇī of the Mother of Planets. Āryagrahamātṛkānāmadhāraṇī. 'Phags ma gza' rnams kyi yum zhes bya ba'i gzungs. Dg.K. rgyud, *ba* (Toh. 660).

Dhāraṇī of the Ten Stages. Daśabhūmidhāraṇī. Sa bcu pa'i gzungs. Dg.K. rgyud, *tsa* (Toh. 688).

First Section of The Supreme Great Glorious Uniform Nondual King Tantra, the Victorious Great Secret Yoga of All Tathāgatas. Śrīsarvatathāgataguhyatantrayogamahārājādvayasamatāvijayanāmavajraśrīparamamahākalādi. dPal de bzhin gshegs pa thams cad kyi gsang ba rnal 'byor chen po rnam par rgyal ba zhes bya ba mnyam pa nyid gnyis su med pa'i rgyud kyi rgyal po rdo rje dpal mchog chen po brtag pa dang po. Dg.K. rgyud, *cha* (Toh. 453).

Four Places Great Yoginī King Tantra. Śrīcaturpīṭhamahāyoginītantrarāja. rNal 'byor ma'i rgyud kyi rgyal po chen po dpal gdan bzhi pa. Dg.K. rgyud, *nga* (Toh. 428).

Gaṇḍīsūtra. Gaṇ ḍī'i mdo. Dg.K. mdo, *sha* (Toh. 298).

Glorious First One's Section of the Mantra Divisions. Śrīparamādyamantrakalpakhaṇḍa. dPal mchog dang po'i sngags kyi rtog pa'i dum bu. Dg.K. rgyud, *ta* (Toh. 488).

Great Illusion Tantra. Śrīmahāmāyātantrarāja. dPal sgyu 'phrul chen po zhes bya ba'i rgyud kyi rgyal po. Dg.K. rgyud, *nga* (Toh. 425).

Guhyasamāja Tantra. Sarvatathāgatakāyavākcittarahasyoguhyasamājanāmamahākalparāja. De bzhin gshegs pa thams cad kyi sku gsung thugs kyi gsang chen gsang ba 'dus pa zhes bya ba brtag pa'i rgyal po chen po. Dg.K. rgyud, *ca* (Toh. 442).

[*Guhyasamāja*] *Uttaratantra. Phyi ma'i rgyud.* Dg.K. rgyud, *ca* (Toh. 443).

Hevajra Tantra. Hevajratantrarāja. Kye'i rdo rje zhes bya ba rgyud kyi rgyal po. Dg.K. rgyud, *nga* (Toh. 417).

High King of Yoginī Great King Tantras Called The Essence of Gnosis. Śrījñānagarbhanāmayoginīmahātantrarājayatirāja. dPal ye shes snying po zhes bya ba rnal 'byor ma chen mo'i rgyud kyi rgyal po'i rgyal po. Dg.K. rgyud, *nga* (Toh. 421).

Lamp of Principles Great Yoginī King Tantra. Śrītattvapradīpaṃnāmamahāyoginītantrarājā. dPal de kho na nyid kyi sgron ma zhes bya ba'i rnal 'byor chen mo'i rgyud kyi rgyal po. Dg.K. rgyud, *nga* (Toh. 423).

Meeting of the Father and Son Sutra. Āryapitāputrasamāgamananāmamahāyānasūtra. 'Phags pa yab dang sras mjal ba zhes bya ba theg pa chen po'i mdo. Dg.K. dkon, *nga* (Toh. 60).

Ornament of Gnosis Supremely Marvelous Yoginī King Tantra. Śrījñānatilakayoginītantrarājāparamamahādbhutaṃ. dPal ye shes thig le rnal 'byor ma'i rgyud kyi rgyal po chen po mchog tu rmad du byung ba. Dg.K. rgyud, *nga* (Toh. 422).

Ornament of Mahāmudra. Śrīmahāmudrātilakaṃnāmayoginītantrarājadhipati. dPal phyag rgya chen po'i thig le zhes bya ba rnal 'byor ma chen mo'i rgyud kyi rgyal po'i mnga' bdag. Dg.K. rgyud, *nga* (Toh. 420).

Praise of the Black Śrīdevī King Tantra. Śrīdevīkālīpramarājatantra. dPal lha mo nag mo'i bstod pa rgyal po'i rgyud. Dg.K. rgyud, *ba* (Toh. 671).

Rice Seedling Sutra. *Āryaśālistambanāmamahāyānasūtra*. *'Phags pa sā lu'i ljang pa zhes bya ba theg pa chen po'i mdo*. Dg.K. mdo, *tsha* (Toh. 210).

Saṃpūṭa Tantra. *Saṃpūṭanāmamahātantra*. *Yang dag par sbyor ba zhes bya ba'i rgyud chen po*. Dg.K. rgyud, *ga* (Toh. 381).

Secret Jewel Ornament Sutra. *Āryaguhyamaṇitilakanāmasūtra*. *'Phags pa gsang ba nor bu thig le zhes bya ba'i mdo*. Dg.K. rgyud, *tha* (Toh. 493).

Secret Tantra of General Rites. *Sarvamaṇḍalasāmānyavidhiguhyatantra*. *dKyil 'khor thams cad kyi spyi'i cho ga gsang ba'i rgyud*. Dg.K. rgyud, *wa* (Toh. 806).

Supremacy of Vajravārāhi's Inconceivable Gnostic Nondual Mind of all Ḍākinīs. *Ḍākinīsarvacittādvayācintyajñānavajravārāhiabhibhāvatantrarāja*. *mKha' 'gro ma thams cad kyi thugs gnyis su med pa bsam gyis mi khyab pa'i ye shes rdo rje phag mo mngon par 'byung ba'i rgyud kyi rgyal po*. Dg.K. rgyud, *ga* (Toh. 378).

Sutra of Advice to the King. *Āryarājāvavādakanāmamahāyānasūtra*. *'Phags pa rgyal po la gdams pa zhes bya ba theg pa chen po'i mdo*. Dg.K. mdo, *dza* (Toh. 221).

Sutra on Entering Lanka. *Āryalaṅkāvatāramahāyānasūtra*. *'Phags pa lang kar gshegs pa'i theg pa chen po'i mdo*. Dg.K. mdo, *ca* (Toh. 107).

Sutra That Explains the Two Truths. *Āryasaṃvṛtiparamārthasatyanirdeśanāmamahāyānasūtra*.*'Phags pa kun rdzob dang don dam pa'i bden pa bstan pa zhes bya ba theg pa chen po'i mdo*. Dg.K. mdo, *ma* (Toh. 179).

Tantra of the Vajra Array of the Essential Ultimate Secret Gnosis of the Mind of All Tathāgatas, the Extract of the Yoga of Accomplishment, the Sutra of the Knowledge That Unifies Everything, the Sutra of the Array That Is a Dharma Division for the Direct Realization of Mahāyāna. *Sarvatathāgatacittajñānaguhyārthagarbhavyūhavajratantrasiddhiyogāgamasamājasarvavidyāsūtramahāyānābhisamayadharmaparyāyavivyūhanāmasūtra*. *De bzhin gshegs pa thams cad kyi thugs gsang ba'i ye shes don gyi snying po rdo rje bkod pa'i rgyud rnal 'byor grub pa'i lung kun 'dus rig pa'i mdo theg pa chen po mngon par rtogs pa chos kyi rnam grangs rnam par bkod pa zhes bya ba'i mdo*. Dg.K. rnying, *ka* (Toh. 829).

Vajra Garland Great Yoga Exposition Tantra That Differentiates the Secret Heart of All Tantras. *Śrīvajramālābhidhānamahāyogatantrasarvatantrahṛdayarahasyavibhaṅgaiti*. *rNal 'byor chen po'i rgyud dpal rdo rje phreng ba mngon par brjod pa rgyud thams cad kyi snying po gsang ba rnam par phye ba*. Dg.K. rgyud, *ca* (Toh. 445).

Vajrapañjara Tantra. *Āryaḍākinīvajrapañjaramahātantrarājakalpa*. *'Phags pa mkha' 'gro ma rdo rje gur zhes bya ba'i rgyud kyi rgyal po chen po'i brtag pa*. Dg.K. rgyud, *nga* (Toh. 419).

Tengyur (Treatises)

Abhayadatta. *Chronicle of the Eighty-Four Mahāsiddhas*. *Caturaśītisiddhapravṛtti*. *Grub thob brgyad cu rtsa bzhi'i rnam thar*. Nar.T. rgyud, *lu* (N 3095).

Alaṃkakalaśa. *Commentary on the Profound Meaning: The Extensive Commentary on the Vajra Garland Tantra*. *Śrīvajramālāmahāyogatantraṭīkagaṃbhīrārthadīpikā*. *rNal 'byor chen po'i rgyud dpal rdo rje phreng ba'i rgya cher 'grel pa zab mo'i don gyi 'grel pa*. Dg.T. rgyud, *gi* (Toh. 1795).

Ānandagarbha. *Glorious First One's Extensive Explanation. Śrīparamādiṭīkā. dPal mchog dang po'i rgya cher bshad pa.* Dg.T. rgyud, *li–shi* (Toh. 2510).

Anonymous. *Sādhana Method of Śrīdevīkālī. Śrīdevīkālīsādhanopāyikā. dPal lha mo nag mo sgrub pa'i thabs kyi cho ga.* Dg.T. rgyud, *sha* (Toh. 1766).

Āryadeva. *Madhyamaka Four Hundred Verses. Catuḥśatakaśāstranāmakārikā. bsTan bcos bzhi brgya pa zhes bya ba'i tshig le'ur byas pa.* Dg.T. dbu ma, *tsha* (Toh. 3846).

———. *Lamp of the Compendium of Practices. Caryāmelāpakapradīpa. Spyod pa bsdus pa'i sgron ma.* Dg.T. rgyud, *ngi* (Toh. 1803).

Aśvaghoṣa. *Fifty Verses on the Guru. Gurupañcāśikā. bLa ma lnga bcu pa.* Dg.T. rgyud, *tshu* (Toh. 3721).

———. *Great Charnel Ground Commentary on the Fierce Section of the Śrī Mahākāla Tantra. Śrīmahākālatantrarudrakalpamahāśmaśānanāmaṭīkā. dPal nag po chen po'i rgyud drag po'i brtag pa dur khrod chen po zhes bya ba'i 'grel pa.* Dg.T. rgyud, *sha* (Toh. 1753).

Avalokitavrata. *The Lamp of Wisdom Extensive Commentary. Prajñāpradīpaṭīkā. Shes rab sgron ma rgya cher 'grel pa.* Dg.T. dbu ma, *wa–za* (Toh. 3859).

Candragomin. *Letter to a Disciple. Śiṣyalekha. sLob ma la springs pa'i spring yig.* Dg.T. spring yig, *nge* (Toh. 4183).

Candrakīrti. *Introduction to Madhyamaka. Madyamakāvatāra. Dbu ma la 'jug pa.* Dg.T. dbu ma, *'a* (Toh. 3861).

Dārika. *The Compendium of Principles Sādhana of Śrī Cakrasaṃvara Śrīcakrasaṃvarasādhanatattvasaṃgraha. dPal 'khor lo sdom pa'i sgrub thabs de kho na nyid kyis bsdus pa.* Dg.T. rgyud, *wa* (Toh. 1429).

Devakulamahāmati. *Expansion of Principles: The Commentary on the Difficult Points of the Ḍākinī Vajra Latticed Pavilion King Tantra. Ḍākinīvajrajālapañjaratantrarājasyapañjikātattvapauṣṭika. rGyud kyi rgyal po mkha' 'gro ma rdo rje dra ba'i dka' 'grel de kho na nyid rgyas pa.* Dg.T. rgyud, *ca* (Toh. 1196).

Durjayacandra. *Jasmine Commentary on Difficult Points. Kaumudīnāmapañjikā. Kau mu di zhes bya ba'i dka' 'grel.* Dg.T. rgyud, *ga* (Toh. 1185).

———. *Sādhana of the Maṇḍala Rite Called Holding the Good. Suparigrahanāmamaṇḍalopāyikāvidhi. dKyil 'khor gyi cho ga'i sgrub thabs bzang po yongs su gzung ba.* Dg.T. rgyud, *nya* (Toh. 1240).

———. *Six-limb Sādhana. Ṣaḍaṅganāmasādhana. Yan lag drug pa zhes bya ba'i sgrub thabs.* Dg.T. rgyud, *nya* (Toh. 1239).

Gambhīravajra. *Marvelous Clear Profound Meaning. Śrīguhyārthaprakāśamahādbhūta. dPal zab mo'i don gsal ba rmad du byung ba chen po.* Dg.T. rgyud, *ja* (Toh. 1200).

Huṃkara. *True Accomplishment Sādhana of Great Śrī Heruka. Saṃsiddhimahāśrīherukopāyikānāma. dPal khrag 'thung chen po'i sgrub thabs yang dag par grub pa.* Dg.T. rgyud, *la* (Toh. 1678).

Kāmadhenupa. *Gathering the Vajra Stanzas: A Commentary on the Difficult Points of Hevajra. Śrīhevajrasyapañjikāvajrapadoddharaṇa. dPal dgyes pa'i rdo rje'i dka' 'grel rdo rje'i tshig btu ba.* Dg.T. rgyud, *ca* (Toh. 1192).

Kambala. *The Prolegomena of the Sādhana: A Commentary on Difficult Points of Cakrasaṃvara. Sādhananidānanāmaśrīcakrasaṃvarapañjikā. dPal 'khor lo sdom pa'i dka' 'grel sgrub pa'i thabs kyi gleng gzhi.* Dg.T. rgyud, *ma* (Toh. 1401).

———. *The Bright Precious Lamp on the Maṇḍala Rite of the Cakrasamvara Maṇḍala. Śrīcakrasambaramaṇḍalopāyikāratnapradīpodyotanāma. dPal 'khor lo bde mchog gi dkyil 'khor gyi cho ga rin po che rab tu gsal ba'i sgron ma.* Dg.T. rgyud, *wa* (1444).

Kotalipa (Kuddālīpāda). *The Intimate Instruction on the Stages of the Inconceivable. Acantyakramopadeśanāmaḥ. bSam gyis mi khyab pa'i rim pa'i man ngag.* In *DNZ.* vol. 6 (*ca*), pp. 81–95. Second source: *P*, pp. 347–62.

———. *The Intimate Instruction on the Stages of the Inconceivable. Acintyakramopadeśa. bSam gyis mi khyab pa'i rim pa'i man ngag.* Dg.T. rgyud, *wi* (Toh. 2228).

Kṛṣṇa Paṇḍita. *Clarifying the Principles Hevajra Sādhana Hevajrasādhanatattvoddyotakara. Gyes pa'i rdo rje sgrub pa'i thabs de kho na nyid gsal bar byed pa.* Dg.T. rgyud, *nya* (Toh. 1253).

———. *Maṇḍala Rite Textual Commentary on Hevajra. Śrīhevajrapaddhatimaṇḍalavidhi. dPal dgyes pa'i rdo rje'i gzhung 'grel gyi dkyil 'khor gyi cho ga.* Dg.T. rgyud, *nya* (Toh. 1254).

Maitreyanātha. *Ornament of Direct Realization. Abhisamayālaṃkāranāmaprajñāpāramitopadeśaśāstrakārikā. Shes rab phyi pha rol tu phyin pa'i man ngag gi bstan bcos mngon par rtogs pa'i rgyan zhes bya ba'i tshig le'ur byas pa.* Dg.T. shes phyin, *ka* (Toh. 3786).

Munidatta. *Commentary on the Songs of Conduct. Caryāgītikoṣavṛtti. Spyod pa'i glu'i mdzod kyi 'grel pa.* Dg.T. rgyud, *zhi* (Toh. 2293).

Nāgārjuna. *Benedictory Verses. Maṅgalagāthā. Bkra shis kyi tshigs su bcad pa.* Dg.T. bstan bcos sna tshogs, *nyo* (Toh. 4410).

———. *Five Stages. Pañcakrama. Rim pa lnga pa.* Dg.T. rgyud, *ngi* (Toh. 1802).

———. *Letter to a Friend. Suhṛllekha. bShes pa'i spring yig.* Dg.T. spring yig, *ge* (Toh. 4182).

———. *Necklace of Gems. Rājaparikathāratnāvali. rGyal po la gtam bya ba rin po che'i phreng ba,* Dg.T. spring yig, *ge* (Toh. 4158).

———. *Praise to the Incomparable. Nirupamastava. dPe med par bstod pa.* Dg.T. bstod, *ka* (Toh. 1119).

———. *Verses on the Heart of Dependent Origination. Pratītyasamutpādahṛdayakārikā. rTen cing 'brel bar 'byung ba'i snying po'i tshig le'ur byas pa.* Dg.T. dbu ma, *tsa* (Toh. 3836).

———. *Verses on the Rice Seedling Sutra. Āryaśālistambakakārikā. 'Phags pa sā lu ljang pa'i tshig le'ur byas pa.* Dg.T. mdo 'grel, *ngi* (Toh. 3985).

Padmavajra (Saroruha). *Hevajra Sādhana. Śrīhevajrasādhana. dPal dgyes pa rdo rje'i sgrub thabs.* Dg.T. rgyud, *nya* (Toh. 1218).

———. *Stages of the Activity of the Maṇḍala Rite of Hevajra. Hevajramaṇḍalakarmakramavidhi. Kye rdo rje'i dkyil 'khor gyi las kyi rim pa'i cho ga.* Dg.T. rgyud, *nya* (Toh. 1219).

Prajñendraruci. *Blazing Jewel Sādhana. Ratnajvālanāmasādhana. Rin chen 'bar ba zhes bya ba'i sgrub pa'i thabs.* Dg.T. rgyud, *nya* (Toh. 1251).

Rāhulaśrīmitra. *The Clarification of Union: Activity of Empowerment. Yuganaddhaprakāśanāmasekaprakriyā. Zung du 'jug pa gsal ba zhes bya ba'i dbang gi bya ba.* Dg.T. rgyud, *ngi* (Toh. 1818).

Samayavajra. *Jeweled Garland of Yoga Commentary on Difficult Points of the Hevajra Tantra. Śrīhevajrapañjikāyogaratnamālā. dPal dgyes pa'i rdo rje'i dka' 'grel rin po che sbyor ba'i 'phreng ba.* Nar.T. rgyud 'grel, *phu* (N 3482).

———. *Jeweled Garland of Yoga Commentary on Difficult Points of the Hevajra Tantra. Śrīhevajrapañjikāyogaratnamālā. dPal dgyes pa'i rdo rje'i dka' 'grel rin po che sbyor ba'i 'phreng ba.* Q, rgyud 'grel, *phu* (Q 4687).

Śāntideva. *Introduction to the Conduct of Awakening. Bodhicaryāvatāra. Byang chub sems dpa'i spyod pa la 'jug pa.* Dg.T. mdo, *la* (Toh. 3871).

Saroruha (Padmavajra). *Praise to Hevajra. Kye rdo rje'i bstod pa.* Dg.T. rgyud, *nya* (Toh. 1222).

———. *Padminī Commentary on the Difficult Points of the Hevajra Tantra. Hevajratantrapañjikāpadminī. Kye'i rdo rje'i rgyud kyi dka' 'grel padma can.* Dg.T. rgyud, *ka* (Toh. 1181).

———. *Ritual Procedure for the Hevajra Maṇḍala. Hevajramaṇḍalakarmakramavidhi. Kye'i rdo rje'i dkyil 'khor gyi las kyi rim pa'i cho ga.* Dg.T. rgyud, *ta* (Toh. 1263).

Sönyompa (bSod snyom pa). *Maṇḍala Rite. Maṇḍalavidhi. dKyil khor gyi cho ga.* Dg.T. rgyud, *pi*, (Toh. 1882).

Śraddhākaravarman. *Medium Rite in Three Parts. Cha gsum 'bring po'i cho ga.* Dg.T. rgyud, *tshu* (Toh. 3774).

Subhūticandra. *The Milk Cow Extensive Commentary on the Treasury of Immortality. Amarakoṣaṭīkākāmadhenu. Chi ba med pa'i mdzod kyi rgya cher 'grel pa 'dod 'jo'i ba mo.* Dg.T. mdo, *se* (Toh. 4300).

Vajraghanta. *Concise Activities of the Empowerment of Śrī Cakrasamvara. Śrīcakrasaṃvaraṣekaprakriyopadeśa. dPal 'khor lo sdom pa'i dbang gi bya ba mdor bsdus pa.* Dg.T. rgyud, *wa* (Toh. 1431).

Vajragarbha. *Extensive Commentary That Summarizes the Meaning of Hevajra. Hevapiṇḍārthaṭīkā. Kye'i rdo rje bsdus pa'i don gyi rgya cher 'grel pa.* Dg.T. rgyud, *ka* (Toh. 1180).

Vajrāsana. *Supplication to the Eighty-Four Mahāsiddhas. Grub thob brgyad cu rtsa bzhi'i gsol 'debs.* Dg.T. rgyud, *tshu* (Toh. 3758).

Vararuci. *Praise to Śrīmahākālī. Śrīmahākālīdevīstotrāṣṭakanāma. dPal lha mo nag mo chen mo la bstod pa brgyad pa.* Dg.T. rgyud, *sha* (Toh. 1777).

Vasubandhu. *Commentary on the Treasury of Abhidharma. Abhidharmakośabhāṣya. Chos mngon pa'i mdzod kyi bshad pa.* Dg.T. mngon pa, *ku* (Toh. 4090).

———. *Treasury of Abhidharma. Abhidharmakośakārikā. Chos mngon pa'i mdzod kyi tshig le'ur byas pa.* Dg.T. mngon pa, *ku* (Toh. 4089).

———. *The Treatise Called the Meaningful Compendium of Stanzas. Gāthāsaṃgra-*

haśāstrārthanāma. Tshigs su bcad pa'i don bsdus pa zhes bya ba'i bstan bcos. Dg.T. mngon pa, *thu* (Toh. 4103).

Indic Works

Padmakāra. *Sādhana of the Monbu Putra Siblings with Intimate Instructions Composed by Ācarya Padmakāra. Mon bu pu tra ming sring gi sgrub thabs man ngag dang bcas pa slob dpon chen po padma 'byung gnas kyis mdzad pa.* In *Rin chen gter mdzod chen mo* 61, pp. 269–77. Paro: Ngodrup and Sherab Drimay, 1976–1980. BDRC W20578.

Śrīdevi Black Butcher Tantra. Śrīdevisritakālitantra. dPal lha mo shan pa nag mo'i rgyud. In *rNying ma rgyud 'bum* 42, pp. 393–432. Thimphu: Royal Government of Bhutan National Library, 1982. BDRC W21521.

Tibetan Works

Collections

Collected Tantras of Nyingma. rNying ma rgyud 'bum. 46 vols. Thimphu: Royal Bovernment of Bhutan National Library, 1982. BDRC W21521.

Collected Works of Sakya. Sa skya bka' 'bum (*SKB*). 15 vols. Dehra Dun: Sakya Centre, 1992–1993. BDRC W22271.

Jamgön Kongtrul. *The Great Treasury of Precious Treasures. Rin chen gter mdzod chen mo.* 111 vols. Paro: Ngodrub and Sherab Drimay, 1976–1980. BDRC W20578.

Loter Wangpo (Blo gter dbang po), ed. *Collection of All Sādhanas. Sgrub thabs kun btus.* 14 vols. Kangara: Dzongsar Institute for Advanced Studies, n.d. BDRC W23681.

———. *Collection of All Tantras. rGyud sde kun btus.* 30 vols. Delhi: N. Lungtok & N. Gyaltsan, 1971–1972. BDRC W21295. Second source: 43 vols. Kathmandu: Sachen International, 2004. BDRC W27883.

———. *Explanation of the Path with Its Result for Disciples. Lam 'bras slob bshad.* 21 vols. Dehra Dun: Sakya Centre, 1983–1985. BDRC W23649.

———. *Explanation of the Path with Its Result for the Assembly. Lam 'bras tshogs bshad.* 6 vols. Dehra Dun: Sakya Centre, 1985. BDRC W23648.

Tibetan Authors

Amezhab (Ngag dbang kun dga' bsod nams). *Clarification That Is Joyful to Behold: The Meaning Commentary and Historical Context of Chögyal Phakpa's Definitive Reply to the Inquiry of Denma Chukbum. Chos kyi rgyal po 'phags pa rin po che la ldan ma phyug 'bum gyis dris ba zhus pa'i dris lan rnam par nges pa zhes bya ba'i don 'grel khog phub mthong ba rab dga'i gsal byed.* In *Collected Works of Ngawang Kunga Sönam. Ngag dbang kun dga' bsod nams gsung 'bum* 22, pp. 625–728. Kathmandu: Sa skya rgyal yongs gsung rab slob gnyer khang, 2000. BDRC W29307.

———. *Opening the Eye to the Concealed: The Detailed Explanation of Gyal Lhakhang Lodrö Senge's Notes on the Key Points of the Time When the Dharma Lord Palden Lama Dampa Taught the Path with Its Result. Chos rje dpal ldan bla ma dam pas lam 'bras gsung dus kyi gnad kyi zin bris rgyal lha khang blo gros seng ges mdzad pa rnams zhib tu bshad pa sbas pa mig 'byed.* In *Collected Works of Ngawang Kunga Sönam. Ngag dbang kun dga' bsod nams gsung 'bum* 22, pp. 99–118. Kathmandu: Sa skya rgyal yongs gsung rab slob gnyer khang, 2000. BDRC W29307.

———. *Marvelous Beautiful Waves That Arise from the Ocean of Clear Faith: The Liberation of the Lord Master of Scholars, Könchok Lhundrub. rJe btsun mkhas pa'i dbang po dkon mchog lhun grub kyi rnam par thar pa dwang 'dod dad pa'i chu gter las 'ong ba'i ngo mtshar rba rlabs kyi 'phreng mdzes.* In *Collected Works of Ngawang Kunga Sönam. Ngag dbang kun dga' bsod nams gsung 'bum* 4, pp. 577–624. Kathmandu: Sa skya rgyal yongs gsung rab slob gnyer khang, 2000. BDRC W29307.

———. *The Ocean of Intimate Instructions: The Ambrosial Speech of the Forerunner, the Manual of the Explanation of the Concealed Path. Lam sbas bshad kyi khrid yig gong ma'i gsung gi bdud rtsi man ngag gi rgya mtsho.* In *Collected Works of Ngawang Kunga Sönam. Ngag dbang kun dga' bsod nams gsung 'bum* 22, pp. 367–408. Kathmandu: Sa skya rgyal yongs gsung rab slob gnyer khang, 2000. BDRC W29307.

———. *The Ocean That Gathers Excellent Explanations: The Extensive Explanation of the Origins and Historical Context of the Precious Oral Instruction of the Practice of the Precious Complete Doctrine. Yongs rdzogs bstan pa rin po che'i nyams len gyi man ngag gsung ngag rin po che'i byon tshul khog phub dang bcas pa rgyas par bshad pa legs bshad 'dus pa'i rgya mtsho.* In *Collected Works of Ngawang Kunga Sönam. Ngag dbang kun dga' bsod nams gsung 'bum* 21, pp. 339–700. Kathmandu: Sa skya rgyal yongs gsung rab slob gnyer khang, 2000. BDRC W29307.

———. *The Source of All Needs and Wants: The Precious Treasury of the Marvelous Hagiographies, the Rise of the Precious Dynasty of of the Glorious Sakyapa, the Regents of the Sage in Northern Jambudvipa. Dzam gling byang phyogs kyi thub pa'i rgyal tshab chen po dpal ldan sa skya pa'i gdung rabs rin po che ji ltar byon pa'i tshul gyi rnam par thar pa ngo mtshar rin po che'i bang mdzod dgos 'dod kun 'byung.* In *Collected Works of Ngawang Kunga Sönam. Ngag dbang kun dga' bsod nams gsung 'bum* 3, pp. 13–662. Kathmandu: Sa skya rgyal yongs gsung rab slob gnyer khang, 2000. BDRC W29307.

———. *The Sun That Illuminates All the Guardians of the Doctrine: The Excellent Explanation of the Profound Dharma Cycle of Śrī Vajramahākāla. dPal rdo rje nag po chen po'i zab mo'i chos skor rnams byung ba'i tshul legs par bshad pa bstan srung chos kun gsal ba'i nyin byed.* In *Collected Works of Ngawang Kunga Sönam. Ngag dbang kun dga' bsod nams gsung 'bum* 25, pp. 7–498. Kathmandu: Sa skya rgyal yongs gsung rab slob gnyer khang, 2000. BDRC W29307.

Chögyal Phakpa Lodrö Gyaltsen (Chos rgyal 'phags pa blo gros rgyal mtshan). *Entry into the Empowerment: The Rite of Self-Admittance of Hevajra. Kyai rdo rje'i bdag 'jug gi cho ga dbang la 'jug pa.* In *SKB* 13, pp. 458–89. Dehra Dun: Sakya Centre, 1992–1993. BDRC W22271.

———. *Illuminating the Empowerment: The Maṇḍala Rite of Akṣobhya Guhyasamāja. dPal gsang ba 'dus pa mi bskyod rdo rje dkyil 'khor gyi cho ga dbang rab tu gsal ba.*

In *SKB* 14, pp. 353–434. Dehra Dun: Sakya Centre, 1992–1993. BDRC W22271.

———. *Drogön Phakpa's Explanation of the Path with Its Result Vajra Verses. Lam 'bras rdo rje'i tshig rkang gi rnam par bshad pas 'gro mgon 'phags pas mdzad pa.* In *Sakya Lamdre. Sa skya'i lam 'bras* 43, pp. 1–158. Kathmandu: Sachen International, 2008. BDRC W1KG13617.

Dorje Gyalpo (rDo rje rgyal po). *Collected Works of Dorje Gyalpo. rDo rje rgyal po gsung 'bum.* 9 vols. Kathmandu: Khenpo Shedrub Tenzin and Lama Thinley Namgyal, 2003. BDRC W23891.

Drakpa Gyaltsen (Grags pa rgyal mtshan). *Catalog of the Hevajra Dharma Cycle. Kyai rdo rje chos skor gyi dkar chag.* In *SKB* 7, pp. 420–22. Dehra Dun: Sakya Centre, 1992–1993. BDRC W22271.

———. *Chronicle of the Indian Gurus. bLa ma rgya gar ba'i lo rgyus.* In *SKB* 6, pp. 691–707. Dehra Dun: Sakya Centre, 1992–1993. BDRC W22271.

———. *Ornament of the Vajrapañjara Commentary. Phags pa rdo rje gur gyi rgyan zhes bya ba'i rnam 'grel.* In *SKB* 7, pp. 11–156. Dehra Dun: Sakya Centre, 1992–1993. BDRC W22271.

———. *Four Great Trees of the Treatise. gZhung shing chen po bzhi.* In *P*, pp. 300–23. Dehra Dun: Sakya Centre, 1983–1985. BDRC W23649.

———. *Six-Limb Direct Realization of Śrī Hevajra. dPal kyai rdo rje mngon rtogs yan lag drug pa.* In *SKB* 7, pp. 181–97. Dehra Dun: Sakya Centre, 1992–1993. BDRC W22271.

———. *Seven Topics in the All-Basis Cause Continuum. Kun gzhi rgyu rgyud la don bdun.* In *P*, pp. 128–31. Dehra Dun: Sakya Centre, 1983–1985. BDRC W23649.

———. *Annotated Hevajra King Tantra. Kye'i rdo rje zhes bya ba'i rgyud kyi rgyal po.* In *SKB* 18, pp. 531–710. Lhasa: s.n., 1999. BDRC W20751.

———. *Light Rays That Benefit Others (The Rite of Sarvavid). Kun rig gi cho ga gzhan phan 'od zer.* In *SKB* 9, pp. 1–118. Dehra Dun: Sakya Centre, 1992–1993. BDRC W22271.

———. *The Origin of Śrī Heruka. dPal he ru ka'i byung tshul.* In *SKB* 7, pp. 515–22. Dehra Dun: Sakya Centre, 1992–1993. BDRC W22271.

———. *Twenty-Two Ancillary Short Texts. sKabs gyi yig nyer gnyis. P*, pp. 128–31. Dehra Dun: Sakya Centre, 1983–1985. BDRC W23649.

———. *Jetsun's Annotated Vajrapañjara Tantra. rDo rje gur gyi rgyud rje btsun gyi mchan dang bcas pa.* In *SKB* 7, pp. 449–648. Dehra Dun: Sakya Center, 1992–1993. BDRC W22271.

———. *Yantras of the Thirty-Two Activities. Phrin las sum cu rtsa gnyis kyi 'khrul 'khor.* In *P*, pp. 288–92. Dehra Dun: Sakya Centre, 1983–1985. BDRC W23649.

Gyaltsen Pal (rGyal mtshan dpal). *The Concealed Explanation of the Vajra Body. rDo rje lus kyi sbas bshad.* In *Sakya Lamdre. Sa skya'i lam 'bras* 42, pp. 779–864. Kathmandu: Sachen International, 2008. BDRC W1KG13617.

Könchok Gyaltsen (dKon mchog rgyal mtshan). *The Six Limbs: The Medium Length Direct Realization of the Intimate Instruction Tradition of Śrī Hevajra. dPal kye rdo rje man ngag lugs kyi mngon par rtogs pa 'bring du bya ba yan lag drug pa.* In

Evaṃ Kabum. E wam bka' 'bum 10, pp. 51–90. Beijing: Krung go'i bod rig pa dpe skrun khang, 2009–2010. BDRC W1KG8320.

Könchok Lhundrub (dKon mchog lhun grub). *The Beautiful Ornament of the Body Maṇḍala. Lus dkyil mdzes rgyan.* In *L*, 18, pp. 275–91. Dehra Dun: Sakya Centre, 1983–1985. BDRC W23649.

———. *Beautiful Ornament of the Three Appearances. Lam 'bras bu dang bcas pa'i gdams ngag gi gzhung shing rgyas pa gzhung ji ltar ba bzhin bkri ba'i lam gyi sngon 'gro'i khrid yig snang gsum mdzes par byed pa'i rgyan.* In *LT*, 4, pp. 75–269. Dehra Dun, U.P.: Sakya Centre, 1985. BDRC W23648.

———. *Beautiful Ornament of the Three Tantras. Lam 'bras bu dang bcas pa'i gdams ngag gi gzhung shing rgyas pa gzhung ji ltar ba bzhin bkri ba'i lam gyi dngos gzhi'i khrid yig rgyud gsum mdzes par byed pa'i rgyan.* In *LT*, 4, pp. 75–269. Dehra Dun: Sakya Centre, 1985. BDRC W23648.

———. *Condensed Essential Citations and Intimate Instructions of the Empowerment Rite of the Intimate Instruction Tradition of Śrī Hevajra. Kye rdo rje man ngag lugs kyi dbang gi mtshams sbyor lung dang man ngag gi snying po bsdus pa.* In *Evaṃ Kabum. E wam bka' 'bum* 14, pp. 309–61. Beijing: Krung go'i bod rig pa dpe skrun khang, 2009–2010. BDRC W1KG8320.

———. *Knowledge Mantra of Brahma: The Dispute of The Great Shenyen Muse and the Definitive Analytical Reply. bShes gnyen chen po mus srad pas brgal zhing brtag pa'i lan rnam par nges pa tshangs ba'i rig sngags.* In *Evaṃ Kabum. E wam bka' 'bum* 18, pp. 38–98. Beijing: Krung go'i bod rig pa dpe skrun khang, 2009–2010. BDRC W1KG8320.

———. *Treasury of Citations and Intimate Instructions: The Excellent Explanation of the Words and Meanings of the Śrī Hevajra Empowerment. dPal kye rdo rje'i dbang gi tshig don rnams legs par bshad pa lung dang man ngag gi gter mdzod.* In *Evaṃ Kabum. E wam bka' 'bum* 11, pp. 317–432. Beijing: Krung go'i bod rig pa dpe skrun khang, 2009–2010. BDRC W1KG8320.

Könchok Palden (dKon mchog dpal ldan). *The Ocean of All Wishes: The Explanation of the Glorious Source of All Desires, the Autobiographical Hagiography of Könchok Lhundrub. dKon mchog lhun grub kyi rnam thar rang nyid kyis mdzad pa 'dod dgu'i dpal 'byung gi rnam bshad 'dod dgu'i chu gter dkon mchog dpal ldan gyis mdzad pa.* In *Sakya Lamdre. Sa skya'i lam 'bras* 28, pp. 181–240. Kathmandu: Sachen International, 2008. BDRC W1KG13617.

Kunga Dorje (Kun dga' Rdo rje). *The Red Annals. Deb ther dmar po.* Beijing: Mi rigs dpe skrung khang, 1981. BDRC W1KG5760.

Kunga Gyaltsen, Sakya Paṇḍita (Kun dga' rgyal mtshan). *Hagiography of the Lord Guru. bLa ma rje btsun chen po'i rnam thar.* In *SKB* 10, pp. 584–606. Dehra Dun: Sakya Centre, 1992–1993. BDRC W22271.

———. *The Red Volume. Lam 'bras po ti dmar ma.* Dehra Dun: Sakya Centre, 1985. BDRC W30149.

———. *The Explanation of the Concealed Path. Lam sbas bshad pa.* In *SKB* 12, pp. 227–29. Dehra Dun: Sakya Centre, 1992–1993. BDRC W22271.

———. *The Trio of Outer, Inner, and Secret Maṇḍala Offerings. Phyi nang gsang gsum gyi maṇḍala 'bul chog*. In *SKB* 12, pp. 249–52. Dehra Dun: Sakya Centre, 1992–1993. BDRC W22271.

———. *Differentiation of the Three Vows. sDom pa gsum gyi rab tu dbye ba*. In *SKB* 12, pp. 15–110. Dehra Dun: Sakya Centre, 1992–1993. BDRC W22271.

Kunga Nyingpo (Kun dga' snying po). *Bhayanāsa Protection Cakra. Bhayanāsa'i srung 'khor*. In *SKB* 2, pp. 294–96. Dehra Dun: Sakya Centre, 1992–1993. BDRC W22271.

———. *Chronicle of Ācārya Saroruhavajra. sLob dpon mtsho skyes kyi lo rgyus*. In *SKB* 2, pp. 685–89. Dehra Dun: Sakya Centre, 1992–1993. BDRC W22271.

———. *Commentary on the Difficult Points of the Two-Section Hevajra Root Tantra Composed by Lama Sachen. bLa ma sa chen mdzad kye rdo rje'i rtsa rgyud brtag gnyis kyi dka' 'grel*. In *SKB* 1, pp. 323–491. Dehra Dun: Sakya Centre, 1992–1993. BDRC W22271.

———. *For the Sons. Lam 'bras gzhung bshad sras don ma*. In *L*, 12, pp. 1–446. Dehra Dun: Sakya Centre, 1983–1985. BDRC W23649.

———. *Gathengma*: *The Commentary on the Vajra Verses Treatise Requested by Khampa Gathengma to the Lord of Yogins, The Great Glorious Sakyapa. gZhung rdo rje'i tshig rkang gi 'grel pa rnal 'byor dbang phyug dpal sa skya pa chen po la khams pa sga theng gis zhus pa*. In *Lam 'bras gzhung rdo rje'i tshig rkang gi rnam 'grel bcu gcig* 2, pp. 149–491. Dehra Dun: Sakya Centre, 1985. BDRC W24767.

———. *Protection Cakra of the Ten Wrathful Ones Taught in the* Vajrapañjara. *Rdo rje gur las gsungs pa'i khro bcu'i srung 'khor*. In *SKB* 2, pp. 285–94. Dehra Dun: Sakya Centre, 1992–1993. BDRC W22271.

Kunga Zangpo (Kun dga' bzang po). *Marvelous Ocean: The Origin of Hevajra and the Hagiography of the Lineage Gurus. Kye rdo rje'i byung tshul dang brgyud pa'i bla ma'i rnam thar ngo mtshar rgya mtsho*. In *The Collected Works of Kunga Zangpo. Kun dga' bzang po gsung 'bum* 2, pp. 425–51. Dehra Dun: Sakya Centre, 199?. BDRC W11577.

———. *Victory over the Armies: The Intimate Instructions for Accomplishing the Bali Offering. gTor sgrub kyi man ngag g.yul las rnam rgyal*. In *The Collected Works of Kunga Zangpo. Kun dga' bzang po gsung 'bum* 2, pp. 660–66. Dehra Dun: Sakya Centre, 199?. BDRC W11577.

———. *Moon Rays. Zla zer*. In *L* 14, pp. 1–412. Kathmandu: Sachen International, 2008.

———. *Victory over the Enemies: The Bali Rite of the Sakya Guardians of the Teachings. Sa skya'i bka' srung rnams kyi gtor chog dgra las rnam rgyal*. In *The Collected Works of Kunga Zangpo* 2, pp. 640–60. Dehra Dun: Sakya Centre, n.d. BDRC W11577.

———. *String of Pearls*: *The Supplication to the Lineage Gurus of the Path with Its Result. Lam 'bras bla ma brgyud ba'i gsol 'debs mu tig phreng ba*. In *The Collected Works of Kunga Zangpo* 1, pp. 7–10. Dehra Dun: Sakya Centre, n.d. BDRC W11577.

Losal Gyatso (bLo gsal rgya mtsho). *Necklace of Gorgeous Blue Poppies*: *The Hagi-*

ography of The Great Lord Vajradhara Losal Gyaltsen, the Dharma King of the Three Realms. Khams gsum chos kyi rgyal po bdag chen rdo rje 'chang blo gros rgyal mtshan dpal bzang po'i rnam par thar pa yid 'phrog utpala'i do shal. In *Sakya Lamdre. Sa skya'i lam 'bras* 2, pp. 7–123. Kathmandu: Sachen International, 2008. BDRC W1KG13617.

Loter Wangpo (bLo gter dbang po). *Digest of the Stages of Accomplishing Awakening: The Profound Path of the Nāḍīs, Vāyus, and Yantras, as Well as the Best and Mediocre Heat of Caṇḍalī. rTsa rlung 'khrul 'khor zab lam byang chub sgrub pa'i rim pa bklags chog ma dang gtum mo'i bde drod rab 'bar ma gnyis.* In *L* 20, pp. 193–255. Dehra Dun: Sakya Centre. BDRC W23649.

———. *Great Ganges River of Excellent Virtue: The Limbs of Ripening and Liberation of the Collection of All Sādhanas and the Record of Lineages.* In *Collection of All Sādhanas, Sgrub thabs kun btus* 11, 443–646. Kangara: Dzongsar Institute for Advanced Studies, n.d. BDRC W23681.

Ngawang Chödrak (Ngag dbang chos grags). *Essence of Excellent Explanations: Necessary for Easy Access of the Intelligent to Expertise, the Explanation of Outer Generation Stage of the Intimate Instruction System of Śrī Hevajra. dPal kye rdo rje man ngag lugs kyi phyi bskyed pa'i rim pa'i rnam par bshad pa blo gsal bde 'jug mkhas la nyer mkho snying po'i legs bshad.* In *LT* 5, pp. 401–83. Dehra Dun: Sakya Centre, 1985. BDRC W23648.

———. *Laughing Lotus Patch of the Oral Instruction Doctrine: Notes on the Origin and Historical Context of the Precious Oral Instruction. gSung ngag rin po che'i byung tshul dang khog phubs kyi zin bris gsung ngag bstan pa'i pad tshal bzhad pa.* In *G*, pp. 265–302. Kathmandu: Sachen International, 2004. BDRC W27883.

Ngawang Lekpa (Ngag dbang legs pa). *Commentary on Recalling the Purities and Miscellany. Dag pa dran pa'i 'grel dang gzhan khag.* In *The Collected Works of Ngawang Lekpa. Ngag dbang legs pa gsung 'bum*, pp. 79–109. Kathmandu: Sa skya rgyal yongs gsung rab slob gnyer khang, 2007. BDRC W1KG11942.

Ngawang Namgyal (Ngag dbang rnam rgyal). *The Hagiography of Taklung Thangpa. sTag lung thang pa'i rnam thar.* India: sTag lung chos mdzod dpe skrung khang, 2011. BDRC W8LS20733.

Palden Tsultrim (dPal ldan tshul khrims). *The Hagiography of the Glorious Lama Dama Sönam Gyaltsen. dPal ldan bla ma dam pa bsod nams rgyal mtshan gyi rnam par thar pa.* In *Sakya Lamdre. Sa skya'i lam 'bras* 1, pp. 494–518. Kathmandu: Sachen International, 2008. BDRC W1KG13617.

Sönam Senge (bSod nams seng ge). *Lamp of the Key Points of the Profound Meaning. gSung ngag lam 'bras don bsdus ma'i rnam bshad zab don gnad kyi sgon me.* In *The Collected Works of Sönam Senge. bSod nams seng ge gsung 'bum* 12, pp. 7–42. Dkar mdzes bod rigs rang skyong khul, sde dge rdzong, rdzong sar khams bye'i slob gling: rDzong sar khams bye'i slob gling, 2004–2014. BDRC W1PD1725.

Sönam Gyaltsen (bSod nams rgyal mtshan). *Direct Realization of Hevajra. Kyai rdo rje'i mngon par rtog pa.* In *The Collected Works of Sönam Gyaltsen. bSod nams rgyal mtshan gsung 'bum* 2, pp. 1–60. Kathmandu: Sa skya rgyal yongs gsung rab slob gnyer khang, 2007. BDRC W1KG11900.

Sönam Gyatso (bSod nams rgya mtsho). *Garland of Jewels. bKa' brgyud chos 'byung nor bu'i phreng ba*. BDRC W1KG4232.

———. *The Clear Mirror of Royal Succession. rGyal rabs gsal ba'i me long*. sDe dge: sDe dge dgon chen, n.d. BDRC W00CHZ0103341.

Sönam Tsemo (bSod nams rtse mo). *Garland of Offerings to Śrī Cakrasamvara. dPal 'khor lo bde mchog gi mchod phreng*. In *SKB* 5, pp. 287–322. Dehra Dun: Sakya Centre, 1992–1993. BDRC W22271.

———. *General Presentation of the Tantras. rGyud sde spyi'i rnam par gzhag pa*. In *SKB* 3, pp. 9–156. Dehra Dun: Sakya Centre, 1992–1993. BDRC W22271.

———. *Great River of Empowerment: The Rite of Ripening Disciples into Maṇḍala of Śrī Hevajra. dPal kyai rdo rje'i dkyil 'khor du slob ma smin par byed pa'i cho ga dbang gi chu bo chen mo*. In *SKB* 5, pp. 75–184. Dehra Dun: Sakya Centre, 1992–1993. BDRC W22271.

Tsang Jampa Dorje Gyaltsen (gTsang byams pa rdo rje rgyal mtshan). *Dismissing Attacks against Nyakma. gNyag ma'i rtsod spong.* In The Mantra Cycle of Sakya Scholars of the Past. *sNgon byon pa'i sa skya pa'i mkhas pa rnams kyi sngags skor* 3, pp. 407–612. Kathmandu: Sa skya rgyal yongs gsung rab slob gnyer khang, 2007. BDRC W1KG4312.

Yeshe Gyaltsen (Ye shes rgyal mtshan). *Jeweled Necklace: The Hagiography of the Dharma King Lama Dampa. bLa ma dam pa chos kyi rgyal po rin po che'i rnam par thar pa rin chen phreng ba.* In *L*, 1, pp. 290–338. Dehra Dun: Sakya Centre, 1983–1985. BDRC W23649.

3. Reference Bibliography

Davidson, Ronald M. *Indian Esoteric Buddhism: A Social History of the Tantric Movement*. New York: Columbia University Press, 2002.

———. *Tibetan Renaissance: Tantric Buddhism in the Rebirth of Tibetan Culture.* New York: Columbia University Press, 2005.

Deroche, Marc-Henri. "'Phreng po gter ston Shes rab 'od zer (1518–1584) on the Eight Lineages of Attainment: Research on a Ris med Paradigm." In *Contemporary Visions in Tibetan Studies. Proceedings of the First International Seminar of Young Tibetologists*. Chicago: Serindia, 2009.

Gardner, Alexander. *The Life of Jamgon Kontrul the Great*. Boulder: Snow Lion, 2019.

Gerloff, Torsten. *Saroruhavajra's Hevajra Lineage: A Close Study of the Surviving Sanskrit Works*. PhD diss., Hamburg, 2017.

Gyaltsen, Sönam. *The Clear Mirror: A Traditional Account of Tibet's Golden Age.* Translated by McComas Taylor and Lama Choedak Yuthok. Ithaca: Snow Lion, 1996.

Heimbel, Jörg. *Vajradhara in Human Form: The Life and Times of Ngor chen Kun dga' bzang po.* Nepal: Lumini International Research Institute, 2017.

Jackson, David. *Enlightenement by a Single Means: Tibetan Controversies on the "Single Sufficient White Remedy" (Dkar po chig thub).* Wien: Verlag der Österreichischen Akademie der Wissenschaften, 1994.

Kongtrul, Jamgön. *Buddhist Ethics.* Ithaca: Snow Lion, 1998.

———. *Chöd: The Sacred Teachings on Severance.* In *The Treasury of Precious Instructions,* 14. Translated by Sarah Harding. Boulder: Snow Lion, 2016.

———. *Systems of Buddhist Tantra.* Ithaca: Snow Lion, 2005.

———. *The Treasury of Knowledge, Book 8, Part 4: Esoteric Instructions.* Translated by Sarah Harding, the Kalu Rinpoché Translation Group. Ithaca: Snow Lion Publications, 2007.

———. *The Catalog of The Treasury of Precious Instructions.* Translated by Richard Barron (Chökyi Nyima). New York: Tsadra Foundation, 2013.

Lama Dampa Sönam Gyaltsen and Virupa. *Treasury of Esoteric Instructions: An Explication of the Oral Instructions of the Path with the Result.* Translated by Cyrus Stearns. Ithaca, NY: Snow Lion, 2008.

Lhundrup, Ngorchen Konchog. *The Beautiful Ornament of the Three Visions.* Translated by Lobsang Dagpa and Jay Goldberg. Ithaca: Snow Lion, 1991.

Monier-Williams, Monier. *Sanskrit-English Dictionary.* Ottawa: Laurier Books, 2001.

Murti, K.R. Srikantha. *Vagbhaṭa's Aṣṭāṅgahṛdayam.* Varanasi: Chowkhambha Krishnadas Academy, 2008.

O'Flaherty, Wendy Doniger. "The Submarine Mare in the Mythology of Śiva." *Journal of the Royal Asiatic Society of Great Britain and Ireland,* no. 1 (1971): 9–27. www.jstor.org/stable/25203231.

Reichle, Natasha. *Violence and Serenity: Late Buddhist Sculpture from Indonesia.* Honolulu: University of Hawaii Press, 2007.

Ringu Tulku. *The Ri-me Philosophy of Jamgön Kongtrul the Great: A Study of the Buddhist Lineages of Tibet.* Boston: Shambhala Publications, 2006.

Shakaba, Tsepon Wangchuk Deden. *One Hundred Thousand Moons: An Advanced Political History of Tibet.* 2 vols. Translated by Derek F. Maher. Leiden: Brill, 2010.

Sharrock, Peter D. "Hevajra at Bantéay Chmàr." *The Journal of the Walters Art Museum* 64/65 (2006): 49–64.

Smith, E. Gene. *Among Tibetan Texts: History and Literature of the Himalayan Plateau.* Boston: Wisdom Publications, 2001.

Sobisch, Jan-Ulrich. *Hevajra and Lam 'Bras Literature of India and Tibet as Seen through the Eyes of A-mes-Zhabs.* Wiesbaden: Dr. Ludwig Reichert Verlag, 2008

Stearns, Cyrus. *Luminous Lives: The Story of the Early Masters of the Lam 'bras in Tibet.* Boston: Wisdom Publications, 2001.

———. *Taking the Result as the Path: Core Teachings of the Sakya Lamdré Tradition.* Boston: Wisdom Publications, 2005.

Vasubandhu. *Abhidharmakośabhaṣyaṃ*. Translated by Louis de La Vallée Poiussin. English Translation by Leo M. Pruden. Berkeley: Asian Humanities Press, 1988–1990.

Von Rospatt, Alexander, "The Sacred Origins of the Svayambhūcaitya and the Nepal Valley: Foreign Speculation and Local Myth." *Journal of the Nepal Research Center* 13 (2009): 33–91.

Wedemeyer, Christian K. *Āryadeva's Lamp That Integrates the Practices: (Caryāmelāpakapradipa): The Gradual Path of Vajrayāna Buddhism According to the Esoteric Communion Noble Tradition*. New York: Columbia University Press, 2007.

Index

pure appearances, 33, 42, 65, 402–3
purification, 123
  basis of, familiarization with, 495–96
  forty-two bases of, 116
  objects and agents of, 321–23, 415, 416
  preliminary, 457, 461, 475, 476
purity, natural, 189, 322, 336
Pūrṇavajra, xv
Putra, 184, 199, 200, 206

Rāgavajrā, 157, 168, 170, 171, 176, 313, 323
rakṣa syllable, 8, 118
Rākṣasa, 162, 163, 186, 241, 315, 573–74n16
rākṣasas, 8, 93, 95, 120, 573n8
Rākṣasi, 196
Rākṣasi Ekajati, 184, 199. *See also* Ekajati
Raktayamāri, 148, 367, 481
Rāmāyaṇa, 570n3
rang rig, use of term, 561n9
rasanā
  as body, 123, 139
  in caṇḍālī yoga, 550
  control of, 451, 508
  exhalation and, 70
  four cakras and, 72–73
  in fourth empowerment, 81
  inner syllables of, 510
  of samsara, 92
  at time of death, 494, 495
Ratnaḍāka, 189, 202
Ratnasambhava-Hevajra couple, 257, 270, 325–27
Ratnasambhava/Ratnarāja
  empowerment of, 257–58, 325–27
  limb of, 150
  in maṇḍala drawing, 234
  permission of, 345
  praise to, 189
  samaya of, 305
  symbols of, 171, 175
  visualizations, 172, 219, 524, 525n*
Ratnatārā, 234, 257, 326
Ravana Daśagriva, 570n3
rebirth, 288
  in higher realms, 36
  instructions on, 500
  karma and, 37, 38
  recalling, 13, 137
  release from bad, 277
  transference and, 496
recitation, 469, 471
  approach, 56, 59
  as example, 409–10
  of self-creation, 216–17
  vajra, 423, 424
  visualization and, 474
  yoga of, 176
Red Annals (Kunga Dorje), 513
refuge, 50, 56, 58, 154, 543
  inviting field, 472, 474
  in preliminaries, 151, 372, 541
  uncommon, 291, 292
relatives, 39, 395–96, 498
Remati, 570n3
renunciation
  and attainment, nonduality of, 65
  four correct kinds, 9, 101, 122–23, 124, 265, 339, 457
  generating, 470
  of people, 50
result tantra, 27, 66. *See also* mahāmudrā result tantra
results, 48
  experiences of, 30
  experiential appearance of, 45, 420
  four at time of cause, 102–3
  ripened, 102
  single, 139
  solace of, 274–75, 353–54
  three connate dharmas of, 28
  three modes, 62
  twofold, 14
Rice Seedling Sutra, 410
Rongpa Sherab Senge, 367
root tantra. *See* all-basis cause tantra
Rudra, xvii, 163, 240, 315, 329
Rudra Cakravartin, 479–80
Rupavajrā, 129, 565n80, 566–67n98

Sachen Kunga Nyingpo, 482, 525n*, 584n6 (chap. 16)
  Chronicle of Ācārya Saroruhavajra, xxi
  commentaries by, 21, 61